Understanding the Emotional Disorders

Understanding the Emotional Disorders

A Symptom-Level Approach Based on the IDAS-II

DAVID WATSON

MICHAEL W. O'HARA

OXFORD
UNIVERSITY PRESS

OXFORD
UNIVERSITY PRESS

Oxford University Press is a department of the University of Oxford. It furthers the University's objective of excellence in research, scholarship, and education by publishing worldwide. Oxford is a registered trade mark of Oxford University Press in the UK and certain other countries.

Published in the United States of America by Oxford University Press
198 Madison Avenue, New York, NY 10016, United States of America.

Library of Congress Cataloging-in-Publication Data
Names: Watson, David, 1946– author. | O'Hara, Michael W., author.
Title: Understanding the emotional disorders : a symptom-level approach based on the IDAS-II /
David Watson, Michael W. O'Hara.
Description: Oxford ; New York: Oxford University Press, [2017] |
Includes bibliographical references and index.
Identifiers: LCCN 2017002687 (print) | LCCN 2017005052 (ebook) | ISBN 9780199301096 (hardback) |
ISBN 9780199301102 (updf) | ISBN 9780190668563 (epub)
Subjects: LCSH: Mental illness. | Mental illness—Diagnosis. | Psychology, Pathological. |
BISAC: PSYCHOLOGY / Clinical Psychology. | PSYCHOLOGY / Psychopathology / Depression. |
PSYCHOLOGY / Psychopathology / Anxieties & Phobias.
Classification: LCC RC469 .W378 2017 (print) | LCC RC469 (ebook) | DDC 616.89—dc23
LC record available at https://lccn.loc.gov/2017002687

CONTENTS

Preface vii

1. The Underlying Nature and Structure of the *Emotional Disorders* 1

2. Development of the IDAS and IDAS-II 23

3. The Structure, Specificity, and Validity of Depression Symptoms 61

4. Positive Mood Dysfunction in Psychopathology 87

5. The Nature and Structure of Bipolar Symptoms 119

6. Anger and Psychopathology 146

7. The Structure, Validity, and Specificity of PTSD Symptoms 175

8. Anxiety Symptoms 206

9. The Structure, Validity, and Specificity of OCD Symptoms 232

10. Toward a Comprehensive Symptom-Based Model of Psychopathology 260

References 287
About the Authors 311
Index 313

PREFACE

In the summer of 2002, the National Institute of Mental Health (NIMH) issued an unusual Request for Applications (RFA) that was due later that year. This RFA encouraged mental health researchers to submit proposals for the creation of new, state-of-the-art measures of depression. The RFA mentioned several possible strategies that might be used in the creation of these new psychometric instruments, one of them being the development of a multidimensional measure that would provide separate assessment for specific types of depression symptoms. We were excited by the possibility of creating a novel type of depression measure and developed an assessment strategy based on the concept of homogeneous item composites (HICs), which basically involves creating a set of candidate items for each potential target construct (see Chapter 2 for a more complete description of this approach). We quickly put together a research team and a detailed grant proposal, which was submitted to the NIMH in October 2002.

We were so convinced of the merits of this HIC-based approach that we began writing items for this new instrument in early 2003, well before we learned about the fate of our grant proposal. At this point, we decided to commit ourselves to constructing this new measure, with or without external funding. Fortunately, our proposal was favorably reviewed by the NIMH, which awarded us an R01 grant (with total costs of approximately $1.5 million) later that year. As would be expected, this generous financial support allowed us to be much more ambitious in scope during the scale development and validation process. Among other things, we eventually decided to incorporate prominent symptoms of anxiety in this new measure. This grant-based research eventually led to creation of the original Inventory of Depression and Anxiety Symptoms (IDAS). Buoyed by the success of this original instrument, we subsequently used our remaining grant funds to create an expanded form of the IDAS—the IDAS-II—that included additional anxiety symptoms as well as scales assessing important symptoms of mania. The validation of the IDAS-II extended well beyond the life of our NIMH grant and was supported through various other sources.

This book reveals the lessons we have learned while conducting this symptom-based research over the past decade and a half. The fundamental thesis of the book is that psychopathology is better understood in terms of homogeneous symptom dimensions, rather than from the perspective of more complex disorders (as exemplified by *DSM* diagnoses). We consider a very broad range of psychopathology in the book, but we focus primarily on depression (Chapter 3), bipolar disorder (Chapter 5), posttraumatic stress disorder (PTSD; Chapter 7), the anxiety disorders (Chapter 8), and obsessive-compulsive disorder (OCD; Chapter 9). Other chapters examine the role of positive emotional dysfunction (Chapter 4) and anger (Chapter 6) in psychopathology. The concluding chapter explores a more comprehensive model that also includes homogeneous dimensions related to sleep disturbance, eating- and weight-related problems, personality pathology, psychosis/thought disorder, and hypochondriasis.

In the chapters that follow, we provide a detailed discussion of why a symptom-based approach is preferable to a diagnosis-based strategy for studying psychopathology. There are a number of reasons for this, but the main one is that many disorders—including depression, bipolar disorder, PTSD, and OCD—contain multiple symptom dimensions that clearly can be differentiated from one another. Moreover, we report extensive evidence establishing that these symptom dimensions are highly generalizable and can be identified in multiple types of data, including self-ratings, semistructured interviews, and clinicians' ratings. More important, these differentiable symptom dimensions often have strikingly different correlates and highly distinct properties. As one example, in Chapter 5 we show that measures of bipolar symptoms define two very different factors, which we label *Manic Distress* and *Manic Elation*. Scores on the Manic Distress factor correlate substantially with indicators of neuroticism and negative affectivity, whereas scores on Manic Elation are strongly associated with extraversion and positive emotionality.

Similarly, in Chapter 3, we report evidence establishing that three types of symptoms—dysphoria, lassitude, and suicidality—exhibit strong criterion validity and significant specificity in relation to diagnoses of major depression. In contrast, symptoms of insomnia and appetite disturbance display unimpressive criterion validity and poor specificity. Moreover, these nonspecific symptoms provide little or no incremental information in logistic regression analyses. Taken together, these results suggest that the diagnosis of depression can be improved by focusing primarily on its strong and specific symptoms (such as dysphoria and lassitude) and deemphasizing weak and nonspecific symptoms (i.e., insomnia and appetite disturbance).

The topics discussed in this book should be of considerable interest to clinicians and to a broad range of psychopathology researchers. We assume that readers will approach these issues with an appropriate level of scientific skepticism and will not be satisfied with pat conclusions; rather, they will want to see the relevant evidence so they can draw their own inferences from the data. Accordingly, the book reports an enormous amount of empirical data, much of which is presented in an extensive set of more than 150 tables. We encourage readers to study these data carefully and draw their own conclusions.

This book—and the research reported in it—would not have been possible without substantial financial assistance. We will begin by formally acknowledging the very generous financial support we received from the NIMH (RO1-MH068472). As we already have indicated, the ambitious scope of our research program would not have been possible without their generous assistance. Other reported findings were collected with the help of additional grants from the NIMH (R01-MH083830, Lee Anna Clark, PI; F31-MH084507 to Erin Koffel), as well as grants from the Centers for Disease Control and Prevention (MM-0822, Scott Stuart PI), the University of Minnesota Press (to Roman Kotov), the Feldstein Medical Foundation (also to Roman Kotov), and the American Psychological Association (to Kristin Naragon-Gainey). David Watson also received major research funding from the University of Notre Dame.

In addition, the research reported in this book represents the hard work of a great many people. We particularly would like to acknowledge the tremendous efforts of our key research collaborators; these include Michael Chmielewski, Stephanie Ellickson-Larew, Wakiza Gámez, Joshua Gootzeit, Erin Koffel, Roman Kotov, Elizabeth McDade-Montez, Kristin Naragon-Gainey, Graham Nelson, Jenny Gringer Richards, Camilo Ruggero, Leonard Simms, Kasey Stanton, Sara Stasik-O'Brien, and Scott Stuart. We need to thank many other individuals who played an important part in collecting the reported data; these include Daniel Foti, Catherine Glenn, Greg Hajcak, Annmarie MacNamara, Jill Malik, Maria Rienzi, Nadia Suzuki, and Anna Weinberg. Also, we want to acknowledge our spouses, Lee Anna Clark and Jane Engeldinger, who have supported us in the research and the writing of this book over the past 15 years. Finally, we would like to acknowledge the thousands of people who participated in our studies; they are the real heroes here.

Understanding the Emotional Disorders

1

The Underlying Nature and Structure of the *Emotional Disorders*

Our basic goal in this introductory chapter is to clarify the underlying nature and structure of the *emotional disorders.* Watson (2005) used this term to characterize the symptoms and diagnoses classified within two key diagnostic classes—namely, the mood disorders and anxiety disorders—in the fourth edition of the *Diagnostic and Statistical Manual of Mental Disorders* (*DSM-IV;* American Psychiatric Association, 2000). In the newly revised framework of the *DSM-5* (American Psychiatric Association, 2013), these disorders now fall into five adjacent diagnostic classes: bipolar and related disorders, depressive disorders, anxiety disorders, obsessive-compulsive and related disorders, and trauma- and stressor-related disorders. Although most forms of psychopathology are associated with emotional dysfunction and dysregulation (Mineka, Watson, & Clark, 1998; Watson, 2009), the emotional disorders are characterized by a particularly strong component of affective disturbance (e.g., sad mood in the depressive disorders, fearful, apprehensive mood in the anxiety disorders, elevated mood in the bipolar disorders; see Watson, 2005; Watson, Clark, & Stasik, 2011), a point we develop in greater detail later.

Starting in the 1980s, a large body of research has examined the structure of the emotional disorders. This research has been stimulated by two key taxonomic problems: comorbidity and heterogeneity. Comorbidity can be broadly defined as the co-occurrence of different disorders within the same individual (see Lilienfeld, Waldman, & Israel, 1994; Mineka et al., 1998); it therefore reflects the empirical overlap between constructs that are hypothesized to be distinct from one another. When comorbidity occurs at greater than chance levels in the population (e.g., when many people with generalized anxiety disorder [GAD] also meet diagnostic criteria for major depression), it raises the more general issue of discriminant validity. Evidence of significant—often substantial—comorbidity among *DSM* disorders has led to the development of increasingly sophisticated models that attempt to account for these patterns of co-occurrence (see Mineka et al., 1998; Watson, 2005, 2009).

In contrast, heterogeneity results when phenomena that ordinarily are collapsed together are found to be sufficiently distinctive to warrant their separation. In the nosological context, this frequently results in the creation of diagnostic subtypes, which is an acknowledgment that an existing taxonomic category is too heterogeneous to be maximally informative (Watson, 2003b). This type of evidence has stimulated research into the specific symptom dimensions underlying many of the emotional disorders, including major depression, posttraumatic stress disorder (PTSD), obsessive-compulsive disorder (OCD), and specific phobia (see Watson, 2009; Watson, Gamez, & Simms, 2005; Watson et al., 2007, 2012). The problem of heterogeneity has motivated much of the symptom-based research that we report in subsequent chapters.

THE PROBLEM OF COMORBIDITY

Symptom Co-Occurrence

Self-Report Data

Starting in the 1970s, a large number of studies have reported correlational and factor analyses of prominent anxiety and depression scales. Researchers consistently have identified strong associations between self-report measures of anxiety and depression, with coefficients typically falling in the .50 to .80 range (L. A. Clark & Watson, 1991; Feldman, 1993; Mineka et al., 1998; Watson et al., 1995). This finding is highly robust across different populations and has been observed in college students (Gotlib, 1984; Joiner, 1996; Watson, 2005; Watson & Clark, 1992; Watson et al., 1995), children and adolescents (Brady & Kendall, 1992; Cole, Truglio, & Peeke, 1997; Wolfe et al., 1987), community-dwelling adults (Orme, Reis, & Herz, 1986; Watson, 2005; Watson et al., 1995), and psychiatric patients (D. A. Clark, Steer, & Beck, 1994; L. A. Clark & Watson, 1991; Jolly & Dykman, 1994; Lonigan, Carey, & Finch, 1994; Steer, Clark, Beck, & Ranieri, 1995; Watson, 2005; Watson, O'Hara, & Stuart, 2008). Although some early evidence suggested that somewhat better differentiation was obtained in psychiatric patient samples (for an early review, see L. A. Clark & Watson, 1991), more recent data indicate that the correlations between anxiety and depression scales are quite similar in distressed and nondistressed samples (Watson, 2005, Watson, O'Hara, & Stuart, 2008).

Other Data

This problem is not simply confined to self-report data. In fact, considerable overlap also is found in clinicians' ratings of depression and anxiety, although the level of differentiation in these data tends to be somewhat greater than in self-ratings (L. A. Clark & Watson, 1991; Mineka et al., 1998). It is unclear, however, whether this improved differentiation represents (a) an increased sensitivity to subtle cues that patients themselves discount or are unaware of, which would imply that clinicians' ratings are more valid than self-ratings; or (b) rating biases on the part of clinicians, which would suggest that clinicians' ratings actually may be less valid than self-ratings (see L. A. Clark & Watson, 1991; Mineka et al., 1998).

Relatedly, clinicians', teachers', and parents' ratings of anxiety and depression in children show relatively little differentiation. Indeed, in their review of the literature, Brady and Kendall (1992) concluded that analyses of behavioral and observational ratings typically have yielded a single anxiety-depression factor in children (see also Cole et al., 1997). Again, however, it is unclear whether (a) these syndromes actually are less differentiated in children or (b) the scales used to assess child psychopathology are less valid than those available for adults. Some evidence, however, suggests that child anxiety scales perform particularly poorly, and that ratings of anxiety differentiate less well between depressed and anxious children than do ratings of depression (Brady & Kendall, 1992).

Psychometric Considerations

To some extent, these strong correlations reflect psychometric and taxonomic problems with older measures of depression and anxiety. These older scales were created in an era in which discriminant validity was not a major concern, so that little thought was given to specifying and defining the boundaries of these constructs. For example, Gotlib and Cane (1989) noted that several symptoms (e.g., insomnia, fatigue, irritability, restlessness, difficulty concentrating) are found in the criteria for both GAD and major depression. Not surprisingly, these overlapping symptoms frequently appear in older scales assessing both depression and anxiety, thereby inflating the correlation between them. Furthermore, many older scales contain symptom content that is actually more appropriate to the other syndrome. For instance, the trait form of the State-Trait Anxiety Inventory (Spielberger, Gorsuch, Lushene, Vagg, & Jacobs, 1983) assesses feelings of failure, disappointment, and unhappiness that are more characteristic of depression than anxiety; conversely, the Center for Epidemiological Studies Depression Scale (Radloff, 1977) assesses feelings of fearfulness that are more relevant to anxiety than depression.

It must be emphasized, however, that these conceptual and psychometric problems cannot account entirely for the strong and pervasive association between depression and anxiety scales. Indeed, measures of these syndromes remain substantially intercorrelated even after such problems have been eliminated (L. A. Clark & Watson, 1991).

Diagnostic Comorbidity

Finally, substantial comorbidity has been observed at the diagnostic level; indeed, comorbidity now is widely recognized to be a pervasive problem throughout the *DSM* (L. A. Clark, Watson, & Reynolds, 1995; Krueger & Markon, 2006; Mineka et al., 1998; Widiger & Clark, 2000), including the emotional disorders. For instance, in L. A. Clark's (1989) meta-analysis, 57% of those with major depression also met diagnostic criteria for one or more anxiety disorders. The National Comorbidity Survey (NCS) yielded remarkably similar data: Of those who met criteria for depression, 58% had one or more anxiety disorders during their lifetime, and 51.2% had an anxiety disorder during the preceding year (Kessler et al., 1996). Conversely, L. A. Clark's (1989) meta-analysis revealed that 56% of patients with an anxiety disorder also met diagnostic criteria for depression (see also Alloy, Kelly, Mineka, & Clements, 1990; Kessler et al., 1996; Mineka et al., 1998).

In addition to their co-occurrence with depression, the anxiety disorders in both *DSM-III-R* (American Psychiatric Association, 1987) and *DSM-IV* have been shown to be highly comorbid with each other (e.g., Brown, Campbell, Lehman, Grisham, & Mancill, 2001; Brown & Barlow, 1992). For instance, using lifetime diagnoses in the NCS data, Magee, Eaton, Wittchen, McGonagle, and Kessler (1996) reported that 74.1% of those with agoraphobia, 68.7% of those with simple phobia, and 56.9% of those with social phobia also met criteria for another anxiety disorder.

It is informative to examine the nature and strength of these relations in greater detail. Consequently, we present tetrachoric correlations between six *DSM-III-R/DSM-IV* mood and anxiety disorder diagnoses: major depression, dysthymic disorder, GAD, panic disorder, social phobia, and agoraphobia (these data are adapted from Watson, 2009, Table 1). For readers who are unfamiliar with these coefficients, tetrachoric correlations estimate the associations between normally distributed latent continuous variables when both observed scores are dichotomous (Flora & Curran, 2004; Olsson, Drasgow, & Dorans, 1982). In analyses involving diagnostic variables, tetrachoric correlations offer clear advantages over standard Pearson product-moment correlations, in that they are unaffected by differences in prevalence rates, thereby facilitating cross-diagnosis comparisons.

Table 1.1 presents weighted mean tetrachoric correlations that are computed across four large national epidemiological samples: the NCS (Krueger, 1999;

Table 1.1 WEIGHTED MEAN TETRACHORIC CORRELATIONS AMONG *DSM-III/DSM-IV* MOOD AND ANXIETY DISORDER DIAGNOSES IN FOUR NATIONAL EPIDEMIOLOGICAL SAMPLES

Disorder	1	2	3	4	5	6
1. Major depression	.—					
2. Dysthymic disorder	.74	.—				
3. GAD	.64	.66	.—			
4. Panic disorder	.55	.50	.58	.—		
5. Social phobia	.50	.49	.51	.53	.—	
6. Agoraphobia	.48	.42	.52	.67	.61	.—

NOTE: $N = 29{,}014$. *DSM* = *Diagnostic and Statistical Manual of Mental Disorders*. GAD = generalized anxiety disorder.

N=8,098) and NCS Replication (NCS-R; Kessler et al., 2005; *N*=3,199) data in the United States; Wave 1 of the Netherlands Mental Health Survey and Incidence Study (NEMESIS; W. A. Vollebergh, personal communication, December 15, 2003; *N*=7,076); and the Australian National Survey of Mental Health and Well-Being (NSMHWB; Slade & Watson, 2006; *N*=10,641). Overall, therefore, these tetrachoric correlations are based on a combined *N* of 29,014.

The data shown in Table 1.1 establish moderate to strong levels of comorbidity across all six diagnoses. For example, major depression is strongly comorbid with dysthymic disorder (tetrachoric r=.74); both of these mood disorders, in turn, are highly related to diagnoses of GAD (r=.64 and .66, respectively). Similarly, agoraphobia diagnoses overlap strongly with both panic disorder (r=.67) and social phobia (r=.61). As noted earlier, these comorbidity data raise significant concerns about the distinctiveness and discriminant validity of these *DSM* diagnoses.

STRUCTURAL MODELS OF COMORBIDITY

The Two-Factor Affective Model

The "Big Two" Dimensions of Affect

Why is there such extensive comorbidity among the *DSM* anxiety and depressive disorders? In the 1980s, Watson, Clark, and colleagues developed an explanatory model drawing on well-established findings from the basic mood literature (Watson, Clark, & Carey, 1988), as well as the seminal work of Auke Tellegen (1985). Extensive evidence has established the existence of two broad, higher order dimensions of emotional experience: Negative Affect and Positive Affect (see Watson, 2005; Watson & Clark, 1997; Watson, Clark, & Tellegen, 1988; Watson & Tellegen, 1985; Watson, Wiese, Vaidya, & Tellegen, 1999). Negative Affect is a general dimension of subjective distress and dissatisfaction that subsumes a broad range of specific lower order negative mood states, including fear, sadness, anger, and guilt. Its emergence in structural analyses indicates that these various negative emotions significantly co-occur both within and across individuals. Thus, someone who is feeling sad also is likely to report significant levels of fear, anger, guilt, and so on; we will examine the magnitude of these relations shortly. In parallel fashion, the general Positive Affect dimension reflects important co-occurrences among specific positive mood states; for example, someone who is happy also will report feeling interested, energetic, bold, confident, and alert. These two higher order factors are highly robust and have been identified in both intra- and interindividual analyses; moreover, they emerge consistently across diverse sets of descriptors, time frames, response formats, and languages (Watson & Clark, 1997; Watson et al., 1999).

The Power of the General Negative Affect Factor

Extrapolating from these mood data, Watson, Clark, and Carey (1988) argued that this general Negative Affect dimension was largely responsible for the substantial overlap/comorbidity between depression and anxiety. Put differently, this higher order factor produces strong correlations among different types of negative emotion, including sad/depressed affect and fearful/anxious affect.

Watson, O'Hara, and Stuart (2008) report data that demonstrate both the power and robustness of this general Negative Affect dimension (see also Watson, 2005). Watson, O'Hara, and Stuart (2008) created three scales assessing specific types of negative affect: Depressed Mood (four items; e.g., *I felt sad, I felt depressed, I felt unhappy*), Anxious Mood (seven items; e.g., *I felt tense, I felt fearful, I found myself worrying all the time*), and Angry Mood (seven items; e.g., *I felt angry, I felt grouchy, I was furious*). They reported correlations between these mood scales in eight different samples—247 high school students, 980 college students, 362 community adults, 925 postpartum women, 214 older adults, 131 adolescent patients, and 690 adult psychiatric patients—as well as a combined overall sample (total $N=3{,}549$). Because of the influence of the general Negative Affect factor, we would expect scores on these three scales to be strongly associated with one another. Consistent with this expectation, Angry Mood was consistently and strongly correlated with both Anxious Mood (*r*s ranged from .64 to .75, overall $r=.68$) and Depressed Mood (*r*s ranged from .55 to .72, overall $r=.68$) in all eight samples. Replicating a frequent finding in the mood literature, Anxious Mood and Depressed Mood were even more strongly related to one another, with coefficients ranging from .72 (college students) to .85 (older adults), and an overall correlation of .78 in the combined sample.

These data have crucial implications for our understanding of the emotional disorders, as they establish a very strong link between sad/depressed mood (the core element of *DSM* depressive disorders) and anxious/worried mood (a key feature of *DSM* anxiety disorders). In light of these associations, it is easy to understand the strong comorbidity between these disorders.

The Differentiating Role of Positive Affect

Given this strong link between different types of negative affect, how can clinical manifestations of depression and anxiety be distinguished from one another? Findings from the mood literature also establish that Positive Affect has stronger and more consistent (negative) associations with measures of depression than with indicators of anxiety (see Clark & Watson, 1991; Watson, 2005; Watson, Clark, & Carey, 1988). For example, Watson (2005, Table 1) reports correlations between three scales contained in the Expanded Form of the Positive and Negative Affect Schedule (PANAS-X; Watson & Clark, 1999): Fear (six items; e.g., *afraid, frightened, nervous*), Sadness (five items; e.g., *blue, downhearted, alone*), and Joviality (eight items; e.g., *cheerful, happy, enthusiastic, energetic*). Across 14 different samples (overall $N=9{,}663$), Joviality was weakly related to Fear, with correlations generally falling in the −.05 to −.20 range. In contrast, Joviality was more substantially related to Sadness, with coefficients generally falling in the −.30 to −.45 range.

The Two-Factor Model of Affect

Based on these and other types of data, Watson, Clark, and Carey (1988) proposed that low levels of positive affectivity (i.e., anhedonia) were a specific feature of depression that distinguishes it from the anxiety disorders. Thus, in this two-factor model, Negative Affect represents a nonspecific factor common to depression and anxiety, whereas low Positive Affect is a specific factor that is related primarily to depression. In support of this model, indicators of both depression and anxiety have been found to be strongly related to measures of general negative affectivity; in contrast, measures of positive affectivity are consistently negatively correlated with depressed mood and symptomatology and are more weakly related to anxious mood and symptomatology (e.g., Jolly, Dyck, Kramer, & Wherry, 1994; Mineka et al., 1998; Watson et al., 1988; Watson, O'Hara, Chmielewski et al., 2008).

Subsequent studies have continued to report findings that are quite consistent with the broad outlines of this two-factor model. For example, as we discuss in detail subsequently, measures of positive mood/well-being actually show better diagnostic specificity vis-à-vis diagnoses of depression than do some of the formal *DSM* symptom criteria for major depression. At the same time, however, the accumulating data have highlighted the fact that Positive Affect has a much richer, more complex association with psychopathology than was captured in this early model. We also revisit this issue in Chapter 4.

The Tripartite Model

Development of the Tripartite Model

This affect-based model conceptualized depression and anxiety in terms of two factors, one that is specific and another that is nonspecific. That is, in this scheme, Negative Affect is a nonspecific factor that is common to both depression and anxiety; the influence of this common factor helps to explain the strong association between them. In contrast, (low) Positive Affect is a specific factor that is relatively unique to depression.

One obvious limitation of this model is that it simply characterized anxiety as an undifferentiated state of high Negative Affect. It therefore could not differentiate clearly between fear/anxiety—which, presumably, represents a specific, lower order type of Negative Affect—and the general, higher order dimension itself. This lack of differentiation limited the clinical and heuristic value of the model. Fortunately, L. A. Clark and Watson (1991) were able to expand it by identifying a second specific factor that is relatively unique to anxiety, and that differentiates it from both depression and the general factor. Specifically, based on an extensive review of the literature—which was conducted in their role as Advisors to the *DSM-IV* Anxiety Disorders Work Group—they concluded that symptoms of physiological arousal are more strongly characteristic of anxiety than depression (L. A. Clark & Watson, 1991).

This conclusion was based on three types of evidence. First, content analyses indicated that anxiety scales with the best discriminant validity (i.e., having the lowest correlations with depression) tended to measure somatic symptoms of anxiety, rather than focusing on anxious mood per se. Second, autonomic symptoms of panic disorder (e.g., dizziness, shortness of breath, racing heart) consistently were able to differentiate anxious and depressed patient groups, whereas other types of anxiety symptoms did not. Third, structural analyses identified three replicable symptom factors within this domain. These three dimensions consisted of (a) a general neurotic factor that included feelings of inferiority and rejection, oversensitivity to criticism, and anxious and depressed mood (in other words, general Negative Affect); (b) a specific depression factor that was defined by the loss of interest or pleasure (i.e., anhedonia or low Positive Affect), anorexia, crying spells, and suicidal ideation; and (c) a specific anxiety factor that was defined by items reflecting tension, shakiness, and panic (L. A. Clark & Watson, 1991).

Integrating these data with the older two-factor model, L. A. Clark and Watson (1991) proposed that a *tripartite model* best captures the underlying structure of depression and anxiety. In this model, symptoms of anxiety and depression are grouped into three basic subtypes. First, many symptoms are strong indicators of the general Negative Affect dimension. These symptoms are, therefore, relatively nonspecific—that is, they frequently are experienced by both anxious and depressed individuals. This nonspecific group includes both anxious and depressed mood, as well as other symptoms that are prevalent in both types of disorder, such as insomnia, restlessness, irritability, and poor concentration. In addition, each syndrome is characterized by a cluster of relatively unique symptoms: Somatic tension and hyperarousal (e.g., dizziness and lightheadedness, shortness of breath, racing heart) are relatively specific to anxiety, whereas manifestations of anhedonia and the absence of Positive Affect (e.g., loss of interest, feeling that nothing is interesting or enjoyable) are relatively specific to depression. Thus, in this expanded model, anxiety and depression are conceptualized as consisting of both a nonspecific and a specific factor.

Early Tests of the Model

The articulation of the tripartite model stimulated a new wave of research into the nature and structure of anxious and depressive symptoms (see Mineka et al., 1998; Watson, 2000). Several early studies—which were published within a few years of the formulation of the model—subjected existing symptom measures to exploratory factor analyses. Consistent with the tripartite model, these studies found clear evidence of three factors: a specific anxiety factor, a specific depression factor, and a nonspecific factor that contained both types of symptoms (e.g., Jolly & Dykman, 1994; Jolly & Kramer, 1994).

Unfortunately, these early studies were forced to rely on measures that were not explicitly designed to assess the major symptom groups of the tripartite model; most notably, most of these measures were heavily laden with items assessing general Negative Affect and covered the two specific symptom groups less satisfactorily. The paucity of good hyperarousal and anhedonia indicators (particularly the latter) made it challenging to identify specific dimensions that closely matched the predictions generated by the tripartite model. Nevertheless, several investigators were able to identify structures that strongly supported this model, finding evidence of (a) a general Negative Affect factor, (b) a specific anxiety factor that primarily was marked by symptoms of anxious arousal, and (c) a specific depression factor characterized by anhedonia and hopelessness (D. A. Clark et al., 1994; Steer et al., 1995; Steer, Clark, & Ranieri, 1994). Still, the early literature on this model demonstrates the problems that arise when structural analyses are forced to rely on measures that were not specifically created to assess key constructs of interest.

Development of the Mood and Anxiety Symptom Questionnaire

To address these measure-based problems, Watson and Clark (1991) created the Mood and Anxiety Symptom Questionnaire (MASQ; for a detailed discussion of the development of the MASQ, see Watson et al., 1995). The 90 MASQ items were culled from the symptom criteria for the anxiety and mood disorders in *DSM-III-R* (American Psychiatric Association, 1987). The tripartite model then was used as a framework to group these items into five scales; sample items from each scale are presented in Box 1.1. One scale—General Distress: Mixed Symptoms (15 items)—contains content that appeared in the *DSM-III-R* symptom criteria for both the anxiety and mood disorders (e.g., irritability, insomnia, difficulty

---

Box 1.1

Sample Items From the Mood and Anxiety Symptom Questionnaire (MASQ)

General Distress: Mixed Symptoms
Felt irritable; had trouble falling asleep; had trouble concentrating; got tired or fatigued easily.

General Distress: Anxious Symptoms
Felt afraid; felt nervous; felt keyed up, "on edge"; was unable to relax.

Anxious Arousal
Startled easily; was short of breath; felt faint; was trembling or shaking.

General Distress: Depressive Symptoms
Felt discouraged; felt worthless; felt like a failure; blamed myself for a lot of things.

Anhedonic Depression
Felt really bored; felt like nothing was very enjoyable; felt really happy*;
felt like I had a lot of energy.*

NOTE: Items taken from the Mood and Anxiety Symptom Questionnaire, © 1991 by D. B. Watson & L. A. Clark. Reproduced with permission.

* Reverse-keyed item.

---

concentrating). This scale is not central to our current discussion and will not be considered further.

The MASQ also contains two pairs of anxiety and depression scales. One pair of scales is composed of symptoms that—according to the tripartite model—should be strongly related to general Negative Affect and, therefore, relatively nonspecific to depression and anxiety. Thus, the General Distress: Anxious Symptoms scale (GD: Anxiety; 11 items) contains several indicators of anxious mood, as well as other symptoms of anxiety disorder that were hypothesized to be relatively nondifferentiating (e.g., inability to relax, diarrhea). Conversely, the General Distress: Depressive Symptoms scale (GD: Depression; 12 items) includes several items reflecting depressed mood, along with other relatively nonspecific symptoms of mood disorder (e.g., feelings of disappointment and failure, self-blame, pessimism).

In contrast, the second pair is composed of symptoms that were hypothesized to be relatively specific to either anxiety or depression. Anxious Arousal (17 items) includes various symptoms of somatic tension and hyperarousal (e.g., feeling dizzy or lightheaded, shortness of breath, dry mouth). Conversely, Anhedonic Depression (22 items) contains eight items that directly assess the loss of interest and pleasure (e.g., felt bored, slowed down; felt that nothing was interesting or enjoyable), as well as 14 reverse-keyed items that assess positive emotional experiences (e.g., felt cheerful, optimistic, "up"; had a lot of energy; looked forward to things with enjoyment). Preliminary analyses demonstrated that these two sets of Anhedonic Depression items were strongly intercorrelated, thereby justifying their combination in a single scale (see Watson et al., 1995).

Relations Among the MASQ Scales

Clearly, the tripartite model would predict that the correlation between the two specific scales should be substantially lower than that between the two nonspecific scales. Watson et al. (1995) tested this key prediction in five samples (three student, one adult, one patient). Their results provided strong support for the tripartite model and clearly demonstrated that certain types of anxiety and depression symptoms can be more easily differentiated than others.

It is informative to consider the properties of these MASQ scales in greater detail. Watson (2000) reported MASQ data from eight large samples (six student, one adult, one patient) with a combined *N* of 3,629. We have since collected MASQ data in eight samples of University of Iowa students (combined $N = 2{,}593$), 564 Gulf War veterans, 102 psychiatric outpatients, and 52 patients with OCD. We began by computing correlations among the four MASQ anxiety and depression scales separately in each sample; we then calculated overall weighted mean correlations (after *r*-to-*z* transformation) across all 19 samples (i.e., these 11 new samples, plus the 8 samples previously reported in Watson [2000]).

Table 1.2 reports these weighted mean correlations, based on an overall *N* of 6,940. In discussing these data, we first must consider the crucial issue of *convergent validity* (Campbell & Fiske, 1959). One could plausibly argue that in the process of creating the two specific MASQ scales, Watson and Clark (1991) somehow

Table 1.2 Weighted Mean Correlations Between the MASQ Anxiety and Depression Scales

Scale	1	2	3	4
Anxiety Scales				
1. GD: Anxiety	.—			
2. Anxious Arousal	.73			
Depression Scales				
3. GD: Depression	.70	.55	.—	
4. Anhedonic Depression	.42	.33	.69	.—

NOTE: $N = 6{,}940$. MASQ = Mood and Anxiety Symptom Questionnaire. GD: Anxiety = General Distress: Anxious Symptoms. GD: Depression = General Distress: Depressive Symptoms.

lost the essence of the target underlying constructs (i.e., anxiety and depression). Put differently, it is possible that these specific scales no longer represent valid measures that clearly are recognizable as indicators of anxiety and depression.

The easiest way to address this concern is to correlate these specific scales with other, more traditional measures of the target syndromes. In this regard, the Table 1.2 data are very reassuring: Anxious Arousal had a weighted mean correlation of .73 with GD: Anxiety, whereas Anhedonic Depression had an overall correlation of .69 with GD: Depression.

Watson (2000) further established the convergent validity of the scales by relating them to the Beck Anxiety Inventory (BAI; Beck & Steer, 1990) and the Beck Depression Inventory (BDI; Beck, Rush, Shaw, & Emery, 1979). Across three samples with a combined *N* of 1,616, Watson (2000) reported weighted mean correlations of .74 between the BAI and Anxious Arousal, and .62 between the BDI and Anhedonic Depression. Taken together with the Table 1.2 data, these results demonstrate that the MASQ specific scales show strong convergent validity in relation to more traditional measures of these constructs.

With that context in mind, it is interesting to examine the *discriminant validity* of the different MASQ scales. As noted earlier, the tripartite model predicts that the GD: Anxiety and GD: Depression scales should be highly interrelated and display poor discriminant validity. Table 1.2 indicates that this prediction is strongly confirmed, with an overall weighted mean correlation of .70; this coefficient indicates that these scales share nearly half of their variance with one another (see also Watson, 2005).

The tripartite model further predicts that anxiety and depression symptoms will become better differentiated when assessment is focused more on the specific symptom groups. Table 1.2 indicates that substituting Anxious Arousal for GD: Anxiety reduces the magnitude of the discriminant correlation from .70 to .55 (30% shared variance). We can achieve even better discrimination, however, by substituting Anhedonic Depression for GD: Depression ($r = .42$, 18% shared variance). Clearly, however, the best differentiation is obtained by using both of the specific scales; note that the overall correlation between Anxious Arousal and Anhedonic Depression is only .33. In other words, substituting the specific scales for the nonspecific scales reduces the overlapping variance from 49% to only 11%.

Broader Implications of the Tripartite Model

The data shown in Table 1.2 demonstrate that it is quite possible to distinguish depression from anxiety; the key consideration is to focus assessment primarily on the unique symptoms that define each syndrome. At a more fundamental level, the most important implication of the tripartite model is that *symptoms matter*; that is, differential diagnosis and assessment can be enhanced by focusing more on the specific symptom clusters within a disorder and deemphasizing those symptoms that largely represent nonspecific manifestations of general distress/Negative Affect. This became a fundamental guiding principle in the symptom scale development work we describe in Chapter 2.

Integrative Hierarchical Model

Problems With the Tripartite Model

Subsequent studies have continued to support key elements of the tripartite model (see Watson, 2000, 2005). At the same time, however, accumulating evidence also exposed problems related to each of the specific symptom groups that are posited by the model. First, it became clear that the tripartite model fails to account for the marked heterogeneity among the *DSM-IV* anxiety disorders (in *DSM-5*, this would include disorders in three adjacent diagnostic classes: anxiety disorders, obsessive-compulsive and related disorders, and trauma- and stressor-related disorders). Most notably, it became clear that a single specific factor (i.e., anxious arousal) could not accurately capture the diverse nature of these disorders. In fact, Brown, Chorpita, and Barlow (1998) reported results establishing that the anxious arousal component of the tripartite model was not generally characteristic of the anxiety disorders, but instead represented the specific, unique component of panic disorder; subsequent evidence also has linked anxious arousal to PTSD (due primarily to its component of hyperarousal; see Brown et al., 2001).

Second, as was noted previously, the Positive Affect dimension actually has a much richer, more complex association with psychopathology than was posited in these early models. Several studies have demonstrated that low Positive Affect is not uniquely linked to depression but also is consistently related to indicators of both social anxiety/social phobia (e.g., Brown et al., 1998; Watson, Clark, & Carey, 1988; Watson et al., 2005; Watson & Naragon-Gainey, 2010) and schizophrenia/schizotypy (for a review, see Watson & Naragon-Gainey, 2010). Finally, as we will discuss in Chapter 4, certain types of psychopathology—such as the bipolar disorders—are associated with elevated levels of Positive Affect (see Watson, Clark, Chmielewski, & Kotov, 2013; Watson et al., 2012). Thus, unlike Negative Affect—which is consistently elevated in clinical populations—Positive Affect does not display a consistent directional trend in relation to psychopathology.

Barlow's Hierarchical Model of the Anxiety Disorders

In the 1990s, David Barlow and colleagues proposed a hierarchical model that was more effective in capturing the heterogeneity of the anxiety disorders (Barlow, 1991; Barlow & DiNardo, 1991; Brown & Barlow, 1992; Zinbarg & Barlow, 1996). Barlow asserted that each of the individual anxiety disorders contains a shared component in a two-level hierarchical scheme. This higher order factor originally was labeled *anxious apprehension* (Barlow, 1991; Brown & Barlow, 1992); in subsequent papers, however, Barlow acknowledged that it essentially represents the general Negative Affect component of the tripartite model (Brown et al., 1998; Zinbarg & Barlow, 1996). Consequently, this higher order factor not only is common across the anxiety disorders but also is shared with depression. Consequently, this general factor primarily is responsible for the observed comorbidity both (a) among individual anxiety disorders and (b) between these disorders and depression.

In addition, each of the anxiety disorders also contains a specific, unique component that distinguishes it from all of the others in this hierarchical scheme. Thus, each individual disorder can be decomposed into (a) a common component of general Negative Affect that is shared with all of the others, plus (b) a specific element that uniquely defines it. Around this same time, Spence (1997) proposed a very similar model of anxiety in childhood.

The Integrative Hierarchical Model of Anxiety and Depression

Based on an extensive review of the literature, Mineka et al. (1998) proposed an expanded structural model that integrated key features of the tripartite model with Barlow's hierarchical organization of the anxiety disorders. In this integrative hierarchical model, each individual syndrome can be viewed as containing both a common and a unique component. Following the original logic of the tripartite model, this shared component represents broad individual differences in Negative Affect; it is a pervasive higher order factor that (a) is common to both the mood and anxiety disorders and (b) is primarily responsible for the observed overlap among these disorders. In addition, however, each disorder also includes a unique component that differentiates it from all of the others. For instance, anhedonia, disinterest, and the absence of Positive Affect comprise the core features of the specific component of depression.

These features all are fully consistent with the original tripartite model. The major change in this model was that anxious arousal no longer was viewed as broadly characteristic of all anxiety disorders; rather, it assumed a much more limited role as the specific component of panic disorder (Brown et al., 1998; Mineka et al., 1998). In parallel fashion, each of the other anxiety disorders was postulated to have its own unique component that is distinct from anxious arousal (it should be noted, however, that Mineka et al. did not actually describe the unique components of most disorders). One possible exception is GAD, which is very strongly saturated with nonspecific Negative Affect and, therefore, may not have a well-defined specific component of its own (Barlow & DiNardo, 1991; Brown & Barlow, 1992; Brown et al., 1998).

In articulating this model, Mineka et al. (1998) discussed three additional points that are worth noting here. First, they incorporated an explicitly quantitative component into this integrative scheme. That is, Mineka et al. (1998) summarized a range of evidence indicating that the size of these general and specific components differs markedly across disorders. Specifically, major depression, dysthymic disorder, and GAD all are distress-based disorders that clearly contain an enormous amount of this general factor variance; in contrast, most of the other anxiety disorders (such as social phobia and specific phobia) contain a more modest component of nonspecific Negative Affect (for a further elaboration of this point, see Watson, 2009; Watson et al., 2005). Thus, Mineka et al. (1998) stated that "future research must move beyond the simple truism that each disorder is characterized by both a common and a unique component and specify the proportions of general and specific variance that are characteristic of each syndrome" (p. 397).

Second, consistent with the comorbidity data reviewed previously, Mineka et al. (1998) argued that this general Negative Affect dimension was not restricted to the anxiety and mood disorders but also characterized many other types of psychopathology. Indeed, they summarized evidence indicating that virtually all major forms of psychopathology—"including substance use disorders, somatoform disorders, eating disorders, personality and conduct disorders, and schizophrenia" (p. 398)—were characterized by elevated levels of Negative Affect. Subsequent research has reinforced the validity of this conclusion (see, for example, Caspi et al., 2014; Lahey, 2009; Lahey et al., 2012).

Finally, Mineka et al. (1998) asserted that specificity must be viewed in relative terms, arguing that "It is highly unlikely that any group of symptoms will be found to be unique to a single disorder across the entire *DSM*" (p. 398). Consistent with this argument, they acknowledged the evidence we reviewed earlier establishing that low Positive Affect is not uniquely related to depression.

Failure to Model Comorbidity Accurately

Although the integrative hierarchical model represents a significant improvement over its predecessors, it also has important limitations of its own. Most notably, it posits that a single nonspecific factor—namely, general Negative Affect—essentially is responsible for observed patterns of comorbidity. Specifically, it predicts (a) a high level of comorbidity between two disorders that both have strong components of general distress/negative affectivity, but (b) a weaker level of comorbidity between syndromes containing less of this general factor variance.

This former proposition has received substantial support in the literature. To illustrate this point, consider the comorbidity data presented in Table 1.1. Major depression, dysthymic disorder, and GAD all are distress-based disorders that are strongly saturated with general factor variance (Mineka et al., 1998; Watson, 2005). According to the integrative hierarchical model, these disorders should be strongly comorbid—and they are. As shown in Table 1.1, the weighted mean tetrachoric correlations among these diagnoses ranged from .64 (GAD vs. major depression) to .74 (major depression vs. dysthymic disorder) across the four large national epidemiological samples.

It is the second proposition that has proven to be problematic. For example, according to the integrative hierarchical model, social phobia and agoraphobia—disorders containing lesser amounts of general factor variance—should display a weaker level of comorbidity. As shown in Table 1.1, however, these diagnoses had a weighted mean correlation of .61 across the four national samples. Agoraphobia also was very strongly comorbid with panic disorder (weighted mean $r = .67$) in these data (see also Krueger, 1999; Magee et al., 1996; Vollebergh et al., 2001). These strong correlations are inconsistent with the integrative hierarchical model, and they indicate that more than one nonspecific factor is required to model comorbidity adequately.

To illustrate this important point, we subjected the correlation matrix in Table 1.1 to a confirmatory factor analysis using PROC CALIS in SAS 9.3 (SAS Institute, Inc., 2011). Specifically, we tested whether a single factor could model the correlations among these six diagnoses adequately. Four different fit indices were used to evaluate this model: the standardized root-mean-square residual (SRMR), the root-mean-square error of approximation (RMSEA), the comparative fit index (CFI), and the Tucker-Lewis Index (TLI). In general, fit is considered acceptable if CFI and TLI are .90 or greater and SRMR and RMSEA are .10 or less (Finch & West, 1997; Hu & Bentler, 1998; Hu & Bentler, 1999). However, more stringent cutoffs for these indices have been recommended, including values of .95 for CFI and TLI, .08 for SRMR, and .06 for RMSEA (Hu & Bentler, 1999).

Based on these benchmarks, a one-factor model clearly did not fit these comorbidity data well. Specifically, CFI (.876), TLI (.794), and RMSEA (.210) all indicated a poor fit; only SRMR (.068) suggested an adequate fit. Thus, a single general factor cannot even account for the comorbidities among this very limited set of six diagnoses.

Diagnosis-Based Structural Analyses

Modeling Comorbidities Directly

One could improve the integrative hierarchical model's explanatory power by taking into account the influence of the Positive Affect and anxious arousal dimensions. For instance, a shared component of low Positive Affect most likely contributes to the comorbidity between major depression and social phobia (Watson & Naragon-Gainey, 2010), whereas a common element of anxious arousal may be partly responsible for the observed covariation between panic disorder and PTSD (Brown et al., 2001, 1998). Even so, however, the model still fails to account fully for the overlap between lower distress disorders such as agoraphobia and social phobia. Of course, the model could be further enhanced through the identification of additional dimensions, which would enable it to provide a better fit to the empirical evidence. It is simpler, however, to analyze the comorbidity data directly and then create a structural model that captures these covariations as accurately as possible.

Early Structural Data

A number of investigators have used this approach to develop increasingly comprehensive models of *DSM-III-R*, *DSM-IV*, and *ICD-10* (WHO, 1992) diagnoses. In a seminal study, Krueger (1999) conducted an extensive series of confirmatory factor analyses of *DSM-III-R* diagnoses in the NCS data. He found that a three-factor model—consisting of Externalizing (alcohol dependence, drug dependence, antisocial personality disorder), Anxious-Misery (major depression, dysthymia, GAD), and Fear (panic disorder, agoraphobia, social phobia, simple phobia)—best fit the data; the latter two factors were strongly correlated and so defined a higher order "Internalizing" dimension. It is noteworthy, moreover, that this model (a) replicated across both lifetime and 12-month diagnoses and (b) fit the data better than a structure based on the traditional *DSM* classification, in which the anxiety disorders marked one factor, and depression and dysthymia defined the other. Vollebergh et al. (2001) obtained very similar results in confirmatory factor analyses of the two waves of the NEMESIS data.

B. J. Cox, Clara, and Enns (2002) and Watson (2005) subsequently expanded this structural scheme by establishing that PTSD also loaded on the Anxious-Misery factor in the NCS data. In their analyses of the Australian NSMHWB, Slade and Watson (2006) further extended this evidence by modeling an expanded set of anxiety disorders. They demonstrated that major depression, dysthymic disorder, GAD, and PTSD all defined the Anxious-Misery factor, whereas panic disorder, agoraphobia, social phobia, and OCD were markers of Fear.

This same basic structure has been replicated in several other samples. Most notably, Kendler, Prescott, Myers, and Neale (2003) used twin data to examine major sources of genetic risk for common psychiatric disorders. They concluded that "the structure of these genetic risk factors bears a conspicuous resemblance to the phenotypic structure of adult psychiatric disorders proposed by Krueger et al. and Vollebergh et al." (p. 935). These results are congruent with a broader range of evidence establishing the close similarity between phenotypic and genotypic structures within this domain (see Hettema, Neale, Myers, Prescott, & Kendler, 2006; Mineka et al., 1998; Watson, 2005). The broadband Internalizing-Externalizing structure also has been shown to be invariant between sexes (Eaton et al., 2012; Kramer, Krueger, & Hicks, 2007).

Watson's (2005) Model of the Emotional Disorders

Watson (2005; see also L. A. Clark & Watson, 2006) used this structural evidence to propose a quantitative reorganization of the *DSM-IV* mood and anxiety disorders. This new structural scheme begins by positing an emotional disorders superclass that subsumes all of the *DSM-IV* mood and anxiety disorders, with the possible exception of OCD. This overarching superclass can be decomposed into three correlated subclasses. The first subclass consists of disorders that consistently define the Anxious-Misery factor in structural analyses; it includes major depression, dysthymic disorder, GAD, and PTSD. Watson (2005) labeled these syndromes the *distress disorders* to emphasize that they all involve the experience of pervasive subjective distress and all contain a large component of nonspecific Negative Affect.

The second subclass consists of disorders that consistently define the Fear factor in the structural analyses. This includes panic disorder, agoraphobia, social phobia, and specific phobia. Watson (2005) labeled this group the *fear disorders*.

Finally, Watson (2005) tentatively suggested that the bipolar disorders could constitute a third diagnostic subclass. He noted, however, that structural investigations of these disorders had been hampered by two key problems—low base rates and hierarchical exclusion rules—that we discuss in detail later.

Broader Structural Analyses

Several subsequent studies have attempted to broaden the scope and comprehensiveness of this structural model by clarifying the placement of other types of disorders. For example, in a large ($N = 1{,}434$) sample of female adolescent twins, Forbush et al. (2010) compared the fit of four different models that tested the placement of eating disorders within this Internalizing-Externalizing framework. In these alternative models, eating disorders (a) defined their own separate diagnostic class, (b) represented an additional subclass within Internalizing, (c) formed a subtype within Externalizing, and (d) were allowed to cross-load on both Internalizing and Externalizing. Confirmatory factor analyses indicated that eating disorders formed an additional subclass within Internalizing in the best-fitting model.

Kotov et al. (2011) examined a greatly expanded set of 25 disorders in analyses based on the responses of 2,900 patients, who were evaluated as part of the Rhode Island Methods to Improve Diagnostic and Assessment Services (MIDAS) project. In addition to the emotional disorders, the analyzed variables included thought disorder, eating disorder, various somatoform disorders (e.g., hypochondriasis), substance use disorders (alcohol and drug use), and the Axis II personality disorders (e.g., antisocial personality disorder, borderline personality disorder, schizotypal personality disorder). The best-fitting model consisted of five correlated factors: Internalizing (defined by major depression, various anxiety disorders, and eating disorder), Externalizing (marked by alcohol and drug use, and by antisocial personality disorder), Thought Disorder (defined primarily by psychosis, mania, schizotypal personality disorder, and schizoid personality disorder), Somatoform Disorders (marked by hypochondriasis, undifferentiated somatoform disorder, and pain disorder), and Antagonism (key indicators included narcissistic, histrionic, borderline, and antisocial personality disorders).

Forbush and Watson (2013) also analyzed an expanded set of *DSM-IV* diagnoses that included personality disorders, eating disorders, bipolar disorders, and impulse control disorders, using data from the Collaborative Psychiatric Epidemiological Surveys ($N = 16{,}233$). The best-fitting model yielded an Externalizing factor that was marked by antisocial personality disorder, conduct disorder, attention-deficit/hyperactivity disorder, drug use, alcohol use, intermittent explosive disorder, and pathological gambling. In addition, it contained a higher order Internalizing factor that included five diagnostic subclasses: Distress (major depression, dysthymic disorder, GAD, PTSD), Fear (agoraphobia, social phobia, panic disorder, specific phobia), Eating Pathology (bulimia nervosa, binge eating disorder, anorexia nervosa), Dysphoria (pathological introversion, rigidity, borderline features), and Bipolar (bipolar I disorder, bipolar II disorder).

METHODOLOGICAL PROBLEMS IN DISORDER-BASED ANALYSES

Overview

Diagnosis-based analyses have played an important role in clarifying the nature of the relations among *DSM* and *ICD* disorders. In particular, they have highlighted a basic distinction between internalizing and externalizing forms of psychopathology. However, one faces several daunting problems when conducting analyses based on *DSM* diagnoses. We discuss four general problems that hamper disorder-based analyses and complicate their interpretation (for additional discussion of these and other problems, see Brown et al., 2001; Watson, 2005, 2009).

Low Base Rates

Many *DSM* disorders show very low base rates in nonclinical samples—and even in some patient samples. These low prevalence rates can render statistical analyses problematic or impossible. Among other things, extremely low base rates will attenuate the magnitude of observed correlations with other variables. According to *DSM-IV*, for example, bipolar I and bipolar II have estimated lifetime prevalence rates of only 0.4%–1.6% and 0.5%, respectively, in community samples (American Psychiatric Association, 2000); Merikangas et al. (2007) report very similar lifetime rates of 1.0% and 1.1%, respectively, in the NCS-R data. In a related vein, Forbush and Watson (2013) reported that in their very large (N= 16,233) nationally representative sample, only 31 individuals (0.19%) met full diagnostic criteria for anorexia nervosa, and only 34 participants (0.21%) could be diagnosed with pathological gambling.

Researchers have dealt with these low base rates in a number of different ways. The most common strategy is simply to exclude these low base rate disorders from structural analyses. Within the emotional disorders, for instance, the bipolar disorders were excluded from structural analyses of both the NCS (Krueger, 1999) and NEMESIS (Vollebergh et al., 2001) data because of their very low base rate in the general population. Similarly, although OCD symptomatology is quite common in the general population (see Watson, Wu, & Cutshall, 2004), the full syndrome shows a low prevalence rate and often is excluded from structural analyses (e.g., Vollebergh et al., 2001).

Another approach has been to relax certain diagnostic criteria and, therefore, to include subsyndromal cases in the analyses. For example, Forbush and Watson (2013) diagnosed subthreshold anorexia nervosa if an individual met all *DSM* criteria with the exception of amenorrhea, and scored subsyndromal pathological gambling as present if a respondent had any clinically significant gambling symptoms. Similarly, due to low base rates, Kotov et al. (2011) expanded personality disorder diagnoses to include subthreshold cases; specifically, they relaxed diagnostic rules to require one criterion fewer than specified in *DSM-IV.*

A third strategy has been to collapse conceptually related disorders into a single broad category. For instance, because of low base rates, Forbush et al. (2010) combined bulimia nervosa and binge eating disorder into a broader "bulimic syndromes" variable, and created composite variables reflecting both drug abuse/dependence and alcohol abuse/dependence.

The use of these different strategies for handling low base rate disorders creates two further problems in understanding and interpreting the results of these studies. First, it means that different sets of indicators have been included in these analyses, which can be expected to produce a certain amount of structural instability across studies. Second, as the cited examples demonstrate, some disorders have been assessed differently across studies, which can lead to them being classified somewhat inconsistently in these analyses.

Hierarchical Exclusion Rules

Hierarchical exclusion rules (e.g., criteria stipulating that certain disorders should not be diagnosed if they occur only during the course of a coexisting disorder; see Brown & Barlow, 1992; L. A. Clark et al., 1995) have been an important and longstanding problem in the emotional disorders. For example, *DSM-III* (American Psychiatric Association, 1980) included an extensive set of exclusionary criteria that had the general effect of making it difficult to diagnose anxiety disorders in the presence of clinically significant depression (Mineka et al., 1998). Many of these exclusion rules subsequently were dropped in *DSM-III-R* and *DSM-IV*, but some of them remain in modified form currently.

Hierarchical exclusion rules create two key problems for diagnosis-based analyses. First, if they are strictly applied, they make it impossible for certain disorders to co-occur in the same individual, thereby making it impossible to include both of them in meaningful structural analyses. For instance, several editions of the *DSM* included hierarchical exclusion rules that—if strictly applied—precluded the simultaneous diagnosis of most unipolar and bipolar mood disorders. Indeed, the *DSM-IV* text revision explicitly stated: "A history of a Manic, Mixed, or Hypomanic Episode precludes the diagnosis of Major Depressive Disorder" (APA, 2000, p. 373).

Second, paralleling the situation discussed earlier with regard to low base rates, researchers have dealt with these exclusion rules inconsistently across studies, which can have important effects on the reported results. One strategy has been to relax certain rules. For example, Forbush and Watson (2013) noted: "Although a diagnosis of bipolar II disorder requires that an individual has never had a manic episode, we did not apply this hierarchical exclusion rule to allow for the possibility that bipolar disorders might form their own latent class of disorder"

(p. 3). Similarly, Kotov et al. (2011) eliminated the exclusion rules for GAD in their analyses.

A second strategy has been to create modified diagnostic variables that bypass these exclusion rules. For instance, Kotov et al. (2011) "examined mood episodes (major depressive and manic) rather than mood disorders, as these diagnoses contain exclusion rules" (p. 1005). Similarly, Kotov et al. (2011) created a single psychotic symptoms variable—rather than using formal *DSM* diagnoses—"because individual psychotic disorders incorporate complex hierarchical rules" (p. 1005).

A third—and, we suspect, very common—approach is simply to ignore these exclusion rules. Our own research provides an extreme example that illustrates both the nature and the potential magnitude of this problem. As shown in Table 1.1, the diagnosticians in these four large epidemiological studies generated a very strong level of comorbidity between major depression and dysthymic disorder (weighted mean, $r=.74$). It should be noted, moreover, that this pattern actually was quite consistent across the individual samples: the tetrachoric correlations ranged from .69 in the NCS to .88 in the NCS-R data. In contrast, we reported very different results in a sample of 575 psychiatric patients (Watson, O'Hara, Chmielewski et al., 2008). We obtained *DSM-IV* diagnoses using the Structured Clinical Interview for *DSM-IV* (SCID-IV; First et al., 1997). We assessed interrater reliability using audiotaped interviews and found strong diagnostic agreement for both major depression ($\kappa=.95$) and dysthymic disorder ($\kappa=.80$). Nevertheless, we actually obtained a moderate negative association (tetrachoric $r = -.42$) between major depression and dysthymic disorder. Why this difference? Our interviewers followed the *DSM-IV* exclusion rules very strictly, such that they only diagnosed dysthymic disorder when they could identify a minimum 2-year period of dysphoria that clearly preceded the first onset of a major depressive episode. We strongly suspect that the diagnosticians in the epidemiological studies handled this problem quite differently.

Diagnostic Unreliability

Disorder-based analyses largely are dependent on dichotomous indicators (i.e., the presence versus absence of *DSM* or *ICD* diagnoses). Extensive evidence has established that continuous measures are more reliable and valid than dichotomous variables (Brown & Barlow, 2005; Watson, 2003a; Widiger & Clark, 2000), particularly when the underlying distribution is continuous, rather than categorical (Cohen, 1983). Markon, Chmielewski, and Miller (2011) recently quantified the magnitude of the gains associated with the use of continuous measures of psychopathology. They conducted two meta-analyses involving 58 studies and a total of 59,575 participants. Overall, their findings indicated that the use of continuous measures was associated with a 15% increase in reliability and 37% increase in validity versus discrete measures of psychopathology. They noted, moreover, that "this increase occurs across all types of samples and forms of psychopathology, with little evidence for exceptions" (p. 856). Not surprisingly, therefore, they concluded by stating: "Future research and theory are likely to benefit from increased use of continuous measures of psychopathology" (p. 874).

In a related vein, there is growing evidence that the interrater reliability of common *DSM* diagnoses is unimpressive (see, for example, Chmielewski, Clark, Bagby, & Watson, 2015; Kendler, Karkowski, & Prescott, 1999; Kraemer, Kupfer, Clarke, Narrow, & Regier, 2012; Spitzer, Williams, & Endicott, 2012). In discussing this issue, it must be emphasized that the estimated reliability of *DSM* diagnoses is heavily dependent on the method that is used to assess it (Chmielewski et al., 2015). For example, one widely used approach is to audiotape or videotape the clinical interviews, which then are rated independently by a second diagnostician. Zimmerman (1994) notes that there is only a single source of unreliability in an audiotape analysis, namely, rater variance in the interpretation of diagnostic criteria. Moreover, the audiotape approach is widely used with semistructured interviews—such as the SCID-IV—that employ diagnostic skip outs: Once it is clear that a respondent does not meet full *DSM* criteria for a disorder, the interviewer moves on to a new category without asking further questions. The use of skip outs produces a biased overestimate of interrater reliability; that is, a second diagnostician cannot possibly diagnose a disorder if the original interviewer failed to ask necessary questions because he or she concluded that the respondent did not meet full *DSM* criteria.

The retest method provides a more conservative test of diagnostic reliability (Chmielewski et al., 2015). Here, two different diagnosticians interview each individual independently on two different occasions. There are three important sources of error in a test-retest analysis (Zimmerman, 1994; see also Kraemer, Kupfer, Clarke, Narrow, & Regier, 2012): rater variance in the interpretation of the diagnostic criteria, rater variance in the elicitation of information from the subject of the interview, and subject variance across interviews (this last source of inconsistency can be minimized by using a very short retest interval; see Chmielewski & Watson, 2009; Watson, 2004). Not surprisingly, standard *DSM* diagnoses typically show much poorer interrater reliability using the retest method (Chmielewski et al., 2015; D. L. Foley, Neale, & Kendler, 1998; Kendler, Karkowski, & Prescott, 1999; Kendler, Neale, Kessler, Heath, & Eaves, 1993; Williams et al., 1992; Zimmerman, 1994). In fact, Kendler and colleagues have shown that lifetime diagnoses of many common *DSM* disorders (including major depression and the phobias) are only moderately reliable and contain a substantial amount of measurement error, particularly in epidemiological samples (D. L. Foley et al., 1998; Kendler et al., 1993, 1999).

This problem clearly has not been solved in *DSM-5* (see Chmielewski et al. 2015, for a discussion). Regier et al. (2013) recently presented interrater reliability data from the *DSM-5* Field Trials conducted in the United States and Canada. They reported kappas for 15 adult *DSM-5* diagnoses based on the retest method. Overall, they concluded that three diagnoses had interrater reliabilities in the *very good* range ($\kappa = .60–.79$); seven were in the *good* range ($\kappa = .40-.59$), four were in the *questionable* range ($\kappa = .20–.39$), and one was judged to be *unacceptable* ($\kappa = -.004$). For our purposes, it is particularly noteworthy that the results for emotional disorder diagnoses were quite mixed, but generally unimpressive: PTSD ($\kappa = .67$), bipolar I disorder ($\kappa = .56$), major depression ($\kappa = .28$), GAD ($\kappa = .20$), and mixed anxiety-depressive disorder ($\kappa = -.004$). These results raise serious concerns about the reliability of *DSM* emotional disorder diagnoses.

Diagnostic Heterogeneity

Finally, diagnosis-based analyses fail to capture the marked heterogeneity of many *DSM* disorders (Watson, 2005, 2009). As noted earlier, structural analyses consistently have identified multiple symptom dimensions within both OCD (e.g., Leckman et al., 2010; Mataix-Cols, Rosario-Campos, & Leckman, 2005; Watson, 2009) and PTSD (e.g., Gootzeit & Markon, 2011; Watson, 2009; Yufik & Simms, 2010). Moreover, our own work has established the existence of multiple symptom dimensions within depression (Watson, 2009; Watson et al., 2007; Watson & Stasik, 2014). As we show in subsequent chapters, these symptom dimensions can be quite distinctive and correlate rather differently with other variables. Consequently, symptom-based analyses provide a more precise and nuanced view of psychopathology.

OUR APPROACH: MODELING SYMPTOMS WITHIN DISORDERS

The approach we take in this book represents a synthesis of the lessons learned from these earlier models. In essence, our approach involves examining the specific symptom dimensions that make up the major syndromes within the emotional disorders (e.g., specific symptoms of PTSD). Similar to the integrative hierarchical model, it uses the *DSM* emotional disorders—in particular, the *DSM-IV* mood and anxiety disorders—as its basic organizing framework. This explicit link to the *DSM* eliminates one of the major problems in the tripartite model by capturing the full range of content—as comprehensively as possible—subsumed by the emotional disorders. Moreover, by modeling replicable symptom dimensions that have emerged consistently in structural analyses, this approach bypasses problems associated with diagnostic heterogeneity, as well as other limitations of disorder-based analyses. We describe the development of this symptom-based scheme in Chapter 2.

2

Development of the IDAS and IDAS-II

Over the past decade, we have worked to develop a comprehensive, symptom-based approach to modeling the emotional disorders. This work is centered on the original Inventory of Depression and Anxiety Symptoms (IDAS; Watson et al., 2007) and its expanded second version (IDAS-II; Watson et al., 2012). The original impetus for this research was to create a new, multidimensional measure of depression symptoms that addressed key limitations in traditional self-report scales, such as the Center for Epidemiological Studies Depression Scale (CES-D; Radloff, 1977), the original Beck Depression Inventory (BDI), and the revised second edition of the BDI (the BDI-II; Beck, Steer, & Brown, 1996). These traditional measures have been a mainstay of clinical research for more than 50 years (for reviews, see Joiner, Walker, Pettit, Perez, & Cukrowicz, 2005; Nezu, Nezu, McClure, & Zwick, 2002). Moreover, they have many strong psychometric properties, including excellent internal consistency and impressive convergence with clinical ratings of depression (see L. A. Clark & Watson, 1991; Watson et al., 2007; Watson, O'Hara, Chmielewski, et al., 2008). Nevertheless, several factors limit the usefulness of these traditional measures; we discuss these limitations in the following section.

LIMITATIONS OF TRADITIONAL DEPRESSION SCALES

Poor Discriminant Validity

As was discussed in Chapter 1, older self-report measures of depression tend to show poor discriminant validity vis-à-vis indicators of anxiety. In an extensive review of this literature, L. A. Clark and Watson (1991) reported overall mean correlations between self-reported depression and anxiety ranging from .62 to .70 across different types of instruments and samples. Furthermore, as was noted in Chapter 1, this finding is quite robust and has been observed in children and adolescents (e.g., Brady & Kendall, 1992), college students (e.g., Gotlib, 1984; Watson et al., 1995), community adults (e.g., Watson et al., 1995), and psychiatric patients (e.g., L. A. Clark & Watson, 1991; Steer et al., 1995). To take one specific example, the BDI and BAI are strongly interrelated in student (e.g., Nitschke, Heller, Imig, McDonald, & Miller, 2001; Watson et al., 1995), adult (e.g., Manne et al., 2001; Watson et al., 1995), and patient samples (e.g., Hewitt & Norton, 1993; Steer et al., 1995).

Content Validity

Questionable or Inappropriate Content

Several popular depression measures have been criticized on content grounds. Three content-based concerns are particularly important. First, many instruments contain non-depression-related content. Of particular concern, Gotlib and Cane (1989) documented that several common self-report measures—including the BDI and the CES-D—contain items tapping various types of anxiety; the inclusion of this anxiety-related content obviously contributes to the discriminant validity problems noted earlier. A related issue is that many measures contain content that is not directly related to depression as it is defined in *DSM-IV* and *DSM-5*. For instance, Osman, Kopper, Barrios, Gutierrez, and Bagge (2004) had expert raters evaluate the relevance of individual BDI-II items to the *DSM-IV* symptom criteria for major depression. Their results established that some BDI-II items (e.g., past failure, punishment feelings, loss of interest in sex) do not correspond directly to any of these *DSM-IV* symptoms.

Lack of Comprehensiveness

Second, many instruments have been criticized because their content is not sufficiently comprehensive; that is, they do not contain items tapping all nine *DSM-IV/DSM-5* symptom criteria for major depression (see Dozois, Dobson, & Ahnberg, 1998; Nezu et al., 2002; Penley, Wiebe, & Nwosu, 2003). The CES-D, for example, does not assess suicidal ideation (Criterion 9), and it does not tap content related to either appetite gain (a component of Criterion 3) or hypersomnia (part of Criterion 4). Similarly, Moran and Lambert (1983) concluded that the original BDI measured only six of the *DSM-III* symptom criteria adequately; two additional criteria (appetite and sleep) were assessed partially, and one symptom (Criterion 5: psychomotor disturbance) was not assessed at all. This criticism helped to stimulate the development of the BDI-II, which now contains content related to all of the current *DSM-IV/DSM-5* criteria (see Dozois et al., 1998; Nezu et al., 2002).

Sampling Concerns

The third issue concerns the sampling or representativeness of the assessed content. That is, many instruments contain multiple items assessing certain types of content, but only single indicators to represent other symptoms. For example, the BDI-II contains several items tapping feelings of worthlessness and guilt

(Criterion 7), and two items apiece assessing fatigue and loss of energy (Criterion 6) and cognitive problems (Criterion 8); however, it includes only single items related to appetite disturbance, sleep disturbance, and suicidal ideation. Similarly, the CES-D contains numerous items assessing depressed mood (Criterion 1) and two items apiece reflecting fatigue/loss of energy and interpersonal concerns; however, it includes only single items tapping appetite disturbance, sleep disturbance, and cognitive problems. These sampling issues are important, in part, because they help to explain some of the structural evidence we discuss subsequently. Most notably, the inclusion of multiple items tapping similar content encourages the identification of a corresponding content-based factor; for instance, the presence of two interpersonal items helps to explain why an interpersonal factor frequently is found in analyses of the CES-D. Conversely, content-based factors cannot be identified when only a single relevant marker is included in the item pool (this is a manifestation of the familiar "garbage in garbage out"—or GIGO—problem in factor analysis).

Absence of Well-Defined Subscales

A final limitation is that most traditional measures originally were created to yield a single, overall index of symptom severity (although in some cases, the test developer subsequently has created subscales from an already-existing item pool; see, for example, Radloff, 1977; Reynolds, 2002). It must be emphasized that the use of overall scores is not inherently problematic. Indeed, as was noted earlier, most depression scales display impressive internal consistency, which indicates that these symptoms are characterized by a strong general factor (a point we return to subsequently).

Nevertheless, several researchers have expressed the concern that this focus on overall scores fails to acknowledge the heterogeneous and multidimensional nature of depressive symptoms, and that it hampers the identification of meaningful subtypes. Bedi, Koopman, and Thompson (2001), for instance, argue that the use of an overall index "may lead to a loss of information about the distinct dimensions of depression encased within the total score" (p. 307). In a related vein, Ingram and Siegle (2002) advocate a symptom profile approach that "targets the specific symptoms, or clusters of symptoms, that are considered important, rather than grouping all 'depressed' people together because they have met some threshold of depressive symptoms regardless of the composition of the symptoms" (p. 96).

In other words, meaningful symptom dimensions can be identified within depression. It therefore makes sense—both clinically and scientifically—to assess these specific dimensions separately. This, in turn, has stimulated the emergence of a very large literature on the underlying structure of depression symptoms. We turn now to a brief review of these studies, focusing on analyses of the BDI/BDI-II and CES-D.

THE STRUCTURE OF DEPRESSION SYMPTOMS

BDI/BDI-II

BDI

Beck, Steer, and Garbin (1988) summarized findings from 13 studies that factor analyzed the items included in the original BDI. The extracted structures varied widely, with solutions ranging from one to seven factors. Beck et al. (1988) concluded that the evidence pointed toward a structure defined by three highly correlated factors, which they labeled Negative Attitudes toward the Self, Performance Impairment, and Somatic Disturbance. Beck and Steer (1993) also concluded that a three-factor solution best characterized the item structure of the BDI.

BDI-II

The BDI-II item pool has been factor analyzed in more than two dozen studies, which attests to the continuing interest in this topic (for reviews of this evidence, see Brouwer, Meijer, & Zevalkink, 2013; McPherson & Martin, 2010; Quilty, Zhang, & Bagby, 2010). However, the findings have been inconsistent and have failed to yield a clear, consensual structure. Some investigators have obtained three-factor structures that resemble those reported with the original BDI (e.g., Byrne, Stewart, & Lee, 2004), but other three-factor solutions have emerged as well (e.g., Manian, Schmidt, Bornstein, & Martinez, 2013; Seignourel, Green, & Schmitz, 2008). In addition, several different two-factor solutions have been reported in the literature. For instance, various investigators have found that the cognitive and affective items combine to form a single dimension, with the somatic/vegetative symptoms defining a separate factor (e.g., Bedi et al., 2001; Dozois et al., 1998; Osman, Barrios, Gutierrez, Williams, & Bailey, 2008; Osman et al., 2004). Alternatively, several studies have found that the somatic and affective items jointly define a "Noncognitive" or "Somatic-Affective" factor, with the cognitive items forming their own distinct dimension (e.g., Steer, Ball, Ranieri, & Beck, 1999; Steer, Rissmiller & Beck, 2000). Finally, some analyses have obtained a combined Cognitive-Somatic factor, with the affective items defining a separate dimension (e.g., Storch, Roberti, & Roth, 2004; VanVoorhis & Blumentritt, 2007).

CES-D

In the original article describing the development of the CES-D, Radloff (1977) conducted item-level factor analyses in three different samples. These analyses revealed consistent evidence of an underlying four-factor structure that included two large symptom dimensions (Depressed Affect and Somatic Disturbance), a Positive Affect factor that was defined by all four reverse-keyed items (e.g., "I was happy," "I enjoyed life"), and a small, two-item Interpersonal factor ("People were unfriendly," "I felt that people dislike me").

Many subsequent studies have tested the adequacy of this four-factor structure. The results have been quite mixed. Some analyses have supported Radloff's original structure (e.g., Golding & Anehensel, 1989; Hertzog, Van Alstine, Usala, Hultsch, & Dixon, 1990; Makambi, Williams, Taylor, Rosenberg, & Adams-Campbell, 2009; Olson, Presniak, & MacGregor, 2010). Other studies, however, have obtained inconsistent support, finding that the structure fits well in some groups, but not others (e.g., Crockett, Randall, Shen, Russell, & Driscoll, 2005; Posner, Stewart, Marín, & Pérez-Stable, 2001; for a meta-analytic review, see Kim, DeCoster, Huang, & Chiriboga, 2011). Finally, several investigators have reported alternative structures ranging from two to five factors (e.g., K. L. Foley, Reed, Mutran, & DeVellis, 2002; Leykin, Torres, Aguilera, & Munõz, 2011; Rivera-Medina, Caraballo, Rodríguez-Cordero, Bernal, & Dávila-Marrero, 2010; Thorson & Powell, 1993).

Overall Conclusions

Two broad conclusions can be drawn from this extensive literature. First, most investigators do find evidence of additional content dimensions beyond the general depression factor. This finding suggests that meaningful subfactors potentially can be identified within this domain. Second, analyses of the most frequently examined instruments have failed to identify consistent, replicable factor structures. As we have seen, analyses of the BDI and BDI-II have produced a variety of two-factor and three-factor solutions, whereas analyses of the CES-D items have yielded structures ranging from two to five factors.

Although these results may seem disappointing, they hardly are surprising in light of the sampling/representativeness issues we discussed earlier. Instruments such as the BDI-II and CES-D originally were created to be general measures of depression and were not explicitly constructed to yield meaningful content factors or subscales. Thus, they simply lack the range and sampling of item content necessary to produce replicable symptom dimensions. Put differently, structural analyses will be much more informative when they are based on item pools that were explicitly created to clarify the underlying structure of the domain, rather than on preexisting item pools constructed for other purposes. In this regard, we again emphasize that a specific symptom dimension cannot emerge in a structural analysis when only a single relevant marker has been included in the item pool.

BASIC ASSESSMENT STRATEGY FOR THE ORIGINAL IDAS

We created the original IDAS to complement these older measures and to address their limitations. Unlike instruments such as the BDI-II and CES-D, our explicit goal in developing the IDAS was to create specific symptom scales reflecting distinctive aspects of depression. We highlight three key aspects of our approach. First, because of the discriminant validity problems noted earlier, we included a broad range of anxiety-related symptoms in our item pool. This enabled us to examine the relations between symptoms of anxiety and depression, and to create specific scales with enhanced discriminant validity. It also led to the creation of three anxiety scales in the original IDAS; we subsequently expanded our coverage of anxiety symptoms substantially in the IDAS-II.

Second, in order to be sufficiently comprehensive, we included multiple items for each of the nine *DSM-IV* symptom criteria for a major depressive episode. Moreover, we were careful to include items reflecting different aspects of these criteria. Most notably, we wrote items reflecting (a) appetite loss *and* appetite gain, (b) insomnia *and* hypersomnia, and (c) psychomotor retardation *and* agitation.

Third, in creating this item pool, our basic strategy was to include multiple markers to define all of the symptom dimensions that potentially could emerge in our structural analyses. To ensure that sufficient markers were included for each potential dimension, we rationally organized the candidate items into *homogeneous item composites* (Hogan & Hogan, 1992), or HICs. For instance, our original item pool contained eight items reflecting fatigue and loss of energy (e.g., "I felt exhausted," "I did not have a lot of energy"). The creation of these HICs ensured that the corresponding symptom dimension had a reasonable chance to emerge in our subsequent structural analyses. For example, the inclusion of these fatigue/anergia items made it possible for a corresponding content factor to be identified in our data; in fact, this ultimately led to the creation of the IDAS Lassitude scale. Note, however, that the development of these HICs in no way forces a corresponding factor to emerge; indeed, as we will see, many of these rationally created HICs ultimately failed to define distinctive dimensions in our structural analyses.

DEVELOPMENT OF THE ORIGINAL IDAS

Phase 1

Goals

We developed the original IDAS in two phases (for a more detailed discussion, see Watson et al., 2007). The basic goal of Phase 1 was to evaluate the nature and quality of our initial item pool. For instance, we examined whether certain items were worded too strongly or too mildly. We also used the Phase 1 data to identify highly correlated items that provided redundant information; these unnecessary items were eliminated. Finally, we were interested in identifying potentially interesting symptom dimensions that might be underrepresented in our initial item pool; these analyses then served as the basis for the generation of new items to be used in Phase 2.

Method

The Phase 1 participants were 499 undergraduate students at the University of Iowa. They completed a symptom instrument consisting of 180 items; the participants indicated the extent to which they had experienced each symptom "during the past two weeks, including today" on a 5-point scale ranging from *not at all* to *extremely*.

Initial Measurement Model

As discussed earlier, we rationally organized the candidate items into 20 HICs to ensure proper content coverage (see Table 2.1 for a list of these HICs, plus sample items). Thirteen HICs (a total of 117 items) targeted symptoms that were broadly relevant to depression. Nine HICs (a total of 79 items) corresponded to the basic symptom criteria for major depression in *DSM-IV* (depressed mood, loss of interest or pleasure, appetite disturbance, sleep disturbance, psychomotor problems, fatigue/anergia, worthlessness and guilt, cognitive problems, suicidal ideation). The four remaining HICs tapped symptoms potentially relevant to the hopelessness subtype of depression (Abramson, Metalsky, & Alloy, 1989); the specific symptom features of *DSM-IV* melancholic depression; angry/irritable mood (which can be an alternative expression of depressed mood in children and adolescents; see *DSM-IV*, p. 327); and markers of high energy and positive affect (which have been shown to be specifically related to depression; see Mineka et al.,

Table 2.1 Homogeneous Item Composites (HICs) and Sample Items From the Original IDAS Item Pool

HIC/No. of Items	Sample Items
Depression HICs	
Depressed mood (8)	I felt sad; I was tearful; I felt alone.
Loss of interest (8)	Nothing seemed fun to me; I wasn't interested in doing very much.
Appetite disturbance (10)	My appetite was poor; I ate too much at times.
Sleep disturbance (10)	I had trouble falling asleep; I slept more than usual.
Psychomotor problems (9)	I felt fidgety, restless; I talked more slowly than usual.
Fatigue/anergia (8)	I felt exhausted; I lacked the energy to get things done.
Worthlessness/guilt (9)	I blamed myself for things; I felt like a failure.
Cognitive problems (9)	I had trouble concentrating; I was forgetful.
Suicidal ideation (8)	I hurt myself purposely; I thought about killing myself.
Hopelessness depression (8)	I felt helpless; I felt like giving up.
Melancholic depression (8)	I felt terrible in the morning; I felt like being by myself.
Angry/irritable mood (8)	I got annoyed easily; I felt like breaking things.
High energy/positive affect (14)	I felt cheerful; I felt optimistic; I was proud of myself.
Anxiety HICs	
Anxious mood (8)	I felt afraid; I felt uneasy; I was frightened.
Worry (7)	I worried a lot; I could not stop worrying about things.
Panic (10)	I felt faint; My heart was racing or pounding.
Agoraphobia (6)	I avoided crowded situations; I had trouble leaving my home.
Social anxiety (10)	I felt shy and timid around other people; I avoided certain social situations.
Obsessive-compulsive disorder symptoms (14)	I worried a lot about germs; I found myself checking things, even though I knew it wasn't necessary.
Traumatic intrusions (8)	I had memories of something bad that happened; I was reminded of something awful that happened to me.

1998). The other seven HICs (a total of 63 items) assessed various anxiety-related symptoms; the seven groups were anxious mood, worry, panic, agoraphobia, social anxiety, obsessive-compulsive symptoms, and traumatic intrusions related to posttraumatic stress disorder.

Results

As noted earlier, we were interested in identifying potentially important symptom dimensions that might be underrepresented in our initial item pool. We therefore conducted a series of factor analyses in this pool. Specifically, we subjected the 117 depression items and 63 anxiety items to separate principal factor analyses, using squared multiple correlations as the initial communality estimates; all factors were rotated using both varimax (which constrains them to be orthogonal) and promax (which allows them to be correlated) (for a discussion of the specific advantages associated with using each type of rotation, see Watson, 2012).

Analyses of the 117 depression items suggested the existence of seven meaningful factors. The first dimension—which we tentatively labeled Core Depression—was large and relatively broad, and was marked by items from several different HICs. In contrast, five other factors were specific in nature and essentially defined individual symptom criteria of depression; we tentatively labeled these dimensions Suicidality, Insomnia, Lassitude, Psychomotor Problems, and Appetite Problems. Items reflecting high energy and positive affect marked the final factor, which we labeled Well-Being.

Analyses of the 63 anxiety symptoms revealed five interpretable factors. Four of these dimensions—Panic, Social Anxiety, Obsessive-Compulsive Symptoms, and Traumatic Intrusions—clearly corresponded to our original HICs. The fifth factor ("Anxious Mood") was an amalgam of the anxious mood and worry HICs. Finally, the items comprising our agoraphobia HIC failed to define a distinct factor in these analyses; this dimension therefore was dropped from further consideration (although some of the items were retained because of their potential relevance to other factors, such as Social Anxiety).

As discussed earlier, we also conducted a series of analyses to identify extreme and redundant items. On the basis of these various analyses, we dropped 32 items and wrote 21 new ones, creating a revised item pool of 169 items. This revised pool was then used in Phase 2.

Phase 2

Method

We developed a final set of symptom scales in Phase 2. To ensure that we were identifying highly robust and replicable symptom dimensions, we developed our scales through separate principal factor analyses of the revised pool of 169 items in three large samples: 673 college students, 353 psychiatric patients, and 362 community-dwelling adults (for details regarding these samples, see Watson et al., 2007). As in Phase 1, we used both varimax and promax rotations to explicate the nature of the underlying symptom structure.

Basic Analytic Strategy

In selecting dimensions as targets for scale development, we were guided by three basic principles. First, our goal was to identify the maximum number of factors that were psychologically meaningful, and we were particularly interested in isolating content factors that reflected specific types of symptoms. Accordingly, we concentrated on solutions with relatively large numbers of factors. Second, we wanted to create scales that showed an acceptable level of discriminant validity; we eventually had to drop certain symptom dimensions that failed to emerge as reasonably distinct. Third, we only were interested in dimensions that were robust and generalizable across our three samples; consequently, our final scales reflect factors that emerged in all three data sets.

The 10 Specific Scales

Using this approach, we identified 10 specific content factors that represented distinct, well-defined symptom dimensions. It is noteworthy that seven of these dimensions—Suicidality, Insomnia, Lassitude, Well-Being, Panic, Social Anxiety, and Traumatic Intrusions—also emerged in our Phase 1 analyses. An eighth Phase 1 dimension—Appetite Problems—split into separate Appetite Loss and Appetite Gain factors in these data. The final dimension was Ill Temper (e.g., "I lost my temper and yelled at people"), which did not emerge as a distinct factor in Phase 1.

We created scales to assess these 10 dimensions. In selecting items for the final scales, we were guided by three basic considerations. First, we retained items that tended to be the purest factor markers (i.e., had high loadings on that dimension and very low loadings on all other factors) and, therefore, maximized the discriminant validity of that scale vis-à-vis the others. Second, we minimized redundancy as much as possible and retained maximally distinct and informative items. Third, in making the difficult final choices between items that had very similar psychometric properties, we selected those that optimized the characteristics of the scales in our psychiatric patient sample. On the basis of these considerations, we created eight-item measures of Well-Being and Panic; six-item measures of Suicidality, Lassitude, and Insomnia; five-item measures of Social Anxiety and Ill Temper; a four-item Traumatic Intrusions scale; and three-item measures of Appetite Loss and Appetite Gain.

Three of these scales (Panic, Social Anxiety, and Traumatic Intrusions) assess symptoms that traditionally are linked to anxiety, whereas five others (Suicidality, Insomnia, Lassitude, Appetite Loss, Appetite Gain) represent classic manifestations of depression. With regard to the latter, it is worth noting that the IDAS Suicidality scale essentially represents *DSM-IV/DSM-5* Criterion 9 for a major depressive episode; the Insomnia scale taps the corresponding portion of Criterion 4 (sleep disturbance); and Appetite Loss and Appetite Gain jointly define Criterion 3 (appetite disturbance). The Lassitude scale is more complex, containing content related to both fatigue/anergia (Criterion 6) and the hypersomnia portion of Criterion 4; it also includes an item reflecting circadian variation ("I felt much worse in the morning than later in the day") that originally was part of the HIC designed to tap the symptom features of melancholic depression (see Watson et al., 2007).

Creation of the Dysphoria Scale

In addition to these specific symptom dimensions, our analyses revealed a very large, nonspecific factor that was defined by the core affective/cognitive symptoms of both depression and anxiety. It is particularly noteworthy that items assessing five of the nine *DSM-IV/DSM-5* symptom criteria for a major depressive episode—Criterion 1 (depressed mood), Criterion 2 (anhedonia/loss of interest), Criterion 5 (psychomotor problems), Criterion 7 (worthlessness/guilt), and Criterion 8 (cognitive problems)—were highly interrelated and defined a single common factor. Items assessing anxious mood and worry also were strong markers of this dimension. Thus, these data demonstrate the existence of a broad factor that is strongly saturated with general distress/negative affectivity and that lies at the very core of the emotional disorders (see also Watson, 2005, 2009): It subsumes more than half of the *DSM-IV/DSM-5* symptom criteria for a major depressive episode, as well as the central features of generalized anxiety disorder (GAD).

We constructed a 10-item Dysphoria scale that captures the nature and scope of this diverse dimension. We selected single items to assess depressed mood, anhedonia, worry, worthlessness, and guilt. We also selected two markers apiece tapping psychomotor problems (one reflecting retardation, the other agitation) and cognitive problems. Finally, we included one item from the original hopelessness HIC ("I felt discouraged about things").

Creation of the General Depression Scale

The Dysphoria scale assesses the core emotional and cognitive symptoms of depression (and anxiety), and it obviously is broad and nonspecific in its content. Nevertheless, it is narrower in scope than most traditional measures of depression, such as the BDI-II and the CES-D. We therefore felt it was desirable to create an expanded measure that more closely resembles these traditional measures and that includes a comprehensive range of depression-related content. This led us to develop the 20-item General Depression scale. This scale includes all 10 Dysphoria items, as well as two items apiece from Suicidality, Lassitude, Insomnia, Appetite Loss, and Well-Being (these items are reverse-keyed). Consequently, the General Depression scale contains content related to all nine *DSM-IV/DSM-5* criteria for a major depressive episode.

DEVELOPMENT OF THE IDAS-II

Rationale for the IDAS-II

Based on an accumulation of reliability and validity data that we present later, it gradually became clear that the original IDAS measures a large number of distinctive symptom dimensions in a relatively efficient manner (a total of 64 items). These encouraging results further suggested that it would be desirable to expand the instrument in order to assess symptoms of the emotional disorders more comprehensively. This led to the creation of the expanded version of the IDAS, or

IDAS-II. Our basic goal in developing the IDAS-II was to create new scales assessing other important aspects of the anxiety disorders (e.g., obsessive-compulsive disorder [OCD], agoraphobia), as well as key symptoms of bipolar disorder.

Method

Scale development data were collected in two samples. Participants were 307 undergraduate students at the University of Iowa and 355 community-dwelling adults living in Eastern Iowa. They completed a 169-item symptom instrument, which included the final, 64-item version of the original IDAS, plus a 6-item measure of anxious mood (Watson et al., 2007). Following the logic used in the creation of the original IDAS, we wrote 99 new items that were organized into 12 rational HICs (see Table 2.2) assessing symptoms of posttraumatic stress disorder (PTSD) (two HICs: traumatic avoidance and numbing), OCD (three HICs: cleaning, checking/counting, and ordering/rituals), social phobia (two HICs: social interaction anxiety and performance/evaluation anxiety), specific phobia (three HICs: animal phobia, blood-injection phobia, and situational phobia), agoraphobia (one HIC), and mania (one HIC). The rationale for these 12 new target

Table 2.2 Homogeneous Item Composites (HICs) and Sample Items From the IDAS-II Item Pool

HIC/No. of Items	Sample Items
Traumatic avoidance (7)	I avoided situations that bring up bad memories; I tried not to think about bad things from my past.
Numbing (7)	I felt cut off from others; I felt emotionally numb.
Cleaning (9)	I washed my hands excessively; I avoided using public restrooms.
Checking/counting (8)	I checked things repeatedly; I felt compelled to count things.
Ordering/rituals (7)	I rearranged things so that they were in a certain order; I had little rituals or habits that took up a lot of my time.
Social interaction anxiety (6)	I felt nervous making small talk; I avoided social situations.
Performance/evaluation anxiety (6)	I was anxious about talking in public; I felt uncomfortable eating or drinking in front of other people.
Animal phobia (11)	I was afraid of spiders; I avoided handling slimy things.
Blood-injection phobia (4)	I avoided the sight of blood; I felt faint at the sight of blood.
Situational phobia (8)	I felt anxious in small spaces; I avoided bridges.
Agoraphobia (6)	I avoided crowded stores; I had trouble leaving my home.
Bipolar symptoms (20)	I had intense mood swings; I was elated for no special reason.

dimensions is discussed in detail in Watson et al. (2012); we also will discuss many of these target dimensions in subsequent chapters.

Basic Analytic Strategy

We followed the same basic analytic strategy that was used in the creation of the original IDAS. As before, we conducted a separate series of principal factor analyses in each sample, using both varimax and promax rotations. In selecting dimensions as targets for scale development, we again sought to identify the maximum number of factors (and scales) that were both (a) psychologically meaningful and (b) robust and generalizable; consequently, our final scales reflect factors that emerged clearly in both samples. Specifically, to be retained for scale development, a dimension had to have at least three consistent markers across both samples; a marker was defined as a variable that (a) loaded at least |.35| on the target factor and (b) had loadings below |.30| on all other factors.

Results

Preliminary Analyses

Preliminary analyses of the candidate items revealed two problems related to poor construct differentiation/discriminant validity. First, the numbing items were very strongly related to the existing Dysphoria scale and failed to define a distinct dimension in our structural analyses. For example, a scale created by summing the seven candidate numbing items correlated .84 and .83 with Dysphoria in the student and community samples, respectively. This dimension therefore was dropped from further consideration.

Second, we initially had hoped to create scales assessing two distinguishable dimensions within social phobia. However, the social interaction and performance/evaluation anxiety items were strongly correlated with both (a) each other and (b) the existing IDAS Social Anxiety scale. For instance, the summed social interaction candidate items correlated .79 and .84 with the performance items in the student and adult samples, respectively. Similarly, these summed scores had correlations with the existing Social Anxiety scale that ranged from .75 to .80 across the two samples. We therefore abandoned the idea of creating separate social interaction and performance anxiety scales.

Additional analyses, however, indicated that we could enhance the psychometric properties of the existing Social Anxiety scale by adding in one of the performance items ("I was anxious about talking in public"). We therefore added this item, thereby creating an expanded, six-item version of Social Anxiety in the IDAS-II.

Creation of the IDAS-II Anxiety Scales

Next, we conducted item-level principal factor analyses of the 80 remaining candidate symptoms; these analyses revealed eight clear, replicable content dimensions. Six of these factors tapped anxiety symptoms. Five factors closely resembled our rational HICs: Cleaning, Ordering, Checking, Traumatic Avoidance, and Animal Phobia. The sixth factor included items from both the agoraphobia and situational phobia HICs. This dimension makes good sense clinically; indeed, both the *DSM-IV* (Craske et al., 1994) and *DSM-5* (LeBeau et al., 2010; Wittchen, Gloster, Beesdo-Baum, Fava, & Craske, 2010) Anxiety Disorders Work Groups acknowledged the close connection between agoraphobia and the situational subtype of specific phobia. We labeled this hybrid dimension "Claustrophobia" to (a) reflect the core content of its strongest markers (e.g., "I felt anxious in small spaces") and (b) emphasize its significant links to both agoraphobia and situational phobia (for a discussion of how claustrophobia relates to these disorders, see Craske et al., 1994). Finally, the blood-injection items failed to define a replicable factor in these samples; consequently, they were not considered further.

We created scales to assess these six robust dimensions. In selecting items for the final scales, we again retained items that were (a) the purest factor markers (i.e., had high loadings on that dimension and very low loadings on all other factors) and (b) maximally distinct and informative (i.e., minimized redundancy with one another). On the basis of these considerations, we created a seven-item measure of Cleaning; five-item Ordering and Claustrophobia scales; a four-item measure of Traumatic Avoidance; and a three-item Checking scale. The final five-item Claustrophobia scale included three items from the original situational phobia HIC and two items from the agoraphobia HIC; the other scales drew all of their items from the corresponding HIC.

We also created a provisional nine-item Animal Phobia scale. Although this scale showed good internal consistency (coefficient alpha = .85 and .86 in the student and adult samples, respectively), it performed poorly in analyses of convergent and discriminant validity. It therefore was dropped from further consideration, leaving us with five new anxiety scales.

Creation of the IDAS-II Bipolar Scales

The bipolar items defined two replicable factors. The first dimension had 11 consistent markers; these robust markers reflected talkativeness/pressure of speech, flight of ideas, affective lability, and the negative sequelae of excessive goal-directed activity; we labeled this dimension *Mania*. The second factor had seven consistent markers representing elevated mood, heightened energy, and grandiosity/excessive self-esteem; we labeled this dimension *Euphoria*.

We subsequently conducted correlational and factor analyses examining these 18 remaining items in relation to the original IDAS scales. Two types of Mania items—namely, those reflecting (a) affective lability and (b) the negative sequelae of excessive goal-related activity—showed poor discriminant validity in relation to Dysphoria; we dropped these items, creating a reduced five-item Mania scale. Similar analyses revealed that two Euphoria markers showed poor discriminant validity vis-à-vis the IDAS Well-Being scale. They therefore were dropped, creating the final five-item version of Euphoria.

Thus, the expanded IDAS-II contains 99 items that are organized into 18 nonoverlapping scales, plus General Depression (which, as noted, contains items from several other scales). In the following sections, we examine the basic psychometric properties of these scales; we present additional validity evidence (including convergent, discriminant, criterion, and incremental validity) in subsequent chapters.

RELIABILITY EVIDENCE

Estimating the Reliability of Symptom Measures

We begin by examining two types of evidence—internal consistency and short-term temporal stability—that traditionally have been used to estimate the reliability of measures. Joiner et al. (2005), for example, state: "With regard to reliability, appropriate assessment devices display internal consistency (the extent to which each item measures the same construct) and short-term test-retest stability (the extent to which a measure yields the same score across repeated administrations)" (p. 269). Joiner et al. (2005) then go further and offer specific guidelines for evaluating the adequacy of depression symptom measures: "We recommend the following psychometric criteria as a minimum standard for selecting depression assessment devices: (a) internal consistency and short-term test-retest reliabilities ≥ .70" (p. 269).

These are reasonable guidelines for interpreting the properties of symptom measures. Moreover, Joiner et al. (2005) are correct in arguing that (a) internal consistency estimates (such as coefficient alpha) and (b) test-retest correlations provide valuable information about the construct validity of symptom scales. At the same time, however, it must be emphasized that neither type of evidence provides a clear, unambiguous estimate of *reliability*, which can be defined as the ratio of true score variance to total variance in a measure (see Watson, 2012).

In fact, it is well established that conventional indices of internal consistency—such as coefficient alpha—are best viewed as indicators of the consistency of measurement across various conditions, rather than reliability per se. Indeed, coefficient alpha can either overestimate or underestimate the true level of reliability under different assessment conditions (see Becker, 2000; Green, 2003; McCrae, Kurtz, Yamagata, & Terracciano, 2011; Osburn, 2000; Schmidt, Le & Ilies, 2003; Schmitt, 1996; Watson, 2012). Alpha will underestimate the true reliability of a measure that is heterogeneous and multidimensional (Cronbach, 1951; Osburn, 2000; Schmitt, 1996). This is because coefficient alpha was derived from classical reliability theory, which equates inconsistency in responding with measurement error. In many cases, however, inconsistency reflects the heterogeneity of item content, rather than error per se. Conversely, alpha will overestimate reliability when there are systematic errors of measurement (e.g., response biases, transient error). Unlike random errors, systematic measurement errors are significantly correlated across assessments, thereby producing consistent responding. Consequently, they are misclassified as "true score" variance in classical reliability theory.

Similarly, test-retest coefficients can either underestimate or overestimate reliability depending on the circumstances (Watson, 2012). In the context of symptom scales, retest correlations generally can be expected to *underestimate* the true reliability of a measure. This is because retest correlations only represent clear, unambiguous indices of reliability when it is reasonable to assume that there has been no actual change on the assessed variable, such that the underlying true score remains perfectly invariant. Cattell (1964a, 1964b; Cattell, Eber, & Tatsuoka, 1970) emphasized this point several decades ago, arguing for the importance of distinguishing between *dependability* and *stability*. Cattell defined dependability as "the correlation between two administrations of the same test *when the lapse of time is insufficient for people themselves to change* with respect to what is being measured" (Cattell et al., 1970, p. 30). In contrast, he defined stability as the correlation between two administrations of a test across a retest interval that is lengthy enough for true change to occur (Cattell et al., 1970, p. 31).

This distinction is crucial: It makes it quite clear that dependability correlations provide an unambiguous index of reliability, whereas stability coefficients do not. When applied to symptom measures, however, the problem is that true change rarely can be completely ruled out, even over very brief time intervals. Suppose, for example, that a respondent reports extremely elevated depressed mood at an initial assessment, but only moderate dysphoria at a second assessment 1 week later: Does this inconsistency in reporting reflect measurement error—or true change in the level of depression?

Internal Consistency Evidence

Original IDAS Scales (Now Subsumed Within the IDAS-II)

With these caveats in mind, we now examine the internal consistency of the IDAS-II scales. We will begin by considering evidence for the 12 original IDAS scales. The top portion of Table 2.3 presents coefficient alphas and average interitem correlations (AICs) for these scales in large aggregate samples of clinical patients (N = 1,914), community adults (N = 1,837), and college students (N = 4,055). Table 2.4 reports parallel data in high school students (N = 247), postpartum women (N = 1,070), and older adults (N = 214; M age = 73.5; range = 57–92 years).

Given their factor analytic origin, one would expect these scales to be internally consistent. The data reported in Tables 2.3 and 2.4 confirm this expectation. Overall, 71 of the 72 coefficients (98.6%) are ≥ .75, thereby easily exceeding the minimum criterion recommended by Joiner et al. (2005). The only real anomaly is that Suicidality had a low coefficient alpha (.55) in the older adult sample. This reduced value primarily is attributable to the very low levels of Suicidality—and, hence, the reduced variability of the item responses—in these participants (see Table 2.11).

Ideally, the AIC for a measure should be moderate, falling between .15 and .50 (L. A. Clark & Watson, 1995; Watson, 2012). Furthermore, given that most of the IDAS-II scales are specific in scope, one would expect their AICs to fall in the upper part of this range (i.e., from .35 to .50). With a few exceptions, eight

Table 2.3 Internal Consistencies (Coefficient Alphas) and Average Interitem Correlations (AICs) for the IDAS-II Scales in Clinical Patient, Community Adult, and College Student Samples

	Patients		**Adults**		**Students**	
IDAS-II Scale	α	AIC	α	AIC	α	AIC
Original IDAS Scales						
General Depression (20)	.91	.35	.92	.36	.90	.31
Dysphoria (10)	.90	.47	.90	.49	.89	.44
Well-Being (8)	.89	.50	.90	.52	.87	.45
Panic (8)	.84	.39	.84	.39	.83	.38
Lassitude (6)	.81	.42	.84	.48	.80	.40
Insomnia (6)	.87	.54	.85	.48	.82	.43
Suicidality (6)	.85	.49	.81	.41	.83	.45
Social Anxiety (5)[a]	.86	.54	.85	.54	.83	.49
Ill Temper (5)	.87	.58	.87	.57	.83	.49
Traumatic Intrusions (4)	.86	.60	.85	.58	.82	.53
Appetite Loss (3)	.86	.67	.85	.65	.84	.64
Appetite Gain (3)	.82	.60	.81	.58	.78	.54
IDAS-II Scales						
Cleaning (7)	.89	.54	.87	.49	.85	.46
Social Anxiety (6)	.86	.51	.86	.50	.85	.49
Claustrophobia (5)	.89	.62	.88	.59	.85	.53
Mania (5)	.86	.56	.82	.48	.82	.47
Ordering (5)	.85	.54	.80	.45	.79	.43
Euphoria (5)	.79	.43	.72	.34	.75	.38
Traumatic Avoidance (4)	.88	.65	.88	.65	.88	.65
Checking (3)	.90	.74	.87	.68	.85	.65

NOTE: For the original IDAS scales, $N = 1{,}914$ (Patients), 1,837 (Adults), 4,055 (Students). For the IDAS-II scales, $N = 908$ (Patients), 1,091 (Adults), 2,781 (Students). The number of items in each scale is shown in parentheses. AIC = average interitem correlation.

[a] Original five-item version of scale.

scales—General Depression (median AIC = .35), Panic (median AIC = .39), Lassitude (median AIC = .43), Suicidality (median AIC = .43), Well-Being (median AIC = .46), Dysphoria (median AIC = .47), Insomnia (median AIC = .51), and Social Anxiety (median AIC = .51)—have values broadly within this moderate range; overall, the AICs for these eight scales range from .20 to .60 across the six samples. These data establish that these scales tap a range of moderately related content; it is particularly noteworthy that we were able to write clusters of moderately correlated items to assess three of the specific symptoms of major depression (Lassitude, Suicidality, and Insomnia). The AICs for Ill Temper (median = .55) and Traumatic Intrusions (median = .55) also tend to be moderate in magnitude. In contrast, the values for Appetite Gain (median AIC = .58) and Appetite Loss (median AIC = .65) are higher, indicating that these scales subsume a narrower range of symptom content.

Table 2.4 Internal Consistencies (Coefficient Alphas) and Average Interitem Correlations (AICs) for the IDAS-II Scales in High School Student, Postpartum, and Older Adult Samples

	High School Students		Postpartum		Older Adults	
IDAS-II Scale	α	AIC	α	AIC	α	AIC
Original IDAS Scales						
General Depression (20)	.92	.36	.91	.35	.91	.35
Dysphoria (10)	.90	.47	.90	.47	.90	.49
Well-Being (8)	.86	.44	.88	.47	.86	.43
Panic (8)	.85	.42	.81	.35	.75	.28
Lassitude (6)	.80	.40	.82	.44	.84	.46
Insomnia (6)	.81	.42	.87	.53	.88	.54
Suicidality (6)	.90	.60	.75	.34	.55	.20
Social Anxiety (5)[a]	.84	.52	.82	.49	.76	.39
Ill Temper (5)	.85	.54	.88	.59	.76	.39
Traumatic Intrusions (4)	.82	.53	.84	.57	.79	.48
Appetite Loss (3)	.84	.63	.88	.70	.75	.50
Appetite Gain (3)	.77	.52	.87	.69	.80	.58

NOTE: $N=247$ (High School Students), 1,070 (Postpartum), 214 (Older Adults). The number of items in each scale is shown in parentheses. AIC = average interitem correlation.

[a] Original five-item version of scale.

IDAS-II Scales

The lower portion of Table 2.3 presents coefficient alphas and AICs for the scales that were revised or newly created in the IDAS-II; these values are based on subsets of the clinical patient ($N=908$), community adult ($N=1,091$), and college student ($N=2,781$) samples that completed the entire IDAS-II. All 24 alpha coefficients exceed Joiner et al.'s (2005) recommended minimum of .70; indeed, 20 coefficients (83.3%) are ≥ .80. Euphoria consistently shows the lowest alphas in these data, with values ranging from .72 (adults) to .79 (patients) across samples.

Five of the eight scales—Euphoria (median alpha = .38), Ordering (median alpha = .45), Mania (median alpha = .48), Cleaning (median alpha = .49), and Social Anxiety (median alpha = .50)—generally have AICs in the target range of .15 to .50, establishing that they are composed of moderately correlated items. In contrast, the AICs for Claustrophobia (median = .59), Traumatic Avoidance (median = .65), and Checking (median = .68) are higher, indicating that these scales are quite narrow and specific in scope.

Retest Evidence

Original IDAS Scales (Now Subsumed Within the IDAS-II)

We now consider both (a) short-term retest and (b) longer term temporal stability evidence for our symptom scales, beginning with data collected on the original IDAS scales. To date, we have obtained four sets of relevant evidence. First, we collected retest data from 250 psychiatric patients who were assessed at two sessions spaced approximately 1 week apart (these results are reported in Watson et al., 2007). The first column of Table 2.5 ("1 Week") presents the retest correlations from this sample. The 12 original IDAS scales all displayed strong short-term temporal stability in these data, with retest coefficients ranging from .72 (Ill Temper) to General Depression (.84); the mean correlation (after *r*-to-*z* transformation) was .80. Two additional aspects of these results are worth noting. First, these values all exceed the minimum benchmark of .70 for short-term test-retest coefficients recommended by Joiner et al. (2005). Second, the coefficients show little variability and are tightly clustered around the mean; indeed, with the exception of Ill Temper, the remaining correlations range narrowly from .75 to .84. Thus, different types of symptoms all show very similar levels of temporal stability in this patient sample.

Table 2.5 SHORT-TERM RETEST AND LONG-TERM STABILITY CORRELATIONS FOR THE IDAS-II SCALES

Scale	1 Week	2 Weeks	9 Months	4 Years
Original IDAS Scales				
General Depression	.84	.76	.67	.—
Social Anxiety[a]	.82	.74	.68	.51
Dysphoria	.83	.74	.66	.64
Lassitude	.78	.69	.62	.44
Well-Being	.78	.67	.55	.52
Suicidality	.77	.66	.62	.—
Traumatic Intrusions	.76	.64	.60	.35
Appetite Gain	.81	.64	.49	.45
Panic	.83	.63	.67	.34
Insomnia	.75	.61	.61	.51
Ill Temper	.72	.61	.63	.57
Appetite Loss	.82	.54	.48	.28
IDAS-II Scales				
Social Anxiety	.—	.76	.68	.—
Cleaning	.—	.69	.74	.—
Ordering	.—	.69	.66	.—
Traumatic Avoidance	.—	.68	.55	.—
Mania	.—	.68	.69	.—
Checking	.—	.67	.60	.—
Euphoria	.—	.65	.59	.—
Claustrophobia	.—	.59	.70	.—

NOTE: For the original IDAS scales, *N* = 250 (1 Week), 1,338 (2 Weeks; except for General Depression and Suicidality, where *N* = 646), 294 (9 Months), 227 (4 Years). For the IDAS-II scales, *N* = 841 (2 Weeks), 294 (9 Months).

[a] Original five-item version of scale.

Second, we report 2-week retest correlations on 1,338 college students; the results presented here are based on a combined sample representing the responses of 319 students from the University of Iowa, 327 students from the University of North Texas, and 692 students from the University of Notre Dame (General Depression and Suicidality were not assessed in the Notre Dame subsample, so $N = 646$ for these scales). Retest correlations from this sample are presented in the second column of Table 2.5 ("2 Weeks"). Clearly, these coefficients tend to be lower than those in the patient sample: Only three scales meet the minimum benchmark of .70, and the mean correlation is .67 (versus .80 in the patients). Even more striking is the increased variability of the correlations, which now range from a high of .76 (General Depression) to a low of only .54 (Appetite Loss).

Third, we present longer term stability correlations from 294 adult participants (age range = 18–77 years, mean age = 45.0 years; for more information regarding this sample, see Watson, Stasik, Ellickson-Larew, & Stanton, 2015a, 2015b). These participants were assessed on the complete IDAS-II on two different occasions roughly 9.5 months apart (mean interval = 286.6 days). Note that a substantial amount of true change can be expected in symptom levels over a time interval of this extended duration, such that these now clearly are stability—rather than dependability—correlations. Stability coefficients from this sample are displayed in the third column in Table 2.5 ("9 Months"). These retest correlations are somewhat lower than those in the 2-week data and again are quite variable; coefficients ranged from .48 to .68, with a mean value of .61. It is noteworthy that the three scales that had the highest coefficients in the 2-week data—General Depression, Social Anxiety, and Dysphoria (*r*s ranged from .74 to .76, mean $r = .75$)—also were strongly stable here, with retest correlations ranging from .66 to .68 (mean $r = .67$). At the other extreme, Appetite Loss had the lowest correlation both in this sample ($r = .48$) and in the 2-week data ($r = .54$).

Finally, we present very long-term stability data from 227 participants in the Iowa Longitudinal Personality Project (ILPP), a study of personality development in young adulthood (for more information about ILPP, see Vaidya, Gray, Haig, & Watson, 2002; Vaidya, Gray, Haig, Mroczek, & Watson, 2008; Watson et al., 2007). The ILPP participants initially were assessed in the fall of 1996 when they were enrolled in an introductory psychology course at the University of Iowa; at that time, their average age was approximately 18 years. The participants subsequently were retested in 1999 (Time 2), 2002 (Time 3), 2005 (Time 4), and 2009 (Time 5). The original IDAS scales[1] were included in the fourth and fifth waves of ILPP; thus, these data represent roughly 4-year stability correlations obtained when participants were between the ages of 27 and 31, on average.

These long-term stability correlations are displayed in the last column of Table 2.5 ("4 Years"). As would be expected, these coefficients are systematically lower than those observed over shorter time intervals; overall, the mean stability correlation is only .47 in this sample. It is noteworthy, however, that the pattern of the coefficients

1. General Depression and Suicidality were not assessed in the fifth wave of ILPP; consequently, retest data are not available for these scales.

is broadly consistent with that seen in other samples. For instance, Dysphoria ($r = .64$) and Social Anxiety ($r = .51$) again display relatively strong levels of stability in these data, whereas Appetite Loss again has the lowest retest coefficient ($r = .28$).

At the same time, however, it is clear that the stability correlations vary even more dramatically in this sample, ranging all the way from a high of .64 (Dysphoria) to a low only .28 (Appetite Loss). At the upper end, Dysphoria displays a level of stability that is broadly comparable to that exhibited by some of the personality scales that were included in ILPP. For example, trait versions of the general, higher order PANAS-X scales (Watson & Clark, 1999) had ILPP stability correlations of .67 (Negative Affect) and .61 (Positive Affect) across this same 4-year time interval. Thus, scores on Dysphoria essentially appear to be trait-like in character. At the other extreme, three scales (Appetite Loss, Panic, and Traumatic Intrusions) had correlations $\leq .35$ in this sample, thereby displaying a very modest level of long-term stability.

IDAS-II Scales

The lower portion of Table 2.5 presents stability data for the eight scales that were revised or newly created in the IDAS-II. The second column of Table 2.5 presents 2-week retest correlations; these results are based on a subset of the student participants who were administered the complete IDAS-II ($N = 841$; this includes 692 students from the University of Notre Dame and 149 students from the University of North Texas). Generally speaking, these results are quite similar to those presented earlier for the original IDAS scales. For example, the mean retest correlation for these scales (.68 after r-to-z transformation) is virtually identical to that reported earlier for the 12 original scales (.67). Although only one scale meets the minimum benchmark of .70 (Social Anxiety, $r = .76$), most of them come close. Finally, we again see substantial variability across scales, with stability coefficients ranging from a low of .59 (Claustrophobia) to a high of .76 (the revised six-item Social Anxiety scale).

As noted earlier, the adult participants were assessed on the complete IDAS-II; consequently, retest coefficients for the newly developed scales are displayed in the third column of Table 2.5. Once again, we see considerable variability across scales, with individual coefficients ranging from .55 (Traumatic Avoidance) to .74 (Cleaning). It is noteworthy, however, that these scales showed virtually the same average level of stability across this 9.5-month interval (mean $r = .66$) as they did in the 2-week data ($r = .67$). Furthermore, their average level of stability was somewhat higher than that observed for the 12 original scales (mean $r = .61$) in this same sample. On the basis of these results, it seems reasonable to conclude that these newly developed measures are at least as stable as the original IDAS scales.

RELATIONS WITH PERSONALITY

In discussing our stability data, we suggested that scores on the Dysphoria scale—which consistently produces strong retest coefficients across time intervals ranging from 1 week ($r = .83$) to 4 years ($r = .64$)—essentially are trait-like in character. This raises the related issue of whether certain IDAS-II scales have a stronger personality component than others. We examined this issue by correlating the IDAS-II scales with the general higher order traits—neuroticism, extraversion, openness to experience, agreeableness, and conscientiousness—included in the prominent five-factor or "Big Five" model of personality (Markon, Krueger & Watson, 2005, Watson, Clark, & Harkness, 1994). The Big Five traits were assessed using the 44-item version of the Big Five Inventory (BFI; John & Srivastava, 1999), which includes eight-item Neuroticism and Extraversion scales, nine-item measures of Agreeableness and Conscientiousness, and a ten-item Openness scale.

Correlations between the IDAS-II and BFI scales are presented in Table 2.6; the final column of the table displays multiple correlations that demonstrate the combined ability of the Big Five to predict each symptom. Data for the 12 original IDAS scales are based on a very large combined sample ($N = 3{,}714$), which included 635 clinical outpatients, 732 community adults, 1,863 college students, 271 young adults, and 213 older adults (*M* age = 73.5; range = 57–92 years). Results for the

Table 2.6 Correlations Between the BFI and IDAS-II Symptom Scales

Symptom Scale	Neur	Extra	Open	Agree	Con	Overall *R*
Original IDAS Scales						
Dysphoria	**.64**	−.30	−.09	−.29	**−.37**	**.67**
General Depression	**.57**	−.28	−.09	−.27	−.34	**.60**
Social Anxiety[a]	**.48**	**−.46**	−.13	−.26	−.30	**.58**
Well-Being	**−.46**	**.39**	.23	.27	.30	**.55**
Ill Temper	**.43**	−.10	−.04	**−.38**	−.24	**.50**
Lassitude	**.44**	−.22	−.07	−.21	−.34	**.49**
Panic	**.38**	−.14	−.04	−.25	−.25	**.42**
Traumatic Intrusions	**.39**	−.10	.02	−.21	−.20	**.41**
Suicidality	.33	−.18	−.04	−.25	−.26	**.39**
Insomnia	.31	−.10	−.03	−.18	−.18	.33
Appetite Loss	.28	−.11	−.01	−.12	−.15	.29
Appetite Gain	.25	−.08	−.07	−.16	−.21	.29
IDAS-II Scales						
Social Anxiety	**.48**	**−.47**	−.14	−.28	−.30	**.59**
Traumatic Avoidance	**.35**	−.11	−.03	−.21	−.21	**.37**
Euphoria	−.21	.27	.18	.03	.07	.33
Mania	.26	.01	.04	−.17	−.17	.32
Claustrophobia	.21	−.12	−.08	−.22	−.16	.27
Checking	.26	−.14	−.07	−.16	−.10	.27
Ordering	.25	−.10	−.06	−.16	−.01	.27
Cleaning	.19	−.08	−.04	−.21	−.13	.24

Note: For the original IDAS scales, $N = 3{,}714$. For the IDAS-II scales, $N = 1{,}616$. Correlations $\geq |.35|$ are in bold. BFI = Big Five Inventory. Neur = Neuroticism. Extra = Extraversion. Open = Openness. Agree = Agreeableness. Con = Conscientiousness.
[a] Original five-item version of scale.

new IDAS-II scales are based on a combined sample of 1,616 participants (732 adults, 884 students). In both of these combined samples, we eliminated mean-level differences in symptom and trait levels across populations (e.g., patients generally report higher levels of symptoms than community adults) by standardizing the scores on a within-population basis and then combining them to permit a single overall analysis.

As would be expected based on previous results (e.g., Watson et al., 2005; Watson & Naragon-Gainey, 2014), Neuroticism is the strongest and broadest predictor of symptoms of the emotional disorders: It had 10 correlations ≥ .35, and it demonstrated the strongest individual association in 17 of 20 cases (85%). Consistent with earlier findings, it correlated particularly strongly with Dysphoria ($r = .64$) and General Depression ($r = .57$). These data clearly demonstrate that Neuroticism is very strongly linked to the general distress/negative affectivity dimension that lies at the core of the emotional disorders. Extraversion correlated positively with Well-Being ($r = .39$) and negatively with Social Anxiety ($r = -.46$ and −.47 with the original five-item and revised six-item versions, respectively). Agreeableness and Conscientiousness correlated negatively with Ill Temper ($r = -.38$) and Dysphoria ($r = -.37$), respectively. Finally, replicating previous research, Openness consistently was weakly related to the symptom scores.

At the multivariate level, the final column of Table 2.6 establishes that certain IDAS-II scales have much stronger overall associations with personality than others. At one extreme, four scales—Dysphoria (.67), General Depression (.60), Social Anxiety (.58 and .59 for the original and revised versions, respectively), and Well-Being (.55)—had multiple *R*s ≥ .55. At the other extreme, six scales—Cleaning (.24), Ordering (.27), Checking (.27), Claustrophobia (.27), Appetite Loss (.29), and Appetite Gain (.29)—had *R*s < .30. Based on these results, it is clear that some IDAS-II scales have a much stronger personality component than others.

INTERNAL STRUCTURE OF THE IDAS-II

Scale Intercorrelations

We now consider the internal structure of the IDAS-II, beginning with an examination of the individual scale correlations. Table 2.7 presents the correlations between the 18 nonoverlapping scales in the final version of the IDAS-II (General Depression was omitted from these analyses because it shares items with several other scales, thereby artifactually raising its associations with them). For ease of presentation, we report these data on a standardized combined sample ($N = 4{,}780$) consisting of 908 patients, 1,091 community adults, and 2,781 college students. Once again, to eliminate mean-level differences across populations (i.e., patients vs. adults vs. students), we standardized the scale scores on a within-population basis and then combined them to permit a single overall analysis.

We discuss other aspects of these relations in subsequent chapters. For now, we will highlight three key findings. First, Dysphoria shows the strongest overall

Table 2.7 Correlations Among the IDAS-II Scales (Standardized Combined Sample)

Scale	**1**	**2**	**3**	**4**	**5**	**6**	**7**	**8**	**9**	**10**	**11**	**12**	**13**	**14**	**15**	**16**	**17**	**18**
1. Dysphoria	.—																	
2. Lassitude	**.69**	.—																
3. Suicidality	**.56**	.35	.—															
4. Insomnia	**.53**	.43	.34	.—														
5. Appetite Loss	.48	.36	.33	.43	.—													
6. Appetite Gain	.40	.42	.22	.25	−.04	.—												
7. Ill Temper	**.63**	.46	**.51**	.43	.33	.33	.—											
8. Well–Being	−.40	−.24	−.29	−.15	−.16	−.02	−.21	.—										
9. Mania	**.56**	.42	.37	.43	.36	.33	.46	.02	.—									
10. Euphoria	.08	.07	.11	.14	.14	.18	.18	**.51**	.45	.—								
11. Panic	**.66**	**.54**	**.55**	**.50**	.47	.34	**.58**	−.17	**.54**	.24	.—							
12. Social Anxiety	**.65**	.47	.45	.40	.33	.37	.45	−.23	.45	.15	**.55**	.—						
13. Claustrophobia	.39	.27	.40	.35	.29	.24	.37	−.12	.39	.21	**.51**	**.51**	.—					
14. Traumatic Intrusions	**.63**	.46	**.52**	.44	.38	.29	**.56**	−.20	.44	.14	**.59**	.49	.40	.—				
15. Traumatic Avoidance	**.54**	.39	.38	.38	.33	.26	.44	−.14	.44	.20	.47	.47	.41	**.63**	.—			
16. Checking	.43	.34	.28	.33	.27	.28	.35	.00	.49	.29	.43	.44	.40	.38	.40	.—		
17. Ordering	.40	.31	.29	.33	.27	.30	.35	.03	.49	.33	.41	.45	.41	.37	.39	**.64**	.—	
18. Cleaning	.33	.26	.31	.28	.24	.27	.33	−.00	.38	.27	.43	.40	**.50**	.35	.37	.49	**.52**	.—

NOTE: $N = 4{,}780$. Correlations of ≥ |.50| are in bold. Correlations ≥ |.03| are significant at $p < .05$.

associations with the other scales; Table 2.7 indicates that 9 of its 17 correlations (52.9%) are ≥ |.50|; in marked contrast, only 17 of the 136 correlations (12.5%) among the other scales reach this same magnitude. These data establish that this broad scale taps crucial content that lies at the core of the emotional disorders; moreover, they suggest that Dysphoria exists at a higher structural level than the others (i.e., it shows some properties of a general factor). Having said that, however, we also should note that several of the new IDAS-II scales (Euphoria, Cleaning, Claustrophobia, Ordering, Checking) are more weakly related to Dysphoria, with correlations ranging from only .08 to .43. These data indicate that these new scales are less strongly saturated with the nonspecific general distress variance that is assessed by Dysphoria.

Second, one would expect to see particularly strong correlations between (a) the two PTSD scales (Traumatic Intrusions and Traumatic Avoidance) and (b) the three OCD scales (Checking, Ordering, and Cleaning); Table 2.7 confirms this expectation. Nevertheless, the correlations between the two trauma scales ($r = .63$) and between Checking and Ordering ($r = .64$) are high enough to raise potential discriminant validity concerns that we address in Chapters 7 (PTSD symptoms) and 9 (OCD symptoms).

Third, Euphoria correlated weakly with the other scales, with two exceptions: It was substantially positively related to both Well-Being ($r = .51$) and Mania ($r = .45$). Indeed, a multiple regression analysis—with Mania and Well-Being as predictors and Euphoria as the criterion—yielded an R of .67, indicating that these scales jointly accounted for 45% of its variance. On the basis of these results, it seems reasonable to suggest that Euphoria taps a form of positive affect (which explains its strong link to Well-Being) that is specifically related to bipolar disorder (which explains its strong association with Mania).

These findings are unusual for two reasons. First, Well-Being and Mania are completely unrelated to one another ($r = .02$). Second, Euphoria has a substantial *positive* correlation with both scales, despite the fact that Mania and Well-Being tend to relate oppositely to other variables; for example, Dysphoria has a strong positive correlation (.56) with Mania, but a moderate negative correlation (–.40) with Well-Being. We explore the implications of this curious pattern subsequently.

Factor Structure

Original IDAS Scales

We now examine the factor structure of the instrument, beginning with analyses of the original IDAS scales (see also Watson et al., 2007). We conducted separate principal factor analyses of the scales (with squared multiple correlations in the diagonal) in each of six samples (patients, community adults, college students, postpartum women, high school students, and older adults). Our initial prediction was that these analyses would yield a two-factor structure, with some scales (e.g., Lassitude, Suicidality) defining a depression factor and others (e.g., Panic, Social Anxiety) marking an anxiety factor. This expectation was

Table 2.8 Loadings of the Original IDAS Scales on the First Principal Factor Across Six Samples

Scale	Patients	Community Adults	College Students	Postpartum	High School Students	Older Adults
Dysphoria	.90	.91	.89	.92	.92	.92
Panic	.74	.77	.78	.71	.76	.73
Lassitude	.63	.76	.71	.74	.69	.78
Traumatic Intrusions	.70	.72	.72	.67	.77	.67
Social Anxiety[a]	.70	.73	.71	.76	.68	.65
Ill Temper	.64	.73	.72	.72	.78	.57
Suicidality	.66	.67	.64	.53	.75	.65
Insomnia	.59	.60	.61	.66	.62	.58
Appetite Loss	.51	.51	.53	.40	.59	.59
Appetite Gain	.25	.43	.46	.40	.28	.37
Well-Being	−.37	−.46	−.33	−.52	−.46	−.50
Common Variance (%)	89.1	97.1	96.1	92.7	91.4	89.0

NOTE: N = 1,914 (Patients), 1,837 (Community Adults), 4,055 (College Students), 1,070 (Postpartum), 247 (High School Students), 214 (Older Adults). Loadings ≥ |.70| are in bold; loadings ≥ |.60| are in italics.

[a] Original five-item version of scale.

strongly disconfirmed, however. Instead, these analyses established the presence of a dominant general factor. In fact, the first factor accounted for 89.0% (older adults) to 97.1% (community adults) of the common variance across these six samples (see Table 2.8). Not surprisingly, no other interpretable dimension reliably emerged in these analyses.

Table 2.8 presents general factor loadings of the scales in each sample. Two aspects of these data are noteworthy. First, all 11 scales have moderate to strong loadings on this general dimension (although Appetite Gain has loadings of only .25 and .28 in the patients and high school students, respectively). Thus, it truly represents a general factor that underlies all of the scales comprising the original IDAS. Second, Dysphoria easily is the strongest marker of this general dimension. Indeed, it had loadings of .89 to .92 across the six samples. Because factor loadings represent correlations between observed variables and the underlying latent dimensions, these very high values indicate that Dysphoria essentially is equivalent to the general factor underlying the IDAS (i.e., it correlates approximately .90 with this factor). These data support our earlier suggestion that Dysphoria shows properties of a higher order factor.

IDAS-II

As noted earlier, several of the new IDAS-II scales have somewhat weaker associations with Dysphoria. This, in turn, suggests that the power of the general

Table 2.9 LOADINGS OF THE IDAS-II SCALES ON THE FIRST PRINCIPAL FACTOR ACROSS THREE SAMPLES

Scale	Patients	Community Adults	College Students
Dysphoria	**.83**	**.85**	**.84**
Panic	**.74**	**.77**	**.81**
Traumatic Intrusions	**.73**	**.71**	**.73**
Social Anxiety	**.70**	*.69*	**.73**
Mania	**.70**	*.67*	*.69*
Ill Temper	*.66*	*.66*	**.71**
Traumatic Avoidance	*.68*	*.66*	*.65*
Lassitude	.51	*.68*	*.68*
Suicidality	*.60*	*.60*	*.63*
Checking	*.62*	.58	*.63*
Ordering	*.61*	.57	*.63*
Insomnia	*.63*	.57	*.61*
Claustrophobia	*.67*	.53	*.61*
Cleaning	.55	.51	.59
Appetite Loss	.54	.47	.52
Appetite Gain	.23	.46	.51
Euphoria	.35	.22	.32
Well-Being	−.23	−.30	−.18
Common Variance (%)	72.6	76.3	79.1

NOTE: *N*=908 (Patients), 1,091 (Community Adults), 2,781 (Students). Loadings ≥ |.70| are in bold; loadings ≥ |.60| are in italics.

factor has been somewhat diminished in the revised and expanded instrument. We tested this possibility by subjecting the 18 nonoverlapping IDAS-II scales to separate principal factor analyses in each of three samples (patients, community adults, students). We began by again extracting a single general factor; findings from this one-factor solution are presented in Table 2.9. Dysphoria clearly remains the strongest marker of this general factor, with loadings ranging from .83 to .85 across samples. Consistent with expectation, however, the power of this general dimension has been substantially weakened by the inclusion of these additional scales: Whereas it accounted for 89.0% to 97.1% of the common variance in the original instrument, it now explains only 72.6% (patients) to 79.1% (college students) of the common variance in the IDAS-II.

This, in turn, suggests that additional dimensions potentially can be identified in the expanded instrument. We tested this idea using the standardized combined sample (*N*=4,780) that also was used to generate the correlational data shown in Table 2.7. These analyses revealed the presence of three interpretable factors, which were rotated to oblique simple structure using promax (with power=3); loadings from this solution are presented in Table 2.10. Factor I—which we labeled “Distress”—closely resembled the general factor of the original

Table 2.10 Promax Loadings of the IDAS-II Scales (Standardized Combined Sample)

IDAS-II Scale	Factor I	II	III
Dysphoria	**.87**	.03	−.14
Lassitude	**.71**	−.03	−.04
Panic	**.69**	.14	.06
Ill Temper	**.67**	.05	.01
Traumatic Intrusions	**.66**	.11	−.03
Appetite Loss	**.62**	−.10	.08
Insomnia	**.61**	.02	.06
Mania	**.54**	.17	**.33**
Suicidality	**.54**	.13	−.12
Traumatic Avoidance	**.46**	.25	.01
Cleaning	−.04	**.71**	−.00
Ordering	.00	**.71**	.09
Checking	.05	**.67**	.07
Claustrophobia	.13	**.58**	−.08
Social Anxiety	**.38**	**.44**	−.15
Appetite Gain	.23	.27	.03
Euphoria	.16	.10	**.70**
Well-Being	−.26	−.03	**.68**

NOTE: $N = 4{,}780$. Loadings ≥ |.30| are in bold. Factor correlations: .65 (I vs. II), −.05 (I vs. III), .26 (II vs. III).

instrument and again essentially was defined by Dysphoria (which had a loading of .87). Factor II ("Obsessions/Fear") was marked primarily by the three OCD scales (loadings ranged from .67 to .71); Claustrophobia (.58) and Social Anxiety (.44) also had salient loadings on this dimension. Factor III ("Positive Mood") was defined primarily by Euphoria (.70) and Well-Being (.68); Mania also had a significant secondary loading (.33) on this dimension. Thus, the inclusion of the new scales—which provided most of the markers for Factors II and III—has expanded the scope and complexity of the instrument considerably.

NORMS AND GROUP COMPARISONS

Descriptive Statistics

Next, we present basic descriptive statistics for the scales in various groups. Table 2.11 reports means and standard deviations for the original IDAS scales in six aggregated samples: patients, high school students, college students, community adults, postpartum women, and older adults (see also Watson et al., 2007). To facilitate comparisons across scales, the mean scores are presented as averages (i.e., as the average response per item), rather than sums.

Table 2.11 Descriptive Statistics for the Original IDAS Scales Across Different Types of Respondents

	Patients		High School Students		College Students		Community Adults		Postpartum		Older Adults	
Scale	*M*	*SD*	*M*	*SD*	*M*	*SD*	*M*	*SD*	*M*	*SD*	*M*	*SD*
General Depression	2.79	0.79	2.21	0.73	2.15	0.64	2.03	0.66	1.95	0.63	1.89	0.62
Dysphoria	2.84	0.94	2.13	0.84	2.09	0.78	1.97	0.79	1.79	0.74	1.77	0.74
Lassitude	2.74	0.97	2.47	0.90	2.38	0.85	2.11	0.86	2.07	0.82	1.85	0.78
Insomnia	2.63	1.10	2.11	0.88	2.07	0.84	1.95	0.85	2.04	0.93	2.04	0.89
Social Anxiety[a]	2.42	1.11	2.06	0.95	1.86	0.84	1.70	0.82	1.60	0.76	1.44	0.59
Traumatic Intrusions	2.39	1.17	1.87	0.95	1.69	0.85	1.57	0.82	1.51	0.78	1.46	0.67
Appetite Gain	2.27	1.14	2.15	0.99	2.11	0.96	2.08	0.97	2.10	1.09	1.81	0.85
Appetite Loss	2.22	1.12	1.96	1.02	1.81	0.91	1.55	0.77	1.55	0.83	1.52	0.71
Ill Temper	2.11	1.04	2.05	0.97	1.74	0.80	1.63	0.78	1.81	0.88	1.32	0.50
Panic	1.91	0.79	1.70	0.72	1.52	0.60	1.37	0.53	1.26	0.43	1.40	0.49
Suicidality	1.67	0.84	1.49	0.82	1.24	0.50	1.22	0.45	1.11	0.30	1.20	0.29
Well-Being	2.31	0.87	2.87	0.85	2.98	0.80	2.93	0.85	2.84	0.86	2.95	0.82

NOTE: $N = 1{,}914$ (Patients), 247 (High School Students), 4.055 (College Students), 1,837 (Community Adults), 1,070 (Postpartum), 214 (Older Adults).

[a] Original five-item version of scale.

Table 2.12 Descriptive Statistics for the New IDAS-II Scales Across Different Types of Respondents

Scale	Patients		College Students		Community Adults	
	M	*SD*	*M*	*SD*	*M*	*SD*
Dysphoria	2.78	0.93	2.11	0.79	1.94	0.76
Traumatic Avoidance	2.58	1.17	1.91	0.97	1.66	0.85
Social Anxiety	2.31	1.04	1.85	0.83	1.67	0.76
Mania	2.14	1.04	1.84	0.82	1.61	0.73
Checking	1.95	1.09	1.85	0.94	1.51	0.78
Ordering	1.85	0.95	1.83	0.79	1.60	0.71
Claustrophobia	1.83	1.06	1.30	0.58	1.21	0.53
Cleaning	1.58	0.82	1.49	0.66	1.29	0.53
Euphoria	1.58	0.73	1.82	0.71	1.65	0.63

NOTE: $N = 908$ (Patients), 2,781 (College Students), 1,091 (Community Adults).

Table 2.12 presents parallel values for the new IDAS-II scales in subsets of the patient, college student, and community adult samples (see also Watson et al., 2012). In interpreting these data, one issue that arises is whether these subsamples are representative of the overall groups displayed in Table 2.11. We therefore include results for the Dysphoria scale in Table 2.12, which provides a basis for comparing the two sets of data. It is noteworthy that the mean Dysphoria scores are virtually identical across the two sets of patients (2.84 vs. 2.78), college students (2.09 vs. 2.11) and adults (1.97 vs. 1.94) in Tables 2.11 and 2.12, respectively, which establishes that these subsamples are quite representative of the overall groups.

Group Comparisons

As would be expected, Tables 2.11 and 2.12 indicate that patients consistently report the highest levels of psychopathology. We conducted follow-up analyses to quantify the magnitude of the group differences in our three largest samples (i.e., patients, college students, community adults). Specifically, we computed effect sizes using Cohen's *d* (Cohen, 1992) by (a) calculating the difference between the mean scale scores of two groups and then (b) dividing this value by the pooled standard deviation; these *d* values are reported in Table 2.13. Cohen (1992, Table 1) proposed that *d* values from $|0.20|$ to $|0.49|$ represent small effect sizes; those ranging from $|0.50|$ to $|0.79|$ reflect medium effect sizes; and values of $|0.80|$ or greater indicate large effect sizes. Based on these cutoffs, the patients reported substantially greater levels of psychopathology (i.e., medium or large effect sizes) in 15 of 20 comparisons involving the adults, and in 11 of the 20 comparisons with

Table 2.13 Mean Score Comparisons (Expressed as Cohen's *d*) on the IDAS-II Scales Across Samples

IDAS-II Scale	Patients-College Students	Patients-Adults	College Students-Adults
Original IDAS Scales			
General Depression	**0.85**	**0.93**	0.19
Dysphoria	**0.83**	**0.89**	0.15
Traumatic Intrusions	*0.68*	*0.74*	0.15
Suicidality	*0.65*	*0.63*	0.05
Social Anxiety[a]	*0.58*	*0.69*	0.19
Insomnia	*0.58*	*0.65*	0.14
Panic	*0.55*	*0.74*	0.26
Lassitude	0.41	*0.65*	0.31
Ill Temper	0.41	*0.50*	0.14
Appetite Loss	0.40	*0.66*	0.30
Appetite Gain	0.16	0.18	0.03
Well-Being	*−0.76*	*−0.67*	0.06
IDAS-II Scales			
Traumatic Avoidance	*0.63*	**0.84**	0.27
Claustrophobia	*0.69*	*0.70*	0.15
Social Anxiety	*0.50*	*0.67*	0.22
Mania	0.34	*0.57*	0.28
Cleaning	0.13	0.41	0.31
Checking	0.11	0.47	0.37
Ordering	0.03	0.30	0.30
Euphoria	−0.32	−0.10	0.24

Note: For the original IDAS scales, $N = 1{,}914$ (Patients), 4,055 (Students), 1,837 (Adults). For the IDAS-II scales, $N = 908$ (Patients), 2,781 (Students), 1,091 (Adults). Large effect sizes ($d \geq |.80|$ are in bold; medium effect sizes ($d = |.50|$ to $|.79|$ are in italics.

[a] Original five-item version of scale.

the students; in contrast, mean-level differences between the students and adults consistently were small in magnitude.

General Depression and Dysphoria showed large effect sizes in both patient comparisons (*d*s ranged from 0.83 to 0.93); these clearly are the two scales that differ most strongly across clinical versus nonclinical samples. Traumatic Avoidance displayed a large effect size in the comparison with adults ($d = 0.84$), but only a medium effect size ($d = 0.63$) in the student analyses. Eight scales (Traumatic Intrusions, Suicidality, Social Anxiety [both versions], Insomnia, Panic, Claustrophobia, and Well-Being) had medium effect sizes in both patient comparisons, with *d*s ranging from $|0.50|$ to $|0.76|$. In addition, four scales (Lassitude, Ill Temper, Appetite Loss, Mania) showed medium effect sizes in the adult analyses, but small effects in the student comparisons. Finally, five scales (Cleaning, Checking, Ordering, Euphoria, Appetite Gain) produced consistently small effects. These last analyses raise potential concerns about the validity and clinical utility of these five scales that we address in subsequent chapters.

Nationally Representative Norms

Finally, we collected normative data on the IDAS-II from a large community sample that could be weighted on important demographic characteristics in order to be nationally representative (for more details about this study and sample, see Nelson, O'Hara, & Watson, 2016). Participants were recruited using Amazon's Mechanical Turk. A total of 1,836 individuals completed the online survey, which consisted of the 99 IDAS-II items, plus a brief demographic questionnaire. In terms of gender, 52.4% of participants were female (N = 962), and 47.6% were male (N = 874). The mean age of participants was 35.6 years (SD = 13.1). The sample was 72.8% White/Caucasian (N = 1,347), 8.4% Black/African American (N = 152), 8.3% Asian/Pacific Islander/Native Hawaiian (N = 154), and 10.4% Multiracial/Other (N = 192). With regard to ethnicity, 11.0% (N = 203) of the sample reported being of Hispanic, Latino, or Spanish origin. The sample was fairly representative in terms of gender and race/ethnicity, but it was markedly younger than the US population. For instance, whereas 42.4% of our sample was ages 18–29 and 12.7% was 55 or older, the 2013 American Community Survey (ACS; United States Census Bureau, 2013) estimates that 22.7% of Americans are 18–29 and 34.6% are over 55.

Given that these participants were not fully representative of the United States at large, it was necessary to calculate sample weights in order to make the data a less biased estimation of normative scores. The data were weighted according to age, gender, and race/ethnicity, using the 2013 ACS 3-year estimates. Participant age was collapsed into four categories: 18–29, 30–44, 45–54, and 55+. Participant race was also collapsed into four categories: White, Black/African American, Asian/Pacific Islander, and Multiracial/Other. The sample also was weighted to reflect Hispanic ethnicity. A total of 1,836 participants provided complete demographic information, allowing their data to be used to construct the sample weights.

To calculate the sample weights, the percentage of individuals with a given combination of demographic traits (e.g., female, Asian/Pacific Islander, and ages 30–44) in the US population as estimated by the ACS was divided by the percentage of participants who reported having the same combination of traits in the sample. As a result, weights <1.0 indicate that a given combination of traits was overrepresented in our sample, whereas weights >1.0 indicate that these traits were underrepresented relative to the US population. Because the ACS did not publish data on the combination of age, gender, race, and Hispanic ethnicity, additional steps were required in order to weight the sample to be representative on each of these demographic characteristics. After constructing a weighted frequency table for the sample according to age, gender, and race, additional weights for Hispanic ethnicity were calculated using the weighted data.

However, once the data were weighted by Hispanic ethnicity, the sample was no longer representative on the characteristics of age, sex, and race. As a result, an iterative solution was used in which the data were reweighted repeatedly until the weights for both age/gender/race and Hispanic ethnicity converged. The convergence criterion was that the weighted frequency of a given characteristic (either an age/gender/race combination or the presence or absence of Hispanic ethnicity) be within one tenth of 1% of the frequency of that characteristic in the US population. The data converged after five iterations.

Means (presented here as sums, rather than averages) and standard deviations for each of the IDAS-II scales are presented in Table 2.14. The table reports both the raw and weighted values for each scale in this normative sample. It is noteworthy that the weighting process resulted in the weighted means being lower than the raw values. This primarily is due to the overrepresentation of younger adults—who tend to report higher symptom scores than older adults (see Tables 2.11 through 2.13)—in the sample.

Because psychopathology symptom measures typically do not yield normally distributed results (Crawford & Garthwaite, 2009), using simple T or z scores based on means and standard deviations is unlikely to lead to accurate assessment of symptom severity. As a result, percentiles were calculated using the weighted data for each of the IDAS-II scales. To compute these percentiles, we used the formula $((m + 0.5k)/N)$, where m is the weighted number of people with

Table 2.14 Normative Statistics for the IDAS-II Scales in a Nationally Representative Sample

	Raw		Weighted	
IDAS-II Scale	*M*	*SD*	*M*	*SD*
General Depression	41.94	14.75	39.02	14.42
Dysphoria	19.90	8.61	18.31	8.34
Lassitude	13.14	5.23	11.96	5.12
Insomnia	12.43	5.54	11.80	5.52
Suicidality	8.35	3.93	7.88	5.24
Appetite Loss	5.06	2.82	4.68	2.57
Appetite Gain	6.19	2.87	5.89	2.82
Ill Temper	8.15	4.01	7.44	3.66
Well-Being	22.40	7.42	22.92	7.38
Social Anxiety	10.86	5.51	9.84	5.12
Panic	11.92	5.69	11.14	5.85
Claustrophobia	7.25	3.70	6.91	3.49
Cleaning	11.83	5.05	10.99	4.72
Checking	6.18	2.86	5.60	2.65
Ordering	8.78	3.93	8.19	3.56
Mania	9.24	4.34	8.39	4.08
Euphoria	8.84	3.55	8.61	4.81
Traumatic Intrusions	6.60	3.50	6.11	3.22
Traumatic Avoidance	7.85	3.86	7.39	3.66

NOTE: $N = 1{,}836$.

scores below a given score, k is the weighted number of people who obtained the given score, and N is the total sample size. Table 2.15 presents normative percentiles for the 18 nonoverlapping IDAS-II scales; Table 2.16 provides corresponding data for the composite General Depression scale.

An examination of Tables 2.15 and 2.16 demonstrates the value of using percentiles to account for the nonnormal distribution of psychopathology symptoms. As an example, the weighted mean (7.88) and standard deviation (5.24) of the Suicidality scale suggest that an individual scoring a 10 on this scale would be in the 66th percentile if the data were normally distributed. However, a score of 10 actually places an individual in the 86th percentile, a full quintile higher. Given the skewed nature of these symptom scores, using percentiles provides a more accurate picture of the severity of psychopathology.

DESCRIPTION OF PRIMARY SAMPLES

Overview

In the chapters that follow, we present extensive validity evidence (including convergent, discriminant, criterion, and incremental validity) on a wide range of measures assessing symptoms of the emotional disorders. In doing so, we will report data collected from a large number of samples. Our validity analyses will draw particularly heavily on samples that include both self-report symptom scales and various interview-based measures. For the sake of convenience and to facilitate the efficient presentation of these data, we have given these samples arbitrary numerical designations (Sample 1, Sample 2, and so on). In this concluding section of Chapter 2, we briefly describe these 11 samples (Table 2.17 presents summary characteristics for each one). Note that specific sample sizes in later chapters will vary due to missing data. For information regarding the interrater reliability of these various interview measures, see Watson et al. (2007, 2012, 2015a, 2015b) and Watson, O'Hara, Chmielewski, et al. (2008).

Samples

Sample 1 consisted of 337 outpatients who were recruited from the Community Mental Health Center of Mideastern Iowa, the Adult Psychiatry Clinic of the University of Iowa Hospitals and Clinics, and the Seashore Psychology Clinic in the Department of Psychological and Brain Sciences at the University of Iowa (this sample is described in greater detail in Watson et al., 2007, Study 3). All participants completed the original IDAS. In addition, most patients (a) received current *DSM-IV* diagnoses using the Structured Clinical Interview for DSM-IV (SCID-IV; First, Spitzer, Gibbon, & Williams, 1997) and (b) were rated on various emotional disorder symptoms using the Clinician Rating version of the IDAS (IDAS-CR; Watson, O'Hara, Chmielewski, et al., 2008; Koffel, 2011; Watson et al., 2012). The IDAS-CR will be described in Chapter 3.

Participants in Sample 2 were 316 outpatients who were recruited from the same sites as Sample 1 (these participants are described in Watson, O'Hara,

Table 2.15 PERCENTILE NORMS FOR THE NONOVERLAPPING IDAS-II SCALES

Score	Dysphoria	Lassitude	Insomnia	Suicidality	Appetite Loss	Appetite Gain	Ill-Temper	Well-Being	Social-Anxiety
3					50	12			
4					62	33			
5					67	48	22		
6		5	9	25	75	60	51		18
7		15	24	60	83	71	65		42
8		26	33	74	87	78	73	1	53
9		37	40	81	91	85	78	3	61
10	9	46	47	86	95	89	82	5	67
11	22	53	54	89	97	93	85	7	71
12	29	60	60	90	98	96	88	9	76
13	35	66	66	92	99	98	90	11	79
14	42	71	71	93	99.2	99	92	13	82
15	47	75	75	94	99.7	99.6	94	16	84
16	51	79	78	95			96	20	87
17	55	82	81	95			97	24	89
18	59	85	85	97			98	27	91
19	64	88	87	98			98	31	93
20	67	90	90	98			99	35	94
21	70	93	92	99			99	40	95
22	73	95	94	99.2			99.2	45	96
23	75	96	96	99.4			99.4	49	97
24	77	97	96	99.7			99.6	54	97
25	79	98	97	99.8			99.9	60	98
26	81	99.1	98	99.9				64	98
27	83	99.3	99	99.9				68	99
28	85	99.5	99	99.9				71	99.1
29	87	99.6	99.3	99.9				75	99.4
30	88	99.9	99.7	99.9				80	99.8
31	90							84	
32	91							89	
33	93							92	
34	94							95	
35	95							96	
36	96							97	
37	96							98	
38	97							99	
39	97							99	
40	98							99.6	
41	98								
42	99								
43	99								
44	99.3								
45	99.6								
46	99.8								
47	99.9								
48	99.9								
49	99.9								
50	99.9								

Panic	Checking	Ordering	Cleaning	Euphoria	Mania	Traumatic Intrusions	Traumatic Avoidance	Claustrophobia
	13							
	35					26	16	
	52	14		10	17	57	36	32
	65	35		27	41	67	47	39
	75	49	11	39	53	74	56	74
22	82	60	31	52	60	80	65	78
52	88	69	47	64	66	84	72	81
64	92	76	57	72	72	87	78	84
71	95	81	65	78	78	89	82	87
76	97	85	72	83	82	92	86	89
79	98	88	77	88	86	94	91	91
82	99	91	81	92	89	96	93	93
84	99.6	93	84	94	92	97	95	94
86		96	87	96	93	98	97	96
88		97	89	98	95	99	98	98
89		98	90	99	96	99.2	99	99
91		99	92	99.2	97	99.5	99.3	99.1
92		99.1	93	99.6	98	99.8	99.7	99.3
93		99.3	94	99.8	99			99.5
94		99.6	96	99.8	99.3			99.6
95		99.8	97	99.9	99.5			99.8
96		99.8	98	99.9	99.7			99.8
97		99.9	98	99.9	99.9			99.9
97			99					
98			99					
98			99.2					
99			99.4					
99			99.5					
99			99.7					
99			99.9					
99.3			99.9					
99.5			99.9					
99.6			99.9					
99.8								
99.9								
99.9								
99.9								
99.9								

Table 2.16 Percentile Norms for the IDAS-II General Depression Scale

Score	Percentile	Score	Percentile	Score	Percentile	Score	Percentile
20	0.4	40	60	60	89	80	99.1
21	1	41	63	61	91	81	99.2
22	3	42	65	62	91	82	99.4
23	6	43	67	63	92	83	99.5
24	11	44	69	64	93	84	99.5
25	16	45	71	65	94	85	99.5
26	20	46	73	66	94	86	99.6
27	22	47	74	67	95	87	99.7
28	28	48	76	68	95	88	99.7
29	31	49	78	69	96	89	99.7
30	33	50	79	70	96	90	99.7
31	37	51	80	71	96	91	99.8
32	41	52	81	72	97	92	99.9
33	44	53	82	73	97	93	99.9
34	46	54	83	74	98	94	99.9
35	49	55	84	75	98	95	99.9
36	52	56	85	76	98	96	99.9
37	54	57	86	77	99	97	99.9
38	56	58	87	78	99	98	99.9
39	58	59	88	79	99	99	99.9
						100	99.9

Chmielewski, et al., 2008). We also report IDAS, IDAS-CR, and SCID-IV data from this sample.

Sample 3 included 296 outpatients who were recruited from the same sites as Samples 1 and 2 (this is Patient Sample 4 in Watson et al., 2012). These participants rated themselves on selected IDAS-II scales. Most of them were interviewed, which also yielded data on the SCID-IV, IDAS-CR, and Personality, Cognitions, Consciousness, and Perceptions Interview (PCCP; Chmielewski & Watson, 2008b; Koffel, 2011; Watson et al., 2012); the PCCP is described in Chapter 9.

The participants in Sample 4 were 412 community adults who completed the IDAS-II (these participants are described in Watson et al., 2015a, 2015b). Although this sample is not fully clinical in nature, roughly half of the participants (46.3%) were either currently receiving treatment for mental health issues or had received it in the past. Consequently, these participants exhibited a relatively high level of psychopathology. These adult participants were interviewed using an adapted version (with the authorization of the author) of the Mini-International Neuropsychiatric Interview (M.I.N.I; Sheehan et al., 1998) that incorporated diagnostic changes for *DSM-5* (see Watson et al., 2015a, 2015b); thus, we report *DSM-5* diagnoses in this sample.[2]

2. Data collection in Sample 4 was ongoing when *DSM-5* was finalized. This study used a version of the M.I.N.I. that included proposed changes for GAD that later were rejected by the American Psychiatric Association. Thus, the GAD diagnosis differs slightly from that in *DSM-5*.

Table 2.17 SUMMARY CHARACTERISTICS OF PRIMARY SAMPLES USED IN LATER CHAPTERS

Sample	*N*	Population	Main Measures	Primary Reference
1	337	Outpatients	IDAS, IDAS-CR, SCID-IV	Watson et al. (2007)
2	316	Outpatients	IDAS, IDAS-CR, SCID-IV	Watson, O'Hara, Chmielewski, et al. (2008)
3	296	Outpatients	IDAS-II*, IDAS-CR, PCCP, SCID-IV	Watson et al. (2012)
4	412	Community	IDAS-II, M.I.N.I.	Watson et al. (2015a, 2015b)
5	394	Outpatients	IDAS-II, IMAS, SCID-IV	Watson et al. (2012)
6	200	Outpatients	IDAS-II, IDAS-CR, PCCP	Watson et al. (2012)
7	1,070	Postpartum	IDAS, HRSD, SCID-IV	Watson, Clark, et al. (2013)
8	307	Students	IDAS, IDAS-CR, SCID-IV	Watson, O'Hara, Chmielewski, et al. (2008)
9	373	Students	IDAS-II*, IDAS-CR, PCCP	Watson et al. (2012)
10	219	Students	IDAS-II, IDAS-CR, PCCP	Watson et al. (2012)
11	402	Students	IDAS-II, IMAS	[Not previously reported]

NOTE: IDAS = Inventory of Depression and Anxiety Symptoms. IDAS-II = Expanded Version of the Inventory of Depression and Anxiety Symptoms. IDAS-CR = Clinician Rating Version of the IDAS. SCID-IV = Structured Clinical Interview for DSM-IV. PCCP = Personality, Cognitions, Consciousness, and Perceptions Interview. IMAS = Interview of Mood and Anxiety Symptoms. M.I.N.I. = Mini-International Neuropsychiatric Interview. HRSD = Hamilton Rating Scale for Depression.
*Participants completed only selected IDAS-II scales.

Sample 5 included 394 outpatients who were recruited from outpatient Psychology and Psychiatry clinics at Stony Brook University and from other local area facilities (this is Patient Sample 3 in Watson et al., 2012). All of the patients rated themselves on the IDAS-II. In addition, subsets of these participants were assessed using the SCID-IV and the Interview for Mood and Anxiety Symptoms (IMAS; Gamez, Kotov, & Watson, 2010; Ruggero et al., 2014; Watson & Naragon-Gainey, 2014; Watson et al., 2007, 2012). The IMAS is described in Chapter 3.

Sample 6 consisted of 200 outpatients who were recruited from the same eastern Iowa sites as Samples 1–3 (this is Patient Sample 2 in Watson et al., 2012). IDAS-II, IDAS-CR, and PCCP data are available for these participants.

The participants in Sample 7 were 1,070 postpartum women who rated themselves on the original IDAS (this sample is described in Watson, Clark, Chmielewski, & Kotov, 2013; it is an expanded version of a sample that is discussed in Watson et al., 2007). Subsets of these women also were assessed on two interview measures: the SCID-IV and the Hamilton Rating Scale for Depression (HRSD; Hamilton, 1960).

Sample 8 consisted of 307 students who were enrolled in an introductory psychology course at the University of Iowa (see Watson, O'Hara, Chmielewski, et al., 2008). These participants completed the original IDAS. Interview data are available on both the SCID-IV and IDAS-CR.

The participants of Sample 9 also were University of Iowa psychology students ($N=373$; this is Student Sample 7 in Watson et al., 2012). They completed the same subset of IDAS-II scales as the Sample 3 participants. In addition, most of these students were interviewed, which produced ratings on the IDAS-CR and PCCP.

Sample 10 consisted of 219 University of Iowa psychology students (this is Student Sample 3 in Watson et al., 2012). IDAS-II, IDAS-CR, and PCCP data are available for these participants.

Finally, Sample 11 included 402 undergraduate students from Stony Brook University in New York. It should be noted, however, that the majority of these students ($N=281$, or 70.1%; treatment history was missing for one participant) had a history of treatment for mental health issues. Accordingly, these participants displayed a relatively high level of psychopathology. We present IDAS-II and IMAS data collected from these students; findings from this sample have not been reported previously.

3

The Structure, Specificity, and Validity of Depression Symptoms

In this chapter, we examine the structure, specificity, and validity (including convergent, discriminant, criterion, and incremental validity) of depression symptoms. As we discussed in Chapter 2, progress in this area was stymied for decades by the absence of measures that assessed specific types of depression symptoms in a reliable and valid manner. Our scale development work with the IDAS, however, has opened up a promising new era in depression research by offering a comprehensive, psychometrically sound measurement model for these symptoms.

We begin by highlighting the major features and key implications of this new measurement model. We then examine the convergent and discriminant validity of these scales to establish that (a) our key findings replicate across measures and methods and (b) specific depression symptoms can be meaningfully distinguished from one another. Next, we explore the specificity and incremental validity of individual depression symptoms and discuss the broader diagnostic and nosological implications of these findings. We then compare the criterion validity of various general depression scales vis-à-vis *DSM-IV/DSM-5* diagnoses of major depression. Finally, we conclude with an examination of sex differences in depression symptoms.

A COMPREHENSIVE MEASUREMENT MODEL FOR DEPRESSION

Explicating the Nature of the General Depression Factor (Dysphoria)

As was noted in Chapter 2, it is well established that depression symptoms are characterized by a strong general factor (e.g., Beck et al., 1988; Brouwer et al., 2013). Nevertheless, our IDAS scale development analyses have played an important role in explicating the nature of this general factor; it therefore will be informative to consider these data in greater detail. As we will see, this factor actually is (a) stronger but (b) less general than was previously thought.

To model the nature and scope of the symptom content subsumed within this broad factor, Watson et al. (2007) obtained ratings from 23 experts (13 faculty, 10 graduate students) who were members of clinical psychology doctoral training programs at the University of Iowa and the University at Buffalo. These experts were given a list of the nine *DSM-IV* symptom criteria for a major depressive episode, as well as the depression symptoms from the IDAS item pool. The raters were asked to read each item and then indicate which of these nine *DSM-IV* criteria—if any—it assessed. Watson et al. (2007) used these data to create *DSM*-based scales reflecting each of these criteria; an item was included on a scale if it was judged to assess that criterion by at least 18 experts (78.3%). This yielded a 5-item scale for Criterion 1 (Depressed Mood); 7-item scales for Criterion 6 (Lassitude), Criterion 7 (Worthlessness/Guilt), Criterion 8 (Cognitive Problems), and Criterion 9 (Suicidality); a 10-item scale for Criterion 5 (Psychomotor Problems); and a 13-item scale for Criterion 2 (Anhedonia). Watson et al. (2007) created separate measures of Appetite Loss (five items) and Appetite Gain (five items) for Criterion 3, and separate measures of Insomnia (eight items) and Hypersomnia (three items) for Criterion 4.

Table 3.1 presents correlations among five of these *DSM* scales (those for Criteria 1, 2, 5, 7 and 8) in our three original IDAS scale development samples (353 patients, 362 community adults, 673 college students). Clearly, these symptoms all are very strongly related to one another. In fact, the average correlations (after *r*-to-*z* transformation) were .71 (patients), .75 (adults), and .72 (students). Thus, these symptoms essentially are interchangeable, at least in self-report data. Moreover, as was noted in Chapter 2, items assessing anxious mood and worry also correlated strongly with these five types of symptoms; specifically, a nine-item Anxious Mood scale had average correlations of .74 (patients), .78 (adults), and .76 (students) with the criterion scales in these same samples. As was discussed in Chapter 2, we created the broad Dysphoria scale to capture the core content defining this general dimension.

The Specific IDAS Depression Scales

Despite the strength and scope of this general factor, it does not exhaust the meaningful variance that can be identified within depression symptoms. Indeed, as was noted in Chapter 2, several specific symptom dimensions consistently emerged in our structural analyses and were used to create corresponding IDAS scales. Five of these scales assess specific symptoms of depression. The composition of four scales is quite straightforward and can be directly linked to individual HICs that were created for the initial IDAS item pool. Specifically, Suicidality assesses *DSM-IV/DSM-5* Criterion 9 (recurrent thoughts of death) for a major depressive episode; Insomnia measures the corresponding portion of Criterion 4 (sleep disturbance); and Appetite Loss and Appetite Gain jointly capture Criterion 3 (appetite disturbance).

Table 3.1 Correlations Among Selected *DSM*-Based Content Scales in the Original IDAS Scale Development Samples

Scale	1	2	3	4	5
Psychiatric Patients					
1. Depressed Mood	.—				
2. Anhedonia	.79	.—			
3. Worthlessness/Guilt	.74	.74	.—		
4. Cognitive Problems	.68	.71	.71	.—	
5. Psychomotor Problems	.66	.69	.63	.74	.—
Community Adults					
1. Depressed Mood	.—				
2. Anhedonia	.80	.—			
3. Worthlessness/Guilt	.80	.79	.—		
4. Cognitive Problems	.67	.70	.73	.—	
5. Psychomotor Problems	.72	.75	.71	.79	.—
College Students					
1. Depressed Mood	.—				
2. Anhedonia	.73	.—			
3. Worthlessness/Guilt	.79	.73	.—		
4. Cognitive Problems	.65	.70	.74	.—	
5. Psychomotor Problems	.66	.71	.70	.75	.—

NOTE: $N = 353$ (Psychiatric Patients), 362 (Community Adults), 673 (College Students). All correlations are significant at $p < .01$. Correlations $\geq .70$ are in bold. Mean correlations = .71 (Patients), .75 (Adults), .72 (Students). Adapted from Watson et al. (2007), Table 1.

In contrast, the Lassitude scale is more complicated, and its composition provides further insight into the complex structure of depression symptoms. As discussed in Chapter 2, it includes a single item reflecting circadian variation in symptom course ("I felt much worse in the morning than later in the day") that originally was part of the HIC designed to tap the features of melancholic depression. Its remaining items reflect content related to both fatigue/anergia (Criterion 6; e.g. "I felt exhausted," "It took a lot of effort to get me going") and the hypersomnia portion of Criterion 4 ("I slept more than usual"). This is because our structural data consistently showed that hypersomnia symptoms actually correlate much more strongly with fatigue/anergia than with insomnia.

We have continued to find this same basic pattern in subsequent samples. To document this point more fully, Table 3.2 presents data on three additional *DSM* criterion scales that were included in the 99-item version of the original IDAS (see Watson et al., 2007, Appendix G): a five-item measure of the Insomnia portion of Criterion 4, a two-item index of the Hypersomnia portion of Criterion 4, and a four-item measure of Criterion 6 (Lassitude). Table 3.2 reports correlations in six different types of respondents (patients, community adults, college students,

Table 3.2 Correlations Among the *DSM*-Based Criterion 4 and Criterion 6 Scales in Various Samples

Sample	**C4: Insomnia with C4: Hypersomnia**	**C4: Insomnia with C6: Lassitude**	**C4: Hypersomnia with C6: Lassitude**
Patients	.01	**.46**	**.45**
Community Adults	.18	**.53**	**.60**
College Students	.10	**.45**	**.49**
Postpartum	.08	**.55**	.38
High School Students	.11	**.52**	.37
Older Adults	.17	**.44**	**.49**
Overall	.08	**.49**	**.45**

NOTE: $N=1{,}006$ (Patients), 362 (Community Adults), 980 (College Students), 1,070 (Postpartum), 247 (High School Students), 214 (Older Adults), 3,879 (Overall), C4 = Criterion 4; C6 = Criterion 6. Correlations ≥ .40 are in bold.

postpartum women, high school students, older adults). It also presents overall correlations based on a standardized combined sample ($N=3{,}879$); to eliminate mean-level differences across populations, we standardized the scores on a within-population basis and then combined them to permit a single overall analysis.

Lassitude and Insomnia are moderately related in these data, with correlations ranging from .44 to .55 (overall $r=.49$) across the six samples. Lassitude also is moderately related to Hypersomnia, with coefficients ranging from .37 to .60 (overall $r=.45$). Note, however, that the two basic subcomponents of *DSM-IV*/*DSM-5* Criterion 4—Insomnia and Hypersomnia—are virtually unrelated, with correlations ranging from only .01 to .17 (overall $r=.08$) across the six samples. These data clearly demonstrate why content related to hypersomnia was included in the IDAS Lassitude scale, rather than Insomnia. More fundamentally, these results (see also Koffel & Watson, 2009) suggest that it might be advantageous to move hypersomnia from Criterion 4 to Criterion 6 in a future revision of the *DSM*.

Relations Among Depression Symptoms

Self-Report Data

Six IDAS scales—Dysphoria, Suicidality, Insomnia, Appetite Loss, Appetite Gain, and Lassitude—jointly capture all of the symptom content included in the nine *DSM-IV*/*DSM-5* diagnostic criteria for a major depressive episode. We can further explicate the structure of depression symptoms by examining the relations among these scales. Table 3.3 presents these correlations in large aggregate samples of psychiatric patients ($N=1{,}914$) and college students ($N=4{,}055$). Two aspects of these data are noteworthy. First, consistent with the factor analytic results reported in Chapter 2, the specific symptom scales correlate quite differently with

Table 3.3 Correlations Among the IDAS Depression Symptom Scales in Psychiatric Patient and College Student Samples

Scale	1	2	3	4	5	6
1. Dysphoria	.—	**.69**	**.54**	**.53**	.48	.44
2. Lassitude	**.64**	.—	.35	.46	.37	.45
3. Suicidality	**.60**	.34	.—	.32	.33	.23
4. Insomnia	**.53**	.33	.31	.—	.42	.29
5. Appetite Loss	.44	.27	.32	.41	.—	.03
6. Appetite Gain	.26	.32	.16	.13	−.26	.—

NOTE: $N = 1{,}914$ (Psychiatric Patients), 4,055 (College Students). Patient correlations are shown below the diagonal; student correlations are displayed above the diagonal. Correlations ≥ .50 and are in bold. IDAS = Inventory of Depression and Anxiety Symptoms.

Dysphoria and clearly contain different amounts of general distress variance. That is, Dysphoria correlates most strongly with Lassitude ($r = .64$ and .69 in patients and students, respectively; overall standardized $r = .67$); more moderately with Suicidality (overall $r = .56$), Insomnia (overall $r = .53$), and Appetite Loss (overall $r = .47$); and more modestly with Appetite Gain (overall $r = .38$). Thus, specific depression symptoms vary substantially in the strength of their general distress components.

Second, the five specific depression scales are only modestly related to one another. In the patients, these correlations range from |.13| to |.41|, with a mean value (ignoring sign) of only .29. Similarly, in students, these coefficients range from |.03| to |.46|, with a mean value of .33. These results clearly establish that it is possible to distinguish specific symptom dimensions within depression. Moreover, taken together with the data presented in Table 3.1, they demonstrate that depression symptoms display a curious structure: Whereas more than half of the *DSM-IV/DSM-5* symptom criteria (e.g., depressed mood, anhedonia, worthlessness) are so strongly correlated as to be virtually interchangeable, the remaining symptoms (e.g., insomnia, appetite loss) are only weakly to moderately interrelated.

Clinicians' Ratings

The data in Table 3.3 are based on self-report. How well do these findings generalize across methods? We can examine this issue using the Clinician Rating version of the IDAS (IDAS-CR), which we created to evaluate the convergent and discriminant validity of these symptom dimensions (Watson, O'Hara, Chmielewski, et al., 2008; see also Koffel, 2011; Watson et al., 2012). The IDAS-CR consists of a series of single-item ratings representing each of the IDAS scales. Each rating is made on a 3-point scale (*absent, subthreshold, present*). To rate each symptom, the clinicians asked a standard initial probe question, as well as several standard follow-up questions. For the IDAS-CR Dysphoria rating, for example, the interviewers began with the standard probe question, "Did you feel sad, depressed, or down over the past two weeks?" They then asked a number of follow-up questions, including "Have you felt inadequate?" "Have you had trouble concentrating?" and "Have you found yourself worrying much of the time?" The interviewers also clarified whether or not reported symptoms had been present "more days than not" over the past 2 weeks, and whether they had (a) been noticed by others or (b) interfered with the patient's day-to-day activities. The interviewers also were free to ask additional questions to ensure that they had enough information to rate the individual confidently on the dimension. Watson, O'Hara, Chmielewski, et al. (2008) established strong interrater reliability for these ratings in both students (intraclass correlations ranged from .65 to .95, median = .87) and patients (range = .74 to .99, median = .89).

Table 3.4 reports parallel IDAS-CR correlations among the six depression symptoms in aggregated samples of patients ($N = 804$; this is a combination of Samples 1, 2, and 6 [see Table 2.14]) and college students ($N = 522$; this is an aggregation of Samples 8 and 10). Consistent with previous results (see Clark & Watson, 1991), the correlations generally are lower in the clinicians' ratings than in the self-report data. It is noteworthy, however, that the general pattern remains the same. That is, corroborating the self-report results, Dysphoria again correlated more strongly with Lassitude (overall standardized $r = .37$) than with Suicidality (overall $r = .28$), Appetite Loss (overall $r = .25$), Insomnia (overall $r = .23$), and Appetite Gain ($r = .13$) in the clinicians' ratings. Furthermore, the five specific depression scales again are weakly related in these data. In the patients, these correlations range from $|.00|$ to $|.36|$, with a mean value (ignoring sign) of only .17. Similarly, in college students, these coefficients range from $|.03|$ to $|.31|$, with a mean value of .15. Taken together with the self-report results, it seems reasonable to conclude that specific depression symptoms are only weakly to moderately related to one another.

Table 3.4 CORRELATIONS AMONG THE IDAS-CR DEPRESSION RATINGS IN PSYCHIATRIC PATIENT AND COLLEGE STUDENT SAMPLES

Scale	1	2	3	4	5	6
1. Dysphoria	.—	**.40**	.19	.26	.24	.15
2. Lassitude	**.36**	.—	.08	**.31**	.10	.20
3. Suicidality	**.34**	.22	.—	.15	.10	.15
4. Insomnia	.22	.22	.10	.—	.19	.03
5. Appetite Loss	.25	.18	.17	.24	.—	−.17
6. Appetite Gain	.11	.13	.08	−.00	**−.36**	.—

Note: $N = 804$ (Psychiatric Patients), 522 (College Students). Patient correlations are shown below the diagonal; student correlations are displayed above the diagonal. Correlations ≥ .30 and are in bold. IDAS-CR = Clinician Rating Version of the Inventory of Depression and Anxiety Symptoms.

CONVERGENT VALIDITY ANALYSES

Self-Report Scales

General Measures of Depression

We turn now to analyses that are designed to establish the convergent validity of the IDAS depression scales and to explicate the nature and scope of the content they assess. We begin by examining the convergent validity of the two broad scales: General Depression and Dysphoria.

The top portion of Table 3.5 reports correlations between General Depression and Dysphoria and three widely used, general measures of depressive symptoms: the 21-item second edition of the Beck Depression Inventory (BDI-II; Beck et al., 1996), the 20-item Center for Epidemiological Studies Depression Scale

Table 3.5 Convergent Validity Analyses: Correlations Between the IDAS-II General Depression and Dysphoria Scales and General Measures of Depression

Scale/Sample	***N***	**General Depression**	**Dysphoria**
BDI-II			
Patients	971	.82	.81
Community Adults	743	.87	.85
College Students	675	.80	.77
Postpartum Women	1,056	.83	.82
Adolescents	376	.81	.81
Older Adults	213	.88	.86
Diabetics	222	.86	.83
Overall	4,256	.83	.82
CES-D			
Patients	302	.88	.86
Community Adults	384	.87	.85
Diabetics	222	.88	.84
Overall	908	.88	.85
MASQ GD:D			
Community Adults	382	.86	.88
Diabetics	220	.83	.83
Overall	602	.85	.86
RADS-2	377	.82	.80
EPDS	1,070	.83	.85
GDS	214	.88	.89

Note: BDI-II = Beck Depression Inventory-II. CES-D = Center for Epidemiological Studies Depression Scale. MASQ GD:D = Mood and Anxiety Symptoms Questionnaire General.
Distress: Depressive Symptoms Scale. RADS-2 = Reynolds Adolescent Depression Scale–Second Edition. EPDS = Edinburgh Postnatal Depression Scale. GDS = Geriatric Depression Scale.

(CES-D; Radloff, 1977), and the 12-item General Distress: Depressive symptoms scale (GD: Depression) from the Mood and Anxiety Symptom Questionnaire (MASQ; Watson et al., 1995). Table 3.5 reports both individual correlations computed on specific types of respondents (e.g., patients, community adults, college students), as well as overall correlations based on standardized combined samples.

These results establish a very strong level of convergent validity; in fact, they are high enough to suggest that all of these measures are virtually indistinguishable from one another. General Depression had overall correlations of .83, .88, and .85 with the BDI-II, CES-D, and MASQ GD: Depression scales, respectively; the corresponding values for IDAS Dysphoria were .82, .85, and .86, respectively. Clearly, these IDAS scales tap virtually all of the reliable variance that is contained in these commonly used scales.

Specialized Measures of Depression

In addition to these general scales, several popular self-report measures have been created to assess depressive symptoms in specialized populations. The lower portion of Table 3.5 reports correlations with three widely used specialty measures of depression. First, the Second Edition of the Reynolds Adolescent Depression Scale (RADS-2; Reynolds, 2002) is a widely used self-report measure of depression in adolescents. Respondents indicate the frequency they have experienced each of 30 items on a 4-point scale ranging from *almost never* to *most of the time*. RADS-2 data were available on a sample of 377 adolescents (mean age = 16.4 years; range = 13–19 years); this included 247 high school students and 130 adolescent patients.

Second, the postpartum women of Sample 7 (N = 1,070; mean age = 27.9 years; range = 18–45 years) completed the 10-item Edinburgh Postnatal Depression Scale (EPDS; J. L. Cox, Holden, & Sagovsky, 1987). For each item, participants chose the response (from four options) that best described their experience over the previous week. Substantial evidence has established the validity of the EPDS as a tool to screen for depression in the postpartum period (J. L. Cox & Holden, 2003; Eberhard-Gran, Eskild, Tambs, Opjordsmoen, & Samuelson, 2001).

Third, 214 older adults (mean age = 73.5 years; range = 57–92 years) were assessed on the Geriatric Depression Scale (GDS; Yesavage et al., 1983). The GDS contains 30 true-false items that are specifically designed to measure depression in elderly respondents.

As can be seen in Table 3.5, the results for these specialty scales closely parallel those seen earlier for the general depression measures, and again suggest that all of these measures essentially are interchangeable with one another. The IDAS General Depression scale had correlations of .82, .83, and .88 with the RADS-2, EPDS, and GDS, respectively; the corresponding values for Dysphoria were .80, .85, and .89, respectively.

These data establish that these IDAS scales capture virtually all of the reliable variance tapped by the RADS-2, EPDS, and GDS. They further suggest that these IDAS scales are appropriate and valid for use across a very wide age range (note that the respondents in Table 3.5 ranged in age from 13 to 92). At a more fundamental level, they challenge the value of—and need for—these types of specialty measures.

The correlations with the three specialty scales in these samples ranged from .80 (Dysphoria vs. the RADS-2) to .89 (Dysphoria vs. the GDS), with a median value of .84. Correlations of this magnitude indicate that these specialty measures produce results that are virtually indistinguishable from those obtained using standard, general depression scales. This being the case, it seems simpler and more straightforward to use the same standard scales across various types of respondents.

Specific Depression Scales

We now examine the convergent validity of the specific IDAS depression scales. Table 3.6 reports correlations—including both (a) coefficients computed on individual types of respondents and (b) overall coefficients based on standardized combined samples—with five self-report symptom scales. First, the Expanded Form of

Table 3.6 Convergent Validity Analyses: Correlations Between IDAS-II Depression Scales and Self-Report Measures of Specific Depression Symptoms

Scale/Sample	*N*	Dysphor	Lass	Suic	Insomn	App Loss	App Gain
PANAS-X Fatigue							
Patients	390	.54	**.77**	.24	.41	.24	.27
Adults	352	.58	**.76**	.29	.38	.19	.40
Students	670	.55	**.72**	.31	.42	.31	.37
Overall	1,412	.55	**.75**	.29	.41	.26	.35
ASIQ							
Patients	330	.55	.35	**.74**	.25	.25	.17
Students	300	.36	.27	**.61**	.22	.14	.20
Older Adults	213	.45	.30	**.71**	.20	.31	.11
Overall	843	.45	.31	**.69**	.23	.22	.16
WHIIRS							
Patients	249	.34	.15	.16	**.77**	.38	.09
Older Adults	213	.35	.39	.22	**.82**	.28	.27
SD Patients	201	.35	.34	.18	**.84**	.18	.16
Overall	663	.35	.28	.19	**.81**	.29	.17
EPSI Restricting							
Patients	303	.24	.04	.22	.30	.58	–.21
ED Patients	158	.17	.06	.10	.21	**.63**	–.44
Overall	461	.22	.05	.18	.27	**.60**	–.29
EPSI Binge Eating							
Patients	303	.25	.36	.09	.12	–.17	**.65**
ED Patients	158	.25	.27	.15	.00	–.40	**.72**
Overall	461	.25	.33	.11	.08	–.25	**.68**

NOTE: Correlations ≥ |.60| are in bold. Dysphor = Dysphoria. Lass = Lassitude. Suic = Suicidality. Insomn = Insomnia. App Loss = Appetite Loss. App Gain = Appetite Gain. PANAS-X = Expanded Form of the Positive and Negative Affect Schedule. ASIQ = Adult Suicidal Ideation Questionnaire. WHIIRS = Women's Health Initiative Insomnia Rating Scale. SD = Sleep Disorder. EPSI = Eating Pathology Symptoms Inventory. ED = Eating Disorder.

the Positive and Negative Affect Schedule (PANAS-X; Watson & Clark, 1999) contains a four-item Fatigue scale (*sleepy, tired, sluggish, drowsy*). Participants rated the extent to which they experienced each mood descriptor over the past week on a 5-point scale ranging from *very slightly or not at all* to *extremely*.

Second, the Adult Suicidal Ideation Questionnaire (Reynolds, 1991a, 1991b) is a 25-item, self-report measure of the severity of suicidal ideation. Each item is rated on a 7-point scale indicating the frequency of suicidal ideation over the past month, with responses ranging from 0 (*I never had this thought*) to 6 (*almost every day*).

Next, the Women's Health Initiative Insomnia Rating Scale (WHIIRS; Levine et al., 2003) is a five-item measure assessing nighttime sleep complaints over the past 4 weeks, including early, middle, and late insomnia. Respondents are asked to indicate how often they have experienced each item on a 5-point scale (ranging from *no, not in the past 4 weeks* to *yes, 5 or more times a week*).

Finally, the Eating Pathology Symptoms Inventory (EPSI; Forbush et al., 2013) is a comprehensive, 45-item measure of eating disorder symptoms. Respondents indicate how frequently they have experienced each symptom over the past 4 weeks on a 5-point scale ranging from *never* to *very often*. We report data here on the six-item Restricting scale (e.g., "People told me that I do not eat very much," "People encouraged me to eat more") and the eight-item Binge Eating scale (e.g., "I ate until I was uncomfortably full," "I stuffed myself with food to the point of feeling sick"). Forbush et al. (2013) report that both of these scales had strong convergent validity with established measures of eating pathology, as well as broad links to general indicators of psychopathology. The IDAS results we report here are taken from Forbush et al. (2013, Table 8).

Table 3.6 establishes strong links between each of these measures and the five specific depression scales of the IDAS. Specifically, Lassitude correlated strongly with PANAS-X Fatigue (overall $r = .75$); Suicidality was substantially related to the ASIQ (overall $r = .69$); Insomnia displayed strong convergence with the WHIIRS (overall $r = .81$); Appetite Loss was highly related to EPSI Restricting (overall $r = .60$); and Appetite Gain was strongly associated with EPSI Binge Eating (overall $r = .68$).

These last two associations merit comment. As we will discuss in greater detail subsequently, the two IDAS appetite scales do not show particularly strong or specific associations with indicators of depression, including *DSM-IV* diagnoses of major depression. The data reported in Table 3.6 indicate that these scales actually may be more informative in assessing other types of psychopathology, such as symptoms of eating pathology. We currently are collecting additional data to explicate the psychopathological correlates of these scales more fully.

Relations With the HRSD

The data shown in Tables 3.5 and 3.6 establish that the IDAS depression scales converge strongly with conceptually related self-report measures. Watson et al. (2007) further established their validity by reporting correlations with clinicians' ratings on the widely used Hamilton Rating Scale for Depression (HRSD; Hamilton, 1960) in a subset of the Sample 7 participants ($N = 293$); we present these correlations in Table 3.7. Three aspects of these data are particularly noteworthy. First, consistent with previous research (Beck & Steer, 1993; Clark & Watson, 1991)—and with other data we will be reporting shortly—these results demonstrate strong associations between self-rated and clinician-rated symptoms.

Second, all of the IDAS depression scales were significantly correlated with the HRSD, establishing some degree of convergent validity for each of them. As would be expected, the two broad scales—General Depression ($r = .67$) and Dysphoria ($r = .64$)—had the strongest associations with the HRSD, whereas the specific scales—Insomnia ($r = .51$), Lassitude ($r = .50$), Suicidality ($r = .34$), Appetite Loss ($r = .30$), and Appetite Gain ($r = .30$)—displayed more moderate relations.

Third, the IDAS General Depression and Dysphoria scales had correlations with the HRSD that were very comparable to those of the BDI-II ($r = .62$) and EPDS ($r = .61$). These results—which hardly are surprising given the very strong correlations between these scales that were reported in Table 3.5—demonstrate that the convergent validity of these general IDAS scales is very similar to that of more traditional measures of depression. Moreover, given that these data were

Table 3.7 Correlations Between the HRSD and Self-Report Symptom Scales in Sample 7

Scale	Correlation
IDAS Scales	
General Depression	.67
Dysphoria	.64
Panic	.60
Social Anxiety	.53
Insomnia	.51
Lassitude	.50
Ill Temper	.49
Traumatic Intrusions	.45
Well-Being	−.38
Suicidality	.34
Appetite Loss	.30
Appetite Gain	.30
Other Scales	
BAI	.64
BDI-II	.62
EPDS	.61

NOTE: $N = 293$. All correlations are significant at $p < .01$. HRSD = Hamilton Rating Scale for Depression. IDAS = Inventory of Depression and Anxiety Symptoms. BAI = Beck Anxiety Inventory. BDI-II = Beck Depression Inventory-II. EPDS = Edinburgh Postnatal Depression Scale. Adapted from Watson et al. (2007, Table 9).

obtained in a postpartum sample, these findings again raise questions regarding the value of—and need for—specialty depression measures such as the EPDS.

ANALYSES OF CONVERGENT AND DISCRIMINANT VALIDITY

Overview

Convergent correlations are necessary—but not sufficient—to establish the construct validity of measures; it also is essential to establish that scales show discriminant validity vis-à-vis "near neighbor" indicators of closely related constructs. Convergent/discriminant validity analyses are particularly important in establishing that specific depression symptoms can be meaningfully distinguished from one another across methods. Consequently, we will present multitrait-multimethod matrices examining the self-report IDAS depression scales in relation to their counterparts on two parallel interview measures: the IDAS-CR and the Interview for Mood and Anxiety Symptoms (IMAS; Gamez, Kotov, & Watson, 2010; Ruggero et al., 2014; Watson & Naragon-Gainey, 2014; Watson et al., 2007, 2012).

IDAS-CR Analyses

As discussed earlier, the IDAS-CR consists of a series of single-item ratings representing each of the IDAS scales; ratings are made on a 3-point scale (*absent, subthreshold, present*). Table 3.8 presents separate sets of correlations between the IDAS depression scales and parallel IDAS-CR ratings in aggregate samples of outpatients ($N = 804$; this a combination of Samples 1, 2, and 6) and students ($N = 522$; this is an aggregate of Samples 8 and 10) in the form of a heteromethod block (Campbell & Fiske, 1959); it should be noted that the data reported here represent a modified version of results reported earlier by Watson and Stasik (2014).

Looking first at convergent validity, all of the IDAS scales were significantly related to their IDAS-CR counterparts in both samples. Convergent correlations in the patient sample ranged from .59 (Lassitude, Insomnia) to .71 (Appetite Loss), with a mean coefficient of .63; parallel values in the student data ranged from .48 (Suicidality) to .62 (Appetite Loss), with a mean coefficient of .55. These results are particularly impressive given that the IDAS-CR consists of a series of single ratings with only three response options. Thus, consistent with previous research (e.g., Beck et al., 1988; Clark & Watson, 1991; Watson et al., 2007), these data demonstrate substantial associations between self-report and interview-based symptom measures.

We turn now to discriminant validity. A classic test of discriminant validity is that each of the convergent correlations should be higher than any of the other values in its row or column of the heteromethod block (Campbell & Fiske, 1959). Table 3.8 indicates that all of the symptom measures met this criterion. We further

Table 3.8 Convergent/Discriminant Validity Analyses: Correlations Between the IDAS Scales and IDAS-CR Ratings in Patient and Student Samples

IDAS Scale	IDAS-CR Rating 1	2	3	4	5	6
Patients						
1. Appetite Loss	**.71**	.22	.27	−.32	.21	.27
2. Suicidality	.22	**.67**	.37	.06	.25	.14
3. Dysphoria	.29	.42	**.60**	.10	.43	.25
4. Appetite Gain	−.30	.08	.13	**.60**	.19	.00
5. Lassitude	.14	.22	.37	.16	**.59**	.13
6. Insomnia	.25	.19	.27	.02	.28	**.59**
Students						
1. Appetite Loss	**.62**	.07	.25	−.14	.13	.11
2. Suicidality	.12	**.48**	.31	.12	.24	.18
3. Dysphoria	.20	.21	**.61**	.20	.46	.31
4. Appetite Gain	−.12	.16	.23	**.51**	.26	.08
5. Lassitude	.14	.17	.44	.22	**.55**	.22
6. Insomnia	.18	.12	.29	.09	.33	**.51**

NOTE: $N = 804$ (Patients), 522 (Students). Convergent correlations are in bold. IDAS = Inventory of Depression and Anxiety Symptoms. IDAS-CR = Clinician Rating version of the IDAS.

quantified these relations by conducting significance tests (using the Williams modification of the Hotelling test for two correlations involving a common variable; see Kenny, 1987) comparing these convergent correlations to each of the 10 discriminant coefficients in the same row or column of the block; this yields a total of 60 tests of discriminant validity across these six symptom dimensions in each sample. All 120 comparisons were significant ($p < .05$, one-tailed) across the two samples, which offers impressive evidence of discriminant validity.

IMAS Analyses

We report IMAS data in Samples 5 ($N = 390$ outpatients) and 11 ($N = 381$ students). Results for the patients were reported previously in Watson and Stasik (2014); the college student data are newly reported here.

The IMAS assesses current (i.e., past month) symptoms; individual items are scored on a 3-point rating scale (*absent, subthreshold, above threshold*). Items were derived from the mood and anxiety disorder modules of the Composite International Diagnostic Interview (CIDI; Kessler & Üstün, 2004) and were designed to cover all *DSM-IV* mood and anxiety disorder symptom criteria. Based on data from prior studies (Gamez et al., 2010; Watson et al., 2007), the IMAS was revised to improve its symptom coverage. The revised version includes five-item measures of Dysphoria and Lassitude, four-item Insomnia and Suicidality scales, and a three-item measure of Appetite Loss (the IMAS does not contain a standalone index of appetite gain).

Extensively trained lay interviewers administered the IMAS. All patient interviews were recorded; a randomly selected interviewer rescored 34 tapes. Interrater reliability consistently was excellent in this sample, with ICCs ranging from .97 to .99 across the various scales (see Watson et al., 2012).

Table 3.9 presents correlations between the IDAS and IMAS scales in the form of a heteromethod block. We again see strong evidence of convergent validity, with correlations ranging from .61 (Lassitude) to .74 (Insomnia) in Sample 5 (mean $r = .68$), and from .64 (Lassitude) to .79 (Insomnia, Appetite Loss) in Sample 11 (mean $r = .73$).

With regard to discriminant validity, we again conducted significance tests comparing each of the convergent correlations to the eight other values in its row or column of the heteromethod block. In Sample 5, 39 of the 40 comparisons (97.5%) were significant ($p < .05$, one-tailed); the sole exception was that the convergent correlation for Lassitude ($r = .61$) was not significantly higher than the discriminant correlation between IDAS Dysphoria and IMAS Lassitude ($r = .57$). Similarly, 39 of the 40 comparisons (97.5%) were significant in Sample 11; once again, the single exception was that the convergent correlation for Lassitude ($r = .64$) was not significantly greater than the discriminant correlation between IDAS Dysphoria and IMAS Lassitude ($r = .61$).

Table 3.9 Convergent/Discriminant Validity Analyses: Correlations Between the IDAS and IMAS Scales in Patient and Student Samples

	IMAS Scale				
IDAS Scale	1	2	3	4	5
Sample 5					
1. Insomnia	**.74**	.27	.40	.43	.39
2. Suicidality	.21	**.71**	.20	.45	.30
3. Appetite Loss	.31	.24	**.70**	.32	.35
4. Dysphoria	.37	.45	.35	**.64**	.57
5. Lassitude	.14	.26	.24	.44	**.61**
Sample 11					
1. Insomnia	**.79**	.20	.46	.32	.49
2. Suicidality	.16	**.71**	.24	.47	.39
3. Appetite Loss	.42	.34	**.79**	.36	.42
4. Dysphoria	.42	.46	.44	**.69**	.61
5. Lassitude	.43	.33	.39	.42	**.64**

NOTE: $N = 390$ Patients (Sample 5), 381 Students (Sample 11). Convergent correlations are in bold. IDAS = Inventory of Depression and Anxiety Symptoms. IMAS = Interview for Mood and Anxiety Symptoms.

Overall, these data offer compelling evidence of convergent and discriminant validity. All of the convergent correlations were significant and at least moderate in magnitude, with mean coefficients of .55 (IDAS-CR student analyses), .63 (IDAS-CR patient analyses), .68 (IMAS patient analyses), and .73 (IMAS student analyses). The scales also generally showed excellent discriminant validity; indeed, 198 of the 200 individual comparisons (99%) were significant ($p < .05$, one-tailed) across these multitrait-multimethod analyses. Thus, our data demonstrate that specific depression symptoms—such as lassitude, insomnia, suicidality, and appetite loss—can be distinguished from one another across methods.

SPECIFICITY TO DEPRESSION

Relations With the Beck Inventories

In establishing the construct validity of these scales, another important issue is specificity, that is, whether or not it is appropriate to view them as indicators of depression, as opposed to something broader (e.g., internalizing psychopathology). Put differently, how specific are these symptoms to depression, as opposed to anxiety or some other form of psychopathology? This issue can be analyzed in a number of different ways and from several different perspectives. One approach is to compare how the scales relate to general measures of depression and anxiety, such as the BDI-II and the Beck Anxiety Inventory (BAI; Beck & Steer, 1990). We examined these correlations in a very large standardized combined sample ($N = 4{,}251$) consisting of 968 patients, 743 community adults, 674 college students, 1,056 postpartum women, 375 adolescents, and 222 diabetics (portions of these data were reported previously in Watson, 2009, and Watson et al., 2007).

Three IDAS scales showed a reasonable degree of specificity in these data, clearly correlating more strongly with the BDI-II than with the BAI: Dysphoria ($rs = .82$ and .71, respectively; difference = .110), Lassitude ($rs = .63$ and .53, respectively; difference = .093), and Suicidality ($rs = .58$ and .48, respectively; difference = .092). In contrast, the three remaining scales—Insomnia, Appetite Loss, and Appetite Gain—showed much poorer specificity. Indeed, Insomnia ($rs = .51$ and .49, respectively; difference = .023) and Appetite Loss ($rs = .42$ and .42, respectively; difference = .002) had virtually identical correlations with the two Beck inventories. Appetite Gain had relatively weak associations with both scales ($rs = .31$ and .25, respectively; difference = .060) in these data.[1]

One striking aspect of these results is that the three scales displaying greater specificity to depression actually tended to have stronger associations with the BAI (mean $r = .58$) than did those showing poor specificity (mean $r = .39$). Thus, they achieved greater specificity not by correlating more weakly with the BAI, but

1. IDAS General Depression—which draws items from several of these scales—also showed good specificity in these analyses, correlating more strongly with the BDI-II ($r = .83$) than with the BAI ($r = .71$; difference = .127).

by correlating more strongly with the BDI-II (mean *rs* = .69 and .42 for the more and less specific scales, respectively). It also is noteworthy that the Dysphoria, Lassitude, and Suicidality scales tend to have higher loadings on the general factor underlying the IDAS and IDAS-II (see Tables 2.8 and 2.9 in Chapter 2) and to have a stronger component of general distress. These results therefore support a key element of the quadripartite model proposed by Watson (2009), namely, that the specificity of a scale is not directly related to—or dependent on—the size of its general distress component. Indeed, as we see here, the three scales with a stronger distress component (Dysphoria, Lassitude, Suicidality) actually show greater specificity than those with a weaker distress component (Insomnia, Appetite Loss, Appetite Gain).

Diagnostic Specificity

Prior Data

Next, we examine the key issue of *diagnostic specificity*, that is, whether these symptoms are more strongly related to major depression than to *DSM-IV* anxiety disorders (for earlier discussions of this issue, see Watson, 2009; Watson, O'Hara, Chmielewski, et al., 2008; Watson & Stasik, 2014). Although the available evidence on this topic is quite limited, there is reason to question the diagnostic specificity of some depression symptoms. For instance, Benazzi (2006) examined the prevalence of depression symptoms in samples of patients diagnosed with bipolar-II (BP-II) disorder and major depression; his results indicated that several symptoms (as assessed by the Structured Clinical Interview for DSM-IV [SCID-IV]; First et al., 1997) showed poor diagnostic specificity. More specifically, symptoms of weight gain, increased eating, hypersomnia, psychomotor agitation, worthlessness, and poor concentration actually were significantly more common in BP-II patients than in those with major depression. Such an overlap in symptom presentation poses problems for discriminating between diagnoses and could lead to the underdiagnosis or misdiagnosis of BP-II (Benazzi, 2006).

Another important consideration is that several of the symptom criteria for major depression are also part of the criterion sets for other mental disorders. For example, insomnia/sleep disturbance is one of the Criterion E symptoms of posttraumatic stress disorder (PTSD), and difficulty concentrating is included in the diagnostic criteria for both PTSD and generalized anxiety disorder (GAD) in *DSM-5*. In a related vein, Carney, Ulmer, Edinger, Krystal, and Knauss (2009) noted that self-report measures of depression typically include symptoms that are also essential features of *DSM-IV* primary insomnia (e.g., insomnia, mood disturbance, irritability, fatigue, impaired concentration, and motivation/anergia; this condition now is labeled *insomnia disorder* in *DSM-5*). Accordingly, Carney et al. (2009) assessed the accuracy of the BDI-II in detecting major depression in patients known to meet *DSM-IV* diagnostic criteria for insomnia. They found that several BDI-II items failed to differentiate (a) those with insomnia from (b) those with insomnia and comorbid depression. More specifically, there were no significant differences between groups on insomnia, irritability, suicidal ideation, increased appetite, decreased concentration, fatigue, decreased libido, and self-critical and punishment-related thoughts. The items that did successfully demonstrate group differences included those related to depressed mood, pessimism, past failure, anhedonia, guilt, self-dislike, crying, agitation, indecision, worthlessness, energy, hypersomnia, and loss of appetite. Thus, on the basis of this limited evidence, it appears that some symptoms are better, purer indicators of depression than are others.

IDAS Data

To examine this issue more fully, we report seven analyses of diagnostic specificity that enable us to evaluate the robustness of these patterns across methods, measures, and populations (six of these analyses are adapted from data reported previously in Watson and Stasik, 2014; findings from Sample 4 are newly presented here). As was noted in Chapter 2, the Sample 4 participants received *DSM-5* diagnoses using an adapted version of the M.I.N.I. (Sheehan et al., 1998) (for interrater reliability data, see Watson et al., 2015a, 2015b). In all other analyses, current *DSM-IV* diagnoses were obtained using the SCID-IV (for interrater reliability data, see Watson, O'Hara, Chmielewski, et al., 2008; Watson et al., 2012).

To examine diagnostic specificity, we computed polyserial correlations between depression symptom measures and various depressive and anxiety disorder diagnoses. Similar to the tetrachoric correlations that were discussed in Chapter 1, polyserial correlations estimate the linear association between two normally distributed latent continuous variables when one of the observed variables is ordinal and the other is continuous (Flora & Curran, 2004; Olsson, Drasgow, & Dorans, 1982). They retain the relative rank order information provided by Pearson correlations (i.e., the same scales will be relatively strong—or weak—predictors of particular variables), but they are unaffected by differences in prevalence rates, thereby facilitating cross-diagnosis comparisons. The interview variables were scored as 0 = *absent*, 1 = *present*, so that positive correlations indicate that higher scores on a factor were associated with an increased likelihood of receiving that rating.

In the first three analyses, we present polyserial correlations between the IDAS ($N = 894$; see Table 3.10), IDAS-CR ($N = 604$; see Table 3.11), and IMAS ($N = 293$; see Table 3.12) depression scales and eight *DSM-IV* mood and anxiety disorder diagnoses (major depression, GAD, PTSD, panic disorder, agoraphobia, social phobia, specific phobia, obsessive-compulsive disorder [OCD]) in outpatient samples. Note that the IDAS analyses use data collapsed across Samples 1, 2, and 5 (see Table 2.14); the IDAS-CR results combine Samples 1 and 2, whereas the IMAS findings are based on Sample 5. The fourth analysis (see Table 3.13) examines how the IDAS scales correlate with *DSM-5* versions of these same diagnoses (except for specific phobia, which was not assessed in these participants) in Sample 4 ($N = 407$). The fifth analysis involves correlations between the IDAS scales and *DSM-IV* diagnoses of (a) major depression and (b) GAD in

Table 3.10 Polyserial Correlations Between the IDAS Depression Scales and *DSM-IV* Diagnoses in a Combined Outpatient Sample

IDAS Scale	MDD	GAD	PTSD	Panic	Agora	Social Phobia	Specific Phobia	OCD
Dysphoria	**.71**	**.45**	**.41**	**.43**	.32	.26	.19	.23
Lassitude	**.49**	.28	.29	.26	.21	.15	.10	.12
Suicidality	**.46**	.20	.25	.20	.17	.12	.07	.16
Insomnia	**.41**	.29	.39	.32	.22	.20	.21	.23
Appetite Loss	.36	.17	.35	.30	.17	.15	.12	.12
Appetite Gain	.12	.06	.06	−.05	.02	.03	.11	.07

NOTE: $N = 894$. Correlations ≥ |.40| are in bold. IDAS = Inventory of Depression and Anxiety Symptoms. MDD = major depression. GAD = generalized anxiety disorder. PTSD = posttraumatic stress disorder. Agora = agoraphobia. OCD = obsessive-compulsive disorder. These results are based on a combined sample that includes data from Samples 1, 2, and 5 (see Table 2.14).

337 postpartum women from Sample 7 (see Table 3.14). The final two analyses (see Table 3.15) evaluate how the IDAS scales ($N = 307$) and IDAS-CR ratings ($N = 303$) correlate with *DSM-IV* diagnoses of (a) major depression and (b) any anxiety disorder in the students of Sample 8 (for more details regarding these samples, see Watson et al., 2007, 2012, 2014; Watson, O'Hara, Chmielewski, et al., 2008).

What do these analyses tell us about the specificity of depression symptoms? To make sense of these complex results, we provide brief summaries of the results for each symptom dimension.

Table 3.11 Polyserial Correlations Between IDAS-CR Depression Symptom Ratings and *DSM-IV* Diagnoses in a Combined Outpatient Sample

IDAS-CR Rating	MDD	GAD	PTSD	Panic	Agora	Social Phobia	Specific Phobia	OCD
Dysphoria	**.58**	**.40**	.31	**.45**	.34	.26	.18	.29
Lassitude	**.48**	.23	.25	.36	.32	.24	.14	.36
Suicidality	**.41**	.19	.16	.22	.17	.16	.07	.20
Insomnia	.24	.20	.26	.28	.20	.15	.02	.15
Appetite Loss	.28	.18	.26	.26	.04	.16	.04	.08
Appetite Gain	.18	−.01	.02	-.09	.01	−.06	.05	.06

NOTE: $N = 604$. Correlations ≥ |.40| are in bold. IDAS-CR = Clinician Rating version of the IDAS. MDD = major depression. GAD = generalized anxiety disorder. PTSD = posttraumatic stress disorder. Agora = agoraphobia. OCD = obsessive-compulsive disorder. These results are based on a combined sample that includes data from Samples 1 and 2 (see Table 2.14).

Table 3.12 Polyserial Correlations Between the IMAS Depression Symptom Scales and *DSM-IV* Diagnoses in Sample 5

IMAS Scale	MDD	GAD	PTSD	Panic	Agora	Social Phobia	Specific Phobia	OCD
Dysphoria	**.58**	.22	**.40**	.16	.04	.15	.12	.07
Lassitude	**.57**	.26	.27	.29	.21	.18	.19	.01
Suicidality	**.45**	.12	.20	.10	.04	.07	.17	.16
Insomnia	.31	.08	.26	.21	.20	.18	.27	.14
Appetite Loss	.36	.09	**.43**	.24	.24	.07	.17	.21

NOTE: $N=293$ outpatients. Correlations $\geq |.40|$ are in bold. IMAS = Interview for Mood and Anxiety Symptoms. MDD = major depression. GAD = generalized anxiety disorder. PTSD = posttraumatic stress disorder. Agora = agoraphobia. OCD = obsessive-compulsive disorder.

Dysphoria

The dysphoria measures showed both (a) the strongest overall association with major depression and (b) impressive diagnostic specificity in these analyses. Specifically, they had the strongest single correlation with major depression in all seven analyses (*r*s ranged from .58 to .77), and in every case correlated more strongly with depression than with any other disorder. To quantify these effects further, we computed weighted mean correlations across all of these analyses. Overall, the dysphoria measures had a mean polyserial correlation of .66 with major depression; in marked contrast, their average correlations with specific anxiety disorder diagnoses were only .45 (GAD), .41 (panic disorder), .40 (PTSD), .30 (agoraphobia), .28 (social phobia), .28 (OCD), and .18 (specific phobia). Thus, consistent with the results obtained earlier with the Beck inventories—and with the quadripartite model of Watson (2009)—we again see

Table 3.13 Polyserial Correlations Between the IDAS Depression Scales and *DSM-5* Diagnoses in Sample 4

IDAS Scale	MDD	GAD	PTSD	Panic	Agora	Social Phobia	Specific Phobia	OCD
Dysphoria	**.71**	**.61**	**.49**	**.48**	**.40**	**.46**	.—	**.54**
Lassitude	**.55**	**.52**	**.45**	**.41**	.38	**.44**	.—	.38
Suicidality	**.45**	.28	.34	.20	.20	.26	.—	.34
Insomnia	**.53**	**.43**	**.41**	.33	.36	.26	.—	.33
Appetite Loss	**.43**	.31	.30	.18	.23	.22	.—	.20
Appetite Gain	.27	.31	.21	.24	.18	.26	.—	.28

NOTE: $N=407$ adults. Correlations $\geq |.40|$ are in bold. IDAS = Inventory of Depression and Anxiety Symptoms. MDD = major depression. GAD = generalized anxiety disorder. PTSD = posttraumatic stress disorder. Agora = agoraphobia. OCD = obsessive-compulsive disorder.

Table 3.14 Polyserial Correlations Between the IDAS Depression Scales and *DSM-IV* Diagnoses in Sample 7

IDAS Scale	MDD	GAD
Dysphoria	**.61**	**.51**
Lassitude	**.53**	**.40**
Suicidality	.38	.19
Insomnia	.38	**.45**
Appetite Loss	.33	.10
Appetite Gain	.20	.27

NOTE: $N = 337$ postpartum women. Correlations ≥ |.40| are in bold. IDAS = Inventory of Depression and Anxiety Symptoms. MDD = major depression. GAD = generalized anxiety disorder. These results are based on an expanded version of the postpartum sample described in Watson et al. (2007).

evidence that symptoms containing a very strong general distress component still can display considerable specificity.

Lassitude

Indicators of lassitude also were strongly related to depression (*r*s ranged from .48 to .57) and displayed substantial diagnostic specificity in these analyses. With regard to the latter, lassitude correlated more strongly with depression than with any other disorder in all seven analyses. Overall, lassitude symptoms had a weighted mean correlation of .51 with major depression, whereas their average correlations with specific anxiety diagnoses ranged from only .13 (specific phobia) to .32 (GAD, panic

Table 3.15 Polyserial Correlations Between the IDAS Depression Scales, IDAS-CR Depression Symptom Ratings, and *DSM-IV* Diagnoses in Sample 8

	IDAS		IDAS-CR	
Symptom	MDD	Any AD	MDD	Any AD
Dysphoria	**.77**	**.55**	**.60**	**.44**
Lassitude	**.51**	.33	**.52**	**.40**
Suicidality	**.42**	.27	.19	.13
Insomnia	.38	.23	.25	.21
Appetite Loss	.31	.16	.15	.19
Appetite Gain	.17	.15	.16	.17

NOTE: $N = 307$ students (IDAS analyses), 303 students (IDAS-CR analyses). Correlations ≥ |.40| are in bold. IDAS = Inventory of Depression and Anxiety Symptoms. IDAS-CR = Clinician Rating version of the IDAS. MDD = major depression. AD = anxiety disorder.

disorder). These findings are consistent with results reported earlier by Watson (2009) and establish that lassitude is a strong and specific symptom of depression.

Suicidality

Suicidality symptoms also displayed impressive specificity in these data; in all seven analyses, they correlated more strongly with major depression (*r*s ranged from .19 to .46) than with any other disorder. Overall, these suicidality measures had a mean correlation of .41 with major depression, whereas their average correlations with specific anxiety disorder diagnoses ranged from only .09 (specific phobia) to .24 (PTSD). These results indicate that suicidality is a moderately strong and specific symptom of depression (see also Watson, 2009).

Insomnia

Insomnia measures were moderately related to major depression (*r*s ranged from .25 to .53) and showed weak, inconsistent evidence of diagnostic specificity. Overall, in fact, indicators of insomnia had very similar mean correlations with major depression (.36), PTSD (.34), panic disorder (.30), and GAD (.29). Thus, consistent with the results of Watson (2009), these findings indicate that insomnia is a relatively modest and nonspecific indicator of depression.

Appetite Loss

Findings for appetite loss were very similar to those for insomnia: These symptoms had relatively weak correlations with major depression (*r*s ranged from .15 to .43) and showed little specificity. Overall, symptoms of appetite loss had a mean correlation of only .31 with major depression; they correlated similarly with panic disorder (average $r = .26$) and actually had a slightly stronger association with PTSD (mean $r = .33$). Therefore, similar to insomnia, appetite loss emerges as a relatively weak and nonspecific symptom of depression in these analyses.

Appetite Gain

Consistent with previous results (see Watson, 2009; Watson et al., 2007; Watson, O'Hara, & Chmielewski, et al., 2008), indicators of appetite gain had the weakest overall associations with major depression (*r*s ranged from .12 to .27, mean $r = .17$). Their relations with the anxiety disorders were inconsistent across analyses, but they tended to be quite low. Overall, their weighted mean correlations with specific anxiety diagnoses ranged from only .00 (panic disorder) to .12 (GAD). Thus, symptoms of appetite gain do not show strong or consistent associations with any of these emotional disorder diagnoses. Taken together with the data reported in Table 3.6, these results further suggest that indicators of appetite gain actually may be more informative in assessing other types of psychopathology, such as symptoms of eating pathology.

Summary

Taken together, these analyses yield a very clear pattern. The three symptom dimensions that have the strongest associations with major depression—dysphoria (mean $r = .66$), lassitude (mean $r = .51$), and suicidality (mean $r = .41$)—also show the clearest, most compelling evidence of specificity. Put differently, the symptoms that display less impressive specificity—insomnia, appetite loss, and appetite gain—do so, in large part, because of their weaker associations with depression (mean *rs* = .36, .31, and .17, respectively). This, in turn, raises the question of whether these weak and nonspecific symptoms actually are necessary, that is, whether they make significant, incremental contributions to the diagnosis of major depression. We examine this issue in our next series of analyses.

INCREMENTAL VALIDITY

Logistic Regression Analyses

Given that the more specific symptom dimensions had the strongest bivariate associations with major depression, one would expect that they also would emerge as particularly strong contributors in multivariate analyses. To test this expectation, we conducted a series of logistic regression analyses to identify the unique, incremental ability of individual depression symptoms to predict diagnoses of major depression (Watson & Stasik, 2014, report a parallel series of analyses in these same datasets—with the exception of Sample 4—that include the IDAS Well-Being scale as an additional predictor). To facilitate interpretation, the symptom scales were standardized to put them on the same metric.

Table 3.16 presents the odds ratios (ORs) from these analyses. Not surprisingly, dysphoria symptoms—which showed the strongest bivariate association with depression—emerged as a significant predictor in all seven analyses, with ORs ranging from 1.83 to 9.74. In addition, lassitude symptoms contributed significantly in all three analyses based on interview measures (ORs ranged from 1.79 to 2.56). This pattern reflects the fact that lassitude symptoms correlate

Table 3.16 ODDS RATIOS FROM LOGISTIC REGRESSION ANALYSES PREDICTING *DSM-IV* DIAGNOSES OF MAJOR DEPRESSION FROM DEPRESSION SYMPTOMS

	IDAS				IDAS-CR		
Symptom	**Patient**	**Adult**	**Postpartum**	**Student**	**Patient**	**Student**	**IMAS**
Dysphoria	5.08**	6.54**	2.60**	9.74**	2.31**	3.32**	1.83**
Lassitude	1.19	0.80	1.47	1.20	1.79**	2.49**	2.56**
Suicidality	1.06	0.99	1.22	1.19	1.51**	1.21	0.99
Insomnia	1.14	1.57*	0.90	1.08	1.11	1.06	1.26
Appetite Loss	0.96	0.88	1.17	0.78	1.44**	1.11	1.20
Appetite Gain	0.79*	0.88	0.96	0.67	1.45**	1.12	.—

NOTE: *N* = 894 (IDAS: Patient), 407 (IDAS: Adult), 351 (IDAS: Postpartum), 307 (IDAS: Student), 605 (IDAS-CR: Patient), 303 (IDAS-CR: Student), 293 (IMAS). IDAS = Inventory of Depression and Anxiety Symptoms. IDAS-CR = Clinician Rating version of the IDAS. IMAS = Interview for Mood and Anxiety Symptoms.
$^*p < .05$ $^{**}p < .01$

strongly with dysphoria in self-report data (see Table 3.3), but more moderately in clinicians' ratings (see Table 3.4), thereby enhancing their ability to make a unique incremental contribution in the latter. Overall, these two symptom dimensions showed incremental predictive power in 10 of 14 analyses (71.4%). Thus, two of the symptoms that showed substantial specificity in earlier analyses—dysphoria and lassitude—also displayed the strongest predictive power in these data.

In contrast, the three symptoms that exhibited little diagnostic specificity—insomnia, appetite loss, and appetite gain—made significant incremental contributions in only 4 of 20 analyses (20.0%). Insomnia and appetite loss symptoms each added incrementally in only one analysis. Indicators of appetite gain contributed significantly in two cases, but one of these represents a suppressor effect: *Lower* scores on IDAS Appetite Gain were associated with an increased likelihood of major depression in the patient sample (see first column of Table 3.16). Overall, therefore, our results indicate that the nonspecific symptoms of major depression actually contribute very little to its diagnosis.

Implications and Conclusions

In thinking about the implications of these findings, it may be helpful to put them in classic assessment terms. Using this framework as a guide, our data yield three basic conclusions. First, symptoms of insomnia and appetite disturbance show relatively poor discriminant validity (i.e., diagnostic specificity) in comparison to indicators of dysphoria, lassitude, and suicidality. Second, these same symptoms demonstrate unimpressive convergent/criterion validity; that is, they have relatively weak bivariate associations with diagnoses of major depression. Third, these symptom dimensions display little or no incremental validity in logistic regression analyses. These final analyses are particularly noteworthy, in that they suggest that these weak, nonspecific symptoms actually may be superfluous in reaching a diagnosis of major depression. This being the case, it seems reasonable to suggest that the diagnosis of depression might be improved by focusing primarily on strong and specific indicators (such as dysphoria and lassitude) and deemphasizing relatively weak and nonspecific symptoms, such as insomnia and appetite disturbance.

The findings we have presented here are preliminary and they clearly need to be replicated and extended in future research. Still, they suggest that it will be useful to scrutinize the properties of these low distress, nonspecific, and poorly functioning symptoms much more closely in the future.

THE CRITERION VALIDITY OF GENERAL DEPRESSION SCALES

The data reported in Tables 3.10 (combined outpatient sample), 3.13 (Sample 4), 3.14 (Sample 7), and 3.15 (Sample 8) establish that certain IDAS depression scales (i.e., Dysphoria, Lassitude, and Suicidality) display stronger criterion validity vis-à-vis *DSM* diagnoses of major depression than do others (i.e., Insomnia, Appetite Loss, Appetite Gain). Another important and related issue concerns how the criterion validity of the IDAS scales compares to that of other popular self-report measures. We examine this issue in the next series of analyses.

Table 3.17 reports both Pearson product-moment correlations (which are informative here, given that we are not conducting any cross-diagnosis comparisons) and polyserial correlations between *DSM-IV* diagnoses of major depression and five broad depression measures—IDAS General Depression, IDAS Dysphoria, the BDI-II, the CES-D, and the EPDS—in outpatient (*N*= 579 and 245 in the BDI-II and CES-D subsamples, respectively), postpartum (Sample 7, *N*= 348), and college student (Sample 8, *N*= 306) samples. Three aspects of these results are noteworthy. First, the self-report scales generally display impressive criterion validity. The Pearson coefficients range from .44 to .65 across measures and samples; the polyserial correlations range from .57 to .78. Thus, our data strongly support the criterion validity of these scales.

Table 3.17 Pearson and Polyserial Correlations Between General Depression Scales and *DSM-IV* Diagnoses of Major Depression

Sample/Scale	Pearson	Polyserial
BDI-II Patient Subsample		
IDAS General Depression	.62	.74
IDAS Dysphoria	.62	.73
BDI-II	.62	.72
CES-D Patient Subsample		
IDAS General Depression	.64	.76
IDAS Dysphoria	.64	.75
BDI-II	.63	.73
CES-D	.65	.78
Postpartum Women (Sample 7)		
IDAS General Depression	.52	.63
IDAS Dysphoria	.51	.61
BDI-II	.51	.60
EPDS	.49	.61
College Students (Sample 8)		
IDAS General Depression	.49	.69
IDAS Dysphoria	.50	.73
BDI-II	.44	.57

Note: *N*= 579 (BDI-II Patient Subsample), 245 (CES-D Patient Subsample), 348 (Postpartum), 306 (College Students). BDI-II = Beck Depression Inventory-II. CES-D = Center for Epidemiological Studies Depression Scale. EPDS = Edinburgh Postnatal Depression Scale.

Second, as would be expected based on the correlations reported in Table 3.5, these five scales all show very similar levels of criterion validity. For our purposes, it is particularly reassuring that the IDAS scales produced correlations that are virtually identical to those obtained with the BDI-II, CES-D, and EPDS.

Third, the four scales assessed in Sample 7 displayed virtually identical levels of criterion validity: The Pearson correlations ranged from .49 (EPDS) to .52 (IDAS General Depression), whereas the polyserial coefficients ranged from .60 (BDI-II) to .63 (IDAS General Depression). These findings again indicate that specialty depression measures—such as the EPDS—provide little useful information that is not obtainable from standard depression scales, such as the BDI-II and IDAS General Depression.

SEX DIFFERENCES

We conclude this chapter with a brief examination of sex differences in depression. It is well established that the prevalence of major depression is greater in women than in men (American Psychiatric Association, 2000, 2013; Kessler et al., 2003). The *DSM-5* text discussion of major depressive disorder, for example, states: "Females experience 1.5 to 3-fold higher rates than males beginning in early adolescence" (p. 165).

This might lead one to expect that measures of depressive symptoms would display substantial sex differences, but this is not the case. In fact, sex differences on self-report depression measures tend to be relatively small. In the BDI Manual, for instance, Beck and Steer (1993) concluded: "Overall, the revised BDI scores are not meaningfully related to gender and age. However, there are studies reporting significant, but not meaningful, relationships between the BDI and these variables (Beck, Steer, & Garbin, 1988)" (p. 19). Sex differences on the BDI-II and CES-D also tend to be small and inconsistent across studies (e.g., Arnau, Meagher, Norris, & Bramson, 2001; Dozois et al., 1998; Lewinsohn, Seeley, Roberts, & Allen, 1997; Roberts, Andrews, Lewinsohn, & Hops, 1990; Zeiders, Umaña-Taylor, & Derlan, 2013). For example, Lewinsohn et al. (1997) reported that CES-D scores of men and women did not differ significantly in a large (586 women, 419 men) sample of community-residing older adults. Similarly, Dozois et al. (1998) found no sex difference on the BDI-II in a large ($N = 1{,}022$; 67% female) sample of college students.

We have replicated and extended these findings in our own data. Table 3.18 reports relevant findings across a broad range of depression measures—including the IDAS self-report depression scales, the BDI-II, the CES-D, and clinicians' ratings on the IDAS-CR—in patient, community adult, and student samples. Given the size of our samples, we focus here on effect sizes, rather than statistical significance per se. Accordingly, we computed Cohen's d (Cohen, 1992) by (a) calculating the difference between the mean scale scores of men and women in each sample and then (b) dividing this value by the pooled standard deviation in that sample.

Table 3.18 Mean Score Comparisons (Expressed as Cohen's *d*) of Depression Symptoms in Women Versus Men

IDAS-II Scale	Patients	Community Adults	College Students
General Self-Report Scales			
General Depression	0.09	−0.13	0.18
Dysphoria	0.08	−0.09	0.18
BDI-II	0.19	0.13	0.11
CES-D	0.03	0.02	.—
Specific Self-Report Scales			
Lassitude	0.04	−0.09	0.16
Suicidality	−0.02	−0.19	−0.11
Insomnia	−0.06	−0.19	0.14
Appetite Loss	−0.03	−0.11	0.10
Appetite Gain	*0.31*	0.20	0.24
IDAS-CR Ratings			
Dysphoria	−0.03	.—	*0.33*
Lassitude	0.15	.—	*0.36*
Suicidality	0.02	.—	−0.08
Insomnia	−0.01	.—	0.20
Appetite Loss	−0.03	.—	0.12
Appetite Gain	0.18	.—	0.15

NOTE: For the IDAS, *N* = 1,905 Patients (676 men, 1,229 women), 1,832 Adults (529 men, 1,303 women), 4,014 Students (1,381 men, 2,633 women). For the BDI-II, *N* = 966 patients (326 men, 640 women), 740 adults (196 men, 544 women), 674 students (209 men, 465 women). For the CES-D, *N* = 302 patients (110 men, 192 women), 383 adults (79 men, 304 women). For the IDAS-CR, *N* = 802 patients (267 men, 535 women), 521 students (169 men, 352 women). Positive values indicate that women scored higher on the scale; negative values indicate that men had higher scores. Small effect sizes ($d = |.30|$ to $|.49|$ are in italics.

As was noted in Chapter 2, Cohen (1992, Table 1) proposed that *d* values from |0.20| to |0.49| represent small effect sizes; those ranging from |0.50| to |0.79| reflect medium effect sizes; and values of |0.80| or greater indicate large effect sizes. We report 38 effect sizes in Table 3.18, and none of them are medium or large in magnitude according to Cohen's criteria. In fact, only three of them (7.9%) even meet Cohen's threshold for a small effect: Women had higher scores on IDAS Appetite Gain ($d = 0.31$) in patients, and on IDAS-CR Dysphoria ($d = 0.33$) and Lassitude ($d = 0.36$) in college students. Clearly, however, the general conclusion that one should draw from these data is that women and men tend to score very similarly on measures of depressive symptoms. Moreover, our data establish that this pattern is highly robust across measures (e.g., IDAS vs. BDI-II), methods (i.e., self-report vs. clinicians' ratings), and specific types of symptoms (e.g., lassitude vs. appetite loss).

4

Positive Mood Dysfunction in Psychopathology

As we discussed in Chapter 1, factor analytic studies have established the existence of two general, higher order dimensions of emotional experience: Negative Affect and Positive Affect (Watson & Clark, 1997; Watson & Tellegen, 1985; Watson et al., 1999). Both of these dimensions have important links to psychopathology. To date, however, research in this area has focused primarily on dysfunctional manifestations of Negative Affect. This focus is understandable, given that virtually all major forms of psychopathology are characterized by elevated levels of negative emotionality (Chapter 1; see also Caspi et al., 2014; Lahey, 2009; Mineka et al., 1998). Kotov, Gamez, Schmidt, and Watson (2010) reported particularly striking meta-analytic evidence for neuroticism, a personality trait that essentially reflects individual differences in negative affectivity (Watson et al., 1999). Kotov et al. (2010) compared the mean neuroticism scores of individuals with and without unipolar mood, anxiety, and substance use disorders. Neuroticism displayed medium to large effect sizes (expressed as Cohen's *d;* Cohen, 1992) with every analyzed disorder; for example, *d*s (corrected for unreliability) ranged from 1.33 to 2.25 for major depression, generalized anxiety disorder (GAD), posttraumatic stress disorder (PTSD), panic disorder, social phobia, and obsessive-compulsive disorder (OCD).

Although it has received far less attention in the research literature, Positive Affect also has important associations with psychopathology. Thus, the basic goal of this chapter is to explicate the nature of positive mood dysfunction in psychopathology (for an earlier review of this topic, see Watson & Naragon-Gainey, 2010). In Chapter 1, we examined early work in this area that emphasized the existence of a specific positive mood deficit in depression (e.g., Clark & Watson, 1991; Mineka et al., 1998; Watson, Clark, & Carey, 1988). Here, we present more recent data that paint a richer and more complex picture. As we will see, the evidence here differs from that noted earlier for negative mood dysfunction in two important ways. First, in contrast to the pervasiveness of negative emotional disturbance in psychopathology, positive mood dysfunction shows much greater specificity. That is, although many syndromes show substantial links to positive affect, others do not, such that individuals with these disorders experience relatively normal levels of positive mood. Second, unlike Negative Affect—which is consistently elevated in clinical populations—Positive Affect does not display a clear directional trend. Whereas many syndromes are associated with anhedonia and low levels of positive mood, other disorders have been linked to excessive positive emotionality.

We begin by developing a measurement model for positive mood based on the hierarchical structure of emotional experience. In subsequent sections, we examine three types of psychopathology that clearly are associated with anhedonia and deficits in positive emotionality: (a) depression, (b) social anxiety/social phobia, and (c) schizophrenia/schizotypy. We conclude the chapter by examining conditions that are associated with elevated levels of Positive Affect, focusing in particular on the bipolar disorders.

A MEASUREMENT MODEL FOR POSITIVE EMOTIONALITY

The PANAS-X Scales

Early studies in this area—which were summarized in Chapter 1—were based on relatively broad and nonspecific measures of Positive Affect, such as the Positive Emotionality scale from the Multidimensional Personality Questionnaire (Tellegen & Waller, 2008) and the Positive Affect scale from the original Positive and Negative Affect Schedule (PANAS; Watson, Clark, & Tellegen, 1988). We will present some additional data based on these types of measures in this chapter.

It must be emphasized that emotional experience cannot be reduced to the two general dimensions of Negative Affect and Positive Affect. In fact, structural studies consistently have identified specific content factors that correspond to discrete emotions such as sadness, fear, anger, and joy (Tellegen, Watson, & Clark, 1999; Watson & Clark, 1992, 1999). This has led to the articulation of a hierarchical model of affect in which these higher order factors are each composed of several correlated—yet ultimately distinguishable—emotional states (Tellegen et al., 1999; Watson & Clark, 1992). For instance, the higher order Negative Affect dimension can be decomposed into specific emotions such as sadness/depression, fear/anxiety, and anger/hostility (a topic we return to in Chapter 6). In this hierarchical model, the lower level reflects the specific content (and distinctive qualities) of individual affects, whereas the upper level reflects their valence (i.e., whether they represent positive or negative states).

In addition to the general Positive Affect scale of the original PANAS, the Expanded Form of the PANAS—the PANAS-X (Watson & Clark, 1999)—contains three factor analytically derived scales assessing distinctive types of positive mood experience: Joviality (*cheerful, happy, joyful, delighted, excited, enthusiastic, lively, energetic*), Self-Assurance (*strong, proud, confident, bold, daring, fearless*), and Attentiveness (*alert, attentive, concentrating, determined*). Watson and Clark (1999) present extensive data establishing the reliability and validity of these scales. In subsequent sections, we present data establishing that these specific positive mood scales have rather different associations with psychopathology.

The IDAS-II Scales

The development of the expanded version of the IDAS—or IDAS-II—offers exciting new opportunities for explicating the nature of positive mood dysfunction in psychopathology. As noted in Chapter 2, the IDAS-II contains two scales—Well-Being and Euphoria—that correlate strongly with one another (r = .51, N = 4,780; see Table 2.7) and anchor a Positive Mood factor in structural analyses (see Table 2.10). Although they correlate strongly with each other, these two scales relate quite differently to psychopathology. As we will see, the eight-item Well-Being scale assesses a healthy, adaptive form of positive affect (e.g., "I felt cheerful," "I looked forward to things with enjoyment," "I felt hopeful about the future"); it therefore tends to correlate negatively with certain symptoms and disorders. In stark contrast, the five-item Euphoria scale assesses a dysfunctional form of positive affect. It taps content reflecting an elated and expansive mood, heightened energy, and grandiosity/excessive self-esteem (e.g., "I felt like I was 'on top of the world,'" "I had so much energy it was hard for me to sit still," "I felt I could do things that other people couldn't"). Its pathological nature is established by the fact that it tends to correlate *positively* with certain forms of psychopathology, as we demonstrate subsequently.

In later sections, we report data on these self-report IDAS-II scales, as well as their counterparts on the interview-based IDAS-CR (see Chapter 3; see also Koffel, 2011; Watson et al., 2012; Watson, O'Hara, Chmielewski, et al., 2008). It therefore is important to establish the convergent and discriminant validity of these measures. Table 4.1 presents separate sets of correlations between these IDAS-II scales and IDAS-CR ratings in Samples 6 (N = 199 outpatients) and 10 (N = 219 students). Looking first at convergent validity, both IDAS-II scales were significantly related to their IDAS-CR counterparts in both samples, with coefficients

Table 4.1 Convergent/Discriminant Validity Analyses: Correlations Between IDAS-II/IDAS-CR Well-Being and Euphoria in Samples 6 (Patients) and 10 (Students)

Measure	1	2	3	4
IDAS-II Scales				
1. Well-Being	.—	.37	**.43**	.14
2. Euphoria	.36	.—	.13	**.31**
IDAS-CR Ratings				
3. Well-Being	**.56**	.17	.—	.04
4. Euphoria	.27	**.44**	.20	.—

Note: Patient correlations (Sample 6, N = 199) are shown below the diagonal; student data (Sample 10, N = 219) are displayed above the diagonal. Convergent correlations are in bold.

ranging from .31 to .56 (mean $r = .44$). It should be noted that although these correlations are significant and at least moderate in magnitude, they tend to be somewhat lower than those seen earlier with the IDAS depression scales (presented in Chapter 3). This finding reflects, in part, the fact that our interviewers have found it more challenging to evaluate clinically meaningful variations in positive mood than levels of distress/dysfunction (for a discussion of this issue, see Watson, O'Hara, Chmielewski, et al., 2008).

We turn now to discriminant validity. To establish discriminant validity, each of the convergent correlations should be higher than the other values in its row or column of the heteromethod block (Campbell & Fiske, 1959). Table 4.1 indicates that the symptom measures met this criterion in every case. We further quantified these relations by conducting significance tests (using the Williams modification of the Hotelling test for two correlations involving a common variable; see Kenny, 1987). All eight comparisons were significant ($p < .05$, one-tailed) across the two samples, with *z*s ranging from 2.00 to 5.74. Thus, we see clear evidence of discriminant validity.

Relations Between the PANAS-X and IDAS-II Scales

It also is important to consider how the positive mood scales of the PANAS-X and IDAS-II relate to each other. Table 4.2 reports correlations among them—along with two strong markers of negative affectivity, the PANAS-X general Negative Affect scale and the IDAS-II Dysphoria scale—in two large samples of participants who were assessed using different versions of the PANAS-X. Participants in the first sample (Past Week sample, $N = 1{,}113$; this included 91 patients, 352 community adults, and 670 college students) rated their recent mood using "past week" time instructions, whereas those in the second sample (General sample, $N = 917$; this included 372 community adults and 545 college students) completed the PANAS-X using general, trait instructions; as in previous chapters, to

Table 4.2 Correlations Between Selected IDAS-II and PANAS-X Scales

Scale	1	2	3	4	5	6	7
1. IDAS-II Well-Being	.—	**.49**	**.74**	**.59**	**.65**	−.40	−.40
2. IDAS-II Euphoria	**.45**	.—	.38	.38	.29	.09	.03
3. PANAS-X Joviality	**.71**	.37	.—	**.70**	**.65**	−.41	−.38
4. PANAS-X Self-Assurance	**.59**	**.48**	**.70**	.—	**.65**	−.25	−.15
5. PANAS-X Attentiveness	**.57**	.27	**.62**	**.60**	.—	−.37	−.28
6. IDAS-II Dysphoria	−.44	.13	−.47	−.26	−.30	.—	**.74**
7. PANAS-X Negative Affect	−.36	.14	−.34	−.13	−.18	**.75**	.—

NOTE: $N = 1{,}113$ (Past Week), 917 (General). Past Week data are shown below the diagonal; general data are displayed above the diagonal. Correlations ≥ |.09| are significant at $p < .01$. Correlations ≥ |.45| are in bold. PANAS-X = Expanded Form of the Positive and Negative Affect Schedule.

eliminate mean-level differences across populations (i.e., patients vs. adults vs. students), we standardized the scale scores on a within-population basis and then combined them to permit a single overall analysis in each sample.

These data clearly establish a strong, specific link between IDAS-II Well-Being and PANAS-X Joviality, indicating that they tap a very similar construct (i.e., feelings of joy, enthusiasm, energy, and optimism). In fact, follow-up statistical tests showed that Well-Being correlated significantly more strongly with Joviality (r=.71 and .74 in the Past Week and General samples, respectively) than with Self-Assurance and Attentiveness (rs ranged from .57 to .65) in both samples (zs ranged from 4.78 to 8.76, all ps < .01, two-tailed). Consequently, we can expect these two scales to have very similar associations with psychopathology.

In contrast, Euphoria tends to correlate more strongly with Self-Assurance than with other types of positive mood. Follow-up tests indicated that Euphoria correlated significantly more strongly with Self-Assurance (r=.48) than with Joviality (r=.37, z=5.17) and Attentiveness (r=.27, z=8.78) in the Past Week sample. Parallel analyses in the General sample again revealed that Euphoria correlated significantly more strongly with Self-Assurance (r=.38) than with Attentiveness (r=.22, z=3.77); however, the difference with Joviality (r=.38) was nonsignificant (z=0.28) in these data. Overall, it appears that the positive emotional content in Euphoria is tipped in the direction of pride, daring, and self-confidence (i.e., Self-Assurance).

To further explicate these relations, we computed partial correlations between the IDAS-II scales and each of the PANAS-X scales, controlling for the influence of the other two PANAS-X scales. For example, we computed correlations between IDAS-II Euphoria and PANAS-X Attentiveness, partialling out the influence of both Joviality and Self-Assurance. These coefficients are presented in Table 4.3. These results again demonstrate that Well-Being is specifically linked to Joviality, whereas Euphoria tends to be most strongly related to Self-Assurance

Table 4.3 Partial Correlations Between IDAS-II Well-Being and Euphoria and the PANAS-X Positive Affect Scales

Sample/Scale	Well-Being	Euphoria
Past Week Sample		
Joviality	**.44**	.07
Self-Assurance	.14	**.33**
Attentiveness	.20	−.05
General Sample		
Joviality	**.48**	.15
Self-Assurance	.03	.17
Attentiveness	**.31**	−.01

NOTE: N=1,113 (Past Week), 917 (General). Correlations ≥ |.14| are significant at p < .01. Correlations ≥ |.30| are in bold. PANAS-X = Expanded Form of the Positive and Negative Affect Schedule.

(especially in the Past Week sample). These cross-instrument associations should be kept in mind as we explore how these various positive mood scales relate to psychopathology.

It also is interesting to examine how various types of positive mood relate to our two indicators of negative affectivity, which correlated strongly with each other in these data ($r = .75$ and .74 in the Past Week and General samples, respectively). IDAS-II Well-Being and PANAS-X Joviality clearly show the strongest inverse associations with negative affectivity, with correlations ranging from −.34 to −.47 (mean $r = -.40$) in the Past Week sample, and from −.38 to −.41 (mean $r = -.39$) in the General sample. Thus, these two scales clearly contain a secondary component of low negative emotionality (see also Watson, Clark et al., 2013), which suggests that they may be particularly powerful predictors of psychopathology. In contrast, the PANAS-X Self-Assurance and Attentiveness scales had more modest inverse links to negative affectivity, with coefficients ranging from −.13 to −.30 (mean $r = -.22$) in the Past Week sample, and from −.15 to −.37 (mean $r = -.26$) in the General sample.

Finally, consistent with its pathological nature, IDAS-II Euphoria actually had weak *positive* associations with the two negative affectivity scales (rs ranged from .03 to .14, mean $r = .10$). As is discussed at length in Watson, Clark et al. (2013), these weak positive correlations reflect the fact that Euphoria contains two distinct components—a *positive mood* component and a *pathological* component—that work in opposition to one another in many instances. In this particular case, the pathological and positive mood components of Euphoria should correlate in opposite directions—positively and negatively, respectively—with indicators of negative affectivity. These opposing forces largely cancel each other out, such that Euphoria is weakly related to these negative affect scales at the simple zero-order level.

Relations With Extraversion

Among the traits comprising the Big Five model of personality (see Chapter 2), extraversion has the strongest and broadest links to positive emotional experience (Watson & Clark, 1992; Watson & Naragon, 2009; Watson et al., 1999). Accordingly, in some later analyses, we also report results for extraversion. It therefore is informative to review briefly how scores on this trait relate to the positive mood scales of the PANAS-X and IDAS-II. First, with regard to the IDAS-II, data reported previously in Chapter 2 (see Table 2.6) indicate that the BFI Extraversion scale correlates moderately with Well-Being ($r = .39$, $N = 3{,}714$) and more modestly with Euphoria ($r = .27$, $N = 1{,}616$).

Watson and Naragon (2009) reported correlations between extraversion and general, trait versions of the PANAS-X scales in a large undergraduate sample ($N = 3{,}136$). Consistent with earlier data, the general Positive Affect scale of the PANAS-X correlated more strongly with extraversion ($r = .49$) than with any of the other Big Five traits (rs ranged from $|.22|$ to $|.39|$) in this sample. Beyond that, however, these analyses also revealed considerable specificity at the lower order level. That is, extraversion was strongly correlated with Joviality ($r=.60$), moderately correlated with Self-Assurance ($r=.47$), and only modestly related to Attentiveness ($r=.28$). Indeed, Attentiveness scores were much more highly related to conscientiousness ($r=.53$) than to extraversion. Thus, similar to the IDAS Well-Being scale, extraversion shows a specific affinity to Joviality at the lower order level. Once again, these associations should be kept in mind as we explore how these various scales relate to different forms of psychopathology.

Finally, it is informative to consider these relations within the framework of the hierarchical structure of personality (Markon et al., 2005; Naragon-Gainey, Watson, & Markon, 2009; Watson et al., 1994). In this structure, extraversion represents a broad, higher order "Big" trait that can be decomposed into several distinct yet empirically correlated components, including both affective and interpersonal elements. For example, Naragon-Gainey et al. (2009) examined the lower order structure of extraversion in two samples (students and patients) and found replicable evidence for four related but distinguishable facets: sociability, positive emotionality, ascendance, and fun seeking. Thus, from a hierarchical structural perspective, positive emotionality represents a narrower, lower order element within the broader, more encompassing dimension of extraversion.

DEPRESSION

Overview

As we discussed in Chapter 1, early research in this area—which was incorporated into the two-factor, tripartite and integrative hierarchical models—emphasized the existence of a specific positive mood deficit in depression (e.g., Clark & Watson, 1991; Mineka et al., 1998; Watson, Clark, & Carey, 1988). Our ongoing work with the IDAS/IDAS-II and PANAS-X has helped to clarify the nature of positive mood dysfunction in the emotional disorders. This research has yielded two key conclusions related to the depressive disorders. First, although positive affect measures are significantly negatively related to many indicators of anxiety, they are most strongly and systematically associated with depression. Second, low positive affect actually shows greater specificity than traditional indicators of depression, including some of the formal symptom criteria for a *DSM-IV/DSM-5* (American Psychiatric Association, 2000, 2013) major depressive episode. Our data therefore demonstrate that we can enhance the assessment and differential diagnosis of major depression by focusing more on this positive mood deficit and deemphasizing nonspecific aspects of the disorder.

Relations With Specific Negative Affects

Five types of evidence support these conclusions. First, indicators of positive affect correlate more strongly with sad, depressed mood (the core element of the *DSM* depressive disorders) than with other types of negative affect, including anxious/worried mood (a key feature of the *DSM* anxiety disorders). To illustrate this important point, Table 4.4 presents correlations between the PANAS-X/IDAS-II positive affect scales and three specific Negative Affect scales from the PANAS-X—Sadness (*sad, blue, downhearted, alone, lonely*), Fear (*afraid, scared, frightened, nervous, jittery, shaky*), and Hostility (*angry, irritable, hostile, scornful, disgusted, loathing*)—in the Past Week and General samples.

Two aspects of these data are noteworthy. First, with the exception of IDAS-II Euphoria, all of the positive mood scales correlated more strongly with Sadness than with the other negative mood scales in both samples. In fact, follow-up tests indicated that the other five positive affect scales correlated significantly more strongly ($p < .01$, one-tailed) with Sadness than with Fear and Hostility in all 20 comparisons. Second, in terms of specific scales, Well-Being and Joviality (*r*s ranged from −.44 to −.48) correlated more strongly with Sadness than did Self-Assurance and Attentiveness (*r*s ranged from −.22 to −.32). Indeed, follow-up statistical tests indicated that the correlations for Joviality and Well-Being were significantly greater than those for Self-Assurance and Attentiveness in all eight comparisons. Thus, depressed mood displays a particularly strong and specific link to the types of content (i.e., feelings of joy, enthusiasm, energy, and optimism) tapped by Well-Being and Joviality.

Table 4.4 CORRELATIONS BETWEEN POSITIVE AFFECT SCALES AND SPECIFIC NEGATIVE AFFECTS

Sample/Scale	Sadness	Fear	Hostility
Past Week Sample			
PANAS-X Positive Affect	**−.35**	−.20	−.17
PANAS-X Joviality	**−.44**	−.25	−.27
PANAS-X Self-Assurance	−.22	−.12	−.02
PANAS-X Attentiveness	−.23	−.14	−.14
IDAS-II Well-Being	**−.44**	−.29	−.27
IDAS-II Euphoria	.02	.16	.19
General Sample			
PANAS-X Positive Affect	**−.37**	−.20	−.24
PANAS-X Joviality	**−.48**	−.27	−.34
PANAS-X Self-Assurance	−.23	−.10	−.04
PANAS-X Attentiveness	−.32	−.21	−.24
IDAS-II Well-Being	**−.45**	−.30	**−.35**
IDAS-II Euphoria	−.07	.09	.02

NOTE: $N = 1{,}113$ (Past Week), 917 (General). Correlations $\geq |.07|$ are significant at $p < .05$. Correlations $\geq |.35|$ are in bold. PANAS-X = Expanded Form of the Positive and Negative Affect Schedule.

Relations With the Beck Inventories

As we discussed earlier in Chapter 3, a second approach to establishing specificity is to compare how scales relate to general measures of depression and anxiety, such as the BDI-II and the BAI. In Chapter 3, we compared BDI-II versus BAI correlations for the six IDAS depression scales in a very large standardized combined sample (N=4,251). Three of the depression scales showed a reasonable degree of specificity in these data, clearly correlating more strongly with the BDI-II than with the BAI: Dysphoria (rs=.82 and .71, respectively; difference=.110), Lassitude (rs=.63 and .53, respectively; difference=.093), and Suicidality (rs=.58 and .48, respectively; difference=.092). In contrast, the three remaining depression scales—Insomnia, Appetite Loss, and Appetite Gain—showed much poorer specificity. Indeed, Insomnia (rs=.51 and .49, respectively; difference=.023) and Appetite Loss (rs=.42 and .42, respectively; difference=.002) had virtually identical correlations with the two Beck inventories, whereas Appetite Gain had relatively weak associations with both scales (rs=.31 and .25, respectively; difference=.060).

It is noteworthy that Well-Being actually showed much more impressive specificity than any of the depression scales in these data. That is, it correlated much more strongly with the BDI-II (r = –.58) than with the BAI (r = –.33; difference = –.252) in this sample. These results are particularly striking given that the IDAS depression scales all share overlapping item content with the BDI-II, whereas Well-Being does not. Thus, these data strongly demonstrate the specificity of low positive mood to depression.

Diagnostic Specificity

PANAS-X Analyses

Third, positive mood scales show strong specificity in relation to formal *DSM* emotional disorder diagnoses (see also Watson, Clark, & Stasik, 2011; Watson & Naragon-Gainey, 2010; Watson, O'Hara, Chmielewski, et al., 2008; Watson et al., 2012). Indeed, they display far better specificity than most symptoms of depression (recall that the diagnostic specificity of depression symptoms was examined in Chapter 3).

To establish this key point, we first consider data related to the PANAS-X positive mood scales. Table 4.5 presents polyserial correlations (see Chapters 1 and 3) between these scales and eight *DSM-IV/DSM-5* diagnoses—major depression, GAD, PTSD, panic disorder, agoraphobia, social phobia, specific phobia, and OCD—in four samples. Participants in Samples 1 (N=331) and 2 (N=253) were administered the complete PANAS-X using either General (Sample 1) or Past Week (Sample 2) time instructions. Participants in Sample 3 (N=252) completed only the general Positive Affect and Joviality scales using General trait instructions. Finally, the Sample 4 participants (N=250) completed the Joviality, Self-Assurance, and Attentiveness scales using General instructions.

Table 4.5 Polyserial Correlations Between PANAS-X Positive Affect Scales and *DSM* Diagnoses

Scale/Sample	MDD	GAD	PTSD	Panic	Agora	Social Phobia	Specific Phobia	OCD
General Positive Affect								
Sample 1	**–.44**	–.15	–.10	–.22	–.14	–.16	.06	–.11
Sample 2	**–.51**	**–.40**	–.19	–.20	–.29	–.15	.00	–.25
Sample 3	**–.46**	–.03	–.15	–.04	.—	–.28	.—	–.08
Weighted *M*	**–.47**	–.19	–.14	–.16	–.21	–.19	.03	–.14
Joviality								
Sample 1	**–.41**	–.19	–.12	–.22	–.24	–.15	–.04	–.23
Sample 2	**–.59**	**–.42**	–.28	–.28	–.29	–.18	.03	–.28
Sample 3	**–.46**	–.15	–.20	–.10	.—	–.29	.—	–.04
Sample 4	**–.37**	–.30	–.28	–.32	–.18	**–.45**	.—	–.34
Weighted *M*	**–.46**	–.26	–.21	–.23	–.24	–.26	–.01	–.18
Self-Assurance								
Sample 1	–.26	–.07	–.02	–.12	–.20	–.08	.10	–.10
Sample 2	**–.42**	–.33	–.23	–.20	–.28	–.25	.02	–.10
Sample 4	–.30	–.22	–.13	–.32	–.23	**–.36**	.—	–.21
Weighted *M*	–.32	–.20	–.12	–.21	–.23	–.22	.07	–.13
Attentiveness								
Sample 1	**–.40**	–.12	–.10	–.15	–.08	–.16	.05	–.02
Sample 2	**–.43**	–.27	–.03	–.09	–.15	–.03	.04	–.19
Sample 4	–.32	–.29	–.12	–.23	–.16	**–.46**	.—	**–.37**
Weighted *M*	**–.39**	–.22	–.08	–.16	–.13	–.22	.05	–.18

NOTE: $N = 331$ (Sample 1), 253 (Sample 2), 252 (Sample 3), 250 (Sample 4). Correlations ≥ |.35| are in bold. MDD = major depression. GAD = generalized anxiety disorder. PTSD = posttraumatic stress disorder. Agora = agoraphobia. OCD = obsessive-compulsive disorder.

The results shown in Table 4.5 indicate that all four PANAS-X scales demonstrate reasonable specificity, showing a stronger inverse association with major depression than with any other diagnosis. Focusing on the three specific affect scales, Joviality had the strongest overall association with major depression (weighted mean $r = -.46$) and displayed impressive specificity, given that its overall correlations with the seven *DSM-IV* anxiety diagnoses ranged from only –.01 to –.26. The results for Attentiveness were similar: It had a weighted mean correlation of –.39 with major depression, whereas no other values exceeded –.22. Self-Assurance (mean $r = -.32$) had the weakest association with major depression, although it also showed some specificity (its correlations with the anxiety diagnoses ranged from .07 to –.23).

As shown in Table 4.1, scores on the Joviality, Self-Assurance, and Attentiveness scales all correlate strongly with one another. In light of this pattern, much of the predictive power of these scales actually is attributable to their shared variance—which, in turn, reflects the influence of the higher order Positive Affect factor. This, then, raises the question of which specific scales make unique, incremental contributions to the diagnosis of major depression. We examined this issue by conducting separate logistic regression analyses—using the three lower order scales as predictors—in Samples 1, 2, and 4. Joviality contributed significantly ($p < .01$, two-tailed) to the prediction of major depression in both Samples 1 and 2; its effect was marginally significant in Sample 4 ($p < .08$). Attentiveness also added to the prediction of depression in Sample 1, but not Samples 2 or 4; Self-Assurance failed to contribute significantly in any sample.

Overall, these data establish a particularly strong and specific link between major depression and Joviality. Joviality (1) was the strongest overall predictor of major depression, (2) contributed significantly to the prediction of depression diagnoses in two of three logistic regression analyses, and (3) demonstrated impressive diagnostic specificity in these data.

Finally, another noteworthy aspect of these data is that—contrary to earlier findings reviewed in Chapter 1—these positive mood scales did not show a particular strong or specific association with social phobia (weighted mean *r*s ranged from only –.19 to –.26). We revisit this issue subsequently.

IDAS-II/IDAS-CR Analyses

The patients in Samples 1 ($N=337$) and 2 ($N=267$) also were assessed on both (a) the original IDAS and (b) the interview-based IDAS-CR. In addition, complete IDAS-II data are available in Samples 4 ($N=407$) and 5 ($N=290$). Accordingly, Table 4.6 presents polyserial correlations between IDAS-II Well-Being (Samples 1, 2, 4, and 5), IDAS-CR Well-Being (Samples 1 and 2 only), and IDAS-II Euphoria (Samples 4 and 5 only) and various *DSM* emotional disorder diagnoses. Note that participants in Samples 4 and 5 were assessed on an additional diagnosis (current manic episode) related to bipolar disorder.

IDAS-II Well-Being and IDAS-CR Well-Being both displayed substantial negative associations with major depression—and impressive diagnostic specificity—in these data. IDAS-II Well-Being had a weighted mean correlation of –.49 with major depression; in marked contrast, its overall correlations with the seven anxiety diagnoses ranged from only .01 to –.23. The results for IDAS-CR Well-Being are quite similar. It had an overall correlation of –.47 with major depression, whereas its average associations with the seven anxiety diagnoses ranged from only –.04 to –.33. Thus, the specificity of Well-Being is highly robust and replicates across samples (both patients and community adults) and methods (both self-reports and clinician ratings).

Euphoria shows a dramatically different pattern: It is very weakly related to major depression (overall $r = -.01$) and actually correlates more highly with some of the anxiety diagnoses (e.g., mean $r=.22$ with PTSD, .24 with specific phobia). Clearly, however, its strongest association is with current manic episodes (mean $r=.34$); we return to this finding in our subsequent discussion of bipolar disorders.

Table 4.6 Polyserial Correlations Between IDAS-II/IDAS-CR Scales and *DSM* Emotional Disorder Diagnoses

				Specific		Social			
Scale/Sample	**MDD**	**GAD**	**PTSD**	**Panic**	**Agora**	**Phobia**	**Phobia**	**OCD**	**Manic**
IDAS-II Well-Being									
Sample 1	**–.57**	–.26	–.12	**–.30**	**–.30**	–.23	–.00	–.20	.—
Sample 2	**–.51**	**–.36**	–.26	–.21	**–.30**	–.13	.09	–.22	.—
Sample 4	**–.36**	–.26	–.13	–.15	–.19	**–.38**	.—	–.17	–.02
Sample 5	**–.53**	–.03	–.12	–.13	–.13	–.07	–.04	–.05	**.37**
Weighted *M*	**–.49**	–.23	–.15	–.20	–.23	–.22	.01	–.16	.15
IDAS-CR Well-Being									
Sample 1	**–.43**	–.19	–.21	**–.32**	**–.33**	–.12	.05	–.12	.—
Sample 2	**–.52**	**–.30**	–.21	**–.34**	**–.31**	–.10	–.16	–.29	.—
Weighted *M*	**–.47**	–.24	–.21	**–.33**	**–.32**	–.11	–.04	–.20	.—
IDAS-II Euphoria									
Sample 4	.11	.08	.24	.06	.09	.02	.—	.16	**.31**
Sample 5	–.18	.10	.18	.06	.08	.01	.24	.13	**.38**
Weighted *M*	–.01	.09	.22	.06	.09	.02	.24	.15	**.34**

NOTE: *N* = 337 (Sample 1), 267 (Sample 2), 407 (Sample 4), 290 (Sample 5). Correlations ≥ |.35| are in bold. MDD = major depression. GAD = generalized anxiety disorder. PTSD = posttraumatic stress disorder. Agora = agoraphobia. OCD = obsessive-compulsive disorder. Manic = current manic episode.

IMAS Analyses

Next, we examine relations with the interview-based IMAS. As was noted in Chapter 2, we have IDAS-II and IMAS data in Samples 5 ($N = 373$ outpatients) and 11 ($N = 362$ students). Simple zero-order correlations between Well-Being and Euphoria and the 10 general IMAS scales are presented in Table 4.7 (Sample 5) and Table 4.8 (Sample 11). These results further establish the specificity of Well-Being to depression. Well-Being correlated most strongly with IMAS Depression in both the patients ($r = -.36$) and students ($r = -.31$). Follow-up statistical tests indicated that its correlation with Depression was significantly stronger ($p < .05$, one-tailed) than its association with the other IMAS scales in 14 of 18 comparisons across the two samples. The four exceptions involved Mania (ignoring sign) in the patients, and Social Phobia, PTSD, and GAD in the students.

Consistent with the diagnostic results presented earlier, Euphoria correlated weakly with IMAS Depression ($r = .13$ and .21 in the patients and students, respectively) and showed no specificity to it (as would be expected, its strongest association was with IMAS Mania, which we discuss in greater detail later). More generally, the data in both samples display a very curious pattern: Despite the fact that Well-Being and Euphoria are substantially positively correlated with one another ($r = .54$ and .48 in Samples 5 and 11, respectively), the former tends to correlate *negatively* with the IMAS scales, whereas the latter correlates *positively* with them. This suggests that these simple zero-order coefficients are being attenuated by the influence of this shared component of general positive affectivity (for further discussion of this issue, see Watson, Clark et al., 2013). Put differently, these results indicate that the unique component of Well-Being is adaptive (i.e., negatively related to psychopathology), whereas the unique component of Euphoria is maladaptive (i.e., positively related to psychopathology).

Table 4.7 Correlations Between the IDAS-II Well-Being and Euphoria Scales and the IMAS Scales in Sample 5 (Patients)

IMAS Scale	Well-Being Simple	Partial	Euphoria Simple	Partial
Depression	**–.36**	**–.51**	.13	**.41**
Mania	.28	–.10	**.64**	**.60**
Irritability	–.20	**–.33**	.15	**.31**
GAD	–.26	**–.42**	.16	**.37**
PTSD	–.22	**–.38**	.18	**.37**
Panic	–.15	**–.33**	.22	**.37**
Agoraphobia	–.18	–.29	.12	.26
Social Phobia	–.21	–.28	.05	.20
Specific Phobia	–.07	–.15	.10	.17
OCD	–.06	–.19	.17	.25

NOTE: $N = 362$. IMAS = Interview of Mood and Anxiety Symptoms. Correlations ≥ |.30| are in bold.

Table 4.8 Correlations Between the IDAS-II Well-Being and Euphoria Scales and the IMAS Scales in Sample 11 (Students)

	Well-Being		**Euphoria**	
IMAS Scale	**Simple**	**Partial**	**Simple**	**Partial**
Depression	**−.31**	**−.48**	.21	**.43**
Mania	.15	−.23	**.64**	**.65**
Irritability	−.23	**−.37**	.17	**.34**
GAD	−.26	**−.40**	.17	**.35**
PTSD	−.28	**−.44**	.19	**.39**
Panic	−.13	−.26	.20	**.30**
Agoraphobia	−.16	−.22	.06	.16
Social Phobia	**−.30**	**−.36**	.03	.21
Specific Phobia	−.09	−.13	.05	.11
OCD	−.07	−.21	.22	.29

NOTE: $N = 373$. IMAS = Interview of Mood and Anxiety Symptoms. Correlations ≥ |.30| are in bold.

We tested this idea by computing partial correlations that controlled for the influence of the other IDAS-II scale (e.g., we calculated the correlation between Well-Being and Depression, controlling for Euphoria). These partial correlations also are presented in Tables 4.7 and 4.8, and it can be seen that they tend to be substantially stronger than the simple zero-order relations. For instance, only 3 of the 20 (15%) zero-order correlations for Well-Being were −.30 or greater; in contrast, 10 of its partial correlations (50%) exceeded this threshold. The results for Euphoria are even more dramatic: It had 12 partial correlations (60%) ≥ .30, compared to only two simple correlations (10%) of this magnitude. These results establish the unique and distinctive properties of these scales in a striking manner.

Relations With Specific Depression Symptoms

After reviewing an extensive body of evidence, we concluded in Chapter 3 that three types of symptoms—dysphoria, lassitude, and suicidality—show the clearest, most compelling evidence of specificity to depression. In contrast, insomnia and appetite disturbance displayed relatively weak, inconsistent evidence of specificity. We can extend this analysis by establishing that indicators of positive affectivity—which, as we have seen, display impressive specificity themselves—tend to have stronger links to these specific symptoms and correlate more weakly with the nonspecific symptoms of insomnia and appetite disturbance (see Watson & Naragon-Gainey, 2010).

To demonstrate this point, the top portion of Table 4.9 presents correlations—including both (a) coefficients computed on individual types of respondents (viz., patients, community adults, students) and (b) overall coefficients based on a standardized combined sample—between self-ratings on Well-Being and the six

Table 4.9 Correlations Between the IDAS-II/IDAS-CR Well-Being and Depression Scales

Scale	Patients	Adults	Students	Overall
Self-Ratings				
Dysphoria	**–.46**	**–.51**	**–.39**	**–.44**
Lassitude	**–.29**	**–.36**	–.23	**–.28**
Suicidality	**–.31**	**–.35**	**–.28**	**–.30**
Insomnia	–.18	**–.27**	–.16	–.19
Appetite Loss	–.15	–.22	–.17	–.18
Appetite Gain	.01	–.15	–.03	–.05
Clinician Ratings				
Dysphoria	**–.42**	.—	**–.31**	**–.37**
Lassitude	**–.25**	.—	**–.31**	**–.27**
Suicidality	**–.27**	.—	–.15	–.22
Insomnia	–.14	.—	–.21	–.17
Appetite Loss	–.23	.—	–.13	–.19
Appetite Gain	.02	.—	–.15	–.04

NOTE: For IDAS-II, $N = 1{,}914$ (Patients), 1,837 (Adults), 4,055 (Students), 7,806 (Overall). For IDAS-CR, $N = 804$ (Patients), 522 (Students), 1,326 (Overall). Correlations $\geq |.25|$ are in bold.

IDAS depression scales. These results indicate that Well-Being correlated most strongly with Dysphoria (overall $r = -.44$), more moderately with Lassitude (overall $r = -.28$) and Suicidality (overall $r = -.30$), and more modestly with Insomnia and the two Appetite scales (overall *r*s ranged from –.05 to –.19). Follow-up statistical tests indicated that Well-Being's correlations with the three specific scales (viz., Dysphoria, Lassitude, and Suicidality) were significantly stronger ($p < .05$, two-tailed) than its associations with the three nonspecific scales (i.e., Insomnia, Appetite Loss, and Appetite Gain) in all 36 comparisons.

How well do these findings replicate across method? To examine this issue, the lower portion of Table 4.9 reports parallel findings based on the clinician-rated IDAS-CR. Once again, Well-Being showed consistently stronger correlations with Dysphoria (overall $r = -.37$) and Lassitude (overall $r = -.27$) than with the three nonspecific scales (overall *r*s ranged from –.04 to –.17). Follow-up tests indicated that these associations were significantly greater in 17 of 18 comparisons (the one exception was that the correlation for Lassitude was not significantly higher than that for Appetite Loss in the patient sample). In contrast, however, the results for Suicidality (overall $r = -.22$) were much less consistent here; follow-up tests revealed that only three of nine comparisons with the nonspecific scales were significant.

We can further test the generality of this pattern by examining self-ratings on the PANAS-X positive mood scales. Table 4.10 reports correlations between them and the six IDAS depression scales. Replicating previous results, the PANAS-X

Table 4.10 Correlations Between the PANAS-X Positive Affect and Joviality Scales and IDAS-II Depression Scales

Scale	Positive Affect	Joviality
Past Week Sample		
Dysphoria	**–.40**	**–.47**
Lassitude	**–.32**	**–.34**
Suicidality	**–.28**	**–.32**
Insomnia	–.16	–.23
Appetite Loss	–.15	–.20
Appetite Gain	–.11	–.09
General Sample		
Dysphoria	**–.37**	**–.41**
Lassitude	**–.32**	**–.33**
Suicidality	**–.25**	**–.31**
Insomnia	–.18	–.23
Appetite Loss	–.16	–.21
Appetite Gain	–.15	–.16

NOTE: $N = 1{,}113$ (Past Week), 918 (General). Correlations $\geq |.25|$ are in bold.

general Positive Affect and Joviality scales consistently correlated more strongly with Dysphoria (*r*s ranged from –.37 to –.47), Lassitude (*r*s ranged from –.32 to –.34), and Suicidality (*r*s ranged from –.25 to –.32) than with the three nonspecific scales (*r*s ranged from –.09 to –.23). Follow-up statistical tests indicated that these associations were significantly greater in 35 of 36 comparisons (the single exception was that the correlation between general Positive Affect and Suicidality did not exceed that for Insomnia in the General sample).

Thus, indicators of positive emotionality show stronger associations with those symptoms—dysphoria, lassitude, and suicidality—that themselves display good specificity to depression. These results further suggest that the enhanced specificity of these various symptoms all reflect—at least in part—some common underlying mechanism. This is an intriguing idea for future research.

SOCIAL ANXIETY/SOCIAL PHOBIA

Overview

We turn now to an examination of social anxiety/social phobia. As we discussed in Chapter 1, positive affect also is consistently negatively related to social anxiety, although the magnitude is weaker than its association with depression. In explicating the nature of these relations, it is helpful to include extraversion, a trait that is both closely linked to positive affect and highly relevant to social anxiety.

Previous reviews of this topic have concluded that whereas depression tends to be more strongly negatively correlated with positive affect than with extraversion, social anxiety shows the opposite pattern (Watson et al., 2005; Watson & Naragon-Gainey, 2010). Consequently, one gets a more complete and accurate view of these relations by including indicators of both positive mood and extraversion in a single integrated analysis.

Disorder-Based Analyses

We begin by reviewing relations with *DSM* diagnoses of social phobia. Here, indicators of extraversion and positive emotionality yield rather different conclusions. The evidence related to positive emotionality is relatively sparse. However, the available data suggest that although low positive emotionality is significantly related to diagnoses of social phobia, this link is neither strong nor specific (Watson, Clark, & Carey, 1988; Watson et al., 2011). As we noted earlier, for example, the PANAS-X positive mood scales had weighted mean correlations ranging from only −.19 to −.26 with diagnoses of social phobia (see Table 4.5), and they had virtually identical associations with GAD (mean *r*s ranged from −.19 to −.26) in these same data. Similarly, our analyses of IDAS/IDAS-CR Well-Being failed to reveal any strong, specific link to social phobia (see Table 4.6).

In marked contrast, an extensive body of evidence has established the existence of a strong negative association between extraversion and social phobia (e.g., Watson et al., 2015b). Kotov et al. (2010) reported meta-analytic data comparing the mean extraversion scores of individuals with and without 14 unipolar mood, anxiety, and substance use diagnoses. Extraversion was significantly negatively related to most of these disorders (mean $d = -0.90$; see Kotov et al., 2010, Table 4), but it was most strongly related to dysthymic disorder ($d = -1.47$) and social phobia ($d = -1.31$). The latter association represents a large effect size (Cohen, 1992), thereby demonstrating the existence of a substantial link between the trait and the disorder.

Symptom-Based Analyses

Prior Evidence

Previous studies have established the existence of significant negative associations between social anxiety symptoms and indicators of both positive emotionality and extraversion. For example, Kashdan (2007) obtained a weighted mean correlation of −.36 between social anxiety and positive affect in a meta-analysis of 19 studies. Watson et al. (2005) reported multiple analyses indicating that social anxiety symptoms had a strong inverse association with extraversion and correlated more moderately with measures of positive emotionality. For instance, Watson et al. (2005) computed correlations between the Social fears scale of the Phobic Stimuli Response Scales (PSRS; Cutshall & Watson, 2004) and

(a) the general Positive Affect scale of the PANAS-X and (b) the BFI Extraversion scale in a sample of 358 students (see their Table 6). PSRS Social had a significantly stronger association with Extraversion ($r = -.54$) than with Positive Affect ($r = -.29$) in these data.

Given that social phobia is highly comorbid with depression (Chapter 1; see also Watson, 2005, 2009), it is important to determine whether the association between social anxiety and positive affect is largely due to this shared, nonspecific variance. In his meta-analytic review, Kashdan (2007) found that positive affect remained significantly related to social anxiety, even after controlling for depression and general negative affectivity (mean partial $r = -.21$). Similarly, Naragon-Gainey et al. (2009) used structural equation modeling to examine four facets of extraversion (sociability, positive emotionality, ascendance, and fun seeking) in relation to social anxiety and depressive symptoms. After controlling for shared variance among these constructs, positive emotionality remained significantly related to social anxiety in two independent samples. Thus, the social anxiety–positive affect association appears to extend beyond comorbidity with depression and beyond shared variance with the interpersonal components of extraversion. Taken together, these results suggest that social anxiety is specifically associated with a positive affect deficit.

Self-Report Data

We have replicated and extended these findings in a group of participants ($N = 666$) who completed multiple measures of various types of anxiety and depression symptoms. These multiple indicators then were aggregated into composite scores for each construct. The use of these multimeasure composites allows us to eliminate idiosyncratic aspects of specific assessment instruments. This aggregated sample included 294 outpatients from Sample 3 and 372 students from Sample 9. Once again, we standardized scale scores on a within-population basis and then combined them in a single overall analysis. The standardized measures of each construct then were averaged to produce an overall composite score for each symptom.

Participants completed three measures of GAD symptoms: (1) the seven-item IDAS Anxious Mood scale (Watson et al., 2007); (2) the nine-item Generalized Anxiety Disorder Questionnaire-IV (Newman et al., 2002); and (3) the ten-item Worry Domains Questionnaire–Short Form (Stöber & Joormann, 2001). Correlations among these measures ranged from .56 to .72 (mean $r = .62$) in this sample.

The battery included four indicators of depression: (1) a nine-item version of the IDAS Dysphoria scale, omitting the worry item that overlaps with Anxious Mood; (2) the CES-D (Radloff, 1977); (3) the Patient Health Questionnaire-9 (PHQ-9; Kroenke, Spitzer, & Williams, 2001); and (4) the eight Loss of Interest items from the MASQ Anhedonic Depression scale (Watson et al., 1995). Correlations among these scales ranged from .67 to .78 (mean $r = .74$).

The participants completed three measures of social phobia: (1) the five-item Social Phobia scale from the Fear Questionnaire (Marks & Mathews, 1979); (2) the ten-item Social Phobia scale from the Albany Panic and Phobia Questionnaire (Rapee, Craske, & Barlow, 1994/1995); and (3) the six-item IDAS-II Social Anxiety scale. Correlations among these measures ranged from .55 to .70 (mean $r = .65$).

The battery contained two indicators of panic: (1) the 17-item Anxious Arousal scale of the Mood and Anxiety Symptom Questionnaire (Watson et al., 1995) and (2) the 13-item Panic Attack Symptom Questionnaire (Watson, 2000b). These scales correlated .70 with one another.

Participants were assessed on two measures of PTSD symptoms: (1) the 17-item PTSD Checklist-Civilian Version (Weathers, Litz, Herman, Huska, & Keane, 1993); and (2) an aggregate score based on the IDAS-II Traumatic Intrusions and Traumatic Avoidance scales. These indicators correlated .72 with one another. In addition to this global measure of PTSD, we computed scores representing each of the symptom dimensions in the influential four-factor model proposed by Simms, Watson, and Doebbeling (2002; see Chapter 7). In our battery, we had two markers of Intrusions (PCL Intrusions, IDAS-II Traumatic Intrusions; $r = .74$), two indicators of Avoidance (PCL Avoidance, IDAS-II Traumatic Avoidance; $r = .69$), and single markers of both Dysphoria (PCL Dysphoria) and Hyperarousal (PCL Hyperarousal).

Finally, participants completed three measures of OCD: (1) the 18-item Obsessive-Compulsive Inventory-Revised (Foa et al., 2002); (2) a total score based on the Obsessive Checking (14 items), Obsessive Cleanliness (12 items), Compulsive Rituals (8 items), and Hoarding (5 items) scales from the Schedule of Compulsions, Obsessions, and Pathological Impulses (SCOPI; Watson & Wu, 2005); and (3) a combined score based on the IDAS-II Checking, Ordering, and Cleaning scales. Correlations among these scales ranged from .62 to .72 (mean $r = .69$). In addition to this global index, we modeled specific symptoms within OCD (for a review of these dimensions, see Chapter 9). Specifically, our battery included three indicators of Checking (OCI-R Checking, SCOPI Obsessive Checking, IDAS-II Checking; *r*s ranged from .67 to .76, mean $r = .72$), three indicators of Ordering (OCI-R Ordering, SCOPI Compulsive Rituals, IDAS-II Ordering; *r*s ranged from .67 to .72, mean $r = .70$), three indicators of Cleaning (OCI-R Washing, SCOPI Obsessive Cleanliness, IDAS-II Cleaning; *r*s ranged from .69 to .73, mean $r = .70$), and two indicators of Hoarding (OCI-R Hoarding, SCOPI Hoarding; $r = .78$).

Table 4.11 presents correlations between these symptom composites and (a) trait versions of the general Positive Affect and Joviality scales of the PANAS-X and (b) the BFI Extraversion scale; the table also includes two markers of negative affectivity (BFI Neuroticism and the general Negative Affect scale of the PANAS-X) for comparison purposes. Replicating previous results (see Watson & Naragon-Gainey, 2010), the Depression composite correlated significantly more strongly ($p < .01$, two-tailed) with the two positive affectivity scales ($r = -.47$ and $-.55$ with Positive Affect and Joviality, respectively) than with Extraversion ($r = -.38$). Moreover, Positive Affect and Joviality both correlated more strongly with Depression than with any other symptom measure. Follow-up statistical tests established that the positive emotionality scales had a significantly stronger

Table 4.11 Correlations Between Personality and Affectivity Scales and Self-Rated Symptom Composites (Standardized Combined Sample)

Symptom Score	PosAff	Jovial	Extra	NegAff	Neur
Depression	**–.47**	**–.55**	–.38	**.72**	**.66**
GAD	–.39	**–.45**	–.34	**.72**	**.72**
Social Phobia	–.37	**–.41**	**–.54**	**.51**	**.52**
Panic	–.24	–.29	–.25	**.66**	**.52**
PTSD	–.26	–.36	–.24	**.68**	**.52**
Dysphoria	–.33	**–.42**	–.30	**.67**	**.55**
Hyperarousal	–.11	–.22	–.19	**.63**	**.47**
Intrusions	–.18	–.27	–.16	**.61**	**.43**
Avoidance	–.21	–.30	–.21	**.54**	**.42**
OCD	–.08	–.14	–.15	**.44**	**.40**
Checking	–.13	–.19	–.20	**.46**	**.42**
Ordering	–.05	–.11	–.10	.35	.33
Hoarding	–.14	–.17	–.15	.31	.25
Cleaning	–.00	–.05	–.08	.25	.24

NOTE: $N = 666$. Correlations ≥ |.40| are in bold. PosAff = Positive Affect. Jovial = Joviality. Extra = Extraversion. NegAff = Negative Affect. Neur = Neuroticism. GAD = generalized anxiety disorder. PTSD = posttraumatic stress disorder. OCD = obsessive-compulsive disorder.

association ($p < .01$, two-tailed) with Depression than with the other symptoms in all 26 comparisons.

Also consistent with previous data, Social Anxiety had a significantly stronger association ($p < .01$, two-tailed) with Extraversion ($r = -.54$) than with the two positive emotionality scales ($r = -.37$ and $-.41$ with Positive Affect and Joviality, respectively). Furthermore, Extraversion had a significantly stronger ($p < .01$, two-tailed) association with Social Anxiety than with the other symptoms in all 13 comparisons. Overall, these data again demonstrate that depression tends to be strongly negatively correlated with indicators of positive mood, whereas social anxiety has a more substantial link to extraversion.

Interview Data

Once again, it is important to establish that these findings replicate across methods. In addition to completing these self-report measures, the participants were interviewed and rated using the IDAS-CR and PCCP (see Chapter 2). Interview data were available on 625 of the 666 participants (252 patients, 373 students). As before, we standardized the scores on a within-population basis and then combined them in a single overall analysis.

We obtained IDAS-CR ratings on six specific anxiety symptoms. The assessed variables included Generalized Anxiety, Social Anxiety and Panic, and three types of PTSD symptoms (Hyperarousal, Intrusions, Avoidance), which also were summed to create an overall PTSD composite. In addition, the PCCP was used to obtain OCD symptom ratings. The PCCP is modeled after the IDAS-CR and uses the same 3-point rating scale (*absent, subthreshold, present*). To assess each symptom, the interviewer asks a standard probe question and three to five follow-up questions. We obtained PCCP ratings on five specific types of OCD symptoms: Checking, Cleaning, Ordering, Rituals, and Obsessive Intrusions; these ratings also were summed to create a general OCD composite.

Table 4.12 presents correlations between these IDAS-CR/PCCP ratings and the same set of trait scales that were included in the self-report analyses. Recall that in the self-report data, social anxiety correlated significantly more strongly with extraversion than with positive affectivity. The Table 4.12 results differ in that IDAS-CR Social Anxiety correlated very similarly with Extraversion ($r = -.36$) and the two indicators of positive emotionality ($r = -.30$ and $-.33$ with general Positive Affect and Joviality, respectively). More generally, however, these data again demonstrate a specific link between social anxiety symptoms and positive emotionality/extraversion. Extraversion, Joviality, and general Positive Affect all correlated more strongly with IDAS-CR Social Anxiety than with any other symptom; follow-up statistical tests revealed that the comparisons were significant ($p < .05$, two-tailed) in 35 of 36 cases (the one exception was that the correlation for Joviality did not exceed its association with Generalized Anxiety; $z = -1.79$, $p < .10$, two-tailed).

Table 4.12 Correlations Between Personality and Affectivity Scales and IDAS-CR/PCCP Ratings (Standardized Combined Sample)

Symptom Score	PosAff	Jovial	Extra	NegAff	Neur
Generalized Anxiety	−.20	−.26	−.15	**.41**	**.45**
Social Anxiety	**−.30**	**−.33**	**−.36**	**.35**	**.39**
Panic	−.16	−.18	−.12	**.38**	**.31**
PTSD	−.13	−.21	−.10	**.42**	**.30**
Hyperarousal	−.12	−.20	−.09	**.36**	.25
Intrusions	−.10	−.16	−.08	**.36**	.26
Avoidance	−.12	−.18	−.09	**.35**	.26
OCD	−.13	−.18	−.15	**.38**	**.35**
Obsessive Intrusions	−.18	−.24	−.21	**.43**	**.37**
Checking	−.07	−.11	−.09	.24	.22
Ordering	.01	−.04	.00	.19	.17
Hoarding	−.12	−.12	−.09	.17	.15
Cleaning	.01	−.01	−.05	.09	.11

NOTE: $N = 625$. Correlations ≥ |.30| are in bold. IDAS-CR = Clinician Rating Version of the Inventory of Depression and Anxiety Symptoms. PCCP = Personality, Cognitions, Consciousness, and Perceptions Interview. PosAff = Positive Affect. Jovial = Joviality. Extra = Extraversion. NegAff = Negative Affect. Neur = Neuroticism. GAD = generalized anxiety disorder. PTSD = posttraumatic stress disorder. OCD = obsessive-compulsive disorder.

SCHIZOPHRENIA/SCHIZOTYPY

The Hedonic Deficit in Schizophrenia/Schizotypy

Overview

There has been extensive research on—as well as integrative reviews of— emotional dysfunction in schizophrenia and related conditions (including schizotypy and schizotypal personality). The accumulating evidence yields two broad conclusions (Watson & Naragon-Gainey, 2010). First, schizophrenia and schizotypy clearly are associated with a marked deficit in positive affect, although the nature of this deficit differs somewhat from that observed in depression and social anxiety. Second, more limited evidence suggests that this deficit is not as great as that observed in depression, which further supports the specificity of low positive affect to depression.

The Expressive Deficit

One striking aspect of schizophrenia—which distinguishes it from depression and other disorders—is that it is associated with a specific deficit in emotional expression. That is, individuals with schizophrenia display a reduced capacity to communicate their feelings both facially and vocally. Kring and Moran (2008) reviewed 23 studies and concluded: "Compared to individuals without schizophrenia, individuals with schizophrenia display fewer positive and negative emotional expressions in response to emotionally evocative film clips, foods, and social interactions. Moreover, schizophrenia patients' diminished facial and vocal expression distinguishes them from other patient groups, including individuals with depression" (p. 821).

The Experiential Deficit

This expressive deficit partly accounts for clinical reports of anhedonia in the disorder (i.e., inexpressiveness can be misinterpreted as flat, constricted affect). Clearly, however, there is an experiential deficit as well (Strauss, 2013). Horan, Blanchard, Clark, and Green (2008) reviewed 13 studies that compared schizophrenia patients and nonclinical controls on trait measures of neuroticism/negative affectivity and extraversion/positive affectivity. Compared to the nonclinical controls, the schizophrenia patients showed a consistent pattern of higher neuroticism/negative affectivity and lower extraversion/positive affectivity. Nine of the reviewed studies used measures of extraversion, but the remaining four were based on direct indicators of positive affectivity. These four studies reported standardized group differences (Cohen's d) ranging from −0.68 to −0.78 (median = −0.72), which reflects a medium effect size. Similarly, Barch, Yodkovik, Sypher-Locke, and Hanewickel (2008) reported a medium-sized difference ($d = -0.61$) in positive affectivity between individuals with schizophrenia and healthy controls.

Positive Versus Negative Symptoms

Multiple studies have shown that self-report measures of schizotypy and schizotypal personality are associated with higher neuroticism/negative affectivity and lower extraversion/positive emotionality (Chmielewski & Watson, 2008a; Kerns, 2006; Ross, Lutz, & Bailley, 2002; for a review, see Horan et al., 2008). It is noteworthy, moreover, that neuroticism/negative affectivity is broadly related to both the negative (e.g., constricted affect, social aloofness) and positive (e.g., magical thinking, perceptual aberrations, suspiciousness) symptoms of schizotypy, whereas extraversion/positive emotionality shows greater specificity: It is consistently associated with the former but only weakly related to the latter (Watson & Naragon-Gainey, 2010).

To illustrate this point, we report results from a large sample of college students, who were assessed twice across a 2-week interval (this sample is described in Chmielewski & Watson, 2008a). Participants completed the BFI, the PANAS-X (using general trait instructions), and the Schizotypal Personality Questionnaire (SPQ; Raine, 1991) at each assessment. The SPQ contains nine scales that mirror the nine diagnostic criteria for schizotypal personality disorder in *DSM-III* (American Psychiatric Association, 1987).

Correlations between the SPQ scales and markers of extraversion/positive emotionality and neuroticism/negative emotionality are presented in Table 4.13 (Time 1) and Table 4.14 (Time 2). Replicating previous data, the negative affectivity scales were broadly related to the SPQ. Across the two assessments, they had overall mean correlations (after r-to-z transformation) of .39 and .31 with the negative and positive symptoms, respectively. In marked contrast, the extraversion/positive emotionality scales clearly had much stronger inverse associations with the negative symptoms than with the positive symptoms. This pattern was particularly striking for BFI Extraversion and PANAS-X Joviality: They were substantially correlated with the negative symptoms (average $r = -.46$), but were only weakly related to the positive symptoms (mean $r = -.10$). The other two specific positive affect scales—Self-Assurance and Attentiveness—showed somewhat lower associations with the negative symptoms (mean $r = -.28$) and were largely unrelated to the positive symptoms (average $r = -.06$). These results therefore extend previous data by establishing that some types of positive affect (viz., Joviality) are more strongly linked to the negative symptoms of schizotypy than are others (i.e., Self-Assurance and Attentiveness).

The Anticipatory Deficit

Surprisingly, however, despite these established links to low positive emotionality/extraversion, individuals with schizophrenia have an undiminished *capacity* to experience pleasure; that is, they show no impairment in positive affect following a pleasant mood induction (interestingly, however, schizotypy scores *are* associated with an hedonic deficit in this paradigm; for discussions of this issue, see A. S. Cohen, Callaway, Najolia, Larsen, & Strauss, 2012; A. S. Cohen & Minor, 2010; Kring & Moran, 2008; Strauss, 2013; Strauss & Gold, 2012). A. S. Cohen and Minor (2010) conducted a meta-analysis of 14 studies that compared the positive affect levels of (a) patients with schizophrenia versus (b) nonclinical controls in response to positive stimuli. The group difference was small (Hedges $D = -0.16$) and nonsignificant, leading them to conclude that

Table 4.13 CORRELATIONS BETWEEN AFFECTIVITY AND PERSONALITY COMPOSITES AND SCHIZOTYPAL PERSONALITY QUESTIONNAIRE (SPQ) SCALES (TIME 1 DATA)

SPQ Scale	Positive Affect	Jovial	Assur	Atten	Extra	Negative Affect	Neur
Negative Symptoms							
No Close Friends	**–.41**	**–.50**	**–.30**	–.24	**–.49**	**.37**	**.30**
Constricted Affect	**–.40**	**–.46**	–.28	–.23	**–.44**	**.40**	**.33**
Social Anxiety	**–.35**	**–.36**	**–.42**	–.22	**–.53**	**.43**	**.45**
Positive Symptoms							
Odd Speech	–.21	–.20	–.03	–.23	–.09	**.42**	.28
Odd Behavior	–.10	–.16	.07	–.15	–.06	**.33**	.19
Suspiciousness	–.18	–.25	–.09	–.12	–.10	**.49**	**.41**
Ideas of Reference	–.05	–.07	.02	–.05	–.00	**.38**	.27
Unusual Perceptual Experiences	–.06	–.10	.03	–.08	–.04	**.30**	.19
Odd Beliefs/Magical Thinking	.03	.03	.14	–.05	.08	.20	.11

NOTE: $N = 555$. Correlations ≥ |.09| are significant at $p < .05$. Correlations ≥ |.30| are in bold. Jovial = Joviality. Assur = Self-Assurance. Atten = Attentiveness. Extra = Extraversion. Neur = Neuroticism.

Table 4.14 CORRELATIONS BETWEEN AFFECTIVITY AND PERSONALITY COMPOSITES AND SCHIZOTYPAL PERSONALITY QUESTIONNAIRE (SPQ) SCALES (TIME 2 DATA)

SPQ Scale	Positive Affect	Jovial	Assur	Atten	Extra	Negative Affect	Neur
Negative Symptoms							
No Close Friends	**–.34**	**–.44**	–.26	–.24	**–.46**	**.42**	**.35**
Constricted Affect	**–.36**	**–.44**	–.28	–.27	**–.47**	**.40**	**.32**
Social Anxiety	**–.32**	**–.33**	**–.41**	–.23	**–.54**	**.45**	**.49**
Positive Symptoms							
Odd Speech	–.16	–.20	–.08	–.18	–.10	**.38**	.29
Odd Behavior	–.09	–.15	.03	–.14	–.06	.24	.16
Suspiciousness	–.26	**–.33**	–.13	–.23	–.14	**.52**	**.44**
Ideas of Reference	–.05	–.08	–.01	–.11	–.06	**.37**	**.36**
Unusual Perceptual Experiences	–.09	–.15	.00	–.11	–.09	**.32**	.27
Odd Beliefs/Magical Thinking	–.04	–.06	.06	–.10	–.02	.22	.16

NOTE: $N = 441$. Correlations ≥ |.09| are significant at $p < .05$. Correlations ≥ |.30| are in bold. Jovial = Joviality. Assur = Self-Assurance. Atten = Attentiveness. Extra = Extraversion. Neur = Neuroticism.

"there was little evidence to suggest that patients were anhedonic in response to laboratory stimuli" (p. 147).

Why, then, do schizophrenia patients consistently report anhedonia/low positive affect on trait measures (Horan et al., 2008)? There is growing evidence that schizophrenia is associated with an anticipatory pleasure deficit, such that individuals with the disorder do not expect to experience positive affect when engaging in future goal-directed activities (A. S. Cohen & Minor, 2010; Kring & Moran, 2008; Strauss, 2013). For example, Gard, Kring, Gard, Horan, and Green (2007) found that schizophrenia patients anticipated less pleasure from future activities than did healthy controls, particularly in relation to goal-directed activities. Furthermore, this anticipatory deficit was associated with a reduction in goal-directed activity in the schizophrenia group. These results suggest that although individuals with schizophrenia experience normal levels of pleasure in response to rewarding activities, this anticipatory deficit causes them to engage in these activities less frequently, thereby leading to lower levels of positive affect.

In support of this argument, experience-sampling studies suggest that individuals with schizophrenia do report lower levels of positive affect in their everyday lives (Gard et al., 2007; Kimhy et al., 2006). Kimhy et al. (2006), for instance, collected repeated mood ratings from 10 hospitalized schizophrenia patients and 10 healthy controls over the course of a single day. Compared to the controls, the patients reported elevated levels of sadness/depression and loneliness and lower levels of cheerfulness.

Specificity of the Deficit in Relation to Depression

To determine the size and specificity of this hedonic deficit, however, one must compare (a) patients with schizophrenia versus (b) those with other disorders. Myin-Germeys et al. (2003) reported the best available evidence to date. They obtained experience sampling data from 42 patients with nonaffective psychosis (a total of 1,890 momentary assessments), 46 patients with current major depression (2,070 assessments), and 49 healthy controls (2,499 assessments). Analyses were based on a three-item measure of positive affect (*happy, cheerful, satisfied*). As would be expected, the schizophrenia group reported substantially lower levels of positive affect (overall mean = 4.4) than the healthy controls (mean = 5.5); using the standard deviation of the psychosis patients, this translates into a d of −1.10.

It is important to note, however, that the schizophrenia patients also reported substantially *higher* positive affect than the depressed patients (mean = 2.2; again using the standard deviation of the psychotic patients, this translates into a $d = 2.20$). These results suggest that although schizophrenia is associated with a reduction in positive affect, this hedonic deficit is not as great as that observed in depression. It should be noted, however, that whereas all of the depressed patients currently were experiencing an acute episode, most of the schizophrenia patients were (a) in remission and (b) on medication. Thus, these findings very likely exaggerate the true magnitude of the difference between these groups.

Joiner, Brown, and Metalsky (2003) compared the BDI scores of 50 patients with major depression and 52 patients with schizophrenia. They created two scales from the BDI, one using three items assessing anhedonic symptoms and the other based on the 18 remaining items. It is noteworthy that the two groups did not differ significantly on the nonanhedonic items or on the BDI total score. Consistent with the results of Myin-Germeys et al. (2003), however, patients with major depression obtained significantly higher scores on the anhedonia scale than the patients with schizophrenia. Overall, the available data suggest that anhedonia/low positive affect is more strongly linked to depression than to schizophrenia.

IDAS Analyses

The data we have reviewed clearly establish that schizophrenia and schizotypy are associated with a marked deficit in positive affect. One limitation of these findings, however, is that they are based on measures assessing healthy, adaptive forms of positive emotionality. As noted earlier, the development of the IDAS-II offers intriguing new opportunities for explicating the nature of positive mood dysfunction in psychopathology, in that it includes a measure (viz., Euphoria) of dysfunctional positive affect.

In an earlier section, for example, we showed that measures of positive emotionality tend to be inversely related to the negative symptoms of schizotypy, but they are largely uncorrelated with the positive symptoms. It is informative to reconsider this issue from the perspective of the IDAS-II positive mood scales. We examined these relations in a standardized combined sample that consisted of 220 outpatients, 411 adults, and 277 college students (overall $N = 908$). In addition to the IDAS-II, participants completed the Personality Inventory for *DSM-5* (PID-5; Krueger, Derringer, Markon, Watson, & Skodol, 2012), which assesses the 25 specific facets in the trait dimensional model of personality pathology that was newly developed for Section III of *DSM-5*. The PID-5 includes three measures of negative symptoms that are similar to those assessed in the SPQ: Withdrawal (e.g., "I keep my distance from people"), Intimacy Avoidance (e.g., "I break off relationships if they start to get close"), and Restricted Affectivity (e.g., "I don't get emotional"). It also contains four measures of positive symptoms: Suspiciousness (e.g., "Plenty of people are out to get me"), Eccentricity (e.g., "I often say things that others find odd or strange"), Cognitive and Perceptual Dysregulation (e.g., "I have periods in which I feel disconnected from the world or from myself"), and Unusual Beliefs and Experiences (e.g., "I have seen things that weren't really there").

Correlations between these PID-5 scales and IDAS-II Well-Being and Euphoria are reported in Table 4.15. The results for Well-Being are broadly similar to those seen earlier with the SPQ scales. Replicating previous results, Well-Being correlated negatively with these schizotypy scales and tended to have somewhat stronger associations with the negative symptoms (average $r = -.23$) than with the positive symptoms (mean $r = -.16$). Within the negative symptoms, it was most strongly related to Withdrawal ($r = -.33$) and Intimacy Avoidance ($r = -.24$). However, it

Table 4.15 CORRELATIONS BETWEEN THE IDAS-II WELL-BEING AND EUPHORIA SCALES AND PID-5 MARKERS OF PSYCHOTICISM/SCHIZOTYPY (STANDARDIZED COMBINED SAMPLE)

PID-5 Scale	Well-Being Simple	Well-Being Partial	Euphoria Simple	Euphoria Partial
Negative Symptoms				
Withdrawal	**–.33**	**–.40**	.05	.24
Intimacy Avoidance	–.24	**–.32**	.09	.23
Restricted Affectivity	–.11	–.21	.16	.24
Positive Symptoms				
Suspiciousness	–.24	**–.36**	.17	**.33**
Eccentricity	–.16	**–.34**	.28	**.41**
Cog & Percept Dysreg	–.19	**–.39**	**.31**	**.45**
Unusual Beliefs & Exper	–.06	–.28	**.37**	**.45**

NOTE: $N = 908$. PID-5 = Personality Inventory for *DSM-5*. Cog & Percept Dysreg = Cognitive and Perceptual Dysregulation. Unusual Beliefs & Exper = Unusual Beliefs and Experiences. Correlations ≥ |.30| are in bold.

also correlated negatively with the positive symptoms of Suspiciousness ($r = -.24$), Cognitive and Perceptual Dysregulation ($r = -.19$), and Eccentricity ($r = -.16$), which differs somewhat from the SPQ results discussed earlier.

In marked contrast, Euphoria displays a pattern that differs dramatically from that seen with any other positive mood scale: It was weakly related to the negative symptoms (*r*s ranged from .05 to .16) and was moderately *positively* correlated with the positive symptoms (*r*s ranged from .17 to .37). More specifically, it displayed particularly strong positive associations with Unusual Beliefs and Experiences ($r = .37$), Cognitive and Perceptual Dysregulation ($r = .31$), and Eccentricity ($r = .28$). Thus, high scores on Euphoria are associated with the eccentric cognitions, unusual perceptual experiences, and odd behaviors that characterize the positive symptoms of schizotypy.

The Well-Being and Euphoria scales again displayed strikingly different patterns, despite being substantially positively correlated in this combined sample ($r = .46$). As discussed earlier, this unusual pattern suggests that these simple zero-order coefficients are being attenuated by the influence of their shared component of general positive affectivity (see also Watson, Clark et al., 2013). As before, we tested this idea by computing partial correlations that controlled for the influence of the other IDAS-II scale. These partial correlations also are presented in Table 4.15, and it can be seen that they tend to be substantially stronger than the simple zero-order relations. Most notably, the partial correlations between Euphoria and the positive symptom scales are higher and now range from .32 to .45 (mean $r = .41$).

These findings further clarify the unusual nature of the IDAS-II Euphoria scale. Based on these results, it appears that its unique component has an irrational, unrealistic quality that leads to a distorted view of the world—and of oneself—and that can be expected to create significant real-world problems in functioning. It will be interesting to explicate these maladaptive aspects of Euphoria in future research.

DISORDERS ASSOCIATED WITH ELEVATED POSITIVE AFFECT

Bipolar Disorders

State Associations

Thus far, we have focused on disorders that are associated with low levels of positive affect. We conclude this chapter with an examination of conditions associated with excessive positive mood, beginning with the bipolar disorders. Heightened positive affect clearly is linked to mania in an important way, in that the definition of manic episodes includes "abnormally and persistently elevated, expansive, or irritable mood" (APA, 2013, p. 124). Manic symptoms are, in fact, associated with the experience of elevated positive mood, with one daily diary study reporting a strong positive correlation between mean levels of manic symptoms and positive affect over a period of several weeks ($r = .54$; T. D. Meyer & Hofmann, 2005).

The IDAS-II Euphoria scale was designed to assess the elevated, expansive mood that characterizes many manic episodes. The scale has demonstrated impressive criterion validity and specificity to mania in numerous analyses. In the IMAS analyses presented earlier (see Tables 4.7 and 4.8), for example, it correlated .64 and .64 with IMAS Mania in Samples 5 and 11, respectively. Euphoria had no other coefficients exceeding .22 in either sample, establishing strong discriminant validity. Follow-up significance tests indicated that its convergent correlations with IMAS Mania were significantly stronger ($p < .01$, one-tailed) than the discriminant coefficients in all 18 comparisons.

Similarly, Euphoria displays good diagnostic specificity. As shown in Table 4.6, it had a mean polyserial correlation of .34 with diagnoses of current manic episodes; its other diagnostic correlations ranged from only −.01 to .24 in these data.

Current manic episodes clearly are associated with elevated levels of positive affect. Because current mania also is likely to impact ratings of trait positive affect (see Johnson, Gruber, & Eisner, 2007), we emphasize findings in remitted patients or nonclinical analogues in the following section.

Trait Associations

Self-report data based on trait positive affect scales have yielded mixed results for those at risk for mania. Studies have found that trait positive affect levels among currently remitted individuals diagnosed with bipolar I disorder do not differ from those of normal controls (e.g., Bagby et al., 1996, 1997). Likewise, in a daily diary study, mean levels of daily positive affect over 28 days among those with a lifetime diagnosis of cyclothymia were similar to levels reported by normal controls (Lovejoy & Steuerwald, 1995). However, other results suggest atypical levels of trait positive affect among those with a bipolar disorder or who are at risk for developing a bipolar disorder. For instance, when shown positive, neutral, and

Table 4.16 Correlations Between the PANAS-X Specific Positive Affect Scales and Total Scores on (a) the Hypomanic Personality Scale and (b) Narcissistic Personality Inventory in Sample 4

PANAS-X Scale	HPS	NPI
Joviality	.16*	.35**
Self-Assurance	.28**	**.48****
Attentiveness	−.01	.25**

NOTE: $N = 245$. Correlations ≥ .30 are in bold.
PANAS-X = Expanded Form of the Positive and Negative Affect Schedule. HPS = Hypomanic Personality Scale.
NPI = Narcissistic Personality Inventory.
*$p < .05$ **$p < .01$.

negative film clips, those at high risk for mania (as identified using a self-report measure) reported greater levels of positive mood than those at low risk for mania regardless of the valence of the clip (Gruber, Johnson, Oveis, & Keltner, 2008). In contrast, Gruber et al. (2009) reported unexpectedly low levels of positive affect among individuals in recovery from either (a) bipolar I or (b) a bipolar spectrum disorder, as compared to normal controls ($d = -1.5$). In interpreting these conflicting results, it should be noted that because individuals with bipolar disorders experience extreme levels of positive affect during mania and depression, their subjective scale for rating positive affect might differ from those who have never been manic (Johnson et al., 2007).

These conflicting findings also might be due, in part, to differential associations between bipolar disorder and specific types of positive emotionality. To test this possibility, Table 4.16 reports correlations between (a) general trait versions of the specific PANAS-X positive affect scales and (b) total scores on the Hypomanic Personality Scale (HPS; Eckblad & Chapman, 1986) in Sample 4 ($N = 245$). Whereas Joviality has the strongest negative associations with depression, it is noteworthy that Self-Assurance (i.e., feeling proud, confident, bold, and daring) has the most substantial link to the HPS. Follow-up tests indicated that the HPS had a significantly stronger correlation with Self-Assurance ($r = .28$) than with Attentiveness ($r = -.01$; $z = 4.52$, $p < .01$, two-tailed); however, the comparison with Joviality ($r = .16$) was only marginally significant ($z = 1.92$; $p < .06$, two-tailed). These results suggest that it would be useful to examine specific lower order relations between positive emotionality and bipolar disorder in future research.

Behavioral Activation System Hypersensitivity

Although a few studies have reported data on direct measures of positive affect, most research relating mania to positive emotions has focused on a different but related construct: the Behavioral Activation System (BAS, also referred to as the Behavioral Approach System; for a review of this literature, see Johnson, Edge, Holmes & Carver, 2012). Positive affect represents the subjective component of the goal-oriented BAS, which directs organisms toward situations and experiences that potentially may yield pleasure and reward. This system is adaptive in that it ensures the procuring of resources (e.g., food and water, shelter, the cooperation of others, sexual partners) that are essential to the survival of both the individual and the species (Watson, 2000a; Watson et al., 1999).

Depue and colleagues hypothesized that the affective dysfunction characteristic of the bipolar disorders may be due to dysregulation of the BAS. In the case of manic episodes, the BAS becomes overly sensitive to minor signals of reward, leading to excessive positive affect and an increase in goal-seeking/approach behavior. In contrast, during depressive episodes, the BAS shuts down and fails to respond properly to reward incentives, resulting in anhedonia, lethargy, and hopelessness (e.g., Depue & Iacono, 1989).

Several lines of research provide support for the theory that greater BAS sensitivity increases one's vulnerability to the bipolar disorders. First, there is a concurrent association between symptoms of mania and self-reported BAS scores among students diagnosed with a lifetime bipolar spectrum disorder ($r = .18$; Alloy et al., 2008), and between daily reported mean levels of the two constructs in a student sample ($r = .38$; T. D. Meyer & Hofmann, 2005). In addition, recovered individuals diagnosed with bipolar I report higher levels of BAS responsivity than do normal controls (Salavert et al., 2007); conversely, individuals with high BAS levels are significantly more likely to have a lifetime bipolar spectrum diagnosis than those with low BAS levels (Alloy et al., 2008). Compared to controls, nonclinical analogues with elevated levels of hypomanic symptoms (e.g., Carver & White, 1994) and individuals diagnosed with current bipolar I (B. Meyer, Johnson, & Winters, 2001) also have higher BAS sensitivity scores.

The association between BAS sensitivity and mania remains significant in prospective studies, in which higher BAS levels predicted first onset of bipolar spectrum disorder (Alloy et al., 2012) and a shorter time to onset of a manic episode among those with a lifetime bipolar spectrum disorder (Alloy et al., 2008). Individuals with bipolar I disorder who also had higher BAS scores when asymptomatic were more likely than those with lower BAS levels to subsequently enter a manic episode (Salavert et al., 2007). Taken together, there is evidence that elevated positive affect—when operationalized as heightened BAS activity that promotes goal-seeking behavior —is a risk factor for mania, as well as a concomitant of these symptoms (for a more extensive review of this evidence, see Johnson et al., 2012).

Consistent with the BAS hypersensitivity hypothesis, events relevant to goal attainment (e.g., marriage, a major promotion) often precede the development of mania. For instance, in a sample of individuals with bipolar I disorder, goal-attainment events predicted an increase in manic symptoms over the subsequent 2 months. Supporting the specificity of this association, non-goal-attainment positive events (e.g., receiving a tax refund) were not predictive of changes in manic symptoms (Johnson et al., 2000). Similarly, goal-attainment events predicted an increase in manic symptoms among those with bipolar I over the course of a 2-year longitudinal study (Johnson et al., 2008). In a study of bipolar spectrum college students, those who took final exams (a goal-attainment event) exhibited more hypomanic episodes than did those who were not taking exams at that time; in contrast, normal controls did not show an increase in hypomanic symptoms when taking exams (Nusslock, Abramson, Harmon-Jones, Alloy, & Hogan, 2007). Thus, events relevant to the attainment of goals may be a proximal trigger of manic symptoms in vulnerable groups. Indeed, after reviewing this evidence, Johnson et al. (2012) recently concluded: "People with bipolar disorder and those at risk for disorder respond differently to goal progress and success feedback than do other people. Whether measured by self-reports or laboratory paradigms, mania proneness appears related to longer-lasting excitement, confidence, energy, and goal pursuit in response to success" (p. 255).

Personality Disorder

In recent years, it has become evident that elevated positive mood is not uniquely characteristic of the bipolar disorders. Most notably, considerable data have established positive associations between extraversion and both narcissistic personality disorder (NPD) and histrionic personality disorder (HPD). For example, several studies have reported that self-report measures of narcissism have substantial positive correlations with extraversion (e.g., Ackerman et al., 2011; Miller et al., 2011; Miller, Gentile, & Campbell, 2013). In a meta-analytic review of the literature, Saulsman and Page (2005) reported significant positive associations between extraversion and diagnoses of both HPD ($r = .42$) and NPD ($r = .20$). In a subsequent meta-analysis, Samuel and Widiger (2008) replicated this finding for HPD ($r = .33$) but obtained a nonsignificant association between extraversion and NPD ($r = .09$).

Do these associations extend to direct measures of positive affect? Samuel and Widiger (2008) reported that the positive emotionality facet of extraversion was significantly positively related to HPD ($r = .23$), but not NPD ($r = -.02$). As a further test of these relations, the second column of Table 4.16 reports correlations between (a) the specific PANAS-X positive affect scales and (b) total scores on the 40-item Narcissistic Personality Inventory (NPI; Raskin & Hall, 1981; Raskin & Terry, 1988) in the Sample 4 participants. It is noteworthy that all three positive affect scales had significant positive correlations with the NPI. Moreover, paralleling the HPS results reported earlier, the NPI correlated significantly more strongly with Self-Assurance ($r = .48$) than with Joviality ($r = .35$; $z = 2.01$, $p < .05$, two-tailed) and Attentiveness ($r = .25$; $z = 3.46$, $p < .01$, two-tailed). These results suggest that the affective states tapped by Self-Assurance (i.e., feelings of confidence, strength, boldness, and daring) have a particularly strong link to disorders characterized by excessive positive mood.

We can further examine this issue in the standardized combined sample of participants ($N = 908$) who completed both the IDAS-II and the PID-5. In addition to the schizotypy markers described earlier, the PID-5 contains scales assessing Grandiosity (e.g., "To be honest, I'm just more important than other people") and

Attention Seeking (e.g., "I do things to make sure people notice me"); the former measures the excessive self-esteem/self-confidence and sense of entitlement that is characteristic of NPD, whereas the latter taps the exhibitionism and egocentrism of HPD (APA, 2013). Consistent with other results we have presented, both of these scales had significantly stronger ($p < .01$, two-tailed) positive correlations with Euphoria ($r = .39$ and .33 with Grandiosity and Attention Seeking, respectively) than with Well-Being ($r = .17$ and .14, respectively).

Based on these data, it seems reasonable to conclude that positive mood—at least the dysfunctional forms of positive affect that are assessed by Self-Assurance (in the PANAS-X) and Euphoria (in the IDAS-II)—is elevated in both NPD and HPD. It is likely that other disorders are associated with excessive positive affect as well. This is an exciting area for future research.

5

The Nature and Structure of Bipolar Symptoms

In this chapter, we explicate the nature and structure of symptoms related to the bipolar disorders. Bipolar symptoms are unusual in that they tend to be associated with elevated levels of both distress/negative emotionality and energy/positive emotionality (Watson, Clark et al., 2013; Watson & Naragon-Gainey, 2014). As we will see, individual symptom measures assess these two components in varying degrees—such that some place greater weight on elevated negative emotionality, whereas others focus more on excessive positive emotionality—leading them to display strikingly different correlates with other variables. In subsequent sections, we will examine the value of a two-factor structural model that reflects whether the negative or positive emotional component is dominant within a scale.

In Chapter 4, we presented extensive data establishing the validity of the IDAS-II Euphoria scale, which assesses a dysfunctional form of positive affect (and which, therefore, has a dominant component of high positive emotionality). As was discussed in Chapter 2, however, the IDAS-II also contains a second measure of bipolar symptoms: the five-item Mania scale. This scale assesses such bipolar symptoms as talkativeness/pressure of speech, flight of ideas, and restlessness/agitation (e.g., "It felt like my mind was moving 'a mile a minute,'" "I kept racing from one activity to the next"). We begin our examination of bipolar symptoms by reporting data to establish the construct validity of this scale.

ESTABLISHING THE VALIDITY OF IDAS-II MANIA

IDAS-CR Analyses

We first examine the convergent and discriminant validity of the Mania scale vis-à-vis ratings on the interview-based IDAS-CR. Discriminant validity analyses are maximally informative when they involve near-neighbor constructs that are strongly related to one another (Watson, 2012); due to this overlap, they are most likely to present problems in differentiation. As shown in Chapter 2 (see

Table 2.7), IDAS-II Mania correlates most strongly with seven other IDAS-II scales: Dysphoria ($r = .56$), Panic ($r = .54$), Checking ($r = .49$), Ordering ($r = .49$), Ill Temper ($r = .46$), Euphoria ($r = .45$), and Social Anxiety ($r = .45$). We therefore included these IDAS-II/IDAS-CR symptom dimensions in the present analyses.

Table 5.1 presents separate sets of correlations between these IDAS-II scales and parallel IDAS-CR ratings in Samples 6 ($N = 198$ outpatients) and 10 ($N = 219$ students) in the form of a heteromethod block (Campbell & Fiske, 1959). Given that we have examined the convergent and discriminant validity of some of these other scales already—and will discuss others subsequently—we focus here on the data related to Mania. Looking first at convergent validity, self-ratings on Mania were strongly related to their IDAS-CR counterparts in both patients ($r = .59$) and students ($r = .53$), establishing a substantial level of convergence.

We turn now to discriminant validity. As has been discussed in previous chapters, a key test of discriminant validity is that a convergent correlation should be higher than the other values in its row or column of the heteromethod block (Campbell & Fiske, 1959). Table 5.1 indicates that the convergent correlations for Mania met this criterion in every case. We further quantified these relations by conducting formal significance tests. All 28 comparisons were significant ($p < .05$,

Table 5.1 Convergent/Discriminant Validity Analyses: Correlations Between the IDAS-II Scales and IDAS-CR Ratings in Samples 6 and 10

	IDAS-CR Rating							
IDAS Scale	1	2	3	4	5	6	7	8
Patients (Sample 6)								
1. Mania	**.59**	.22	.19	.23	.22	.12	.08	.05
2. Dysphoria	.33	**.63**	.30	.21	.08	.25	–.10	.33
3. Panic	.21	.25	**.51**	.09	.13	.19	.06	.18
4. Checking	.18	.18	.03	**.49**	.35	.09	–.03	.13
5. Ordering	.21	.19	.03	.39	**.66**	.20	–.02	.19
6. Ill Temper	.17	.28	.27	.21	.13	**.60**	–.08	.19
7. Euphoria	.33	.07	–.02	.06	.17	.08	**.44**	–.05
8. Social Anxiety	.12	.28	.22	.17	.21	.15	.00	**.57**
Students (Sample 10)								
1. Mania	**.53**	.30	.22	.18	.37	.13	.05	.14
2. Dysphoria	.40	**.59**	.30	.28	.21	.18	–.02	.35
3. Panic	.24	.37	**.26**	.20	.26	.14	.02	.30
4. Checking	.20	.13	.17	**.50**	.32	.06	.09	.19
5. Ordering	.29	.12	.16	.39	**.65**	.11	–.02	.19
6. Ill Temper	.18	.35	.19	.24	.19	**.54**	.03	.22
7. Euphoria	.16	.03	–.08	–.06	.16	.11	**.31**	.02
8. Social Anxiety	.21	.29	.11	.26	.22	.15	–.07	**.66**

Note: $N = 198$ patients (Sample 6), 219 students (Sample 10). Convergent correlations are in bold. IDAS-II = Expanded version of the Inventory of Depression and Anxiety Symptoms. IDAS-CR = Clinician Rating version of the IDAS.

one-tailed) across the two samples, with *z*s ranging from 2.28 to 6.63. Thus, we see clear, strong evidence of discriminant validity in these data.

IMAS Analyses

Next, we examine relations with the interview-based IMAS. In Chapter 4, we showed that the IDAS-II Euphoria scale correlated .64 and .64 with IMAS Mania in Samples 5 and 11, respectively. Euphoria had no other coefficients exceeding .22 in either sample, establishing a strong level of discriminant validity. Follow-up significance tests indicated that its convergent correlations with IMAS Mania were significantly stronger ($p < .01$, one-tailed) than the discriminant coefficients in all 18 comparisons.

Table 5.2 presents parallel findings for IDAS-II Mania in these same two samples. It is noteworthy that Mania showed the same level of convergence with IMAS Mania in both Sample 5 ($r = .63$) and Sample 11 ($r = .68$); in fact, its overall mean convergent correlation ($r = .65$) is virtually identical to that reported earlier for Euphoria ($r = .64$).

Although IDAS-II Mania was moderately correlated with several other IMAS scales, these coefficients clearly were lower in magnitude than those with IMAS Mania. Follow-up significance tests indicated that its convergent correlations with IMAS Mania were significantly stronger ($p < .01$, one-tailed) than the discriminant coefficients in all 18 comparisons across the two samples (*z*s ranged from 2.71 to 11.01). Thus, the scale again displays impressive discriminant validity in these data.

Table 5.2 Correlations Between IDAS-II Mania and the IMAS Scales in Samples 5 and 11

IMAS Scale	Sample 5	Sample 11
Mania	**.63**	**.68**
Generalized Anxiety Disorder	**.51**	.47
Posttraumatic Stress Disorder	.48	.47
Depression	.47	.47
Irritability	.44	.37
Panic	.41	.41
Obsessive-Compulsive Disorder	.32	.37
Agoraphobia	.30	.20
Social Phobia	.22	.23
Specific Phobia	.19	.14

Note: $N = 362$ patients (Sample 5), 373 students (Sample 11). IMAS = Interview of Mood and Anxiety Symptoms. Correlations ≥ .50 are in bold.

Table 5.3 Polyserial Correlations Between the IDAS-II Mania Scale and *DSM* Emotional Disorder Diagnoses

Diagnosis	Sample 4	Sample 5	Weighted *M*
Major Depression	**.44**	.26	**.37**
Generalized Anxiety Disorder	**.46**	.21	**.36**
Posttraumatic Stress Disorder	**.49**	.23	**.39**
Panic Disorder	**.34**	.18	.28
Agoraphobia	**.33**	.03	.21
Social Phobia	**.30**	.03	.19
Specific Phobia	.—	**.30**	**.30**
Obsessive-Compulsive Disorder	**.44**	.13	**.32**
Current Manic Episode	**.47**	.29	**.40**

NOTE: $N = 407$ adults (Sample 4), 290 outpatients (Sample 5). Correlations ≥ .30 are in bold.

Diagnostic Analyses

In Chapter 4, we reported that the IDAS-II Euphoria scale displayed good diagnostic specificity. Specifically, it had polyserial correlations of .31 (Sample 4, $N = 407$ adults) and .38 (Sample 5, $N = 290$ outpatients) with diagnoses of current manic episodes, with an overall weighted mean correlation of .34 (see Table 4.6); in contrast, its other diagnostic correlations ranged from only −.01 to .24.

Table 5.3 presents parallel results for IDAS-II Mania in these same two samples. It is noteworthy that Mania showed a very similar level of criterion validity. It correlated significantly with diagnoses of current manic episodes in both Samples 4 ($r = .47$) and 5 ($r = .29$), with a weighted mean correlation of .40. Clearly, however, it did not display the same level of diagnostic specificity. In fact, it had very similar mean correlations with panic disorder ($r = .39$), major depression ($r = .37$), and generalized anxiety disorder (GAD; $r = .36$). As we will see, this nonspecific pattern reflects the fact that Mania contains a much larger general distress/negative emotionality component than does Euphoria.

CLARIFYING THE NATURE OF BIPOLAR SYMPTOM SCALES

IDAS-II Item-Level Analyses

As noted earlier, bipolar symptom scales assess distress/negative emotionality and energy/positive emotionality to varying degrees, with some emphasizing the former, and others focusing more on the latter (Watson, Clark et al., 2013; Watson & Naragon-Gainey, 2014). We can illustrate this key point quite clearly using the Mania and Euphoria scales of the IDAS-II. We conducted a principal factor analysis (using squared multiple correlations as the initial communality estimates) of the 10 items contained in these two scales, along with the items included in IDAS-II Dysphoria (a strong marker of distress/negative emotionality; see Chapter 3) and Well-Being (a good indicator of positive emotionality; see Chapter 4). These results are based on the overall standardized combined sample of participants who were assessed on the complete IDAS-II (N=4,780; as noted in Chapter 2, this group included 908 patients, 1,091 community adults, and 2,781 college students); as in previous chapters, to eliminate mean-level differences across populations (i.e., patients vs. adults vs. students), we standardized the item responses on a within-population basis and then combined them to permit a single overall analysis.

This analysis revealed the presence of two clear factors, which we rotated to orthogonal simple structure using varimax. The resulting loadings (see Table 5.4) indicate that these factors can be labeled Negative Affect and Positive Affect, respectively.

As would be expected, the Dysphoria items are strong markers of the Negative Affect factor (mean loading=.61) and also tend to have negative secondary loadings on Positive Affect (mean loading = –.21). The Well-Being items basically show the opposite pattern: They strongly define the Positive Affect factor (mean loading=.66) and tend to load negatively on Negative Affect (mean loading = –.15). In marked contrast, the items contained in the two bipolar scales all have *positive* loadings on both factors, indicating that they tap elevated levels of both negative and positive emotionality. Clearly, however, the items in these scales weight these two elements quite differently. The Mania items are strong markers of the Negative Affect dimension (mean loading=.62) and tend to have more modest loadings on Positive Affect (mean loading=.19). Conversely, the Euphoria items strongly define the Positive Affect factor (mean loading=.51) and load more weakly on Negative Affect (mean loading=.28). Overall, these analyses demonstrate that the negative emotionality component is predominant in IDAS-II Mania, whereas the content in Euphoria is tipped in the direction of elevated positive emotionality.

Relations With Other Symptom Scales

Description of Other Bipolar Measures

We can extend this framework by examining how the IDAS-II scales relate to other measures of bipolar symptoms. We next consider associations with three other measures of mania symptoms: the General Behavior Inventory (GBI; Depue, Krauss, Spoont, & Arbisi, 1989; Depue et al., 1981), the Hypomanic Personality Scale (HPS; Eckblad & Chapman, 1986), and the Hypomania Checklist-32 (HCL-32; Angst et al., 2005). First, the GBI was designed to assess an individual's likelihood of risk for bipolar disorder (see Depue et al., 1981). The 21-item GBI Hypomania scale taps a broad range of bipolar symptoms (e.g., distractibility, reduced need for sleep, pressure of speech), whereas the 7-item Biphasic scale

Table 5.4 VARIMAX-ROTATED FACTOR LOADINGS OF THE IDAS-II DYSPHORIA, WELL-BEING, MANIA, AND EUPHORIA ITEMS (STANDARDIZED COMBINED SAMPLE)

Paraphrased Item	I	II
Dysphoria Items		
Worried all the time	**.68**	−.24
Felt discouraged about things	**.68**	**−.36**
Had trouble concentrating	**.67**	−.16
Felt inadequate	**.66**	**−.33**
Blamed myself for things	**.66**	−.23
Felt depressed	**.60**	**−.39**
Felt fidgety, restless	**.59**	−.06
Had trouble making up my mind	**.56**	−.08
Had little interest in usual activities	**.52**	−.27
Talked more slowly than usual	**.47**	.02
Mania Items		
Thoughts jumped rapidly	**.72**	.15
Hard to keep up with thoughts	**.71**	.14
Mind was moving "a mile a minute"	**.70**	.16
Spoke so rapidly others couldn't follow	**.51**	.18
Raced from one activity to the next	**.48**	**.30**
Euphoria Items		
Felt I was "on top of the world"	.08	**.68**
Had much more energy than usual	.28	**.53**
Felt elated for no special reason	**.32**	**.46**
Had so much energy it was hard to sit still	**.43**	**.45**
Felt I could do things others couldn't	.27	**.43**
Well-Being Items		
Felt I had a lot to look forward to	−.15	**.70**
Felt I had lots of interesting things to do	−.09	**.69**
Felt like I had a lot of energy	.04	**.68**
Felt hopeful about the future	−.18	**.67**
Felt I had accomplished a lot	−.18	**.66**
Was proud of myself	−.24	**.65**
Looked forward to things with enjoyment	−.19	**.62**
Felt optimistic	−.24	**.60**

NOTE: $N = 4{,}780$. Loadings $\geq |.30|$ are in bold.

focuses more narrowly on affective lability (e.g., rapid shifts in mood or energy) and behavioral volatility (e.g., changes in eating patterns). Respondents rate how often they experience each item on a 4-point scale ranging from *never or hardly* to *very often or almost constantly.* GBI data were available on a total of 1,706 participants (713 community adults, 993 college students).

Similar to the GBI, the HPS measures long-term manic/hypomanic tendencies, rather than current symptoms. The items are rated using a true-false format. In addition to creating a total score, we also examined the three HPS subscales developed by Schalet, Durbin, and Revelle (2011): Mood Volatility (13 items[1]; e.g., "When I feel an emotion, I usually feel it with extreme intensity"), Social Vitality (19 items; e.g. "In unfamiliar surroundings, I am often so assertive and sociable that I surprise myself"), and Excitement (7 items; e.g. "I often feel excited and happy for no apparent reason"). HPS data were available on 1,432 participants (363 adults, 1,069 students).

The HCL-32 consists of 32 items that are rated using a dichotomous yes/no format. Respondents are asked to indicate how they felt during "a period when you were in a 'high' state." Sample items include "I am more self-confident," "I am less shy or inhibited," and "I think faster." We obtained HCL data from 706 participants (364 adults, 342 students).

Results

Table 5.5 presents correlations—once again, based on combined samples that were standardized on a within-population basis—between the GBI, HPS, and HCL-32 and the IDAS-II bipolar symptom scales. The most striking aspect of these data is the marked variability in the strength and pattern of the associations. More specifically, the correlations with Mania ranged from .19 (HPS Social Vitality) to .56 (GBI Hypomania), whereas those for Euphoria ranged from .25 (GBI Biphasic) to .45 (HPS Total, HPS Excitement).

With regard to the pattern of associations, follow-up statistical tests indicated that the HPS Mood Volatility (.53 vs. .29; $z = 9.56$), GBI Biphasic (.51 vs. .25; $z = 11.47$), and GBI Hypomania scales (.56 vs. 44; $z = 5.25$) all correlated

Table 5.5 Correlations Between IDAS-II Mania, Euphoria, and Dysphoria Scales and Self-Report Mania Measures

Mania Scale	Mania	Euphoria
GBI Biphasic	**.51**	.25
GBI Hypomania	**.56**	**.44**
HPS Total	**.44**	**.45**
HPS Mood Volatility	**.53**	.29
HPS Excitement	.33	**.45**
HPS Social Vitality	.19	.34
HCL-32	.29	.31

NOTE: $N = 1{,}706$ (GBI), 1,432 (HPS), 706 (HCL-32). Correlations ≥ .40 are in bold. GBI = General Behavior Inventory. HPS = Hypomanic Personality Scale. HCL-32 = Hypomania Checklist-32.

1. Watson et al. (2012) reported results based on a 12-item version of this subscale that omitted the item "I seem to be a person whose mood goes up and down easily." This item is included in the scoring of the Mood Volatility scale in all analyses reported in this chapter.

significantly more strongly with Mania than with Euphoria. The data for HPS Volatility and GBI Biphasic are consistent with a broad range of evidence indicating that mood variability is a core feature of neuroticism/negative emotionality (Watson et al., 1994). In fact, Watson et al. (1994) included affective lability as a facet within neuroticism in their hierarchical model of personality (see their Table 3); similarly, it has been included as a component of the higher order negative affectivity domain in the trait dimensional model in Section III of *DSM-5* (Krueger et al., 2012; Watson, Stasik, Ro, & Clark, 2013). Thus, it makes good sense that these scales contain a dominant component of negative emotionality.

HPS Excitement (.45 vs. 33; $z = 4.85$) and Social Vitality (.34 vs. .19; $z = 5.77$) showed the opposite pattern, correlating significantly more strongly with Euphoria than with Mania; consequently, these scales appear to focus more on individual differences in positive emotionality. The final two scales—the HCL-32 and the HPS Total score—had very similar correlations with Mania (.44 and .29, respectively) and Euphoria (.45 and .31, respectively) that did not differ significantly from one another.

THE TWO-FACTOR STRUCTURE OF BIPOLAR SYMPTOMS

Factor Analyses of the Bipolar Scales

The data presented in Table 5.5 suggest that there are two basic types of bipolar symptom scales, depending on whether the negative emotional component (e.g., HPS Mood Volatility, GBI Biphasic, IDAS-II Mania) or the positive emotional component (e.g., HPS Excitement, HPS Social Vitality, IDAS-II Euphoria) predominates. We tested this idea more formally by conducting separate principal factor analyses (using squared multiple correlations as the initial communality estimates) in two samples of participants—361 community adults and 341 college students—who were assessed on all the measures displayed in Table 5.4. Note that the HPS Total score was omitted from these structural analyses because it shares items with the HPS subscales (see also Watson & Naragon-Gainey, 2014, who reported similar results based on a standardized combined sample).

Two factors emerged in each sample and were rotated to orthogonal simple structure using varimax; the resulting loadings are presented in Table 5.6. The GBI Biphasic, GBI Hypomania, HPS Mood Volatility, and IDAS-II Mania scales defined Factor 1 in both samples. This dimension taps individual differences in affective lability, restlessness, and cognitive manifestations of mania (e.g., pressure of speech), and should be more strongly related to indicators of negative emotionality; we therefore labeled it Manic Distress. Conversely, IDAS-II Euphoria, HPS Excitement, HPS Social Vitality, and HCL-32 marked Factor 2 in both samples. This dimension appears to reflect individual differences in elation, excitement, and manic energy/activation, and so should relate more strongly to indicators of positive emotionality; accordingly, we labeled it Manic Elation. We computed regression-based factor scores to model these two dimensions in subsequent analyses.

Table 5.6 Varimax Factor Loadings of the Bipolar Symptom Scales in Adult and Student Samples

	Adults		Students	
Scale	**I**	**II**	**I**	**II**
GBI Biphasic	**.84**	.11	**.83**	.04
GBI Hypomania	**.78**	.36	**.71**	.38
HPS Mood Volatility	**.72**	**.40**	**.69**	**.43**
IDAS-II Mania	**.48**	.34	**.48**	.37
IDAS-II Euphoria	.08	**.65**	.15	**.63**
HPS Excitement	.36	**.60**	.27	**.63**
HPS Social Vitality	.25	**.52**	.12	**.55**
HCL-32	.30	**.43**	.27	**.47**

NOTE: $N = 361$ (Adults), 341 (Students). Loadings ≥ |.40| are in bold. GBI = General Behavior Inventory. HPS = Hypomanic Personality Scale. IDAS-II = Expanded Version of the Inventory of Depression and Anxiety Symptoms. HCL-32 = Hypomania Checklist-32.

Assessment of Factor Similarity

Congruence Coefficients

Before examining these dimensions in greater detail, it is important to establish that the same set of factors emerged in each solution. We examined this issue using both of the basic approaches to measuring factor similarity (Everett & Entrekin, 1980): (a) calculating congruence coefficients based on the factor loadings (Lorenzo-Seva & ten Berge, 2006) and (b) computing comparability coefficients (Finn, 1986), which involves deriving regression-based factor scores for each solution (Everett & Entrekin, 1980; Finn, 1986; Gorsuch, 1983; Harman, 1976). We first computed congruence coefficients, which provide a quantitative estimate of the similarity of the factor loadings across solutions. Based on an extensive series of analyses, Lorenzo-Seva and ten Berge (2006) concluded that congruence coefficients in the .85–.94 range indicate that the two compared factors display fair similarity, whereas values ≥ .95 indicate good similarity. We obtained congruence coefficients of .994 (Manic Distress) and .998 (Manic Elation), which establishes good factor similarity across samples.

Comparability Coefficients

Next, we calculated comparability coefficients, which generally represent a more stringent test of factor similarity (Everett & Entrekin, 1980). As noted earlier, the two-factor solutions each generated a set of regression-based factor scoring weights, which then can be applied to the participants' actual responses in each sample. Consequently, we have a total of four factor scores—two representing the adult factors and two representing the student factors—that can be compared. If the two solutions are highly similar, then the corresponding weights for each

Table 5.7 ANALYSES OF FACTOR SIMILARITY: COMPARABILITY COEFFICIENTS

Sample/Factor	**1**	**2**	**3**	**4**
Community Sample				
1. Adult Factor I	.—			
2. Student Factor I	**.998**	.—		
3. Adult Factor II	.218	.236	.—	
4. Student Factor II	.266	.282	**.995**	.—
Student Sample				
1. Adult Factor I	.—			
2. Student Factor I	**.998**	.—		
3. Adult Factor II	.144	.161	.—	
4. Student Factor II	.180	.194	**.996**	.—

NOTE: $N = 361$ (Community Sample), 341 (Student Sample). Convergent correlations between parallel factors are in bold.

factor (e.g., the Manic Distress weights in the adult data vs. the parallel weights in the student sample) will produce scores that are very highly correlated.

Table 5.7 presents the comparability correlations between these two sets of factor scores in both the adult ($N = 361$) and the student ($N = 341$) data. These results demonstrate an impressive level of factor similarity across samples. In fact, the comparability coefficients (which all are > .99) easily exceed Everett's (1983) factor similarity benchmark of .90. Taken together with the congruence coefficients, these data establish that the same two factors clearly emerged in both samples.

Relations With the Big Five

FACTOR CORRELATIONS

These two symptom factors correlate quite differently with other variables; these differential associations demonstrate the heuristic and practical value of this structural scheme. This differential pattern is strikingly illustrated in Table 5.8, which reports correlations between regression-based factor scores and the five higher order traits assessed in the 44-item version of the BFI (John & Srivastava, 1999; for more details regarding the BFI, see Chapter 2). In addition to the simple bivariate relations, the final column of Table 5.7 displays multiple correlations that demonstrate the combined ability of the Big Five to predict each symptom factor.

As would be expected, the Manic Distress factor correlated strongly with BFI Neuroticism in both the adults ($r = .52$) and the students ($r = .58$). It also had moderate inverse associations with both agreeableness and conscientiousness (*rs* ranged from −.25 to −.35 across the two samples), and generally showed weak links to extraversion and openness (*rs* ranged from −.07 to .20). Thus,

Table 5.8 Correlations Between the BFI Scales and Bipolar Symptom Factors

Sample/Factor	Neur	Extra	Open	Agree	Con	Overall *R*
Adults						
Manic Distress	**.52**	.02	.20	−.35	−.31	.63
Manic Elation	−.20	**.53**	.31	−.15	.01	.60
Students						
Manic Distress	**.58**	−.07	.08	−.33	−.25	.63
Manic Elation	−.24	**.52**	.18	.02	−.03	.54

NOTE: $N = 359$ (Adults), 339 (Students). Correlations ≥ |.40| are in bold. BFI = Big Five Inventory. Neur = Neuroticism. Extra = Extraversion. Open = Openness. Agree = Agreeableness. Con = Conscientiousness.

consistent with its label, this dimension primarily reflects individual differences in negative emotionality.

In marked contrast, Manic Elation had strong positive correlations with extraversion ($r = .53$ and .52 in the adults and students, respectively), indicating that it taps individual differences in positive emotionality to a considerable degree. It also showed moderate associations with both openness ($r = .31$ and .18, respectively) and (low) neuroticism ($r = -.20$ and −.24, respectively), and it was weakly related to agreeableness and conscientiousness (*r*s ranged from .02 to −.15 across the two samples).

These results clearly demonstrate the dysfunctional nature of the Manic Distress factor: Individuals who score highly on this dimension tend to be sad and depressed (i.e., high neuroticism), aggressive and self-centered (i.e., low agreeableness), and impulsive and unreliable (i.e., low conscientiousness). But how can we interpret individual differences in Manic Elation? High scores on this dimension are associated with elevated levels of extraversion and somewhat lower levels of neuroticism, an affective signature that would seem to be largely adaptive in nature. In Chapter 4, we established the dysfunctional nature of the IDAS-II Euphoria scale (e.g., it had a weighted mean correlation of .34 with diagnoses of current manic episodes; see Table 4.6) and showed that it basically represents a pathological form of positive affect. The findings in Table 5.8, however, raise potential validity concerns about some of the other markers of the Manic Elation factor, suggesting that they tap largely adaptive processes. We explore this issue in detail later in the chapter.

HPS Analyses

One further implication of these results is that they demonstrate that it can be rather misleading to use global scale scores that subsume important content related to both bipolar symptom factors. This can be seen quite clearly in the case of the HPS, which contains strong markers of both Manic Distress (Mood Volatility) and Manic Elation (Excitement, Social Vitality). For example, the HPS Total score correlated weakly with BFI Neuroticism in both the adult ($r = .14$) and the student ($r = .06$) samples. However, this overall score masks the fact that the

HPS contains distinctive types of content that correlate quite differently with the trait: At the subscale level, Neuroticism was moderately positively correlated with Mood Volatility (*r* = .40 and .42 in the adults and students, respectively), unrelated to Excitement (*r* = .05 and -.01, respectively), and significantly negatively associated with Social Vitality (*r* = –.14 and –.23, respectively).

Relatedly, the HPS Total score had a moderate positive correlation with BFI Extraversion in both samples (*r* = .45 and .45 in the adults and students, respectively). As would be expected, however, the HPS subscales correlated quite differently with this trait: BFI Extraversion was strongly positively correlated with Social Vitality (*r* = .58 and .60, respectively), moderately associated with Excitement (*r* = .40 and .40, respectively), and weakly related to Mood Volatility (*r* = .19 and .08, respectively).

These results demonstrate the importance of analyzing these subscales—and, more fundamentally, the two bipolar symptom factors—separately from each other. Returning to our earlier point, they also raise particular validity concerns related to the HPS Social Vitality subscale, given its very strong links to extraversion. We revisit this issue subsequently.

BIS/BAS Relations

As was discussed in Chapter 4, the bipolar disorders have been linked to hypersensitivity of the Behavioral Activation System (BAS; see Johnson et al., 2012), a motivational system that directs organisms toward situations and experiences that potentially may yield pleasure and reward. The BAS is substantially associated with individual differences in positive emotionality (Watson, 2000a; Watson et al., 1999), although more recent evidence indicates that it also is linked to elevated levels of anger (Carver & Harmon-Jones, 2009; Watson, 2009b). Conversely, individual differences in negative emotionality are associated with the withdrawal-oriented Behavioral Inhibition System (BIS; Watson, 2000a; Watson et al., 1999), which is designed to keep organisms out of danger by inhibiting behavior that might lead to pain, punishment, or some other undesirable consequence. Given the nature and correlates of the two bipolar symptom factors, it seems plausible to suggest that Manic Elation would be more strongly associated with the BAS, whereas Manic Distress would be more substantially linked to individual differences in the BIS.

We can test these hypotheses using the Behavioral Inhibition System/Behavioral Activation System (BIS/BAS) scales that were developed by Carver and White (1994). The BIS scale contains seven items that were designed to reflect concerns over the possibility of a bad occurrence (e.g., "I worry about making mistakes") and a heightened sensitivity to such events when they do occur (e.g., "Criticism or scolding hurts me quite a bit"). BAS sensitivity is assessed via three subscales, which we will analyze separately here: Drive (four items; e.g., "If I see a chance to get something I want, I move on it right away"), Reward Responsiveness (five items; e.g., "When I get something I want, I feel excited and energized"), and Fun Seeking (four items; e.g., "I crave excitement and new sensations").

Table 5.9 Correlations Between the BIS/BAS Scales and Bipolar Symptom Factors

Mania Factor	**BIS**	**BAS Scales** Reward	Drive	Fun Seeking
Adults				
Manic Distress	.25	.19	**.31**	.24
Manic Elation	−.14	.18	.26	**.45**
Students				
Manic Distress	**.30**	.10	.12	.14
Manic Elation	−.20	.18	**.32**	**.45**

NOTE: $N = 359$ (Adults), 339 (Students). Correlations ≥ |.30| are in bold. BIS = Behavioral Inhibition System. BAS = Behavioral Activation System. Reward = Reward Responsiveness.

Table 5.9 reports correlations between these BIS/BAS scales and the bipolar factor scores in the adult and student samples. These results partly support our predictions. Consistent with expectation, Manic Distress was moderately correlated with the BIS scale ($r = .30$)—and had significantly weaker associations with the three BAS subscales (*r*s ranged from .10 to .14, *z*s ranged from 2.30 to 2.33, all *p*s < .05, one-tailed)—in the student data. Contrary to prediction, however, Manic Distress had similar, moderate links to all four scales in the adult sample, with correlations ranging from .19 (BAS Reward Responsiveness) to .31 (BAS Drive).

Consistent with our hypotheses, Manic Elation tended to correlate more strongly with the BAS subscales than with the BIS. Moreover, it displayed marked specificity vis-à-vis these three subscales; that is, it correlated moderately with Fun Seeking ($r = .45$ and .45 in the adults and students, respectively), more modestly with Drive ($r = .26$ and .32, respectively), and only weakly with Reward Responsiveness ($r = .18$ and .18, respectively). Follow-up statistical tests indicated that Manic Elation correlated significantly more strongly ($p < .05$, two-tailed) with Fun Seeking than with Drive ($z = 4.02$ and 2.42 in the adults and students, respectively), Reward Responsiveness ($z = 5.24$ and 5.11, respectively), and the BIS scale (ignoring sign; $z = 4.74$ and 3.67, respectively) in both samples. Thus, scores on this factor are particularly related to individual differences in BAS Fun Seeking, a scale that contains items reflecting both (a) a desire to pursue new rewards and (b) an impulsive willingness to approach potentially rewarding events on the spur of the moment (see Carver & White, 1994).

TAI Analyses

Temperament and Affectivity Inventory

Finally, the student participants also completed the newly developed Temperament and Affectivity Inventory (TAI; Watson, Stasik, Chmielewski, & Naragon-Gainey, 2014). The TAI consists of 12 factor analytically derived scales that jointly provide a comprehensive assessment of individual differences in emotionality. It therefore provides a particularly rich and differentiated picture of how these bipolar symptom factors relate to individual differences in negative and positive emotionality.

The TAI contains a series of statements that are rated on a 5-point scale ranging from *strongly disagree* to *strongly agree*. The 12 factor-based scales are Anxiety (8 items; e.g., "I worry about terrible things that might happen"), Depression (7 items; e.g., "I have a gloomy outlook on life"), Regret (5 items; e.g., "I've made a lot of mistakes in my life"), Anger (12 items; e.g., "I tend to be rather irritable"), Lassitude (7 items; e.g., "I sometimes feel too tired to do anything"), Self-Doubt (6 items; e.g., "I wish I had more self-confidence"), Mistrust (9 items; e.g., "I am suspicious of others"), Attentiveness (6 items; e.g., "It is easy for me to concentrate for long periods of time"), Experience Seeking (9 items; e.g., "I like to stir things up when I am bored"), Vigor (5 items; e.g., "My life is fast-paced"), Geniality (10 items; e.g., "It is easy for me to laugh"), and Shyness (9 items; e.g., "I get nervous at social gatherings").

RESULTS

Table 5.10 presents correlations between the TAI scales and the bipolar symptom factors in the student sample. Replicating and extending other findings, Manic Distress was broadly related to indicators of negative emotionality in these data: It correlated most strongly with Anxiety ($r = .53$) and Depression ($r = .51$), and more moderately with Regret, Anger, Lassitude, Self-Doubt, and Mistrust (*r*s ranged from .38 to .46). Conversely, Manic Elation was moderately associated with indicators of positive emotionality. Consistent with the Table 5.9 results, it correlated particularly strongly ($r = .47$) with TAI Experience Seeking, a scale that taps individual differences in adventurousness (e.g., "I'm an adventurous person"), risk taking (e.g., "People have told me that I am reckless"), fearlessness

Table 5.10 CORRELATIONS BETWEEN THE BIPOLAR SYMPTOM FACTORS AND TAI SCALES IN THE STUDENT SAMPLE

TAI Scale	Manic Distress	Manic Elation
Anxiety	**.53**	−.14
Depression	**.51**	−.27
Regret	**.46**	−.06
Anger	**.43**	.08
Lassitude	**.42**	−.06
Self-Doubt	**.41**	−.27
Mistrust	**.38**	−.01
Attentiveness	**−.34**	.03
Experience Seeking	.15	**.47**
Vigor	.02	**.39**
Geniality	−.14	**.33**
Shyness	.19	**−.41**

NOTE: $N = 339$. TAI = Temperament and Affectivity Inventory. Correlations ≥ |.30| are in bold.

(e.g., "I enjoy things that others might find scary"), and novelty seeking (e.g., "I enjoy trying new things"). Follow-up statistical tests indicated that Manic Elation correlated significantly more strongly with Experience Seeking than with Geniality ($r = .33$, $z = 2.25$, $p < .05$, two-tailed); however, the difference with Vigor ($r = .39$; $z = 1.38$) was not significant. Taken together with the BIS/BAS results, these data indicate that the Manic Elation factor displays a particular affinity to a form of positive emotionality that is tipped in the direction of recklessness, impulsivity, and novel experience seeking.

REPLICATION AND EXTENSION IN AN MTURK SAMPLE

Measurement Model

Next, we test the generality of this two-factor structure in a new sample of participants who were assessed using a somewhat different set of measures (see also Stanton, Gruber, & Watson, in press, who report a more detailed version of these results in their Study 1). We recruited this community sample ($N = 329$) online from the Mechanical Turk (MTurk) system hosted by Amazon Web Services (https://www.mturk.com). The participants included 177 men and 151 women (the sex of one participant was unspecified) with a mean age of 32.2 years (range = 18–66 years).

As in the two previous samples, the participants completed both the IDAS-II and the HPS. In place of the GBI and the HCL-32, however, they were assessed on two new measures of bipolar symptoms. First, the Altman Self-Rating Mania Scale (ASRM; Altman, Hedeker, Peterson & Davis, 1997) contains five items. Each item consists of five statements; participants are asked to choose the statement "that best describes the way you have been feeling for the past week." The five items tap feelings of happiness and cheerfulness, self-confidence, the need for sleep, talkativeness, and overall level of activity. Altman et al. (1997) demonstrated the validity of the ASRM by showing that scores were significantly higher for manic patients than for all other diagnostic groups.

Second, the Mood Disorder Questionnaire (MDQ; Hirschfeld et al., 2000) is a widely used measure that was designed to serve as a screening instrument for bipolar spectrum disorders. The respondents are asked to indicate whether there ever was "a period of time when you were not your usual self" and if they experienced each of 14 bipolar symptoms (e.g., were more talkative than usual, needed less sleep than usual, engaged in risky behavior, got into trouble because of excessive spending) on a yes-no basis.

Factor Analysis of the Bipolar Scales

Altogether, we have seven measures of bipolar symptoms (ASRM, HPS Excitement, HPS Mood Volatility, HPS Social Vitality, IDAS-II Euphoria, IDAS-II Mania,

Table 5.11 VARIMAX FACTOR LOADINGS OF THE BIPOLAR SYMPTOM SCALES IN THE MTURK SAMPLE

Bipolar Symptom Scale	I	II
IDAS-II Euphoria	**.84**	.35
Altman Self-Rating Mania Scale	**.75**	.24
HPS Social Vitality	**.59**	.28
HPS Mood Volatility	.25	**.77**
IDAS-II Mania	**.55**	**.64**
Mood Disorder Questionnaire	.22	**.60**
HPS Excitement	**.52**	**.55**

NOTE: $N = 329$. Loadings ≥ |.40| are in bold. MTurk = Mechanical Turk. IDAS-II = Expanded Version of the Inventory of Depression and Anxiety Symptoms. HPS = Hypomanic Personality Scale.

MDQ) available in this MTurk sample. To examine their structure, we subjected these measures to a principal factor analysis. Replicating prior results, we identified two clear factors in these data; these factors were rotated orthogonally using varimax. The resulting loadings are presented in Table 5.11. It is noteworthy that these two factors reflect the same basic dimensions as those found in the previous samples. Factor 1 was defined primarily by the IDAS-II Euphoria, ASRM, and HPS Social Vitality scales; IDAS-II Mania and HPS Excitement also had loadings > .50 on this factor. This dimension appears to focus on individual differences in energy and positive emotionality, and so it can be identified as Manic Elation. In contrast, HPS Mood Volatility and the MDQ were the clearest markers of Factor 2; IDAS-II Mania and HPS Excitement also had strong loadings on this dimension. This factor appears to tap individual differences in affective lability, recklessness, and the cognitive manifestations of mania, and so it can be identified as Manic Distress. Once again, we computed regression-based factor scores to model these two dimensions in subsequent analyses.

Relations With Personality and Affectivity

DESCRIPTION OF MEASURES

The participants in the MTurk sample completed an extensive battery of questionnaires tapping individual differences in positive and negative emotionality. Several of these measures were described earlier; these included (a) the IDAS-II Dysphoria and Well-Being scales; (b) the Neuroticism and Extraversion scales of the 44-item BFI; (c) trait versions of the general Negative Affect and Positive Affect scales of the PANAS-X; and (d) the TAI Attentiveness, Geniality, Experience Seeking, and Vigor scales.

In addition, the battery included the 11-item Positive Emotions and 9-item Negative Emotions scales from the modified trait version of the Differential

Emotions Scale (mDES; Fredrickson, Tugade, Waugh, & Larkin, 2003). The participants rated the extent to which they experienced various positive affects (e.g., glad, happy, joyful; interested, alert, curious) and negative affects (scared, fearful, afraid; sad, downhearted, unhappy) "on the average, or in general" on a 5-point scale ranging from *not at all* to *extremely.*

Next, the participants were assessed on the Affect Valuation Index (AVI; Tsai, 2007; Tsai, Knutson, & Fung, 2006). They were asked to rate how often they experience various emotions "over the course of a typical week" on a 5-point scale ranging from *never* to *all the time.* The battery in this MTurk sample included a three-item measure of High Arousal Positive Affect (*elated, enthusiastic, excited*) and a four-item measure of Low Arousal Positive Affect (*calm, peaceful, relaxed, serene*).

The participants also completed the widely used Satisfaction with Life Scale (SWLS; Diener, Emmons, Larsen, & Griffin, 1985). The SWLS is a five-item measure of general life satisfaction (e.g., "So far I have gotten the important things I want in life"). Items are rated on a 7-point scale ranging from *strongly disagree* to *strongly agree.*

The battery also included the Subjective Happiness Scale (SHS; Lyubomirsky & Lepper, 1999). The SHS assesses general feelings of happiness; it consists of four items that are rated on 7-point response scales.

Finally, the Positive Urgency Measure (PUM; Cyders et al., 2007) assesses individual differences in the tendency to act rashly when one is experiencing a state of high positive affect. The PUM consists of 14 items (e.g., "When I am really excited, I tend not to think of the consequences of my actions") that are rated on a 4-point scale ranging from *agree strongly* to *disagree strongly.*

Results

Table 5.12 presents correlations between these scales and scores on the Manic Elation and Manic Distress factors. These results are broadly consistent with those observed in previous samples and again demonstrate the strikingly different nature of the two factors. Once again, Manic Distress clearly is substantially related to individual differences in negative emotionality. It correlated strongly with IDAS-II Dysphoria ($r=.60$) and the PUM ($r=.60$), and more moderately with BFI Neuroticism ($r=.41$), PANAS-X Negative Affect ($r=.39$), and mDES Negative Emotions ($r=.38$) in this sample.

Conversely, Manic Elation is more strongly and consistently linked to individual differences in positive emotionality. Its strongest correlates included IDAS-II Well-Being ($r=.74$), PANAS-X Positive Affect ($r=.65$), BFI Extraversion ($r=.58$), the SWLS ($r=.51$), and the SHS ($r=.47$) in these data. It also is informative to examine how it related to individual scales within the same instrument. Consistent with the results shown in Table 5.10, Manic Elation correlated significantly more strongly with TAI Vigor ($r=.66$) and Experience Seeking ($r=.63$) than with Geniality ($r=.32$; $z=7.64$ and 6.23, respectively) and Attentiveness ($r=.24$; $z=9.35$ and 7.03, respectively). Moreover, it had a significantly stronger association with AVI High Arousal Positive Affect ($r=.73$) than with Low Arousal Positive Affect ($r=.40$; $z=8.56$) in these data. Finally, it is noteworthy that

Table 5.12 Correlations Between the Bipolar Symptom Factors and Personality and Affectivity Scales in the MTurk Sample

Scale	Manic Elation	Manic Distress
IDAS-II Well-Being	**.74**	.00
AVI High Arousal Positive Affect	**.73**	.12
TAI Vigor	**.66**	.08
PANAS-X Positive Affect	**.65**	.04
TAI Experience Seeking	**.63**	.27
BFI Extraversion	**.61**	.05
mDES Positive Emotions	**.58**	.01
Satisfaction with Life Scale	**.51**	−.16
Subjective Happiness Scale	**.47**	−.25
AVI Low Arousal Positive Affect	**.40**	−.09
TAI Geniality	**.32**	−.02
IDAS-II Dysphoria	−.01	**.60**
Positive Urgency	**.31**	**.60**
BFI Neuroticism	**−.39**	**.41**
PANAS-X Negative Affect	−.10	**.39**
mDES Negative Emotions	−.13	**.38**
TAI Attentiveness	.24	**−.38**

NOTE: $N = 329$. MTurk = Mechanical Turk. BFI = Big Five Inventory. PANAS-X = Expanded Form of the Positive and Negative Affect Schedule. mDES = Modified Differential Emotions Scale. IDAS-II = Expanded version of the Inventory of Depression and Anxiety Symptoms. AVI = Affect Valuation Index. TAI = Temperament and Affectivity Inventory. Correlations ≥ |.30| are in bold.

this factor correlated *positively* with the PUM ($r = .31$); thus, high scores on this dimension are associated with a tendency to act rashly when experiencing positive affect. Taken together with previous results, these data indicate that the Manic Elation factor displays a particular affinity to forms of positive emotionality that are tipped in the direction of high energy/arousal, recklessness, impulsivity, and novel experience seeking.

SAMPLE 4 ANALYSES

Factor Analysis of the Bipolar Scales

The Sample 4 data provide a rich opportunity to explicate the distinctive nature of these bipolar symptom factors more fully. A subset of these adult participants completed both the IDAS-II and the HPS. As already noted, these two instruments jointly yield five indicators (IDAS-II Euphoria and Mania; HPS Mood Volatility, Social Vitality, and Excitement) that can be used to model bipolar symptom dimensions in structural analyses.

Table 5.13 Varimax Factor Loadings of the Bipolar Symptom Scales in Sample 4

Bipolar Symptom Scale	I	II
HPS Mood Volatility	**.73**	.29
IDAS-II Mania	**.71**	.18
HPS Excitement	**.58**	**.50**
HPS Social Vitality	.12	**.55**
IDAS-II Euphoria	.35	**.47**

NOTE: $N = 246$. Loadings ≥ |.40| are in bold. CAMPP = IDAS-II =Expanded Version of the Inventory of Depression and Anxiety Symptoms. HPS = Hypomanic Personality Scale.

Following the procedure used in previous samples, we subjected the bipolar scales to a principal factor analysis; we extracted two factors and rotated them using varimax. The loadings from this two-factor solution are presented in Table 5.13. Given the smaller number of indicators that were available in this sample, the factors were not as clearly defined as in previous analyses. Nevertheless, the dimensions that emerged are easily interpretable and correspond well to those seen earlier. Factor 1 is most strongly defined by HPS Mood Volatility (.73) and IDAS-II Mania (.71) and clearly represents Manic Distress. Conversely, Factor 2 has HPS Social Vitality (.55), HPS Excitement (.50), and IDAS-II Euphoria (.47) as its strongest markers and can be identified as Manic Elation. Once again, we computed regression-based factor scores to model these two dimensions in subsequent analyses.

Facet-Level Relations With Personality

We examine the correlates of these factor scores in three series of analyses. First, we previously showed that Manic Distress and Manic Elation are strongly correlated with general measures of neuroticism and extraversion, respectively. The Sample 4 data allow us to examine these relations more precisely at the lower order facet level. Participants in Sample 4 were assessed on the 240-item NEO Personality Inventory-3 (NEO-PI-3; McCrae, Costa, & Martin, 2005), which is an updated version of the widely used NEO PI-R (Costa & McCrae, 1992); the only change was that 38 items were revised to lower the reading level, thereby making the instrument more appropriate for younger examinees and adults with lower educational levels. Items are rated on a 5-point Likert scale ranging from *strongly disagree* to *strongly agree*. The NEO-PI-3 contains six 8-item facet scales to assess each higher order trait domain. The Neuroticism facets are Anxiety, Angry Hostility, Depression, Self-Consciousness, Impulsiveness, and Vulnerability; the facets for Extraversion are Warmth, Gregariousness, Assertiveness, Activity, Excitement Seeking, and Positive Emotions.

Table 5.14 Correlations Between the Bipolar Symptom Factors and NEO-PI-3 Neuroticism and Extraversion Scales in Sample 4

NEO-PI-3 Scale	Manic Distress	Manic Elation
Neuroticism	**.67**	−.02
Angry Hostility	**.62**	.19
Anxiety	**.58**	−.09
Depression	**.58**	−.01
Self-Consciousness	**.49**	−.12
Vulnerability	**.49**	−.09
Impulsiveness	**.45**	.04
Extraversion	−.17	**.52**
Assertiveness	−.15	**.44**
Excitement Seeking	−.03	**.43**
Activity	.00	**.43**
Positive Emotions	−.11	.38
Gregariousness	−.20	.25
Warmth	−.23	.21

NOTE: $N = 243$. Correlations ≥ .40 are in bold.
NEO-PI-3 = NEO Personality Inventory-3.

Table 5.14 presents correlations between the bipolar symptom factors and the NEO-PI-3 Neuroticism and Extraversion scales (both general domain scores and specific facet scales). Replicating previous findings, scores on Manic Distress correlated strongly with NEO-PI-3 Neuroticism ($r = .67$) in this sample. It is noteworthy that Manic Distress was broadly related to all of the facets of Neuroticism, with correlations ranging from .62 (Angry Hostility) to .45 (Impulsiveness); thus, this dimension shows largely nonspecific associations with neuroticism.

As expected, Manic Elation correlated substantially with NEO-PI-3 Extraversion ($r = .52$) in these data. However, it showed greater specificity at the facet level. It had particularly strong associations with the more agentic aspects of Extraversion; specifically, its highest coefficients were with Assertiveness ($r = .44$), Excitement Seeking ($r = .43$), and Activity ($r = .43$). In contrast, it was modestly related to the more communal aspects of the trait, correlating only .25 and .21 with Gregariousness and Warmth, respectively. Thus, consistent with other results we have presented, Manic Elation displays a particular affinity to the components of extraversion reflecting energy, dominance, and intense experience seeking.

Relations With Personality Pathology

Next, we examine the broader psychopathological correlates of these factors. The Sample 4 participants also completed two measures of personality pathology.

First, they were assessed on the PID-5 (Krueger et al., 2012). As was discussed in Chapter 4, the PID-5 assesses the 25 specific facets in the trait dimensional model of personality pathology that was newly developed for Section III of *DSM-5* (American Psychiatric Association, 2013). The PID-5 is ideal for our purposes because its scales tap an extremely wide range of psychopathology, including multiple indicators of internalizing (e.g., Anhedonia, Anxiousness, and Depressivity), externalizing (e.g., Callousness, Impulsivity, and Irresponsibility), and psychoticism/schizotypy (e.g., Eccentricity, Unusual Beliefs and Experiences, Cognitive and Perceptual Dysregulation).

Second, the participants completed the 40-item version of the Narcissistic Personality Inventory (NPI; Raskin & Hall, 1981) that was developed by Raskin and Terry (1988). The NPI is a widely used measure that was created to assess individual differences in narcissism, based on the diagnostic criteria for NPD in *DSM-III* (American Psychiatric Association, 1980). The NPI uses a forced-choice response format. Respondents are presented with a series of paired statements, each of which includes both a narcissistic (e.g., "I think I am a special person") and a nonnarcissistic (e.g., "I am no better or worse than most people") option. As was discussed in Chapter 4, NPD has been linked to elevated levels of extraversion and positive emotionality. Consequently, we expected that NPI scores would be particularly related to individual differences in Manic Elation.

Table 5.15 reports correlations between these factor scores and the personality pathology scales. These results further explicate the distinctive nature of the two symptom dimensions. Manic Distress displays a much broader range of associations in these data; it correlates most strongly with indicators of internalizing psychopathology (e.g., $r=.66$ with Distractibility, $r=.64$ with Anxiousness, $r=.64$ with Perseveration, and $r=.56$ with Depressivity) and psychoticism/schizotypy (e.g., $r=.65$ with Cognitive and Perceptual Dysregulation, $r=.65$ with Eccentricity, $r=.54$ with Suspiciousness, and $r=.53$ with Unusual Beliefs and Experiences). Not surprisingly, this dimension also correlates strongly with PID-5 Emotional Lability ($r=.66$), a scale that contains the same type of content as Manic Distress markers such as HPS Mood Volatility and GBI Biphasic. Overall, these findings indicate that high scores on the factor are associated with elevated levels of distress and internalizing psychopathology that can take on a somewhat peculiar and paranoid character.

It is noteworthy that Manic Elation consistently showed *positive* associations with personality pathology; indeed, Table 5.15 indicates that 24 of its 26 correlations (92.3%) were positive in sign (the two exceptions were PID-5 Anhedonia and Submissiveness). These results clearly demonstrate the pathological nature of this dimension. Manic Elation correlated most strongly with narcissism on the NPI ($r=.68$), as well as PID-5 Attention Seeking ($r=.56$), Grandiosity ($r=.46$), Risk Taking ($r=.46$), and Manipulativeness ($r=.44$). These results both replicate and extend previous findings. They demonstrate that high scores on this factor are associated with excessive self-regard and an inflated sense of self-importance, as well as grandiosity, exhibitionism, and the reckless pursuit of rewarding activities.

Table 5.15 Correlations Between the Bipolar Symptom Factors and Personality Pathology Measures in Sample 4

Personality Pathology Scale	**Manic Distress**	**Manic Elation**
PID-5 Emotional Lability	**.66**	.19
PID-5 Distractibility	**.66**	.11
PID-5 Cognitive and Perceptual Dysregulation	**.65**	.27
PID-5 Eccentricity	**.65**	.31
PID-5 Anxiousness	**.64**	.08
PID-5 Perseveration	**.64**	.24
PID-5 Hostility	**.59**	.29
PID-5 Impulsivity	**.58**	.35
PID-5 Depressivity	**.56**	.07
PID-5 Suspiciousness	**.54**	.22
PID-5 Unusual Beliefs & Experiences	**.53**	.33
PID-5 Withdrawal	**.52**	.06
PID-5 Rigid Perfectionism	**.49**	.25
PID-5 Irresponsibility	**.49**	.24
PID-5 Separation Insecurity	**.46**	.14
PID-5 Intimacy Avoidance	**.46**	.14
PID-5 Anhedonia	**.43**	−.17
PID-5 Callousness	**.42**	.35
PID-5 Deceitfulness	.37	.36
PID-5 Restricted Affectivity	.31	.09
PID-5 Submissiveness	.24	−.02
Narcissistic Personality Inventory	.14	**.68**
PID-5 Attention Seeking	.27	**.56**
PID-5 Grandiosity	.32	**.46**
PID-5 Risk Taking	.28	**.46**
PID-5 Manipulativeness	.28	**.44**

NOTE: $N = 241$. Correlations ≥ .40 are in bold. PID-5 = Personality Inventory for *DSM-5*.

Relations With *DSM* Diagnoses

Finally, we examine links with formal *DSM-5* diagnoses of the emotional disorders. Table 5.16 presents polyserial correlations between the factor scores and eight *DSM* disorders: major depression, GAD, posttraumatic stress disorder (PTSD), panic disorder, agoraphobia, social phobia, obsessive-compulsive disorder (OCD), and lifetime diagnoses of mania. Manic Distress clearly displays much stronger associations in these data. As would be expected, it correlated most strongly with mania ($r = .62$). However, it had similar associations with PTSD ($r = .57$) and GAD ($r = .56$), and correlated ≥ .38 with every disorder. Overall, it showed substantial links to the emotional disorders but only a limited level of specificity.

Table 5.16 Polyserial Correlations Between the Bipolar Symptom Factors and *DSM* Emotional Disorder Diagnoses in Sample 4

Diagnosis	Manic Distress	Manic Elation
Major Depression	**.47**	.01
Generalized Anxiety Disorder	**.56**	.06
Posttraumatic Stress Disorder	**.57**	.19
Panic Disorder	**.41**	−.03
Agoraphobia	**.38**	.01
Social Phobia	**.51**	−.07
Obsessive-Compulsive Disorder	**.52**	.11
Mania	**.62**	.19

NOTE: $N = 242$. Correlations ≥ .30 are in bold.

In marked contrast, Manic Elation exhibited consistently weak associations with these disorders. In fact, its only significant correlation was with diagnoses of mania ($r = .19$), which offers some modest support for the criterion validity of this dimension.

IMPLICATIONS AND FUTURE DIRECTIONS

The Two-Factor Structure of Bipolar Symptoms

Most symptom measures are associated with higher levels of negative affect and, to a lesser extent, lower levels of positive affect (Watson, Clark et al., 2013; Watson & Naragon-Gainey, 2014). As we have seen, bipolar symptoms are unusual in that they tend to be associated with elevated levels of both distress/negative emotionality and energy/positive emotionality. However, individual symptom measures assess these two components in varying degrees, such that some place greater weight on elevated negative emotionality, whereas others focus more on excessive positive emotionality.

In this chapter, we have established that bipolar symptom measures define a two-factor structure that reflects which of these two components is dominant within a scale; this structure is highly robust and replicates well across varying sets of indicators and different types of participants. Scales tapping affective lability, psychomotor restlessness, and cognitive manifestations of mania (e.g., pressure of speech, flight of ideas) primarily reflect individual differences in negative emotionality and jointly define a dimension we have labeled Manic Distress. Conversely, scales that focus primarily on symptoms such as euphoria, excitement, and manic energy/activation primarily reflect individual differences in positive emotionality and are strong markers of a factor we have termed Manic Elation.

Research Implications

We believe that the identification of this robust two-factor structure has important implications that should inform future work in this area. Most notably, these two factors are highly distinctive and correlate quite differently with other variables. The Manic Distress factor is strongly positively correlated with the personality trait of neuroticism, diverse markers of distress/negative emotionality, scales assessing internalizing psychopathology and psychoticism/schizotypy, and *DSM* diagnoses of the emotional disorders; it also is negatively related to the personality traits of agreeableness and conscientiousness. In marked contrast, Manic Elation is strongly linked to the personality trait of extraversion (particularly its more agentic aspects, such as dominance and excitement seeking), various indicators of positive emotionality, and personality pathology scales assessing narcissism, recklessness, grandiosity, exhibitionism, and novel experience seeking.

The distinctive properties of these two types of scales should be kept in mind in generating hypotheses and when selecting measures to assess bipolar symptoms. Clearly, one should expect to obtain different results depending on which type of symptom is the primary focus of assessment. Moreover, our results show that global scores can be quite misleading if they conflate these two types of symptoms. This is seen most clearly in the case of the HPS, which contains three highly distinctive subscales. As discussed earlier, neuroticism scores were moderately positively correlated with Mood Volatility, unrelated to Excitement, and significantly negatively associated with Social Vitality; conversely, individual differences in extraversion were strongly positively correlated with Social Vitality, moderately associated with Excitement, and weakly related to Mood Volatility. On the basis of these results, we encourage future researchers to focus on these HPS subscales—rather than the total score—in their analyses.

We also reported results on two GBI subscales—Hypomania and Biphasic—that sometimes are combined to yield an overall Mania score (e.g., Murray, Goldstone, & Cunningham, 2007; Nusslock et al., 2012). This practice makes good sense, in that these scales (a) are strongly interrelated ($r = .68$ and .76 in our student and adult samples, respectively) and (b) both are strong markers of the Manic Distress factor (see Table 5.6). Nevertheless, GBI Biphasic—which assesses affective lability (e.g., rapid shifts in mood or energy) and behavioral volatility (e.g., changes in eating patterns)—tends to correlate more strongly with indicators of neuroticism/negative emotionality. For example, BFI Neuroticism correlated significantly more strongly with GBI Biphasic ($r = .61$ and .49 in the student and adult samples, respectively) than with Hypomania ($r = .19$ and .27, respectively; $z = 13.40$ and 7.08, respectively, both $ps < .01$, two-tailed) in our data.

These findings again highlight the distinctive nature of different types of bipolar symptoms. Moreover, as was noted earlier, they are consistent with a broad range of evidence indicating that mood variability/affective lability is a core feature of neuroticism/negative emotionality (Krueger et al., 2012; Watson et al.,

1994; Watson, Stasik, et al., 2013). Future work is needed to establish the convergent, discriminant, and criterion validity of these different types of symptoms. For instance, as was discussed in Chapter 1, neuroticism/negative emotionality is a pervasive general factor in psychopathology that is responsible for much of the observed overlap/comorbidity between different symptoms and disorders. It therefore seems likely that focusing on symptoms that are particularly strong markers of neuroticism—such as items tapping emotional lability—may lead to the creation of bipolar measures that show limited specificity and poor discriminant validity. We return to this issue shortly.

Assessment Implications

In a related vein, future research should explicate the construct validity of existing symptom measures more fully. For example, as noted earlier, our data raise significant validity concerns regarding the HPS Social Vitality subscale, which correlated strongly with BFI Extraversion in both the student ($r = .60$) and adult ($r = .58$) samples (see also Schalet et al., 2011, who reported a .58 correlation between Social Vitality and extraversion). These concerns are exacerbated by the fact that Social Vitality actually correlated significantly more strongly with BFI Extraversion than with any of the other bipolar scales that were assessed in these samples (*r*s ranged from .11 to .43, *z*s ranged from 2.89 to 7.34, all *p*s $< .01$). Furthermore, Social Vitality was even more strongly related to BFI Extraversion ($r = .67$) in the MTurk sample.

These data suggest that Social Vitality might be better viewed as a measure of extraversion than of bipolar symptomatology per se. In this regard, it is noteworthy that in the original HPS scale development article, Eckblad and Chapman (1986) stated: "A trait specification was written describing the hypomanic personality. Such persons were characterized as upbeat, gregarious, confident, and energetic people who sometimes display these attributes to a maladaptive extreme, becoming euphoric, hypersociable, grandiose, and overactive, with occasional episodic hypomanic symptoms" (p. 216). The first part of this statement provides an excellent description of an extravert; this suggests that extraversion-related content (such as gregariousness, confidence, and energy) may have been included in the final scale. In fact, several HPS items (e.g., "In unfamiliar surroundings, I am often so assertive and sociable that I surprise myself"; "At social gatherings, I am usually the 'life of the party' ") appear to assess extraversion, rather than hypomania per se.

To investigate this issue further, we conducted two additional sets of analyses in the Sample 4 data. First, we correlated the three HPS subscales with the NEO-PI-3 extraversion facet scales ($N = 245$); these results are presented in Table 5.17. Social Vitality again was strongly associated with overall Extraversion scores in these data ($r = .54$). It also showed impressive specificity at the lower order level, correlating more strongly with Assertiveness ($r = .55$) and Excitement Seeking ($r = .44$)

Table 5.17 Correlations Between the HPS Subscales and NEO-PI-3 Extraversion Scales in Sample 4

NEO-PI-3 Scale	Social Vitality	Excitement	Mood Volatility
Extraversion	**.54**	.17	−.12
Assertiveness	**.55**	.13	−.06
Excitement Seeking	**.44**	.18	.03
Gregariousness	.35	.01	−.15
Activity	.34	.20	.00
Positive Emotions	.32	.14	−.10
Warmth	.20	.02	−.21

NOTE: $N = 245$. Correlations ≥ .40 are in bold. HPS = Hypomanic Personality Scale. NEO-PI-3 = NEO Personality Inventory-3.

than with the other facets within this domain (*r*s ranged from .20 to .35). These results indicate that Social Vitality contains item content specifically related to dominance and experience seeking.

Second, we computed polyserial correlations between the HPS subscales and the same eight *DSM-5* diagnoses examined earlier; these coefficients are reported in Table 5.18. Paralleling the results seen earlier at the factor level (see Table 5.16), Mood Volatility clearly was the strongest overall predictor of psychopathology in these analyses, as all of its correlations were ≥ .37. It also displayed some degree of diagnostic specificity, as it correlated more strongly with mania ($r = .59$) than with disorders such as GAD ($r = .52$), PTSD ($r = .48$), OCD ($r = .48$), and major depression ($r = .47$). Thus, consistent with our earlier suggestion, Mood Volatility is very broadly related to the emotional disorders.

HPS Excitement also showed some diagnostic specificity in these data. It correlated moderately with both mania ($r = .44$) and PTSD ($r = .44$) and more modestly with all of the other diagnoses (*r*s ranged from .15 to .35).

Table 5.18 Polyserial Correlations Between the HPS Subscales and *DSM* Emotional Disorder Diagnoses in Sample 4

DSM Diagnosiss	Social Vitality	Excitement	Mood Volatility
Major Depression	−.09	.27	**.47**
Generalized Anxiety Disorder	−.02	**.34**	**.52**
Posttraumatic Stress Disorder	.01	**.44**	**.48**
Panic Disorder	−.15	.20	**.37**
Agoraphobia	.01	.15	**.38**
Social Phobia	−.20	.22	**.42**
Obsessive-Compulsive Disorder	−.04	**.35**	**.48**
Mania	.07	**.44**	**.59**

NOTE: $N = 242$. Correlations ≥ .30 are in bold. HPS = Hypomanic Personality Scale. NEO-PI-3 = NEO Personality Inventory-3.

Finally, Social Vitality was very weakly related to these disorders; in fact, none of its correlations differed significantly from 0. It is particularly noteworthy that it correlated only .07 with lifetime diagnoses of mania. These results suggest that the scale has very limited predictive validity vis-à-vis the emotional disorders—including the bipolar disorders. Moreover, they are consistent with the argument that Social Vitality basically is a measure of extraversion. It will be important to clarify the construct validity of this subscale in the future.

6

Anger and Psychopathology

In this chapter, we explore how individual differences in anger are linked to a broad range of psychopathology. As was discussed in Chapter 1, anger correlates strongly with other types of negative mood, such as feelings of sadness/depression, fear/anxiety, and dissatisfaction/guilt. It therefore is a strong indicator of the broad, higher order Negative Affect dimension that consistently emerges in analyses of emotional experience (see Watson, 2009b; Watson et al., 1988; Watson, O'Hara, & Stuart, 2008; Watson & Tellegen, 1985; Watson et al., 1999). Similarly, anger represents a specific facet—once again, along with other types of negative emotionality, including fear/anxiety and sadness/depression—of the higher order trait of neuroticism in hierarchical models of personality, although it shows substantial links to (low) agreeableness as well (Costa & McCrae, 1992; Krueger et al., 2012; Watson, 2000a; Watson, Stasik, et al., 2013).

Anger's place in the development, course, and structure of psychopathology is less clearly defined than is the case with other types of negative mood. As was noted in Chapter 1, anxious/fearful mood is a core element of the *DSM-5* (American Psychiatric Association, 2013) anxiety disorders. Indeed, *DSM-5* defines anxiety disorders as "disorders that share features of excessive fear and anxiety and related behavioral disturbances" (p. 189). In parallel fashion, sad/depressed mood is recognized as a central feature of the *DSM-5* depressive disorders.

It is noteworthy, however, that *DSM-5* does not include a corresponding class of *anger disorders* (for discussions of the placement of anger within the *DSM*, see Eckhardt & Deffenbacher, 1995; Kassinove & Tafrate, 2006). Nevertheless, anger, irritability, and hostility are part of the symptom criteria for numerous disorders. For instance, *DSM-5* explicitly states that the depressive disorders all share the common feature of "sad, empty, or irritable mood" (p. 155), and it further lists irritable mood as part of the symptom criteria for major depression (specifically, it can represent an alternative expression of depressed mood in children and adolescents; see *DSM-5*, p. 160). Within the bipolar disorders, "elevated, expansive and irritable mood" is part of the symptom criteria for both manic (p. 124) and hypomanic episodes (p. 132). Irritability is included in the symptom criteria for generalized anxiety disorder (GAD), and "irritable behavior and angry outbursts" form part of Criterion E in posttraumatic stress disorder (PTSD) (p. 272). Oppositional defiant disorder (p. 462) is defined by angry/irritable mood (often loses temper, is often touchy or easily annoyed, is often angry and resentful) and argumentative/defiant behavior (e.g., often argues with authority figures, often deliberately annoys others). Intermittent explosive disorder (p. 466) involves "recurrent behavioral outbursts representing a failure to control aggressive impulses" that may be based on feelings of anger. Within the personality disorders (PDs), paranoid PD (p. 649) includes the criterion "perceives attacks on his or her character or reputation that are not apparent to others and is quick to react angrily or to counterattack," antisocial PD (p. 659) contains "irritability and aggressiveness, as indicated by repeated physical fights or assaults," and borderline PD (p. 663) involves "inappropriate, intense anger or difficulty controlling anger (e.g., frequent displays of temper, constant anger, recurrent physical fights)."

Consequently, one would expect anger, irritability, and hostility to show broad and relatively nonspecific associations with psychopathology, although it seems reasonable to predict that they should display particularly strong associations with those disorders that include them as part of their formal diagnostic criteria. We review relevant evidence in this chapter, focusing on symptoms and diagnoses within three broad classes of psychopathology (see Caspi et al., 2014): internalizing (e.g., indicators of depression and anxiety), externalizing (e.g., substance abuse, antisocial behavior), and psychoticism (e.g., schizophrenia, schizotypy, and mania). In doing so, we will present data based on both state and trait measures of anger and hostility. It therefore is necessary to establish that these measures converge well and define the same basic construct. Accordingly, we begin our examination of this topic by examining the convergent and discriminant validity of relevant measures of anger and hostility, focusing in particular on the IDAS-II Ill Temper scale.

ESTABLISHING THE VALIDITY OF IDAS-II ILL TEMPER

IDAS-II Ill Temper

The original IDAS item pool contained a number of items tapping anger, irritability, and temperamental outbursts. Structural analyses indicated that the items assessing irritable mood showed poor discriminant validity vis-à-vis other indicators of negative mood (in particular, the Dysphoria scale); they therefore were dropped during the scale development process. The final, five-item Ill Temper scale contains more extreme, high activation items that assess feelings of anger and rage ("I was furious," "I felt enraged," "Little things made me mad") and related behavioral outbursts ("I lost my temper and yelled at people," "I felt like breaking things").

IDAS-CR Analyses

We first examine the convergent and discriminant validity of the Ill Temper scale in relation to ratings on the interview-based IDAS-CR. As we noted in Chapter 5, discriminant validity analyses are maximally informative when they involve near-neighbor constructs that are strongly related to one another (Watson, 2012) and, therefore, are most likely to present problems in differentiation. As shown in Chapter 2 (see Table 2.7), Ill Temper correlates most strongly with seven other IDAS-II scales: Dysphoria ($r = .63$), Panic ($r = .58$), Traumatic Intrusions ($r = .56$), Suicidality ($r = .51$), Lassitude ($r = .46$), Mania ($r = .46$), and Social Anxiety ($r = .45$). We therefore included these IDAS-II/IDAS-CR symptom dimensions in the present analyses. Following the logic discussed in Chapter 5, however, we focus exclusively here on aspects of the data that specifically involve Ill Temper.

Table 6.1 presents separate sets of correlations between these IDAS-II scales and parallel IDAS-CR ratings in Samples 6 ($N = 198$ outpatients) and 10 ($N = 219$ students) in the form of a heteromethod block (Campbell & Fiske, 1959). Looking first at convergent validity, self-ratings on Ill Temper were strongly related to their IDAS-CR counterparts in both the patients ($r = .60$) and the students ($r = .54$), establishing a substantial level of convergence.

As has been discussed in previous chapters, a key test of discriminant validity is that a convergent correlation should be higher than all of the other values in its row or column of the heteromethod block (Campbell & Fiske, 1959). Table 6.1

Table 6.1 CONVERGENT/DISCRIMINANT VALIDITY ANALYSES: CORRELATIONS BETWEEN THE IDAS-II SCALES AND IDAS-CR RATINGS IN SAMPLES 6 AND 10

	IDAS-CR Rating							
IDAS-II Scale	**1**	**2**	**3**	**4**	**5**	**6**	**7**	**8**
Patients (Sample 6)								
1. Ill Temper	**.60**	.29	.27	.12	.19	.20	.17	.20
2. Dysphoria	.26	**.63**	.31	.20	.35	.35	.34	.32
3. Panic	.19	.25	**.52**	.13	.24	.28	.21	.18
4. Traumatic Intrusions	.17	.16	.17	**.60**	.21	.13	.09	.17
5. Suicidality	.20	.32	.33	.24	**.68**	.10	.07	.24
6. Lassitude	.12	.44	.26	.18	.26	**.59**	.18	.23
7. Mania	.11	.23	.19	−.00	.13	.22	**.59**	.06
8. Social Anxiety	.17	.28	.23	.04	.22	.21	.13	**.56**
Students (Sample 10)								
1. Ill Temper	**.54**	.35	.19	.33	−.01	.36	.18	.22
2. Dysphoria	.18	**.59**	.30	.34	.21	.47	.40	.35
3. Panic	.14	.37	**.26**	.35	.13	.31	.24	.30
4. Traumatic Intrusions	.24	.25	.26	**.64**	.01	.25	.17	.13
5. Suicidality	.03	.21	.12	.17	**.49**	.29	.08	.32
6. Lassitude	.13	.36	.15	.39	.17	**.47**	.26	.28
7. Mania	.13	.30	.22	.18	.04	.19	**.53**	.14
8. Social Anxiety	.15	.29	.11	.23	.23	.30	.21	**.66**

NOTE: $N = 198$ patients (Sample 6), 219 students (Sample 10). Convergent correlations are in bold. IDAS-II = Expanded version of the Inventory of Depression and Anxiety Symptoms. IDAS-CR = Clinician Rating version of the IDAS.

indicates that the convergent correlations for Ill Temper met this criterion in every case. We further quantified these relations by conducting significance tests, using the Williams modification of the Hotelling test for two correlations involving a common variable (Kenny, 1987). All 28 comparisons were significant ($p < .05$, one-tailed) across the two samples, with *z*s ranging from 2.39 to 7.48. Thus, we see strong evidence of discriminant validity in these data. Based on these results, it seems reasonable to conclude that IDAS-II Ill Temper and IDAS-CR Ill Temper are valid indicators of the same underlying construct.

IMAS Analyses

Next, we examine relations with the interview-based IMAS. If Ill Temper is a valid indicator of anger and hostility, it should correlate more strongly with the six-item IMAS Irritability scale than with the other IMAS scales. Table 6.2 presents correlations with the IMAS in Samples 5 ($N = 362$ patients) and 11 ($N = 373$ students). These results provide evidence of excellent convergent validity, as Ill Temper correlated very strongly with Irritability in both the patients ($r = .72$) and the students ($r = .77$). Furthermore, Ill Temper showed impressive discriminant validity, as its correlations with the nine remaining IMAS scales ranged from only .15 to .56. Follow-up significance tests indicated that its convergent correlations with Irritability were significantly stronger ($p < .01$, one-tailed) than the discriminant coefficients in all 18 comparisons across the two samples (*z*s ranged from 6.06 to 13.36). Consequently, IDAS-II Ill Temper and IMAS Irritability also can be viewed as measures of the same basic construct.

Table 6.2 CORRELATIONS BETWEEN IDAS-II ILL TEMPER AND THE IMAS SCALES IN SAMPLES 5 AND 11

IMAS Scale	Sample 5	Sample 11
Irritability	**.72**	**.77**
Generalized Anxiety Disorder	**.53**	**.56**
Depression	**.50**	**.56**
Posttraumatic Stress Disorder	.48	**.55**
Mania	.40	.49
Panic	.38	.44
Obsessive-Compulsive Disorder	.26	.34
Agoraphobia	.25	.33
Social Phobia	.22	.34
Specific Phobia	.15	.22

NOTE: $N = 362$ patients (Sample 5), 373 students (Sample 11). Correlations $\geq .50$ are in bold. All correlations are significant at $p < .01$. IDAS-II = Expanded version of the Inventory of Depression and Anxiety Symptoms. IMAS = Interview of Mood and Anxiety Symptoms.

PANAS-X Analyses

We will present data on other self-report measures of anger and hostility, so it is important to establish their convergent and discriminant validity as well. In Chapter 4, we reported extensive results on the three specific positive affect scales—Joviality, Self-Assurance, and Attentiveness—of the PANAS-X (Watson & Clark, 1999). The PANAS-X also contains four factor analytically derived scales assessing distinct types of negative emotional experience: Fear (*afraid, frightened, scared, nervous, jittery, shaky*), Sadness (*sad, blue, downhearted, alone, lonely*), Guilt (*guilty, ashamed, blameworthy, angry at self, disgusted with self, dissatisfied with self*), and Hostility (*angry, irritable, hostile, scornful, disgusted, loathing*). If IDAS-II Ill Temper is a valid measure of anger, it should correlate more strongly with PANAS-X Hostility than with the other negative affect scales.

Table 6.3 presents these correlations in two large samples that were described in Chapter 4; these participants rated their mood either "over the past week" (Past Week Sample, $N = 1{,}113$) or "in general, that is, on average" (General Sample, $N = 917$). As expected, Ill Temper correlated strongly with Hostility in both the Past Week ($r = .73$) and the General ($r = .66$) sample. Its discriminant correlations with the other three negative affect scales were substantial but clearly lower, ranging from .51 to .57. Follow-up tests confirmed that Ill Temper had a significantly stronger correlation with Hostility than with the other PANAS-X scales in all six comparisons (*z*s ranged from 7.15 to 12.36, all *p*s < .01, one-tailed).

Table 6.3 Simple and Partial Correlations Between IDAS-II Ill Temper and the PANAS-X Negative Affect Scales

Sample/Scale	**Simple *r***	**Partial *r***
Past Week Sample		
Fear	.51	.03
Sadness	.57	.10
Guilt	.57	.04
Hostility	**.73**	**.52**
General Sample		
Fear	.51	.07
Sadness	.52	.07
Guilt	.51	.03
Hostility	**.66**	**.43**

NOTE: $N = 1{,}113$ (Past Week), 917 (General). Correlations $\geq |.10|$ are significant at $p < .01$. Correlations $\geq |.40|$ are in bold. IDAS-II = Expanded version of the Inventory of Depression and Anxiety Symptoms. PANAS-X = Expanded Form of the Positive and Negative Affect Schedule.

Table 6.3 also includes partial correlations that control for the influence of the other three PANAS-X scales; for example, the partial correlations with Fear control for Sadness, Guilt, and Hostility. It is noteworthy that Ill Temper remained substantially related to Hostility in these analyses, with partial correlations of .52 and .43 in the Past Week and General samples, respectively. In marked contrast, its associations with the three remaining scales now were quite weak, ranging from only .03 to .10. Thus, the substantial zero-order associations between Ill Temper and Fear, Sadness and Guilt essentially reflect the nonspecific influence of the higher order Negative Affect factor: Once this variance is controlled, these relations basically disappear. In contrast, Ill Temper and Hostility clearly share some specific lower order variance that cannot be attributed to general Negative Affect. These results further establish the construct validity of Ill Temper and demonstrate that it assesses the same basic construct as PANAS-X Hostility.

Relations With Trait Measures

As noted earlier, anger/hostility represents a specific facet trait within the general personality domain of neuroticism (Costa & McCrae, 1992; Krueger et al., 2012; Watson, 2000; Watson, Stasik, et al., 2013). The Sample 4 participants completed four trait measures that include parallel sets of scales assessing three key negative emotional facets of neuroticism: anxiety, depression, and hostility. First, they were assessed on the PID-5 (Krueger et al., 2012; see Chapters 4 and 5), which measures the 25 specific facets in the trait dimensional model of personality pathology that is included of Section III of *DSM*-5 (American Psychiatric Association, 2013). We report results here on the 10-item Hostility scale, the 9-item Anxiousness scale, and the 14-item Depressivity scale.

Second, the participants completed the NEO-PI-3 (McCrae et al., 2005; see Chapter 5), a widely used measure of the five-factor model of personality. As noted in Chapter 5, the NEO-PI-3 contains six facets of neuroticism, each of which is assessed using eight items. We present data here on the Angry Hostility, Anxiety, and Depression scales.

Third, the participants were assessed on the TAI (Watson et al., 2015; see Chapter 5), which was designed to provide comprehensive assessment of individual differences in emotionality. We report data on the Anger (12 items), Anxiety (8 items), and Depression (7 items) scales.

Finally, the Faceted Inventory of the Five-Factor Model (FI-FFM; E. Simms, 2009; see also Naragon-Gainey et al., 2009; Watson, Stasik et al., 2013; Watson et al., 2015a, 2015b) is a factor analytically derived, 247-item self-report inventory that assesses specific lower order traits within the framework of the five-factor model. The items are sentences that are rated on a 5-point Likert scale ranging from *strongly disagree* to *strongly agree*. We present results for three 10-item neuroticism facet scales: Anger Proneness, Anxiety, and Depression.

Simple zero-order correlations between Ill Temper and these trait scales are presented in the first column of Table 6.4. One would expect Ill Temper to correlate more strongly with indicators of trait hostility than with scales assessing

Table 6.4 Simple and Partial Correlations Between IDAS-II Ill Temper and Trait Measures of Negative Affect

Trait Scale	Simple	Partial
Anger/Hostility		
PID-5 Hostility	**.71**	**.53**
FI-FFM Anger Proneness	**.64**	**.48**
TAI Anger	**.60**	**.43**
NEO-PI-3 Angry Hostility	**.58**	**.42**
Anxiety		
PID-5 Anxiousness	**.53**	.07
TAI Anxiety	**.47**	.05
FI-FFM Anxiety	**.42**	−.11
NEO-PI-3 Anxiety	**.40**	−.05
Depression		
FI-FFM Depression	**.55**	.10
PID-5 Depressivity	**.53**	.14
NEO-PI-3 Depression	**.47**	.08
TAI Depression	**.47**	.01

NOTE: $N = 406$. Correlations ≥ .40 are in bold. Correlations ≥ |.14| are significant at $p < .01$. IDAS-II = IDAS-II = Expanded version of the Inventory of Depression and Anxiety Symptoms. PID-5 = Personality Inventory for *DSM-5*. FI-FFM = Faceted Inventory of the Five Factor Model. TAI = Temperament and Affectivity Inventory. NEO-PI-3 = NEO Personality Inventory-3.

other types of negative affectivity. Consistent with this expectation, Ill Temper was strongly related to all four trait anger scales (*r*s ranged from .58 to .71, mean $r = .64$) and had somewhat lower associations with indicators of anxiety (*r*s ranged from .40 to .53, mean $r = .46$) and depression (*r*s ranged from .47 to .55, mean $r = .51$). Follow-up statistical tests revealed that the anger/hostility correlations were significantly stronger ($p < .05$, one-tailed) than those for anxiety and depression in 28 of 32 comparisons (87.5%). The four exceptions were that the coefficient for TAI Anger ($r = .60$) was not significantly greater than that for FI-FFM Depression ($r = .55$), and that the association with NEO Angry Hostility ($r = .58$) was not higher than those for FI-FFM Depression ($r = .55$), PID-5 Depressivity ($r = .53$), and PID-5 Anxiousness ($r = .53$).

Once again, we computed partial correlations that control for the influence of other types of negative emotionality; for example, the partial correlation between Ill Temper and PID-5 Hostility controlled for the influence of all eight anxiety and depression scales. These partial correlations are reported in the second column of Table 6.4. Paralleling the PANAS-X results, Ill Temper remained substantially related to the trait anger/hostility scales in these analyses, with partial correlations ranging from .42 to .53 (mean value = .47). In marked contrast, its associations with the depression and anxiety scales now were quite weak, ranging from only −.11 to .14 (mean value = .04). These results establish that Ill Temper shares some specific lower order variance with the trait anger/hostility scales that cannot be attributed to the influence of the higher order Neuroticism factor.

ESTABLISHING THE VALIDITY OF THE TRAIT NEGATIVE AFFECT SCALES

Finally, because we will be reporting an extensive series of analyses based on the trait negative affect scales in Sample 4, it is important to establish the broader convergent and discriminant validity of these measures. Accordingly, Table 6.5 presents the correlations among these 12 scales in the form of a heterotrait-heteromethod matrix. With regard to convergent validity, Table 6.5 confirms that the four indicators of anger/hostility (*r*s ranged from .65 to .81, mean *r* = .76), anxiety (*r*s ranged from .68 to .81, mean *r* = .74), and depression (*r*s ranged from .69 to .83, mean *r* = .75) all were highly related to each other. Thus, we do see a very strong level of convergent validity in these data.

Table 6.5 CORRELATIONS AMONG THE TRAIT NEGATIVE AFFECT SCALES IN SAMPLE 4

Measure	1	2	3	4	5	6	7	8	9	10	11	12
NEO-PI-3												
1. Angry Hostility	.—											
2. Anxiety	.53	.—										
3. Depression	.57	.68	.—									
FI-FFM												
4. Anger Proneness	**.79**	.58	.58	.—								
5. Anxiety	.56	**.81**	.64	.67	.—							
6. Depression	.58	.66	**.81**	.70	.73	.—						
TAI												
7. Anger	**.81**	.51	.54	**.83**	.54	.61	.—					
8. Anxiety	.54	**.78**	.69	.58	**.75**	.70	.56	.—				
9. Depression	.61	.65	**.77**	.66	.64	**.83**	.65	.75	.—			
PID-5												
10. Hostility	**.65**	.44	.45	**.69**	.45	.56	**.74**	.47	.52	.—		
11. Anxiousness	.47	**.68**	.61	.53	**.68**	.64	.47	**.72**	.60	.55	.—	
12. Depressivity	.43	.51	**.69**	.47	.52	**.70**	.43	.58	**.69**	.54	.70	.—

NOTE: $N = 406$. Convergent correlations are in bold. All correlations are significant at $p < .01$. NEO-PI-3 = NEO Personality Inventory-3. FI-FFM = Faceted Inventory of the Five Factor Model. TAI = Temperament and Affectivity Inventory. PID-5 = Personality Inventory for *DSM-5*.

As in previous analyses, we examined discriminant validity by comparing each of the convergent correlations to all other values in its row and column of the heteromethod block. In the current case, this yields an overall total of 72 comparisons (12 per block x 6 heteromethod blocks). Follow-up statistical tests indicated that the convergent correlations were significantly greater ($p < .05$, one-tailed) than the relevant discriminant coefficients in 71 of 72 analyses (98.6%), establishing a strong degree of discriminant validity. The only exception was that PID-5 Anxiousness did not correlate more strongly with FI-FFM Anxiety (.68) than with FI-FFM Depression (.64) ($z=1.53$, n.s.).

Based on these results, it seems reasonable to conclude that these scales are valid indicators of their target constructs. More generally, the data presented in Tables 6.1 have demonstrated the construct validity of eight different measures of anger/hostility: IDAS-II and IDAS-CR Ill Temper, IMAS Irritability, PANAS-X Hostility, NEO-PI-3 Angry Hostility, FI-FFM Anger Proneness, PID-5 Hostility, and TAI Anger. In the following sections, we examine how these scales relate to a broad range of psychopathology.

ANGER AND INTERNALIZING PSYCHOPATHOLOGY

PANAS-X Analyses

We begin by examining relations with internalizing psychopathology, focusing in particular on the *DSM-IV* depressive and anxiety disorders (in *DSM-5*, these are included in the depressive disorders, anxiety disorders, obsessive-compulsive and related disorders, and trauma- and stressor-related disorders). Table 6.6 presents polyserial correlations between the four specific negative affect scales of the PANAS-X and eight *DSM-IV* diagnoses—major depressive disorder (MDD), GAD, PTSD, panic disorder, agoraphobia, social phobia, specific phobia, and obsessive-compulsive disorder (OCD)—in Samples 1 through 3. Participants in Samples 1 (N=331) and 2 ($N=253$) were administered the complete PANAS-X using either General (Sample 1) or Past Week (Sample 2) time instructions. The patients in Sample 3 ($N=252$) completed only the Fear, Sadness, and Hostility scales using General instructions.

The Sadness and Guilt scales both demonstrated impressive specificity vis-à-vis MDD in these data. Sadness had a weighted mean polyserial correlation of .64 with MDD; its next highest coefficient was only .40 (with PTSD). Similarly, Guilt had an overall correlation of .59 with MDD; no other coefficient exceeded .50. Fear displayed a rather different pattern, showing substantial but nonspecific mean associations with MDD ($r=.53$), agoraphobia ($r=.51$), panic disorder ($r=.50$), GAD ($r=.47$), and PTSD ($r=.46$). Finally, in comparison to the other scales, Hostility clearly showed much weaker associations with internalizing diagnoses; its strongest overall associations were with MDD ($r=.40$), GAD ($r=.32$), and PTSD ($r=.30$).

Table 6.6 Polyserial Correlations Between the PANAS-X Negative Affect Scales and *DSM-IV* Internalizing Diagnoses

Scale/Sample	MDD	GAD	PTSD	Panic	Agora	Social Phobia	Specific Phobia	OCD
Fear								
Sample 1	**.57**	**.51**	**.42**	**.52**	**.50**	.19	.25	.24
Sample 2	**.57**	**.44**	**.51**	**.46**	**.53**	**.41**	.22	**.43**
Sample 3	**.44**	**.43**	**.46**	**.51**	.—	.33	.—	**.40**
Weighted *M*	**.53**	**.47**	**.46**	**.50**	**.51**	.31	.24	.35
Sadness								
Sample 1	**.60**	.39	.36	**.51**	.39	.31	−.05	.24
Sample 2	**.65**	.36	.37	.34	**.40**	.25	.02	.30
Sample 3	**.69**	.37	**.47**	.28	.—	.30	.—	.29
Weighted *M*	**.64**	.37	**.40**	.39	.39	.29	−.02	.27
Guilt								
Sample 1	**.58**	.38	.37	**.50**	.31	.24	.03	.21
Sample 2	**.61**	**.41**	**.41**	**.42**	.37	.36	.06	.35
Weighted *M*	**.59**	.39	.39	**.47**	.34	.29	.04	.27
Hostility								
Sample 1	.38	.33	.29	.30	.27	.20	.17	.15
Sample 2	**.41**	.38	.29	.30	.25	.26	.16	.36
Sample 3	**.41**	.24	.32	.28	.—	.20	.—	.38
Weighted *M*	**.40**	.32	.30	.29	.26	.22	.17	.29

Note: $N = 331$ (Sample 1), 253 (Sample 2), 252 (Sample 3). Correlations $\geq |.40|$ are in bold. Sample correlations $\geq .17$ are significant at $p < .05$. MDD = major depression. GAD = generalized anxiety disorder. PTSD = posttraumatic stress disorder. Agora = agoraphobia. OCD = obsessive-compulsive disorder.

As we discussed at the beginning of this chapter, anger/hostility ratings correlate strongly with other types of negative mood, including fear, sadness, and guilt. It therefore seems likely that these modest to moderate bivariate associations between PANAS-X Hostility and internalizing psychopathology largely are due to shared variance reflecting the influence of the higher order Negative Affect factor. We examined this issue by conducting a series of logistic regression analyses in each sample, using all available negative affect scales as predictors and the various diagnoses as criteria. It should be noted that the predictor variables were entered simultaneously in all of the regression analyses reported in this chapter.

Table 6.7 reports the odds ratios (ORs) from these regression analyses. The results are striking. The PANAS-X Fear scale showed impressive incremental predictive power in these analyses, contributing significantly in 18 of 22 analyses (81.8%). Note, moreover, that it was a significant predictor in every analysis involving GAD, PTSD, panic disorder, agoraphobia, and specific phobia. Consistent with the bivariate analyses, Sadness and Guilt both displayed marked specificity to MDD: They jointly made significant incremental contributions in

Table 6.7 Odds Ratios From Logistic Regression Analyses Predicting *DSM* Internalizing Diagnoses From the PANAS-X Negative Affect Scales

Scale/Sample	MDD	GAD	PTSD	Panic	Agora	Social Phobia	Specific Phobia	OCD
Fear								
Sample 1	**1.98**	**2.36**	**1.87**	**2.42**	**2.87**	0.96	**2.38**	1.35
Sample 2	1.52	**1.72**	**2.70**	**2.29**	**2.97**	**2.07**	**2.13**	**2.04**
Sample 3	1.24	**1.85**	**1.88**	**2.75**	.—	**1.52**	.—	**1.77**
Sadness								
Sample 1	**2.08**	1.32	1.21	1.68	1.74	**1.79**	**0.54**	1.41
Sample 2	**2.57**	1.03	0.90	0.81	1.12	0.72	0.65	0.89
Sample 3	**4.53**	**1.46**	**1.85**	0.92	.—	1.38	.—	0.98
Guilt								
Sample 1	**1.61**	0.92	1.29	1.48	0.62	0.99	0.74	0.99
Sample 2	**1.95**	1.32	1.35	1.64	1.10	1.54	0.72	1.15
Hostility								
Sample 1	0.76	1.07	0.95	0.75	0.99	1.15	1.45	0.99
Sample 2	0.83	1.37	1.02	1.06	0.91	1.03	1.40	1.46
Sample 3	1.05	0.94	1.05	1.14	.—	0.98	.—	1.67

NOTE: $N = 331$ (Sample 1), 253 (Sample 2), 252 (Sample 3). Significant effects ($p < .05$) are in bold. MDD = major depression. GAD = generalized anxiety disorder. PTSD = posttraumatic stress disorder. Agora = agoraphobia. OCD = obsessive-compulsive disorder.

all five analyses involving this disorder, but in only 4 of 33 regressions (12.1%) related to other diagnoses. In stark contrast, PANAS-X Hostility produced nonsignificant ORs in all 22 analyses. It is particularly noteworthy that it failed to add significantly in any analysis involving GAD and PTSD, given that these diagnoses formally include anger and irritability as part of their symptom criteria. These results clearly establish that the moderate bivariate associations shown in Table 6.6 are entirely attributable to the higher order Negative Affect factor.

IDAS-II Analyses

Next, we consider relations between the IDAS-II Ill Temper scale and these same eight *DSM-IV/DSM-5* disorders. Table 6.8 presents polyserial correlations with these diagnoses in Samples 1 ($N = 337$), 2 ($N = 267$), 4 ($N = 407$), and 5 ($N = 290$). These results closely resemble those reported earlier for PANAS-X Hostility. As in the earlier analyses, Ill Temper displayed modest to moderate bivariate associations with internalizing; its strongest overall links were with MDD (mean $r = .38$), PTSD (mean $r = .33$), panic disorder (mean $r = .33$), and OCD (mean $r = .30$).

Table 6.8 Polyserial Correlations Between the IDAS-II Ill Temper Scale and Current *DSM* Diagnoses

Diagnosis	Sample 1	Sample 2	Sample 4	Sample 5	Weighted Mean
Internalizing Disorders					
Major Depression	**.36**	**.32**	**.43**	**.40**	**.38**
Generalized Anxiety Disorder	.28	**.39**	**.35**	.13	.29
Posttraumatic Stress Disorder	**.30**	**.31**	**.40**	**.30**	**.33**
Panic Disorder	**.33**	**.30**	**.37**	**.30**	**.33**
Agoraphobia	.27	.21	**.31**	.18	.25
Social Phobia	.22	.24	.27	.13	.22
Specific Phobia	.19	.22	.—	.23	.21
Obsessive-Compulsive Disorder	.25	.26	**.43**	.18	**.30**
Other Disorders					
Any Substance Use Disorder	.25	.28	.25	.07	.21
Current Manic Episode	.—	.—	**.40**	.07	.27
Psychotic Disorder/ Psychosis	.—	.—	**.34**	.00	.20
Mood Disorder-Psychotic	.—	.—	**.31**	.—	**.31**

Note: $N = 337$ (Sample 1), 267 (Sample 2), 407 (Sample 4), 290 (Sample 5). Correlations $\geq .30$ are in bold. Correlations $\geq .19$ are significant at $p < .05$. Mood Disorder-Psychotic = Mood Disorder with Psychotic Features.

Once again, we conducted a series of logistic regression analyses to examine the incremental predictive power of Ill Temper. To control for the influence of the higher order Negative Affect factor, we used the IDAS-II Dysphoria scale—which is a strong marker of distress/negative emotionality (see Chapters 3 and 5)—as a second predictor in these analyses. The resulting ORs are reported in Table 6.9. Similar to the PANAS-X results, Ill Temper made a significant incremental contribution in only 2 of 31 analyses (6.5%), adding to the prediction of MDD (OR = 0.66) and GAD (OR = 1.41) in Sample 2. However, neither of these effects replicated in another sample; indeed, Ill Temper actually displayed ORs less than 1.00 with GAD in the other three samples, which indicates that these associations were not even in the same direction. Furthermore, its one significant relation with MDD represents a suppressor effect (Watson, Clark, et al., 2013), such that higher scores on Ill Temper were associated with a *reduced* likelihood of receiving the diagnosis. Finally, it is noteworthy that Ill Temper failed to contribute significantly to the prediction of PTSD in all four samples. Thus, the modest to moderate bivariate associations shown in Table 6.8 largely reflect the underlying influence of the higher order Negative Affect factor.

Table 6.9 Odds Ratios From Logistic Regression Analyses Predicting Current *DSM* Diagnoses From the IDAS-II Ill Temper Scale

Diagnosis	Sample 1	Sample 2	Sample 4	Sample 5
Internalizing Disorders				
Major Depression	0.74	**0.66**	0.88	0.96
Generalized Anxiety Disorder	0.93	**1.41**	0.81	0.77
Posttraumatic Stress Disorder	1.19	1.22	1.44	1.35
Panic Disorder	0.77	1.20	1.34	1.28
Agoraphobia	1.10	0.96	1.20	1.20
Social Phobia	1.14	1.10	0.91	1.05
Specific Phobia	0.80	1.41	.—	1.18
Obsessive-Compulsive Disorder	1.44	1.18	1.41	1.50
Other Disorders				
Any Substance Use Disorder	1.37	**1.72**	**1.48**	0.93
Current Manic Episode	.—	.—	1.48	1.71
Psychotic Disorder/Psychosis	.—	.—	1.30	0.87
Mood Disorder-Psychotic	.—	.—	0.98	.—

NOTE: $N = 337$ (Sample 1), 267 (Sample 2), 407 (Sample 4), 290 (Sample 5). Significant effects ($p < .05$) are in bold. The IDAS-II Dysphoria scale was included as a second predictor in these analyses. Mood Disorder-Psychotic = Mood Disorder with Psychotic Features.

IDAS-CR Analyses

Thus far, all of the analyses we have reported were based on self-ratings of anger and hostility. We now examine interview-based indicators of anger, starting with the single-item Ill Temper rating on the IDAS-CR. The first two columns of Table 6.10 present polyserial correlations between IDAS-CR Ill Temper and these same eight *DSM-IV* diagnoses in Samples 1 ($N = 339$) and 2 ($N = 268$). These associations are even weaker than those discussed earlier. In fact, only 2 of the 16 correlations (12.5%)—namely, those with OCD ($r = .35$) and panic disorder ($r = .33$) in Sample 2—exceed .30.

Following the logic of previous analyses, we conducted a series of logistic regression analyses that controlled for the nonspecific influence of the higher order Negative Affect factor; to model its effects, the IDAS-CR Dysphoria scale was included as a second predictor. The resulting ORs for Ill Temper are provided in the third and fourth columns of Table 6.10. Consistent with previous results, Ill Temper made a significant incremental contribution in only 3 of 16 analyses (18.8%)—PTSD in Sample 1 (OR = 1.59), and panic disorder (OR = 1.62) and OCD (OR = 1.71) in Sample 2—and none of them replicated across samples. Once again, the significant bivariate relations between anger and internalizing are largely attributable to the nonspecific influence of the higher order Negative Affect factor.

Table 6.10 RELATIONS BETWEEN IDAS-CR ILL TEMPER RATINGS AND CURRENT *DSM* DIAGNOSES

Diagnosis	Polyserial Correlations Sample 1	Sample 2	Odds Ratios Sample 1	Sample 2
Internalizing Disorders				
Major Depression	**.20**	.19	1.15	1.06
Generalized Anxiety Disorder	**.21**	**.22**	1.30	1.23
Posttraumatic Stress Disorder	**.29**	.16	**1.59**	1.14
Panic Disorder	**.19**	**.33**	1.22	**1.62**
Agoraphobia	**.20**	.06	1.34	0.96
Social Phobia	**.21**	.13	1.40	1.09
Specific Phobia	.07	**.21**	1.14	1.34
Obsessive-Compulsive Disorder	.16	**.35**	1.29	**1.71**
Externalizing Disorders				
Any Substance Use Disorder	.07	**.28**	1.06	**1.58**

NOTE: $N=339$ (Sample 1), 268 (Sample 2). Significant effects ($p < .05$) are in bold. IDAS-CR Dysphoria was included as a second predictor in the logistic regression analyses.

IMAS Analyses

The IMAS Irritability scale provides another opportunity to examine how interview ratings of anger/hostility are linked to internalizing. The first column of Table 6.11 reports polyserial correlations between Irritability and the same eight *DSM-IV* anxiety and depression diagnoses in Sample 5 ($N=313$). Similar to previous results, Irritability showed modest to moderate bivariate relations with internalizing in these data; its strongest associations were with panic disorder ($r=.43$), MDD ($r=.36$), specific phobia ($r=.34$), and agoraphobia ($r=.32$).

Next, we conducted a series of logistic regression analyses using the IMAS Depression and Generalized Anxiety scales as additional predictors to control for general Negative Affect. The resulting ORs are presented in the second column of Table 6.11. In comparison to previous analyses of anger/hostility, IMAS Irritability displayed somewhat stronger predictive power in these data, contributing significantly in three of eight analyses (37.5%): panic disorder (OR = 1.75), specific phobia (OR = 1.57), and agoraphobia (OR = 1.56). However, it again is noteworthy that it failed to contribute significantly to those disorders that include anger and irritability as part of their symptom criteria (OR = 1.04 with GAD and 0.80 with PTSD).

NEO Analyses

A number of studies have reported bivariate associations between the NEO-PI-R Neuroticism facets and various internalizing disorders (e.g., Bagby et al., 1997;

Table 6.11 Relations Between the IMAS Irritability Scale and Current *DSM* Diagnoses in Sample 5

Diagnosis	Polyserial Correlations	Odds Ratios
Internalizing Disorders		
Major Depression	.36	0.87
Generalized Anxiety Disorder	.25	1.04
Posttraumatic Stress Disorder	.23	0.80
Panic Disorder	.43	**1.75**
Agoraphobia	.32	**1.56**
Social Phobia	.21	1.08
Specific Phobia	.34	**1.57**
Obsessive-Compulsive Disorder	.17	1.10
Other Disorders		
Any Substance Use Disorder	−.02	0.85
Current Manic Episode	.22	1.46
Psychosis	.14	1.17

NOTE: $N = 313$. Significant effects ($p < .05$) are in bold. The IMAS Depression and Generalized Anxiety Disorder scales were included as additional predictors in the logistic regression analyses.

Rector, Hood, Richter, & Bagby, 2002). To date, the most complete and informative study was conducted by Bienvenu et al. (2004), who reported associations with eight lifetime *DSM-III-R* mood and anxiety disorder diagnoses. Scores on NEO Angry Hostility were significantly elevated (in comparison with individuals without a mood or anxiety disorder diagnosis) in individuals with MDD, panic disorder, agoraphobia, social phobia, and simple phobia; no significant effects were observed for dysthymia, GAD, and OCD. However, Bienvenu et al. (2004) did not conduct multivariate analyses that controlled for the influence of the other Neuroticism facets; consequently, it is unclear whether Angry Hostility contributed significant incremental information in relation to any of these diagnoses.

Trait Affect Analyses

Initial Factor Analyses

As discussed earlier, the Sample 4 participants completed four trait inventories—the PID-5, the NEO-PI-3, the FI-FFM, and the TAI—that include facet measures of anxiety, depression, and anger/hostility (see Table 6.5). These data provide a unique opportunity to examine how these neuroticism facets relate to psychopathology. We began by subjecting these 12 trait scales to a principal factor analysis, using squared multiple correlations as the initial communality estimates. As expected, three clear factors emerged and were rotated to oblique simple

Table 6.12 PROMAX LOADINGS OF THE TRAIT NEGATIVE AFFECT MEASURES IN SAMPLE 4

Scale	I	II	III
TAI Anger	**.92**	.00	−.00
NEO-PI-3 Angry Hostility	**.82**	.10	−.03
FI-FFM Anger Proneness	**.80**	.18	−.02
PID-5 Hostility	**.71**	−.13	.24
NEO-PI-3 Anxiety	.00	**.85**	.05
FI-FFM Anxiety	.08	**.84**	.00
TAI Anxiety	.03	**.68**	.23
PID-5 Anxiousness	−.00	**.44**	**.43**
PID-5 Depressivity	−.02	−.03	**.87**
NEO-PI-3 Depression	.05	.27	**.61**
FI-FFM Depression	.17	.24	**.59**
TAI Depression	.21	.19	**.58**

NOTE: $N = 408$. Loadings ≥ |.40| are in bold.
TAI = Temperament and Affectivity Inventory.
NEO-PI-3 = NEO Personality Inventory-3. FI-FFM = Faceted Inventory of the Five-Factor Model.
PID-5 = Personality Inventory for *DSM-5*.

structure using promax (power = 3). The resulting factor loadings are displayed in Table 6.12. The three extracted factors clearly can be identified as Anger (marked by TAI Anger, NEO-PI-3 Angry Hostility, FI-FFM Anger Proneness, and PID-5 Hostility), Anxiety (defined most clearly by NEO-PI-3 Anxiety, FI-FFM Anxiety, and TAI Anxiety), and Depression (marked by PID-5 Depressivity, NEO-PI-3 Depression, FI-FFM Depression, and TAI Depression), respectively. We computed regression-based factor scores to model these three dimensions in subsequent analyses.

INDICATORS OF INTERNALIZING

We related these factor scores to a broad range of both self-report and interview-based indicators of internalizing. Current *DSM-5* diagnoses were available for eight internalizing disorders: MDD, dysthymic disorder, GAD, PTSD, panic disorder, agoraphobia, social anxiety disorder, and OCD.

In addition, the Sample 4 participants completed an extensive battery of self-report psychopathology measures that included many redundant, highly correlated scales. Whenever possible, we aggregated them into symptom composites; in each case, the variables were standardized before being combined so that they would be equally weighted.

First, we created a composite collapsing across three measures of depression: (1) the 9-item PHQ-9 (Kroenke et al., 2001); (2) the 20-item IDAS-II General Depression Scale (see Chapter 2); and (3) the 8-item PID-5 Anhedonia scale. Correlations among these scales ranged from .73 to .82 (mean $r = .76$).

Next, the GADQ-IV (Newman et al., 2002) provides comprehensive assessment of GAD symptoms (e.g., "Do you experience excessive worry?"). The GADQ-IV was designed originally to provide an analogue diagnosis of GAD, and it therefore closely follows the diagnostic criteria for the disorder. However, the items also can be scored dimensionally, and this scoring is used in the results that follow.

Participants completed two measures of PTSD symptoms: (1) the five intrusions items and two avoidance items from the PTSD Checklist-Civilian Version (PCL; Weathers, Litz, Herman, Huska, & Keane, 1993); and (2) an aggregate score based on the Traumatic Intrusions (four items) and Traumatic Avoidance (four items) scales of the IDAS-II. These indicators correlated .74 with one another.

The battery contained three indicators of panic: (1) the eight-item IDAS-II Panic scale; (2) a reduced, nine-item version of the MASQ Anxious Arousal scale (see Chapter 1); and (3) an abbreviated, six-item version of the Panic Attack Symptom Questionnaire (Watson, 2000b). These scales had correlations ranging from .59 to .68 (mean $r = .64$).

The participants completed four measures of social anxiety: (1) the five-item Social Phobia scale from the Fear Questionnaire (FQ; Marks & Mathews, 1979); (2) the ten-item Social Phobia scale from the Albany Panic and Phobia Questionnaire (APPQ; Rapee et al., 1994/1995); (3) the six-item IDAS-II Social Anxiety scale; and (4) a factor analytically derived ten-item Social Anxiety scale from the Schizotypal Personality Questionnaire (SPQ; Chmielewski & Watson, 2008a). Correlations among these measures ranged from .54 to .69 (mean $r = .64$).

Next, the participants completed (1) the nine-item APPQ Agoraphobia scale and (2) the five-item FQ Agoraphobia scale. These measures correlated .67 with each other.

Finally, the battery included three indicators of OCD: (1) the 18-item Obsessive-Compulsive Inventory-Revised (OCI-R; Foa et al., 2002); (2) a total score based on the Obsessive Checking (14 items), Obsessive Cleanliness (12 items), Compulsive Rituals (8 items), and Hoarding (5 items) scales from the SCOPI (Watson & Wu, 2005); and (3) a combined score based on the IDAS-II Checking (3 items), Ordering (5 items), and Cleaning (7 items) scales. Correlations among these measures ranged from .65 to .77 (mean $r = .71$).

Bivariate Relations

Table 6.13 reports the bivariate associations (standard Pearson product-moment correlations for the self-report psychopathology measures, polyserial correlations for the dichotomous interview variables) between the trait affect factor scores and indicators of depression and anxiety. Overall, we see strong associations between these neuroticism facets and internalizing psychopathology. The trait Anxiety facet has 11 correlations ≥ .50 (73.3%); moreover, it has the strongest individual association with the self-rated Agoraphobia composite, as well as several *DSM* diagnoses (PTSD, panic disorder, social anxiety disorder, agoraphobia, and OCD). Similarly, the Depression facet has nine coefficients ≥ .50 (60.0%) and has the strongest link to several self-report variables (the Depression composite,

Table 6.13 Correlations Between the Trait Negative Affect Factor Scores and Indicators of Internalizing in Sample 4

Scale	Anger	Anxiety	Depression
Self-Report			
Depression Composite	**.57**	**.67**	**.88**
GADQ-IV	.49	**.70**	**.71**
PTSD Composite	**.51**	**.62**	**.66**
Panic Composite	**.54**	**.61**	**.67**
Social Anxiety Composite	.44	**.63**	**.68**
Agoraphobia Composite	.32	.47	.41
OCD Composite	.44	.47	.47
Interview			
Major Depressive Disorder	.40	**.56**	**.68**
Dysthymic Disorder	.33	.45	**.62**
GAD	.41	**.62**	**.63**
PTSD	.47	**.56**	**.51**
Panic Disorder	.37	**.51**	.40
Social Anxiety Disorder	.28	**.54**	.49
Agoraphobia	.34	.44	.36
OCD	.42	**.61**	.46

NOTE: $N = 403$ (Self-report), 401 (Interview). Self-report results are Pearson correlations; interview results are polyserial correlations. Correlations $\geq |.50|$ are in bold. All correlations are significant at $p < .05$. GADQ-IV = Generalized Anxiety Disorder Questionnaire-IV. GAD = Generalized Anxiety Disorder. PTSD = Posttraumatic Stress Disorder. OCD = Obsessive-Compulsive Disorder.

the GADQ-IV, the PTSD composite, the Panic composite, and the Social Anxiety composite), as well as diagnoses of MDD, dysthymic disorder, and GAD. In contrast, trait Anger has only three correlations ≥ .50 (20.0%), and it never is the strongest individual predictor of internalizing. Consistent with previous results, these findings suggest that Anger's moderate bivariate relations with internalizing primarily reflect the influence of nonspecific Neuroticism.

Multivariate Relations

Next, we conducted a series of regression analyses to determine the amount of unique incremental information provided by each neuroticism facet. For the self-report scales, we report standardized β weights from multiple regression analyses; for the dichotomous interview ratings, we present odds ratios (ORs) from logistic regression analyses. These results are reported in Table 6.14. Consistent with the bivariate results, the Anxiety and Depression facets both were strong predictors of psychopathology, making significant incremental contributions in 12 (80%) and 10 (66.7%) analyses, respectively. Note, moreover, that all of these significant effects represent positive relations, indicating that higher scores on these traits consistently were associated with elevated levels of psychopathology.

Table 6.14 Regression Results: Trait Negative Affect Factor Scores and Indicators of Internalizing in Sample 4

Scale	**Anger**	**Anxiety**	**Depression**
Self-Report			
Depression Composite	–.01	–.03	**.91**
GADQ-IV	–.07	**.41**	**.43**
PTSD Composite	.07	**.23**	**.43**
Panic Composite	**.13**	**.19**	**.44**
Social Anxiety Composite	**–.10**	**.29**	**.52**
Agoraphobia Composite	–.03	**.40**	.12
OCD Composite	**.18**	**.19**	**.21**
Interview			
Major Depressive Disorder	0.66	1.16	**6.82**
Dysthymic Disorder	0.63	0.92	**6.87**
GAD	0.73	**2.30**	**2.91**
PTSD	1.44	**2.33**	1.45
Panic Disorder	1.14	**3.09**	1.01
Social Anxiety Disorder	**0.53**	**3.63**	**1.99**
Agoraphobia	1.19	**2.40**	1.10
OCD	1.28	**4.35**	1.01

NOTE: $N = 403$ (Self-report), 401 (Interview). Self-report results are standardized β weights; interview results are odds ratios. Significant effects ($p < .05$) are in bold. GADQ-IV = Generalized Anxiety Disorder Questionnaire-IV. GAD = Generalized Anxiety Disorder. PTSD = Posttraumatic Stress Disorder. OCD = Obsessive-Compulsive Disorder.

In sharp contrast, the Anger facet produced only four significant effects (26.7%). Furthermore, two of these significant associations were positive (greater Anger was associated with higher scores on the Panic and OCD symptom composites), but the other two were negative (increasing Anger was linked to lower scores on the self-rated Social Anxiety composite and with a reduced likelihood of receiving a social anxiety disorder diagnosis). Overall, we see little evidence that Anger makes an important incremental contribution to internalizing psychopathology.

Summary

In bivariate analyses, indicators of anger/hostility—including both self-report and interview-based measures—tend to show weak to moderate associations with internalizing psychopathology. At first glance, these associations might seem to suggest that anger plays a key role in internalizing. However, they invariably are weaker than those observed for other types of negative affect, such as fear/anxiety and sadness/depression.

The pattern observed at the bivariate level suggests that the associations between anger and internalizing largely reflect the underlying influence of the higher order Negative Affect factor. This consistently was confirmed in the regression analyses. Overall, we reported 92 regression analyses involving relations with internalizing. Anger indicators made a significant incremental contribution in only 12 of these analyses (13.0%). Moreover, only nine of these significant effects reflected positive associations; the others represent suppressor effects in which positive bivariate relations were transformed into negative associations in the multivariate analyses. Furthermore, anger failed to show consistent relations with any specific form of psychopathology. For example, we had expected that anger would show particularly strong associations with GAD and PTSD, both of which include anger and irritability in their formal diagnostic criteria. Across all of our measures, we reported 11 analyses apiece involving GAD and PTSD diagnoses. Contrary to our expectation, indicators of anger/hostility made significant incremental contributions in only two of these 22 analyses (9.1%; one each for GAD and PTSD).

Thus, our data do not support recent analyses that appeared to highlight the importance of anger and hostility in the anxiety disorders (e.g., Hawkins & Cougle, 2011; Olatunji, Ciesielski, & Tolin, 2010). It is noteworthy, however, that these earlier analyses examined anger in isolation, without considering the influence of other types of negative mood (or of the higher order Negative Affect factor). Our results illustrate how misleading it can be to examine single types of affect in isolation; one gets a much clearer sense of the true nature of these associations by investigating multiple affects in a single integrated analysis.

ANGER AND EXTERNALIZING PSYCHOPATHOLOGY

PANAS-X Analyses

We now examine how anger relates to externalizing forms of psychopathology. The participants in Samples 1 ($N=331$) and 2 ($N=253$) were interviewed using the substance use disorders module of the SCID-IV. The PANAS-X Hostility scale had significant positive polyserial correlations with diagnoses of any substance use disorder in both Sample 1 ($r=.19$) and Sample 2 ($r=.32$).

To control for the influence of the general Negative Affect factor, we again conducted logistic regression analyses using all four PANAS-X Negative Affect scales as predictors. Hostility made a significant incremental contribution to the prediction of substance use diagnoses in Sample 2 (OR = 1.90, $p < .01$), but not Sample 1 (OR = 1.11, n.s.). Thus, we see some evidence that anger/hostility is specifically associated with elevated levels of substance use.

IDAS-II Analyses

We have parallel data on the IDAS-II Ill Temper scale in four samples (see Tables 6.8 and 6.9). Ill Temper was significantly positively linked to diagnoses of any substance use disorder in Samples 1 ($r = .25$), 2 ($r = .28$), and 4 ($r = .25$); it also was positively related to substance use pathology in Sample 5, but this association was weak and nonsignificant ($r = .07$).

Next, we conducted logistic regression analyses using IDAS-II Dysphoria to control for the influence of nonspecific Negative Affect. Ill Temper contributed significantly to the prediction of substance use disorder in Samples 2 (OR = 1.72) and 4 (OR = 1.48), but not Samples 1 (OR = 1.37) or 5 (OR = 0.93). Consequently, we again see mixed evidence that indicators of anger/hostility have a specific positive association with problematic substance use.

IDAS-CR Analyses

We have corresponding data for IDAS-CR Ill Temper in Samples 1 and 2. This interview-based rating yielded the same basic results and conclusions as the self-report scales (see Table 6.10). IDAS-CR Ill Temper was significantly positively linked to diagnoses of any substance use disorder in Sample 2 ($r = .28$), but not Sample 1 ($r = .07$). Similarly, logistic regression analyses (using IDAS-CR Dysphoria as a second predictor) indicated that Ill Temper made a significant incremental contribution in Sample 2 (OR = 1.58), but not Sample 1 (OR = 1.06). Once again, these data provide some evidence that anger/hostility is specifically associated with elevated substance use.

IMAS Analyses

Table 6.11 presents parallel results for the IMAS Irritability scale in Sample 5. Irritability was unrelated to diagnoses of any substance use disorder at both the bivariate ($r = -.02$) and multivariate (OR = 0.85) level.

NEO Analyses

Two studies have reported meta-analytic associations between the NEO PI-R facets and indicators of externalizing. The data from these studies clearly establish that anger/hostility is significantly positively linked to at least some forms of externalizing. First, Ruiz, Pincus, and Schinka (2008) presented meta-analytic results indicating that NEO PI-R Angry Hostility was moderately positively related to both antisocial behavior ($r = .30$) and substance use pathology ($r = .29$). It is noteworthy, moreover, that among the six NEO-PI-R Neuroticism facets, Angry Hostility had the strongest bivariate association with the former, but not with the latter. This pattern suggests that Angry Hostility has a specific link to antisocial behavior, but not to substance use pathology.

Second, Samuel and Widiger (2008) examined meta-analytic relations with *DSM-IV* PDs. Among the Cluster B disorders, Angry Hostility was strongly linked to borderline PD ($r=.48$); moderately associated with antisocial PD ($r=.27$) and narcissistic PD ($r=.23$); and weakly linked to histrionic PD ($r=.08$). Furthermore, among the Neuroticism facets, it had the strongest individual association with both narcissistic PD and antisocial PD (in the latter case, it was tied with Impulsiveness, which also correlated .27 with the disorder), suggesting the presence of specific links beyond the effects of general neuroticism.

Trait Affect Analyses

Indicators of Externalizing

Earlier, we examined associations between the three trait affect factor scores—viz., Anger, Anxiety, and Depression—and indicators of internalizing in Sample 4. We now report parallel results for externalizing. Interview data were available for two externalizing diagnoses: alcohol use disorder and (nonalcohol) substance use disorder.

In addition, we report results on two self-report indicators of substance use. First, we created an Alcohol Use composite by combining scores on the 10-item Alcohol Use Disorders Test (AUDIT; Saunders, Aasland, Babor, de la Fuente, & Grant, 1993) and the 10-item Short Michigan Alcoholism Screening Test (SMAST; Selzer, Vinoker, & van Rooijen, 1975). These scales correlated .64 with each other. Second, the Drug Use Survey (DUS; Clark & Watson, 1999) assesses the overall frequency of drug use. Participants rate the 10 items on a 7-point scale, ranging from 1 (*never*) to 7 (*40 times or more*), indicating how many times they have used marijuana, cocaine, amphetamines, diet pills, tranquilizers, psychedelics, narcotics, amyl/butyl nitrates, inhalants, and ecstasy.

As noted earlier, the Sample 4 participants also completed the PID-5 (Krueger et al., 2012). We examined five scales falling within the broad domain of antagonism (Krueger et al., 2012; Watson, Stasik, Ro, & Clark, 2013) that have been linked to various forms of externalizing, such as antisocial PD and narcissistic PD (American Psychiatric Association, 2013): Callousness (14 items; e.g., "I really don't care if I make other people suffer"), Deceitfulness (10 items; e.g., "Lying comes easily to me"), Manipulativeness (5 items; e.g., "It is easy for me to take advantage of others"), Attention Seeking (8 items; e.g., "I do things to make sure people notice me"), and Grandiosity (6 items; e.g., "To be honest, I'm just more important than other people"). In addition, we report results on three markers of the broad disinhibition domain that also have been linked to externalizing: Impulsivity (6 items; e.g., "Even though I know better, I can't stop making rash decisions"), Irresponsibility (7 items; e.g., "I've skipped town to avoid responsibilities"), and Risk Taking (14 items; e.g., "People would describe me as reckless").

Bivariate Relations

Table 6.15 reports the bivariate associations (standard Pearson product-moment correlations for the self-report psychopathology measures, polyserial correlations for the dichotomous interview-based diagnoses) between the trait affect factor

Table 6.15 Correlations Between the Trait Negative Affect Factor Scores and Indicators of Externalizing in Sample 4

Scale	Anger	Anxiety	Depression
Self-Report			
PID-5 Callousness	**.58**	.26	.45
PID-5 Impulsivity	**.54**	.39	**.53**
PID-5 Irresponsibility	**.53**	.40	**.60**
PID-5 Deceitfulness	.47	.26	.42
PID-5 Manipulativeness	.38	.10	.26
Alcohol Use Composite	.30	.22	.32
PID-5 Grandiosity	.29	.09	.17
PID-5 Attention Seeking	.27	.08	.17
PID-5 Risk Taking	.25	−.01	.13
Drug Use Survey	.21	.13	.21
Interview			
Substance Use Disorder	.36	.32	.30
Alcohol Use Disorder	.35	.19	.23

NOTE: $N = 403$ (Self-report), 401 (Interview). Self-report results are Pearson correlations; interview results are polyserial correlations. Correlations ≥ |.50| are in in bold. Correlations ≥ |.10| are significant at $p < .05$. PID-5 = Personality Inventory for *DSM-5*. IDAS-II = Expanded Version of the Inventory of Depression and Anxiety Symptoms.

scores and indicators of externalizing. Consistent with findings from other measures, the Anger factor had significant, moderate associations with substance use, with correlations ranging from .21 (Drug Use Survey) to .36 (substance use disorder diagnoses) and a mean value of .31. It should be noted, moreover, that substance use tended to correlate more strongly with Anger than with Anxiety (*r*s ranged from .13 to .32, mean $r = .22$) and Depression (*r*s ranged from .21 to .32, mean $r = .27$) in these data.

Anger correlated more strongly with the PID-5 antagonism and disinhibition scales, with coefficients ranging from .25 to .58 (mean $r = .42$). Its strongest associations were with Callousness ($r = .58$), Impulsivity ($r = .54$), Irresponsibility ($r = .53$), Deceitfulness ($r = .47$), and Manipulativeness ($r = .38$). Furthermore—and paralleling the substance use data—these PID-5 scales tended to correlate more strongly with Anger than with Anxiety (*r*s ranged from −.01 to .40, mean $r = .20$) and Depression (*r*s ranged from .13 to .60, mean $r = .35$).

Multivariate Relations

Next, we conducted a series of regression analyses to determine the unique incremental information provided by each neuroticism facet. Once again, for the self-report scales, we report standardized β weights from multiple regression analyses; for the dichotomous interview ratings, we present ORs from logistic regression

Table 6.16 Regression Results: Trait Negative Affect Factor Scores and Indicators of Externalizing in Sample 4

Scale	Anger	Anxiety	Depression
Self-Report			
PID-5 Callousness	**.62**	−.46	.40
PID-5 Impulsivity	**.40**	−.21	.43
PID-5 Irresponsibility	**.31**	−.26	.59
PID-5 Deceitfulness	**.42**	−.34	.40
PID-5 Manipulativeness	**.49**	−.44	.28
Alcohol Use Composite	**.19**	−.13	.29
PID-5 Grandiosity	**.39**	−.26	.12
PID-5 Attention Seeking	**.36**	−.28	.15
PID-5 Risk Taking	**.42**	−.45	.20
Drug Use Survey	**.16**	−.14	.21
Interview			
Substance Use Disorder	**1.77**	1.25	1.04
Alcohol Use Disorder	**2.12**	0.74	1.18

NOTE: $N = 403$ (Self-report), 401 (Interview). Self-report results are standardized β weights; interview results are odds ratios. Significant effects ($p < .05$) are in bold. PID-5 = Personality Inventory for *DSM-5*. IDAS-II = Expanded Version of the Inventory of Depression and Anxiety Symptoms.

analyses. These results are reported in Table 6.16. They offer a striking contrast to those observed earlier with internalizing: Anger had a positive incremental association with externalizing in all 12 analyses. Consequently, these data demonstrate that anger/hostility is broadly associated with elevated levels of externalizing.

Summary

We previously established that indicators of anger/hostility tend to show weak to moderate bivariate associations with internalizing that generally disappear at the multivariate level. The data we have reviewed for externalizing provide an interesting contrast. Anger/hostility measures tend to have moderate positive associations with substance abuse pathology, with correlations typically in the .20 to .35 range. It is noteworthy, moreover, that these positive associations often—but not always—remained significant at the multivariate level. Overall, Anger made a significant incremental contribution to the prediction of substance use in 8 of our 13 analyses (61.5%).

Furthermore, anger/hostility consistently displays moderate to strong associations with the types of externalizing pathology captured in the Cluster B PDs. For instance, previous meta-analyses have demonstrated that NEO PI-R Angry Hostility is moderately related to antisocial behavior ($r = .30$; Ruiz et al., 2008) and to diagnoses of borderline, antisocial, and narcissistic PD (*rs* ranged from .23 to .48; Samuel & Widiger, 2008). Similarly, our own data revealed substantial associations with several PID-5 antagonism and disinhibition scales, with particularly strong links to Callousness, Impulsivity, Irresponsibility, Deceitfulness, and Manipulativeness (*rs* ranged from .38 to .58). Moreover, all of these associations remained significant in the regression analyses. Overall, the accumulating evidence establishes that anger/hostility has broader and more substantial links to externalizing than to internalizing psychopathology.

ANGER AND PSYCHOTICISM

IDAS-II Analyses

We now examine how anger relates to indicators of psychoticism (e.g., psychosis, schizotypy, bipolar disorder), looking first at associations with the IDAS-II Ill Temper scale. We have relevant diagnostic data in Samples 4 (using the M.I.N.I.) and 5 (using the SCID-IV). As shown in Table 6.8, Ill Temper had significant positive polyserial correlations with current manic episodes ($r = .40$), psychotic disorder ($r = .34$), and mood disorder with psychotic features ($r = .31$) in Sample 4. However, it was unrelated to current manic episodes ($r = .07$) and psychosis diagnoses ($r = .00$) in Sample 5.

As before, we used IDAS-II Dysphoria to control for the influence of the general Negative Affect factor in a series of logistic regression analyses. Ill Temper did not make a significant incremental contribution in any of these analyses (see Table 6.9). Thus, we see no evidence of a specific association between anger/hostility and psychoticism in these data.

IMAS Analyses

Table 6.11 presents parallel data for the IMAS Irritability scale in Sample 5. At the bivariate level, Irritability was significantly related to current manic episodes ($r = .22$), but not to psychosis diagnoses ($r = .14$). As with Ill Temper, Irritability failed to contribute significantly in either logistic regression. Consequently, we again see no evidence of a specific association between anger/hostility and diagnostic indicators of psychoticism.

NEO Analyses

Ross, Lutz, and Bailley (2002) examined how the NEO PI-R facets related to both positive (magical thinking and odd/unusual perceptions) and negative (social anhedonia/withdrawal) symptoms of schizotypy. NEO PI-R Angry Hostility was weakly related to the positive symptoms, with correlations ranging from only

.06 to .24 (mean $r=.14$). It was more substantially related to negative schizotypy symptoms, however, with a mean correlation of .35. Moreover, it had the strongest individual association with social anhedonia/withdrawal of any neuroticism facet. Thus, we do see some evidence of specificity in these relations.

Samuel and Widiger (2008) examined meta-analytic relations with the *DSM-IV* Cluster A PDs. Angry Hostility had significant moderate correlations with paranoid PD ($r=.41$), schizotypal PD ($r=.29$), and schizoid PD ($r=.19$). It also had the strongest individual association with paranoid PD of any neuroticism facet, providing suggestive evidence of a specific association with this disorder.

Trait Affect Analyses

Indicators of Psychoticism

Finally, we examine how the three trait affect factor scores relate to indicators of psychoticism in Sample 4. Interview data were available for three relevant diagnoses: mania, psychotic disorder, and mood disorder with psychotic features.

In addition, we report data on six self-report symptom measures. First, the Sample 4 participants completed two measures of bipolar symptoms, namely, the IDAS-II Mania and Euphoria scales.

Next, we formed a Positive Schizotypy composite by aggregating three PID-5 scales: Eccentricity (13 items), Cognitive and Perceptual Dysregulation (12 items), and Unusual Beliefs and Experiences (8 items). These indicators had correlations ranging from .65 to .79 (mean $r=.72$) in this sample.

We combined two indicators into a Suspiciousness composite: (1) the 7-item PID-5 Suspiciousness scale and (2) the 7-item Paranoid Ideation scale from the Schizotypal Traits Questionnaire-Short Form (Jackson & Claridge, 1991). These scales correlated .60 with each other.

We constructed a Social Aloofness composite by combining (1) the 10-item PID-5 Withdrawal scale and (2) a 9-item Social Anhedonia scale created from the Schizotypal Personality Questionnaire (see Chmielewski & Watson, 2008a). These scales correlated .71 with one another.

Finally, the 7-item PID-5 Restricted Affectivity scale assesses the coldness, detachment, and flattened affect characteristic of schizoid and schizotypal personality disorders (e.g., "When it comes to my emotions, people tell me I'm a 'cold fish' "). Along with Social Aloofness, this scale provides a second indicator of the negative symptoms of schizotypy.

Bivariate Relations

Table 6.17 reports the bivariate associations (Pearson product-moment correlations for the self-report psychopathology measures, polyserial correlations for the dichotomous interview-based diagnoses) between the trait affect factor scores and indicators of psychoticism. Anger was significantly positively related to all nine psychoticism measures, with correlations ranging from .22 to .65 (mean $r=.45$). It was most strongly related to the Suspiciousness composite

Table 6.17 Correlations Between the Trait Negative Affect Factor Scores and Indicators of Psychoticism in Sample 4

Scale	Anger	Anxiety	Depression
Self-Report			
Suspiciousness Composite	**.65**	**.57**	**.71**
Positive Schizotypy Composite	**.55**	.46	**.62**
IDAS-II Mania	**.55**	**.51**	**.56**
Social Aloofness Composite	**.52**	.47	**.68**
PID-5 Restricted Affectivity	.28	.12	.35
IDAS-II Euphoria	.22	.03	.09
Interview			
Mania	**.53**	**.58**	**.62**
Mood Disorder-Psychotic	.38	**.54**	**.68**
Psychotic Disorder	.26	.34	.36

NOTE: $N = 403$ (Self-report), 401 (Interview). Self-report results are Pearson correlations; interview results are polyserial correlations. Correlations $\geq |.50|$ are in bold. Correlations $\geq |.10|$ are significant at $p < .05$. IDAS-II = Expanded Version of the Inventory of Depression and Anxiety Symptoms. PID-5 = Personality Inventory for *DSM-5*. Mood Disorder-Psychotic = Mood Disorder with Psychotic Features.

($r = .65$), the Positive Schizotypy composite ($r = .55$), IDAS-II Mania ($r = .55$), mania diagnoses ($r = .53$), and the Social Aloofness composite ($r = .52$). It is noteworthy, however, that Depression (rs ranged from .09 to .71, mean $r = .54$) and Anxiety (rs ranged from .03 to .58, mean $r = .42$) also showed broad and substantial associations with psychoticism. In fact, Depression had the strongest individual association with the psychoticism measures in eight of nine cases; the only exception was that Anger had the highest correlation with IDAS-II Euphoria ($r = .22$). This pattern of results suggests that Anger's significant associations with psychoticism are nonspecific and are largely are attributable to general Neuroticism.

Multivariate Relations

As before, we tested this issue via a series of regression analyses. Once again, we report standardized β weights from multiple regression analyses for the self-report scales and ORs from logistic regression analyses for the dichotomous diagnoses. The results are reported in Table 6.18. Anger made a significant incremental contribution in all six analyses involving self-report symptoms. With the regard to the diagnoses, however, it added significantly only in the case of mania (OR = 1.75); the effects for psychotic disorder (OR = 0.99) and mood disorder with psychotic features (OR = 0.76) were nonsignificant. Overall, these data provide some support for a specific link between anger and certain forms of psychoticism.

Table 6.18 Regression Results: Trait Negative Affect Factor Scores and Indicators of Psychoticism in Sample 4

Scale	**Anger**	**Anxiety**	**Depression**
Self-Report			
Suspiciousness Composite	**.33**	–.09	**.56**
Positive Schizotypy Composite	**.28**	**–.17**	**.56**
IDAS-II Mania	**.29**	.06	**.32**
Social Aloofness Composite	**.19**	**–.22**	**.72**
PID-5 Restricted Affectivity	**.20**	**–.46**	**.57**
IDAS-II Euphoria	**.36**	**–.22**	.03
Interview			
Mania	**1.75**	1.26	**2.75**
Mood Disorder-Psychotic	0.76	0.99	**9.20**
Psychotic Disorder	0.99	1.45	1.75

NOTE: $N = 403$ (Self-report), 401 (Interview). Self-report results are standardized β weights; interview results are odds ratios. Significant effects ($p < .05$) are in bold. IDAS-II = Expanded Version of the Inventory of Depression and Anxiety Symptoms. PID-5 = Personality Inventory for *DSM-5*. Mood Disorder-Psychotic = Mood Disorder with Psychotic Features.

Summary

The data for psychoticism have yielded mixed results. Analyses involving *DSM* diagnoses provide little support for a specific link between anger/hostility and psychoticism. Overall, our assessed indicators of anger/hostility (IDAS-II Ill Temper, IMAS Irritability, trait Anger) had significant bivariate relations with psychoticism in 7 of 10 analyses. However, only one of these associations remained significant at the multivariate level (viz., the link between trait Anger and mania diagnoses in Sample 4). Consequently, these significant bivariate associations appear to be largely nonspecific and attributable to the general Negative Affect factor.

In contrast, the symptom data are more encouraging. On the basis of the evidence we have reviewed, anger appears to have particularly strong associations with paranoia/suspiciousness. Trait Anger scores were strongly correlated with the Suspiciousness composite ($r = .65$) in the Sample 4 data; moreover, this association remained significant in the regression analyses ($\beta = .33$). Furthermore, Samuel and Widiger (2008) reported that NEO PI-R Angry Hostility had the strongest individual correlation with paranoid PD ($r = .41$) of any neuroticism facet.

Anger also seems to have a specific link to social anhedonia/withdrawal. In the analyses of the Sample 4 data, trait Anger was strongly correlated with the Social Aloofness composite ($r = .52$) and made a significant incremental contribution in the regression analyses ($\beta = .19$). Similarly, Ross et al. (2002) reported that

NEO PI-R Angry Hostility had the strongest individual association with social anhedonia/withdrawal (mean $r = .35$) of any neuroticism facet.

Results for other types of symptoms are more limited and/or inconsistent. It will be important for future research to explicate how anger/hostility is related to specific types of psychoticism symptoms.

7

The Structure, Validity, and Specificity of PTSD Symptoms

We now examine the structure, validity (including convergent, discriminant, criterion, and incremental validity), and specificity of symptoms of posttraumatic stress disorder (PTSD). More than any other area of psychopathology, research on this topic is closely tied to the vicissitudes of the diagnosis as it has been formulated in various editions of the *Diagnostic and Statistical Manual of Mental Disorders* (*DSM*). Accordingly, we begin this chapter by presenting a brief history of the PTSD diagnosis; this, then, naturally leads to an examination of the structure defined by its unusually detailed set of symptoms. We then review measures of the basic symptom dimensions that have been identified within PTSD and explore their distinctive properties.

A HISTORY OF THE PTSD DIAGNOSIS

Precursor Diagnoses

PRE-*DSM* DIAGNOSES

Clinical cases involving responses to traumatic stress were first reported more than 2,000 years ago (for an early history of the diagnosis, see Crocq & Crocq, 2000). Most of the early cases represented responses to combat-related stress, but other types of trauma (such as railroad and workplace accidents) came to be recognized as potential etiological factors during the Industrial Revolution of the 19th century. Interest in trauma-based forms of psychopathology was greatly stimulated by the advent of modern warfare in the late 19th and early 20th centuries. Conflicts such as the Russo-Japanese War (1904–1905) and World War I (1914–1918) produced cases of “war neurosis,” “battle fatigue,” “combat hysteria,” and “shell shock” on a previously unimaginable scale (Crocq & Crocq, 2000).

DSM-I

Early conceptualizations of trauma-based disorders in the *DSM* emphasized their transient nature (McNally, 2015); consequently, they are more closely linked to the contemporary diagnosis of acute stress disorder, rather than PTSD per se. *DSM-I* (American Psychiatric Association, 1952), for example, included traumatic stress-based conditions under the label "gross stress reaction," which fell within the broader category of "transient situational personality disorders." *DSM-I* indicated that this condition was to be diagnosed "only in situations in which the individual has been exposed to severe physical demands or extreme emotional stress, such as in combat or in civilian catastrophe (fire, earthquake, explosion, etc.)" (p. 40). The *Manual* further specified that gross stress reaction should only be used as a short-term diagnosis, such that "if the reaction persists, this term is to be regarded as a temporary diagnosis to be used only until a more definitive diagnosis is established" (p. 40).

DSM-II

Traumatic stress conditions were given relatively little attention in *DSM-II* (American Psychiatric Association, 1968). They were classified under "transient situational disturbances," which were subsumed within the overarching category of "adjustment reaction of adult life." Few details were provided, although the *Manual* gives an example of "fear associated with military combat and manifested by trembling, running, and hiding" (p. 49). Again, this was explicitly defined as an acute, transient reaction; in fact, *DSM-II* states that if "the symptoms persist after the stress is removed, the diagnosis of another mental disorder is indicated" (p. 48).

The PTSD Era

DSM-III

American involvement in the Vietnam War in the 1960s and early 1970s created a renewed interest in traumatic stress reactions and led to the explicit recognition that they could be chronic in nature, persisting well after contact with the traumatic event had ended (Crocq & Crocq, 2000; McNally, 2015). Responding to this new sensibility, *DSM-III* (American Psychiatric Association, 1980) introduced PTSD as a formal diagnosis that could be either "acute" (i.e., duration of less than 6 months) or "chronic or delayed" ("duration of symptoms six months or more" and/or "onset of symptoms at least six months after the trauma"; p. 238).

DSM-III specified that PTSD should be diagnosed only in response to "a recognizable stressor that would evoke significant symptoms of distress in almost everyone" (p. 238). In addition, the *Manual* included an unusually long and detailed list of symptoms, which has been a characteristic feature of the disorder ever since. Specifically, it provided a list of 12 symptoms, which were organized into three groups. Criterion B included three symptoms involving reexperiencing the trauma in some form (intrusive recollections of the event, recurrent dreams of the event, feeling as if the event were reoccurring). Criterion C consisted of three symptoms of numbing and reduced involvement with the external world (diminished interest in activities, feeling detached or estranged from others, constricted affect). Finally, Criterion D was a heterogeneous set of six symptoms, containing indicators related to avoidance (avoidance of activities that recalled the event), hyperarousal (hyperalertness or exaggerated startle response), and internalizing (sleep disturbance, guilt, memory or concentration problems, intensification of symptoms through exposure to the event).

This tripartite organization of the symptoms is noteworthy, because it came to be viewed as an implied factor structure; that is, researchers argued that the symptoms within each criterion group should be indicators of the same latent factor in a formal structural analysis. For example, the three Criterion B reexperiencing symptoms should correlate more strongly with each other than with the symptoms included in Criteria C or D, thereby forming a corresponding factor in structural analyses (L. Simms et al., 2002; Taylor, Kuch, Koch, Crockett, & Passey, 1998; Yufik & Simms, 2010) This, in turn, stimulated intense interest in the actual structure of PTSD symptoms, a topic we will examine shortly.

DSM-III-R

DSM-III-R (American Psychiatric Association, 1987) introduced an expanded set of 17 symptoms that subsequently became the subject of intense factor analytic scrutiny. Criterion B now included four manifestations of reexperiencing and traumatic intrusions (intrusive recollections of the event, recurrent dreams of the event, feeling as if the event were reoccurring, intense distress at events related to the trauma). A greatly expanded Criterion C now included seven symptoms related to avoidance (avoiding trauma-related thoughts or feelings, avoiding situations that arouse memories of the trauma) and numbing/dysphoria (amnesia for at least part of trauma, diminished interest in activities, feeling detached or estranged from others, restricted range of affect, sense of foreshortened future). Finally, Criterion D consisted of six symptoms reflecting increased arousal (sleep difficulties, irritability/anger, difficulty concentrating, hypervigilance, exaggerated startle response, physiologic reactivity when exposed to trauma-related events).

DSM-IV

These 17 symptoms essentially remained intact in *DSM-IV* (American Psychiatric Association, 2000). In fact, the only real modification was that one of the *DSM-III-R* Criterion D hyperarousal symptoms (physiologic reactivity on exposure to a trauma-related event) was moved to Criterion B in *DSM-IV*. Consequently, the PTSD diagnosis in *DSM-IV* consisted of five intrusions/reexperiencing symptoms, seven avoidance/numbing/dysphoria symptoms, and five hyperarousal symptoms. The first column of Table 7.1 provides a schematic depiction of the three-factor structure implied by the organization of the symptoms in *DSM-IV*.

Table 7.1 Mapping of *DSM-IV* PTSD Symptoms Onto Various Structural Models

***DSM-IV* PTSD Symptom**	***DSM-IV***	**King**	**Simms**	**Elhai**
B1. Repeated, disturbing memories	I	I	I	I
B2. Repeated, disturbing dreams	I	I	I	I
B3. Reliving a stressful experience	I	I	I	I
B4. Feeling upset when reminded of event	I	I	I	I
B5. Had physical reaction when reminded	I	I	I	I
C1. Avoided thinking/talking about event	A/N	A	A	A
C2. Avoided activities/situations	A/N	A	A	A
C3. Trouble remembering parts of event	A/N	N	D	N
C4. Loss of interest in activities	A/N	N	D	N
C5. Feeling distant or cut off	A/N	N	D	N
C6. Feeling emotionally numb	A/N	N	D	N
C7. Feeling future will be cut short	A/N	N	D	N
D1. Trouble falling or staying asleep	HA	HA	D	DA
D2. Feeling irritable/angry outbursts	HA	HA	D	DA
D3. Difficulty concentrating	HA	HA	D	DA
D4. Being "superalert," watchful	HA	HA	HV	HV
D5. Feeling jumpy, easily startled	HA	HA	HV	HV

NOTE: PTSD = posttraumatic stress disorder. I = Intrusions. A = Avoidance. N = Numbing. D = Dysphoria. HA = Hyperarousal. DA = Dysphoric Arousal. HV = Hypervigilance.

THE STRUCTURE OF PTSD SYMPTOMS

Early Evidence

As noted earlier, the implied *DSM* structure has produced an intense interest in the actual empirical structure that is defined by PTSD symptoms. These studies eventually yielded the important general conclusion that the organization of the symptoms in the *DSM* was less than optimal. Several early studies examined the set of symptoms included in *DSM-III* (for a review of these early studies, see Taylor et al., 1998), but the bulk of the evidence is based on the expanded pool of 17 symptoms presented in *DSM-III-R* and *DSM-IV.* Indeed, Yufik and Simms (2010) reported a meta-analytic investigation of the structure defined by these symptoms based on 40 structural studies with a combined sample size of 14,827.

Some early structural studies found evidence of two broad factors, rather than the three-factor organization implied in *DSM-III-R* and *DSM-IV.* For example, Taylor et al. (1998) factor analyzed PTSD symptoms in samples of (a) 103 civilian victims of car accidents and (b) 419 United Nations peacekeepers stationed in Bosnia. In both samples, they identified factors representing Intrusions/Avoidance (i.e., a mixture of Criterion B and C symptoms) and Hyperarousal/Numbing (i.e., a combination of Criterion C and D symptoms). Buckley, Blanchard, and Hickling (1998) replicated this two-factor structure in a sample of 217 car accident victims.

King's Four-Factor Numbing Model

However, two alternative four-factor models have received the greatest support in this extensive literature. The first model—which originally was proposed by King, Leskin, King, and Weathers (1998)—is depicted in the second column of Table 7.1. It can be seen that this model follows the tripartite *DSM-IV* organization, except that the Criterion C symptoms are split into separate Avoidance (two symptoms) and Numbing (five symptoms) factors. It is noteworthy that this four-factor structure subsequently became the basis for the reorganized model in *DSM-5* (American Psychiatric Association, 2013), which we will describe in more detail later.

Simms's Four-Factor Dysphoria Model

The second four-factor model was proposed and tested by L. Simms et al. (2002); this scheme is depicted in the third column of Table 7.1. As can be seen, this model contains Intrusions and Avoidance factors that are identical to those specified in the King et al. structure. However, its arrangement of the 10 remaining symptoms differs markedly from both the *DSM-IV* and King et al. models. Similar to them, it also includes a Hypervigilance factor, but this now is defined by only two of the *DSM-IV* Criterion D symptoms (hypervigilance, exaggerated startle response).[1] The fourth factor in the Simms et al. structure—Dysphoria—consists of the five Criterion C numbing symptoms (loss of interest, detachment, restricted affect, sense of foreshortened future, inability to recall the trauma) and the three remaining Criterion D symptoms (sleep disturbance, irritability, difficulty concentrating). As is suggested by its name, most of its defining symptoms are relatively nonspecific and closely resemble classic manifestations of internalizing psychopathology. In fact, this cluster contains several indicators (e.g., loss of interest, insomnia, irritability, difficulty concentrating) that also are part of the symptom criteria for other emotional disorders, including depression and generalized anxiety disorder (GAD). These overlapping symptoms have important implications that we will examine subsequently.

Yufik and Simms's Meta-Analysis

As was noted earlier, Yufik and Simms (2010) conducted a meta-analytic investigation based on 40 studies that reported results using the 17 PTSD symptoms included in *DSM-III-R* and *DSM-IV*. They aggregated correlation matrices across these studies and then applied confirmatory factor analysis to test the fit of five

1. L. Simms et al. (2002) actually called this two-item factor *Hyperarousal*. We have renamed it *Hypervigilance* here to avoid confusion and to distinguish it clearly from the broader, five-item dimension included in the *DSM-IV* and King models.

competing structures: (1) a one-factor model positing a single general factor; (2) the two-factor model identified by Taylor et al. (1998); (3) a three-factor model reflecting the organization of the symptoms in *DSM-IV*; (4) the four-factor King Numbing model; and (5) the four-factor Simms Dysphoria model. Their results indicated that both four-factor models (a) fit the data well and, moreover, (b) fit the data better than the three less differentiated structures. Accordingly, we subsequently will report data based on both of these four-factor schemes. Nevertheless, it also should be noted that Yufik and Simms (2010) found that the Simms Dysphoria model generally fit the data better than the King Numbing model across various measures and populations. Consequently, this model has received the strongest overall support in the literature.

Elhai's Five-Factor Dysphoric Arousal Model

A five-factor model—which shares key features with both of these prominent four-factor schemes—also has received some attention in the past few years (e.g., Liu et al., 2014). This structure—which originally was proposed and tested by Elhai, Biehn et al. (2011)—is displayed in the final column of Table 7.1. As shown in the table, this model contains Intrusions and Avoidance factors that are identical to those specified in the King and Simms structures. It also includes a Numbing factor that is identical to that contained in the King model. However, it divides the *DSM-IV* Criterion D symptoms into two factors that can be labeled Dysphoric Arousal (sleep disturbance, feeling irritable, difficulty concentrating) and Hypervigilance (hypervigilance, exaggerated startle response); the latter factor is identical to the Hypervigilance dimension in the Simms Dysphoria model.[2] Consequently, this five-factor scheme shares three dimensions in common with both the King (Intrusions, Avoidance, Numbing) and Simms (Intrusions, Avoidance, Hypervigilance) models. We will report some findings based on this five-factor structure.

DSM-5

Factor analytic evidence rarely has a direct effect on *DSM* diagnoses, but it recently did so in the restructuring of PTSD in *DSM-5*. The *DSM-5* Sub-Work Group on Posttraumatic and Dissociative Disorders was acutely aware of the fact that extensive structural evidence failed to support the tripartite organization in *DSM-IV* (see Friedman, 2013; Friedman, Resick, Bryant, & Brewin, 2011). For example, Friedman et al. (2011) state: "Taken together, most confirmatory factor analyses support a four, rather than a three-factor *DSM-IV* model. . . . Based on these

2. Elhai, Biehn et al. (2011) actually called this two-item factor *Anxious Arousal*. Because it is identical to the Hypervigilance dimension in the Simms et al. model, we have given it the same name here.

findings, a four-factor model for PTSD has been proposed for *DSM-5*" (p. 757). Similarly, Friedman (2013) writes:

> Almost all studies that have used confirmatory factor analysis to investigate the latent structure of PTSD have failed to confirm the *DSM-IV* 3-factor structure. Although intrusion (B) and arousal (D) symptoms have usually emerged as two distinct symptom clusters, the avoidance/numbing (C) cluster has usually emerged as distinct avoidance (C1 and C2) and numbing (C3–C7) clusters, respectively. . . . Given such conclusive evidence, the sub-work group proposed a 4-, rather than 3-factor solution retaining the intrusion (B) and arousal (now E and renamed "arousal and reactivity") clusters and separating the DSM-IV avoidance/numbing into avoidance (C) and negative cognitions and mood (D) clusters. (p. 551)

Thus, *DSM-5* adopted an expanded, 20-symptom version of the four-factor King Numbing model. The 17 *DSM-III-R/DSM-IV* symptoms have been retained (although some have been revised or reworded), with three new items added. The five Criterion B Intrusions symptoms (repeated, disturbing memories of the event; recurrent, distressing dreams; dissociative reactions in which the event seems to be recurring; intense distress at exposure to event-related cues; marked physiological reactions to event-related cues) remain largely unchanged from *DSM-IV* (Friedman, 2013). The two avoidance symptoms (avoiding trauma-related thoughts or feelings; avoiding situations that arouse memories of the trauma) also essentially are the same, except that they now form a separate Criterion C. Criterion D (now labeled "Negative alterations in cognitions and mood") is an expansion and reformulation of the *DSM-IV* numbing symptoms; in *DSM-5,* this group consists of seven symptoms (amnesia for at least part of trauma; exaggerated negative beliefs about oneself or others; distorted cognitions about the cause or consequences of the trauma; persistent negative emotional states, such as fear, horror, anger, or guilt; diminished interest in activities; feeling detached or estranged from others; inability to experience positive emotions). Finally, Criterion E ("Marked alterations in arousal and reactivity") consists of an expanded set of six symptoms (irritable behavior and angry outbursts; reckless or self-destructive behavior; hypervigilance; exaggerated startle response; concentration problems; sleep disturbance).

TWO BASIC PROPERTIES OF PTSD SYMPTOMS

A Strong General Factor

Before discussing specific measures and examining their construct validity, it is helpful to clarify two basic properties of PTSD symptoms. First, despite the existence of specific factors such as Intrusions and Avoidance, PTSD symptoms all tend to be substantially interrelated and, therefore, are characterized by a strong general factor (Watson, 2009a; Yufik & Simms, 2010). In support of this point,

Gootzeit and Markon (2011) reported meta-analytic associations between the factors specified in the King and Simms models (see their Tables 4 and 5). The correlations among the King factors ranged from .67 (Avoidance with Hyperarousal) to .80 (Numbing with Hyperarousal), with a mean value of .72. Similarly, correlations among the Simms model factors ranged from .63 (Avoidance with Hypervigilance) to .77 (Intrusions with Avoidance), with a mean coefficient of .71. In a related vein, Watson (2009a) showed that PTSD symptoms contain a much larger component of general distress/negative affectivity than obsessive-compulsive disorder (OCD) symptoms. Consequently, PTSD symptom measures generally can be expected to correlate strongly with one another.

Differential Specificity

Despite their significant intercorrelations, the individual symptom dimensions within PTSD display some very distinctive properties. One well-established difference concerns their specificity versus nonspecificity to PTSD. Earlier, we noted that several PTSD symptoms—especially indicators of Dysphoria in the Simms model (which are split across the Numbing and Hyperarousal factors in the King model)—also are part of the criteria for other emotional disorders, such as major depression and GAD. Not surprisingly, these shared symptoms show much poorer specificity to PTSD than indicators of Intrusions and Avoidance. For instance, Gootzeit and Markon (2011) present meta-analytic associations between PTSD symptom factors and indicators of anxiety. Analyses based on the King model revealed that measures of anxiety correlated much more strongly with symptoms of Hyperarousal (.59) and Numbing (.54) than with Intrusions (.40) and Avoidance (.33). Results based on the Simms factors indicated that anxiety symptoms correlated more strongly with Dysphoria (.58) than with the other three factors (*r*s ranged from .33 to .49, mean $r = .41$).

PTSD symptoms show even stronger overlap with indicators of depression. To document this point, Table 7.2 presents correlations between depressive symptoms and scores on the four King dimensions that have been reported in various studies. It should be noted that Table 7.2 is an updated version of the findings reported in Watson (2009a, Table 2) and Gootzeit and Markon (2011, Table 4) and incorporates data from both of these earlier reviews. Three aspects of these findings are noteworthy. First, the correlations generally are moderate to strong in magnitude, which is consistent with other evidence establishing substantial overlap/comorbidity between depression and PTSD (Rosen & Lilienfeld, 2008; Watson, 2005, 2009a; Watson & Stasik, 2014). Second, the individual symptom dimensions correlate quite differently with depression. Specifically, the Hyperarousal and Numbing symptoms have much stronger correlations with depression (weighted mean $rs = .71$ and .70, respectively, in the self-report data) than do the Intrusions and Avoidance symptoms ($rs = .55$ and .48, respectively). Third, self-rated and clinician-rated PTSD symptoms yielded similar results. Most notably, depression also correlates more strongly with Hyperarousal and Numbing ($rs = .62$ and .64,

Table 7.2 Correlations Between Depression Symptoms and PTSD Symptom Scores From the King et al. (1998) Four-Factor Structure

Study	*N*	Numbing	Hyper	Intrus	Avoid
Self-Rated PTSD Symptoms					
Boelen & Spuij (2013)	332	.64	.67	.57	.43
Elhai, Contractor et al. (2011)	740	.77	.67	.62	.57
Fetzner et al. (2013)					
Men	1,271	.73	.68	.56	.51
Women	72	.72	.73	.60	.49
Fetzner et al. (2014)	122	.64	.62	.50	.42
Hellmuth et al. (2012)	356	.63	.62	.40	.39
Hukkelberg & Jensen (2011)	312	.70	.75	.67	.62
D. Johnson et al. (2007)	221	.59	.63	.46	.28
Naifeh et al. (2008)	252	.48	.59	.52	.46
Palmieri, Marshall et al. (2007)	488	.86	.85	.77	.63
Palmieri, Weathers et al. (2007)	2,960	.76	.75	.62	.55
Schnurr & Lunney (2011)	253	.44	.34	.32	.18
L. Simms et al. (2002)					
Deployed sample	1,896	.75	.76	.51	.46
Nondeployed sample	1,799	.66	.67	.38	.34
Watson et al. (2012)					
Patient Sample 4	291	.78	.71	.56	.55
Student Sample 7	373	.73	.70	.63	.56
Witteveen et al. (2006)					
Police Officers	833	.58	.63	.51	.46
Firefighters	333	.51	.53	.43	.32
Weighted Mean	**12,904**	.71	.70	.55	**.48**
Clinician-Rated PTSD Symptoms					
J. Beck et al. (2009)	109	.47	.33	.35	.26
McDevitt-Murphy et al. (2005)	55	.69	.56	.46	.34
Palmieri, Weathers et al. (2007)	2,960	.62	.65	.54	.46
Weighted Mean	**3,124**	.62	.64	.53	.45

NOTE: Hyper = Hyperarousal. Intrus = Intrusions. Avoid = Avoidance.

respectively) than with Intrusions and Avoidance (*rs* = .53 and .45, respectively) in the clinicians' ratings. These results highlight the heterogeneity of PTSD symptoms and illustrate the importance of examining these dimensions separately.

Table 7.3 reports findings paralleling those of Table 7.2 for the Simms factors; this table updates results reported in Watson (2009a, Table 3) and Gootzeit and Markon (2011, Table 5). These results are even more striking and offer very strong evidence of the value of examining these relations at the specific symptom level. The Simms model clearly puts all of the most nonspecific, distress-laden symptoms together on the same factor. Thus, indicators of depression correlate much more strongly with Dysphoria (*rs* = .75 and .69 in the self-ratings and clinicians' ratings, respectively) than with all other types of PTSD symptoms (*rs* ranged from

Table 7.3 Correlations Between Depression Symptoms and PTSD Symptom Scores From the Simms et al. (2002) Four-Factor Structure

Study	*N*	Dysphoria	Hyper	Intrus	Avoid
Self-Rated PTSD Symptoms					
Boelen et al. (2008)	347	.81	.44	.63	.38
Boelen & Spuij (2013)	332	.73	.44	.57	.43
Boyes et al. (2012)	1,025	.40	.42	.34	.21
Contractor et al. (2014)	818	.78	.67	.71	.66
Elklit & Shevlin (2007)	1,116	.61	.38	.25	.24
Hukkelberg & Jensen (2011)	312	.79	.58	.67	.62
Marshall et al. (2010)					
Community violence sample	304	.63	.60	.63	.50
Fire sample	235	.75	.72	.64	.68
Meis et al. (2011)					
Sample 1	514	.79	.41	.56	.48
Sample 2	2,385	.77	.47	.50	.48
Naragon-Gainey et al. (2012)	132	.44	.12	.24	.26
Palmieri, Weathers et al. (2007)	2,960	.80	.60	.62	.55
Pietrzak et al. (2010)	272	.85	.66	.66	.67
L. Simms et al. (2002)					
Deployed sample	1,896	.80	.52	.51	.46
Nondeployed sample	1,799	.72	.44	.38	.34
Watson et al. (2012)					
Patient Sample 4	291	.84	.50	.56	.55
Student Sample 7	373	.78	.57	.63	.56
Weighted Mean	**15,111**	**.75**	**.51**	**.52**	**.47**
Clinician-Rated PTSD Symptoms					
Palmieri, Weathers et al. (2007)	2,960	.70	.43	.54	.46
Rytwinski et al. (2014)	200	.59	.24	.39	.24
Weighted Mean	**3,160**	**.69**	**.42**	**.53**	**.45**

Note: Hyper = Hypervigilance. Intrus = Intrusions. Avoid = Avoidance.

.42 to .53, mean $r = .48$). These results clearly raise concerns about the specificity and discriminant validity of Dysphoria symptoms that we will examine further in subsequent analyses.

CONVERGENT AND DISCRIMINANT VALIDITY OF PTSD SYMPTOM SCALES

IDAS-II PTSD Scales

Traumatic Intrusions

We now examine the convergent and discriminant validity of PTSD symptom measures, beginning with the scales included in the IDAS and IDAS-II. The initial version of the IDAS was focused primarily on the assessment of depression symptoms. The original item pool contained only seven HICs assessing anxiety symptoms; one of these HICs was an eight-item group assessing posttraumatic intrusions and reexperiencing symptoms. The items contained in this HIC consistently formed a coherent factor that eventually formed the basis for the four-item Traumatic Intrusions scale (e.g., *I had memories of something scary that happened; I had nightmares that reminded me of something bad that happened*).

Expanded Coverage in the IDAS-II

The IDAS Traumatic Intrusions scale has shown strong convergent, discriminant, and criterion validity in multiple samples; we will review this evidence shortly. Based on these encouraging results, we decided to expand our coverage of PTSD symptoms when developing the IDAS-II (Watson et al., 2012). Specifically, we created two new HICs related to avoidance (seven items; e.g., avoided situations that brought up bad memories) and numbing (seven items; e.g., felt cut off from others) symptoms.

We believed that the addition of these two new HICs would be sufficient to provide comprehensive coverage of the basic PTSD symptom dimensions subsumed within the various structural models discussed earlier. In this regard, the original IDAS already contained a Dysphoria scale (which primarily was designed to assess core symptoms of depression; see Chapter 3), which we assumed would capture the closely related content subsumed within the Dysphoria dimension in the Simms four-factor model. In a related vein, we argued that existing IDAS scales already provided adequate coverage of the hyperarousal/hypervigilance symptoms contained in the various structural models. Specifically, Watson et al. (2012) stated:

> We chose not to create an additional HIC related to hyperarousal because this content already is well-captured in the instrument. That is, DSM-IV criteria D1 (difficulty falling or staying asleep), D2 (irritability or outbursts of anger), and D3 (difficulty concentrating) reflect content contained in the Insomnia, Ill Temper, and Dysphoria scales, respectively; the two remaining DSM-IV arousal symptoms (hypervigilance, exaggerated startle response) are captured by content in the Panic scale. (p. 401)

In a later section, we will examine the validity of these arguments by evaluating the comprehensiveness of the PTSD symptom coverage in the IDAS-II.

Preliminary analyses of these newly written PTSD items revealed a significant problem: The numbing symptoms were very strongly related to the existing Dysphoria scale and failed to define a distinct dimension in our structural analyses. For example, a scale creating by summing the seven candidate numbing items correlated .84 and .83 with Dysphoria in student ($N = 307$) and community ($N = 355$) samples, respectively. Given that these items clearly were redundant with Dysphoria, this dimension was dropped from further consideration.

In contrast, the avoidance items consistently defined a distinct factor in our structural analyses. This robust factor formed the basis of the four-item Traumatic Avoidance scale (e.g., *I tried not to think about bad things from my past; I avoided situations that bring up bad memories*) that was included in the IDAS-II. Thus, the IDAS-II includes two explicit trauma-based scales: Traumatic Intrusions and Traumatic Avoidance.

PCL Analyses

Basic Relations With the PCL

To establish the convergent and discriminant validity of these trauma-based scales, we first examine their associations with self-ratings on the PTSD Checklist-Civilian Version (PCL; Weathers, Litz, Herman, Huska, & Keane, 1993). The PCL is a particularly informative measure for our purposes because it is closely based on the *DSM* symptom criteria for PTSD. The version used in these analyses contains 17 symptoms directly corresponding to the *DSM-IV* symptom criteria for PTSD. For example, *DSM-IV* criterion B1 ("recurrent and intrusive distressing recollections of the event, including images, thoughts, or perceptions") is represented by the PCL item "repeated disturbing *memories, thoughts, or images* of a stressful experience from the past") on the PCL. Similarly, the PCL item "feeling *distant* or *cut off* from other people" corresponds to PTSD criterion C5 ("feeling of detachment or estrangement from others") in *DSM-IV*.

Table 7.4 presents correlations between various PCL and IDAS-II scales in a standardized combined sample (overall $N = 1{,}431$). This aggregate sample contained 198 patients (these are drawn from Sample 6 in Table 2.14; note that these participants are used again in the Table 7.5 analyses), 353 community adults, and 880 college students (this total includes 219 participants from Sample 10, who also are used in the Table 7.5 analyses). As in previous chapters, to eliminate mean-level differences across populations, we standardized all the scale scores on a within-population basis and then combined them to permit a single overall analysis. Table 7.4 presents results for the six IDAS-II scales—Traumatic Intrusions, Traumatic Avoidance, Dysphoria, Panic, Insomnia, and Ill Temper—that we previously argued (Watson et al., 2012) jointly provide comprehensive coverage of PTSD symptoms. The table reports correlations between these scales and all of the basic symptom dimensions included in the Simms four-factor model, the King four-factor model, and the Elhai five-factor model. In addition, the final column of Table 7.4 displays multiple correlations that demonstrate the combined ability of these IDAS scales to predict each PTSD symptom dimension. Note that if the IDAS-II truly provides comprehensive coverage of PTSD symptoms, then all of these multiple correlations should be strong in magnitude.

The Table 7.4 data establish that three pairs of PCL/IDAS-II scales clearly assess the same basic constructs. First, IDAS-II Traumatic Intrusions was very

Table 7.4 Correlations Between PCL Scales and Selected IDAS-II Scales (Standardized Combined Sample)

PCL Scale	IDAS-II Scale Traum Intrus	Traum Avoid	Dysphor	Panic	Insom	Ill Temper	*R*
Intrusions	**.73**	.64	.56	.53	.44	.51	**.78**
Avoidance	.61	**.69**	.52	.43	.36	.44	**.73**
Dysphoria	.58	.50	**.77**	.60	.56	.62	**.81**
Numbing	.55	.49	**.72**	.55	.42	.54	**.74**
Hyperarousal	.54	.46	**.67**	.58	.60	.62	**.77**
Dysphoric Arousal	.48	.40	**.66**	.52	**.65**	.60	**.78**
Hypervigilance	.46	.39	.46	.47	.35	.46	.57

NOTE: $N = 1{,}431$. All correlations are significant at $p < .01$. Correlations ≥ .65 are in bold. PCL = PTSD Checklist. IDAS-II = Expanded Form of the Inventory of Depression and Anxiety Symptoms. Traum Intrus = Traumatic Intrusions. Traum Avoid = Traumatic Avoidance. Dysphor = Dysphoria. Insom = Insomnia.

strongly related ($r = .73$) to PCL Intrusions; moreover, this coefficient was significantly higher ($p < .01$, one-tailed) than any other correlation involving these scales. Similarly, the strong correlation between IDAS-II Traumatic Avoidance and PCL Avoidance ($r = .69$) was significantly higher than all other coefficients involving these two scales. Finally, IDAS-II Dysphoria correlated very strongly ($r = .77$) with the eight-item PCL scale assessing the Dysphoria dimension in the Simms four-factor model; these results confirm Watson et al.'s (2012) contention that an additional PTSD-specific dysphoria scale was not needed in the IDAS-II. It is noteworthy, moreover, that IDAS-II Dysphoria also correlated strongly with the PCL Numbing ($r = .72$), Hyperarousal ($r = .67$), and Dysphoric Arousal ($r = .66$) scales.

Do these IDAS-II scales jointly provide comprehensive assessment of PTSD symptoms? Table 7.4 indicates that six of the seven multiple *R*s were quite high, with values ranging from .73 (PCL Avoidance) to .81 (PCL Dysphoria); consequently, the IDAS-II scales jointly account for 53.8% to 66.3% of the variance in these six PTSD symptom dimensions. The single exception involved the two-item Hypervigilance dimension that is common to the Simms four-factor and Elhai five-factor models. Watson et al. (2012) argued that these arousal symptoms (hypervigilance, exaggerated startle response) would be well captured by content contained in the Panic scale. However, PCL Hypervigilance correlated only .47 with IDAS-II Panic in these data. Moreover, the multiple *R* was only .57, reflecting 32.0% shared variance. Although this represents a substantial level of overlap, it nevertheless suggests that it would be useful to consider developing a scale that specifically targets these hypervigilance symptoms in any subsequent expansion of the IDAS.

Relations With the PCL and IDAS-CR

Next, we report more intensive convergent and discriminant validity analyses involving PTSD symptoms of intrusions and avoidance, each of which was assessed by two self-report scales (IDAS-II, PCL), as well as by clinicians' ratings on the IDAS-CR (Koffel, 2011; Watson et al., 2012; Watson, O'Hara, Chmielewski et al., 2008). Table 7.5 reports correlations among these variables in the form of a multitrait-multimethod matrix. These results are reported separately for patients ($N=448$; this combines data from Samples 3 and 6) and students ($N=591$; this is an aggregate of Samples 9 and 10). These results were reported previously in Watson et al. (2012; see their Table 6).

These analyses provide strong evidence of convergent validity across these symptom dimensions. As would be expected, the convergence was particularly impressive between the self-rated IDAS-II and PCL scales, with an overall mean *r* of .73 across all analyses. Both sets of self-report scales also converged well with clinician ratings on the IDAS-CR, although the coefficients for the IDAS-II (mean $r=.60$) were slightly stronger overall than those for the PCL (mean $r=.56$). Finally, it is worth noting that the convergent correlations were substantial in both the patient (mean $r=.67$) and student (mean $r=.61$) data, and across measures of both intrusions (mean $r=.64$) and avoidance (mean $r=.64$).

As was discussed earlier, PTSD symptom dimensions contain a large component of general distress and tend to be strongly interrelated (Gootzeit & Markon, 2011; Watson, 2009a; Yufik & Simms, 2010). Consistent with this broader trend, the discriminant correlations were relatively high in these data, particularly

Table 7.5 Multitrait-Multimethod Matrix of IDAS-II, PCL, and IDAS-CR Measures of Intrusions and Avoidance

Measure	1	2	3	4	5	6
IDAS-II						
1. Intrusions	.—	.69	**.70**	.63	**.59**	.55
2. Avoidance	.73	.—	.60	**.68**	.48	**.59**
PCL						
3. Intrusions	**.76**	.72	.—	.80	**.51**	.53
4. Avoidance	.61	**.76**	.79	.—	.48	**.53**
IDAS-CR Ratings						
5. Intrusions	**.62**	.51	**.60**	.47	.—	.64
6. Avoidance	.54	**.61**	.59	**.60**	.61	.—

NOTE: Patient correlations ($N=448$) are presented below the diagonal; student correlations ($N=591$) are displayed above the diagonal. Convergent correlations are in bold. All correlations are significant at $p < .05$. IDAS-II = Expanded version of the Inventory of Depression and Anxiety Symptoms. PCL = PTSD Checklist. IDAS-CR = Clinician Rating version of the IDAS. Adapted from Watson et al. (2012), Table 6.

within the self-ratings (*r*s ranged from .60 to .80 across scales and samples); the discriminant correlations in the clinicians' ratings were somewhat lower but still were substantial ($r = .61$ and .64 in the patients and students, respectively). As in previous analyses, we conducted significance tests comparing each of the convergent correlations to the other values in its row or column of the heteromethod block. It is noteworthy that all 16 comparisons involving the IDAS-II Traumatic Intrusions and Traumatic Avoidance scales were statistically significant ($p < .05$, one-tailed). Thus, these IDAS-II scales show consistent evidence of discriminant validity in these data. In contrast, the discriminant validity of the PCL scales was more modest; overall, only 11 of the 16 comparisons involving these scales were significant ($p < .05$, one-tailed).

IMAS Analyses

Next, we report two series of convergent/discriminant validity analyses with the interview-based IMAS scales. If Traumatic Intrusions and Traumatic Avoidance are valid and specific indicators of PTSD, then they should correlate more strongly with the 25-item IMAS PTSD scale than with the other IMAS scales. Table 7.6 presents correlations with the IMAS scales in Samples 5 ($N = 362$ patients) and 11 ($N = 393$ students). These results provide evidence of excellent convergent validity: The IMAS PTSD scale correlated strongly with Traumatic Intrusions ($r = .61$ and .69 in patients and students, respectively; mean $r = .65$) and Traumatic Avoidance ($r = .59$ and .68, respectively; mean $r = .64$) in both samples.

Table 7.6 Correlations Between the IDAS-II PTSD Symptom Scales and the IMAS Scales

	Traumatic Intrusions		**Traumatic Avoidance**	
IMAS Scale	**Sample 5**	**Sample 11**	**Sample 5**	**Sample 11**
Posttraumatic Stress Disorder	**.61**	**.69**	**.59**	**.68**
Depression	**.54**	**.55**	**.54**	**.54**
Generalized Anxiety Disorder	**.53**	**.55**	.49	**.53**
Panic	**.50**	**.53**	.45	**.50**
Irritability	.38	.44	.39	.46
Agoraphobia	.34	.37	.41	.37
Mania	.32	.41	.30	.45
Social Phobia	.32	.37	.37	.37
Obsessive-Compulsive Disorder	.32	.30	.33	.29
Specific Phobia	.29	.25	.32	.30

NOTE: $N = 362$ patients (Sample 5), 393 students (Sample 11). Correlations $\geq .50$ are in bold. All correlations are significant at $p < .01$. IDAS-II = Expanded version of the Inventory of Depression and Anxiety Symptoms. PTSD = posttraumatic stress disorder. IMAS = Interview of Mood and Anxiety Symptoms.

Furthermore, the IDAS-II trauma scales showed impressive discriminant validity, as their correlations with the nine remaining IMAS scales consistently were lower. The mean discriminant correlations for Traumatic Intrusions were .40 and .42 in Samples 5 and 11, respectively; the corresponding values for Traumatic Avoidance were .40 and .43, respectively. Follow-up significance tests indicated that their convergent correlations with IMAS PTSD were significantly stronger ($p < .05$, one-tailed) than the discriminant coefficients in all 36 comparisons across the two samples (*z*s ranged from 1.85 to 9.77).

As was discussed in Chapter 3, the revised version of the IMAS contains content-based subscales within each target syndrome. Multiple PTSD subscales have been developed, including an eight-item measure of Intrusions and a six-item indicator of Avoidance. Table 7.7 presents correlations between these scales and the IDAS-II trauma scales in the form of a multitrait-multimethod matrix; results are presented separately in Samples 5 ($N = 378$) and 11 ($N = 401$). IDAS-II Traumatic Intrusions displayed a strong level of convergence with IMAS Intrusions in both Sample 5 ($r = .55$) and Sample 11 ($r = .63$), with a mean correlation of .59. Similarly, IDAS-II Traumatic Avoidance correlated substantially with IMAS Avoidance in both samples ($r = .49$ and .60, respectively; mean $r = .55$).

Once again, we conducted significance tests comparing each of the convergent correlations to the other values in its row or column of the heteromethod block. Overall, this yielded a total of eight comparisons (four comparisons per sample × two samples); all eight comparisons were statistically significant ($p < .05$, one-tailed). Thus, the IDAS-II trauma scales show consistent evidence of discriminant validity vis-à-vis the IMAS PTSD subscales in these data.

Table 7.7 MULTITRAIT-MULTIMETHOD MATRIX OF IDAS-II AND IMAS MEASURES OF INTRUSIONS AND AVOIDANCE IN SAMPLES 5 AND 11

Measure	**1**	**2**	**3**	**4**
IDAS-II Scales				
1. Traumatic Intrusions	.—	.61	**.63**	.38
2. Traumatic Avoidance	.59	.—	.48	**.60**
IMAS Scales				
3. Intrusions	**.55**	.41	.—	.47
4. Avoidance	.36	**.49**	.47	.—

NOTE: Sample 5 correlations ($N = 378$ patients) are presented below the diagonal; Sample 11 correlations ($N = 401$ students) are displayed above the diagonal. Convergent correlations are in bold. All correlations are significant at $p < .05$. IDAS-II = Expanded version of the Inventory of Depression and Anxiety Symptoms. IMAS = Interview of Mood and Anxiety Symptoms.

ITRI Scales

Development of the ITRI

Gootzeit, Markon, and Watson (2015) recently developed a new instrument—the Iowa Traumatic Response Inventory (ITRI)—that takes an innovative approach to the assessment of PTSD symptoms. Work on the ITRI was informed by the structural evidence described earlier; the target constructs included all of the major symptom dimensions within both the Simms and King four-factor models. The ITRI also was specifically designed to avoid the limitations associated with *DSM*-based measures (e.g., a *DSM*-based measure of avoidance is restricted to only two items).

The initial ITRI item pool consisted of 69 items; participants were asked to rate the extent to which they experienced each symptom during the past month on a 5-point scale, ranging from "not at all" to "extremely." Following the same logic that was used to create the IDAS and IDAS-II, these items were grouped into six rationally organized HICs: traumatic intrusions (10 items), avoidance (10 items), numbing (9 items), dysphoria (13 items), hyperarousal (14 items), and dissociation or detachment (13 items). This last group was included based on evidence indicating that peritraumatic dissociation—that is, dissociation experienced during a traumatic event—is a risk factor for the development of PTSD; moreover, peritraumatic dissociation is important in the diagnosis of acute stress disorder (American Psychiatric Association, 2000). Furthermore, some studies (Briere, Scott, & Weathers, 2005; Murray, Ehlers, & Mayou, 2002) suggest that persistent dissociation following a traumatic event is a stronger predictor of PTSD than peritraumatic dissociation. Items measuring dissociative symptoms therefore were included in the ITRI item pool.

This item pool was administered to a sample of 415 University of Iowa undergraduate students. Factor analyses of their responses indicated that the items from the dysphoria and numbing HICs defined a single common dimension; all of the other HICs formed a separate factor. Consequently, five scales were included in the final version of the ITRI: Intrusions (eight items; e.g., "I had nightmares about something bad in the past"), Avoidance (five items; e.g., "I avoided thinking about a bad experience"), Dysphoria (eight items; e.g., "I felt distant or cut off from other people"), Hyperarousal (eight items; e.g., "Unexpected noises made me jump"), and Dissociation (eight items; e.g., "I felt like I was in a daze").

Convergent and Discriminant Validity of the ITRI Scales

Gootzeit et al. (2015) report extensive data to establish the construct validity of the ITRI scales. Table 7.8 presents an adapted version of their Table 4, which examines convergent and discriminant validity in relation to the PCL scales (these were scored to represent the four dimensions in the Simms model); selected IDAS scales; and the Detachment (6 items; e.g., "Sometimes when I am looking in the mirror, I feel like I am seeing someone else"), Obliviousness (14 items; e.g., "I will sometimes walk into a room, and not remember why I went in there"), and Imagination (7 items; e.g., "If I want to, I can imagine some things so vividly

Table 7.8 Correlations Between the ITRI Scales and Other Self-Report Symptom Measures (Student Sample)

Symptom Scale	ITRI Scale Intrusions	Avoidance	Dysphoria	Hyperarousal	Dissociation
PCL Intrusions	**.85***	**.70**	.64	.62	.51
IDAS-II Intrusions	**.84***	.65	.60	.59	.51
PCL Avoidance	**.71**	**.72**	.52	.47	.39
IDAS-II Dysphoria	.65	.51	**.85***	.61	.60
PCL Dysphoria	**.70**	.54	**.82***	.65	.67
IDAS-II Panic	.58	.44	.50	**.81***	.57
PCL Hypervigilance	.57	.44	.52	.65*	.47
DPS Detachment	.44	.34	.45	.40	**.70***
DPS Obliviousness	.44	.35	.48	.47	.55
DPS Imagination	.37	.25	.36	.31	.45

NOTE: $N = 415$. Correlations ≥ .70 are in bold. ITRI = Iowa Traumatic Response Inventory. PCL = PTSD Checklist. IDAS-II = Expanded Version of the Inventory of Depression and Anxiety Symptoms. DPS = Dissociative Processes Scale. Adapted from Gootzeit et al. (2015), Table 4.
*Correlation is significantly higher ($p < .05$) than any other coefficient in its row.

that they hold my attention like a good movie or book does") subscales from the Dissociative Processes Scale (Harrison & Watson, 1992; see also Watson, 2001, 2003a). These correlations are based on the 415 students included in the original scale development sample.

The Table 7.8 data provide strong support for the convergent and discriminant validity of the ITRI Intrusions scale. This scale correlated very highly with both PCL Intrusions ($r = .85$) and IDAS-II Traumatic Intrusions ($r = .84$), and it had consistently lower correlations with the remaining scales (*r*s ranged from .37 to .71, mean $r = .57$). The ITRI Avoidance scale also displayed strong convergent validity in relation to PCL Avoidance ($r = .72$), but it had very similar associations with both indicators of intrusions ($r = .70$ with PCL intrusions, .65 with IDAS-II Traumatic Intrusions). Thus, it shows little specificity/discriminant validity in these data.

The three remaining ITRI scales (a) displayed very clear convergent/discriminant patterns that (b) strongly suggest that they should not be viewed as specific indicators of PTSD. Not surprisingly, ITRI Dysphoria correlated very strongly with both IDAS-II Dysphoria ($r = .85$) and PCL Dysphoria ($r = .82$), indicating that it assesses the same basic construct and is strongly saturated with general distress variance. Moreover, given the extensive evidence related to IDAS-II Dysphoria that is summarized in Chapter 3, these data suggest that these scales actually are better indicators of major depression than they are of PTSD; we will revisit this issue shortly. As expected, ITRI Hyperarousal was strongly related to PCL Hypervigilance ($r = .65$). However, it correlated even more strongly with IDAS-II Panic ($r = .81$), suggesting that it is better viewed as an indicator of panic disorder than of PTSD per se. Finally, it is noteworthy that ITRI Dissociation correlated strongly with DPS Detachment ($r = .70$), and only moderately with indicators of intrusions, avoidance, and hypervigilance (*r*s ranged from .39 to .51, mean $r = .47$). Thus, it appears to be a better marker of dissociation than of PTSD.

To explore the construct validity of the ITRI scales further, Table 7.9 reports similar data in a combined group of participants collapsed across Samples 3 ($N = 296$ patients) and 9 ($N = 373$ students; overall $N = 669$). Once again, we standardized all the scale scores on a within-population basis and then combined them to permit a single overall analysis. Similar to the results shown in Table 7.8, Table 7.9 presents correlations between the ITRI scales and (a) the PCL scales (once again, these are scored to model the four Simms factors) and (b) selected IDAS-II scales (which now include Traumatic Avoidance as an additional indicator of avoidance symptoms). In addition, these participants were assessed on two general measures of depression: the CES-D (Radloff, 1977; see Chapter 3) and the PHQ-9 (Kroenke et al., 2001; see Chapter 4). Finally, the assessment battery included two additional indicators of panic symptoms: the MASQ Anxious Arousal scale (see Chapter 1) and the Panic Attack Symptom Questionnaire (PASQ; see Chapter 4).

Table 7.9 Correlations Between the ITRI Scales and Other Self-Report Symptom Measures (Standardized Combined Sample)

	ITRI Scale				
Symptom Scale	**Intrusions**	**Avoidance**	**Dysphoria**	**Hyperarousal**	**Dissociation**
PCL Intrusions	**.85***	.77	.59	.58	.48
IDAS-II Intrusions	**.79***	.68	.56	.56	.41
PCL Avoidance	.75	**.83***	.56	.47	.44
IDAS-II Avoidance	.69	**.78***	.54	.45	.35
CES-D	.60	.56	**.86***	.56	.51
IDAS-II Dysphoria	.57	.52	**.83***	.56	.50
PCL Dysphoria	.63	.57	**.80***	.59	.62
PHQ-9	.55	.51	**.76***	.56	.51
MASQ Anxious Arousal	.54	.46	.54	**.79***	.48
PASQ	.56	.49	.64	**.77***	.55
PCL Hypervigilance	.53	.47	.54	.62*	.48

NOTE: $N = 669$. Correlations ≥ .70 are in bold. ITRI = Iowa Traumatic Response Inventory. PCL = PTSD Checklist. IDAS-II = Expanded Version of the Inventory of Depression and Anxiety Symptoms. CES-D = Center for Epidemiological Studies Depression Scale. PHQ-9 = Patient Health Questionnaire-9. MASQ = Mood and Anxiety Symptom Questionnaire. PASQ = Panic Attack Symptom Questionnaire.
*Correlation is significantly higher ($p < .05$) than any other coefficient in its row.

ITRI Intrusions again showed impressive convergent validity and reasonable discriminant validity in these data. It correlated very strongly with both PCL Intrusions ($r = .85$) and IDAS-II Traumatic Intrusions ($r = .79$); its discriminant coefficients tended to be substantially lower (*r*s ranged from .53 to .69, mean $r = .59$), except for its relatively high association with PCL Avoidance ($r = .75$). ITRI Avoidance displayed a very similar pattern in this sample: It correlated very strongly with PCL Avoidance ($r = .83$) and IDAS-II Traumatic Avoidance ($r = .78$) and had substantially lower discriminant coefficients (*r*s ranged from .46 to .68, mean $r = .54$), with the single exception of PCL Intrusions ($r = .77$). ITRI Dysphoria clearly emerged as an indicator of depression in these data: In addition to its strong links to both IDAS-II Dysphoria ($r = .83$) and PCL Dysphoria ($r = .80$), it correlated very highly with both the CES-D ($r = .86$) and the PHQ-9 ($r = .76$). Finally, replicating the Table 7.8 data, ITRI Hyperarousal again correlated more strongly with indicators of panic disorder ($r = .79$ with MASQ Anxious Arousal, $r = .77$ with the PASQ) than with PCL Hypervigilance ($r = .62$).

Summarizing their results, Gootzeit et al. (2015) concluded that "the evidence suggested that intrusions and avoidance symptoms are relatively specific to PTSD, whereas dysphoria, dissociation, and hyperarousal are not" (p. 162). Our more limited examination of the relevant data yields the same basic conclusion. The ITRI Intrusions and Avoidance scales both demonstrate strong convergent validity and adequate discriminant validity and show clear specificity to PTSD. In contrast, the ITRI Dysphoria, Hyperarousal, and Dissociation scales are better viewed as indicators of depression, panic disorder, and dissociation, respectively. These results should be kept in mind when we report subsequent analyses involving these ITRI scales.

CRITERION VALIDITY OF PTSD SYMPTOM SCALES

IDAS-II Trauma Scales

Traumatic Intrusions

We now examine the criterion validity and diagnostic specificity of PTSD symptom scales. We begin by evaluating the IDAS-II trauma scales, for which we have the largest amount of data. The top portion of Table 7.10 presents polyserial correlations between the IDAS-II Traumatic Intrusions scale and nine *DSM* emotional disorder diagnoses (PTSD, major depression, GAD, panic disorder, agoraphobia, social phobia, specific phobia, OCD, current manic episodes) in Samples 1 through 5 (combined $N = 1{,}553$). Traumatic Intrusions consistently displayed impressive criterion validity in these analyses. It had polyserial correlations ranging from .45 to .61 with PTSD diagnoses across the five samples, with an overall weighted mean coefficient of .58.

Traumatic Intrusions also shows strong diagnostic specificity in these data. Its weighted mean correlations with the eight other diagnoses range from only .20

(current manic episodes) to .42 (major depression); moreover, only 4 of the 34 individual discriminant correlations (11.8%) were ≥ .45 across the five samples. Thus, self-rated intrusions and reexperiencing symptoms—as assessed by the IDAS-II—are strongly and specifically related to diagnoses of PTSD.

Traumatic Avoidance

The lower portion of Table 7.10 presents parallel findings for the IDAS-II Traumatic Avoidance scale in Samples 3 through 5 (combined $N = 949$). Traumatic Avoidance yielded results that generally were very similar to Traumatic Intrusions in these data. It also showed a high level of criterion validity: Its correlations with PTSD diagnoses ranged from .47 to .60 across samples, with a weighted mean value of .55. In addition, it displayed impressive diagnostic specificity. Its associations with the eight other diagnoses consistently were substantially lower, with overall mean correlations ranging from only .25 (current manic episodes) to .40 (major depression). Furthermore, only 2 of the 20 individual discriminant correlations (10.0%) were ≥ .45 across the three samples. Accordingly, self-rated avoidance symptoms—as assessed by the IDAS-II—also are strongly and specifically related to PTSD diagnoses in these samples.

Table 7.10 Polyserial Correlations Between IDAS-II PTSD Symptom Scales and *DSM* Emotional Disorder Diagnoses

Scale/Sample	PTSD	MDD	GAD	Panic	Agora	Social Phobia	Specific Phobia	OCD	Manic
IDAS-II Traumatic Intrusions									
Sample 1	**.61**	.42	.35	.44	.30	.19	.18	.15	.—
Sample 2	**.60**	.36	.35	**.45**	.37	.31	.32	.33	.—
Sample 3	**.69**	.30	.24	.42	.—	.14	.—	.14	.—
Sample 4	**.55**	**.52**	**.46**	.41	.44	.39	.—	**.51**	.35
Sample 5	**.45**	.42	.20	.30	.17	.08	.23	.04	−.02
Weighted *M*	**.58**	.42	.34	.41	.33	.24	.24	.26	.20
IDAS-II Traumatic Avoidance									
Sample 3	**.60**	.33	.26	.43	.—	.23	.—	.22	.—
Sample 4	**.56**	**.45**	.39	.33	.35	.28	.—	**.48**	.31
Sample 5	**.47**	.38	.12	.35	.27	.21	.34	.14	.16
Weighted *M*	**.55**	.40	.28	.36	.32	.25	.34	.32	.25

NOTE: $N = 337$ (Sample 1), 267 (Sample 2), 252 (Sample 3), 407 (Sample 4), 290 (Sample 5). Correlations ≥ .45 are in bold. IDAS-II Expanded Version of the Inventory of Depression and Anxiety Symptoms. PTSD = posttraumatic stress disorder. MDD = major depressive disorder. GAD = generalized anxiety disorder. Agora = agoraphobia. OCD = obsessive-compulsive disorder. Manic = current manic episode.

Interview Measures of Intrusions and Avoidance

The data presented in Table 7.10 establish that self-rated intrusions and avoidance symptoms show strong specificity to PTSD diagnoses. It is important to examine whether these findings generalize to interview-based measures of these symptoms. Consequently, Table 7.11 reports parallel findings based on the intrusions and avoidance scores from the IDAS-CR (Samples 1 through 3) and the IMAS (Sample 5). These results yield the same basic pattern as was seen with the self-report scales, thereby further demonstrating the criterion validity and diagnostic specificity of these symptoms. IDAS-CR Traumatic Intrusions had polyserial correlations ranging from .45 to .56 across three samples (overall $N=859$), with a weighted mean value of .51. Moreover, its discriminant correlations with the other diagnoses consistently were lower, with overall mean values ranging from only .15 (social phobia) to .38 (panic disorder). Similarly, IDAS-CR Traumatic Avoidance correlated much more strongly with PTSD diagnoses in Sample 3 ($r=.53$) than with any other disorder (values ranged from .12 to .33). Finally, IMAS Intrusions and Avoidance had substantially stronger associations with PTSD diagnoses (both $rs=.42$) than with all other disorders (rs ranged from only .08 to .29) in Sample 5 ($N=302$).

One other aspect of these data is worth noting. Although the IDAS-CR and IMAS scales displayed moderate to strong criterion validity in these data, these correlations tended to be somewhat lower than the corresponding values in Table 7.10. Thus, IDAS-II Traumatic Intrusions correlated more strongly with PTSD diagnoses than did IDAS-CR Traumatic Intrusions in Samples 1 (.61 vs. .45), 2 (.60 vs. .56), and 3 (.69 vs. .54); moreover, it correlated more highly with

Table 7.11 Polyserial Correlations Between Interview-Based Measures of Intrusions and Avoidance and *DSM* Emotional Disorder Diagnoses

Scale/Sample	PTSD	MDD	GAD	Panic	Agora	Social Phobia	Specific Phobia	OCD	Manic
IDAS-CR Traumatic Intrusions									
Sample 1	**.45**	.25	.25	.38	.25	.13	.22	.09	.—
Sample 2	**.56**	.31	.30	.44	.26	.20	.09	.43	.—
Sample 3	**.54**	.31	.19	.30	.—	.11	.—	.26	.—
Weighted *M*	**.51**	.29	.25	.38	.25	.15	.16	.25	.—
IDAS-CR Traumatic Avoidance									
Sample 3	**.53**	.25	.22	.33	.—	.16	.—	.12	.—
IMAS Intrusions									
Sample 5	.42	.29	.27	.26	.11	.07	.28	.19	.24
IMAS Avoidance									
Sample 5	.42	.19	.23	.08	.10	.10	.20	.15	.21

NOTE: $N=339$ (Sample 1), 268 (Sample 2), 252 (Sample 3), 302 (Sample 5). Correlations ≥ .45 are in bold. IDAS-CR = Clinician Rating version of the IDAS. IMAS = Interview of Mood and Anxiety Symptoms. PTSD = posttraumatic stress disorder. MDD = major depressive disorder. GAD = generalized anxiety disorder. Agora = agoraphobia. OCD = obsessive-compulsive disorder. Manic = current manic episode.

PTSD diagnoses in Sample 5 ($r = .45$) than did IMAS Intrusions ($r = .42$). Similarly, IDAS-II Traumatic Avoidance correlated more highly with PTSD diagnoses in Sample 3 ($r = .60$) than did IDAS-CR Traumatic Avoidance ($r = .53$), and it related more strongly to PTSD in Sample 5 ($r = .47$) than did IMAS Avoidance ($r = .42$). These results are somewhat surprising, as they indicate that heteromethod correlations (i.e., self-rated symptoms vs. interview-based diagnoses) actually were stronger in magnitude than their monomethod counterparts (i.e., interview-based symptoms vs. interview-based diagnoses). These findings therefore provide particularly strong evidence for the validity of these self-rated IDAS-II symptoms.

Comparative Analyses of the IDAS-II and PCL

As we have seen, the IDAS-II trauma scales consistently show somewhat stronger criterion correlations than interview-based measures of the same symptoms. How do they compare to other self-report scales? We can examine this issue in Sample 4 ($N = 406$); these participants completed both the IDAS-II and the seven Intrusions and Avoidance items from the PCL. Table 7.12 presents correlations between these self-report scores and six *DSM-5* diagnoses: PTSD, major depression, GAD, panic disorder, social phobia, and OCD. In addition to the individual scales, Table 7.12 reports results for total PTSD scores that were created by combining the intrusions and avoidance items from the same instrument.

Two aspects of these data are noteworthy. First, the IDAS-II scales consistently display somewhat stronger criterion correlations than their PCL counterparts. Thus, the IDAS-II PTSD total score correlated more highly with PTSD diagnoses ($r = .63$) than did the PCL total score ($r = .50$); IDAS-II Traumatic Intrusions displayed stronger criterion validity ($r = .56$) than did PCL Intrusions ($r = .49$); and IDAS-II Traumatic Avoidance had a stronger association with PTSD diagnoses ($r = .56$) than did PCL Avoidance ($r = .45$) in this sample.

Table 7.12 Polyserial Correlations Between PTSD Symptom Measures and *DSM-5* Diagnoses (Sample 4)

Symptom Measure	PTSD	MDD	GAD	Panic	Social Phobia	OCD
IDAS-II						
PTSD Total Score	**.63**	**.55**	.48	.41	.35	**.54**
Traumatic Intrusions	**.56**	**.53**	.47	.41	.38	**.50**
Traumatic Avoidance	**.56**	.45	.40	.33	.26	.47
PCL						
Total Score	**.50**	**.57**	**.50**	.38	.34	.47
Intrusions	.49	**.58**	.48	.36	.33	.45
Avoidance	.45	.49	.48	.36	.31	.44

NOTE: $N = 406$. Correlations ≥ .50 are in bold. PTSD = posttraumatic stress disorder. MDD = major depressive disorder. GAD = generalized anxiety disorder. OCD = obsessive-compulsive disorder. IDAS-II = Expanded Version of the Inventory of Depression and Anxiety Symptoms. PCL = PTSD Checklist.

Second, the PCL scales tended to show slightly poorer diagnostic specificity in these data. For example, PCL Intrusions and Avoidance had somewhat stronger correlations with diagnoses of major depression (r = .58 and .49, respectively) and GAD (r = .48 and .48, respectively) than did their IDAS-II counterparts (for major depression, r = .53 and .45, respectively; for GAD, r = .47 and .40, respectively). Overall, the IDAS-II trauma scales generally showed better criterion validity and superior diagnostic specificity than their PCL counterparts in this sample.

Comparative Analyses Across Multiple Measures

The Sample 3 data provide a much broader and more comprehensive analysis of the criterion validity and specificity of PTSD symptoms, including indicators of dysphoria/numbing and hyperarousal/hypervigilance. The participants in this sample (N = 245) completed three self-report measures of PTSD symptoms (IDAS-II, ITRI, PCL), as well as the interview-based IDAS-CR. Table 7.13 presents polyserial correlations between all of these measures—including both individual symptom scales and overall PTSD scores computed within each instrument—and six *DSM-IV* diagnoses: PTSD, major depression, GAD, panic disorder, social phobia, and OCD. Before considering specific types of symptoms, it is worth noting that the IDAS-II scales tended to display the strongest criterion validity and the clearest diagnostic specificity in these data. For instance, the IDAS-II PTSD Total score (r = .68) and Traumatic Intrusions (r = .66) had the two highest criterion coefficients in the sample. Furthermore, the discriminant correlations were consistently low for all three IDAS-II scales, ranging from only .14 (Traumatic Intrusions with social phobia) to .43 (PTSD Total score with panic disorder).

With regard to individual symptoms, indicators of intrusions/reexperiencing tended to show the highest level of criterion validity and the best diagnostic specificity. The intrusions scales from the four instruments had criterion correlations ranging from .51 (IDAS-CR) to .66 (IDAS-II), with a mean value of .61. The discriminant correlations consistently were much lower, ranging from only .13 (IDAS-CR Avoidance with social phobia) to .43 (ITRI Avoidance with panic disorder), with an overall mean value of .27.

Avoidance symptoms also tended to show good criterion validity and diagnostic specificity in these data. Across the four instruments, the criterion correlations ranged from .50 (IDAS-CR) to .58 (ITRI), with a mean coefficient of .55. Again, the discriminant correlations consistently were considerably lower, ranging from .13 (IDAS-CR Avoidance with OCD) to .40 (IDAS-II Traumatic Avoidance with panic disorder), with an overall mean value of .27.

In contrast, the hyperarousal/hypervigilance measures generally showed moderate criterion validity but poor diagnostic specificity. ITRI Hyperarousal correlated .40 with PTSD diagnoses, but it had an even stronger association (r = .51) with panic disorder. Similarly, all three PCL arousal scales showed poor diagnostic specificity: The five-item Hyperarousal scale (based on the King model) had a stronger association with major depression (r = .54) than with PTSD (r = .51);

Table 7.13 Polyserial Correlations Between PTSD Symptom Measures and *DSM-IV* Diagnoses (Sample 3)

Symptom Measure	PTSD	MDD	GAD	Panic	Social Phobia	OCD
IDAS-II						
PTSD Total Score	**.68**	.33	.29	.43	.20	.22
Traumatic Intrusions	**.66**	.30	.26	.39	.14	.16
Traumatic Avoidance	**.57**	.32	.27	.40	.22	.23
ITRI						
Total Score	**.61**	**.54**	.38	.47	.31	.37
Intrusions	**.64**	.35	.26	.38	.19	.31
Avoidance	**.58**	.37	.21	.35	.21	.31
Dysphoria	.48	**.68**	.47	.34	.39	.38
Hyperarousal	.40	.35	.28	**.51**	.22	.32
Dissociation	.27	.40	.30	.30	.22	.13
PCL						
Total Score	**.61**	**.55**	.37	.48	.32	.37
Intrusions	**.61**	.31	.24	.43	.21	.33
Avoidance	**.53**	.35	.22	.38	.25	.30
Dysphoria	.47	**.65**	.39	.38	.36	.32
Hypervigilance	.44	.33	.29	.44	.20	.30
Numbing	.44	**.59**	.32	.35	.31	.24
Hyperarousal	**.51**	**.54**	.42	.45	.32	.41
Dysphoric Arousal	.39	**.57**	.41	.33	.33	.37
IDAS-CR						
PTSD Total Score	**.57**	.46	.33	.35	.19	.30
Intrusions	**.51**	.31	.19	.28	.13	.27
Avoidance	**.50**	.25	.22	.30	.15	.13
Dysphoria	.19	**.70**	.40	.22	.20	.28
Hyperarousal	**.51**	.20	.20	.27	.10	.27

NOTE: $N = 245$. Correlations ≥ .50 are in bold. PTSD = posttraumatic stress disorder. MDD = major depressive disorder. GAD = generalized anxiety disorder. OCD = obsessive-compulsive disorder. IDAS-II Expanded Version of the Inventory of Depression and Anxiety Symptoms. ITRI = Iowa Traumatic Response Inventory. PCL = PTSD Checklist. IDAS-CR = Clinician Rating version of the IDAS.

the three-item Dysphoric Arousal scale (based on the Elhai model) correlated much more strongly with major depression ($r = .57$) than with any other diagnosis (rs ranged from .33 to .41, mean $r = .37$); and the two-item Hypervigilance scale (based on the Simms model) had equally strong relations with panic disorder and PTSD (both rs = .44). Only IDAS-CR Hyperarousal showed good specificity in these data: Its criterion coefficient with PTSD ($r = .51$) was substantially higher than any other correlation (rs ranged from .10 to .27, mean $r = .21$).

The data for the dysphoria/numbing scales are even more striking. As would be expected based on the findings discussed in Chapter 3, these symptoms actually displayed diagnostic specificity to major depression, rather than to PTSD. That is, ITRI Dysphoria, PCL Dysphoria, PCL Numbing, and IDAS-CR Dysphoria all correlated strongly with diagnoses of major depression, with coefficients ranging from .59 (PCL Numbing) to .70 (IDAS-CR Dysphoria), and a mean value of .66. In contrast, their associations with the other five disorders consistently were much lower, ranging from .19 (IDAS-CR with PTSD) to .48 (ITRI Dysphoria with PTSD), with an overall mean value of .35. Their mean correlation with PTSD diagnoses was only .40, which clearly establishes that they are neither strong nor specific indicators of this disorder.

Finally, the ITRI Dissociation scale was weakly and nonspecifically associated with PTSD. In fact, it actually correlated more strongly with diagnoses of major depression ($r=.40$), GAD ($r=.30$), and panic disorder ($r=.30$) than with PTSD ($r=.27$). Taken together with the evidence reviewed earlier, our data indicate that this scale is better viewed as an indicator of dissociation, rather than PTSD.

Incremental Predictive Power of PTSD Symptom Dimensions

Total Score Comparisons

The data presented in Table 7.13 indicate that some PTSD symptom dimensions show better psychometric properties than others. Specifically, symptoms related to intrusions/reexperiencing and avoidance display stronger criterion validity and better diagnostic specificity than do indicators of dysphoria/numbing and hyperarousal/hypervigilance.

Furthermore, a close inspection of Table 7.13 raises an important question: Are these poorly functioning symptoms actually needed at all? Consider, for example, the findings for the PCL, an instrument that closely mirrors the *DSM* symptom criteria for PTSD. Table 7.13 indicates that the PCL Total Score had a polyserial correlation of .61 with PTSD diagnoses in Sample 3. It is noteworthy that the PCL Intrusions scale—which includes only 5 of its 17 items—also correlated .61 with PTSD diagnoses in this sample. In other words, the inclusion of the 12 remaining PCL items failed to increase the criterion correlation with PTSD diagnoses at all. In fact, the only real effect of including these other symptoms was to worsen diagnostic specificity by increasing associations with other disorders (e.g., the correlation with major depression increased from .31 to .55). Along these same lines, the ITRI Intrusions scale actually had a stronger criterion correlation (.64) than the ITRI Total Score ($r=.61$), while demonstrating much better diagnostic specificity.

These findings suggest that the information provided by the more poorly functioning items is completely redundant with that provided by the better functioning symptoms. Moreover, they strongly suggest that we can improve the criterion validity of measures such as the PCL and ITRI by dropping the poorly functioning items and focusing exclusively on the intrusions and avoidance symptoms.

We tested this issue by creating modified ITRI, PCL, and IDAS-CR total scores that included only the intrusions and avoidance items from these measures and that eliminated all others. Table 7.14 reports polyserial correlations between the six *DSM* diagnoses and both the original and modified total scores for these three

Table 7.14 Polyserial Correlations Between Alternative Versions of the PTSD Symptom Measures and *DSM-IV* Diagnoses (Sample 3)

Symptom Measure	PTSD	MDD	GAD	Panic	Social Phobia	OCD
IDAS-II						
PTSD Total Score	**.68**	.33	.29	.43	.20	.22
ITRI						
Total Score	**.61**	**.54**	.38	.47	.31	.37
Intrusions/Avoidance Only	**.64**	.37	.24	.38	.21	.33
PCL						
Total Score	**.61**	**.55**	.37	.48	.32	.37
Intrusions/Avoidance Only	**.62**	.34	.25	.44	.24	.34
IDAS-CR						
PTSD Total Score	**.57**	.46	.33	.35	.19	.30
Intrusions/Avoidance Only	**.55**	.31	.23	.31	.15	.22

NOTE: $N = 245$. Correlations ≥ .50 are in bold. PTSD = posttraumatic stress disorder. MDD = major depressive disorder. GAD = generalized anxiety disorder. OCD = obsessive-compulsive disorder. IDAS-II = Expanded Version of the Inventory of Depression and Anxiety Symptoms. ITRI = Iowa Traumatic Response Inventory. PCL = PTSD Checklist. IDAS-CR = Clinician Rating version of the IDAS.

instruments; the table also includes the IDAS-II Total score (which only contains intrusions and avoidance items) for comparison purposes. Generally speaking, the modified total scores demonstrate better validity and diagnostic specificity than the original versions. For both the ITRI and PCL, the modified total score actually produced stronger criterion validity ($r = .64$ and .62, respectively) than the original versions ($r = .61$ and .61, respectively), while exhibiting far better diagnostic specificity. The modified total score for the IDAS-CR also showed better diagnostic specificity than the original version (e.g., the correlation with major depression was reduced from .46 to .31), but its criterion correlation was slightly lower (.55 vs. .57 for the original version).

Logistic Regressions

Logistic regression analyses provide another way to test the incremental predictive power of specific types of PTSD symptoms. We conducted a series of six logistic regression analyses in which various symptom scales were used to predict PTSD diagnoses. In the first analysis, the two IDAS-II trauma scales were used as predictors. The second analysis included the five individual ITRI scales as predictors. The next three analyses used different combinations of PCL scales as predictors, based on the scoring specified in the King, Simms, and Elhai models. The final analysis involved the four IDAS-CR scales. In all of these analyses, the symptom scores were standardized to put them on the same metric.

Intrusions were the only significant predictors of PTSD diagnoses in the IDAS-II, PCL, and ITRI analyses, with odds ratios (ORs) ranging from 2.84

(PCL Elhai analysis) to 3.94 (IDAS-II analysis). In addition, the contribution of Traumatic Avoidance approached significance (OR = 1.68, $p = .0836$) in the IDAS-II analysis. In contrast, Hyperarousal emerged as the only significant predictor (OR = 1.99) in the IDAS-CR analysis; Avoidance also showed a marginal effect in these data (OR = 1.73, $p = .0503$).

Thus, intrusions generally showed the strongest incremental predictive power in these analyses. Hyperarousal and avoidance symptoms also displayed more limited incremental validity in these data. Finally, it is noteworthy that dysphoria/numbing symptoms failed to add significantly in any analysis, which indicates that the information provided by these symptoms is redundant and unnecessary.

Additional IDAS-II Analyses

These results are intriguing, but they are limited to a single sample. It obviously is important to test the generalizability of these findings by attempting to replicate them in other groups of respondents. We can test the robustness of some aspects of these results by conducting additional analyses in the three samples (Samples 3 through 5) in which participants were assessed using the IDAS-II. As was established earlier, the IDAS-II Dysphoria scale is very strongly related to the Dysphoria scales in the PCL and ITRI, with correlations ranging from .77 to .85 (see Tables 7.4, 7.8, and 7.9). Accordingly, this scale can be used to model the dysphoria symptoms included in most self-report PTSD inventories.

We therefore conducted two series of analyses examining relations between PTSD diagnoses and three IDAS-II scales: Traumatic Intrusions, Traumatic Avoidance, and Dysphoria. The first series of analyses addressed the same issue as the data presented in Table 7.14. That is, it examined whether adding in the Dysphoria scale improved the criterion validity of the IDAS-II PTSD total score. Specifically, we compared two alternative sets of PTSD total scores: One score included all three IDAS-II scales, whereas the other version was based only on the two trauma scales (i.e., Traumatic Intrusions and Traumatic Avoidance).

Table 7.15 presents polyserial correlations between PTSD diagnoses and these two sets of PTSD total scores in Samples 3 through 5. The total score based only

Table 7.15 Polyserial Correlations Between Alternative Versions of the IDAS-II PTSD Total Score and PTSD Diagnoses

Sample	***N***	**Trauma Scales Only**	**Including Dysphoria**
Sample 3	252	.71	.73
Sample 4	412	.64	.60
Sample 5	290	.51	.46
Weighted Mean	**954**	**.62**	**.59**

NOTE: See text for details regarding computation of the total scores. IDAS-II = Expanded Version of the Inventory of Depression and Anxiety Symptoms.

Table 7.16 Odds Ratios From Logistic Regression Analyses Predicting PTSD Diagnoses From Selected IDAS-II Scales

Scale	Sample 3	Sample 4	Sample 5
Traumatic Intrusions	**3.57**	**2.49**	**1.81**
Traumatic Avoidance	1.44	**2.13**	**1.91**
Dysphoria	1.79	1.03	0.86

NOTE: $N = 252$ (Sample 3), 412 (Sample 4), 290 (Sample 5). Significant effects ($p < .05$) are in bold. IDAS-II = Expanded Version of the Inventory of Depression and Anxiety Symptoms.

on the two trauma scales showed moderate to strong criterion validity: Its correlations with PTSD diagnoses ranged from .51 to .71 across samples, with an overall weighted mean value of .62. Adding in the Dysphoria scale slightly improved criterion validity in Sample 3 (raising the r from .71 to .73), but actually lowered it in the other two samples. Overall, its weighted mean correlation (.59) was slightly lower than the corresponding value based only on the two trauma scales. Thus, replicating previous results, we see very little evidence that adding in dysphoria items improves the criterion validity of PTSD symptom measures.

In the second series of analyses, we conducted logistic regressions in which the three IDAS-II scales were used to predict PTSD diagnoses in each sample. The ORs from these analyses are presented in Table 7.16. Consistent with previous results, Traumatic Intrusions demonstrated significant incremental predictive power in all three samples, with ORs ranging from 1.81 to 3.57 (all $ps < .05$). Traumatic Avoidance also contributed significantly in Samples 4 (OR = 2.13) and 5 (OR = 1.91), but not Sample 3 (OR = 1.44). Finally, Dysphoria failed to add significantly in any sample, although the effect in Sample 3 approached significance (OR = 1.79, $p = .0603$).

IMAS Analyses in Sample 5

As noted earlier, the revised version of the IMAS contains multiple content-based subscales within PTSD. We already have presented data on the Intrusions and Avoidance subscales. In addition, the IMAS now includes a 6-item measure of Numbing and a 12-item indicator of Hyperarousal. Consequently, the IMAS provides another opportunity to examine the criterion and incremental validity of various types of PTSD symptoms.

Table 7.17 reports polyserial correlations between the IMAS PTSD subscales and nine *DSM-IV* diagnoses (PTSD, major depression, GAD, panic disorder, agoraphobia, social phobia, specific phobia, OCD, current manic episodes) in Sample 5. As was noted earlier (see Table 7.10 and the accompanying discussion), IMAS Intrusions ($r = .42$) and Avoidance ($r = .42$) both show good criterion validity in these data. They also exhibit strong diagnostic specificity. The

Table 7.17 Polyserial Correlations Between the IMAS PTSD Symptom Scales and *DSM-IV* Diagnoses (Sample 5)

Diagnosis	Intrusions	Avoidance	Numbing	Hyperarousal
PTSD	**.42**	**.42**	.29	**.43**
Major Depression	.29	.19	**.31**	**.34**
GAD	.27	.23	.20	**.31**
Panic Disorder	.26	.08	.08	**.35**
Agoraphobia	.11	.10	.17	**.32**
Social Phobia	.07	.10	.14	.19
Specific Phobia	.28	.20	.08	**.32**
OCD	.19	.15	.17	.12
Manic Episodes	.24	.21	.10	.19

NOTE: $N = 302$. Correlations ≥ .30 are in bold. IMAS = Interview of Mood and Anxiety Symptoms. PTSD = posttraumatic stress disorder. GAD = generalized anxiety disorder. OCD = obsessive-compulsive disorder.

discriminant correlations for IMAS Intrusions ranged from .07 (social phobia) to .29 (major depression), with a mean coefficient of .21; the corresponding values for IMAS Avoidance ranged from .08 (panic disorder) to .23 (GAD), with a mean correlation of .16. IMAS Hyperarousal behaved very similarly in this sample, showing good criterion validity ($r = .43$) and adequate diagnostic specificity (its discriminant correlations ranged from .12 to .35, with a mean coefficient of .27). In contrast—but replicating previous results—IMAS Numbing showed relatively weak criterion validity and poor diagnostic specificity in these data; in fact, it actually correlated more strongly with major depression ($r = .31$) than with PTSD ($r = .29$).

Next, we tested the incremental predictive power of these subscales by using them to predict PTSD diagnoses in a logistic regression analysis. Avoidance (OR = 1.68, $p < .05$) and Hyperarousal (OR = 1.67, $p < .01$) both contributed significantly in this analysis; in addition, the effect for Intrusions (OR = 1.57, $p = .064$) approached significance. Finally, Numbing failed to show significant incremental power in this analysis (OR = 1.20, n.s.).

SUMMARY

The PTSD diagnosis within the *DSM* contains an unusually detailed set of symptoms. This, in turn, has created intense interest in the structure defined by these symptoms. The extensive structural evidence in this area has led to the identification of several distinct symptom dimensions within PTSD, such as intrusions/reexperiencing, avoidance, dysphoria/numbing, and hyperarousal/hypervigilance.

Our results strongly demonstrate the value of analyzing these different types of symptoms separately. As we have seen, indicators of intrusions/reexperiencing tended to show the strongest overall criterion validity and impressive diagnostic specificity; they also displayed significant incremental predictive power in most logistic regression analyses. Avoidance symptoms generally behaved similarly and also appear to have a relatively strong and specific association with PTSD diagnoses. The data for hyperarousal symptoms were more mixed: They tended to exhibit moderate to strong criterion validity, with inconsistent evidence of diagnostic specificity and incremental validity. Finally, the data related to the dysphoria/numbing dimension were quite striking: Although these symptoms displayed some criterion validity, they actually showed diagnostic specificity to major depression—not PTSD—and demonstrated virtually no incremental predictive power in the logistic regression analyses. Thus, these symptoms were neither specific to PTSD nor necessary in predicting the diagnosis.

Taken together, our findings suggest that the PTSD diagnosis could be improved by simplifying it to focus more clearly on specific types of symptoms, such as intrusions and avoidance. In particular, our data indicate that we can enhance the diagnosis of PTSD by dropping most indicators of dysphoria and numbing, which could be eliminated with little or no loss of information. This issue merits greater attention in future research.

8

Anxiety Symptoms

In this chapter, we examine symptoms related to the *DSM-5* anxiety disorders, which include panic disorder, agoraphobia, social anxiety disorder/social phobia, specific phobia, and generalized anxiety disorder (GAD). As in several previous chapters, we will use the relevant IDAS-II scales as a basic organizing framework but also will present data from several other instruments.

As was discussed in Chapter 2, the IDAS-II contains three specific scales—Social Anxiety, Panic, and Claustrophobia—that directly target *DSM-5* anxiety disorder symptoms. We begin our examination of this topic by briefly reviewing the development of the IDAS-II anxiety scales; as part of this review, we also will discuss several additional symptom dimensions that were considered for inclusion in the IDAS-II but eventually were dropped for one reason or another. This discussion of the scale development process will help to clarify the nature and structure of symptoms within this area of psychopathology. We then present a series of analyses examining the convergent and discriminant validity of these scales in relation to self-report and interview-based measures from other instruments. Finally, we evaluate the criterion validity and diagnostic specificity of anxiety symptom scales from several different instruments.

DEVELOPMENT OF THE IDAS-II ANXIETY SCALES

Social Anxiety

Initial Five-Item Version

The original IDAS item pool contained a 10-item HIC targeting various aspects of social anxiety. These items provided the core indicators of a readily interpretable factor that consistently emerged in both Phase 1 and Phase 2 of the scale development process (Watson et al., 2007; see also Chapter 2). Items that were robust markers of this factor were included in the initial five-item version of the IDAS Social Anxiety scale. Four of these items (*I felt self-conscious knowing that others were watching me; I was worried about embarrassing myself socially; I found it difficult to make eye contact with people; I found it difficult to talk with people I did not know well*) were drawn from the original social anxiety HIC; the fifth item (*I became anxious in a crowded public setting*) was taken from the agoraphobia HIC, which failed to define a distinct dimension in the Phase 1 analyses. We will report extensive data on this initial version of the Social Anxiety scale.

Revised Six-Item Scale

Several studies have provided evidence for two distinguishable dimensions within social phobia: (1) a social interaction factor centered around fears related directly to interacting with others (e.g., initiating a conversation, making eye contact) and (2) a performance/scrutiny factor that focuses on fears of being watched by others, as well as engaging in activities (such as public speaking, writing, and eating) that would not be stressful if performed in private (Habke, Hewitt, Norton, & Asmundson, 1997; Hughes et al., 2006; LeBeau et al., 2010; Safren, Turk, & Heimberg, 1998). Moreover, these dimensions have shown distinctive correlates in several studies (e.g., Habke et al., 1997; Hughes et al., 2006; LeBeau et al., 2010). In light of this evidence, we created two separate HICs tapping interaction anxiety (e.g., *I worried that I might say the wrong thing*) and performance fears (e.g., *I felt uncomfortable eating or drinking in front of other people*) for inclusion in the IDAS-II item pool.

Unfortunately, as was discussed in Chapter 2, these new social interaction and performance/evaluation anxiety items were strongly correlated with both (a) each other and (b) the original IDAS Social Anxiety scale. We therefore abandoned the idea of creating separate social interaction and performance anxiety scales. However, we added one of these newly written items (*I was anxious about talking in public*) to Social Anxiety, thereby creating an expanded, six-item version of the scale in the IDAS-II. We also report considerable data on this revised version of Social Anxiety.

Panic

The original IDAS item pool included a HIC consisting of 10 items assessing somatic symptoms of anxious arousal (e.g., *I felt dizzy or lightheaded; I was trembling or shaking; I felt like I was choking*). These items consistently formed a distinct factor in both Phase 1 and Phase 2 of the scale development process (Watson et al., 2007; see also Chapter 2). The best indicators of this factor became the eight-item Panic scale in the original IDAS, which remained unchanged in the IDAS-II.

As is discussed in Watson et al. (2007), the IDAS-II Panic scale essentially is a short form of the 17-item Anxious Arousal scale from the MASQ (see Chapter 1). Watson et al. (2007) mention this link explicitly, stating that "10 of the 17 MASQ Anxious Arousal items were adapted to create the panic HIC in the original IDAS item pool" (p. 255). Moreover, as is shown in Appendix A of Watson et al. (2007), all eight IDAS Panic items represent modified versions of corresponding items in Anxious Arousal (see Watson et al., 2007, Table A-1).

More generally, Watson et al. (2007) argue that "in many ways, the IDAS can be viewed as a successor to the Mood and Anxiety Symptom Questionnaire (MASQ)" (p. 255). We can establish the connection between these instruments empirically, using data from two samples: 382 community adults and 220 individuals with diabetes (these samples are described in McDade-Montez & Watson, 2011).

Table 8.1 presents correlations between three IDAS scales—Dysphoria, Panic, and Well-Being—and three related scales from the MASQ: General Distress: Depressive Symptoms (GD: Depression), Anxious Arousal, and High Positive Affect. The MASQ GD: Depression and Anxious Arousal scales were described previously in Chapter 1; High Positive Affect contains the 14 reversed-keyed items from the MASQ Anhedonic Depression scale (see Watson et al., 1995).

Table 8.1 indicates that each of these MASQ scales has a clear, direct counterpart in the IDAS. That is, MASQ GD: Depression correlates very strongly with Dysphoria ($r = .88$ and .83 in the community adults and diabetes patients, respectively); Anxious Arousal is very highly related to Panic ($r = .87$ and .88, respectively); and High Positive Affect is strongly linked to Well-Being ($r = .86$ and .88, respectively).

In a related vein, Watson, Stanton, and Clark (2016) examined relations between these same three IDAS scales and the Mini-MASQ (Casillas & Clark, 2000) in a sample of 448 adult participants (210 men, 238 women; mean age = 35.5 years) who were recruited online through Amazon Mechanical Turk. The Mini-MASQ is a short form of the MASQ consisting of 26 items. It contains a single eight-item General Distress scale, plus reduced versions of Anxious Arousal (10 items)

Table 8.1 CORRELATIONS BETWEEN SELECTED IDAS-II AND MASQ/MINI-MASQ SCALES

	IDAS-II Scale		
MASQ/Mini-MASQ Scale	**Dysphoria**	**Panic**	**Well-Being**
Community Adults			
GD: Depression	**.88**	.53	−.61
Anxious Arousal	.68	**.87**	−.41
High Positive Affect	−.59	−.35	**.86**
Diabetes Patients			
GD: Depression	**.83**	.58	−.60
Anxious Arousal	.66	**.88**	−.37
High Positive Affect	−.61	−.43	**.88**
Amazon Turk Sample			
General Distress	**.88**	.60	−.56
Anxious Arousal	.54	**.87**	−.11
Anhedonic Depression	.61	.25	**−.89**

NOTE: $N = 382$ (Community Adults), 220 (Diabetes Patients), 448 (Amazon Turk Sample). All correlations are significant at $p < .01$; correlations $\geq |.70|$ are in bold. IDAS-II = Expanded version of the Inventory of Depression and Anxiety Symptoms. MASQ = Mood and Anxiety Symptom Questionnaire. GD: Depression = General Distress: Depressive Symptoms.

and Anhedonic Depression (two positively keyed and six negatively keyed items). Correlations between the IDAS and Mini-MASQ scales are presented in the bottom portion of Table 8.1 It is noteworthy that IDAS Dysphoria correlated .88 with Mini-MASQ General Distress; IDAS Panic correlated .87 with Mini-MASQ Anxious Arousal; and IDAS Well-Being correlated −.89 with Mini-MASQ Anhedonic Depression.

The Table 8.1 data clearly establish that the IDAS Panic scale assesses the same underlying construct as MASQ Anxious Arousal. Moreover, they demonstrate that the IDAS contains clear, direct indicators of the three main symptom groups articulated in the tripartite model of Clark and Watson (1991): nonspecific general distress (assessed by Dysphoria), somatic arousal (modeled by Panic), and anhedonia versus positive affect (tapped by Well-Being).

Claustrophobia

As noted in Chapter 2, the original IDAS item pool included a six-item HIC assessing symptoms of agoraphobia (e.g., *I had trouble leaving my home; I avoided crowded situations*). However, these items failed to define a distinct factor in the Phase 1 scale development analyses, so this dimension was dropped from further consideration. Consequently, the original IDAS did not contain a scale directly related to agoraphobia.

Nevertheless, we decided to revisit this issue when writing new items for the IDAS-II. Accordingly, the IDAS-II item pool contained a new six-item HIC tapping agoraphobia symptoms. These items helped to define a hybrid factor in both scale development samples that also was marked by symptoms from the situational phobia HIC (to be discussed shortly). As was discussed in Chapter 2, we labeled this hybrid dimension *Claustrophobia* (a) to reflect the core content of its strongest markers and (b) to emphasize its significant links to both agoraphobia and situational phobia (Watson et al., 2012). The resulting five-item IDAS-II Claustrophobia scale includes two items from the agoraphobia HIC (*I was afraid of getting trapped in a crowd; I avoided tight, enclosed spaces*) and three items from the situational phobia HIC (*I avoided small spaces; I felt anxious in small spaces; I was afraid of tunnels*). Consequently, as we will see, this scale displays significant links to both agoraphobia and certain aspects of specific phobia.

Specific Phobia

DSM-IV and *DSM-5* both formally recognize four subtypes of specific phobia: animal, natural environment (e.g., storms, heights, water), blood-injection-injury, and situational. However, this quadripartite scheme is not supported by structural evidence (see Craske et al., 1994; Watson, 2009c). Indeed, factor analyses of multi-item phobia measures such as the Fear Survey Schedule-III (FSS-III; Wolpe & Lang, 1964, 1974) and the Phobic Stimuli Response Scales (PSRS; Cutshall &

Watson, 2004) provide consistent evidence for only three subtypes of specific phobia: (a) animal fears, (b) blood-injection fears, and (c) some combination of situational and/or agoraphobic fears (Arrindell, Pickersgill, Merckelbach, Ardon, & Cornet, 1991; J. Beck, Carmin, & Henninger, 1998; Cutshall & Watson, 2004; Muris, Schmidt, & Merckelbach, 1999; Watson, 2009c). We therefore included separate HICs representing these three replicated symptom dimensions in the IDAS-II item pool: situational phobia (8 items; e.g. *I was afraid of riding in a car*), animal phobia (11 items; e.g., *I was afraid of spiders; I avoided bugs and insects*), and blood-injection-injury phobia (4 items; e.g., *I felt faint at the sight of blood; I avoided watching gory and gruesome scenes*).

As discussed previously, the situational phobia and agoraphobia items defined a single common dimension and were used to create the IDAS-II Claustrophobia scale. The blood-injection-injury items failed to define a replicable factor and were not considered further. In contrast, the animal phobia items did form a robust factor and were used to create a provisional nine-item scale. However, as was discussed in Chapter 2, this Animal Phobia scale showed poor convergent and discriminant validity and was not retained in the IDAS-II. Consequently, the IDAS-II provides only limited coverage of symptoms directly related to specific phobia.

Anxious Mood and Worry

The original IDAS item pool contained HICs tapping anxious mood (eight items; e.g., *I felt fearful*) and worry (seven items; e.g., *I could not stop worrying about things*). Items from both HICs defined a single common dimension in the Phase 1 scale development analyses and were retained for further consideration. In the Phase 2 analyses, however, these items were clear markers of a large, nonspecific factor that was defined by the core affective/cognitive symptoms of both depression and anxiety (see Chapter 2).

This nonspecific dimension essentially represents the general distress/negative affectivity factor that was discussed in Chapters 1 and 2. To illustrate the nature and strength of this factor, Watson et al. (2007) reported correlations between a 9-item Anxious Mood scale (consisting of items drawn from the original worry and anxious mood HICs) and a 5-item measure of Depressed Mood; 7-item scales assessing Worthlessness/Guilt and Cognitive Problems (e.g., attention and memory difficulties, indecisiveness); a 10-item index of Psychomotor Problems; and a 13-item measure of Anhedonia. Across the three scale development samples (combined $N = 1{,}388$), Anxious Mood had weighted mean correlations of .81 (Worthlessness/Guilt), .77 (Depressed Mood), .76 (Cognitive Problems), .74 (Psychomotor Problems), and .72 (Anhedonia) with these other symptom scales.

In light of these data, it was not possible to create a separate measure of anxious mood and/or worry that would show a reasonable level of discriminant validity. Consequently, a single worry item (*I found myself worrying all the time*) was included in the broad Dysphoria scale that was designed to measure this large, nonspecific factor.

CONVERGENT AND DISCRIMINANT VALIDITY OF ANXIETY SYMPTOM SCALES

Relations With Self-Report Scales

PSRS Analyses

We now examine the convergent and discriminant validity of these anxiety symptom scales. We begin by considering relations with the PSRS (Cutshall & Watson, 2004). The PSRS assesses content related to social phobia, agoraphobia, and specific phobia; items are rated on a 4-point scale ranging from *strongly disagree* to *strongly agree.* The PSRS contains five scales. One scale (Social; 11 items; e.g., *I dislike the feeling of being watched by others*) assesses the interpersonal/evaluative fears characteristic of social phobia. Three other scales—Animal (8 items; e.g., *Rats and mice really bother me*), Blood-Injection (10 items; e.g., *I turn away from the sight of blood*), and Bodily Harm (8 items; e.g., *I get nervous and uneasy during thunderstorms*)—measure various aspects of specific phobia. The final scale—Physical Confinement (9 items)—taps content related to both agoraphobia and situational phobia (e.g., *I dislike crowded places; I would be terrified if locked in a small, dark room*); it therefore should converge particularly well with the IDAS-II Claustrophobia scale.

We report correlations in two large standardized combined samples. The first sample consists of 1,490 participants (this includes 626 outpatients, 663 college students, and 201 older adults) who completed the original IDAS. Accordingly, we report correlations with the Panic scale and the original five-item version of Social Anxiety. The second sample contained 1,023 respondents (including 355 community adults and 668 college students) who completed the expanded IDAS-II; consequently, we report results for Panic, Claustrophobia, and the revised six-item Social Anxiety scale. As in previous chapters, to eliminate mean-level differences across populations, we standardized all the scale scores on a within-population basis and then combined them to permit a single overall analysis.

Table 8.2 presents correlations between these IDAS/IDAS-II scales and the PSRS in both samples. It is noteworthy that the IDAS/IDAS-II Social Anxiety scale correlated strongly with PSRS Social in both Standardized Sample 1 ($r = .64$) and Standardized Sample 2 ($r = .59$), thereby supporting its convergent validity. Moreover, it had a significantly stronger correlation ($p < .01$, one-tailed) with PSRS Social than with any other PSRS scale in both samples (in the first sample, *r*s ranged from .08 to .43, *z*s ranged from 9.44 to 23.17; in the second sample, *r*s ranged from .09 to .40, *z*s ranged from 6.63 to 17.16), which provides strong evidence of discriminant validity. In addition, PSRS Social had a significantly stronger correlation with IDAS/IDAS-II Social Anxiety than with Panic in Standardized Sample 1 ($r = .30$, $z = 15.27$), and with both Panic ($r = .24$, $z = 12.29$) and Claustrophobia ($r = .31$, $z = 9.10$) in Standardized Sample 2; these substantial differences further support its discriminant validity.

As hypothesized, Claustrophobia correlated strongly with PSRS Physical Confinement in Standardized Sample 2 ($r = .51$), which provides significant evidence of convergent validity. In addition, Claustrophobia correlated significantly

Table 8.2 Correlations Between the IDAS-II Anxiety Scales and the Phobic Stimuli Response Scales (PSRS) in Two Standardized Combined Samples

	IDAS-II Scale		
PSRS Scale	**Social Anxiety**	**Panic**	**Claustrophobia**
Standardized Sample 1			
Social	**.64**	.30	.—
Physical Confinement	.43	.34	.—
Bodily Harm	.24	.23	.—
Blood-Injection	.14	.10	.—
Animal	.08	.06	.—
Standardized Sample 2			
Social	**.59**	.24	.31
Physical Confinement	.40	.29	**.51**
Bodily Harm	.24	.24	.32
Blood-Injection	.21	.19	.26
Animal	.09	.07	.14

NOTE: $N = 1{,}490$ (Standardized Sample 1), 1,023 (Standardized Sample 2). All correlations are significant at $p < .05$; correlations $\geq |.50|$ are in bold. IDAS-II = Expanded version of the Inventory of Depression and Anxiety Symptoms. Standardized Sample 1 completed the original IDAS; Standardized Sample 2 completed the IDAS-II.

more strongly with Physical Confinement than with any other PSRS scale (*r*s ranged from .14 to .32, *z*s ranged from 6.47 to 11.96) in this sample. Finally, PSRS Physical Confinement correlated significantly more strongly with Claustrophobia than with both Social Anxiety ($r = .40$, $z = 3.29$) and Panic ($r = .29$, $z = 6.55$) in this sample. Thus, these data yield strong support for the convergent and discriminant validity of the IDAS-II Claustrophobia scale.

Relations With the FQ and APPQ

Next, we examine relations with scales from the Fear Questionnaire (FQ; Marks & Mathews, 1979) and the Albany Panic and Phobia Questionnaire (APPQ; Rapee, Craske, & Barlow, 1994/1995) in community adult ($N = 362$) and college student ($N = 342$) samples. The FQ asks respondents to indicate the extent to which they would avoid various situations. Our participants completed the five-item Agoraphobia scale (e.g., traveling alone by bus or coach; going into crowded shops) and the five-item Social Phobia scale (e.g., being watched or stared at; speaking or acting to an audience).

The APPQ consists of a 9-item Agoraphobia scale (e.g., riding on a subway; going long distances from home alone), a 10-item Social Phobia scale (e.g., meeting strangers; giving a speech), and an 8-item Interoceptive scale that assesses fear of activities that produce somatic sensations (e.g., running up stairs; hiking on a hot day). Respondents use a 9-point scale to describe how much fear that would experience if they were to encounter each activity or situation in the upcoming week.

Table 8.3 Correlations Between the IDAS-II Anxiety Scales and Scales From the Albany Panic and Phobia Questionnaire (APPQ) and the Fear Questionnaire (FQ)

APPQ/FQ Scale	**IDAS-II Scale** **Social Anxiety**	**Panic**	**Claustrophobia**
Community Adults			
APPQ Social Phobia	**.66**	.26	.32
FQ Social Phobia	**.49**	.14	.29
APPQ Agoraphobia	.39	.25	.39
FQ Agoraphobia	.39	.16	.31
APPQ Interoceptive	.23	.18	.24
Students			
APPQ Social Phobia	**.70**	.40	.30
FQ Social Phobia	**.58**	.33	.24
APPQ Agoraphobia	.36	.27	.35
FQ Agoraphobia	.36	.26	.30
APPQ Interoceptive	.35	.35	.28

NOTE: $N=362$ (Community Adults), 342 (Students). All correlations are significant at $p < .01$; correlations $\geq |.45|$ are in bold. IDAS-II = Expanded version of the Inventory of Depression and Anxiety Symptoms.

Table 8.3 presents correlations with the IDAS-II Social Anxiety (six-item version), Panic, and Claustrophobia scales. Social Anxiety was strongly related to both APPQ Social Phobia ($r=.66$ and .70 in the adults and students, respectively; overall mean $r=.68$) and FQ Social Phobia ($r=.49$ and .58, respectively; overall mean $r=.53$), which provides further evidence of its convergent validity. Next, we examined discriminant validity by comparing (a) its convergent correlations with APPQ Social Phobia and FQ Social Phobia with (b) those for all other scales. Eleven of the 12 comparisons (91.7%) were significant ($p < .05$, one-tailed); the sole exception was that Social Anxiety did not correlate more strongly with FQ Social Phobia than with APPQ Agoraphobia ($r=.39$; $z=1.63$, $p < .06$) in the adult sample. Finally, APPQ Social Phobia and FQ Social Phobia correlated significantly more strongly ($p < .01$, one-tailed) with IDAS-II Social Anxiety than with Panic and Claustrophobia in all eight comparisons (all *z*s > 3.37). Overall, these data further establish the convergent and discriminant validity of the IDAS-II Social Anxiety scale.

Somewhat surprisingly, however, the IDAS-II Claustrophobia scale was only moderately correlated with both APPQ Agoraphobia ($r=.39$ and .35 in the adults and students, respectively; overall mean $r=.37$) and FQ Agoraphobia ($r=.31$ and .30, respectively; overall mean $r=.30$) in these samples. It is noteworthy, moreover, that IDAS-II Social Anxiety had correlations of a similar magnitude with both APPQ Agoraphobia (mean $r=.37$) and FQ Agoraphobia (mean $r=.37$). Clearly, IDAS-II Claustrophobia cannot be considered to be a direct, specific indicator of agoraphobia, at least as it has been conceptualized in these other self-report scales.

ASI Analyses

We now examine associations with the Anxiety Sensitivity Index (ASI; Peterson & Reiss, 1987). The ASI is a widely used 16-item measure that assesses individual differences in anxiety sensitivity. Anxiety sensitivity can be defined as a fear that the physiological sensations associated with anxious arousal (e.g., increased heartbeat, rapid respiration, dizziness) have serious negative implications (e.g., "My heart is pounding, I must be having a heart attack"; Reiss, Peterson, Gursky, & McNally, 1986). Anxiety sensitivity is strongly implicated in the development of panic disorder and, to a lesser extent, posttraumatic stress disorder (PTSD), generalized anxiety disorder (GAD), and social phobia (Naragon-Gainey, 2010; Schmidt, Lerew, & Jackson, 1999; Taylor, 2014). Moreover, several studies have shown that the ASI is a significant predictor of panic attacks in both clinical and nonclinical participants (Cox & Taylor, 1999; Ehlers, 1995; Lilienfeld, Turner, & Jacobs, 1993; Maller & Reiss, 1992; Reiss & McNally, 1986; Schmidt, Lerew, & Jackson, 1997; Taylor, 1995a). Consequently, although the ASI is not a direct measure of panic symptoms per se, we would expect it to correlate strongly with the IDAS-II Panic scale.

It now is clearly established that the ASI is multifactorial, with most studies finding a three-factor solution reflecting the physical, mental/psychological, and social consequences of anxiety symptoms (e.g., Stein, Jang, & Livesley, 1999; Stewart, Taylor, & Baker, 1997; Zinbarg, Barlow, & Brown, 1997; Zinbarg, Mohlman, & Hong, 1999). We also report results on corresponding subscales—Physical (eight items; e.g., *It scares me when I feel faint*), Cognitive (three items; e.g., *When I am nervous, I worry that I might be mentally ill*), and Social (three items; e.g., *It is important to me not to appear nervous*)—that contain the best markers of each factor. Based on the meta-analytic findings reported in Naragon-Gainey (2010; see her Table 3), we would expect the IDAS-II Panic scale to correlate more strongly with the Physical and Cognitive subscales than with the Social subscale.

Table 8.4 reports correlations between these ASI scales and the IDAS Panic and Social Anxiety scales in patient ($N = 328$) and student ($N = 266$) samples. The participants in these samples completed the original IDAS, so these results are based on the five-item version of the Social Anxiety scale. In the patient sample, Panic correlated strongly with the ASI Total score ($r = .63$), as well as the Physical ($r = .58$) and Cognitive ($r = .54$) subscales; these results offer significant evidence of convergent validity. In terms of discriminant validity, both the ASI Total score ($z = 2.18$) and the Physical subscale ($z = 3.26$) correlated significantly more strongly ($p < .05$, one-tailed) with Panic than with Social Anxiety; however, the corresponding comparison for the Cognitive subscale did not approach significance (.54 vs. .49; $z = 0.87$, n.s.).

Panic correlated more moderately with these ASI scales in the student sample (rs ranged from .43 to .49), but these results still demonstrate a reasonable level of convergence. Moreover, the Physical subscale correlated significantly more strongly with Panic (.43) than with Social Anxiety (.31) in this sample ($z = 1.75$, $p < .05$, one-tailed); however, the comparisons for the Total score (.49 vs. .41; $z = 1.29$) and the Cognitive subscale (.49 vs. 40; $z = 1.38$) were not significant.

Table 8.4 Correlations Between the IDAS Anxiety Scales and the Anxiety Sensitivity Index (ASI)

ASI Scale	**IDAS-II Scale** **Panic**	**Social Anxiety***
Patient Sample		
Total Score	**.63**	**.51**
Physical	**.58**	.40
Cognitive	**.54**	**.49**
Social	.44	.44
Student Sample		
Total Score	**.49**	.41
Physical	.43	.31
Cognitive	**.49**	.40
Social	.27	.21

NOTE: $N = 328$ (Patients), 266 (Students). All correlations are significant at $p < .01$; correlations $\geq |.45|$ are in bold. IDAS = Inventory of Depression and Anxiety Symptoms.
*Original five-item version of scale.

Finally, it is noteworthy that Social Anxiety was only moderately related to the ASI Social subscale ($r = .44$ and .21 in the patients and students, respectively). Furthermore, Panic had very similar correlations with ASI Social ($r = .44$ and .27, respectively) in these data. These results indicate that the IDAS Social Anxiety scale is not strongly or specifically related to concerns arising from the interpersonal consequences of anxiety symptoms.

Structural Analyses

Next, we report data from three samples in which participants completed multiple measures of both social anxiety and panic symptoms. These responses therefore can be subjected to structural analyses, which yield simple and elegant tests of convergent and discriminant validity: If these measures are valid indicators of their respective constructs, then they should define two distinct factors that clearly reflect these constructs.

The first two groups include Samples 3 ($N = 296$ patients) and 9 ($N = 373$ students). These participants completed an extensive battery of self-report symptom measures. This battery included three measures of social anxiety: (1) the revised six-item version of the IDAS-II Social Anxiety scale, (2) APPQ Social Phobia, and (3) FQ Social Phobia. In addition, participants completed two panic symptom scales: the MASQ Anxious Arousal scale, and the 13-item Panic Attack Symptom Questionnaire (PASQ; Watson, 2000b). The PASQ is a face valid, self-report measure of the 13 *DSM-IV* symptoms of a panic attack (e.g., chest pain or discomfort; feeling of choking; afraid that you were dying). Participants were instructed to indicate the extent to which they had experienced each symptom during the previous month on a 5-point scale ranging from *not at all* to *extremely*.

We began by subjecting these scales to separate principal factor analyses in each sample, using squared multiple correlations as the initial communality estimates. As expected, two interpretable factors emerged in each case and were rotated to oblique simple structure using promax (power = 3). The resulting factor loadings are presented in Table 8.5. In each sample, the two factors clearly can be identified as Social Anxiety and Panic, respectively. All three social anxiety scales are strong markers of the first factor, with loadings ranging from .71 to .90 in Sample 3, and from .66 to .80 in Sample 9. Note, moreover, that all three scales consistently have low loadings on the second factor, with values ranging from only −.07 to .17 across samples. Conversely, both panic scales are strong and clear markers of the second factor. Their loadings on this factor ranged from .71 to .84 across samples, whereas the corresponding values on Factor I ranged from only −.05 to .10. Thus, these results help to establish the convergent and discriminant validity of these scales.

The Sample 4 participants also completed a lengthy battery of self-report psychopathology measures. As was noted in Chapter 6, this battery contained three measures of panic: (1) the IDAS-II Panic scale; (2) a reduced, nine-item version of the MASQ Anxious Arousal scale; and (3) an abbreviated, six-item version of the PASQ. It should be noted that Anxious Arousal and the PASQ both were shortened in order to eliminate overlapping items that would have inflated the correlations between the panic indicators. In addition, the participants were assessed on four measures of social anxiety: (1) the six-item version of IDAS-II Social Anxiety; (2) the FQ Social Phobia scale; (3) the APPQ Social Phobia scale; and (4) a factor analytically derived 10-item Social Anxiety scale from the SPQ (Chmielewski & Watson, 2008a).

We subjected these scales to a principal factor analysis, following the same procedure as before. Two well-defined and readily interpretable factors emerged and were rotated using promax. The loadings from this solution are presented in Table 8.6. Once again, the factors can be identified as Social Anxiety and Panic,

Table 8.5 PROMAX FACTOR LOADINGS OF SOCIAL ANXIETY AND PANIC SYMPTOM SCALES IN PATIENT AND STUDENT SAMPLES

	Sample 3		Sample 9	
Scale	I	II	I	II
APPQ Social Phobia	**.90**	−.03	**.80**	.03
FQ Social Phobia	**.78**	.00	**.73**	−.07
IDAS-II Social Anxiety	**.71**	.17	**.66**	.15
Panic Attack Symptom Questionnaire	.02	**.84**	−.05	**.73**
MASQ Anxious Arousal	.04	**.82**	.10	**.71**

NOTE: $N = 296$ patients (Sample 3), 373 students (Sample 9). Loadings ≥ |.40| are in bold. Factor $r = .55$ (Patient Sample), .54 (Student Sample). APPQ = Albany Panic and Phobia Questionnaire. FQ = Fear Questionnaire. IDAS-II = Expanded version of the Inventory of Depression and Anxiety Symptoms. MASQ = Mood and Anxiety Symptom Questionnaire.

Table 8.6 Promax Factor Loadings of Social Anxiety and Panic Symptom Scales in Sample 4

Scale	I	II
APPQ Social Phobia	**.82**	.05
FQ Social Phobia	**.75**	−.03
SPQ Social Anxiety	**.70**	.09
IDAS-II Social Anxiety	**.54**	.36
MASQ Anxious Arousal	.04	**.78**
IDAS-II Panic	.09	**.76**
Panic Attack Symptom Questionnaire	.02	**.72**

NOTE: $N = 411$. Loadings ≥ |.40| are in bold. Factor $r = .67$. APPQ = Albany Panic and Phobia Questionnaire. FQ = Fear Questionnaire. SPQ = Schizotypal Personality Questionnaire. IDAS-II = Expanded version of the Inventory of Depression and Anxiety Symptoms. MASQ = Mood and Anxiety Symptom Questionnaire.

respectively. The four social anxiety scales all are strong markers of Factor I, with loadings ranging from .54 (IDAS-II Social Anxiety) to .82 (APPQ Social Phobia). Conversely, the three panic scales all clearly define Factor II, with loadings ranging from .72 (PASQ) to .78 (MASQ Anxious Arousal). Note also that the cross-loadings consistently are low, with a single exception: IDAS-II Social Anxiety has a moderate secondary loading (.36) on the Panic factor. Consequently, these data provide further support for the construct validity of these scales.

Relations With Interview Measures

IDAS-CR Analyses

We now evaluate convergent and discriminant validity using interview-based ratings of these constructs. First, we examine the IDAS Social Anxiety and Panic scales in relation to ratings on the IDAS-CR. Following the logic of previous chapters, we began by identifying the IDAS scales that correlate most strongly with our target constructs. As shown in Table 2.7, Panic ($r = .66$) and Social Anxiety ($r = .65$) both correlate strongly with IDAS Dysphoria. In addition, Panic is highly related to both Suicidality ($r = .55$) and Ill Temper ($r = .58$), whereas Social Anxiety is strongly linked to Traumatic Intrusions ($r = .59$). We therefore included these four other IDAS/IDAS-CR symptom dimensions in these validity analyses. Note that these results are based on the original, five-item version of the IDAS Social Anxiety scale.

Table 8.7 presents separate sets of correlations between these six IDAS scales and parallel IDAS-CR ratings in (a) 802 outpatients (this group combines participants from Samples 1, 2, and 6) and (b) 522 college students (this group is an aggregation of Samples 8 and 10) in the form of a heteromethod block (Campbell & Fiske, 1959). With regard to convergent validity, self-ratings on Social Anxiety

Table 8.7 CONVERGENT/DISCRIMINANT VALIDITY ANALYSES: CORRELATIONS BETWEEN THE IDAS SCALES (USING THE FIVE-ITEM VERSION OF SOCIAL ANXIETY) AND IDAS-CR RATINGS IN PATIENT AND STUDENT SAMPLES

	IDAS-CR Rating					
IDAS Scale	1	2	3	4	5	6
Patients						
1. Social Anxiety*	**.62**	.37	.33	.31	.24	.19
2. Panic	.30	**.60**	.32	.27	.32	.24
3. Dysphoria	.41	.44	**.60**	.42	.35	.28
4. Suicidality	.33	.35	.37	**.67**	.29	.25
5. Traumatic Intrusions	.33	.33	.31	.31	**.62**	.27
6. Ill Temper	.22	.32	.31	.30	.28	**.61**
Students						
1. Social Anxiety*	**.59**	.20	.34	.18	.20	.10
2. Panic	.31	**.43**	.36	.14	.26	.09
3. Dysphoria	.39	.36	**.61**	.21	.30	.19
4. Suicidality	.25	.22	.31	**.48**	.16	.09
5. Traumatic Intrusions	.19	.29	.32	.12	**.52**	.19
6. Ill Temper	.19	.18	.36	.12	.26	**.45**

NOTE: $N = 802$ (Patients), 522 (Students). Convergent correlations are in bold. IDAS = Inventory of Depression and Anxiety Symptoms. IDAS-CR = Clinician Rating version of the IDAS.
*Original five-item version of scale.

were strongly related to their IDAS-CR counterparts in both the patients ($r = .62$) and students ($r = .59$), with an overall mean value of .61. The IDAS Panic scale also showed strong convergent validity in the patients ($r = .60$), but its association with IDAS-CR Panic was only moderate in magnitude ($r = .43$) in the students; the weighted mean correlation was .54 across the two samples, which indicates a substantial level of convergence.

As in previous IDAS-CR analyses, we examined discriminant validity by comparing each convergent correlation to all of the other values in its row or column of the heteromethod block (Campbell & Fiske, 1959). Aggregating across both scales and samples, this yields a total of 40 tests of discriminant validity. Overall, 39 of these 40 comparisons (97.5%) were statistically significant ($p < .05$, one-tailed), with *z*s ranging from 2.04 to 13.35. The only exception was IDAS Panic did not correlate more strongly with IDAS-CR Panic ($r = .43$) than with IDAS-CR Dysphoria ($r = .36$) in the student sample. Consequently, we see strong evidence of both convergent and discriminant validity in these data.

We also repeated these analyses using subgroups of participants (197 patients from Sample 6 and 219 students from Sample 10) who completed the revised, six-item version of IDAS-II Social Anxiety. These analyses produced convergent correlations that are similar to those seen in Table 8.7 ($r = .56$ in patients, .66 in students; overall mean $r = .61$). Moreover, all 20 tests of discriminant validity were significant in these subsamples. Thus, this expanded version of the scale also displays impressive convergent and discriminant validity.

IMAS Analyses

Next, we examine relations with the interview-based IMAS. Correlations between the IMAS scales and IDAS-II Social Anxiety (six-item version), Panic, and Claustrophobia are presented in Table 8.8 ($N = 362$ patients from Sample 5) and Table 8.9 ($N = 393$ students from Sample 11). These data yield impressive evidence of convergent validity. Specifically, IDAS-II Social Anxiety correlated strongly with IMAS Social Phobia ($r = .70$ in both samples) and IDAS-II Panic was highly related to IMAS Panic ($r = .65$ and .72 in the patients and students, respectively; overall mean $r = .69$). In addition, it is noteworthy that Claustrophobia was substantially associated with IMAS Agoraphobia ($r = .71$ and .63, respectively; mean $r = .67$) in both samples. These strong correlations are surprising, as they are much higher than those seen previously with self-report measures of agoraphobia (mean $rs = .37$ and .30 with APPQ Agoraphobia and FQ Agoraphobia, respectively; see Table 8.3). These results establish that Claustrophobia has important links to at least some symptom measures of agoraphobia.

As in previous chapters, we evaluated discriminant validity by comparing each convergent correlation with all other values in the same column (e.g., testing whether IDAS-II Social Anxiety correlates more strongly with IMAS Social Phobia than with IMAS Panic); this yields a total of 54 tests of discriminant validity across scales and samples. Overall, 52 of these 54 comparisons (96.3%) were significant ($p < .05$, one-tailed). The only exceptions were that IDAS-II Panic did not have a significantly stronger correlation with IMAS Panic than with IMAS Generalized Anxiety Disorder ($r = .63$, $z = 0.75$, n.s.) and IMAS Posttraumatic Stress Disorder ($r = .58$, $z = 1.63$, $p < .06$) in Sample 5.

Table 8.8 Correlations Between the IDAS-II Anxiety Scales and the IMAS Scales in Sample 5

IMAS Scale	Social Anxiety	Panic	Claustrophobia
Social Phobia	**.70**	.41	.55
Panic	.49	**.65**	.47
Agoraphobia	.59	.42	**.71**
Generalized Anxiety Disorder	.50	**.63**	.47
Posttraumatic Stress Disorder	.50	.58	.48
Depression	.50	.57	.48
Obsessive-Compulsive Disorder	.39	.30	.43
Specific Phobia	.43	.30	.49
Irritability	.34	.43	.33
Mania	.25	.35	.26

NOTE: $N = 362$ patients. Correlations $\geq .60$ are in bold. All correlations are significant at $p < .01$. IDAS-II = Expanded version of the Inventory of Depression and Anxiety Symptoms. IMAS = Interview of Mood and Anxiety Symptoms.

Table 8.9 Correlations Between the IDAS-II Anxiety Scales and the IMAS Scales in Sample 11

IMAS Scale	Social Anxiety	Panic	Claustrophobia
Social Phobia	**.70**	.43	.40
Panic	.53	**.72**	.39
Agoraphobia	.44	.43	**.63**
Generalized Anxiety Disorder	**.60**	**.64**	.40
Posttraumatic Stress Disorder	.53	**.64**	.41
Depression	.52	.58	.33
Obsessive-Compulsive Disorder	.33	.35	.29
Specific Phobia	.25	.24	.35
Irritability	.44	.50	.31
Mania	.36	.47	.32

NOTE: $N = 393$ students. Correlations ≥ .60 are in bold. All correlations are significant at $p < .01$. IDAS-II = Expanded version of the Inventory of Depression and Anxiety Symptoms. IMAS = Interview of Mood and Anxiety Symptoms.

Summary

Social Anxiety

Taken together, the data we have presented offer strong support for the construct validity of the IDAS/IDAS-II Social Anxiety scale. The scale shows strong convergent validity with several other self-report scales, including APPQ Social Phobia (mean $r = .68$), PSRS Social (mean $r = .62$), and FQ Social Phobia (mean $r = .53$). It also correlated highly with corresponding interview-based measures on the IDAS-CR (mean $r = .61$) and the IMAS (mean $r = .70$). In addition, the scale consistently displayed impressive discriminant validity in these analyses. Finally, it is important to note that the original five-item version and the revised six-item version of the scale behaved very similarly in our data, with both demonstrating strong construct validity.

Panic

Our results also strongly support the construct validity of the IDAS Panic scale. The findings presented in Table 8.1 establish that Panic essentially is a short form of the MASQ/Mini-MASQ Anxious Arousal scale (mean $r = .87$). Subsequent analyses demonstrated a strong level of convergence with other self-report measures, including the PASQ and various ASI scales (mean rs = .57, .52, and .51 with ASI Total, ASI Cognitive, and ASI Physical, respectively). Moreover, the scale converged well with its interview-based counterparts on the IDAS-CR (mean $r = .54$) and the IMAS (mean $r = .69$). Finally, similar to Social Anxiety, it also consistently exhibited significant discriminant validity across various analyses.

Claustrophobia

In contrast, the data for IDAS-II Claustrophobia are more complex and challenging to interpret. As expected, Claustrophobia correlated strongly ($r = .51$) with

PSRS Physical Confinement, a scale that contains content related to both agoraphobia and situational phobia. It was only moderately related to both APPQ Agoraphobia (mean $r = .37$) and FQ Agoraphobia (mean $r = .30$), but it was much more strongly linked to the IMAS Agoraphobia scale (mean $r = .67$). In fact, Claustrophobia correlated more strongly with IMAS Agoraphobia than with any self-report measure. Further work is needed to explicate the construct validity of this scale.

CRITERION VALIDITY OF ANXIETY SYMPTOM SCALES

IDAS-II Scales and IDAS-CR Ratings

IDAS-II Social Anxiety

We turn now to an examination of the criterion validity and diagnostic specificity of anxiety symptom scales. We begin by evaluating the IDAS-II Social Anxiety scale. The top portion of Table 8.10 presents polyserial correlations with nine *DSM* emotional disorder diagnoses (social phobia, major depression, GAD, PTSD, panic disorder, agoraphobia, specific phobia, obsessive-compulsive disorder [OCD], current manic episodes) in Samples 1 through 5. It should be noted

Table 8.10 Polyserial Correlations Between IDAS-II and IDAS-CR Social Anxiety and *DSM* Emotional Disorder Diagnoses

Scale/Sample	Social Phobia	MDD	GAD	PTSD	Panic	Agora	Specific Phobia	OCD	Manic
IDAS-II Social Anxiety									
Sample 1*	**.51**	**.47**	.40	.43	.42	**.48**	.31	.10	.—
Sample 2*	**.61**	**.55**	**.45**	.44	**.53**	**.62**	.29	.35	.—
Sample 3	**.63**	**.46**	.25	.33	.34	.—	.—	.26	.—
Sample 4	**.47**	**.51**	**.47**	**.46**	.38	**.45**	.—	**.47**	.37
Sample 5	.44	.32	.23	.31	.41	.33	.34	.23	.01
Weighted *M*	**.52**	**.46**	.37	.40	.41	**.47**	.31	.29	.22
IDAS-CR Social Anxiety									
Sample 1	.37	.35	.34	.33	.29	.36	.27	.09	.—
Sample 2	**.56**	.44	.41	.30	**.51**	**.54**	.24	.44	.—
Sample 3	**.62**	**.46**	.29	.11	.25	.—	.—	.28	.—
Weighted *M*	**.50**	.41	.35	.26	.35	.44	.26	.26	.—

NOTE: $N = 337$ (Sample 1), 267 (Sample 2), 250 (Sample 3), 407 (Sample 4), 290 (Sample 5). Correlations ≥ .45 are in bold. IDAS-II = Expanded Version of the Inventory of Depression and Anxiety Symptoms. MDD = major depressive disorder. GAD = generalized anxiety disorder. PTSD = posttraumatic stress disorder. Agora = agoraphobia. OCD = obsessive-compulsive disorder. Manic = current manic episode.

* Original five-item version of scale.

that participants in Samples 1 and 2 completed the original five-item version of Social Anxiety, whereas those in Samples 3 through 5 were assessed using the expanded six-item scale.

IDAS Social Anxiety consistently exhibited strong criterion validity in these analyses. It had polyserial correlations ranging from .44 to .63 with social phobia diagnoses across the five samples, with an overall weighted mean coefficient ($N = 1{,}551$) of .52. These coefficients are similar in magnitude to those we have observed previously with other IDAS-II scales. For instance, in Chapter 7, we reported that IDAS-II Traumatic Intrusions and Traumatic Avoidance had weighted mean correlations of .58 and .55, respectively, with PTSD diagnoses.

In contrast, however, Social Anxiety does not show the same level of diagnostic specificity that we typically have found with other scales. Although its strongest overall association was with social phobia, it correlated similarly with diagnoses of agoraphobia (overall mean $r = .47$) and major depression (mean $r = .46$); it also had mean correlations $\geq .40$ with both panic disorder ($r = .41$) and PTSD ($r = .40$). The Sample 4 data yielded particularly poor specificity, with numerous disorders (social phobia, major depression, GAD, PTSD, agoraphobia, and OCD) producing polyserial correlations between .45 and .51. Overall, these findings yield mixed but encouraging evidence that further supports the construct validity of this scale.

IDAS-CR Social Anxiety

The lower portion of Table 8.10 presents parallel findings based on IDAS-CR Social Anxiety ratings in Samples 1 through 3 (overall $N = 854$). These data are similar to those obtained with IDAS-II Social Anxiety, demonstrating both strong criterion validity and limited diagnostic specificity. Thus, IDAS-CR Social Anxiety correlated strongly with diagnoses of social phobia ($r = .50$), but it had associations of a similar magnitude with both agoraphobia ($r = .44$) and major depression ($r = .41$). Once again, we see mixed—but supportive—evidence of construct validity. In subsequent analyses, we will examine whether this pattern of limited specificity is unique to these measures or is more broadly characteristic of indicators of social anxiety.

IDAS-II Panic

The top portion of Table 8.11 reports parallel results for the IDAS-II Panic scale in Samples 1, 2, 4, and 5 (overall $N = 1{,}301$). Once again, these data establish both substantial criterion validity and limited diagnostic specificity. With regard to criterion validity, IDAS-II Panic had correlations with panic disorder diagnoses ranging from .38 to .60 across samples, with an overall mean coefficient of .48. However, it had an equally strong association with major depression (rs ranged from .42 to .57, mean $r = .48$). In Samples 4 and 5, in fact, it actually correlated more strongly with major depression ($r = .57$ and .42, respectively) than with panic disorder ($r = .40$ and .38, respectively). IDAS-II Panic also had correlations ranging from .28 to .52 (mean $r = .41$) with diagnoses of agoraphobia in these data. Overall, these results provide inconsistent support for the construct validity of this scale.

IDAS-CR Panic

The lower portion of Table 8.11 reports findings based on IDAS-CR Panic ratings in Samples 1 through 3 (total $N=854$). In contrast to the other measures we have examined, these data demonstrate both strong criterion validity and impressive diagnostic specificity. IDAS-CR Panic had correlations with panic disorder diagnoses that ranged from .60 to .64 across samples, with a weighted mean value of .63; in contrast, its next strongest associations were only .47 (with agoraphobia) and .38 (with major depression). These results strongly support the construct validity of this IDAS-CR rating.

IDAS-II Claustrophobia

Next, we consider findings for the IDAS-II Claustrophobia scale, which was assessed in Samples 4 and 5 (see Table 8.12). As noted earlier, based on its item content, this scale would be expected to have particularly strong associations with two diagnoses: agoraphobia and specific phobia. Consistent with this expectation, Claustrophobia had its strongest overall associations with agoraphobia (mean $r=.47$) and specific phobia ($r=.42$), which provides evidence of both criterion validity and diagnostic specificity. It should be noted, however, that its specificity was somewhat limited, as it also had mean coefficients ≥ .35 with panic disorder ($r=.39$), PTSD ($r=.38$), and OCD ($r=.35$). Overall, these data provide encouraging support for the construct validity of this scale.

Table 8.11 Polyserial Correlations Between IDAS-II and IDAS-CR Panic and *DSM* Emotional Disorder Diagnoses

Scale/Sample	Panic	MDD	GAD	PTSD	Agora	Social Phobia	Specific Phobia	OCD	Manic
IDAS-II Panic									
Sample 1	**.60**	.43	.36	.31	.42	.21	.22	.20	.—
Sample 2	**.55**	**.48**	.32	.43	**.52**	.34	.31	.40	.—
Sample 4	.40	**.57**	**.46**	**.47**	.41	.41	.—	.35	.30
Sample 5	.38	.42	.19	.33	.28	.14	.19	.17	.06
Weighted *M*	**.48**	**.48**	.35	.39	.41	.28	.24	.28	.20
IDAS-CR Panic									
Sample 1	**.64**	.38	.30	.22	**.45**	.11	.13	.10	.—
Sample 2	**.64**	.47	.39	.42	**.50**	.37	.22	.41	.—
Sample 3	**.60**	.27	.33	.30	.—	.19	.—	.30	.—
Weighted *M*	**.63**	.38	.34	.31	**.47**	.21	.17	.26	.—

NOTE: $N=337$ (Sample 1), 267 (Sample 2), 250 (Sample 3), 407 (Sample 4), 290 (Sample 5). Correlations ≥ .50 are in bold. IDAS-II = Expanded Version of the Inventory of Depression and Anxiety Symptoms. MDD = major depressive disorder. GAD = generalized anxiety disorder. PTSD = posttraumatic stress disorder. Agora = agoraphobia. OCD = obsessive-compulsive disorder. Manic = current manic episode.

Table 8.12 Polyserial Correlations Between the IDAS-II Claustrophobia Scale and *DSM* Emotional Disorder Diagnoses

Diagnosis	Sample 4	Sample 5	Weighted *M*
Agoraphobia	**.48**	**.45**	**.47**
Specific Phobia	.—	**.42**	**.42**
Panic Disorder	.38	**.41**	.39
Posttraumatic Stress Disorder	**.41**	.34	.38
Obsessive-Compulsive Disorder	**.41**	.26	.35
Major Depression	**.42**	.23	.34
Social Phobia	.31	.30	.31
Generalized Anxiety Disorder	.27	.21	.25
Current Manic Episode	.21	.11	.17

Note: $N = 407$ (Sample 4: Adults), 290 (Sample 5: Outpatients). Correlations ≥ .40 are in bold.

PSRS Scales

Participants in Samples 1 and 2 also were assessed on the five PSRS scales, which permits an examination of their specificity and criterion validity. Table 8.13 presents polyserial correlations between the PSRS scales and eight *DSM-IV* diagnoses (social phobia, agoraphobia, specific phobia, panic disorder, major depression, GAD, PTSD, and OCD); data from the two samples have been combined here for ease of presentation. Three aspects of these results are noteworthy. First, PSRS Physical Confinement exhibits impressive criterion validity and diagnostic specificity in these data. It correlated .61 with diagnoses of agoraphobia, whereas its next strongest association was only .40 with panic disorder. Second, PSRS Social had strong links to both social phobia ($r = .56$) and agoraphobia ($r = .57$); the former association supports its criterion validity, whereas the latter establishes that its diagnostic specificity is somewhat limited. Finally, the three remaining PSRS scales—Bodily Harm, Blood-Injection, and Animal—all display consistently weak criterion validity in these data, with coefficients ranging from only .02 to .25. It is particularly surprising that these scales all were very weakly related to diagnoses of specific phobia (*r*s ranged from only .11 to .12). These findings raise significant concerns about the construct validity of these scales that need to be addressed in future research.

Comparative Analyses Across Multiple Measures

Sample 3 Data

As noted previously (see Table 8.5 and the accompanying discussion), the Sample 3 participants completed multiple self-report measures of social anxiety (IDAS-II Social Anxiety, APPQ Social Phobia, FQ Social Phobia) and panic symptoms (MASQ Anxious Arousal, PASQ). These data therefore provide a broader

Table 8.13 Polyserial Correlations Between PSRS Scales and *DSM-IV* Emotional Disorder Diagnoses

Scale	**Social Phobia**	**Agora**	**Specific Phobia**	**Panic**	**MDD**	**GAD**	**PTSD**	**OCD**
Social	**.56**	**.57**	.18	.38	.40	.38	.35	.37
Physical Confinement	.31	**.61**	.32	.40	.34	.28	.38	.37
Bodily Harm	.08	.13	.11	.21	.19	.16	.16	.25
Blood-Injection	.15	.16	.12	.14	.02	.13	.08	.08
Animal	.10	.09	.12	.21	.03	.07	.13	.18

NOTE: $N = 579$. Correlations ≥ .50 are in bold. PSRS = Phobic Stimuli Response Scales. Agora = agoraphobia. MDD = major depressive disorder. GAD = generalized anxiety disorder. PTSD = posttraumatic stress disorder. OCD = obsessive-compulsive disorder.

and more comprehensive examination of the criterion validity and diagnostic specificity of these anxiety symptoms. Table 8.14 presents polyserial correlations between these symptom scales and six *DSM-IV* diagnoses: social phobia, panic disorder, major depression, GAD, PTSD, and OCD.

Looking first at the social anxiety scales, it is interesting to note that IDAS-II Social Anxiety yielded the best overall pattern. It had the strongest individual association with social phobia diagnoses ($r = .63$) in these data. Moreover, its correlations with the other disorders ranged from only .26 (with GAD and OCD) to .46 (with major depression), establishing an impressive level of diagnostic specificity. APPQ Social Phobia and FQ Social Phobia also showed reasonable specificity in this sample, but they showed somewhat lower criterion validity vis-à-vis social

Table 8.14 Polyserial Correlations Between Social Anxiety and Panic Symptom Scales and *DSM-IV* Diagnoses (Sample 3)

Symptom Measure	**Social Phobia**	**Panic**	**MDD**	**GAD**	**PTSD**	**OCD**
Social Anxiety Scales						
IDAS-II Social Anxiety	**.63**	.35	**.46**	.26	.33	.26
APPQ Social Phobia	**.52**	.28	.38	.18	.25	.23
FQ Social Phobia	**.49**	.33	.39	.20	.17	.28
Panic Scales						
MASQ Anxious Arousal	.28	**.56**	.42	.32	.42	.37
Panic Attack Symptom Q	.25	**.51**	.42	.42	.39	.27

NOTE: $N = 252$. Correlations ≥ .45 are in bold. MDD = major depressive disorder. GAD = generalized anxiety disorder. PTSD = posttraumatic stress disorder. OCD = obsessive-compulsive disorder. IDAS-II = Expanded Version of the Inventory of Depression and Anxiety Symptoms. APPQ = Albany Panic and Phobia Questionnaire. FQ = Fear Questionnaire. MASQ = Mood and Anxiety Symptom Questionnaire.

phobia diagnoses ($r = .52$ and .49, respectively). Overall, these results strongly support the construct validity of these scales.

The two panic scales displayed similar properties in this sample. They both exhibited strong criterion validity in these data, with coefficients of .56 (MASQ Anxious Arousal) and .51 (PASQ). Both scales also exhibited an adequate level of diagnostic specificity; their correlations with the other disorders ranged from .28 to .42 (MASQ Anxious Arousal), and from .25 to .42 (PASQ). Overall, these data provide good evidence of construct validity.

Sample 4 Data

The Sample 4 data provide an even more comprehensive examination of the comparative validity and specificity of anxiety symptoms. As discussed earlier (see Table 8.6 and the accompanying discussion), these participants completed multiple self-report measures of both social anxiety (IDAS-II Social Anxiety, APPQ Social Phobia, FQ Social Phobia, SPQ Social Anxiety) and panic symptoms (IDAS-II Panic, plus abbreviated versions of MASQ Anxious Arousal and the PASQ). They also were assessed on IDAS-II Claustrophobia, as well as two self-report indicators of agoraphobia (APPQ Agoraphobia, FQ Agoraphobia). Finally, they completed the GADQ-IV (Newman et al., 2002); as discussed in Chapter 6, this scale provides comprehensive assessment of GAD symptoms and, accordingly, should be strongly and specifically linked to that diagnosis.

Table 8.15 reports polyserial correlations between these anxiety scales and seven *DSM-5* diagnoses: social phobia, panic disorder, agoraphobia, GAD, major depression, PTSD, and OCD. Looking first at criterion validity, it can be seen that the magnitude of the correlations varied widely across scales. The GADQ-IV clearly showed the strongest criterion validity, correlating .67 with GAD diagnoses. Among the social anxiety scales, SPQ Social Anxiety had the strongest link to social phobia ($r = .50$), followed by IDAS-II Social Anxiety ($r = .46$), APPQ Social Phobia ($r = .43$), and FQ Social Phobia ($r = .38$).[1] The panic symptom scales all had similar, moderate associations with panic disorder, with coefficients ranging from .40 (IDAS-II Panic, MASQ Anxious Arousal) to .43 (PASQ). Finally, diagnoses of agoraphobia actually were more strongly linked to IDAS-II Claustrophobia ($r = .48$) than to either FQ Agoraphobia ($r = .38$) or APPQ Agoraphobia ($r = .37$).

In contrast, no scale demonstrated an impressive level of diagnostic specificity. In fact, only two scales—IDAS-II Claustrophobia and SPQ Social Anxiety—actually had their strongest correlation with the target disorder. In interpreting these findings, it should be kept in mind that several of these same scales displayed much better diagnostic specificity in Sample 3 (see Table 8.14). Consequently, these unimpressive specificity results may reflect some peculiarity of this sample or in how the disorders were assessed (as noted in Chapter 2, these participants were interviewed using the M.I.N.I., not the SCID).

1. It is interesting to note that the latter three scales displayed the same rank order in their criterion validities in Sample 3 (see Table 8.14). Collapsed across Samples 3 and 4, these scales produced weighted mean criterion validity correlations of .53 (IDAS-II Social Anxiety), .46 (APPQ Social Phobia), and .42 (FQ Social Phobia).

Table 8.15 Polyserial Correlations Between Anxiety Symptom Scales and *DSM-V* Diagnoses (Sample 4)

Symptom Measure	Social Phobia	Panic	Agora	GAD	MDD	PTSD	OCD
Social Anxiety Scales							
SPQ Social Anxiety	**.50**	.34	**.49**	**.45**	**.46**	**.44**	**.40**
IDAS-II Social Anxiety	**.46**	.38	**.45**	**.47**	**.51**	**.46**	**.46**
APPQ Social Phobia	**.43**	.33	.38	**.44**	**.44**	.39	.37
FQ Social Phobia	.38	.34	.29	.33	**.40**	.34	**.48**
Panic Scales							
Panic Attack Symptom Q	**.44**	**.43**	.39	**.54**	**.53**	**.47**	.37
IDAS-II Panic	**.40**	**.40**	**.41**	**.47**	**.58**	**.47**	.33
MASQ Anxious Arousal	**.45**	**.40**	.39	**.47**	**.56**	.37	**.40**
Other Anxiety Scales							
IDAS-II Claustrophobia	.30	.38	**.48**	.27	**.42**	**.41**	.39
FQ Agoraphobia	.27	.33	.38	.26	.36	.38	.37
APPQ Agoraphobia	**.42**	.36	.37	.26	.34	.36	.35
GADQ-IV	**.50**	**.51**	**.46**	**.67**	**.67**	**.48**	**.51**

NOTE: $N = 406$. Correlations ≥ .40 are in bold. Agora = Agoraphobia. GAD = generalized anxiety disorder. MDD = major depressive disorder. PTSD = posttraumatic stress disorder. OCD = obsessive-compulsive disorder. SPQ = Schizotypal Personality Questionnaire. IDAS-II = Expanded Version of the Inventory of Depression and Anxiety Symptoms. APPQ = Albany Panic and Phobia Questionnaire. FQ = Fear Questionnaire. MASQ = Mood and Anxiety Symptom Questionnaire. GADQ-IV = Generalized Anxiety Questionnaire-IV.

Summary

Generally speaking, our data establish that anxiety symptom scales display moderate to strong criterion validity. This was true of the GADQ-IV (which correlated .67 with GAD diagnoses in Sample 4); both self-report and interview-based measures of social anxiety and panic symptoms (which had criterion correlations generally falling in the .40 to .65 range); and IDAS-II Claustrophobia (which had a weighted mean correlation of .47 with agoraphobia). There were two exceptions, however. First, APPQ Agoraphobia ($r = .37$) and FQ Agoraphobia ($r = .38$) had relatively unimpressive associations with agoraphobia diagnoses. Second, the PSRS Animal, Bodily Harm, and Blood-Injection scales had criterion coefficients ranging from only .11 to .12 with diagnoses of specific phobia. These lower criterion correlations may reflect significant validity problems that need to be examined more closely in future research.

In contrast, with a few exceptions (e.g., the IDAS-CR Panic data in Table 8.11), the scales tended to show unimpressive diagnostic specificity. Again, these results may be due to validity issues that need to be explicated in subsequent research. They also may reflect important problems—such as comorbidity (see Chapter 1)—in the diagnoses themselves. It will be important for future work to clarify the main causes of these surprisingly nonspecific associations.

INCREMENTAL VALIDITY

IDAS-II Analyses

Finally, we will examine the incremental predictive power of anxiety symptom scales using logistic regression analysis. In the first series of analyses, we tested the incremental validity of various IDAS-II scales in predicting five *DSM* diagnoses: major depression, social phobia, panic disorder, agoraphobia, and specific phobia. In Samples 1 and 2, we included the IDAS-II Social Anxiety (the original five-item version) and Panic scales as predictors of these disorders. In Samples 4 and 5, we used the Social Anxiety (expanded six-item version), Panic, and Claustrophobia scales as predictors. We included the IDAS-II Dysphoria scale as an additional predictor in all four samples to model the influence of general distress/negative affectivity. In these (and subsequent) analyses, the symptom scores were standardized to put them on the same metric.

Table 8.16 presents the odds ratios (ORs) from these logistic regressions. IDAS-II Social Anxiety made a significant incremental contribution to the prediction of

Table 8.16 ODDS RATIOS FROM LOGISTIC REGRESSION ANALYSES PREDICTING *DSM* DIAGNOSES FROM IDAS-II SYMPTOM SCALES

Sample/Scale	Major Depression	Social Phobia	Panic Disorder	Agora	Specific Phobia
Sample 1					
Dysphoria	**6.76**	0.80	**4.01**	0.93	1.41
Social Anxiety*	0.91	**3.59**	0.63	**2.03**	0.79
Panic	0.84	0.90	**2.64**	**1.68**	1.36
Sample 2					
Dysphoria	**7.77**	0.85	1.33	0.94	0.73
Social Anxiety*	1.12	**4.12**	**1.83**	**3.26**	1.54
Panic	0.96	1.13	**2.20**	**2.02**	**1.72**
Sample 4					
Dysphoria	**6.63**	1.40	**2.43**	1.08	.—
Social Anxiety	0.65	**1.95**	0.88	1.48	.—
Panic	1.27	1.24	0.97	1.01	.—
Claustrophobia	1.21	0.94	**1.56**	**2.28**	.—
Sample 5					
Dysphoria	**6.16**	0.76	0.99	0.64	1.18
Social Anxiety	0.85	**3.13**	1.41	1.13	1.22
Panic	1.01	0.70	1.35	1.33	0.76
Claustrophobia	0.76	1.14	**1.44**	**2.36**	**2.00**

NOTE: $N = 337$ (Sample 1), 267 (Sample 2), 407 (Sample 4), 290 (Sample 5). Significant effects ($p < .05$) are in bold. Agora = Agoraphobia.
*Original five-item version of scale.

social phobia diagnoses in all four samples, with ORs ranging from 1.95 to 4.12. Social Anxiety also contributed significantly in analyses involving agoraphobia in Samples 1 and 2, as well as panic disorder in Sample 2. The IDAS-II Panic scale contributed significantly to the prediction of panic disorder in two of four analyses (Samples 1 and 2). It also made a significant incremental contribution in analyses involving agoraphobia (Samples 1 and 2) and specific phobia (Sample 2). Finally, IDAS-II Claustrophobia added significantly to the prediction of agoraphobia in Samples 4 and 5, and to the prediction of specific phobia in Sample 5; it also displayed incremental power in relation to panic disorder in both Samples 4 and 5. Overall, these results yield impressive evidence of incremental validity and further support the construct validity of these scales.

IDAS-CR Analyses

Next, we conducted a parallel series of analyses using three IDAS-CR ratings—Social Anxiety, Panic, and Dysphoria—as predictors of these same five diagnoses in Samples 1 through 3. Table 8.17 reports the ORs from these analyses. These results provide further evidence of the incremental predictive power of these anxiety symptoms. IDAS-CR Social Anxiety made a significant incremental contribution to the prediction of social phobia diagnoses in all three analyses, with ORs ranging from 2.17 to 3.86. Social Anxiety also contributed significantly in analyses involving major depression (all three samples), agoraphobia (Samples 1 and 2), and panic disorder (Sample 2). IDAS-CR Panic added significantly to the

Table 8.17 Odds Ratios From Logistic Regression Analyses Predicting *DSM* Diagnoses From IDAS-CR Ratings

Sample/Scale	Major Depression	Social Phobia	Panic Disorder	Agora	Specific Phobia
Sample 1					
Dysphoria	**2.38**	1.31	1.99	1.26	1.25
Social Anxiety	**1.50**	**2.17**	1.07	**1.62**	1.11
Panic	**1.53**	0.96	**4.90**	**2.15**	1.12
Sample 2					
Dysphoria	**4.09**	1.32	1.59	1.64	1.32
Social Anxiety	**1.61**	**3.02**	**2.10**	**2.49**	1.37
Panic	**1.67**	**1.49**	**4.01**	**2.19**	1.27
Sample 3					
Dysphoria	**4.04**	0.91	1.09	.—	.—
Social Anxiety	**1.81**	**3.86**	1.22	.—	.—
Panic	1.22	1.10	**3.66**	.—	.—

NOTE: $N = 339$ (Sample 1), 268 (Sample 2), 252 (Sample 3). Significant effects ($p < .05$) are in bold. Agora = Agoraphobia.

Table 8.18 Odds Ratios From Logistic Regression Analyses Predicting *DSM* Diagnoses From IDAS Dysphoria and the PSRS Scales

Scale	Social Phobia	Agoraphobia	Specific Phobia
IDAS Dysphoria	1.30	**1.63**	**4.09**
PSRS Social	**3.32**	**1.85**	1.06
PSRS Physical Confinement	0.94	**3.07**	1.33
PSRS Bodily Harm	0.80	0.67	0.97
PSRS Blood-Injection	1.12	1.18	1.05
PSRS Animal	1.00	0.87	1.30

NOTE: $N = 579$. Significant effects ($p < .05$) are in bold. IDAS = Inventory of Depression and Anxiety Symptoms. PSRS = Phobic Stimuli Response Scales.

prediction of panic disorder in all three samples, with ORs ranging from 3.66 to 4.90. In addition, it provided significant incremental variance in analyses involving agoraphobia (Samples 1 and 2), major depression (Samples 1 and 2), and social phobia (Sample 2).

PSRS Analyses

In the final series of analyses, we tested the incremental predictive power of the five PSRS scales in a combined dataset collapsed across Samples 1 and 2 ($N = 579$). We examined the incremental validity of these scales in predicting three conceptually related *DSM-IV* diagnoses: social phobia, agoraphobia, and specific phobia. Once again, we included the IDAS-II Dysphoria scale as an additional predictor to model the influence of general distress/negative affectivity.

The ORs from these analyses are presented in Table 8.18. PSRS Social made a significant incremental contribution to the prediction of both social phobia (OR = 3.32) and agoraphobia (OR = 1.85), whereas Physical Confinement added significantly in the analysis of agoraphobia (OR = 3.07). These findings provide further support for the construct validity of these scales. It is noteworthy, however, that the three remaining PSRS scales—Bodily Harm, Blood-Injection, and Animal—failed to contribute significantly in any analysis, including the prediction of specific phobia (ORs ranged from 0.97 to 1.30). These results raise further concerns about the validity of these scales.

CONCLUDING SUMMARY

We have presented data on a large number of self-report and interview-based measures of anxiety symptoms. Our analyses included measures assessing symptoms of social anxiety/social phobia (e.g., IDAS-II Social Anxiety, APPQ Social Phobia), panic disorder (e.g., IDAS-II Panic, MASQ Anxious Arousal), agoraphobia (e.g., FQ Agoraphobia, APPQ Agoraphobia), claustrophobia (IDAS-II

Claustrophobia), specific phobia (e.g., PSRS Animal, PSRS Blood-Injection), and GAD (GADQ-IV). Generally speaking, these symptom measures exhibited impressive construct validity. Specifically, they tended to show strong convergent validity and significant discriminant validity vis-à-vis both self-report and interview-based measures, as well as substantial criterion validity and impressive incremental validity in relation to conceptually linked *DSM* diagnoses. These results support the continued use of these scales.

However, we also have noted some problems along the way that merit further attention in future research. We will highlight two problems that are particularly deserving of closer scrutiny. First, anxiety symptom measures tended to show poor diagnostic specificity. That is, although they typically had moderate to strong polyserial correlations with their target diagnoses, they often displayed equally strong relations with at least some other disorders. Second, self-report measures of agoraphobia and specific phobia (particularly the latter) generally showed unimpressive criterion and incremental validity in our analyses. Future research should include a broader array of predictors and outcomes to provide more exhaustive tests of the validity of these symptom measures.

9

The Structure, Validity, and Specificity of OCD Symptoms

In this chapter, we examine symptoms of obsessive-compulsive disorder (OCD). Beginning in *DSM-5* (American Psychiatric Association, 2013), OCD is the centerpiece of a new diagnostic class: obsessive-compulsive and related disorders (OCRDs). However, in *DSM-III, DSM-III-R*, and *DSM-IV*, OCD was included within the anxiety disorders. Most of the research presented here was developed within the framework of *DSM-IV*, so we will emphasize how OCD symptoms relate to various indicators of anxiety and depression. For example, later in the chapter we examine how OCD symptom measures relate to diagnoses of OCD, as well as major depression and various anxiety disorders. We will present extensive data related to hoarding, but we will not consider other *DSM-5* OCRDs (e.g., body dysmorphic disorder, trichotillomania, excoriation disorder) in any detail.

It is noteworthy that the *DSM* has never presented a specific, detailed list of OCD symptoms. For instance, *DSM-5* simply defines OCD as the "presence of obsessions, compulsions, or both" (p. 237) and then provides brief examples of each (e.g., hand washing, ordering, and checking are provided as exemplars of compulsions). Nevertheless, similar to posttraumatic stress disorder (PTSD; see Chapter 7), there is a rich literature examining the nature and correlates of specific symptom dimensions within OCD. We will begin this chapter by reviewing early attempts to assess OCD symptoms, as well as the structural evidence that eventually led to the identification of core, consensual dimensions within the disorder. We then review instruments that have been developed to assess these core symptom dimensions and discuss the validity (including convergent, discriminant, criterion, and incremental validity) and specificity of the scales included in these measures.

SELF-REPORT SYMPTOM MEASURES

Early Assessment Instruments

Several self-report OCD symptom inventories were developed during the 1970s and 1980s, including the Leyton Obsessional Inventory (LOI; Cooper, 1970), the

Compulsive Activity Checklist (CAC; Marks, Hallam, Connolly, & Philpott, 1977), the Maudsley Obsessive-Compulsive Inventory (MOCI; Hodgson & Rachman, 1977), and the Padua Inventory (Sanavio, 1988). Although these older instruments had some attractive features, they also were limited in significant ways (for detailed critiques of these early self-report measures, see Foa, Kozak, Salkovskis, Coles, & Amir, 1998; Taylor, 1995b; Thordarson et al., 2004). For instance, the three subscales of the LOI are very strongly interrelated (with correlations ranging between .70 and .91), raising serious concerns about their discriminant validity (Taylor, 1995b). The CAC does not provide a comprehensive assessment of this domain, in that it focuses narrowly on checking and washing rituals and does not measure important types of obsessions (Foa et al., 1998). Similarly, the Padua Inventory also has been criticized for failing to measure important groups of symptoms (see Foa et al., 1998; Thordarson et al., 2004).

The Structure of OCD Symptoms

The most significant limitation of these early measures, however, is that they were developed prior to the publication of structural analyses that clarified the underlying structure of the OCD domain. OCD subsumes a broad range of symptoms, and researchers increasingly recognized that the disorder is phenotypically—perhaps even genotypically—heterogeneous (Baer, 1994; Calamari et al., 2004; Eapen, Robertson, Alsobrook, & Pauls, 1997; Leckman et al., 1997; Summerfeldt, Richter, Antony, & Swinson, 1999). Structural analyses have documented the existence of several replicable symptom dimensions, each of which is characterized by prominent obsessions and compulsions (e.g., Baer, 1994; Leckman et al., 1997, 2010; Summerfeldt et al., 1999). Mataix-Cols, Rosario-Campos, and Leckman (2005) reviewed 12 major factor analytic studies and established the existence of four highly replicable symptom dimensions: (1) symmetry and ordering, (2) cleaning and contamination, (3) obsessions and checking, and (4) hoarding.

Furthermore, in an international survey of 187 OCD experts (Mataix-Cols et al., 2007), 89% of the respondents agreed that OCD is heterogeneous and consists of distinct symptom dimensions. Moreover, the experts explicitly acknowledged the existence of these same four symptom dimensions: cleaning (92% endorsement), symmetry/order (87%), hoarding (85%), and obsessions and checking (85%). A majority of the experts (69%) also supported the existence of a fifth dimension related to sexual and religious obsessions, but this factor has not consistently emerged in structural analyses.

OCI and OCI-R

OCI

The Obsessive-Compulsive Inventory (OCI; Foa et al., 1998) was the first self-report instrument to provide systematic coverage of these replicable symptom dimensions. The original version of the OCI contained seven subscales: Obsessing,

Mental Neutralizing, Checking, Doubting, Washing, Ordering, and Hoarding. However, analyses of the OCI scales quickly revealed some significant problems (see Wu & Watson, 2003). The most serious problem was the very poor discriminant validity of the original Checking and Doubting scales. In two large student samples, Wu and Watson (2003) obtained correlations of .81 and .78 between these scales, suggesting that they actually assess a single underlying construct. This problem reflects the fact that the original OCI subscales were created on rational grounds, rather than through rigorous structural analyses.

OCI-R

Foa and her colleagues corrected this problem, however, when they constructed the revised OCI (OCI-R; Foa et al., 2002). To create this new version of the instrument, Foa et al. (2002) subjected the OCI items to factor analyses, which identified six underlying dimensions, rather than the hypothesized seven. Accordingly, the original Doubting scale was dropped, thereby eliminating its problematic relation to Checking. In addition, each of the six remaining scales was shortened to three items apiece, yielding an overall instrument with 18 items. We report extensive data on the OCI-R scales in this chapter.

SCOPI

Development of the SCOPI

Around this same time, Watson and Wu began developing the Schedule of Compulsions, Obsessions, and Pathological Impulses (SCOPI; see Watson & Wu, 2005). The SCOPI scales were created from factor analyses of data from two large student samples (*N*s = 482; 466). These analyses resulted in a final 47-item measure containing five scales; participants indicate their level of agreement with each item using a 5-point response format (1 = strongly disagree, 5 = strongly agree).

The SCOPI contains three core OCD symptom scales. Obsessive Checking is the longest (14 items) and broadest scale; it is composed of items assessing recurring and intrusive thoughts (e.g., "I sometimes find that I cannot get rid of unpleasant thoughts that have popped into my mind"), obsessions of doubt (e.g., "I often am plagued by the nagging doubt that I've failed to do something important"), checking (e.g., "I spend a lot of time checking things over and over again"), and counting (e.g., "I sometimes count things over and over again"). Next, high scorers on Obsessive Cleanliness (12 items) express considerable concern about germs and contamination (e.g., "I worry a lot about germs"); they report that cleanliness is very important to them (e.g., "I don't like wearing clothes that are dirty"), and that they wash themselves frequently. Third, Compulsive Rituals (eight items) assesses individual differences in the need to perform common tasks in a fixed, ritualistic manner (e.g., "I have little rituals that I follow even though I know they are silly"; "If I don't do certain tasks in a particular order, I feel uncomfortable"). We will examine these three scales in detail.

These core OCD scales are strongly interrelated and clearly define a common underlying construct. For example, Table 9.1 presents correlations among the

Table 9.1 Correlations Among the SCOPI Scales in a Combined Student Sample

SCOPI Scale	1	2	3	4
1. Obsessive Checking	.—			
2. Obsessive Cleanliness	**.50**	.—		
3. Compulsive Rituals	**.56**	**.50**	.—	
4. Hoarding	.42	.21	.26	.—
5. Pathological Impulses	.37	.14	.20	.25

NOTE: $N = 2{,}837$. All correlations are significant at $p < .01$, two-tailed. Correlations of |.50| and greater are in bold. SCOPI = Schedule of Compulsions, Obsessions, and Pathological Impulses. Adapted from Watson and Wu (2005, Table 1).

SCOPI scales in a very large student sample ($N = 2{,}837$; these data are adapted from Watson & Wu, 2005, Table 1). Correlations among the three core SCOPI scales ranged from .50 to .56 (mean $r = .52$) in this sample.

The SCOPI also includes a five-item Hoarding scale (e.g., "I find it difficult to throw things away even when I know I don't need them"). It is important to note that Hoarding is only weakly to moderately correlated with the core OCD scales. For instance, Table 9.1 reports correlations ranging from .21 to .42 (mean $r = .30$) with the three core scales. Other data indicate that hoarding is linked to a broad range of psychopathology and is not specific to OCD (Watson & Wu, 2005; Wu & Watson, 2005). Indeed, Mataix-Cols et al. (2010) concluded that "the phenomenological differences between hoarding and OCD outweigh the similarities" (p. 570). Based on this evidence, hoarding disorder now is listed as a separate OCRD in *DSM-5*. Nevertheless, because this symptom dimension has been included in many widely used OCD measures, we will examine it here.

Finally, the eight-item Pathological Impulses scale contains content related to kleptomania (e.g., "Occasionally I will have a sudden urge to steal something"), pyromania (e.g., "I find that I am fascinated by fire"), and other types of dysfunctional impulses (e.g., "While driving, I sometimes have the impulse to do something crazy"). However, Watson and Wu (2005) found that Pathological Impulses correlated only modestly with the other SCOPI scales. For example, Table 9.1 reports correlations ranging from only .14 to .37, with a mean value of .24. Furthermore, Pathological Impulses displayed relatively weak associations with other OCD measures; for instance, correlations with the OCI-R scales ranged from .18 to .42 (mean $r = .25$) in a sample of 2,228 students. Consequently, it will not be discussed in this chapter.

Relations With the OCI-R

The accumulated data indicate that the SCOPI and OCI-R assess four common symptom dimensions: checking, ordering/rituals, washing/cleaning, and hoarding. Table 9.2 presents correlations between paired OCI-R and SCOPI scales in a

Table 9.2 Multitrait-Multimethod Matrix of Selected SCOPI and OCI-R Scales in a Combined Student Sample

Scale	1	2	3	4	5	6	7	8
SCOPI Scales								
1. Obsessive Checking	.—							
2. Compulsive Rituals	.54	.—						
3. Obsessive Cleanliness	.49	.49	.—					
4. Hoarding	.43	.28	.21	.—				
OCI-R Scales								
5. Checking	**.73**	.44	.40	.27	.—			
6. Ordering	.45	**.64**	.42	.24	.50	.—		
7. Washing	.46	.40	**.64**	.20	.56	.50	.—	
8. Hoarding	.42	.27	.20	**.77**	.41	.35	.33	.—

NOTE: $N = 2{,}228$. Convergent correlations are in bold. All correlations are significant at $p < .01$. SCOPI = Schedule of Compulsions, Obsessions, and Pathological Impulses. OCI-R = Obsessive-Compulsive Inventory–Revised. Adapted from Watson and Wu (2005, Table 4).

very large student sample ($N = 2{,}228$). These data establish that SCOPI Obsessive Checking maps onto OCI-R Checking ($r = .73$), SCOPI Obsessive Cleanliness converges strongly with OCI-R Washing ($r = .64$), SCOPI Compulsive Rituals is linked to OCI-R Ordering ($r = .64$), and SCOPI Hoarding assesses the same underlying construct as OCI-R Hoarding ($r = .77$). Moreover, each of these convergent correlations is significantly higher than all of the other coefficients in its row and column of the heteromethod block (*zs* ranged from 10.96 to 34.88; all *ps* < .01, two-tailed), indicating a strong level of discriminant validity. These clear convergent/discriminant relations further establish that specific types of OCD symptoms can be meaningfully distinguished from one another.

What about the other two OCI-R scales? As noted earlier, Obsessive Checking is the broadest SCOPI scale. Not surprisingly, therefore, OCI-R Obsessing ($r = .52$) and Mental Neutralizing ($r = .47$) both correlated most strongly with Obsessive Checking in this sample and had weaker associations with the other SCOPI scales (*rs* ranged from .23 to .42, mean $r = .30$). These results demonstrate that Obsessive Checking contains content related to obsessive intrusions that overlaps with these OCI-R scales.

Relations With the Y-BOCS

Watson and Wu (2005) also examined relations between the SCOPI and the self-report version of the Yale-Brown Obsessive-Compulsive Scale (Y-BOCS) Symptom Checklist, which was developed by Baer (1991). Participants completed a modified version of this instrument, in which the traditional checklist format was replaced with a 5-point Likert scale (ranging from *strongly disagree* to *strongly agree*); this change was made because the checklist format is highly susceptible to response biases (see Clark & Watson, 1995). Structural analyses of the Y-BOCS

Table 9.3 Multitrait-Multimethod Matrix of Selected SCOPI and Y-BOCS Scales

Scale	1	2	3	4	5	6	7	8
SCOPI Scales								
1. Obsessive Checking	.—	.74	.62	.44	**.55**	.66	.47	.35
2. Compulsive Rituals	.67	.—	.60	.30	.40	**.60**	.41	.30
3. Obsessive Cleanliness	.57	.59	.—	.32	.36	.45	**.59**	.30
4. Hoarding	.39	.24	.22	.—	.23	.23	.22	**.60**
Y-BOCS Scales								
5. Obsessions/Checking	**.57**	.38	.32	.29	.—	.68	.69	.44
6. Symmetry/Ordering	.57	**.56**	.41	.26	.61	.—	.57	.46
7. Contamination/Cleaning	.46	.43	**.58**	.19	.63	.60	.—	.51
8. Hoarding	.36	.22	.19	**.62**	.48	.48	.38	.—

NOTE: Student correlations ($N = 419$) are shown below the diagonal; patient correlations ($N = 149$) are displayed above the diagonal. Convergent correlations are in bold. All correlations are significant at $p < .01$. SCOPI = Schedule of Compulsions, Obsessions, and Pathological Impulses. Y-BOCS = Yale-Brown Obsessive-Compulsive Scale. Adapted from Watson and Wu (2005, Tables 5 and 6).

(Leckman et al., 1997; Summerfeldt et al., 1999) have identified four distinctive symptom factors, which were used to create corresponding scales: Obsessions and Checking (21 items), Contamination and Cleanliness (12 items), Symmetry and Ordering (5 items), and Hoarding (2 items).

Table 9.3 presents correlations between the SCOPI and Y-BOCS scales in student ($N = 419$) and patient ($N = 149$) samples. Following the pattern observed earlier with the OCI-R, it can be seen that these two inventories generally converge well and assess this domain similarly. Two scale pairs show very clear convergent/discriminant patterns in both samples. Specifically, Y-BOCS Contamination/Cleaning converges with SCOPI Obsessive Cleanliness ($r = .58$ and .59 in the student and patient samples, respectively), whereas Y-BOCS Hoarding is strongly linked to SCOPI Hoarding ($r = .62$ and .60, respectively). Furthermore, each of these convergent correlations is significantly higher than all of the other coefficients in its row and column of the heteromethod block in both samples (*z*s ranged from 2.07 to 9.88; all *p*s < .05, two-tailed), demonstrating clear discriminant validity.

The remaining scales show more complex patterns, however. As would be expected, Y-BOCS Obsessions/Checking correlates strongly with SCOPI Obsessive Checking ($r = .57$ and .55, respectively). This convergent association is significantly higher than all of the other coefficients in its row or column of the heteromethod block in both samples (*z*s ranged from 2.72 to 6.64; all *p*s < .01, two-tailed), except that it did not exceed the correlation between Y-BOCS Symmetry/Ordering and SCOPI Obsessive Checking in either sample ($z = 0.00$ and −2.23, respectively). Similarly, the Y-BOCS Symmetry/Ordering scale correlated substantially with SCOPI Compulsive Rituals ($r = .56$ and .60, respectively).

This coefficient is significantly higher than all of the other correlations in its row or column of the heteromethod block (*zs* ranged from 2.53 to 8.14; all $ps < .05$, two-tailed), except that it did not exceed the association between Y-BOCS Symmetry/Ordering and SCOPI Obsessive Checking ($z = 0.00$ and -1.36, respectively).

Overall, these data indicate that the SCOPI and the Y-BOCS assess very similar content, although this content is arranged somewhat differently. Both instruments contain clear, direct measures of washing/cleaning and hoarding. In addition, they both include items assessing checking, obsessive intrusions, counting, ordering, and rituals; however, these symptoms are grouped somewhat differently in the two instruments.

IDAS-II

Development of the IDAS-II OCD Scales

The original IDAS item pool contained a single 14-item HIC assessing various types of OCD symptoms. These items marked a distinct and interpretable dimension in the initial Phase 1 scale development analyses. However, they failed to define a replicable factor in the main Phase 2 structural analyses (see Watson et al., 2007, Study 2). Consequently, the original version of the IDAS did not contain any OCD-related content.

We suspected that our initial approach was problematic, however, in that we assessed OCD-related content in an undifferentiated manner, rather than targeting specific symptom dimensions (e.g., checking, cleaning) systematically. We therefore adopted a very different strategy in developing the IDAS-II. Specifically, we expanded our coverage in the IDAS-II item pool to include three distinct HICs related to cleaning (nine items; e.g., worried a lot about germs), checking/counting (eight items; e.g., checked things repeatedly), and ordering/rituals (seven items; e.g., needed to do things in a fixed, specific order). Based on evidence that was summarized earlier, we concluded that hoarding was not specific to OCD and, therefore, decided not to create a HIC to assess these types of symptoms.

These three sets of OCD-related items marked clear, replicable factors in both of our scale development samples. This led to the creation of corresponding scales that we labeled Cleaning (seven items), Checking (three items), and Ordering (five items).

Relations With the SCOPI and OCI-R

Based on their content, these three IDAS-II OCD scales appear to tap the same basic symptoms as corresponding measures in the SCOPI and OCI-R. We can test the convergence between these three instruments using data from Sample 4. Table 9.4 presents correlations between corresponding checking, ordering, and cleaning scales from the IDAS-II, SCOPI, and OCI-R in the form of a multitrait-multimethod matrix. These results establish a strong level of convergent validity across the three sets of scales. Specifically, correlations among the three checking scales ranged from .64 to .74, with a mean value of .68; correlations among the

Table 9.4 Multitrait-Multimethod Matrix of Parallel OCD Symptom Scales From the IDAS-II, SCOPI, and OCI-R (Sample 4)

Measure	1	2	3	4	5	6	7	8	9
IDAS-II Scales									
1. Checking	.—								
2. Ordering	.75	.—							
3. Cleaning	.62	.63	.—						
SCOPI Scales									
4. Checking	**.64**	.58	.50	.—					
5. Rituals	.54	**.66**	.44	.73	.—				
6. Cleaning	.44	.48	**.71**	.59	.58	.—			
OCI-R Scales									
7. Checking	**.66**	.54	.50	**.74**	.55	.49	.—		
8. Ordering	.56	**.64**	.46	.61	**.70**	.46	.60	.—	
9. Cleaning	.48	.51	**.70**	.58	.49	**.69**	.61	.53	.—

NOTE: $N = 411$. Convergent correlations are in bold. All correlations are significant at $p < .05$. OCD = obsessive-compulsive disorder. IDAS-II = Expanded version of the Inventory of Depression and Anxiety Symptoms. SCOPI = Schedule of Compulsions, Obsessions, and Pathological Impulses. OCI-R = Obsessive-Compulsive Inventory–Revised.

ordering scales ranged from .64 to .70, with an average coefficient of .67; and correlations among the cleaning/washing scales ranged from .69 to .71, with a mean value of .70.

As in previous analyses, we can examine the key issue of discriminant validity by comparing each convergent coefficient to all of the other values in its row or column of the heteromethod block. Overall, the Table 9.4 data yield 36 tests of discriminant validity (12 comparisons per block *x* three heteromethod blocks). All 36 comparisons were significant ($p < .05$, one-tailed), with z values ranging from 2.11 to 8.67.

Based on these data, we can conclude that the OCI-R, SCOPI, and IDAS-II all contain parallel indicators of checking, ordering/rituals, and washing/cleaning. The SCOPI and OCI-R also contain highly correlated measures of hoarding, whereas the IDAS-II does not.

CONVERGENCE WITH INTERVIEW MEASURES

IMAS Analyses

Relations With IMAS Scales

Thus far, we only have presented convergent/discriminant validity analyses between different sets of self-report scales. We now broaden our scope by

Table 9.5 Correlations Between the IDAS-II OCD Scales and the IMAS Scales in Sample 5

IMAS Scale	Checking	Ordering	Cleaning
Obsessive-Compulsive Disorder	**.66**	**.68**	**.68**
Posttraumatic Stress Disorder	.37	.39	.35
Agoraphobia	.34	.31	.43
Generalized Anxiety Disorder	.34	.36	.34
Depression	.34	.34	.34
Specific Phobia	.27	.31	.40
Panic	.32	.31	.32
Social Phobia	.28	.27	.37
Irritability	.29	.28	.26
Mania	.27	.30	.22

NOTE: $N = 362$ patients. Correlations ≥ .50 are in bold. All correlations are significant at $p < .01$. IDAS-II = Expanded version of the Inventory of Depression and Anxiety Symptoms. OCD = obsessive-compulsive disorder. IMAS = Interview of Mood and Anxiety Symptoms.

examining convergent and discriminant validity vis-à-vis interview-based measures of these same symptoms. We begin by reporting two series of convergent/discriminant validity analyses between the IDAS-II OCD scales and the interview-based IMAS. If these IDAS-II scales are valid and specific indicators of OCD, then they should correlate more strongly with the 19-item IMAS OCD scale than with the other IMAS scales. These correlations are presented in Table 9.5 (using data from Sample 5, $N = 362$ patients) and Table 9.6 (Sample 11, $N - 393$ students).

Table 9.6 Correlations Between the IDAS-II OCD Scales and the IMAS Scales in Sample 11

IMAS Scale	Checking	Ordering	Cleaning
Obsessive-Compulsive Disorder	**.67**	**.69**	**.54**
Posttraumatic Stress Disorder	.32	.36	.19
Agoraphobia	.32	.30	.27
Generalized Anxiety Disorder	.34	.29	.16
Depression	.33	.30	.13
Specific Phobia	.18	.15	.22
Panic	.32	.30	.17
Social Phobia	.24	.23	.19
Irritability	.28	.29	.11
Mania	.32	.29	.19

NOTE: $N = 393$ students. Correlations ≥ .50 are in bold. All correlations are significant at $p < .01$. IDAS-II = Expanded version of the Inventory of Depression and Anxiety Symptoms. OCD = obsessive-compulsive disorder. IMAS = Interview of Mood and Anxiety Symptoms.

These results provide evidence of excellent convergent validity. In the patient sample, the convergent correlations ranged from .66 to .68, with a mean value of .67; in the students, the convergent coefficients ranged from .54 to .69, with an average value of .64.

Furthermore, the IDAS-II OCD scales showed impressive discriminant validity, as their correlations with the nine remaining IMAS scales consistently were much lower. Across the two samples, the IDAS-II scales had mean discriminant correlations of .30 (Checking), .30 (Ordering), and .26 (Cleaning). Follow-up significance tests indicated that their convergent correlations with IMAS OCD were significantly stronger ($p < .01$, one-tailed) than these discriminant coefficients in all 54 comparisons across the two samples (*z*s ranged from 5.21 to 11.07).

Relations With IMAS OCD Subscales

The revised IMAS contains multiple OCD content scales, including measures of Checking (four items), Rituals (six items), and Cleaning (five items). Table 9.7 presents correlations between these narrower content scales and the IDAS-II OCD scales in the form of a multitrait-multimethod matrix; these coefficients are presented separately in Samples 5 ($N = 390$ patients) and 11 ($N = 402$ students). The two sets of scales displayed an impressive level of convergent validity in these data. The convergent coefficients in the patient sample ranged from .66 to .73, with a mean value of .69; corresponding values in the student data ranged from .65 to .67, with an average coefficient of .66.

Once again, we conducted significance tests comparing each of the convergent correlations to all of the other values in its row or column of the heteromethod block. Overall, this yielded a total of 24 comparisons (12 comparisons per sample × two

Table 9.7 Multitrait-Multimethod Matrix of IDAS-II and IMAS OCD Symptom Scales

Measure	1	2	3	4	5	6
IDAS-II Scales						
1. Checking	.—	.63	.47	**.66**	.52	.35
2. Ordering	.69	.—	.54	.49	**.65**	.36
3. Cleaning	.60	.60	.—	.36	.29	**.67**
IMAS Scales						
4. Checking	**.67**	.52	.46	.—	.52	.37
5. Rituals	.53	**.66**	.50	.62	.—	.34
6. Cleaning	.39	.42	**.73**	.44	.49	.—

NOTE: Sample 5 correlations ($N = 390$ patients) are presented below the diagonal; Sample 11 correlations ($N = 402$) are displayed above the diagonal. Convergent correlations are in bold. All correlations are significant at $p < .05$. IDAS-II = Expanded version of the Inventory of Depression and Anxiety Symptoms. IMAS = Interview of Mood and Anxiety Symptoms. OCD = obsessive-compulsive disorder.

samples); all 24 tests were statistically significant ($p < .01$, one-tailed), with z values ranging from 3.96 to 10.88. Thus, the IDAS-II OCD scales show strong and consistent evidence of discriminant validity vis-à-vis the IMAS OCD subscales in these samples.

PCCP Analyses

Correlational Analyses

Next, we report more intensive convergent and discriminant validity analyses involving multiple measures of checking, ordering, and cleaning. In the first series of analyses, each symptom dimension was assessed by two self-report scales (IDAS-II, SCOPI), as well as by clinicians' ratings on the Personality, Cognitions, Consciousness, and Perceptions Interview (PCCP; Chmielewski & Watson, 2008b; Koffel, 2011; Watson et al., 2012). The PCCP is modeled after the IDAS-CR and uses the same 3-point rating scale (*absent, subthreshold, present*). To assess each symptom, the interviewer asks a standard probe question and three to five follow-up questions (interrater reliability data are reported in Watson et al., 2012).

Table 9.8 presents correlations among these three instruments in the form of a multitrait-multimethod matrix. These results are displayed separately for patients ($N = 448$; this combines data from Samples 3 and 6) and students ($N = 591$; this aggregates responses from Samples 9 and 10). It should be noted that these findings were reported previously in Watson et al. (2012; see their Table 5).

We see strong evidence of convergent validity in these data. As one would expect, the level of convergence is particularly impressive between the two sets of

Table 9.8 Multitrait-Multimethod Matrix of Parallel Symptom Measures From the IDAS-II, SCOPI, and PCCP

Measure	1	2	3	4	5	6	7	8	9
IDAS-II									
1. Checking	.—	.65	.42	**.69**	.49	.37	**.51**	.31	.21
2. Ordering	.59	.—	.52	.55	**.69**	.43	.37	**.55**	.30
3. Cleaning	.26	.39	.—	.42	.43	**.73**	.23	.24	**.59**
SCOPI									
4. Checking	**.69**	.51	.36	.—	.65	.53	**.53**	.35	.29
5. Rituals	.45	**.76**	.37	.57	.—	.56	.35	**.59**	.32
6. Cleaning	.23	.36	**.77**	.44	.46	.—	.21	.28	**.58**
PCCP Ratings									
7. Checking	**.55**	.42	.24	**.59**	.41	.24	.—	.36	.21
8. Ordering	.38	**.67**	.29	.42	**.67**	.33	.46	.—	.26
9. Cleaning	.17	.24	**.68**	.27	.29	**.64**	.25	.30	.—

NOTE: Patient correlations ($N = 448$) are shown below the diagonal; student correlations ($N = 591$) are displayed above the diagonal. Convergent correlations are in bold. All correlations are significant at $p < .05$. IDAS-II = Expanded version of the Inventory of Depression and Anxiety Symptoms. SCOPI = Schedule of Compulsions, Obsessions, and Pathological Impulses. PCCP = Personality, Cognitions, Consciousness, and Perceptions Interview. Adapted from Watson et al. (2012), Table 5.

self-report scales, which produced an overall mean r of .72 across all symptoms and samples. It also is noteworthy that the IDAS-II (mean convergent $r = .59$) and SCOPI (mean $r = .59$) scales showed similarly strong correlations with the clinicians' ratings. Finally, it is reassuring to see that the convergent correlations were substantial across all three types of symptoms (for cleaning, mean $r = .67$; for ordering, mean $r = .66$; for checking, mean $r = .59$) and in both the patient (mean $r = .67$) and student (mean $r = .61$) data.

With regard to discriminant validity, all of the convergent correlations were at least .14 greater than the discriminant coefficients in the same row or column of the heteromethod block. Once again, we tested these differences formally. There are six different heteromethod blocks in Table 5, which yield a total of 72 individual comparisons (12 per block). All 72 comparisons were significant ($p < .01$, one-tailed; zs ranged from 4.55 to 11.49). Thus, we see clear and consistent evidence of discriminant validity in these data.

Factor Analyses

The participants in Samples 3 ($N = 252$ patients) and 9 ($N = 373$ students) also completed the OCI-R. Consequently, these participants were assessed on three self-report indicators (OCI-R, SCOPI, IDAS-II) and one interview measure (PCCP) of each target construct (i.e., checking, ordering, cleaning). Given the large number of indicators in each sample, we subjected them to structural analyses, which yield elegant tests of convergent and discriminant validity: If these measures are valid indicators of their target constructs, then they should define three readily interpretable factors that clearly represent these constructs.

We subjected these measures to separate principal factor analyses in each sample, using squared multiple correlations as the initial communality estimates. As would be expected, three interpretable factors emerged in each case and were rotated to oblique simple structure using promax (power = 3). The resulting factor loadings are presented in Table 9.9 (Sample 3) and Table 9.10 (Sample 9). Looking first at the patient data (see Table 9.9), the three factors obviously represent Cleaning, Ordering, and Checking, respectively. All four cleaning/washing measures were clear markers of Factor I, with loadings ranging from .79 (SCOPI Obsessive Cleanliness, IDAS-II Cleaning) to .88 (PCCP Cleaning); note also that all of the secondary loadings on the other two factors were less than $|.15|$. Next, the four indicators of ordering/rituals strongly defined Factor II, with loadings ranging from .75 (PCCP Ordering, OCI-R Ordering) to .84 (IDAS-II Ordering); the highest secondary loading was only .15 (OCI-R Ordering on Factor III). Finally, the four checking scales had loadings ranging from .62 (PCCP Checking) to .83 (IDAS-II Checking, OCI-R Checking) on Factor III; the strongest secondary loading was only .10 (PCCP Checking on Factor II). Not surprisingly, these factors were moderately to strongly interrelated, indicating that they define a common underlying domain (viz., OCD): the factor correlations were .44 (Cleaning with Checking), .47 (Cleaning with Ordering), and .64 (Ordering with Checking).

In the student sample (see Table 9.10), the three factors clearly can be identified as Checking, Cleaning, and Ordering, respectively. All four checking scales were relatively pure markers of Factor I, with loadings ranging from .68 (PCCP

Table 9.9 PROMAX FACTOR LOADINGS OF THE OCD SYMPTOM SCALES IN SAMPLE 3

Scale	I	II	III
PCCP Cleaning	**.88**	−.05	−.04
OCI-R Washing	**.86**	−.04	.07
IDAS-II Cleaning	**.79**	.04	.04
SCOPI Obsessive Cleanliness	**.79**	.14	−.01
IDAS-II Ordering	.03	**.84**	.06
SCOPI Compulsive Rituals	.06	**.80**	.04
OCI-R Ordering	−.05	**.75**	.15
PCCP Ordering	.02	**.75**	.01
OCI-R Checking	.05	.01	**.83**
IDAS-II Checking	−.07	.07	**.83**
SCOPI Obsessive Checking	.06	.05	**.81**
PCCP Checking	.03	.10	**.62**

NOTE: $N = 252$ patients. OCD = obsessive-compulsive disorder. Loadings ≥ |.40| are in bold. PCCP = Personality, Cognitions, Consciousness, and Perceptions Interview. OCI-R = Obsessive-Compulsive Inventory–Revised. IDAS-II = Expanded version of the Inventory of Depression and Anxiety Symptoms. SCOPI = Schedule of Compulsions, Obsessions, and Pathological Impulses.

Table 9.10 PROMAX FACTOR LOADINGS OF THE OCD SYMPTOM SCALES IN SAMPLE 9

Scale	I	II	III
OCI-R Checking	**.84**	.02	−.03
SCOPI Obsessive Checking	**.81**	.05	.05
IDAS-II Checking	**.78**	.04	.00
PCCP Checking	**.68**	−.12	.07
IDAS-II Cleaning	.07	**.90**	−.11
SCOPI Obsessive Cleanliness	−.02	**.81**	.09
PCCP Cleaning	−.16	**.75**	.04
OCI-R Washing	.20	**.63**	.05
PCCP Ordering	−.10	−.03	**.82**
SCOPI Compulsive Rituals	.13	.11	**.67**
OCI-R Ordering	.25	−.04	**.65**
IDAS-II Ordering	.26	.18	**.48**

NOTE: $N = 373$ students. OCD = obsessive-compulsive disorder. Loadings ≥ |.40| are in bold. OCI-R = Obsessive-Compulsive Inventory–Revised. SCOPI = Schedule of Compulsions, Obsessions, and Pathological Impulses. IDAS-II = Expanded version of the Inventory of Depression and Anxiety Symptoms. PCCP = Personality, Cognitions, Consciousness, and Perceptions Interview.

Checking) to .84 (OCI-R Checking). It is noteworthy that all of the secondary loadings on the other factors were less than |.15|. Similarly, the four indicators of cleaning/washing had loadings ranging from .63 (OCI-R Washing) to .90 (IDAS-II Cleaning) on Factor II; the highest secondary loading was only .20 (OCI-R Washing on Factor I). Finally, the four ordering/rituals measures had loadings ranging from .48 (IDAS-II Ordering) to .82 (PCCP Ordering) on Factor III; the strongest secondary loadings were only .26 (IDAS-II Ordering on Factor I) and .25 (OCI-R Ordering on Factor I). As would be expected, these three factors were strongly interrelated: the factor correlations were .52 (Cleaning with Ordering), .53 (Checking with Cleaning), and .65 (Checking with Ordering).

SPECIFICITY OF OCD SYMPTOMS

Symptom Specificity

Relations With Depression Symptoms

We now consider the key issue of specificity, that is, the extent to which symptom dimensions such as checking and cleaning are specific to OCD versus more broadly related to psychopathology. We begin by examining their associations with self-rated symptoms of depression. Watson (2009a) reported weighted mean correlations between the SCOPI and OCI-R scales and two widely used measures of depression: (1) the Beck Depression Inventory (Beck & Steer, 1993) or Beck Depression Inventory-II (Beck et al., 1996) and (2) the MASQ GD: Depression scale. Table 9.11 reproduces the mean coefficients from this review (these results are adapted from Watson, 2009a, Table 4). It is noteworthy that these correlations are much lower than those observed in Chapter 7 for PTSD: Whereas the correlations between PTSD symptoms and self-rated depression typically were in the .45 to .75 range (see Tables 7.2 and 7.3), the corresponding values in Table 9.11 generally fall between .25 and .45. In other words, the strongest correlations observed with OCD symptoms are similar in magnitude to the weakest associations obtained with PTSD symptoms. Clearly, OCD symptoms tend to be more weakly related to depression and are less saturated with general distress/negative affectivity than are PTSD symptoms.

As with PTSD, the individual OCD symptom dimensions display differential correlations with depression. Specifically, depression correlates more strongly with OCI-R Obsessions (overall mean $r=.42$) and SCOPI Obsessive Checking (overall mean $r=.43$) than with any other scale (mean *r*s ranged from .24 to .27). As discussed earlier, although SCOPI Obsessive Checking is broader in content than OCI-R Obsessing, both scales contain items assessing intrusive and recurring thoughts; for example, the former includes the item "I sometimes find that I cannot get rid of unpleasant thoughts that have popped into my mind," whereas the latter contains the item "I frequently get nasty thoughts and have difficulty getting rid of them." Consequently, the data in Table 9.11 indicate that these types of obsessive intrusions are most strongly linked to depression.

Table 9.11 Weighted Mean Correlations Between OCD Symptoms and Depression

OCD Scale	BDI	MASQ GD: D	Weighted *M*
OCI-R			
Obsessions	**.38**	**.46**	**.42**
Washing	.28	.26	.27
Checking	.23	**.32**	.27
Ordering	.21	**.31**	.26
Hoarding	.19	**.33**	.26
Neutralizing	.18	**.33**	.26
SCOPI			
Obsessive Checking	**.42**	**.43**	**.43**
Hoarding	.11	.27	.25
Compulsive Rituals	.04	.26	.24
Obsessive Cleanliness	.09	.26	.24

Note: $N = 1{,}531–1{,}535$ (OCI-R vs. BDI), 1,532 (OCI-R vs. MASQ GD: D), 291 (SCOPI vs. BDI-II), 2,273 (SCOPI vs. MASQ GD: D). Correlations of |.30| and greater are in bold. OCD = obsessive-compulsive disorder. OCI-R = Obsessive-Compulsive Inventory–Revised. SCOPI = Schedule of Compulsions, Obsessions, and Pathological Impulses. BDI = Beck Depression Inventory. MASQ GD:D = MASQ General Distress: Depressive Symptoms. Adapted from Watson (2009a, Table 4).

One limitation of Watson's (2009a) review is that it did not include any data clarifying the specificity of the IDAS-II OCD scales. We can examine this issue using the data from Sample 4. As already noted (see Table 9.4 and the accompanying discussion), the Sample 4 participants were assessed on three OCD symptom inventories: the IDAS-II, SCOPI, and OCI-R. They also completed three self-report measures of depression symptoms: IDAS-II Dysphoria, the Patient Health Questionnaire (PHQ-9; Kroenke et al., 2001), and the Depressivity scale from the Personality Inventory for *DSM-5* (PID-5; Krueger et al., 2012). In addition to the individual scales, we created a Depression Composite by standardizing these three measures and then combining them.

Table 9.12 presents correlations between these depression and OCD symptom scores. Three aspects of these data are noteworthy. First, these correlations tend to be somewhat higher than those displayed in Table 9.11: Whereas only one of those coefficients was greater than .45, several of the current correlations exceed .50.

Second, the OCI-R and SCOPI results essentially replicate the findings reported earlier by Watson (2009a). For example, the Depression Composite correlated significantly more strongly ($p < .01$, one-tailed) with OCI-R Obsessing ($r = .61$) than with any other OCI-R scale (*r*s ranged from .35 to .42; *z*s ranged from 5.01 to 6.73). Similarly, the Depression Composite had a significantly stronger correlation with

Table 9.12 Correlations Between Self-Report Measures of OCD and Depression Symptoms (Sample 4)

Symptom Measure	IDAS-II Dysphoria	PHQ-9	PID-5 Depressivity	Composite
OCI-R Scales				
Obsessing	**.56**	**.57**	**.56**	**.61**
Checking	**.42**	.39	.34	**.42**
Neutralizing	.36	.38	.34	.39
Hoarding	.36	.38	.32	.38
Washing	.35	.32	.31	.35
Ordering	.33	.31	.31	.35
SCOPI Scales				
Obsessive Checking	**.51**	**.47**	**.48**	**.53**
Hoarding	.31	.26	.28	.30
Compulsive Rituals	.25	.22	.27	.27
Obsessive Cleanliness	.20	.15	.14	.18
IDAS-II Scales				
Checking	**.46**	.35	.31	**.41**
Ordering	**.44**	.32	.32	.39
Cleaning	.39	.27	.28	.34

NOTE: $N = 408$. Correlations ≥ .40 are in bold. OCD = obsessive-compulsive disorder. IDAS-II = Expanded Version of the Inventory of Depression and Anxiety Symptoms. PHQ-9 = Patient Health Questionnaire. PID-5 = Personality Inventory for *DSM-5*. OCI-R = Obsessive-Compulsive Inventory–Revised. SCOPI = Schedule of Compulsions, Obsessions, and Pathological Impulses.

SCOPI Obsessive Checking ($r = .53$) than with any other SCOPI scale (*r*s ranged from .18 to .30, *z*s ranged from 5.36 to 9.19). Consequently, these data again indicate that depression is more strongly linked to obsessive intrusions than to other types of OCD symptoms.

Third, unlike the other OCD instruments, the IDAS-II scales do not display a clear differential pattern. For instance, all three scales correlated similarly with the Depression Composite, with coefficients ranging from .34 (Cleaning) to .41 (Checking). Follow-up significance tests indicated that none of these coefficients differed significantly ($p < .05$, two-tailed) from the others (*z*s ranged from 0.53 to 1.66).

Relations With Anxiety Symptoms

The Sample 4 data also can be used to examine how various OCD symptoms relate to prominent symptoms of anxiety. In Chapter 6, we reported results on five anxiety scores that were derived from the Sample 4 data. We briefly review these measures here (see Chapter 6 for more details):

(1) The GADQ-IV (Newman et al., 2002) closely follows the diagnostic criteria for generalized anxiety disorder (GAD) and provides comprehensive assessment of GAD symptoms.
(2) We created a PTSD Composite based on (a) the intrusions and avoidance items from the PTSD Checklist; and (b) an aggregate score based on the Traumatic Intrusions and Traumatic Avoidance scales of the IDAS-II.
(3) We constructed a Panic Composite using (a) the IDAS-II Panic scale; (b) a reduced, nine-item version of the MASQ Anxious Arousal scale; and (3) an abbreviated, six-item version of the Panic Attack Symptom Questionnaire (Watson, 2000b).
(4) We created a Social Anxiety Composite by averaging four measures: (a) the Social Phobia scale from the Fear Questionnaire (FQ; Marks & Mathews, 1979); (2) the Social Phobia scale from the Albany Panic and Phobia Questionnaire (APPQ; Rapee et al., 1994/1995); (3) the IDAS-II Social Anxiety scale; and (4) a factor analytically derived Social Anxiety scale from the Schizotypal Personality Questionnaire (Chmielewski & Watson, 2008a).
(5) We constructed an Agoraphobia Composite by aggregating (a) the APPQ Agoraphobia scale and (b) the FQ Agoraphobia scale.

Table 9.13 presents correlations between these five symptom scores and the OCI-R, SCOPI, and IDAS-II OCD scales. The OCI-R findings replicate and extend those observed earlier with depression. It is particularly noteworthy that—as with depression—the anxiety symptoms tended to correlate more strongly with Obsessing than with the other OCI-R scales. Obsessing had correlations ranging from .52 to .65 (mean $r = .59$) with the GAD, PTSD, panic, and social anxiety symptoms; in contrast, the other OCI-R scales tended to be more moderately linked to these types of anxiety, with correlations ranging from .35 to .53 (mean $r = .43$). Follow-up tests indicated that these four anxiety symptom scores correlated significantly more strongly ($p < .05$, one-tailed) with Obsessing than with the other OCI-R scales in 19 of 20 comparisons (95%; z values ranged from 1.81 to 6.90); the sole exception was that the Panic Composite did not correlate more highly with Obsessing ($r = .58$) than with Checking ($r = .53$; $z = 1.35$, n.s.).

In contrast to the other anxiety scores, the Agoraphobia Composite yielded a nonspecific pattern of moderate correlations. Thus, it correlated similarly with Checking ($r = .47$), Obsessing ($r = .42$), Washing ($r = .42$), and Mental Neutralizing ($r = .40$). Generally speaking, however, the Table 9.13 data—together with the results seen earlier with depression—establish that Obsessing shows greater nonspecificity and has a stronger component of general distress/negative affectivity than the other OCI-R scales.

As would be expected based on previous results, anxiety symptoms correlated more strongly with Obsessive Checking than with the other SCOPI scales. Obsessive Checking had correlations ranging from .47 to .58 (mean $r = .53$) with

Table 9.13 Correlations Between Self-Report Measures of OCD and Anxiety Symptoms (Sample 4)

Symptom Measure	Composites				
	GADQ-IV	PTSD	Panic	Social Anxiety	Agora
OCI-R Scales					
Obsessing	**.61**	**.65**	**.58**	**.52**	.42
Checking	.43	**.50**	**.53**	.45	.47
Neutralizing	.37	**.50**	**.50**	.42	.40
Hoarding	.39	.40	.38	.37	.36
Washing	.35	.46	.43	.39	.42
Ordering	.40	.46	.42	.35	.37
SCOPI Scales					
Obsessive Checking	**.52**	**.58**	**.56**	**.53**	.47
Hoarding	.31	.30	.31	.33	.29
Compulsive Rituals	.31	.37	.34	.32	.33
Obsessive Cleanliness	.25	.37	.34	.29	.40
IDAS-II Scales					
Checking	.36	**.53**	.48	.43	.40
Ordering	.38	**.50**	.46	.41	.36
Cleaning	.30	.47	.45	.43	.44

NOTE: $N = 408$. Correlations ≥ .50 are in bold. OCD = obsessive-compulsive disorder. GADQ-IV = Generalized Anxiety Disorder Questionnaire-IV. Agora = Agoraphobia. OCI-R = Obsessive-Compulsive Inventory–Revised. SCOPI = Schedule of Compulsions, Obsessions, and Pathological Impulses. IDAS-II = Expanded Version of the Inventory of Depression and Anxiety Symptoms.

the five anxiety scores; in contrast, the other SCOPI scales were more moderately linked to these anxiety symptoms, with correlations ranging from .25 to .40 (mean $r = .33$). Follow-up tests indicated that all five anxiety symptom scores correlated significantly more strongly ($p < .05$, one-tailed) with Obsessive Checking than with the other SCOPI scales in 14 of 15 comparisons (93.3%; z values ranged from 4.04 to 7.39); the single exception was that the Agoraphobia Composite did not correlate more highly with Obsessive Checking ($r = .47$) than with Obsessive Cleanliness ($r = .40$; $z = 1.58$, $p < .06$, one-tailed). Thus, Obsessive Checking shows substantially greater nonspecificity than the other SCOPI scales in relation to both depression and anxiety symptoms.

Finally, consistent with the results observed earlier with depression, the IDAS-II OCD scales all tended to have similar, moderate associations with the anxiety symptoms. For Checking, the correlations ranged from .36 to .53, with a mean value of .44. Similarly, the correlations for Ordering ranged from .36 to .50, with an average coefficient of .42. Finally, the correlations for Cleaning ranged from .30 to .47, with a mean value of .42. Consequently, unlike the pattern seen with the other instruments, the IDAS-II OCD scales all show similar levels of nonspecificity vis-à-vis both depression and anxiety symptoms.

Table 9.14 Polyserial Correlations Between the SCOPI Scales and *DSM-IV* Emotional Disorder Diagnoses in Sample 2

Scale	OCD	MDD	GAD	PTSD	Panic	Agora	Social Phobia	Specific Phobia
Obsessive Checking	**.71**	**.46**	**.43**	**.40**	**.53**	.35	**.45**	.14
Compulsive Rituals	**.46**	.07	.03	.11	.22	.07	.24	.01
Hoarding	**.44**	.13	.05	−.10	.18	.06	.07	−.12
Obsessive Cleanliness	.34	.09	.16	.12	.28	.09	.19	.14

NOTE: $N = 251$. Correlations ≥ .40 are in bold. SCOPI = Schedule of Compulsions, Obsessions, and Pathological Impulses. OCD = obsessive-compulsive disorder. MDD = major depressive disorder. GAD = generalized anxiety disorder. PTSD = posttraumatic stress disorder. Agora = agoraphobia.

Diagnostic Specificity

Sample 2

We now examine the criterion validity and diagnostic specificity of various OCD symptom measures. In doing so, we will first discuss the results of individual samples separately, and then conclude by reporting summary findings collapsed across all of the samples. We begin with Sample 2 ($N = 251$). Table 9.14 presents polyserial correlations between the SCOPI scales and eight *DSM-IV* diagnoses: OCD, major depression, GAD, PTSD, panic disorder, agoraphobia, social phobia, and specific phobia. As would be expected based on the symptom results (see Tables 9.11 through 9.13), Obsessive Checking clearly displays the strongest and broadest relations with these diagnoses. In fact, it has polyserial correlations ≥ .40 with six different diagnoses. Nevertheless, it shows impressive criterion validity and diagnostic specificity in these data. It easily is the strongest predictor of OCD diagnoses, with a polyserial correlation of .71; its next highest correlation is only .53 with panic disorder.

Compulsive Rituals and Hoarding both demonstrate a reasonable level of criterion validity and specificity in this sample. Compulsive Rituals correlated .46 with OCD diagnoses, whereas its associations with the other seven disorders ranged from only .01 to .22 (mean $r = .11$). Similarly, Hoarding had a polyserial correlation of .44 with OCD; in contrast, its other coefficients ranged from only −.12 to .18, with a mean value (ignoring sign) of $|.10|$.

Finally, SCOPI Obsessive Cleanliness produced the least impressive validity results in these data. Although it correlated significantly with OCD diagnoses, this coefficient ($r = .34$) was the weakest of any SCOPI scale. Moreover, it had an association of similar magnitude ($r = .28$) with panic disorder. However, its associations with the other six diagnoses were quite weak (*r*s ranged from .09 to .19, mean $r = .13$), indicating some degree of specificity.

SAMPLE 5

The Sample 5 participants provide a more extensive examination of these issues. These patients rated themselves on the IDAS-II ($N=290$) and also were assessed on the interview-based IMAS ($N=314$). Consequently, these data allow us to compare the criterion validity and specificity of the same set of symptoms assessed via two different methods (i.e., self-report vs. interview).

Table 9.15 presents polyserial correlations between (a) the three IDAS-II OCD scales and their IMAS counterparts and (b) the same eight *DSM-IV* diagnoses examined in Sample 2. Before discussing specific scales, it is noteworthy that the two instruments displayed very similar levels of criterion validity in these data. The IDAS-II scales had polyserial correlations with OCD diagnoses that ranged from .41 to .46, with a mean value of .44; the corresponding values for the IMAS scales ranged from .44 to .50, with an average coefficient of .47. Consequently, the level of criterion validity essentially was invariant across assessment method.

Turning now to individual symptom dimensions, the indicators of checking and ordering/rituals all showed moderate criterion validity and a reasonable level of diagnostic specificity in this sample. Their correlations with OCD diagnoses ranged from .41 (IDAS-II Checking) to .50 (IMAS Rituals), with an average coefficient of .46. In contrast, their associations with the other seven diagnoses consistently were lower, ranging from .02 to .32 (mean $r=.17$).

The two cleaning scales show a comparable level of criterion validity, as they had correlations of .45 (IDAS-II) and .44 (IMAS) with OCD diagnoses. However, they had associations of a similar magnitude with specific phobia diagnoses (for IDAS-II Cleaning, $r=.44$; for IMAS Cleaning, $r=.38$). Their associations with the other six diagnoses consistently were weaker (rs ranged from .08 to .28, mean $r=.17$), which demonstrates some degree of specificity.

Table 9.15 POLYSERIAL CORRELATIONS BETWEEN OCD SYMPTOM SCALES AND *DSM-IV* EMOTIONAL DISORDER DIAGNOSES IN SAMPLE 5

Scale	OCD	MDD	GAD	PTSD	Panic	Agora	Social Phobia	Specific Phobia
IDAS-II Scales								
Ordering	**.46**	.16	.12	.18	.15	.09	.09	.29
Cleaning	**.45**	.10	.14	.17	.28	.26	.23	**.44**
Checking	**.41**	.15	.14	.20	.17	.11	.07	.32
IMAS Scales								
Rituals	**.50**	.02	.13	.18	.18	.16	.11	.27
Checking	**.46**	.17	.16	.27	.22	.16	.08	.29
Cleaning	**.44**	.08	.08	.10	.21	.21	.20	.38

NOTE: $N=290$ (IDAS-II scales), 314 (IMAS scales). Correlations ≥ .40 are in bold. IDAS-II = Expanded version of the Inventory of Depression and Anxiety Symptoms. IMAS = Interview of Mood and Anxiety Symptoms. OCD = obsessive-compulsive disorder. MDD = major depressive disorder. GAD = generalized anxiety disorder. PTSD = posttraumatic stress disorder. Agora = agoraphobia.

Sample 4

As noted previously, the participants of Sample 4 (*N* = 406) completed three self-report OCD measures: the IDAS-II, SCOPI, and OCI-R. These data yield an even more extensive examination of criterion validity and diagnostic specificity. Table 9.16 presents polyserial correlations between these self-report scales and seven *DSM-5* diagnoses: OCD, major depression, GAD, PTSD, panic disorder, agoraphobia, and social phobia. Before examining specific types of symptoms, it is important to compare the criterion validities of these three instruments. As we established earlier (see Tables 9.4, 9.9, and 9.10), the IDAS-II, SCOPI, and OCI-R all contain strongly correlated measures of checking, order/rituals, and washing/cleaning. It is instructive to compare the predictive power of these overlapping sets of scales. Overall, the IDAS-II OCD scales showed the strongest level of criterion validity. They had polyserial correlations with OCD diagnoses that ranged from .45 to .56, with a mean value of .50. Their counterparts on the OCI-R did nearly as well: Their criterion correlations with OCD ranged from .41 to .53, with an average coefficient of .45. Finally, the criterion coefficients for the three parallel SCOPI scales ranged from .35 to .53, with a mean value of .43. Thus, the three instruments generally performed comparably, with the IDAS-II scales slightly outperforming the others.

Table 9.16 Polyserial Correlations Between OCD Symptom Scales and *DSM-5* Diagnoses (Sample 4)

Symptom Measure	**OCD**	**MDD**	**GAD**	**PTSD**	**Panic**	**Agora**	**Social Phobia**
IDAS-II Scales							
Ordering	**.56**	.36	.27	**.44**	.25	.23	.21
Checking	**.49**	**.44**	.32	**.49**	.27	.32	.24
Cleaning	**.45**	.34	.22	.38	.22	.21	.15
SCOPI Scales							
Obsessive Checking	**.53**	**.49**	**.45**	**.45**	.28	.23	.34
Compulsive Rituals	**.41**	.29	.22	.29	.12	.11	.23
Obsessive Cleanliness	.35	.21	.11	.25	.14	.11	.16
Hoarding	.08	.22	.26	.25	.10	.07	.16
OCI-R Scales							
Ordering	**.53**	.36	.26	.32	.27	.16	.24
Obsessing	**.42**	**.50**	**.41**	.35	.33	.32	.33
Washing	**.42**	.34	.23	.25	.12	.18	.10
Checking	**.41**	**.46**	.32	.32	.22	.29	.26
Neutralizing	.26	.32	.27	.20	.12	.20	.17
Hoarding	.06	.28	.27	.23	.17	.14	.14

NOTE: *N* = 406. Correlations ≥ .40 are in bold. OCD = obsessive-compulsive disorder. MDD = major depression. GAD = generalized anxiety disorder. PTSD = posttraumatic stress disorder. Agora = agoraphobia. IDAS-II = Expanded Version of the Inventory of Depression and Anxiety Symptoms. SCOPI = Schedule of Compulsions, Obsessions, and Pathological Impulses. OCI-R = Obsessive-Compulsive Inventory–Revised.

We now consider specific symptom dimensions within OCD. Overall, the indicators of ordering/rituals displayed the most impressive combination of criterion validity and diagnostic specificity in this sample. It is noteworthy that they tended to show the strongest criterion validity, with correlations ranging from .41 to .53 (mean $r=.50$). Moreover, they consistently displayed specificity to OCD. IDAS-II Ordering correlated .56 with OCD diagnoses; its other coefficients ranged from only .21 to .44, with an average value of .29. Similarly, OCI-R Ordering had a criterion correlation of .53; its associations with the other disorders ranged from .16 to .36, with a mean coefficient of .27. Finally, SCOPI Compulsive Rituals correlated more strongly with OCD ($r=.41$) than with any other disorder (*r*s ranged from .11 to .29, mean $r=.21$).

The checking scales exhibited a similar level of criterion validity in these data, with coefficients ranging from .41 to .53 (mean $r=.48$). However, they all showed associations of the same magnitude with other disorders. SCOPI Obsessive Checking correlated .53 with OCD but also correlated .49 with major depression, .45 with GAD, and .45 with PTSD. IDAS-II Checking had correlations of .49 with both OCD and PTSD, and it also had a similar association with major depression ($r=.44$). OCI-R Checking actually had a stronger association with major depression ($r=.46$) than with OCD ($r=.41$). Averaging across all three scales, the criterion validities for OCD (mean $r=.48$) and major depression (mean $r=.46$) were virtually identical, and the coefficient for PTSD (mean $r=.42$) was nearly as high.

The washing/cleaning scales showed a more moderate level of criterion validity, with correlations ranging from .35 to .45 (mean $r=.41$). In contrast to the checking scales, however, they exhibited a reasonable level of specificity in these data. IDAS-II Cleaning correlated more strongly with OCD ($r=.45$) than with any other disorder (*r*s ranged from .15 to .38, mean $r=.25$). Similarly, OCI-R Washing had a criterion correlation of .42 with OCD; its associations with the other diagnoses ranged from .10 to .34, with an average coefficient of .20. Finally, SCOPI Obsessive Cleanliness correlated more modestly with OCD ($r=.35$), but this still was its strongest association (*r*s with other disorders ranged from .11 to 25; mean $r=.16$).

The remaining scales all showed unimpressive validity in this sample. It is particularly noteworthy that SCOPI Hoarding ($r=.08$) and OCI-R Hoarding ($r=.06$) both had nonsignificant correlations with OCD in these data. OCI-R Obsessing had a significant moderate criterion correlation ($r=.42$). However, it had a similar association with GAD ($r=.41$), and it actually showed a somewhat stronger link to major depression ($r=.50$). Consequently, it showed no specificity in this sample. Finally, OCI-R Mental Neutralizing had similar, modest associations with major depression ($r=.32$), GAD ($r=.27$), and OCD ($r=.26$).

Sample 3

The Sample 3 outpatients ($N=252$) also rated themselves on the IDAS-II, SCOPI, and OCI-R. In addition, they were assessed using the PCCP, which yielded clinicians' ratings of Checking, Ordering, Cleaning, Hoarding, and Obsessing. Consequently, this sample includes four measures apiece of checking, ordering/rituals, and cleaning/washing (one from each measure); three indicators of

Table 9.17 Polyserial Correlations Between OCD Symptom Scales and *DSM-IV* Diagnoses (Sample 3)

Symptom Measure	OCD	MDD	GAD	PTSD	Panic	Social Phobia
IDAS-II Scales						
Checking	**.45**	.31	.22	.22	.19	.15
Ordering	**.43**	.09	.18	.12	.14	.07
Cleaning	.25	.23	.15	.14	.17	.08
SCOPI Scales						
Obsessive Checking	**.52**	.37	.30	.27	.33	.28
Compulsive Rituals	**.41**	.04	.11	.06	.18	.01
Hoarding	.36	.08	.09	.15	.23	.17
Obsessive Cleanliness	.27	.13	.11	.09	.13	.04
OCI-R Scales						
Obsessing	**.46**	**.41**	.33	.38	.38	.28
Checking	**.43**	.22	.10	.21	.27	.18
Ordering	.39	.11	.11	.11	.16	.06
Hoarding	.37	.13	.12	.17	.19	.18
Neutralizing	.26	.13	.05	.11	.20	.06
Washing	.23	.17	.07	.05	.02	.12
PCCP Ratings						
Ordering	**.45**	.01	.19	.12	.15	.12
Checking	**.40**	.14	.16	.10	.15	.24
Obsessing	.37	.33	.30	.32	.27	.36
Hoarding	.32	.02	.09	.08	.18	.14
Cleaning	.26	.21	.08	.03	.02	.10

NOTE: $N = 252$. Correlations ≥ .40 are in bold. OCD = obsessive-compulsive disorder. MDD = major depressive disorder. GAD = generalized anxiety disorder. PTSD = posttraumatic stress disorder. IDAS-II = Expanded Version of the Inventory of Depression and Anxiety Symptoms. SCOPI = Schedule of Compulsions, Obsessions, and Pathological Impulses. OCI-R = Obsessive-Compulsive Inventory–Revised. PCCP = Personality, Cognitions, Consciousness, and Perceptions Interview.

hoarding (SCOPI, OCI-R, PCCP); two measures of obsessing (OCI-R, PCCP); and a single index of mental neutralizing (OCI-R).

Table 9.17 presents polyserial correlations between these symptom measures and six *DSM-IV* diagnoses: OCD, major depression, GAD, PTSD, panic disorder, and social phobia. As in previous analyses, we can compare the overall criterion validities of the four instruments by examining the three sets of symptoms they all have in common. This comparison yielded mean criterion correlations of .40 for the SCOPI (range = .27 to .52); .38 for the IDAS-II (range = .25 to .45); .37 for the PCCP (range = .26 to .45); and .35 for the OCI-R (range = .23 to .43). Thus, the four measures generally displayed similar levels of criterion validity, with the SCOPI yielding the highest correlations on average.

Looking now at the individual symptom dimensions, the checking and ordering/rituals scales demonstrated the strongest overall pattern of criterion validity and diagnostic specificity in these data. The four indicators of checking had criterion correlations ranging from .40 to .52, with an average value of .45. Their associations with the other disorders consistently were weaker, ranging from .10 to .37 (mean r = .22). Similarly, the four ordering/rituals scales had criterion coefficients with OCD that ranged from .37 to .45, with a mean value of .42. Their discriminant correlations ranged from .04 to .18, with an average coefficient of only .11.

In contrast, the indicators of washing/cleaning all displayed surprisingly weak criterion validity in this sample. Their correlations with OCD diagnoses ranged from only .23 to .27, with a mean coefficient of .25. Every scale did have its strongest association with OCD, which indicates a modest level of specificity. Averaging across all four measures, their mean discriminant correlations were .19 (major depression), .10 (GAD), .08 (PTSD), .08 (panic disorder), and .08 (social phobia).

The hoarding measures fared much better in these data than in the Sample 4 analyses. Their criterion coefficients ranged from .32 to .37, with an average value of .35. Moreover, their associations with the other diagnoses tended to be rather low, ranging from .02 to .23 (mean r = .13). Thus, they show moderate criterion validity and good diagnostic specificity in this sample.

Replicating the Sample 4 results, the indicators of obsessing displayed moderate criterion validity but very limited specificity. Specifically, they had criterion correlations of .46 (OCI-R Obsessing) and .37 (PCCP Obsessing), with a mean value of .41. However, they also correlated moderately with major depression (mean r = .37), PTSD (mean r = .35), panic disorder (mean r = .32), social phobia (mean r = .32), and GAD (mean r = .31).

Finally, as in Sample 4, OCI-R Mental Neutralizing had a significant but surprisingly weak correlation (r = .26) with OCD diagnoses, demonstrating only a modest level of criterion validity. It did show some limited specificity to OCD, as its discriminant coefficients consistently were lower (rs ranged from .05 to .20, mean r = .11).

Summary of Findings: Composite Scores

Given the variability of the results across the four samples, it will be helpful to examine summary findings using all of the available data. We began by creating composite scores that were constructed using all of the indicators available in a given sample. More specifically, we first standardized the symptom scores—so that they would be weighted equally in the aggregates—and then averaged them to create the composite. For the checking, ordering/rituals, and cleaning/washing symptoms, we had single indicators in Sample 2, two indicators in Sample 5, three indicators in Sample 4, and four indicators in Sample 3. For hoarding, we had a single indicator in Sample 2, two indicators in Sample 4, and three indicators in Sample 3. For obsessing symptoms, we had a single indicator in Sample 4 and two indicators in Sample 3. Finally, we had a single measure of mental neutralizing in both Sample 4 and Sample 3.

After creating the composites, we correlated them with the six disorders that were diagnosed in all four samples: OCD, major depression, GAD, PTSD, panic disorder, and social phobia. We computed these correlations separately in each

Table 9.18 Weighted Mean Polyserial Correlations Between OCD Symptom Dimensions and *DSM* Diagnoses

Symptom Measure	OCD	MDD	GAD	PTSD	Panic	Social Phobia
Checking	**.54**	.37	.31	.35	.31	.27
Ordering/Rituals	**.51**	.18	.17	.23	.21	.18
Obsessing	**.44**	**.47**	.38	.37	.34	.34
Washing/Cleaning	.39	.19	.16	.19	.20	.17
Hoarding	.32	.24	.21	.23	.12	.11
Neutralizing	.26	.25	.18	.17	.15	.13

NOTE: N = 1,226 (Checking, Ordering/Rituals, Washing/Cleaning), 909 (Hoarding), 658 (Obsessing, Neutralizing). Correlations ≥ .40 are in bold. OCD = obsessive-compulsive disorder. MDD = major depressive disorder. GAD = generalized anxiety disorder. PTSD = posttraumatic stress disorder.

sample, and then computed weighted mean coefficients using all available data. Consequently, these summary correlations are based on 1,226 observations for checking, ordering/rituals, and washing/cleaning; 909 observations for hoarding; and 658 observations for obsessing and mental neutralizing.

Table 9.18 presents these summary correlations between the six symptom dimensions and the six *DSM* diagnoses. Checking symptoms showed the strongest overall association with OCD diagnoses (r = .54). They also displayed a reasonable level of diagnostic specificity, as their associations with the other disorders were considerably lower (rs ranged from .27 to .37, mean r = .32). Ordering symptoms also exhibited strong criterion validity (r = .51) and demonstrated the most impressive specificity, as they were only weakly related to all other disorders (rs ranged from .17 to .23, mean r = .19). Overall, the data from our four samples strongly support the validity and specificity of these two symptom dimensions.

The summary data also support the validity of washing/cleaning symptoms. Although these scales correlated only moderately with OCD diagnoses (r = .39), this easily was their strongest association overall; in fact, all of their other correlations were quite low, ranging from .16 to .20 (mean r = .18).

Indicators of obsessing also produced moderate criterion correlations with OCD diagnoses (r = .44). Clearly, however, they showed no specificity to this disorder. Obsessing symptoms actually had a slightly stronger association (r = .47) with major depression, and they also had correlations of a similar magnitude with GAD (r = .38) and PTSD (r = .37).

The hoarding scales had a relatively modest association with OCD (r = .32), although this was their single highest correlation (other rs ranged from .11 to .24, mean r = .18). These findings are consistent with the argument that hoarding is better conceptualized as a distinct disorder, rather than representing a symptom dimension within OCD (Mataix-Coles et al., 2010; Wu & Watson, 2005).

Finally, these data offer little support for the validity of the OCI-R Mental Neutralizing scale, which was our only indicator of this symptom dimension.

Mental Neutralizing had weak and virtually identical correlations with OCD ($r = .26$) and major depression ($r = .25$). Thus, it is neither a strong nor a specific predictor of OCD diagnoses.

SUMMARY OF FINDINGS: INDIVIDUAL SCALES

We also computed overall weighted mean correlations to examine the criterion validity of individual self-report symptom scales (note that the IMAS scales were only assessed in Sample 5, and the PCCP ratings were only available in Sample 3). These summary correlations are based on 948 observations for the IDAS-II, 909 observations for the SCOPI, and 658 observations for the OCI-R.

Overall, SCOPI Obsessive Checking had the highest overall criterion correlation with OCD diagnoses ($r = .58$). Seven other scales also had criterion coefficients $\geq .40$: IDAS-II Ordering ($r = .49$), OCI-R Ordering ($r = .48$), IDAS-II Checking ($r = .45$), OCI-R Obsessing ($r = .44$), SCOPI Compulsive Rituals ($r = .42$), OCI-R Checking ($r = .42$), and IDAS-II Cleaning ($r = .40$). Two other scales had criterion validities $\geq .30$: OCI-R Washing ($r = .35$) and SCOPI Obsessive Cleanliness ($r = .33$). The three remaining scales had relatively weak criterion correlations (for OCI-R Mental Neutralizing, $r = .26$; for SCOPI Hoarding, $r = .26$; for OCI-R Hoarding, $r = .18$).

INCREMENTAL VALIDITY

Overview

Finally, we examine the incremental power of individual self-report scales to predict OCD diagnoses using logistic regression analyses. We conducted three separate series of analyses, using the IDAS-II scales (in Samples 3, 4, and 5), SCOPI scales (in Samples 2, 3, and 4), and OCI-R scales (in Samples 3 and 4) as predictors. We included the IDAS-II Dysphoria scale as an additional predictor in every analysis to model the influence of general distress/negative affectivity. In all of these analyses, the symptom scores were standardized to put them on the same metric.

IDAS-II Analyses

Table 9.19 presents the odds ratios (ORs) from these logistic regressions. Looking first at the IDAS-II analyses, it is noteworthy that all three scales made a significant incremental contribution in at least one sample. IDAS-II Ordering displayed the most impressive predictive power: It added significantly in both Sample 3 (OR = 1.67) and Sample 5 (OR = 2.09), and it also showed a marginal effect in Sample 4 (OR = 1.89, $p < .09$). Checking added significantly (OR = 1.70) in the Sample 3 analyses, whereas Cleaning made an incremental contribution in Sample 5 (OR = 2.24). Thus, there is at least some evidence indicating that higher scores on all three scales are associated with an increased likelihood of being diagnosed with OCD, which supports their construct validity.

Table 9.19 Odds Ratios From Logistic Regression Analyses Predicting OCD Diagnoses From OCD Symptom Scales and IDAS-II Dysphoria

Scale	Sample 2	Sample 3	Sample 4	Sample 5
IDAS-II Analyses				
Checking	.—	**1.70**	1.14	1.22
Ordering	.—	**1.67**	1.89	**2.09**
Cleaning	.—	1.03	1.31	**2.24**
Dysphoria	.—	1.58	**2.32**	**0.41**
SCOPI Analyses				
Obsessive Checking	**4.76**	**2.03**	2.18	.—
Compulsive Rituals	1.15	1.57	1.05	.—
Obsessive Cleanliness	0.93	0.96	1.46	.—
Hoarding	1.43	1.29	**0.45**	.—
Dysphoria	1.25	1.59	**3.08**	.—
OCI-R Analyses				
Obsessing	.—	**1.96**	1.42	.—
Checking	.—	**1.82**	1.39	.—
Ordering	.—	1.38	**2.12**	.—
Washing	.—	0.94	1.64	.—
Neutralizing	.—	0.83	0.63	.—
Hoarding	.—	1.48	**0.48**	.—
Dysphoria	.—	1.17	**2.72**	.—

NOTE: $N = 251$ (Sample 2), 252 (Sample 3), 411 (Sample 4), 290 (Sample 5). Significant effects ($p < .05$) are in bold. OCD = obsessive-compulsive disorder. IDAS-II = Expanded Version of the Inventory of Depression and Anxiety Symptoms. SCOPI = Schedule of Compulsions, Obsessions, and Pathological Impulses. OCI-R = Obsessive-Compulsive Inventory–Revised.

SCOPI Analyses

The SCOPI analyses produced a very different pattern. Obsessive Checking was the only scale to show a positive association with OCD diagnoses: It made a significant incremental contribution in both Samples 2 (OR = 4.76) and 3 (OR = 2.03), and it showed a marginal effect in Sample 4 (OR = 2.18, $p < .08$). Neither Compulsive Rituals (ORs ranged from 1.05 to 1.57) nor Obsessive Cleanliness (ORs ranged from 0.93 to 1.46) added significantly in any analysis. Finally, SCOPI Hoarding had nonsignificant associations in both Samples 2 (OR = 1.43) and 3 (OR = 1.29), and it produced a significant suppressor effect in Sample 4 (OR = 0.45): Higher scores on Hoarding were associated with a *reduced* likelihood of being diagnosed with OCD in this sample.

OCI-R Analyses

Three OCI-R scales made significant positive contributions in one of the two samples: Obsessing (OR = 1.96 in Sample 3), Checking (OR = 1.82 in Sample 3), and Ordering (OR = 2.12 in Sample 4). Neither Washing nor Mental Neutralizing had a significant effect in either sample (ORs ranged from 0.63 to 1.64). Hoarding showed a marginal positive relation to OCD in Sample 3 (OR = 1.48, $p < .10$), but it displayed a suppressor effect in Sample 4 (OR = 0.48): Replicating the finding observed with SCOPI Hoarding, higher scores on OCI-R Hoarding were associated with a reduced likelihood of receiving an OCD diagnosis in this sample.

Summary of Findings

These results are largely congruent with our earlier analyses of criterion validity. Generally speaking, indicators of checking and ordering/rituals tended to display the greatest predictive power in these analyses. Across the three instruments, checking scales produced significant positive effects in four of eight analyses, and they showed a marginal effect in a fifth case. Indicators of ordering/rituals did almost as well, yielding three significant effects and one marginal effect. In contrast, the cleaning/washing scales exhibited only one significant association (IDAS-II Cleaning in Sample 5) across the eight analyses. The hoarding scales produced one marginal positive association and two suppressor effects in five analyses; thus, hoarding symptoms tended to be associated with a reduced likelihood of being diagnosed with OCD. Finally, OCI-R Obsessing contributed significantly in one of two analyses, whereas Mental Neutralizing failed to add incremental variance in either sample.

CONCLUSION

In this chapter, we have examined the validity (including convergent, discriminant, criterion, and incremental validity) and specificity of OCD symptom scales. Our results demonstrate the value of analyzing these specific types of OCD symptoms separately. As we have seen, indicators of checking and ordering/rituals produced the most impressive results: They tended to show the strongest criterion validity, good diagnostic specificity, and significant incremental validity in the logistic regression analyses. Washing/cleaning symptoms also showed good diagnostic specificity, but they displayed more moderate criterion validity and limited incremental predictive power in the logistic regressions. Findings for the hoarding scales generally support the conclusion that they are better viewed as manifestations of a separate disorder rather than as symptoms of OCD: They displayed modest criterion validity and failed to contribute positively to the prediction of OCD diagnoses. Obsessing indicators exhibited moderate criterion validity, but they clearly were not specific to OCD, as they displayed similar associations with major depression, GAD, and PTSD. Finally, our data provide little support for the validity of the OCI-R Mental Neutralizing scale, which was weakly correlated with both OCD and major depression.

10

Toward a Comprehensive Symptom-Based Model of Psychopathology

In Chapter 1, we reviewed several significant problems associated with disorder-based approaches to psychopathology. These problems included comorbidity between disorders and heterogeneity within diagnoses; the low base rates of many disorders; and the unimpressive reliability of judgments based on *DSM* diagnoses (see also Chmielewski et al., 2015; Watson, 2005, 2009a). In light of these problems, we argued for the value of an alternative approach that focuses on the specific symptom dimensions that make up the major syndromes within the emotional disorders (e.g., specific symptom dimensions within obsessive-compulsive disorder [OCD] and posttraumatic stress disorder [PTSD]). This approach uses the *DSM* emotional disorders—in particular, the *DSM-IV* mood and anxiety disorders—as its basic organizing framework, while bypassing heterogeneity and other problems associated with disorder-based models. In Chapters 2 through 9, we explored the nature and implications of this symptom-based approach, using the IDAS-II scales as a basic organizing framework.

REVIEW OF MAJOR FINDINGS

Identification of Robust Symptom Dimensions

Convergent Validity

These symptom-based analyses yielded several important findings and conclusions. First, we were able to establish that specific symptom dimensions are highly robust and can be clearly differentiated from one another across measures and methods. For example, we showed in Chapter 9 that corresponding self-report symptom scales from the IDAS-II, OCI-R, and SCOPI were strongly and systematically related to one another.

More important, we were able to show that self-report symptom scales displayed strong convergent validity and significant discriminant validity vis-à-vis parallel interview-based ratings from the IDAS-CR, PCCP, and IMAS. Table 10.1 summarizes the convergent validity data presented in Chapters 3 through 9 by reporting weighted mean correlations—computed over all available data—between the IDAS-II scales and their interview-based counterparts. The data reported here all are based on results that were presented in earlier chapters, with two exceptions. In Chapters 4 and 5, we reported convergent correlations between (a) the IDAS-II Mania and Euphoria scales and (b) the overall IMAS Mania scale (mean *rs* = .65 and .64, respectively). Here, we report weighted mean correlations with two IMAS Mania subscales that show a clear convergent/discriminant pattern

Table 10.1 Weighted Mean Convergent Correlations Between IDAS-II Scales and Interview Ratings

Symptom Dimension	IDAS-CR/PCCP	IMAS
Depressive Disorders		
Dysphoria	.61	.66
Suicidality	.60	.71
Lassitude	.58	.62
Insomnia	.56	.77
Appetite Loss	.68	.75
Appetite Gain	.56	.—
Bipolar Disorders		
Mania	.56	.71
Euphoria	.37	.67
Anxiety Disorders		
Social Anxiety	.61	.70
Panic	.54	.69
Claustrophobia	.—	.67
PTSD		
Traumatic Intrusions	.60	.60
Traumatic Avoidance	.60	.55
OCD		
Checking	.53	.66
Ordering	.60	.65
Cleaning	.63	.70
Other		
Ill Temper	.57	.75
Well-Being	.49	.—

NOTE: IDAS-II = Expanded version of the Inventory of Depression and Anxiety Symptoms. IDAS-CR = Clinician Rating version of the IDAS. PCCP = Personality, Cognitions, Consciousness, and Perceptions Interview. IMAS = Interview of Mood and Anxiety Symptoms. PTSD = posttraumatic stress disorder. OCD = obsessive-compulsive disorder.

vis-à-vis their IDAS-II counterparts (for a description of these IMAS Mania subscales, see Ruggero et al. 2014). Specifically, we present convergent correlations (a) between IDAS-II Mania and IMAS Hyperactive Cognition (weighted mean $r=.71$) and (b) IDAS-II Euphoria and IMAS Euphoric Activation (mean $r=.67$).

Table 10.1 establishes an impressive level of convergence between these self-report and interview-based symptom measures. As shown in the first column of the table, average correlations with the single-item IDAS-CR/PCCP ratings ranged from .37 to .68, with an overall mean value of .57 (median $r=.58$). As would be expected, the level of convergence with the multi-item IMAS scales is substantially higher; here, average correlations ranged from .55 to .75, with an overall mean value of .68 (median $r=.68$). Clearly, the self-report dimensions we identified in the IDAS-II converge quite well with interview-based ratings of these same symptoms.

Discriminant Validity

Substantial convergent correlations are necessary—but not sufficient—to establish the existence of meaningful symptom dimensions that are robust and generalizable across methods; it also is essential to demonstrate that these symptom scores can be meaningfully distinguished from one another through an examination of their discriminant validity. In Chapters 3 through 9, we reported an extensive series of discriminant validity analyses by conducting significance tests comparing (a) each convergent coefficient with (b) all of the other values in its row or column of the heteromethod block (following the logic articulated by Campbell & Fiske, 1959). These analyses consistently yielded impressive evidence of discriminant validity. Across Chapters 3 through 9, we reported 256 individual tests comparing specific IDAS-II scales to their single-item counterparts on the IDAS-CR and PCCP; 255 of these comparisons (99.6%) were statistically significant ($p < .05$, one-tailed). Similarly, 306 of the 310 comparisons (98.7%) involving the IMAS scales and subscales were statistically significant. Consequently, our data demonstrate that specific symptom dimensions—even highly correlated dimensions with depression, PTSD, and OCD—can be meaningfully distinguished from one another across methods.

Multiple Symptoms Within Disorders

Identification of Specific Symptom Dimensions

Second, we were able to demonstrate the existence of multiple symptom dimensions within several disorders. Previous structural work has established replicable symptom dimensions within both PTSD (see Chapter 7) and OCD (see Chapter 9). Consistent with this prior work, the IDAS-II contains scales assessing two different types of PTSD symptoms (Traumatic Intrusions and Traumatic Avoidance) and three specific types of OCD symptoms (Checking, Ordering, and Cleaning). These scales all displayed strong convergent and discriminant validity in the analyses summarized earlier.

In addition, our work on the IDAS extended previous evidence by identifying several distinguishable symptom dimensions within major depression. Thus, the IDAS-II contains six specific symptom scales—Dysphoria, Suicidality, Lassitude, Insomnia, Appetite Gain, and Appetite Loss—that jointly capture the content subsumed within all nine symptom criteria for a major depressive episode in *DSM-IV/DSM-5*. These scales also displayed strong convergent and discriminant validity in our data. However, their criterion validity and diagnostic specificity varied widely; we will return to this topic shortly.

Finally, the IDAS-II contains two scales assessing key symptoms of bipolar disorder: Mania and Euphoria. These scales exhibited substantial convergent and discriminant validity, and a comparable level of criterion validity. Nevertheless, they also showed some strikingly different associations with other variables; we will examine this topic in greater detail subsequently.

Differential Organization of Symptom Domains

Before leaving this topic, it is worth noting that these various symptom domains are structured quite differently from one another. As was discussed in Chapter 7, PTSD symptom dimensions all tend to be substantially interrelated and are characterized by a strong general factor (Watson, 2009a; Yufik & Simms, 2010). For example, Gootzeit and Markon (2011) reported mean meta-analytic correlations of .72 and .71 between the PTSD symptom factors included in the four-factor King and Simms models, respectively. Consistent with this broader trend, the two IDAS-II PTSD scales correlated .63 with each other in our data (see Table 2.7).

Similarly, the core symptom dimensions within OCD all tend to be moderately to strongly correlated with one another (see Chapter 9) and clearly define a common underlying domain (this statement excludes hoarding, a non-OCD symptom dimension that has been included in many popular OCD inventories). For instance, the correlations among the three IDAS-II OCD scales ranged from .49 to .64 in our data (see Table 2.7), with a mean value of .55.

In marked contrast, depression symptoms display a much more complex—and rather curious—internal structure. As we discussed in Chapters 2 and 3, depression symptoms show clear evidence of a strong underlying factor that is only quasi-general in scope. In fact, during the IDAS scale development process, we found that more than half of the *DSM-IV/DSM-5* symptom criteria for a major depressive episode—including depressed mood, anhedonia, worthlessness/guilt, cognitive problems, and psychomotor disturbance—were so strongly correlated as to be virtually interchangeable in self-report data. Accordingly, these affective, cognitive, and psychomotor symptoms all were collapsed together into the broad IDAS Dysphoria scale. It is noteworthy, furthermore, that all of the other IDAS depression scales are moderately to strongly associated with Dysphoria. For example, in Chapter 3 (see Table 3.3) we reported mean correlations of .67 (Lassitude), .56 (Suicidality), .53 (Insomnia), .47 (Appetite Loss), and .38 (Appetite Gain) with Dysphoria.

All of this might lead one to expect that these specific depression scales also are moderately to strongly linked to one another, but they are not; rather, they tend to be only modestly related to each other (see Table 3.3). In our patient sample, correlations among these five specific IDAS depression scales ranged from |.13| to |.41|, with a mean value (ignoring sign) of only .29. Similarly, in our student sample, these coefficients ranged from |.03| to |.46|, with a mean value of .33. Looking at some specific examples, IDAS Lassitude correlated only .27 and .37 with Appetite Loss in the patients and students, respectively; similarly, Suicidality correlated only .31 and .32, respectively, with Insomnia. These relatively modest associations raise questions regarding whether these symptoms all should be subsumed within the diagnosis of major depression; we will revisit this issue later.

Finally, mania symptoms clearly do not define a single general factor. Although the two bipolar symptom scales in the IDAS-II correlate moderately to strongly with each other ($r = .45$ in Table 2.7), we found consistent evidence that commonly used self-report mania scales actually define two distinct factors, which we labeled Manic Distress (defined by such indicators as GBI Biphasic, GBI Hypomania, HPS Mood Volatility, and IDAS-II Mania) and Manic Elation (marked by such scales as HPS Social Vitality and IDAS-II Euphoria). Moreover, these factors showed strikingly different correlates with other variables; we examine this issue in greater detail in the following section.

Differential Symptom Correlates

Differential Correlates of the Mania Factors

It would not be particularly interesting to identify multiple symptom dimensions within a disorder if these symptoms subsequently were shown to correlate similarly with other variables. In many cases, however, we were able to show that symptom dimensions within the same disorder had very different patterns of correlates. The two mania factors offer an excellent illustration of these differential correlates, and they help to establish the theoretical and practical value of examining psychopathology at the specific symptom level. Consistent with its name, the Manic Distress factor correlated strongly with various indicators of negative affectivity. For instance, as was shown in Chapter 5 (see Tables 5.8, 5.12, and 5.14), it was strongly linked to the broad personality dimension of neuroticism, with correlations ranging from .41 to .67 (mean $r = .54$) across four samples. This factor also was strongly associated with trait anxiety and depression scales from the TAI ($r = .53$ and .51, respectively), the NEO-PI-3 (both $rs = .58$), and the PID-5 ($r = .64$ and .56, respectively), and was more moderately related to the PANAS-X Negative Affect scale ($r = .39$). In addition, Manic Distress was a nonspecific predictor of *DSM-5* emotional disorder diagnoses, correlating particularly strongly with mania ($r = .62$), PTSD ($r = .57$), generalized anxiety disorder ($r = .56$), OCD ($r = .52$), and social phobia ($r = .51$). Finally, it essentially was unrelated to the general personality trait of extraversion, with correlations ranging from only −.17 to .05 (mean $r = -.03$).

In marked contrast, Manic Elation was strongly linked to extraversion, with correlations ranging from .52 to .61 (mean $r = .55$). It also showed moderate to strong positive correlations with indicators of positive emotionality, displaying a particular affinity to forms of positive affectivity that involved high energy and arousal, recklessness, impulsivity, and novel experience seeking. Thus, it correlated .73 with AVI High Arousal Positive Affect and had overall mean correlations of .55, .54, and .45 with TAI Experience Seeking, TAI Vigor, and BAS Fun Seeking, respectively. Manic Elation also correlated strongly with scores on the Narcissistic Personality Inventory (r = .58) and with PID-5 Attention Seeking (r = .56). Unlike Manic Distress, it was largely unrelated to *DSM-5* emotional disorder diagnoses (rs ranged from −.07 to .19) and was only modestly linked to neuroticism (rs ranged from −.02 to −.39, mean r = −.23). These data establish the importance of assessing and analyzing these two types of mania symptoms separately.

Differential Correlates of the IDAS-II Positive Mood Scales

In a related vein, the IDAS-II positive mood scales provide an excellent illustration of how strongly related scales can display strikingly different correlates. As shown in Table 2.7, Well-Being and Euphoria correlated .51 with each other in our data; moreover, they jointly defined a Positive Mood factor in structural analyses of the IDAS-II scales (see Chapter 2). Nevertheless, they showed very different associations with various indicators of psychopathology. Analyses of the IMAS scales provided an excellent illustration of their differential correlates (see Tables 4.7 and 4.8). Euphoria was strongly positively related to IMAS Mania (mean r = .64) and displayed a much weaker positive association with IMAS Depression (mean r = .17). In contrast, Well-Being was negatively associated with IMAS Depression (mean r = −.33) and more weakly related to IMAS Mania (mean r = .21). As another example, IDAS-II Well-Being had a weighted mean correlation of −.49 with *DSM* diagnoses of major depression (see Table 4.6); in marked contrast, Euphoria was completely unrelated to these diagnoses (r = −.01). Clearly, these two scales tap very different forms of positive mood.

Differential Criterion Validity

Another noteworthy finding is that symptom dimensions showed very different levels of criterion validity in relation to their target *DSM* diagnosis. Table 10.2 summarizes the criterion validity data reported in previous chapters for the IDAS-II, IDAS-CR/PCCP, and IMAS scales; the table displays mean criterion correlations (e.g., associations between depression symptom scales and diagnoses of major depression; relations between PTSD symptoms and PTSD diagnoses) computed across all available data. Table 10.2 demonstrates that the overall criterion validity of OCD symptom scales varied widely, ranging from a low of .26 (PCCP Cleaning) to a high of .50 (IDAS-II Ordering and IMAS Rituals). The PTSD scales also showed considerable variation, with coefficients ranging from .42 (IMAS Avoidance) to .58 (IDAS-II Traumatic Intrusions).

Clearly, however, depression symptoms displayed the most dramatic variation, with coefficients ranging from the very weak (r = .17 for IDAS-II Appetite Gain)

Table 10.2 CRITERION VALIDITY OF SYMPTOM SCALES: WEIGHTED MEAN POLYSERIAL CORRELATIONS WITH *DSM* DIAGNOSES

Scale	*N*	Mean Criterion *r*
Major Depression		
IDAS-II Dysphoria	1,945	.70
IDAS-CR Dysphoria	907	.59
IMAS Dysphoria	293	.58
IMAS Lassitude	293	.57
IDAS-II Lassitude	1,945	.51
IDAS-CR Lassitude	907	.49
IDAS-II Well-Being	1,301	−.49
IDAS-CR Well-Being	604	−.47
IMAS Suicidality	293	.45
IDAS-II Suicidality	1,945	.44
IDAS-II Insomnia	1,945	.43
IDAS-II Appetite Loss	1,945	.36
IMAS Appetite Loss	293	.36
IDAS-CR Suicidality	907	.34
IMAS Insomnia	293	.31
IDAS-CR Insomnia	907	.24
IDAS-CR Appetite Loss	907	.23
IDAS-CR Appetite Gain	907	.18
IDAS-II Appetite Gain	1,945	.17
Current Manic Episodes		
IDAS-II Mania	697	.40
IDAS-II Euphoria	697	.34
Posttraumatic Stress Disorder		
IDAS-II Traumatic Intrusions	1,553	.58
IDAS-II Traumatic Avoidance	949	.55
IDAS-CR Traumatic Avoidance	252	.53
IDAS-CR Traumatic Intrusions	859	.51
IMAS Intrusions	302	.42
IMAS Avoidance	302	.42
Social Phobia		
IDAS-II Social Anxiety	1,551	.52
IDAS-CR Social Anxiety	854	.50
Panic Disorder		
IDAS-CR Panic	854	.63
IDAS-II Panic	1,551	.48
Agoraphobia		
IDAS-II Claustrophobia	697	.47
Specific Phobia		
IDAS-II Claustrophobia	290	.42
Obsessive-Compulsive Disorder		
IDAS-II Ordering	948	.50
IMAS Rituals	314	.50

Table 10.2 CONTINUED

Scale	*N*	Mean Criterion *r*
IDAS-II Checking	948	.46
IMAS Checking	314	.46
PCCP Ordering	252	.45
IMAS Cleaning	314	.44
IDAS-II Cleaning	948	.40
PCCP Checking	252	.40
PCCP Cleaning	252	.26

NOTE: IDAS-II = Expanded version of the Inventory of Depression and Anxiety Symptoms. IDAS-CR = Clinician Rating version of the IDAS. IMAS = Interview of Mood and Anxiety Symptoms. PCCP = Personality, Cognitions, Consciousness, and Perceptions Interview.

to the very strong ($r = .70$ with IDAS-II Dysphoria). Moreover, these data clearly establish the differential validity of specific types of symptoms within depression. The three indicators of dysphoria have the strongest overall level of criterion validity, with coefficients ranging from .58 to .70. The three lassitude scales also show substantial criterion validity, with correlations ranging from .49 to .57. Indicators of well-being (*r*s ranged from −.47 to −.49) and suicidality (*r*s ranged from .34 to .45) come next; they exhibited more moderate levels of criterion validity. Finally, indicators of insomnia (*r*s ranged from .24 to .43), appetite loss (*r*s ranged from .23 to .36), and appetite gain (*r*s ranged from .17 to .18) generally displayed unimpressive levels of criterion validity. Based on these data, it is obvious that certain symptoms (such as dysphoria and lassitude) are better indicators of depression than others (such as insomnia and appetite disturbance).

Differential Diagnostic Specificity

We also established a clear link between criterion validity and diagnostic specificity: Generally speaking, scales that correlated more strongly with the criterion diagnosis also tended to show better specificity. Not surprisingly, therefore, the diagnostic specificity of symptom scales also varied dramatically. We will focus here on the specificity of depression (discussed previously in Chapter 3) and PTSD (see Chapter 7) measures, which provide particularly striking illustrations of the differential validity of specific symptom dimensions.

In Chapter 7 (see Table 7.13), we examined the criterion validity and diagnostic specificity of a large number of PTSD symptom scales, using data collected in Sample 3. We revisit these issues in Table 10.3, which reports polyserial correlations with *DSM-IV* diagnoses of major depression and PTSD in these same participants. Unlike our earlier analysis of the Sample 3 data—which focused exclusively on PTSD scales—Table 10.3 also includes several indicators of depression symptoms (e.g., the PHQ-9, IDAS-II Dysphoria) for comparison purposes. As we discussed earlier in Chapter 7, indicators of traumatic intrusions and

Table 10.3 Analyses of Diagnostic Specificity: Polyserial Correlations Between Symptom Measures and *DSM-IV* Diagnoses of Major Depression and PTSD (Sample 3)

Symptom Measure	MDD	PTSD
CES-D	**.76***	.51
PHQ-9	**.73***	.43
MASQ Loss of Interest	**.70***	.37
IDAS-CR Dysphoria	**.68***	.23
IDAS-II Dysphoria	**.66***	.57
ITRI Dysphoria	**.66***	.52
PCL Dysphoria	**.64***	.50
ITRI Dissociation	.40*	.27
IDAS-II Traumatic Intrusions	.30	**.69***
ITRI Intrusions	.35	**.66***
PCL Intrusions	.33	**.63***
ITRI Avoidance	.37	**.61***
IDAS-II Traumatic Avoidance	.33	**.60***
PCL Avoidance	.36	.56*
IDAS-CR Traumatic Intrusions	.31	.54*
IDAS-CR Traumatic Avoidance	.25	.53*
IDAS-CR Hyperarousal	.19	.52*
PCL Hypervigilance	.33	.46*
ITRI Hyperarousal	.36	.42*

NOTE: $N = 245$. Correlations ≥ .60 are in bold. The stronger correlation in each row is marked with an asterisk. PTSD = posttraumatic stress disorder. MDD = major depressive disorder. CES-D = Center for Epidemiological Studies Depression Scale. PHQ-9 = Patient Health Questionnaire-9. MASQ = Mood and Anxiety Symptom Questionnaire. IDAS-CR = Clinician Rating version of the IDAS. IDAS-II = Expanded Version of the Inventory of Depression and Anxiety Symptoms. ITRI = Iowa Traumatic Response Inventory. PCL = PTSD Checklist.

avoidance generally demonstrated strong criterion validity and excellent diagnostic specificity in these data. Thus, they had correlations ranging from .53 to .69 (mean $r = .60$) with diagnoses of PTSD, and coefficients varying from only .25 to .37 (mean $r = .33$) with major depression. Measures of hypervigilance and hyperarousal displayed more moderate criterion validity (correlations with PTSD ranged from .42 to .52, mean $r = .47$) and adequate diagnostic specificity (*r*s with depression ranged from .19 to .36, mean $r = .29$).

In marked contrast, PTSD-based measures of dysphoria symptoms (as defined in the Simms four-factor model) actually correlated more strongly with major depression than with PTSD. In fact, it is noteworthy that these PTSD scales (from the PCL and ITRI) were virtually indistinguishable from dysphoria scales that were developed in the context of depression (i.e., IDAS-II and IDAS-CR

Dysphoria). These four indicators of dysphoria had correlations ranging from .64 to .68 (mean $r = .66$) with major depression, and from only .23 to .57 (mean $r = .46$) with PTSD. Based simply on these data, one would be forced to conclude that ITRI Dysphoria and PCL Dysphoria actually should be viewed as measures of depression, rather than PTSD.

Next, we consider the diagnostic specificity of depression symptom scales. Table 10.4 reports correlations between (a) depression scales from the IDAS-II, IDAS-CR, and IMAS and (b) diagnoses of both major depression and PTSD. It should be noted that these analyses were restricted to those samples that provided ratings on both diagnoses (for a description of these samples, see Chapters 2 and 3); thus, the criterion correlations with major depression that are reported here differ somewhat from those presented earlier in Table 10.2.

Indicators of dysphoria, lassitude, suicidality, and well-being all show clear diagnostic specificity in these data. Thus, the dysphoria scales had mean polyserial correlations of .62 and .38 with major depression and PTSD, respectively;

Table 10.4 Analyses of Diagnostic Specificity: Weighted Mean Polyserial Correlations Between Depression Symptom Measures and *DSM-IV* Diagnoses of Major Depression and PTSD

Symptom Measure	*N*	MDD	PTSD
IDAS-II Dysphoria	1,301	**.71***	**.44**
IDAS-CR Dysphoria	604	**.58***	.31
IMAS Dysphoria	293	**.58***	**.40**
IMAS Lassitude	293	**.57***	.27
IDAS-CR Well-Being	604	**−.54***	−.18
IDAS-II Lassitude	1,301	**.51***	.34
IDAS-CR Lassitude	604	**.48***	.25
IDAS-II Well-Being	1,301	**−.46***	−.16
IDAS-II Suicidality	1,301	**.46***	.28
IMAS Suicidality	293	**.45***	.20
IDAS-II Insomnia	1,301	**.45***	**.40**
IDAS-CR Suicidality	604	**.41***	.16
IDAS-II Appetite Loss	1,301	.39*	.34
IMAS Appetite Loss	293	.36	**.43***
IMAS Insomnia	293	.31*	.26
IDAS-CR Appetite Loss	604	.28*	.26
IDAS-CR Insomnia	604	.24	.26*
IDAS-CR Appetite Gain	604	.18*	.02
IDAS-II Appetite Gain	1,301	.17*	.11

Note: Correlations ≥ .40 are in bold. The stronger correlation in each row is marked with an asterisk. PTSD = posttraumatic stress disorder. MDD = major depressive disorder. IDAS-II = Expanded Version of the Inventory of Depression and Anxiety Symptoms. IDAS-CR = Clinician Rating version of the IDAS. IMAS = Interview of Mood and Anxiety Symptoms.

indicators of lassitude had average coefficients of .52 and .29, respectively; the suicidality measures had mean correlations of .44 and .21, respectively; and the IDAS-II and IDAS-CR Well-Being scales had average coefficients of –.50 and –.17, respectively.

In contrast, the remaining symptoms fared more poorly. The insomnia scales had moderate correlations with both diagnoses that were very similar in magnitude (mean $rs = .33$ and .31 with major depression and PTSD, respectively). Indicators of appetite loss displayed a very similar pattern, producing mean coefficients of .34 with both disorders. Finally, IDAS-II and IDAS-CR Appetite Gain correlated very weakly with both major depression (mean $r = .17$) and PTSD (mean $r = .07$). Overall, these symptom scales show no clear evidence of diagnostic specificity.

Differential Incremental Validity

Thus, symptoms displaying relatively weak criterion validity also tend to show poor diagnostic specificity. This, then, might suggest that we can improve the diagnosis of major depression and PTSD by eliminating these poorly performing symptoms. On the other hand, it still could be argued that these weaker symptoms nevertheless provide clinically useful information that enhances their respective diagnoses.

We tested this idea by conducting logistic regression analyses to identify the unique, incremental validity of individual symptom dimensions in the prediction of their respective diagnoses. With regard to major depression (see Chapter 3), indicators of dysphoria (seven significant effects) and lassitude (three significant effects) showed incremental predictive power in 10 of 14 analyses (71.4%). In contrast, the three symptoms that exhibit little diagnostic specificity—insomnia (one significant effect), appetite loss (one significant effect), and appetite gain (one significant effect)—made significant positive contributions to depression diagnoses in only 3 of 20 cases (15.0%). Overall, therefore, our results indicate that the nonspecific symptoms of major depression actually contribute very little to its diagnosis.

Our analyses of PTSD symptoms (see Chapter 7) yielded the same basic findings and conclusions. Measures of intrusions generally showed the strongest incremental predictive power in our logistic regressions. Hyperarousal and avoidance symptoms also displayed more limited incremental validity in these data. In contrast, dysphoria/numbing symptoms failed to add significantly in any analysis. Other analyses revealed that the information provided by the more poorly functioning PTSD symptoms is completely redundant with that provided by indicators of intrusions and avoidance. In fact, we showed that dropping these poorly functioning symptoms—thereby focusing assessment exclusively on indicators of intrusions and avoidance—yielded much better diagnostic specificity while fully maintaining criterion validity (see Tables 7.14 and 7.15). Thus, the information provided by these poorly functioning PTSD symptoms is both unnecessary (i.e., it does not enhance criterion validity) and counterproductive (i.e., it reduces diagnostic specificity).

Taken together, our data strongly suggest that we can improve the diagnoses of both major depression and PTSD by focusing on their strongest and most specific symptoms and eliminating the more poorly functioning criteria. In the case of depression, it would make sense to concentrate primarily on indicators of dysphoria, lassitude, suicidality, and anhedonia/low positive affect, and to deemphasize—or eliminate altogether—insomnia and appetite disturbance. With regard to PTSD, our data indicate that it would be better to focus primarily on indicators of intrusions and avoidance, and to drop most symptoms of dysphoria and numbing. As we have seen, dropping these poorly functioning symptoms would enhance diagnostic specificity with little or no loss of information.

DEVELOPING A COMPREHENSIVE SYMPTOM-BASED MODEL OF PSYCHOPATHOLOGY

Overview

Our data have demonstrated the many advantages of a symptom-based approach to studying psychopathology. As we have seen, one of these advantages is that symptom-based analyses can be used to improve various *DSM* diagnoses, such as major depression and PTSD. Given the many problems associated with disorder-based approaches that we discussed earlier (see especially Chapter 1), however, perhaps it is time to move away from diagnosis-based models altogether and to focus primarily at the level of homogeneous symptom dimensions.

In Chapters 2 through 9, we used the IDAS-II scales as a basic organizing framework for studying psychopathology. Although we believe the IDAS-II is a valuable research and assessment tool, it obviously does not provide a comprehensive assessment of psychopathology. Rather, it offers reasonably comprehensive coverage of five major diagnostic classes within *DSM-5:* bipolar and related disorders, depressive disorders, anxiety disorders, obsessive-compulsive and related disorders (OCRDs), and trauma- and stressor-related disorders.

Fortunately, researchers recently have developed a number of other state-of-the-art measures assessing several other major domains of psychopathology. Jointly, these instruments assess most—but not all—major forms of psychopathology. In this next section, we discuss various instruments that significantly extend the range of coverage provided by the IDAS-II. To move toward a comprehensive model of symptom-based psychopathology, we again will use the IDAS-II as a central organizing framework; in doing so, we will examine how these other measures relate to the IDAS-II scales. These analyses will allow us to (a) identify major points of overlap between the IDAS-II and these other measures and (b) explicate the ways in which these other instruments expand the coverage provided by the IDAS-II.

Iowa Sleep Disturbances Inventory (ISDI)

Description of the ISDI

The Iowa Sleep Disturbances Inventory (ISDI; Koffel, 2011; Koffel & Watson, 2010) contains 95 items. These items are grouped into 13 factor analytically derived scales that jointly provide comprehensive assessment of the major forms of sleep-related problems: Nightmares (e.g., have frequent nightmares), Initial Insomnia (e.g., takes a long time to fall asleep), Fatigue (e.g., usually feel tired during the day), Fragmented Sleep (e.g., wake up early and can't get back to sleep), Nonrestorative Sleep (e.g., have a hard time waking up), Anxiety at Night (e.g., have trouble sleeping due to nervousness), Light Sleep (e.g., easily awakened by noises), Movement at Night (e.g., move arms or legs a lot while sleeping), Sensations at Night (e.g., have unusual feelings in legs at night), Excessive Sleep (e.g., take long naps), Irregular Schedule (e.g., bedtime is irregular), Sleep Paralysis (e.g., sometimes feel paralyzed when falling asleep), and Sleep Hallucinations (e.g., experience dreamlike images when falling asleep). Participants respond to the ISDI items using a dichotomous true-false format. Koffel and Watson (2010) and Koffel (2011) report extensive data establishing that the ISDI scales are internally consistent, show good retest reliability over a 2-week period, and demonstrate substantial convergent, discriminant, and criterion validity.

Factor Structure of the ISDI

We have complete ISDI and IDAS-II data in patients (this is Sample 6; see Chapter 2) and students (this is Sample 10). We began by subjecting the ISDI scales to separate principal factor analyses in each sample, using squared multiple correlations as the initial communality estimates. Three clearly interpretable factors emerged in each sample and were rotated to oblique simple structure using promax (power = 3). The resulting factor loadings are presented in Table 10.5 (these data are adapted from Koffel, 2011, Table 2). The first factor in each solution represents various nighttime sleep problems; it therefore can be labeled Insomnia. The Insomnia factor has four clear and consistent markers across samples: Initial Insomnia, Fragmented Sleep, Light Sleep, and Anxiety at Night. In contrast, Factor II primarily reflects fatigue and sleepiness during the day; accordingly, we will call it Lassitude. Its consistent markers include Fatigue, Nonrestorative Sleep, Irregular Schedule, and Excessive Sleep. Finally, Factor III—which we will label Unusual Sleep Experiences—taps various types of anomalous sleep experiences (for a discussion of these types of experiences, see Watson et al., 2015a). Unusual Sleep Experiences has three consistent markers: Sleep Hallucinations, Sleep Paralysis, and Nightmares. We created regression-based factor scores to model these three ISDI dimensions in subsequent analyses.

Bivariate Analyses

Correlations between these ISDI factor scores and the IDAS-II scales are presented in Table 10.6 (patients) and Table 10.7 (students). As would be expected, the ISDI Insomnia factor correlated very strongly with the IDAS-II Insomnia scale in both

Table 10.5 PROMAX LOADINGS OF THE ISDI SCALES IN PATIENT AND STUDENT SAMPLES

ISDI Scale	Patients I	II	III	Students I	II	III
Initial Insomnia	**.67**	.26	–.06	**.73**	.11	–.07
Fragmented Sleep	**.59**	–.04	.13	**.52**	.02	.19
Light Sleep	**.56**	–.12	–.06	**.46**	.01	–.05
Anxiety at Night	**.53**	.17	.08	**.61**	–.12	.05
Fatigue	–.10	**.68**	.04	.12	**.72**	–.03
Nonrestorative Sleep	.13	**.61**	–.06	.13	**.67**	–.10
Irregular Schedule	.10	**.52**	–.09	.11	**.40**	.06
Excessive Sleep	**–.36**	**.45**	.22	**–.33**	**.54**	.11
Sleep Hallucinations	.13	–.06	**.61**	.06	.12	**.52**
Nightmares	.12	.02	**.60**	.17	.04	**.51**
Sleep Paralysis	–.05	.04	**.34**	–.14	.11	**.52**
Movement at Night	–.01	–.04	**.33**	–.01	–.04	.27
Sensations at Night	.24	–.10	.16	.05	–.11	**.51**

NOTE: $N = 200$ (Patients), 219 (Students). Loadings ≥ |.30| are in bold. ISDI = Iowa Sleep Disturbances Inventory. Adapted from Koffel (2011, Table 2).

Table 10.6 CORRELATIONS BETWEEN THE ISDI FACTOR SCORES AND IDAS-II SCALES (PATIENT SAMPLE)

IDAS-II Scale	Insomnia	Lassitude	Unusual Sleep Experiences
Insomnia	**.76***	.37	.30
Mania	.32*	.30	.25
Appetite Loss	.32*	.21	.25
Claustrophobia	.23*	.09	.13
Checking	.19*	.17	.14
Euphoria	.12*	.03	–.02
Lassitude	.16	**.75***	.28
Dysphoria	.25	**.55***	.23
Social Anxiety	.18	**.40***	.17
Panic	.23	.37*	.29
Well-Being	–.12	–.33*	–.11
Ill Temper	.17	.32*	.22
Appetite Gain	–.10	.28*	.05
Suicidality	.14	.25*	.18
Traumatic Intrusions	.22	.27	**.47***
Traumatic Avoidance	.23	.27	.35*
Cleaning	.10	.14	.15*
Ordering	.07	.04	.13*

NOTE: $N = 200$. Correlations ≥ |.40| are in bold. The highest correlation in each row is marked with an asterisk. ISDI = Iowa Sleep Disturbances Inventory. IDAS-II = Expanded version of the Inventory of Depression and Anxiety Symptoms.

Table 10.7 CORRELATIONS BETWEEN THE ISDI FACTOR SCORES AND IDAS-II SCALES (STUDENT SAMPLE)

IDAS-II Scale	Insomnia	Lassitude	Unusual Sleep Experiences
Insomnia	**.70***	**.51**	**.49**
Claustrophobia	.25*	.24	.19
Lassitude	.33	**.75***	.37
Dysphoria	**.45**	**.53***	.36
Well-Being	−.33	**−.40***	−.14
Social Anxiety	.34	.36*	.28
Suicidality	.32	.36*	.28
Ill Temper	.19	.35*	.34
Appetite Loss	.18	.31*	.24
Appetite Gain	.07	.19*	.13
Traumatic Intrusions	.29	.36	**.51***
Traumatic Avoidance	.19	.33	**.45***
Panic	.27	.38	.39*
Mania	.29	.27	.30*
Checking	.17	.12	.25*
Euphoria	−.10	−.06	.16*
Ordering	.14*	.07	.14*
Cleaning	.05*	.03	.05*

NOTE: $N=219$. Correlations ≥ |.40| are in bold. The highest correlation in each row is marked with an asterisk. ISDI = Iowa Sleep Disturbances Inventory. IDAS-II = Expanded version of the Inventory of Depression and Anxiety Symptoms.

patients ($r=.76$) and students ($r=.70$). In addition, ISDI Insomnia correlated .45 with IDAS-II Dysphoria in the students; no other correlation exceeded |.35| in either sample. Similarly, the ISDI Lassitude factor was strongly linked to IDAS-II Lassitude in both patients ($r=.75$) and students ($r=.75$). ISDI Lassitude also correlated strongly with IDAS-II Dysphoria in both samples ($r=.55$ and .53 in patients and students, respectively). Although the IDAS-II clearly does not contain the detailed assessment of sleep-related pathology provided by the ISDI, these data indicate that it does model the core dysfunction modeled by its Insomnia and Lassitude factors quite well.

In contrast, the ISDI Unusual Sleep Experiences factor does not have a clear, direct counterpart on the IDAS-II. Its strongest associations were with Traumatic Intrusions ($r=.47$ and .51 in patients and students, respectively), Traumatic Avoidance ($r=.35$ and .45, respectively), and Insomnia ($r=.30$ and .49, respectively). Based on these results, it appears that the IDAS-II provides more limited assessment of the content subsumed within this factor.

REGRESSION ANALYSES

We can use multiple regression analyses to quantify the level of shared variance between the IDAS-II and ISDI more precisely. We conducted separate regression analyses in each sample, using the 18 nonoverlapping IDAS-II scales as predictors and the three ISDI factors as criteria. The top portion of Table 10.8 presents R and R^2 values from these analyses. The IDAS-II scales jointly provide excellent coverage of both ISDI Lassitude (R =.81 and .82 in patients and students, respectively) and Insomnia (R=.79 and .77, respectively), with R^2 values ranging from .586 to .671. Consistent with the bivariate analyses, they predicted Unusual Sleep Experiences less well, but even here we see a reasonable degree of shared variance between the instruments (R=.57 and .67, respectively). Clearly, this is the area

Table 10.8 Regression Results Showing the Combined Ability of IDAS-II Scales to Predict Scores on Other Psychopathology Measures

Instrument/Score	***R***	***R*²**
ISDI (Patients)		
Lassitude	.81	.658
Insomnia	.79	.623
Unusual Sleep Experiences	.57	.327
ISDI (Students)		
Lassitude	.82	.671
Insomnia	.77	.586
Unusual Sleep Experiences	.67	.452
EPSI		
Disinhibited Eating	.63	.394
Restrained Eating	.55	.307
Fitness Concerns	.46	.210
PID-5		
Negative Affectivity	.82	.674
Detachment	.74	.543
Psychoticism	.70	.487
Disinhibition	.67	.446
Antagonism	.51	.261
SPQ		
Mistrust	.70	.493
Social Anxiety	.67	.449
Eccentricity/Oddity	.63	.393
Social Anhedonia	.62	.381
Unusual Beliefs and Experiences	.52	.271
MIHT		
Hypochondriacal Alienation	.53	.286
Hypochondriacal Worry	.49	.242
Hypochondriacal Reassurance	.29	.083
Hypochondriacal Absorption	.25	.063

Note: ISDI = Iowa Sleep Disturbances Inventory. EPSI = Eating Pathology Symptoms Inventory. PID-5 = Personality Inventory for *DSM-5*. SPQ = Schizotypal Personality Questionnaire. MIHT = Multidimensional Inventory of Hypochondriacal Traits.

in which the ISDI most significantly expands the content coverage offered by the IDAS-II.

Eating Pathology Symptoms Inventory (EPSI)

Description of the EPSI

Paralleling the ISDI, the Eating Pathology Symptoms Inventory (EPSI; Forbush et al., 2013) is a comprehensive, 45-item measure of eating disorder symptoms. Respondents indicate how frequently they have experienced each symptom over the past 4 weeks on a 5-point scale ranging from *never* to *very often*. In Chapter 3, we reported results on two EPSI scales. Here, we examine the full instrument, which contains eight factor analytically derived scales: Body Dissatisfaction (e.g., wished the shape of my body was different), Binge Eating (e.g., ate until I was uncomfortably full), Purging (e.g., made myself vomit to lose weight), Excessive Exercise (e.g., pushed myself very hard when exercising), Cognitive Restraint (e.g., tried to avoid high-calorie foods), Restricting (e.g., people encouraged me to eat more), Muscle Building (e.g., considered taking a muscle-building supplement), and Negative Attitudes Toward Obesity (e.g., thought that obese people lack self-control). Forbush et al. (2013) report extensive data establishing that the ISDI scales are internally consistent, show good retest reliability over a 2- to 4-week period, and demonstrate substantial convergent and discriminant validity.

Factor Structure of the EPSI

We have complete EPSI and IDAS-II data in 217 outpatients (this sample is described in Watson et al., 2013). To clarify the structure of the EPSI, we subjected its scales to a principal factor analysis. This analysis yielded three interpretable factors; the resulting promax loadings are presented in Table 10.9. We labeled these three factors Disinhibited Eating (marked by Body Dissatisfaction, Binge Eating, and Purging), Fitness Concerns (defined by Muscle Building, Excessive Exercise, and Negative Attitudes Toward Obesity), and Restrained Eating (marked

Table 10.9 Promax Loadings of the EPSI Scales in an Outpatient Sample

EPSI Scale	I	II	III
Body Dissatisfaction	**.67**	−.15	.17
Binge Eating	**.56**	.08	**−.33**
Purging	**.46**	.20	.18
Muscle Building	−.01	**.64**	.07
Excessive Exercise	−.08	**.50**	.11
Negative Attitudes Toward Obesity	.22	**.38**	−.06
Cognitive Restraint	.15	.02	**.42**
Restricting	−.06	.13	**.42**

NOTE: $N = 217$. Loadings ≥ |.30| are in bold. EPSI = Eating Pathology Symptoms Inventory.

by Cognitive Restraint and Restricting), respectively. As in the ISDI analyses, we created regression-based factor scores to model these dimensions in subsequent analyses.

Bivariate Analyses

Table 10.10 presents correlations between these EPSI factor scores and the IDAS-II scales. In contrast to the ISDI results, these data reveal only one strong association: Disinhibited Eating correlated .54 with Appetite Gain. Disinhibited Eating also correlated moderately with Lassitude (r=.38) and Traumatic Intrusions (r=.33). Conversely, Restrained Eating had a moderate positive correlation with Appetite Loss (r=.38) and a comparable negative association with Appetite Gain (r = −.33). Finally, Fitness Concerns correlated moderately with Mania (r=.33). Thus, we do see some points of overlap between these instruments. Not surprisingly, this shared variance centers on the two IDAS-II appetite scales, which have moderate to strong links with the Disinhibited Eating and Restrained Eating factors.

Regression Analyses

Once again, we conducted multiple regression analyses—using the IDAS-II scales as predictors and the EPSI factor scores as criteria—to quantify the level of shared variance between the instruments. R and R^2 values from these analyses

Table 10.10 Correlations Between the EPSI Factor Scores and IDAS-II Scales

IDAS-II Scale	Disinhibited Eating	Fitness Concerns	Restrained Eating
Appetite Gain	**.54***	.01	**−.33**
Lassitude	**.38***	.12	−.09
Traumatic Intrusions	**.33***	.24	.20
Panic	.29*	.19	.13
Dysphoria	.28*	.21	.09
Ill Temper	.25*	.13	.03
Claustrophobia	.25*	.13	.06
Social Anxiety	.23*	.20	.06
Suicidality	.19*	.19*	.15
Well-Being	−.09*	−.03	.02
Mania	.23	**.33***	.22
Traumatic Avoidance	.20	.26*	.19
Euphoria	.03	.23*	.16
Ordering	.12	.23*	.11
Insomnia	.16	.20*	.17
Cleaning	.14	.18*	.16
Appetite Loss	−.04	.25	**.38***
Checking	.11	.12	.14*

NOTE: N=216. Correlations ≥ |.30| are in bold. The highest correlation in each row is marked with an asterisk. EPSI = Eating Pathology Symptoms Inventory. IDAS-II = Expanded version of the Inventory of Depression and Anxiety Symptoms.

are presented in Table 10.8. These results indicate that the IDAS-II scales jointly account for roughly 40% of the variance in Disinhibited Eating ($R = .63$, $R^2 = .394$), approximately 30% of the variance in Restrained Eating ($R = .55$, $R^2 = .307$), and roughly 20% of the variance in Fitness Concerns ($R = .46$, $R^2 = .210$). Overall, we see less much overlap here than was observed previously with the ISDI. Clearly, the EPSI substantially extends the symptom coverage provided by the IDAS-II.

Personality Inventory for *DSM-5* (PID-5)

Description of the PID-5

Researchers recently have developed two different inventories that provide comprehensive assessment of the basic traits underlying the *DSM* personality disorders: the Computerized Adaptive Test of Personality Disorder (CAT-PD; L. Simms et al., 2011) and the Personality Inventory for *DSM-5* (PID-5; Krueger et al., 2012). Although these instruments were developed independently of one another, they are very similar in content and, in fact, assess many of the same trait dimensions (Wright & Simms, 2014). Given their similarity—and because we have more data on the PID-5—we will focus on it here.

The PID-5 consists of 220 items that are rated on a 4-point scale ranging from 0 (very false or often false) to 3 (very true or often true). As was noted in Chapter 4, it assesses the 25 specific facet traits in the alternative model of personality pathology that was newly developed for Section III of *DSM-5*. These facet traits, in turn, define five higher order domains of pathological personality. It should be noted that four of these five domains have close parallels in the prominent five-factor model of personality (see Krueger & Markon, 2014). More specifically, PID-5 Negative Affectivity closely corresponds to neuroticism; PID-5 Detachment taps a dimension similar to (low) extraversion; PID-5 Antagonism parallels (low) agreeableness; and PID-5 Disinhibition is strongly linked to (low) conscientiousness. The final PID-5 domain—Psychoticism—is more tangentially related to openness. Although it is a relatively new instrument, the PID-5 already has been very widely used in research; in fact, the original Krueger et al. (2012) scale development article has been cited more than 375 times according to Google Scholar (as of December 3, 2016).

Factor Structure of the PID-5

We have complete PID-5 and IDAS-II data in three samples: 220 outpatients (this sample is described in Watson et al., 2013), 277 students from the University of North Texas, and 411 community adults from Sample 4. As in previous chapters, for ease of presentation, we report these data on a standardized combined sample ($N = 908$); we created this composite group by standardizing all of the scale scores on a within-sample basis and then aggregating them to permit a single overall analysis.

Next, we subjected the PID-5 scales to a principal factor analysis. Consistent with previous research (see Krueger & Markon, 2014), this analysis yielded five interpretable factors; the resulting promax loadings are presented in Table 10.11. We used the standard PID-5 domain names to label these factors: Negative Affectivity (marked most strongly by Anxiousness, Emotional Lability, Separation Insecurity,

Table 10.11 PROMAX LOADINGS OF THE PID-5 SCALES (STANDARDIZED COMBINED SAMPLE)

PID-5 Scale	I	II	III	IV	V
Anxiousness	**.83**	.05	−.03	−.10	.12
Emotional Lability	**.77**	−.12	−.01	.07	.14
Separation Insecurity	**.77**	−.19	.14	−.01	.01
Depressivity	**.60**	.39	−.07	.08	−.10
Submissiveness	**.53**	−.10	.03	−.10	.11
Perseveration	**.48**	.14	.02	.08	.38
Distractibility	**.42**	.19	−.11	.39	.02
Suspiciousness	.32	.29	.15	−.00	.13
Withdrawal	.13	**.78**	−.06	−.17	.15
Restricted Affectivity	−.26	**.68**	.18	−.02	.19
Intimacy Avoidance	−.12	**.66**	−.06	.05	.13
Anhedonia	**.43**	**.61**	−.07	−.05	−.19
Manipulativeness	.03	−.00	**.80**	.03	.01
Deceitfulness	.17	.10	**.74**	.10	−.11
Grandiosity	−.06	.05	**.59**	−.11	.33
Callousness	−.13	**.44**	**.58**	.12	−.01
Attention Seeking	.20	**−.40**	**.53**	.23	.12
Hostility	.32	.24	.38	.09	.04
Impulsivity	.19	−.05	.09	**.70**	−.03
Risk Taking	−.28	−.12	.29	**.65**	−.00
Irresponsibility	.18	.25	.16	**.47**	−.12
Unusual Beliefs and Experiences	.09	.19	.03	.21	**.53**
Rigid Perfectionism	.33	.11	.12	−.28	**.53**
Cognitive and Perceptual Dysregulation	.26	.23	−.05	.25	**.48**
Eccentricity	.17	.21	.03	.37	.32

NOTE: $N = 908$. Loadings ≥ |.40| are in bold. PID-5 = Personality Inventory for *DSM-5*.

Depressivity, and Submissiveness), Detachment (defined by Withdrawal, Restricted Affectivity, Intimacy Avoidance, and Anhedonia), Antagonism (marked by Manipulativeness, Deceitfulness, Grandiosity, Callousness, and Attention Seeking), Disinhibition (defined primarily by Impulsivity, Risk Taking, and Irresponsibility), and Psychoticism (marked by Unusual Beliefs and Experiences, Rigid Perfectionism, and Cognitive and Perceptual Dysregulation). As in previous analyses, we created regression-based factor scores to model these five dimensions in subsequent analyses.

BIVARIATE ANALYSES

Table 10.12 presents correlations between these PID-5 factors and the IDAS-II scales. It is noteworthy that four of the five PID-5 factors correlate strongly with multiple IDAS-II scales. Negative Affectivity clearly exhibited the greatest overlap

Table 10.12 CORRELATIONS BETWEEN PID-5 FACTOR SCORES AND IDAS-II SCALES (STANDARDIZED COMBINED SAMPLE)

IDAS-II Scale	NA	DET	ANT	DIS	PSY
Dysphoria	**.77***	**.61**	.18	**.50**	.30
Social Anxiety	**.64***	**.60**	.12	.33	.37
Traumatic Intrusions	**.64***	**.45**	.19	**.45**	**.41**
Panic	**.61***	**.51**	.22	**.47**	**.41**
Lassitude	**.61***	**.45**	.24	**.43**	.28
Ill Temper	**.57***	**.47**	.36	**.53**	.38
Mania	**.57***	**.42**	.32	**.54**	**.49**
Suicidality	**.56***	**.53**	.19	**.42**	.31
Traumatic Avoidance	**.53***	**.42**	.15	.29	.38
Insomnia	**.47***	**.40**	.18	.36	.30
Claustrophobia	**.45***	**.44**	.17	.33	**.42**
Appetite Loss	**.42***	.38	.15	.34	.33
Appetite Gain	.32*	.24	.20	.25	.24
Well-Being	**–.40**	**–.46***	.06	–.18	.15
Ordering	.37	.34	.26	.25	**.57***
Checking	**.43**	.37	.20	.27	**.56***
Cleaning	.37	.35	.17	.21	**.48***
Euphoria	.11	.04	.38	.32	**.47***

NOTE: $N = 908$. Correlations ≥ |.40| are in bold. The highest correlation in each row is marked with an asterisk. PID-5 = Personality Inventory for *DSM-5*. IDAS-II = Expanded version of the Inventory of Depression and Anxiety Symptoms. NA = Negative Affectivity. DET = Detachment. ANT = Antagonism. DIS = Disinhibition. PSY = Psychoticism.

with the IDAS-II, correlating particularly strongly with Dysphoria ($r = .77$), Social Anxiety ($r = .64$), Traumatic Intrusions ($r = .64$), Panic ($r = .61$), and Lassitude ($r = .61$). Detachment had its strongest links with Dysphoria ($r = .61$), Social Anxiety ($r = .60$), Suicidality ($r = .53$), and Panic ($r = .51$). Disinhibition displayed strong associations with Mania ($r = .54$), Ill Temper ($r = .53$), and Dysphoria ($r = .50$). Finally, Psychoticism displayed particularly strong links to the three OCD scales (*r*s ranged from .48 to .57) and the two bipolar scales ($r = .49$ and .47 with Mania and Euphoria, respectively).

In contrast, PID-5 Antagonism was more weakly related to the IDAS-II. In fact, it had only three associations ≥ .30: .38 with Euphoria, .36 with Ill Temper, and .32 with Mania. It obviously shares the least amount of variance with the IDAS-II.

REGRESSION ANALYSES

Once again, we conducted multiple regression analyses, using the IDAS-II scales as predictors and the PID-5 factor scores as criteria. R and R^2 values from these analyses are presented in Table 10.8. The IDAS-II scales jointly provide excellent coverage of PID-5 Negative Affectivity ($R = .82$, $R^2 = .674$). They also display a relatively strong level of overlap with Detachment, Psychoticism, and Disinhibition, accounting for roughly 45% to 55% of the variance in these factors (*R*s ranged from .67 to .74, R^2 values ranged from .446 to .543). Consistent with the bivariate analyses, the IDAS-II predicted Antagonism less well, but even here there is a considerable amount of shared variance between the instruments ($R=.51$, $R^2=.261$). Overall, however, Antagonism is the PID-5 domain that most significantly expands the content coverage offered by the IDAS-II.

Schizotypal Personality Questionnaire (SPQ)

Description of the SPQ

The PID-5 provides considerable coverage of characteristics related to psychosis and thought disorder, particularly through its Psychoticism (positive symptoms) and Detachment (negative symptoms) domains. In addition, the Schizotypal Personality Questionnaire (SPQ; Raine, 1991) contains 74 items that assess a broad range of content related to the Cluster A personality disorders; respondents answer these items using a dichotomous yes/no format.

Chmielewski and Watson (2008a) identified five replicable factors in structural analyses of the SPQ items in two large samples. We used the best markers of these dimensions to create corresponding factor-based scales: Mistrust (9 items; e.g., people are talking behind my back), Eccentricity/Oddity (10 items; e.g., other people think I am strange), Unusual Beliefs and Experiences (10 items; e.g., have communicated with others telepathically), Social Anxiety (10 items; e.g., get anxious when meeting people for the first time), and Social Anhedonia (9 items; e.g., have little interest in getting to know other people). These five scales jointly provide a reasonably comprehensive assessment of characteristics related to psychosis and thought disorder.

Bivariate Analyses

Table 10.13 presents correlations between these five factor-based SPQ scales and the IDAS-II in 295 adult participants from Sample 4. Mistrust exhibited the strongest and broadest overlap with the IDAS-II; it had particularly substantial links with Mania ($r=.60$), Panic ($r=.58$), Dysphoria ($r=.57$), and Ill Temper ($r=.57$). As would be expected, SPQ Social Anxiety correlated strongly with IDAS-II Social Anxiety ($r=.62$); it also had moderate associations with Dysphoria ($r=.47$) and Panic ($r=.41$). Eccentricity/Oddity correlated most highly with Dysphoria ($r=.54$), Mania ($r=.53$), and Social Anxiety ($r=.50$). Social Anhedonia had several moderate associations in the .40 to .50 range. Finally, SPQ Unusual Beliefs and Experiences displayed the least amount of overlap with the IDAS-II: Its highest coefficient was only .40 (with Suicidality).

Regression Analyses

We again conducted a series of multiple regression analyses, using the IDAS-II scales as predictors and the five SPQ factor scales as criteria. *R* and R^2 values from these analyses are presented in Table 10.8. The IDAS-II scales jointly accounted for

Table 10.13 Correlations Between SPQ Factor Scales and IDAS-II Scales (Sample 4)

IDAS-II Scale	Mistrust	Oddity	Unusual	Social Anxiety	Social Anhedonia
Mania	**.60***	**.53**	.38	.27	.36
Panic	**.58***	**.48**	.37	**.41**	**.46**
Dysphoria	**.57***	**.54**	.33	**.47**	**.48**
Ill Temper	**.57***	**.48**	.36	.28	**.46**
Traumatic Intrusions	**.51***	**.43**	.39	.35	**.43**
Checking	**.49***	**.44**	.26	.24	.30
Ordering	**.48***	**.44**	.23	.21	.26
Claustrophobia	**.48***	.35	.27	.28	.33
Cleaning	**.48***	.34	.26	.20	.32
Traumatic Avoidance	**.46***	.33	.29	.36	**.42**
Suicidality	**.45***	.37	**.40**	.33	**.40**
Insomnia	**.43***	**.40**	.24	.30	.35
Euphoria	**.42***	**.40**	.27	−.01	.15
Appetite Gain	**.40***	.33	.19	.25	.26
Lassitude	**.42**	**.47***	.24	.38	**.42**
Appetite Loss	.33	.28	.34*	.28	.32
Social Anxiety	**.60**	**.50**	.28	**.62***	**.47**
Well-Being	−.10	−.06	−.01	−.27*	−.24

NOTE: $N = 295$. Correlations ≥ |.40| are in bold. The highest correlation in each row is marked with an asterisk. SPQ = Schizotypal Personality Questionnaire. IDAS-II = Expanded version of the Inventory of Depression and Anxiety Symptoms. Oddity = Eccentricity/Oddity. Unusual = Unusual Beliefs and Experiences.

approximately 40% to 50% of the variance in four of the five SPQ scales: Mistrust, Social Anxiety, Eccentricity/Oddity, and Social Anhedonia (*R*s ranged from .62 to .70, R^2 values ranged from .381 to .493). In contrast, they accounted for less than 30% of the variance in Unusual Beliefs and Experiences ($R = .52$, $R^2 = .271$). Consistent with the bivariate analyses, this content area shows the least amount of shared variance with the IDAS-II.

Multidimensional Inventory of Hypochondriacal Traits (MIHT)

The Multidimensional Inventory of Hypochondriacal Traits (MIHT; Longley, Watson, & Noyes, 2005) is a 31-item measure assessing characteristics related to hypochondriasis (which is now called illness anxiety disorder in *DSM-5*). The MIHT consists of four factor analytically derived scales: Hypochondriacal Alienation (seven items; e.g., wish others took my health complaints more seriously), Hypochondriacal Worry (seven items; e.g., worry a lot about my health), Hypochondriacal Reassurance (eight items; e.g., turn to others for support when not feeling well), and Hypochondriacal Absorption (nine items; e.g., am sensitive to changes in my body). Respondents answer each item using a 5-point scale ranging from *strongly disagree* to *strongly agree.* Longley et al. (2005) present extensive data establishing that the MIHT scales are internally consistent, show strong retest reliability over an 8-week period, and demonstrate substantial convergent, discriminant, and criterion validity.

Bivariate Analyses

Table 10.14 presents correlations between these four MIHT scales and the IDAS-II in 411 adult participants from Sample 4. Hypochondriacal Alienation and Hypochondriacal Worry both displayed a moderate level of overlap with the IDAS-II, as each scale had several coefficients in the .30 to .40 range. In marked contrast, Hypochondriacal Reassurance and Hypochondriacal Absorption were very weakly related to the IDAS-II. In fact, neither scale had a correlation as high as .20 with any IDAS-II scale. These two MIHT scales clearly contain content that is not well captured by the IDAS-II.

Regression Analyses

We again conducted multiple regression analyses in which the IDAS-II scales were the predictors and the four MIHT scales served as criteria. R and R^2 values from these analyses are presented in the bottom portion of Table 10.8. As would be

Table 10.14 Correlations Between the MIHT and IDAS-II Scales (Sample 4)

IDAS-II Scale	Alienation	Worry	Reassurance	Absorption
Dysphoria	**.40***	**.36**	.17	.14
Lassitude	**.40***	**.31**	.19	.15
Panic	**.39***	**.35**	.14	.08
Appetite Loss	**.36***	.27	.05	.07
Suicidality	**.36***	.24	.08	.03
Traumatic Intrusions	**.34***	**.30**	.14	.12
Mania	**.34***	**.30**	.15	.13
Ill Temper	**.30***	.27	.14	.09
Insomnia	.26*	.24	.04	.11
Well-Being	−.25*	−.13	−.01	.09
Euphoria	.15*	.15*	.15*	.08
Traumatic Avoidance	**.33**	**.40***	.15	.17
Social Anxiety	**.35**	**.39***	.17	.10
Checking	**.33**	**.35***	.15	.11
Cleaning	.26	**.35***	.13	.07
Ordering	.26	**.32***	.12	.11
Claustrophobia	**.30**	**.31***	.10	.06
Appetite Gain	.22	.25*	.18	.13

NOTE: $N = 411$. Correlations ≥ |.30| are in bold. The highest correlation in each row is marked with an asterisk. MIHT = Multidimensional Inventory of Hypochondriacal Traits. IDAS-II = Expanded version of the Inventory of Depression and Anxiety Symptoms.

expected based on the bivariate analyses, the IDAS-II scales jointly accounted for approximately 25% to 30% of the variance in MIHT Hypochondriacal Alienation and Hypochondriacal Worry (*R*s ranged from .49 to .53, R^2 values ranged from .242 to .286). Consistent with the Table 10.14 results, however, they shared very little variance with either Hypochondriacal Reassurance ($R=.29$, $R^2=.083$) or Hypochondriacal Absorption ($R=.25$, $R^2=.063$). Overall, we see only a modest to moderate level of overlap between the two instruments.

Further Extension of the Model

DSM-5 contains 19 classes of mental disorders. The instruments we have reviewed thus far provide detailed symptom coverage of most of these classes, including schizophrenia spectrum and other psychotic disorders; bipolar and related disorders; depressive disorders; anxiety disorders; OCRDs; trauma- and stressor-related disorders; somatic symptom and related disorders; feeding and eating disorders; sleep-wake disorders; disruptive, impulse-control, and conduct disorders; and personality disorders.

Researchers have developed many other psychometrically sophisticated measures that substantially extend the symptom-level coverage that currently is available. Some instruments provide relatively broad assessment of psychopathology. For example, the Achenbach System of Empirically Based Assessment (ASEBA; Achenbach & Rescorla, 2001) was initially constructed to assess a broad range of symptoms in youth via self-, parent-, and teacher-ratings. Self- and informant-report versions subsequently were developed for use in both adults (Achenbach & Rescorla, 2003) and the elderly (Achenbach, Newhouse, & Rescorla, 2004).

As another example, the Externalizing Spectrum Inventory (ESI; Krueger, Markon, Patrick, Benning, & Kramer, 2007) provides detailed and comprehensive assessment of externalizing psychopathology; it exists both in its original 415-item version and in a 160-item Brief Form (ESI-BF; Patrick, Kramer, Krueger, & Markon, 2013). The ESI and ESI-BF contain 23 homogeneous scales assessing various types of aggression, alienation, impulsivity, irresponsibility, antisocial behavior (e.g., theft, fraud), rebelliousness, and multiple forms of substance abuse.

In addition, many instruments provide reliable and valid assessment of a narrower range of symptoms. A complete discussion of these measures is beyond the scope of this chapter, but we will present a few illustrations. The Curious Experiences Survey (Goldberg, 1999), the Multiscale Dissociation Inventory (Briere, 2002), and the Dissociative Processes Scale (Harrison & Watson, 1992) all assess multiple homogeneous symptom dimensions within the dissociative disorders. The Massachusetts General Hospital Hair Pulling Scale (Keuthen, O'Sullivan, Ricciardi, & Shera, 1995) and the Milwaukee Inventory for Subtypes of Trichotillomania (Flessner et al., 2008) both provide symptom-level assessment of trichotillomania (hair-pulling disorder), which is one of the OCRDs in *DSM-5*. The Skin Picking Scale (Keuthen et al., 2001) and the Milwaukee Inventory for the Dimensions of Adult Skin Picking (Walther et al., 2009) both measure symptoms associated with excoriation (skin-picking) disorder, which is another OCRD. The Yale Global Tic Severity Scale-Self Report (Best, 2009) and the MOVES (Gaffney, Sieg, & Hellings, 1994) both assess symptoms related to neurodevelopmental disorders. Finally, instruments exist to measure various types of sexual dysfunctions (e.g., Forbes, Baillie, & Schniering, 2015) and paraphilic disorders (e.g., Mokros, Schilling, Weiss, Nitschke, & Eher, 2014).

CONCLUSION

Given these recent advances in assessment, we now can measure virtually all major forms of psychopathology at the symptom level. Consequently, although much more work remains to be done, it now is feasible to transition away from disorder-based models and to focus instead at the level of homogeneous symptom dimensions. We hope that this book will serve as a useful organizing framework as we enter this exciting new era of psychopathology research.

REFERENCES

Abramson, L. Y., Metalsky, G. L., & Alloy, L. B. (1989). Hopelessness depression: A theory based subtype of depression. *Psychological Review, 96*, 358–372.

Achenbach, T. M., Newhouse, P. A., & Rescorla, L. A. (2004). *Manual for ASEBA Older Adult Forms & Profiles*. Burlington, VT: University of Vermont. Research Center for Children, Youth, & Families.

Achenbach, T. M., & Rescorla, L. A. (2001). *Manual for the ASEBA school-age forms and profiles*. Burlington, VA: University of Vermont Research Center for Children, Youth, and Families.

Achenbach, T. M., & Rescorla, L. A. (2003). *Manual for the ASEBA adult forms and profiles*. Burlington, VT: University of Vermont.

Ackerman, R. A., Witt, E.A., Donnellan, M. B., Trzesniewski, K. H., Robins, R. W., & Kashy, D. A. (2011). What does the Narcissistic Personality Inventory really measure? *Assessment, 18*, 67–87.

Alloy, L. B., Abramson, L. Y., Walshaw, P. D., Cogswell, A., Grandin, L. D., Hughes, M. E., . . . Hogan, M. E. (2008). Behavioral approach system and behavioral inhibition system sensitivities and bipolar spectrum disorders: Prospective prediction of bipolar mood episodes. *Bipolar Disorders, 10*, 310–322.

Alloy, L. B., Bender, R. E., Whitehouse, W. G., Wagner, C. A., Liu, R. T., Grant, D. A., . . . Abramson, L. Y. (2012). High Behavioral Approach System (BAS) sensitivity, reward responsiveness, and goal-striving predict first onset of bipolar disorders: A prospective behavioral high-risk design. *Journal of Abnormal Psychology, 121*, 339–351.

Alloy, L. B., Kelly, K. A., Mineka, S., & Clements, C. M. (1990). Comorbidity of anxiety and depressive disorders: A helplessness-hopelessness perspective. In J. Maser & R. C. Cloninger (Eds.), *Comorbidity of mood and anxiety disorders* (pp. 499–543). Washington, DC: American Psychiatric Press.

Altman, E. G., Hedeker D., Peterson, J. L., & Davis, J. M. (1997). The Altman Self-Rating Mania Scale. *Biological Psychiatry, 42*, 948–955.

American Psychiatric Association. (1952). *Diagnostic and statistical manual of mental disorders* (1st ed.) Washington, DC: Author.

American Psychiatric Association. (1968). *Diagnostic and statistical manual of mental disorders* (2nd ed.) Washington, DC: Author.

American Psychiatric Association. (1980). *Diagnostic and statistical manual of mental disorders* (3rd ed.) Washington, DC: Author.

American Psychiatric Association. (1987). *Diagnostic and statistical manual of mental disorders* (3rd ed., rev.). Washington, DC: Author.

American Psychiatric Association. (2000). *Diagnostic and statistical manual of mental Disorders* (4th ed., text rev.). Washington, DC: Author.

American Psychiatric Association. (2013). *Diagnostic and statistical manual of mental disorders* (5th ed.). Washington, DC: Author.

Angst, J., Adolfsson, R., Benazzi, F., Gamma, A., Hantouche, E., Meyer, T. D., . . . Scott, J. (2005). The HCL-32: Towards a self-assessment tool for hypomanic symptoms in outpatients. *Journal of Affective Disorders, 88*, 217–233.

Arnau, R. C., Meagher, M. W., Norris, M. P., & Bramson, R. (2001). Psychometric evaluation of the Beck Depression Inventory-II with primary care medical patients. *Health Psychology, 20*, 112–119.

Arrindell, W. A., Pickersgill, M. J., Merckelbach, H., Ardon, M. A., & Cornet, F. C. (1991). Phobic dimensions: III. Factor analytic approaches to the study of common phobic fears; an updated review of findings obtained with adult subjects. *Advances in Behaviour Research and Therapy, 13*, 73–130.

Baer, L. (1991). *Getting control: Overcoming your obsessions and compulsions.* Boston, MA: Little, Brown, & Co.

Baer, L. (1994). Factor analysis of symptom subtypes of obsessive compulsive disorder and their relation to personality and tic disorders. *Journal of Clinical Psychiatry, 55* (Suppl 3), 18–23.

Bagby, R. M., Bindseil, K. D., Schuller, D. R., Rector, N. A., Young, L. T., Cooke, R. G., . . . Joffe, R. (1997). Relationship between the five-factor model of personality and unipolar, bipolar and schizophrenic patients. *Psychiatry Research, 70*, 83–94.

Bagby, R. M., Young, L. T., Schuller, D. R., Bindseil, K. D., Cooke, R. G., Dickens, S. E., . . . Joffe, R. T. (1996). Bipolar disorder, unipolar depression and the five factor model of personality. *Journal of Affective Disorders, 41*, 25–32.

Barlow, D. H. (1991). The nature of anxiety: Anxiety, depression, and emotional disorders. In R. M. Rapee & D. H. Barlow (Eds.), *Chronic anxiety: Generalized anxiety disorder and mixed anxiety-depression* (pp. 1–28). New York, NY: Guilford Press.

Barch, D. M., Yodkovik, N., Sypher-Locke, H., & Hanewickel, M. (2008). Intrinsic motivation in schizophrenia: Relationships to cognitive function, depression, anxiety and personality. *Journal of Abnormal Psychology, 117*, 776–787.

Barlow, D. H., & DiNardo, P. A. (1991). The diagnosis of generalized anxiety disorder: Development, current status, and future directions. In R. M. Rapee & D. H. Barlow (Eds.), *Chronic anxiety: Generalized anxiety disorder and mixed anxiety-depression* (pp. 95–118). New York, NY: Guilford Press.

Beck, A. T., Rush, A. J., Shaw, B. F., & Emery, G. (1979). *Cognitive therapy of depression.* New York, NY: Guilford Press.

Beck, A. T., & Steer, R. A. (1990). *Beck Anxiety Inventory manual.* San Antonio, TX: Psychological Corporation.

Beck, A. T., & Steer, R. A. (1993). *Beck Depression Inventory manual* (1993 edition). San Antonio, TX: The Psychological Corporation.

Beck, A. T., Steer, R. A., & Brown, G. K. (1996). *Beck Depression Inventory manual* (2nd ed.). San Antonio, TX: Psychological Corporation.

Beck, A. T., Steer, R., & Garbin, M. (1988). Psychometric properties of the Beck Depression Inventory: Twenty-five years of evaluation. *Clinical Psychology Review, 8*, 77–100.

Beck, J. G., Carmin, C. N., & Henninger, N. J. (1998). The utility of the Fear Survey Schedule-III: An extended replication. *Journal of Anxiety Disorders, 12*, 177–182.

Beck, J. G., & Grant, D. M., Clapp, J. D., & Palyo, S. A. (2009). Understanding the interpersonal impact of trauma: Contributions of PTSD and depression. *Journal of Anxiety Disorders, 23*, 443–450.

Becker, G. (2000). How important is transient error in estimating reliability? Going beyond simulation studies. *Psychological Methods, 5*, 370–379.

Bedi, R. P., Koopman, R. F., & Thompson, J. M. (2001). The dimensionality of the Beck Depression Inventory-II and its relevance for tailoring the psychological treatment of women with depression. *Psychotherapy, 38*, 306–318.

Benazzi, F. (2006). Symptoms of depression as possible markers of bipolar II disorder. *Progress in Neuro-Psychopharmacology & Biological Psychiatry, 30*, 471–477.

Best, S. H. (2009). *Experiential avoidance in chronic tic disorders: An online survey and pilot treatment study using habit reversal and Acceptance and Commitment Therapy.* (Doctoral dissertation). Retrieved from ProQuest Dissertations and Theses.

Bienvenu, O. J., Samuels, J. F., Costa, P. T., Reti, I. M., Eaton, W. W., & Nestadt, G. (2004). Anxiety and depressive disorders and the five-factor model of personality: A higher- and lower-order personality trait investigation in a community sample. *Depression and Anxiety, 20*, 92–97.

Boelen, P. A., & Spuij, M. (2013). Symptoms of post-traumatic stress disorder in bereaved children and adolescents: Factor structure and correlates. *Journal of Abnormal Child Psychology, 41*, 1097–1108.

Boelen, P. A., van den Hout, M. A., & van den Bout, J. (2008). The factor structure of Posttraumatic Stress Disorder symptoms among bereaved individuals: A confirmatory factor analysis study. *Journal of Anxiety Disorders, 22*, 1377–1383.

Boyes, M. E., Cluver, L. D., & Gardner, F. (2012). Psychometric properties of the Child PTSD Checklist in a community sample of South African children and adolescents. *PloS ONE, 7*, e46905.

Brady E. U., & Kendall, P. C. (1992). Comorbidity of anxiety and depression in children and adolescents. *Journal of Consulting and Clinical Psychology, 111*, 244–255.

Briere, J. (2002). Multiscale Dissociation Inventory (MDI). Odessa, FL: Psychological Assessment Resources.

Briere, J., Scott, C., & Weathers, F. (2005). Peritraumatic and persistent dissociation in the presumed etiology of PTSD. *American Journal of Psychiatry, 162*, 2295–2301.

Brouwer, D., Meijer, R. R., & Zevalkink, J. (2013). On the factor structure of the Beck Depression Inventory-II: G is the key. *Psychological Assessment, 25*, 136–145.

Brown, T. A., & Barlow, D. H. (1992). Comorbidity among anxiety disorders: Implications for treatment and DSM-IV. *Journal of Consulting and Clinical Psychology, 60*, 835–844.

Brown, T. A., & Barlow, D. H. (2005). Dimensional versus categorical classification of mental disorders in the fifth edition of the *Diagnostic and Statistical Manual of Mental Disorders* and beyond: Comment on the Special Section. *Journal of Abnormal Psychology, 114*, 551–556.

Brown, T. A., Campbell, L. A., Lehman, C. L., Grisham, G. R., & Mancill, R. B. (2001). Current and lifetime comorbidity of the *DSM-IV* anxiety and mood disorders in a large clinical sample. *Journal of Abnormal Psychology, 110*, 585–599.

Brown, T. A., Chorpita, B. F., & Barlow, D. H. (1998). Structured relationships among dimensions of the *DSM-IV* anxiety and mood disorders and dimensions of negative affect, positive affect, and autonomic arousal. *Journal of Abnormal Psychology, 107*, 179–192.

Buckley, T. C., Blanchard, E. B., & Hickling, E. J. (1998). A confirmatory factor analysis of posttraumatic stress symptoms. *Behavioural Research and Therapy, 36*,1091–1099

Byrne, B. M., Stewart, S. M., & Lee, P. W. H. (2004). Validating the Beck Depression Inventory-II for Hong Kong community adolescents. *International Journal of Testing, 43*, 199–216.

Calamari, J. E., Wiegartz, P. S. Riemann, B. C., Cohen, R. J., Greer, A., Jacobi, D. M., . . . Carmin, C. (2004). Obsessive-compulsive disorder subtypes: An attempted replication and extension of a symptom-based taxonomy. *Behaviour Research and Therapy, 42*, 647–670.

Campbell, D. T., & Fiske, D. W. (1959). Convergent and discriminant validation by the multitrait-multimethod matrix. *Psychological Bulletin, 56*, 81–105.

Carney, C. E., Ulmer, C., Edinger, J. D., Krystal, A. D., & Knauss, F. (2009). Assessing depression symptoms in those with insomnia: An examination of the Beck Depression Inventory second edition (BDI-II). *Journal of Psychiatric Research, 43*, 576–582.

Carver, C. S., & Harmon-Jones, E. (2009). Anger is an approach-related affect: Evidence and implications. *Psychological Bulletin, 135*, 183–204.

Carver, C. S., & White, T. L. (1994). Behavioral inhibition, behavioral activation, and affective responses to impending reward and punishment: The BIS/BAS Scales. *Journal of Personality and Social Psychology, 67*, 319–333.

Casillas, A., & Clark, L. A. (2000, May). *The Mini Mood and Anxiety Symptom Questionnaire (Mini-MASQ)*. Poster presented at the 72nd Annual Meeting of the Midwestern Psychological Association, Chicago, IL.

Caspi, A., Houts, R. M., Belsky, D. W., Goldman-Mellor, S. J. Harrington, H., Israel, S., . . . Moffitt, T. E. (2014). The p factor: One general psychopathology factor in the structure of psychiatric disorders? *Clinical Psychological Science, 2*, 119–137.

Cattell, R. B. (1964a). Beyond validity and reliability: Some further concepts and coefficients for evaluating tests. *Journal of Experimental Education, 33*, 133–143.

Cattell, R. B. (1964b). Validity and reliability: A proposed more basic set of concepts. *Journal of Educational Psychology, 55*, 1–22.

Cattell, R. B., Eber, H. W., & Tatsuoka, M. M. (1970). *Handbook for the Sixteen Personality Factor Questionnaire (16PF)*. Champaign, IL: Institute for Personality and Ability Testing.

Chmielewski, M., Clark, L. A., Bagby, R. M., & Watson, D. (2015). Method matters: Understanding diagnostic reliability in *DSM-IV* and *DSM-5*. *Journal of Abnormal Psychology, 124*, 764–769.

Chmielewski, M., & Watson, D. (2008a). The heterogeneous structure of schizotypal personality disorder: Item-level factors of the Schizotypal Personality Questionnaire and their associations with obsessive-compulsive disorder symptoms, dissociative tendencies, and norma personality. *Journal of Abnormal Psychology, 117*, 364–376.

Chmielewski, M., & Watson, D. (2008b, October). *Oddity: The third higher order factor of psychopathology*. Poster session presented at the annual meeting of the Society for Research in Psychopathology, Iowa City, IA.

Chmielewski, M., & Watson D. (2009). What is being assessed and why it matters: The impact of transient error on trait research. *Journal of Personality and Social Psychology, 97*, 186–202.

Clark, D. A., Steer, R. A., & Beck, A. T. (1994). Common and specific dimensions of self-reported anxiety and depression: Implications for the cognitive and tripartite models. *Journal of Abnormal Psychology, 103*, 645–654.

Clark, L. A. (1989). The anxiety and depressive disorders: Descriptive psychopathology and differential diagnosis. In P. C. Kendall & D. Watson (Eds.), *Anxiety and depression: Distinctive and overlapping features* (pp. 83–129). San Diego, CA: Academic Press.

Clark, L. A., & Watson, D. (1991). Tripartite model of anxiety and depression: Psychometric evidence and taxonomic implications. *Journal of Abnormal Psychology, 100*, 316–336.

Clark, L. A., & Watson, D. (1995). Constructing validity: Basic issues in objective scale development. *Psychological Assessment, 7*, 309–319.

Clark, L. A., & Watson D. (1999). Temperament: A new paradigm for trait psychology. In L. A. Pervin & O. P. John (Eds.), *Handbook of personality* (2nd ed., pp. 102–138). New York, NY: Guilford Press.

Clark, L. A., & Watson, D. (2006). The distress and fear disorders: An alternative empirically based taxonomy of the "mood" and "anxiety" disorders. *British Journal of Psychiatry, 189*, 481–483.

Clark, L. A., Watson, D., & Reynolds, S. (1995). Diagnosis and classification of psychopathology: Challenges to the current system and future directions. *Annual Review of Psychology, 46*, 121–153.

Cohen, A. S., Callaway, D. A., Najolia, G. M., Larsen, J. T., & Strauss, G. P. (2012). On "risk" and reward: Investigating state anhedonia in psychometrically defined schizotypy and schizophrenia. *Journal of Abnormal Psychology, 121*, 407–415.

Cohen, A. S., & Minor, K. S. (2010). Emotional experience in patients with schizophrenia revisited: Meta-analysis of laboratory studies. *Schizophrenia Bulletin, 36*, 143–150.

Cohen, J. (1983). The cost of dichotomization. *Applied Psychological Measurement, 7*, 249–253.

Cohen, J. (1992). A power primer. *Psychological Bulletin, 112*, 155–159.

Cole, D. A., Truglio, R., & Peeke, L. (1997). Relation between symptoms of anxiety and depression in children: A multitrait-multimethod-multigroup assessment. *Journal of Consulting and Clinical Psychology, 65*, 110–119.

Contractor, A. A., Mehta, P., Tiamiyu, M. F., Hovey, J. D., Geers, A. L., Charak, R., . . . Elhai, J. D. (2014). Relationship between PTSD and distress dimensions in an Indian child/adolescent sample following the 2008 Mumbai terrorist attacks. *Journal of Abnormal Child Psychology, 42*, 925–935.

Cooper, J. (1970). The Leyton Obsessional Inventory. *Psychological Medicine, 1*, 48–64.

Costa, P. T., Jr., & McCrae, R. R. (1992). *Revised NEO Personality Inventory (NEO-PI-R) and NEO Five-Factor Inventory (NEO-FFI) professional manual.* Odessa, FL: Psychological Assessment Resources.

Cox, B. J., Clara, I. P., & Enns, M. W. (2002). Posttraumatic stress disorder and the structure of common mental disorders. *Depression and Anxiety, 15*, 168–171.

Cox, B. J., & Taylor, S. (1999). Anxiety disorders: Panic and phobias. In T. Millon, P. H. Blaney, & R. D. Davis (Eds.). *Oxford textbook of psychopathology* (pp. 81–113). New York, NY: Oxford University Press.

Cox, J. L., & Holden, J. (2003). *Perinatal mental health: A guide to the Edinburgh Postnatal Depression Scale.* London, UK: Gaskell.

Cox, J. L., Holden, J. M., & Sagovsky, R. (1987). Detection of postnatal depression: Development of the 10-item Edinburgh Postnatal Depression Scale. *British Journal of Psychiatry, 150*, 782–786.

Craske, M. G., Barlow, D. H., Clark, D. M., Curtis, G. C., Hill, E. M., Himle, J. A., . . . Warwick, H. M. C. (1994). Specific (simple) phobia. In T. A. Widiger, A. J. Frances, H. A. Pincus, R. Ross, M. B. First, & W. W. Davis (Eds.), *DSM-IV sourcebook* (Vol. 2, pp. 473–506). Washington, DC: American Psychiatric Press.

Crawford, J. R., & Garthwaite, P. H. (2009). Percentiles please: The case for expressing neuropsychological test scores and accompanying confidence limits as percentile ranks. *The Clinical Neuropsychologist, 23*, 193–204.

Crockett, L. J., Randall, B. A., Shen, Y.-L., Russell, S. T., & Driscoll, A. K. (2005). Measurement equivalence of the Center for Epidemiological Studies Depression Scale for Latino and Anglo adolescents: A national study. *Journal of Consulting and Clinical Psychology, 73*, 47–58.

Crocq, M.-A., & Crocq, L. (2000). From shell shock and war neurosis to posttraumatic stress disorder: A history of psychotraumatology. *Dialogues in Clinical Neuroscience, 2*, 47–55.

Cronbach, L. J. (1951). Coefficient alpha and the internal structure of tests. *Psychometrika, 16*, 297–334.

Cutshall, C., & Watson, D. (2004). The Phobic Stimuli Response Scales: A new self-report measure of fear. *Behaviour Research and Therapy, 42*, 1193–1201.

Cyders, M. A., Smith, G. T., Spillane, N. S., Fischer, S., Annus, A. M., & Peterson, C. (2007). Integration of impulsivity and positive mood to predict risky behavior: Development and validation of a measure of positive urgency. *Psychological Assessment, 19*, 107–118.

Depue, R. A., & Iacono, W. G. (1989). Neurobehavioral aspects of affective disorders. *Annual Review of Psychology, 40*, 457–492.

Depue, R. A., Krauss, S., Spoont, M. R., & Arbisi, P. (1989). General Behavior Inventory identification of unipolar and bipolar affective conditions in a nonclinical university population. *Journal of Abnormal Psychology, 98*, 117–126.

Depue, R. A., Slater, J. F., Wolfstetter-Kausch, H., Klein, D., Goplerud, E., & Farr, D. (1981). A behavioral paradigm for identifying persons at risk for bipolar depressive disorder: A conceptual framework and five validation studies. *Journal of Abnormal Psychology, 90*, 381–437.

Diener, E., Emmons, R. A., Larsen, R. J., & Griffin, S. (1985). The Satisfaction with Life Scale. *Journal of Personality Assessment, 49*, 71–75.

Dozois, D. J. A., Dobson, K. S., & Ahnberg, J. L. (1998). A psychometric evaluation of the Beck Depression Inventory-II. *Psychological Assessment, 10*, 83–89.

Eapen, V., Robertson, M. M., Alsobrook, J. P., & Pauls, D. L. (1997). Obsessive compulsive symptoms in Gilles de le Tourette syndrome and obsessive compulsive disorder: Differences by diagnosis and family history. *American Journal of Medical Genetics, 74*, 432–438.

Eaton, N. R., Keyes, K. M., Krueger, R. F., Balsis, S., Skodol, A. E., Markon, K. E., Grant, B. F., & Hasin, D. S. (2012). An invariant dimensional liability model of gender differences in mental disorder prevalence: Evidence from a national sample. *Journal of Abnormal Psychology, 121*, 282–288.

Eberhard-Gran, M., Eskild, A., Tambs, K., Opjordsmoen, S., Samuelsen, S. O. (2001). Review of validation studies of the Edinburgh Postnatal Depression Scale. *Acta Psychiatrica Scandinavica, 104*, 243–249.

Eckblad, M., & Chapman, L. J. (1986). Development and validation of a scale for hypomanic personality. *Journal of Abnormal Psychology, 95*, 214–222.

Eckhardt, C. I., & Deffenbacher, J. L. (1995). Diagnosis of anger disorders. In H. Kassinove (Ed.), *Anger disorders: Definition, diagnosis, and treatment* (pp. 27–47). Philadelphia, PA: Taylor & Francis.

Ehlers, A. (1995). A 1-year prospective study of panic attacks: Clinical course and factors associated with maintenance. *Journal of Abnormal Psychology, 104*, 164–172.

Elhai, J. D., Biehn, T. L., Armour, C., Klopper, J. J., Frueh, B. C., & Palmieri, P. A. (2011). Evidence for a unique PTSD construct represented by PTSD's D1-D3 symptoms. *Journal of Anxiety Disorders, 25*, 340–345.

Elhai, J. D., Contractor, A. A., Palmieri, P. A., Forbes, D., & Richardon, J. D. (2011). Exploring the relationship between underlying dimensions of posttraumatic stress disorder and depression in a national, trauma-exposed military sample. *Journal of Affective Disorders, 133*, 477–480.

Elklit, A., & Shevlin, M. (2007). The structure of PTSD symptoms: A test of alternative models using confirmatory factor analysis. *British Journal of Clinical Psychology, 46*, 299–313.

Everett, J. E. (1983). Factor comparability as a means of determining the number of factors and their rotation. *Multivariate Behavioral Research, 18*, 197–218.

Everett, J. E., & Entrekin, L. V. (1980). Factor comparability and the advantages of multiple group factor analysis. *Multivariate Behavioral Research, 2*, 165–180.

Feldman, L. A. (1993). Distinguishing depression from anxiety in self-report: Evidence from confirmatory factor analysis on nonclinical and clinical samples. *Journal of Consulting and Clinical Psychology, 61*, 631–638.

Fetzner, M. G., Abrams, M. P., & Asmundson, G. J. G. (2013). Symptoms of posttraumatic stress disorder and depression in relation to alcohol-use and alcohol-related problems among Canadian forces veterans. *Canadian Journal of Psychiatry, 58*, 417–425.

Fetzner, M. G., Peluso, D. L., & Asmundson, G. J. G. (2014). Tolerating distress after trauma: Differential associations between distress tolerance and posttraumatic stress symptoms. *Journal of Psychopathology and Behavioral Assessment, 36*, 475–484.

Finch, J. F., & West, S. G. (1997). The investigation of personality structure: Statistical models. *Journal of Research in Personality, 31*, 439–485.

Finn, S. E. (1986). Structural stability of the MMPI in adult males. *Journal of Consulting and Clinical Psychology, 54*, 703–707.

First, M. B., Spitzer, R. L., Gibbon, M., & Williams, J. B. W. (1997). *Structured Clinical Interview for DSM-IV Axis I Disorders—Patient edition (SCID-I/P)*. New York, NY: Biometrics Research, New York State Psychiatric Institute.

Flessner, C. A., Woods, D. W., Franklin, M. E., Cashin, S. E., Keuthen, N. J., & The Trichotillomania Learning Center-Scientific Advisory Board (2008). The Milwaukee Inventory for Subtypes of Trichotillomania-Adult Version (MIST-A): Development of an instrument for the assessment of "focused" and "automatic" hair pulling. *Journal of Psychopathology and Behavioral Assessment, 30*, 20–30.

Flora, D. B., & Curran, P. J. (2004). An empirical evaluation of alternative methods of estimation for confirmatory factor analysis with ordinal data. *Psychological Methods, 9*, 466–491.

Foa, E. B., Huppert, J. D., Leiberg, S., Langner, R., Kichic, R., Hajcak, G., & Salkovskis, P. M. (2002). The Obsessive-Compulsive Inventory: Development and validation of a short version. *Psychological Assessment, 14*, 485–496.

Foa, E. B., Kozak, M. J., Salkovskis, P. M., Coles, M. E., & Amir, N. (1998). The validation of a new obsessive-compulsive disorder scale: The Obsessive-Compulsive Inventory. *Psychological Assessment, 10*, 206–214.

Foley, D. L., Neale, M. C., & Kendler, K. S. (1998). Reliability of a lifetime history of major depression: Implications for heritability and co-morbidity. *Psychological Medicine, 28*, 857–870.

Foley, K. L., Reed, P. S., Mutran, E. J., & DeVellis, R. F. (2002). Measurement adequacy of the CES-D among a sample of older African-Americans. *Psychiatry Research, 109*, 61–69.

Forbes, M. K., Baillie, A. J., & Schniering, C. A. (November 20, 2015). Where do sexual dysfunctions fit into the meta-structure of psychopathology? A factor mixture analysis. *Archives of Sexual Behavior*. Advance online publication.

Forbush, K. T., South, S. C., Krueger, R. F., Iacono, W. G., Clark, L. A., Keel, P. K, Legrand, L. N., & Watson, D. (2010). Locating eating pathology within an empirical diagnostic taxonomy: Evidence from a community-based sample. *Journal of Abnormal Psychology, 119*, 282–292.

Forbush, K. T., & Watson, D. (2013). The structure of common and uncommon mental disorders. *Psychological Medicine, 43*, 97–108.

Forbush, K. T., Wildes, J. E., Pollack, L. O., Dunbar, D., Luo, J., Patterson, K., . . . Watson, D. (2013). Development and validation of the Eating Pathology Symptoms Inventory (EPSI). *Psychological Assessment, 25*, 859–878.

Fredrickson, B. L., Tugade, M. M., Waugh, C. E., & Larkin, G. R. (2003). What good are positive emotions in crises? A prospective study of resilience and emotions following the terrorist attacks on the United States on September 11th, 2001. *Journal of Personality and Social Psychology, 84*, 365–376.

Friedman, M. (2013). Finalizing PTSD in *DSM-5:* Getting here from there and where to go next. *Journal of Traumatic Stress, 26*, 548–556.

Friedman, M., Resick, P. A., Bryant, R. A., & Brewin, C. R. (2011). Considering PTSD for *DSM-5. Depression and Anxiety, 28*, 750–769.

Gaffney, G. R., Sieg, K., & Hellings, J. (1994). The MOVES: A self-rating scale for Tourette's Syndrome. *Journal of Child and Adolescent Psychopharmacology, 4*, 269–280.

Gamez, W., Kotov, R., & Watson, D. (2010). The validity of self-report assessment of avoidance and distress. *Anxiety, Stress & Coping: An International Journal, 23*, 87–99.

Gard, D. E., Kring, A. M., Gard, M. G., Horan, W. P., & Green, M. F. (2007). Anhedonia in schizophrenia: Distinctions between anticipatory and consummatory pleasure. *Schizophrenia Research, 93*, 253–260.

Goldberg, L. R. (1999). The Curious Experiences Survey, a revised version of the Dissociative Experiences Scale: Factor structure, reliability, and relations to demographic and personality variables. *Psychological Assessment, 11*(2), 134–145.

Golding, J. M., & Anehensel, C. S. (1989). Factor structure of the Center for Epidemiological Studies Depression Scale among Mexican Americans and non-Hispanic whites. *Psychological Assessment, 1*, 163–168.

Gootzeit, J., & Markon, K. (2011). Factors of PTSD: Differential specificity and external correlates. *Clinical Psychology Review, 31*, 993–1003.

Gootzeit, J., Markon, K., & Watson, D. (2015). Measuring dimensions of PTSD: The Iowa Traumatic Response Inventory. *Assessment. 22*, 152–166.

Gorsuch, R. L. (1983). *Factor analysis* (2nd ed.). Hillsdale, NJ: Erlbaum.

Gotlib, I. H. (1984). Depression and general psychopathology in university students. *Journal of Abnormal Psychology, 93*, 19–30.

Gotlib, I. H., & Cane, D. B. (1989). Self-report assessment of depression and anxiety. In P. C. Kendall & D. Watson (Eds.), *Anxiety and depression: Distinctive and overlapping features* (pp. 131–169). San Diego, CA: Academic Press.

Green, S. B. (2003). A coefficient alpha for test-retest data. *Psychological Methods, 8*, 88–101.

Gruber, J., Culver, J. L., Johnson, S. L., Nam, J. Y., Keller, K. L., & Ketter, T. A. (2009). Do positive emotions predict symptomatic change in in bipolar disorder? *Bipolar Disorders, 11*, 330–336.

Gruber, J., Johnson. S. L., Oveis, C., & Keltner, D. (2008). Risk for mania and positive emotional responding: Too much of a good thing? *Emotion, 8*, 23–33.

Habke, A. M., Hewitt, P. L., Norton, G. R., & Asmundson, G. (1997). The Social Phobia and Social Interaction Anxiety Scales: An exploration of the dimensions of social anxiety and sex differences in structure and relations with pathology. *Journal of Psychopathology and Behavioral Assessment, 19*, 21–39.

Hamilton, M. (1960). A rating scale for depression. *Journal of Neurology, Neurosurgery and Psychiatry, 12*, 56–62.

Harman, H. H. (1976). *Modern factor analysis* (3rd ed.). Chicago, IL: University of Chicago Press.

Harrison, J. A., & Watson, D. (1992). *The Dissociative Processes Scale*. Unpublished manuscript, Department of Psychology, University of Iowa, Iowa City.

Hawkins, K. A., and Cougle, J. R. (2011). Anger problems across the anxiety disorders: Findings from a population-based study. *Depression and Anxiety, 28*, 145–152.

Hellmuth, J. C., Stappenbeck, C. A., Hoerster, K. D., Jakupcak, M. (2012). Modeling PTSD symptom clusters, alcohol misuse, anger, and depression as they relate to aggression and suicidality in returning U.S. veterans. *Journal of Traumatic Stress, 25*, 527–534.

Hertzog, C., Van Alstine, J., Usala, P. D., & Hultsch, D. F., & Dixon, R. (1990). Measurement properties of the Center for Epidemiological Studies Depression Scale (CES-D) in older populations. *Psychological Assessment, 2*, 64–72.

Hettema, J. M., Neale, M. C., Myers, J. M., Prescott, C. A., & Kendler, K. S. (2006). A population-based twin study of the relationship between neuroticism and internalizing disorders. *American Journal of Psychiatry, 163*, 857–864.

Hewitt, P. L., & Norton, G. R. (1993). The Beck Anxiety Inventory: A psychometric analysis. *Psychological Assessment, 5*, 408–412.

Hirschfeld, R. M. A., Williams, J. B. W., Spitzer, R. L., Calabrese, J. R., Flynn, L., Keck, P. E., Jr., . . . Zajecka, J. (2000). Development and validation of a screening instrument for bipolar spectrum disorder: The Mood Disorder Questionnaire. *American Journal of Psychiatry, 157*, 1873–1875.

Hodgson, R. J., & Rachman, S. (1977). Obsessional-compulsive complaints. *Behaviour Research and Therapy, 15*, 389–395.

Hogan, R., & Hogan, J. (1992). *Hogan Personality Inventory Manual*. Tulsa, OK: Hogan Assessment Systems.

Horan, W. P., Blanchard, J. J., Clark, L. A., & Green, M. F. (2008). Affective traits in schizophrenia and schizotypy. *Schizophrenia Bulletin, 34*, 856–874.

Hu, L., & Bentler, P. M. (1998). Fit indices in covariance structure modeling: Sensitivity to underparameterized model misspecification. *Psychological Methods, 3*, 424–453.

Hu, L., & Bentler, P. M. (1999). Cutoff criteria for fit indexes in covariance structure analysis: Conventional criteria versus new alternatives. *Structural Equation Modeling, 6*, 1–55.

Hughes, A. A., Heimberg, R. G., Coles, M. E., Gibb, B. E., Liebowitz, M. R., & Schneier, F. R. (2006). Relations of the factors of the tripartite model of anxiety and depression to types of social anxiety. *Behaviour Research and Therapy, 44*, 1629–1641.

Hukkelberg, S. S., & Jensen, T. K. (2011). The dimensionality of posttraumatic stress symptoms and their relationship to depression in children and adolescents. *Journal of Traumatic Stress, 24*, 326–333.

Ingram, R. E., & Siegle, G. J. (2002). Contemporary methodological issues in the study of depression: Not your father's Oldsmobile. In I. H. Gotlib & C. L. Hammen (Eds.), *Handbook of depression* (pp. 86–114). New York, NY: Guilford Press.

Jackson, M., & Claridge, G. (1991). Reliability and validity of a psychotic traits questionnaire (STQ). *British Journal of Clinical Psychology, 30*, 311–323.

John, O. P., & Srivastava, S. (1999). The Big Five trait taxonomy: History, measurement, and theoretical perspectives. In L. A Pervin & O. P. John (Eds.), *Handbook of personality* (2nd ed.) (pp. 102–138). New York, NY: Guilford.

Johnson, D. M., Palmieri, P. A., Jackson, A. P., & Hobfoll, S. E. (2007). Emotional numbing weakens abused inner-city women's resiliency resources. *Journal of Traumatic Stress, 20*, 197–206.

Johnson, S. L., Cueller, A. K., Ruggero, C., Winett-Perlman, C., & Goodnick, P. (2008). Life events as predictors of mania and depression in bipolar I disorder. *Journal of Abnormal Psychology, 117*, 268–277.

Johnson, S. L., Edge, M. D., Holmes, M. K., & Carver, C. S. (2012). The behavioral activation system and mania. *Annual Review of Clinical Psychology, 8*, 243–267.

Johnson, S. L., Gruber, J., & Eisner, L. R. (2007). Emotion and bipolar disorder. In Rottenberg, J., & Johnson, S. L. (Eds.), *Emotion and psychopathology: Bridging affective and clinical science* (pp. 123–150). Washington, D.C.: American Psychological Association.

Johnson, S. L., Sandrow, D., Meyer, B., Winters, R., Miller, I., Keitner, G., & Solomon, D. (2000). Increases in manic symptoms following life events involving goal attainment. *Journal of Abnormal Psychology, 109*, 721–727.

Joiner, T. E. (1996). A confirmatory factor-analytic investigation of the tripartite model of depression and anxiety in college students. *Cognitive Therapy and Research, 20*, 521–539.

Joiner, T. E., Brown, J. S., & Metalsky, G. I. (2003). A test of the tripartite model's prediction of anhedonia's specificity to depression: Patients with major depression versus patients with schizophrenia. *Psychiatry Research, 119*, 243–250.

Joiner, T. E., Jr., Walker, R. L., Pettit, J. W., Perez, M., & Cukrowicz, K. C. (2005). Evidence-based assessment of depression in adults. *Psychological Assessment, 17*, 267–277.

Jolly, J. B., Dyck, M. J., Kramer, T. A., & Wherry, J. N. (1994). Integration of positive and negative affectivity and cognitive content-specificity: Improved discrimination of anxious and depressive symptoms. *Journal of Abnormal Psychology, 103*, 544–552.

Jolly, J. B., & Dykman, R. A. (1994). Using self-report data to differentiate anxious and depressive symptoms in adolescents: Cognitive content specificity *and* global distress? *Cognitive Therapy and Research, 18*, 25–37.

Jolly, J. B., & Kramer, T. A. (1994). The hierarchical arrangement of internalizing cognitions. *Cognitive Therapy and Research, 18*, 1–14.

Kashdan, T. B. (2007). Social anxiety spectrum and diminished positive experiences: Theoretical synthesis and meta-analysis. *Clinical Psychology Review, 27*, 348–365.

Kassinove, H., & Tafrate, R. C. (2006). Anger-related disorders: Basic issues, models, and diagnostic considerations. In E. L. Feindler (Ed.), *Anger related disorders: A practitioner's guide to comparative treatments* (pp. 1–27). New York, NY: Springer.

Kendler, K. S., Karkowski, L. M., & Prescott, C. A. (1999). Fears and phobias: Reliability and heritability. *Psychological Medicine, 29*, 539–553.

Kendler, K. S., Neale, M. C., Kessler, R. C., Heath, A. C., & Eaves, L. J. (1993). The lifetime history of major depression in women: Reliability of diagnosis and heritability. *Archives of General Psychiatry, 50*, 863–870.

Kendler, K. S., Prescott, C. A., Myers, J., & Neale, M. C. (2003). The structure of genetic and environmental risk factors for common psychiatric and substance use disorders in men and women. *Archives of General Psychiatry, 60*, 929–937.

Kenny, D. A. (1987). *Statistics for the social and behavioral sciences.* Boston, MA: Little, Brown and Company.

Kerns, J. G. (2006). Schizotypy facets, cognitive control, and emotion. *Journal of Abnormal Psychology, 115*, 418–427.

Kessler, R. C., Berglund, P., Demler, O., Jin, R., Koretz, D., Merikangas, K. R., . . . Wang, P. S. (2003). The epidemiology of major depressive disorder: Results from the National Comorbidity Survey Replication (NCS-R). *JAMA: Journal of the American Medical Association, 289*, 3095–3105.

Kessler, R. C., Chiu, W. T., Demler, O., & Walters, E. E. (2005). Prevalence, severity, and comorbidity of 12-month *DSM-IV* disorders in the National Comorbidity Survey Replication. *Archives of General Psychiatry, 62*, 617–627.

Kessler, R. C., Nelson, C. B., McGonagle, K. A., Liu, J., Swartz, M., & Blazer, D. G. (1996). Comorbidity of *DSM-III-R* major depressive disorder in the general population: Results from the US National Comorbidity Survey. *British Journal of Psychiatry, 168 (Suppl. 30)*, 17–30.

Kessler, R. C., & Üstün, T. B. (2004). The World Mental Health (WMH) Survey Initiative Version of the World Health Organization (WHO) Composite International Diagnostic Interview (CIDI). *International Journal of Methods in Psychiatric Research, 13*, 93–121.

Keuthen, N. J., O'Sullivan, R. L., Ricciardi, J. N., & Shera, D. (1995). The Massachusetts General Hospital (MGH) Hairpulling Scale: I. Development and factor analyses. *Psychotherapy and Psychosomatics, 64*, 141–145.

Keuthen, N. J., Wilhelm, S., Deckersbach, T., Engelhard, I. M., Forker, A. E., Baer, L., & Jenike, M. A. (2001). The Skin Picking Scale: Scale construction and psychometric analyses. *Journal of Psychosomatic Research, 50*, 337–341.

Kim, G., DeCoster, J., Huang, C.-H., & Chiriboga, D. A. (2011). Race/ethnicity and the factor structure of the Center for Epidemiological Studies Depression Scale: A meta-analysis. *Cultural Diversity and Ethnic Minority Psychology, 17*, 381–396.

Kimhy, D., Delespaul, P., Corcoran, C., Ahn, H., Yale, S., & Malaspina, D. (2006). Computerized experience sampling method (ESMc): Assessing feasibility and validity among individuals with schizophrenia. *Journal of Psychiatric Research, 40*, 221–230.

King, D. W., Leskin, G. A., King, L. A., & Weathers, F. W. (1998). Confirmatory factor analysis of the Clinician-Administered PTSD Scale: Evidence for the dimensionality of posttraumatic stress disorder. *Psychological Assessment, 10*, 90–96.

Koffel, E. (2011). Further validation of the Iowa Sleep Disturbances Inventory. *Psychological Assessment, 23*, 587–598. doi: 10.1037/a0022818.

Koffel, E., & Watson, D. (2009). The two-factor structure of sleep complaints and its relation to depression and anxiety. *Journal of Abnormal Psychology, 118*, 183–194.

Koffel, E., & Watson, D. (2010). Development and initial validation of the Iowa Sleep Disturbances Inventory. *Assessment, 17*, 423–439.

Kotov, R., Gamez, W., Schmidt, F., & Watson, D. (2010). Linking "big" personality traits to anxiety, depressive, and substance use disorders: A meta-analysis. *Psychological Bulletin, 136*, 768–821.

Kotov, R., Ruggero, C. J., Krueger, R. F., Watson, D., Yuan, Q., & Zimmerman, M. (2011). New dimensions in the quantitative classification of mental illness. *Archives of General Psychiatry, 68*, 1003–1011.

Kraemer, H. C., Kupfer, D. J., Clarke, D. E., Narrow, W. E., & Regier, D. A. (2012). DSM-5: How reliable is reliable enough? *American Journal of Psychiatry, 169*, 13–15.

Kramer, M. D., Krueger, R. F., & Hicks, B. M. (2007). The role of internalizing and externalizing liability factors in accounting for gender differences in the prevalence of common psychopathological syndromes. *Psychological Medicine, 38*, 1–11.

Kring, A. M., & Moran, E. K. (2008). Emotional response deficits in schizophrenia: Insights from affective science. *Schizophrenia Bulletin, 34*, 819–834.

Kroenke, K., Spitzer, R. L., & Williams, J. B. W. (2001). The PHQ-9: Validity of a brief depression severity measure. *Journal of General Internal Medicine, 16*, 606–613.

Krueger, R. F. (1999). The structure of common disorders. *Archives of General Psychiatry, 56*, 921–926.

Krueger, R. F., Derringer, J., Markon, K. E., Watson, D., & Skodol, A. E. (2012). Initial construction of a maladaptive personality trait model and inventory for *DSM-5*. *Psychological Medicine, 42*, 1879–1890.

Krueger, R. F., & Markon, K. E. (2006). Reinterpreting comorbidity: A model-based approach to understanding and classifying psychopathology. *Annual Review of Clinical Psychology, 2*, 111–133.

Krueger, R. F., & Markon, K. E. (2014). The role of the DSM-5 personality trait model in moving toward a quantitative and empirically based approach to classifying personality and psychopathology. *Annual Review of Clinical Psychology, 10*, 477–501.

Krueger, R. F., Markon, K. E., Patrick, C. J., Benning, S. D., & Kramer, M. D. (2007). Linking antisocial behavior, substance use, and personality: An integrative quantitative model of the adult externalizing spectrum. *Journal of Abnormal Psychology, 116*, 645–666.

Lahey, B. B. (2009). Public health significance of neuroticism. *American Psychologist, 64*, 241–256.

Lahey, B. B. Applegate, B., Hakes, J. K., Zald, D. H., Hariri, A. R., & Rathouz, P. J. (2012). Is there a general factor of prevalent psychopathology during adulthood? *Journal of Abnormal Psychology, 121*, 971–977.

LeBeau, R. T., Glenn, D., Liao, B., Wittchen, H.-U., Beesdo-Baum, K., Ollendick, T., & Craske, M. G. (2010). Specific phobia: A review of *DSM-IV* specific phobia and preliminary recommendations for *DSM-V*. *Depression and Anxiety, 27*, 148–167.

Leckman, J. F., Denys, D., Simpson, H. B., Mataix-Cols, D., Hollander, E., Saxena, S., . . . Stein, D. J. (2010). Obsessive-compulsive disorder: A review of diagnostic criteria and possible subtypes and dimensional specifiers for *DSM-V*. *Depression and Anxiety, 27*, 507–527.

Leckman, J. F., Grice, D. E., Boardman, J., Zhang, H., Vitale, A., Bondi, C., . . . Pauls, D. L. (1997). Symptoms of obsessive-compulsive disorder. *American Journal of Psychiatry, 154*, 911–917.

Levine, D. W., Kripke, D. F., Kaplan, R. M., Lewis, M. A., Naughton, M. J., Bowen, D. J., & Shumaker, S. A. (2003). Reliability and validity of the Women's Health Initiative Insomnia Rating Scale. *Psychological Assessment, 15*, 137–148.

Lewinsohn, P. M., Seeley, J. R., Roberts, R. E., & Allen, N. B. (1997). Center for Epidemiologic Studies Depression Scale (CES-D) as a screening instrument for depression among community-residing older adults. *Psychology and Aging, 12*, 277–287.

Leykin, Y., Torres, L. D., Aguilera, A., & Munõz, R. F. (2011). Factor structure of the CES-D in a sample of Spanish- and English-speaking smokers on the Internet. *Psychiatry Research, 185*, 269–274.

Lilienfeld, S. O., Turner, S. M., & Jacob, R. G. (1993). Anxiety sensitivity: An examination of theoretical and methodological issues. *Advances in Behavior Research and Therapy, 15*, 147–183.

Lilienfeld, S. O., Waldman, I. D., & Israel, A. C. (1994). Critical examination of the use of the term and concept of comorbidity in psychopathology research. *Clinical Psychology: Science and Practice, 1*, 71–83.

Liu, P., Wang, L., Cao, C., Wang, R., Zhang, J., Zhang, B., . . . Elhai, J. D. (2014). The underlying dimensions of *DSM-5* posttraumatic stress disorder symptoms in an epidemiological sample of Chinese earthquake survivors. *Journal of Anxiety Disorders, 28*, 345–351.

Longley, S. L., Watson, D., & Noyes, R., Jr. (2005). Assessment of the hypochondriasis domain: The Multidimensional Inventory of Hypochondriacal Traits (MIHT). *Psychological Assessment, 17*, 3–14.

Lonigan, C. J., Carey, M. P., & Finch, A. J., Jr. (1994). Anxiety and depression in children and adolescents: Negative affectivity and the utility of self-reports. *Journal of Consulting and Clinical Psychology, 62*, 1000–1008.

Lorenzo-Seva, U., & ten Berge, J. M. F. (2006). Tucker's congruence coefficient as a meaningful index of factor similarity. *Methodology: European Journal of Research Methods for the Behavioral and Social Sciences, 2*, 57–64.

Lovejoy, M. C., & Steuerwald, B. L. (1995). Subsyndromal unipolar and bipolar disorders: Comparisons on positive and negative affect. *Journal of Abnormal Psychology, 104*, 381–384.

Lyubomirsky, S., & Lepper, H. S. (1999). A measure of subjective happiness: Preliminary reliability and construct validation. *Social Indicators Research, 46*, 137–155.

Magee, W. J., Eaton, W. W., Wittchen, H.-U., McGonagle, K. A., & Kessler, R. C. (1996). Agoraphobia, simple phobia, and social phobia in the National Comorbidity Survey. *Archives of General Psychiatry, 53*, 159–168.

Makambi, K. H., Williams, C. D., Taylor, T. R., Rosenberg, L., & Adams-Campbell, L. L. (2009). An assessment of the CES-D scale factor structure in black women: The Black Women's Health Study. *Psychiatry Research, 168*, 163–170.

Maller, R. G., & Reiss, S. (1992). Anxiety sensitivity in 1984 and panic attacks in 1987. *Journal of Anxiety Disorders, 4*, 241–247.

Manian, N., Schmidt, E., Bornstein, M. H., & Martinez, P. (2013). Factor structure and clinical utility of BDI-II factor scores in postpartum women. *Journal of Affective Disorders, 149*, 259–268.

Manne, S., Nereo, N., DuHamel, K., Ostroff, J., Parsons, S., Martini, R., . . . Redd, W. H. (2001). Anxiety and depression of mothers of children undergoing bone marrow transplant: Symptom prevalence and use of the Beck Depression and Beck Anxiety Inventories as screening instruments. *Journal of Consulting and Clinical Psychology, 69*, 1037–1047.

Markon, K. E., Chmielewski, M., & Miller, C. J. (2011). The reliability and validity of discrete and continuous measures of psychopathology: A quantitative review. *Psychological Bulletin, 137*, 856–879.

Markon, K. E, Krueger, R. F., & Watson, D. (2005). Delineating the structure of normal and abnormal personality: An integrative hierarchical approach. *Journal of Personality and Social Psychology*, *88*, 139–157.

Marks, I. M., Hallam, R. S., Connolly, J., & Philpott, R. (1977). *Nursing in behavioral psychotherapy.* London, UK: Royal College of Nursing.

Marks, I. M., & Mathews, A. M. (1979). Brief standard self-rating for phobic patients. *Behaviour Research and Therapy*, *23*, 563–569.

Marshall, G. N., Schell, T. L., & Miles, J. N. V. (2010). All PTSD symptoms are highly associated with general distress: Ramifications for the dysphoria symptom cluster. *Journal of Abnormal Psychology*, *119*, 126–135.

Mataix-Cols, D., Frost, R. O., Pertusa, A., Clark, L. A., Saxena, S., Leckman, J. F., . . . Wilhelm, S. (2010). Hoarding disorder: A new diagnosis for *DSM-V? Depression and Anxiety*, *27*, 556–572.

Mataix-Cols, D., Pertusa, A., & Leckman, J. F. (2007). Issues for DSM-V: How should obsessive-compulsive and related disorders be classified? *American Journal of Psychiatry*, *164*, 1313–1314.

Mataix-Cols, D., Rosario-Campos, M. C., & Leckman, J. F. (2005). A multidimensional model of obsessive-compulsive disorder. *American Journal of Psychiatry*, *162*, 228–238.

McCrae, R. R., Costa, P. T., Jr., & Martin, T. A. (2005). The NEO-PI-3: A more readable Revised NEO Personality Inventory. *Journal of Personality Assessment*, *84*, 261–270.

McCrae, R. R., Kurtz, J. E., Yamagata, S., & Terracciano, A. (2011). Internal consistency, retest reliability, and their implications for personality scale validity. *Personality and Social Psychology Review*, *15*, 28–50.

McDade-Montez, E. A., & Watson, D. (2011). Examining the potential influence of diabetes on depression and anxiety symptoms via multiple sample confirmatory factor analysis. *Annals of Behavioral Medicine*, *42*, 341–351.

McDevitt-Murphy, M. E., Weathers, F. W., Adkins, J. W., & Daniels, J. B. (2005). Use of the Personality Assessment Inventory in assessment of posttraumatic stress disorder in women. *Journal of Psychopathology and Behavioral Assessment*, *27*, 57–65.

McNally, R. C. (2015). Posttraumatic stress disorder and dissociative disorders. In P. H. Blaney, R. F. Krueger, & T. Millon (Eds.), *Oxford textbook of psychopathology* (3rd ed.) (pp. 191–204). New York, NY: Oxford University Press.

McPherson, A., & Martin, C. R. (2010). A narrative review of the Beck Depression Inventory (BDI) and implications for its use in an alcohol-dependent population. *Journal of Psychiatric and Mental Health Nursing*, *17*, 19–30.

Meis, L. A., Erbes, C. R., Kaler, M. E., Arbisi, P. A., & Polusny, M. A. (2011). The structure of PTSD among two cohorts of returning soldiers: Before, during, and following deployment to Iraq. *Journal of Abnormal Psychology*, *120*, 807–818.

Merikangas, K. R., Akiskal, H. S., Angst, J., Greenberg, P. E., Hirschfeld, R. M. A., Petukhova, M., & Kessler, R. C. (2007). Lifetime and 12-month prevalence of bipolar spectrum disorder in the National Comorbidity Survey Replication. *Archives of General Psychiatry*, *64*, 543–552.

Meyer, B., Johnson, S. L., & Winters, R. (2001). Responsiveness to threat and incentive in bipolar disorder: Relations of the BIS/BAS scales with symptoms. *Journal of Psychopathology and Behavioral Assessment*, *23*, 133–143.

Meyer, T. D., & Hofmann, B. U. (2005). Assessing the dysregulation of the behavioral activation system: The Hypomanic Personality Scale and the BIS-BAS Scales. *Journal of Personality Assessment*, *85*, 318–324.

Miller, J. D., Gentile, B., & Campbell, W. K. (2013). A test of the construct validity of the Five-Factor Narcissism Inventory. *Journal of Personality Assessment, 95*, 377–387.

Miller, J. D., Hoffman, B. J., Gaughan, E. T., Gentile, B., Maples, J., & Campbell, W. K. (2011). Grandiose and vulnerable narcissism: A nomological network analysis. *Journal of Personality, 79*, 1013–1042.

Mineka, S., Watson, D., & Clark, L. A. (1998). Comorbidity of anxiety and unipolar mood disorders. *Annual Review of Psychology, 49*, 377–412.

Mokros, A., Schilling, F., Weiss, K., Nitschke, J., & Eher, R. (2014). Sadism in sexual offenders: Evidence for dimensionality. *Psychological Assessment, 26*, 138–147.

Moran, P. W., & Lambert, M. J. (1983). A review of current assessment tools for monitoring changes in depression. In M. S. Lambert, E. R., Christensen, & S. S. DeJulio (Eds.), *The assessment of psychotherapy outcome* (pp. 263–303). New York, NY: Wiley.

Muris, P., Schmidt, H., & Merckelbach, H. (1999). The structure of specific phobic symptoms among children and adolescents. *Behaviour Research and Therapy, 37*, 863–868.

Murray, G., Goldstone, E., & Cunningham, E. (2007). Personality and the predisposition(s) to bipolar disorder: Heuristic benefits of a two-dimensional model. *Bipolar Disorders, 9*, 453–461.

Murray, J., Ehlers, A., & Mayou, R. A. (2002). Dissociation and post-traumatic stress disorder: Two prospective studies of road traffic accident survivors. *British Journal of Psychiatry, 180*, 363–368.

Myin-Germeys, I., Peeters, F., Havermans, R., Nicolson, N. A. deVries, M. W., Delespaul, P., & van Os, J. (2003). Emotional reactivity to daily life stress in psychosis and affective disorder: An experience sampling study. *Acta Psychiatrica Scandinavica, 107*, 124–131.

Naifeh, J. A., Elhai, J. D., Kashdan, T. B., & Grubaugh, A. L. (2008). The PTSD Symptom Scale's latent structure: An examination of trauma-exposed medical patients. *Journal of Anxiety Disorders, 22*, 1355–1368.

Naragon-Gainey, K. (2010). Meta-analysis of the relations of anxiety sensitivity to the depressive and anxiety disorders. *Psychological Bulletin, 136*(1), 128–150.

Naragon-Gainey, K., Simpson, T. L., Moore, S. A., Varra, A. A., & Kaysen, D. L. (2012). The correspondence of daily and retrospective PTSD reports among female victims of sexual assault. *Psychological Assessment, 24*, 1041–1047.

Naragon-Gainey, K., Watson, D., & Markon, K. E. (2009). Differential relations of depression and social anxiety symptoms to the facets of extraversion/positive emotionality. *Journal of Abnormal Psychology, 118*, 299–310.

Nelson, G. H., O'Hara, G. W., & Watson, D. (2016). *National norms for the Inventory of Depression and Anxiety Symptoms-II (IDAS-II)*. Manuscript submitted for publication.

Newman, M. G., Zuellig, A. R., Kachin, K. E., Constantino, M. J., Przeworski, A., Erickson, T., & Cashman-McGrath, L. (2002). Preliminary reliability and validity of the GADQ-IV: A revised self-report diagnostic measure of generalized anxiety disorder. *Behavior Therapy, 33*, 215–233.

Nezu, A. M., Nezu, C. M., McClure, K. S., & Zwick, M. L. Assessment of depression In I. H. Gotlib & C. L. Hammen (Eds.), *Handbook of depression* (pp. 61–85). New York, NY: Guilford Press.

Nitschke, J. B., Heller, W., Imig, J. C., McDonald, R. P., & Miller, G. A. (2001). Distinguishing dimensions of anxiety and depression. *Cognitive Therapy and Research, 25*, 1–22.

Nusslock, R., Abramson, L. Y., Harmon-Jones, E., Alloy, L. B., & Hogan, M. E. (2007). A goal-striving life event and the onset of hypomanic and depressive episodes and symptoms: Perspective from the behavioral approach system (BAS) dysregulation theory. *Journal of Abnormal Psychology, 116*, 105–115.

Nusslock, R., Harmon-Jones, E., Alloy, L. B., Urosevic, S., Goldstein, K., & Abramson, L. Y. (2012). Elevated left mid-frontal activity prospectively predicts conversion to Bipolar I Disorder. *Journal of Abnormal Psychology, 121*, 592–601.

Olatunji, B. O., Ciesielski, B. G., and Tolin, D. F. (2010). Fear and loathing: A meta-analytic review of the specificity of anger in PTSD. *Behavior Therapy, 41*, 93–105.

Olson, T. R., Presniak, M. D., & MacGregor, M. W. (2010). Reevaluating positive affect in the Center for Epidemiologic Studies-Depression Scale. *Psychiatry Research, 178*, 545–549.

Olsson, U., Drasgow, F., & Dorans, N. J. (1982). The polyserial correlation coefficient. *Psychometrika, 47*, 337–347.

Orme, J. G., Reis, J., & Herz, E. J. (1986). Factorial and discriminant validity of the Center for Epidemiological Studies Depression (CES-D) Scale. *Journal of Clinical Psychology, 42*, 28–33.

Osburn, H. G. (2000). Coefficient alpha and related internal consistency coefficients. *Psychological Methods, 5*, 343–355.

Osman, A., Barrios, F. X., Gutierrez, P. M., Williams, J. E., & Bailey, J. (2008). Psychometric properties of the Beck Depression Inventory-II in nonclinical adolescent samples. *Journal of Clinical Psychology, 64*, 83–102.

Osman, A., Kopper, B. A., Gutierrez, P. M., & Bagge, C. L. (2004). Reliability and validity of the Beck Depression Inventory-II with adolescent psychiatric inpatients. *Psychological Assessment, 16*, 120–132.

Palmieri, P. A., Marshall, G. N., & Schell, T. L. (2007). Confirmatory factor analysis of posttraumatic stress symptoms in Cambodian refugees. *Journal of Traumatic Stress, 20*, 207–216.

Palmieri, P. A., Weathers, F. W., Difede, J., & King, D. W. (2007). Confirmatory factor analysis of the PTSD Checklist and the Clinician-Administered PTSD Scale in disaster workers exposed to the World Trade Center Ground Zero. *Journal of Abnormal Psychology, 116*, 329–341.

Patrick, C. J., Kramer, M. D., Krueger, R. F., & Markon, K. E. (2013). Optimizing efficiency of psychopathology assessment through quantitative modeling: Development of a brief form of the Externalizing Spectrum Inventory. *Psychological Assessment, 25*, 1332–1348.

Penley, J. A., Wiebe, J. S., & Nwosu, A. (2003). Psychometric properties of the Spanish Beck Depression Inventory-II in a medical sample. *Psychological Assessment, 15*, 569–577.

Peterson, R. A., & Reiss, S. (1987). *Test manual for the Anxiety Sensitivity Index.* Orland Park, IL: International Diagnostic Systems.

Pietrzak, R. H., Goldstein, M. B., Malley, J. C., Rivers, A. J., & Southwick, S. M. (2010). Structure of posttraumatic stress disorder symptoms and psychosocial functioning in Veterans of Operations Enduring Freedom and Iraqi Freedom. *Psychiatry Research, 178*, 323–329.

Posner, S. F., Stewart, A. L., Marín, G., & Pérez-Stable, E. J. (2001). Factor variability of the Center for Epidemiological Studies Depression Scale (CES-D) among urban Latinos. *Ethnicity and Health, 6*, 137–144.

Quilty, L. C., Zhang, K. A., & Bagby, R. M. (2010). The latent symptom structure of the Beck Depression Inventory-II in outpatients with major depression. *Psychological Assessment, 22*, 603–608.

Radloff, L. S. (1977). The CES-D: A self-report depression scale for research in the general population. *Applied Psychological Measurement, 1*, 385–401.

Raine, A. (1991). The SPQ: A scale for the assessment of schizotypal personality based on *DSM-III-R* criteria. *Schizophrenia Bulletin, 17*, 555–564.

Rapee, R. M., Craske, M. G., & Barlow, D. H. (1994/1995). Assessment instrument for panic disorder that includes fear of sensation-producing activities: The Albany Panic and Phobia Questionnaire. *Anxiety, 1*, 114–122.

Raskin, R., & Hall, C. S. (1981). The Narcissistic Personality Inventory: Alternate form reliability and further evidence of construct validity. *Journal of Personality Assessment, 45*, 159–162.

Raskin, R., & Terry, H. (1988). A principal-components analysis of the Narcissistic Personality Inventory and further evidence of its construct validity. *Journal of Personality and Social Psychology, 54*, 890–902.

Rector, N. A., Hood, K., Richter, M. A., & Bagby, R. M. (2002). Obsessive-compulsive disorder and the five-factor model of personality: Distinction and overlap with major depressive disorder. *Behaviour Research and Therapy, 40*, 1205–1219.

Regier, D. A., Narrow, W. E., Clarke, D. E., Kraemer, H. C., Kuramoto, S. J., Kuhl, E. A., & Kupfer, D. J. (2013). *DSM-5* field trials in the United States and Canada, Part II: Test-retest reliability of selected categorical diagnoses. *American Journal of Psychiatry, 170*, 59–70.

Reiss, S., & McNally, R. J. (1986). The expectancy model of fear. In S. Reiss & R. R. Bootzin (Eds.). *Theoretical issues in behavior therapy* (pp. 107–121). New York, NY: Academic Press.

Reynolds, W. M. (1991a). *Adult Suicidal Ideation Questionnaire (ASIQ): Professional manual.* Odessa, FL: Psychological Assessment Resources.

Reynolds, W. M. (1991b). Psychometric characteristics of the Adult Suicidal Ideation Questionnaire in college students. *Journal of Personality Assessment, 56*, 289–307.

Reynolds, W. M. (2002). *Reynolds Adolescent Depression Scale, 2nd ed. (RADS-2) Professional Manual.* Lutz, FL: Psychological Assessment Resources.

Reiss, S., Peterson, R. A., Gursky, D. M., & McNally, R. J. (1986). Anxiety sensitivity, anxiety frequency and the prediction of fearfulness. *Behaviour Research and Therapy, 24*, 1–8.

Rivera-Medina, C. L., Caraballo, J. N., Rodríguez, E. R., Bernal, G., & Dávila-Marrero, E. (2010). Factor structure of the CES-D and measurement invariance across gender for low-income Puerto Ricans in a probability sample. *Journal of Consulting and Clinical Psychology, 78*, 398–408.

Roberts, R. E., Andrews, J. A., Lewinsohn, P. M., & Hops, H. (1990). Assessment of depression in adolescents using the Center for Epidemiologic Studies Depression Scale. *Psychological Assessment, 2*, 122–128.

Rosen, G. M., & Lilienfeld, S. O. (2008). Posttraumatic stress disorder: An empirical evaluation of core assumptions. *Clinical Psychology Review, 28*, 837–868.

Ross, S. R., Lutz, C. J., & Bailley, S. E. (2002). Positive and negative symptoms of schizotypy and the five-factor model: A domain and facet-level analysis. *Journal of Personality Assessment, 79*, 53–72.

Ruggero, C. J., Kotov, R., Watson, D., Kilmer, J. N., Perlman, G., & Liu, K. (2014). Beyond a single index of mania symptoms: Structure and validity of subdimensions. *Journal of Affective Disorders, 161*, 8–15.

Ruiz, M. A., Pincus, A. L., & Schinka, J. A., (2008). Externalizing pathology and the five-factor model: A meta-analysis of personality traits associated with antisocial personality disorder, substance use disorder, and their co-occurrence. *Journal of Personality Disorders, 22*, 365–388.

Rytwinski, N. K., Avena, J. S., Echiverri-Cohen, A. M., Zoellner, L. A., & Feeny, N. C. (2014). The relationship between posttraumatic stress disorder severity, depression severity and physical health. *Journal of Health Psychology, 19*, 509–520.

Safren, S. A., Turk, C. L., & Heimberg, R. G. (1998). Factor structure of the Social Interaction Anxiety Scale and the Social Phobia Scale. *Behaviour Research and Therapy, 36*, 443–453.

Salavert, J., Caseras, X., Torrubia, R., Furest, S., Arranz, B., Duenas, R., & San, L. (2007). The functioning of the behavioral activation and inhibition systems in bipolar I euthymic patients and its influence in subsequent episodes over an eighteen-month period. *Personality and Individual Differences, 42*, 1323–1331.

Samuel, D. B., & Widiger, T. A. (2008). A meta-analytic review of the relationship between the five-factor model and *DSM-IV-TR* personality disorders: A facet level analysis. *Clinical Psychology Review, 28*, 1326–1342.

Sanavio, E. (1988). Obsessions and compulsions: The Padua Inventory. *Behaviour Research and Therapy, 26*, 169–177.

SAS Institute Inc. (2011). *SAS/STAT user's guide* (*SAS* 9.3). Cary, NC: Author.

Saulsman, L. M., & Page, A. C. (2005). Corrigendum to "the five-factor model and personality disorder empirical literature: A meta-analytic review. *Clinical Psychology Review, 25*, 383–394.

Saunders, J. B., Aasland, O. G., Babor, T. F., de la Fuente, J. R., & Grant, M. (1993). Development of the Alcohol Use Disorders Identification Test (AUDIT): WHO collaborative project on early detection of persons with harmful alcohol consumption. II. *Addiction, 88*, 791–804.

Schalet, B. D., Durbin, C. E., & Revelle, W. (2011). Multidimensional structure of the Hypomanic Personality Scale. *Psychological Assessment, 23*, 504–522.

Schmidt, F. L., Le, H., & Ilies, R. (2003). Beyond alpha: An empirical examination of the effects of different sources of measurement error on reliability estimates for measures of individual differences constructs. *Psychological Methods, 8*, 206–224.

Schmidt, N. B., Lerew, D. R., & Jackson, R. J. (1997). The role of anxiety sensitivity in the pathogenesis of panic: Prospective evaluation of spontaneous panic attacks during acute stress. *Journal of Abnormal Psychology, 106*, 355–364.

Schmidt, N. B., Lerew, D. R., & Jackson, R. J. (1999). Prospective evaluation of anxiety sensitivity in the pathogenesis of panic: replication and extension. *Journal of Abnormal Psychology, 108*, 532–537.

Schmitt, N. (1996). Uses and abuses of coefficient alpha. *Psychological Assessment, 8*, 350–353.

Schnurr, P. P., & Lunney, C. A. (2011). Work-related quality of life and posttraumatic stress disorder symptoms among female veterans. *Women's Health Issues, 21-4S*, S169–S175.

Seignourel, P. J., Green, C., & Schmitz, J. M. (2008). Factor structure and diagnostic efficiency of the BDI-II in treatment-seeking substance users. *Drug and Alcohol Dependence, 93*, 271–278.

Selzer, M. L., Vinokur, A., & van Rooijen, L. (1975). A self-administered Short Michigan Alcoholism Screening Test (SMAST). *Journal of Studies on Alcohol, 36*, 117–126.

Sheehan, D. V., Lecrubier, Y., Sheehan, K. H., Amorim, P., Janavas, J., Weiller, E., ... Dunbar, G. C. (1998). The Mini-International Neuropsychiatric Interview

(M.I.N.I.): The development and validation of a structured diagnostic psychiatric interview for DSM-IV and ICD-10. *Journal of Clinical Psychiatry, 59*, 34–57.

Simms, E. E. (2009). *Assessment of the facets of the five factor model: Further development and validation of a new personality measure*. Unpublished doctoral dissertation, University of Iowa.

Simms, L. J., Goldberg, L. R., Roberts, J. E., Watson, D., Welte, J., & Rotterman, J. H. (2011). Computerized adaptive assessment of personality disorder: Introducing the CAT–PD Project. *Journal of Personality Assessment, 93*, 380–389.

Simms, L. J., Watson, D., & Doebbeling, B. N. (2002). Confirmatory factor analyses of posttraumatic stress symptoms in deployed and non-deployed veterans of the Gulf War. *Journal of Abnormal Psychology, 111*, 637–647.

Slade, T., & Watson, D. (2006). The structure of common DSM-IV and ICD-10 mental disorders in the Australian general population. *Psychological Medicine, 36*, 1593–1600.

Spence, S. H. (1997). Structure of anxiety symptoms among children: A confirmatory factor-analytic study. *Journal of Abnormal Psychology, 106*, 280–297.

Spielberger, C. D., Gorsuch, R. L., Lushene, R., Vagg, P. R., & Jacobs, G. A. (1983). *Manual for the State-Trait Anxiety Inventory (Form Y)*. Palo Alto, CA: Consulting Psychologists Press.

Spitzer, R. L., Williams, J. B. W., & Endicott, J. (2012). Standards for *DSM-5* reliability. *American Journal of Psychiatry, 169*, 537.

Stanton, K., Gruber, J., & Watson, D. (June 2, 2016). Basic dimensions defining mania risk: A structural approach. *Psychological Assessment*. Advance online publication.

Steer, R. A., Ball, R., Ranieri, W. F., & Beck, A. T. (1999). Dimensions of the Beck Depression Inventory-II in clinically depressed outpatients. *Journal of Clinical Psychology, 55*, 117–128.

Steer, R. A., Clark, D. A., Beck, A. T., & Ranieri, W. F. (1995). Common and specific dimensions of self-reported anxiety and depression: A replication. *Journal of Abnormal Psychology, 104*, 542–545.

Steer, R. A., Clark, D. A., & Ranieri, W. F. (1994). Symptom dimensions of the SCL-90-R: A test of the tripartite model of anxiety and depression. *Journal of Personality Assessment, 62*, 525–536.

Steer, R. A., Rissmiller, D. J., & Beck, A. T. (2000). Use of the Beck Depression Inventory-II with depressed geriatric inpatients. *Behaviour Research and Therapy, 38*, 311–318.

Stein, M. B., Jang, K. L., & Livesley, W. J. (1999). Heritability of anxiety sensitivity: A twin study. *American Journal of Psychiatry, 156*, 246–251.

Stewart, S. H., Taylor, S., & Baker, J. (1997). Gender differences in dimensions of anxiety sensitivity. *Journal of Anxiety Disorders, 11*, 179—200.

Stöber, J., & Joormann, J. (2001). A short form of the Worry Domains Questionnaire: Construction and factorial validation. *Personality and Individual Differences, 31*, 591–598.

Storch, E. A., Roberti, J. W., & Roth, D. A. (2004). Factor structure, concurrent validity, and internal consistency of the Beck Depression Inventory-Second Edition in a sample of college students. *Depression and Anxiety, 19*, 187–189.

Strauss, G. P. (2013). The emotion paradox of anhedonia in schizophrenia: Or is it? *Schizophrenia Bulletin, 39*, 247–250.

Strauss, G. P., & Gold, J. M. (2012). A new perspective on anhedonia in schizophrenia. *American Journal of Psychiatry, 169*, 364–373.

Summerfeldt, L. J., Richter, M. A., Antony, M. M., & Swinson, R. P. (1999). Symptom structure in obsessive-compulsive disorder: A confirmatory factor-analytic study. *Behaviour Research and Therapy, 37*, 297–311.

Taylor, S. (1995a). Anxiety sensitivity: Theoretical perspectives and recent findings. *Behaviour Research and Therapy, 3*, 243–258.

Taylor, S. (1995b). Assessment of obsessions and compulsions: Reliability, validity, and sensitivity to treatment effects. *Clinical Psychology Review, 15*, 261–296.

Taylor, S. (Ed.). (2014). *Anxiety sensitivity: Theory, research, and treatment of the fear of anxiety*. New York, NY: Routledge.

Taylor, S., Kuch, K., Koch, W. J., Crockett, D. J., & Passey, G. (1998). The structure of posttraumatic stress symptoms. *Journal of Abnormal Psychology, 107*, 154–160.

Tellegen, A. (1985). Structures of mood and personality and their relevance to assessing anxiety, with an emphasis on self-report. In A. H. Tuma & J. D. Maser (Eds.), *Anxiety and the anxiety disorders* (pp. 681–706). Hillsdale, NJ: Erlbaum.

Tellegen, A., & Waller, N. G. (2008). Exploring personality through test construction: Development of the Multidimensional Personality Questionnaire. In G. J. Boyle, G. Matthews, & D. H. Saklofske (Eds.), *The SAGE handbook of personality theory and assessment. Vol. 2: Personality measurement and testing* (pp. 261–292). Thousand Oaks, CA: Sage Publications.

Tellegen, A., Watson, D., and Clark, L. A. (1999). On the dimensional and hierarchical structure of affect. *Psychological Science, 10*, 297–303.

Thordarson, D. S., Radomsky, A. S., Rachman, S., Shafran, R., Sawchuk, C. N., & Hakstian, A. R. (2004). The Vancouver Obsessional Compulsive Inventory. *Behaviour Research and Therapy, 42*, 1289–1314.

Thorson, J. A., & Powell, F. C. (1993). The CES-D: Four or five factors? *Bulletin of the Psychonomic Society, 31*, 577–578.

Tsai, J. L. (2007). Ideal affect: Cultural causes and behavioral consequences. *Perspectives on Psychological Science, 2*, 242–259.

Tsai, J. L., Knutson, B., & Fung, H. H. (2006). Cultural variation in affect valuation. *Journal of Personality and Social Psychology, 90*, 288–307.

United States Census Bureau. (2014). 2013 American Community Survey 3-year estimates. Retrieved from https://www.census.gov/programs-surveys/acs/data.html.

Vaidya, J. G., Gray, E. K., Haig, J. R., Mroczek, D. K., & Watson, D. (2008). Differential stability and individual growth trajectories of Big Five and affective traits during young adulthood. *Journal of Personality, 76*, 267–304.

Vaidya, J. G., Gray, E. K., Haig, J., & Watson, D. (2002). On the temporal stability of personality: Evidence for differential stability and the role of life experiences. *Journal of Personality and Social Psychology, 83*, 1469–1483.

VanVoorhis, C. R. W., & Blumentritt, T. L. (2007). Psychometric properties of the Beck Depression Inventory-II in a clinically-identified sample of Mexican American adolescents. *Journal of Child and Family Studies, 16*, 789–798.

Vollebergh, W. A. M., Iedema, J., Bijl, R. V., de Graaf, R., Smit, F., & Ormel, J. (2001). The structure and stability of common mental disorders: The NEMESIS Study. *Archives of General Psychiatry, 6*, 597–603.

Walther, M. R., Flessner, C. A., Conelea, C. A., & Woods, D. W. (2009). The Milwaukee Inventory for the Dimensions of Adult Skin Picking (MIDAS): Initial development and psychometric properties. *Journal of Behavior Therapy and Experimental Psychiatry, 40*, 127–135.

Watson, D. (2000a). *Mood and temperament.* New York, NY: Guilford Press.

Watson, D. (2000b). *Panic Attack Symptom Questionnaire.* Unpublished physiological hyperarousal measure.

Watson, D. (2001). Dissociations of the night: Individual differences in sleep-related experiences and their relation to dissociation and schizotypy. *Journal of Abnormal Psychology, 110*, 526–535.

Watson, D. (2003a). Investigating the construct validity of the dissociative taxon: Stability analyses of normal and pathological dissociation. *Journal of Abnormal Psychology, 112*, 298–305.

Watson, D. (2003b). Subtypes, specifiers, epicycles, and eccentrics: Toward a more parsimonious taxonomy of psychopathology. *Clinical Psychology: Science and Practice, 10*, 233–238.

Watson, D. (2004). Stability versus change, dependability versus error: Issues in the assessment of personality over time. *Journal of Research in Personality, 38*, 319–350.

Watson, D. (2005). Rethinking the mood and anxiety disorders: A quantitative hierarchical model for *DSM-V*. *Journal of Abnormal Psychology, 114*, 522–536.

Watson, D. (2009a). Differentiating the mood and anxiety disorders: A quadripartite model. *Annual Review of Clinical Psychology, 5*, 221–247.

Watson, D. (2009b). Locating anger in the hierarchical structure of affect: Comment on Carver and Harmon-Jones (2009). *Psychological Bulletin, 135*, 205–208.

Watson, D. (2009c). Rethinking the anxiety disorders in *DSM-V* and beyond: Quantitative dimensional models of anxiety and related psychopathology. In D. McKay, J. S. Abramowitz, S. Taylor, & G. J. G. Asmundson (Eds.), *Current perspectives on the anxiety disorders: Implications for DSM-V and beyond* (pp. 275–302). New York, NY: Springer.

Watson, D. (2012). Objective tests as instruments of psychological theory and research. In H. Cooper, P. M. Camic, D. L. Long, A. T. Panter, D. Rindskopf, & K. J. Sher (Eds.), *APA handbook of research methods in psychology. Volume 1: Foundations, planning, measures, and psychometrics* (pp. 349–369). Washington, DC: American Psychological Association.

Watson, D., & Clark, L. A. (1991). *The Mood and Anxiety Symptom Questionnaire.* Unpublished manuscript, University of Iowa, Iowa City.

Watson, D., & Clark, L. A. (1992). Affects separable and inseparable: On the hierarchical arrangement of the negative affects. *Journal of Personality and Social Psychology, 62*, 489–505.

Watson, D., & Clark, L. A. (1997). Measurement and mismeasurement of mood: Recurrent and emergent issues. *Journal of Personality Assessment, 68*, 267–296.

Watson, D., & Clark, L. A. (1999). *The PANAS-X: Manual for the Positive and Negative Affect Schedule-Expanded Form.* Retrieved from University of Iowa, Department of Psychology Web site: http://www.psychology.uiowa.edu/Faculty/Watson/Watson.html.

Watson, D., Clark, L. A., & Carey, G. (1988). Positive and negative affectivity and their relation to anxiety and depressive disorders. *Journal of Abnormal Psychology, 97*, 346–353.

Watson, D., Clark, L. A., Chmielewski, M., & Kotov, R. (2013). The value of suppressor effects in explicating the construct validity of symptom measures. *Psychological Assessment, 25*, 929–941.

Watson, D., Clark, L. A., & Harkness, A. R. (1994). Structures of personality and their relevance to psychopathology. *Journal of Abnormal Psychology, 103*, 18–31.

Watson, D., Clark, L. A., & Stasik, S. M. (2011). Emotions and the emotional disorders: A quantitative hierarchical perspective. *International Journal of Clinical and Health Psychology, 11*, 429–442.

Watson, D., Clark, L. A., & Tellegen, A. (1988). Development and validation of brief measures of positive and negative affect: The PANAS scales. *Journal of Personality and Social Psychology, 54*, 1063–1070.

Watson, D., Gamez, W., & Simms, L. J. (2005). Basic dimensions of temperament and their relation to anxiety and depression: A symptom-based perspective. *Journal of Research in Personality, 39*, 46–66.

Watson, D., & Naragon, K. (2009). Positive affectivity: The disposition to experience pleasurable emotional states. In C. R. Snyder & S. J. Lopez (Eds.), *The handbook of positive psychology* (2nd ed.) (pp. 207–215). New York, NY: Oxford University Press.

Watson, D., & Naragon-Gainey, K. (2010). On the specificity of positive emotional dysfunction in psychopathology: Evidence from the mood and anxiety disorders and schizophrenia/schizotypy. *Clinical Psychology Review, 30*, 839–848.

Watson, D., & Naragon-Gainey, K. (2014). Personality, emotions, and the emotional disorders. *Clinical Psychological Science, 2*, 422–442.

Watson, D., O'Hara, M. W., Chmielewski, M., McDade-Montez, E. A., Koffel, E., Naragon, K., & Stuart, S. (2008). Further validation of the IDAS: Evidence of convergent, discriminant, criterion, and incremental validity. *Psychological Assessment, 20*, 248–259.

Watson, D., O'Hara, M. W., Naragon-Gainey, K., Koffel, E., Chmielewski, M., Kotov, R., . . . Ruggero, C. J. (2012). Development and validation of new anxiety and bipolar symptom scales for an expanded version of the IDAS (the IDAS-II). *Assessment, 19*, 399–420.

Watson, D., O'Hara, M. W., Simms, L. J., Kotov, R., Chmielewski, M., McDade-Montez, E., . . . Stuart, S. (2007). Development and validation of the Inventory of Depression and Anxiety Symptoms (IDAS). *Psychological Assessment, 19*, 253–268.

Watson, D., O'Hara, M. W., & Stuart, S. (2008). Hierarchical structures of affect and psychopathology and their implications for the classification of emotional disorders. *Depression and Anxiety, 25*, 282–288.

Watson, D., Stanton, K., & Clark, L. A. (October 28, 2016). Self-report indicators of negative valence constructs within the Research Domain Criteria (RDoC): A critical review. *Journal of Affective Disorders*. Advance online publication.

Watson, D., & Stasik, S. M. (2014). Examining the comorbidity between depression and the anxiety disorders from the perspective of the quadripartite model. In C.S. Richards & M.W. O'Hara (Eds.), *The Oxford handbook of depression and comorbidity* (pp. 46–65). New York, NY: Oxford University Press.

Watson, D., Stasik, M. R., Chmielewski, M., & Naragon-Gainey, K. (2015). Development and validation of the Temperament and Affectivity Inventory (TAI). *Assessment, 22*, 540–560.

Watson, D., Stasik, S. M., Ellickson-Larew, S., & Stanton, K. (2015a). Explicating the psychopathological correlates of anomalous sleep experiences. *Psychology of Consciousness: Theory, Research, and Practice, 2*, 57–78.

Watson, D., Stasik, S. M., Ellickson-Larew, S., & Stanton, K. (2015b). Extraversion and psychopathology: A facet-level analysis. *Journal of Abnormal Psychology, 124*, 432–446.

Watson, D., Stasik, S. M., Ro, E., & Clark, L. A. (2013). Integrating normal and pathological personality: Relating the *DSM-5* trait-dimensional model to general traits of personality. *Assessment, 20*, 312–326.

Watson, D., & Tellegen, A. (1985). Toward a consensual structure of mood. *Psychological Bulletin, 98*, 219–235.

Watson, D., Weber, K., Assenheimer, J. S., Clark, L. A., Strauss, M. E., & McCormick, R. A. (1995). Testing a tripartite model: I. Evaluating the convergent and discriminant validity of anxiety and depression symptom scales. *Journal of Abnormal Psychology, 104*, 3–14.

Watson, D., Wiese, D., Vaidya, J., & Tellegen, A. (1999). The two general activation systems of affect: Structural findings, evolutionary considerations, and psychobiological evidence. *Journal of Personality and Social Psychology, 76*, 820–838.

Watson, D., & Wu, K. D. (2005). Development and Validation of the Schedule of Compulsions, Obsessions, and Pathological Impulses (SCOPI). *Assessment, 12*, 50–65.

Watson, D., Wu, K. D., & Cutshall, C. (2004). Symptom subtypes of obsessive-compulsive disorder and their relation to dissociation. *Journal of Anxiety Disorders, 18*, 435–458.

Weathers, F. W., Litz, B. T., Herman, D. S., Huska, J. A., & Keane, T. M. (1993, October). *The PTSD Checklist (PCL): Reliability, validity, and diagnostic utility.* Paper presented at the annual meeting of the International Society for Traumatic Stress Studies, San Antonio, TX.

Widiger, T. A., & Clark, L. A. (2000). Toward *DSM-V* and the classification of psychopathology. *Psychological Bulletin, 126*, 946–963.

Williams, J. B. W., Gibbon, M., First, M. B., Spitzer, R. L., Davies, M., Borus, J., . . . Wittchen, H.-U. (1992). The Structured Clinical Interview for *DSM-III-R* (SCID): II. Multisite test-retest reliability. *Archives of General Psychiatry, 49*, 630–636.

Wittchen, H.-U., Gloster, A. T., Beesdo-Baum, K., Fava, G. A., & Craske, M. G. (2010). Agoraphobia: A review of the diagnostic classificatory position and criteria. *Depression and Anxiety, 27*, 113–133.

Witteveen, A. B., Van der Ploeg, E., Bramsen, I., Huizink, A. C., Slottje, P., Smid, T., & Van der Ploeg, H. M. (2006). Dimensional of posttraumatic stress response among police officers and fire fighters: An evaluation of two self-report scales. *Psychiatry Research, 141*, 213–228.

Wolfe, V. V., Finch, A. J., Jr., Saylor, C. F., Blount, R. L., Pallmeyer, T. P., & Carek, D. J. (1987). Negative affectivity in children: A multitrait/multimethod investigation. *Journal of Consulting and Clinical Psychology, 55*, 245–250.

Wolpe, J., & Lang, P. J. (1964). A fear survey schedule for use in behaviour therapy. *Behaviour Research in Therapy, 2*, 27–30.

Wolpe, J., & Lang, P. J. (1974). A fear survey schedule for use in behavior therapy. In T. J. Edwin (Ed.), *Behavior modification procedures: A sourcebook* (pp. 228–232). New Brunswick, NJ: Aldine Transaction.

World Health Organization. (1992). *International classification of diseases* (10th ed.). Geneva, Switzerland: Author.

Wright, A. G., & Simms, L. J. (2014). On the structure of personality disorder traits: Conjoint analyses of the CAT-PD, PID-5, and NEO-PI-3 trait models. *Personality Disorders: Theory, Research, and Treatment, 5*, 43–51.

Wu, K. D., & Watson, D. (2003). Further investigation of the Obsessive-Compulsive Inventory: Psychometric analysis in two nonclinical samples. *Journal of Anxiety Disorders, 17*, 305–319.

Wu, K. D., & Watson, D. (2005). Hoarding and its relation to obsessive-compulsive disorder. *Behaviour Research and Therapy, 43*, 897–921.

Yesavage, J. A., Brink, T. L., Rose, T. L., Lum, O., Huang, V., Adey, M., & Leirer, V. O. (1983). Development and validation of a geriatric depression screening scale: A preliminary report. *Journal of Psychiatric Research, 17*, 37–49.

Yufik, T., & Simms, L. J. (2010). A meta-analytic investigation of the structure of posttraumatic stress disorder symptoms. *Journal of Abnormal Psychology, 119*, 764–776.

Zeiders, K. H., Umaña-Taylor, & Derlan, C. L. (2013). Trajectories of depressive symptoms and self-esteem in Latino youths: Examining the role of gender and perceived discrimination. *Developmental Psychology, 49*, 951–963.

Zimmerman, M. (1994). Diagnosing personality disorders: A review of issues and research methods. *Archives of General Psychiatry, 51*, 225–245.

Zinbarg, R. E., & Barlow, D. H. (1996). Structure of anxiety and the anxiety disorders: A hierarchical model. *Journal of Abnormal Psychology, 105*, 181–193.

Zinbarg, R. E., Barlow, D. H., & Brown, T. A. (1997). Hierarchical structure and general factor saturation of anxiety sensitivity index: Evidence and implications. *Psychological Assessment, 9*, 277–284.

Zinbarg, R. E., Mohlman, J., & Hong, N. M. (1999). Dimensions of anxiety sensitivity. In S. Taylor (Ed.), *Anxiety sensitivity: Theory, research and treatment of the fear of anxiety* (pp. 83–114). Hillsdale, NJ: Erlbaum.

ABOUT THE AUTHORS

David Watson, PhD, is Andrew J. McKenna Family Professor of Psychology, University of Notre Dame. Dr. Watson is a personality psychologist with specific expertise in clinical and personality assessment. His work investigates the structure and measurement of personality, emotion, and psychopathology, as well as examining how personality traits relate to clinical disorders. The long-term goal of this work is develop comprehensive models that integrate normal-range and pathological processes into a single overarching scheme.

Michael W. O'Hara, PhD, is Professor of Psychological and Brain Sciences, Starch Faculty Fellow, and Director of Clinical Training at the University of Iowa, where he has been for 36 years. He has a long history of scholarship and external support in depression, particularly in the epidemiology of perinatal depression, its consequences for mothers and children, and its prevention and treatment. He has previously served as president of the Society for Research in Psychopathology and the Marcé Society for Perinatal Mental Health.

INDEX

Page numbers followed by *b* and *t* refer to boxes and tables, respectively.

Achenbach System of Empirically Based Assessment (ASEBA), 284
ACS (American Community Survey), 53
Adult Psychiatry Clinic of University of Iowa Hospitals and Clinics, 55
Adult Suicidal Ideation Questionnaire (ASIQ), 69*t*, 70
Affect
  "big two" dimensions of, 5
  two-factor model of, 7
Affectivity measures, relations of bipolar symptom factors and, 134–36, 136*t*
Affect Valuation Index (AVI), 135, 136*t*, 265
Agoraphobia, 4
  criterion validity of symptom scales for, 266*t*
  and OCD symptom measures, 250*t*–252*t*
  predictive power of
    anxiety measures for, 228*t*–230*t*, 229, 230
  tetrachoric correlations, 4*t*, 5
Agoraphobia composite, 162, 163*t*, 164*t*, 248, 249, 249*t*
Agoraphobia symptoms
  correlation of anger measures with, 154, 155, 155*t*–160*t*, 159, 160
  correlation of anxiety measures with, 213, 219, 221*t*, 222–24, 223*t*–225*t*, 226, 227, 227*t*
  correlation of PTSD measures with, 195*t*, 196*t*, 204*t*
  and IDAS-II scales, 35
  negative trait affect scale and, 162, 163*t*, 164*t*
AICs. *see* Average interitem correlations
Albany Panic and Phobia Questionnaire (APPQ), 105, 162, 212–13, 213*t*, 215–17, 219–21, 225–27, 248
Alcohol Use composite, 167, 168*t*, 169*t*
Alcohol use disorder, correlation of anger measures to, 165, 166, 167*t*, 168*t*
Alcohol Use Disorders Test (AUDIT), 167
Altman, E. G., 133
Altman Self-Rating Mania Scale (ASRM), 133, 134*t*
American Community Survey (ACS), 53
Anger, 146–74
  and externalizing psychopathology, 165–70, 168*t*, 169*t*
  Ill Temper scale, validity of, 147–53, 148*t*–150*t*, 152*t*
  and internalizing psychopathology, 154–65, 155*t*–161*t*, 163*t*, 164*t*
  and psychoticism, 170–74, 172*t*, 173*t*
  trait negative affect scales, validity of, 153, 153*t*, 154
Anger disorders, 146
Anger factor
  and indicators of externalizing psychopathology, 168, 168*t*, 169, 169*t*
  and indicators of internalizing psychopathology, 161, 163, 163*t*, 164, 164*t*
Angry Mood scale, 6
Anhedonia, 7
Animal Phobia factor, 35
Animal Phobia scale (IDAS-II), 35
Anticipatory deficit, with schizophrenia/schizotypy, 109, 111
Antisocial personality disorder, anger symptoms in, 147
Anxiety, integrative hierarchical model of, 13–14

Anxiety disorders, convergent validity of IDAS-II for, 261*t*
Anxiety Disorders Work Group, 7–8, 35
Anxiety factor
  and indicators of externalizing psychopathology, 168, 168*t*, 169*t*
  and indicators of internalizing psychopathology, 161–63, 163*t*, 164*t*
  and psychoticism indicators, 171, 172, 172*t*, 173*t*
Anxiety scales (IDAS-II)
  convergent validity of, 211–21, 218*t*
  creation of, 34–35
  criterion validity of, 221–27
  development of, 206–10, 208*t*
  discriminant validity of, 211–21, 218*t*
  incremental validity of, 228–30
Anxiety sensitivity, 214
Anxiety Sensitivity Index (ASI), 214, 215, 215*t*, 220
Anxiety symptoms, 206–31
  Albany Panic and Phobia Questionnaire (APPQ), 212, 213, 213*t*
  Anxiety Sensitivity Index (ASI), 214, 215, 215*t*
  anxious mood and worry, 210
  in children, 3
  Claustrophobia scale, 209, 220–21, 223, 224*t*
  comparative analyses across multiple measures, 224–26, 225*t*, 226*t*
  convergent/discriminant validity of scales, 211–21
  criterion validity of scales, 221–27
  and development of IDAS-II scales, 206–10, 208*t*
  Fear Questionnaire (FQ), 212, 213
  IDAS-CR measures, 217–19, 221*t*, 222, 223*t*, 229, 230
  IMAS analyses, 219, 219*t*, 220*t*
  incremental validity of scales, 228–30
  and interview measures, 217–20, 218*t*
  and OCD symptoms, 247–49, 249*t*, 250*t*
  Panic scale, 207–9, 220, 222–23, 223*t*
  PSRS scales, 211, 212, 212*t*, 224, 225*t*, 230
  and self-report scales, 211–17
  Social Anxiety scale, 206–7, 220, 221–22
  specific phobia, 209–10
  structural analyses for, 215–17, 215*t*, 216*t*
Anxious apprehension, 13
Anxious mood, 210
Anxious Mood factor, 30
Anxious Mood scale, 6
  as depression scale, 62
  as symptom-based analysis, 104
Appetite Gain scale (IDAS and IDAS-II)
  Big Five Inventory correlations with, 43*t*, 44
  convergent/discriminant validity analyses, 72, 73*t*
  convergent validity analyses of, 69, 69*t*, 70
  correlations with Beck inventories, 75, 76, 95
  correlations with *DSM-5* diagnoses, 79*t*
  correlations with *DSM* diagnoses, 266*t*, 269*t*, 270
  correlations with *DSM-IV* diagnoses, 78*t*–80*t*
  correlations with EPSI, 277, 277*t*
  correlations with HRSD and, 71, 71*t*
  correlations with IMAS, 261*t*, 265, 267
  correlations with ISDI, 273*t*, 274*t*
  correlations with MIHT, 283*t*
  correlations with PID-5, 280*t*
  correlations with SPQ, 282*t*
  as depression scale, 62, 64–66, 65*t*, 66*t*
  and depression symptoms, 101, 101*t*, 263, 264
  descriptive statistics across respondent types, 50*t*
  development of, 31
  and diagnostic specificity, 81
  factor structure for, 47, 47*t*, 48*t*, 49*t*
  group comparisons for, 52, 52*t*
  intercorrelations of other scales with, 45*t*
  internal consistency of, 38, 38*t*, 39*t*
  normative statistics for, 54*t*, 56*t*
  sex differences on, 86, 86*t*
  test-retest analyses of, 40*t*
Appetite Loss scale (IDAS and IDAS-II)
  Big Five Inventory correlations with, 43*t*, 44

convergent/discriminant validity analyses, 72, 73*t*, 74, 74*t*
convergent validity analyses of, 69, 69*t*, 70
correlations with Beck inventories, 75, 76, 95
correlations with *DSM-5* diagnoses, 79*t*
correlations with *DSM* diagnoses, 266*t*, 269*t*
correlations with *DSM-IV* diagnoses, 78*t*–80*t*
correlations with EPSI, 277*t*
correlations with HRSD and, 71, 71*t*
correlations with IMAS, 261*t*
correlations with ISDI, 273*t*, 274*t*
correlations with MIHT, 283*t*
correlations with PID-5, 280*t*
correlations with SPQ, 282*t*
as depression scale, 62, 64–66, 65*t*, 66*t*
and depression symptoms, 101, 101*t*, 263, 264
descriptive statistics across respondent types, 50*t*
development of, 31
and diagnostic specificity, 81
factor structure for, 47*t*, 48*t*, 49*t*
and General Depression scale, 32
group comparisons for, 52, 52*t*
intercorrelations of other scales with, 45*t*
internal consistency of, 38, 38*t*, 39*t*
normative statistics for, 54*t*, 56*t*
sex differences on, 86*t*
test-retest analyses of, 40*t*, 41, 42
Appetite Problems factor, 30, 31
APPQ. *see* Albany Panic and Phobia Questionnaire
Apprehension, anxious, 13
Arousal symptoms, in PTSD models, 177, 178*t*, 181
ASEBA (Achenbach System of Empirically Based Assessment), 284
ASI. *see* Anxiety Sensitivity Index
ASIQ (Adult Suicidal Ideation Questionnaire), 69*t*, 70
ASRM (Altman Self-Rating Mania Scale), 133, 134*t*
AUDIT (Alcohol Use Disorders Test), 167
Australian National Survey of Mental Health and Well-Being (NSMHWB), 5, 16
Average interitem correlations (AICs), 37–39, 38*t*, 39*t*
AVI. *see* Affect Valuation Index
Avoidance factor
differential specificity of, 182, 183
in PTSD models, 179, 180
relations of IDAS-II and other measures for, 188, 188*t*, 190, 190*t*
Avoidance symptoms
comparative analyses of, 198
correlations for measures of, 191–94, 192*t*, 193*t*
predictive power of, 202
in PTSD models, 177, 178*t*, 181
self-rated, 195–97

Baer, L., 236
BAI. *see* Beck Anxiety Inventory
Bailley, S. E., 170
Barch, D. M., 108
Barlow, D. H., 12
Barlow, David, 13
Barlow's hierarchical model, 13
Barrios, F. X., 24
BAS. *see* Behavioral Activation System
Base rates, in disorder-based analyses, 18–19
BDI. *see* Beck Depression Inventory
BDI-II. *see* Beck Depression Inventory-II
Beck, A. T., 26, 85
Beck Anxiety Inventory (BAI), 11, 24, 75–76, 95
Beck Depression Inventory (BDI), 11, 23, 24, 26, 27, 75–76, 245, 246*t*
Beck Depression Inventory-II (BDI-II), 23–27, 67, 67*t*, 68, 71, 71*t*, 75, 76, 84, 84*t*, 85, 86*t*, 95, 245
Bedi, R. P., 25
Behavioral Activation System (BAS), 115–17, 130–31, 265
Behavioral Activation System/Behavioral Inhibition System (BIS/BAS) scales, 130–31, 131*t*
Benazzi, F., 76
BFI. *see* Big Five Inventory

Bienvenu, O. J., 160
Big Five Inventory (BFI), 43–44, 43*t*, 104, 105, 109, 128–30, 129*t*, 134, 135, 136*t*, 142, 143
"Big two" dimensions of affect, 5
Bipolar disorder
  symptom dimensions in, 263
Bipolar disorders, 114–17
  behavioral activation system hypersensitivity with, 115–17
  convergent validity of IDAS-II for, 261*t*
  irritability in, 146
  state associations in, 114
  trait associations in, 114–15, 115*t*
Bipolar scales (IDAS-II)
  creation of, 35–36
  factor analysis of, 133–34, 136–37, 137*t*
Bipolar symptoms, 119–45
  item-level analyses, IDAS-II, 122–23, 124*t*
  Mania scale, validity of IDAS-II, 119–22, 120*t*–122*t*
  Mechanical Turk sample, 133–36
  non-IDAS-II measures, 123–26, 125*t*
  relations of personality and affectivity with, 134–36, 136*t*
  Sample4 analyses, 136–41
  two-factor structure of, 126–33
BIS (Behavioral Inhibition System, 130–31
BIS/BAS (Behavioral Activation System/ Behavioral Inhibition System) scales, 130–31, 131*t*
Bivariate analyses
  of ESPI factors and IDAS-II scales, 277, 277*t*
  of ISDI factors and IDAS-II scales, 272–74, 273*t*, 274*t*
  of MIHT factors and IDAS-II scales, 283, 283*t*
  of PID-5 factors and IDAS-II scales, 279, 280, 280*t*
  of SPQ factors and IDAS-II scales, 281, 282*t*
Bivariate relations, for trait negative affect scales, 162–63, 163*t*, 167, 168, 168*t*, 171, 172, 172*t*
Blanchard, E. B., 178
Blanchard, J. J., 108
Borderline personality disorder, 147
Brady E. U., 3
Brown, J. S., 112
Brown, T. A., 12
Buckley, T. C., 178

CAC (Compulsive Activity Checklist), 233
Cane, D. B., 3, 24
Carey, G., 5–6
Carney, C. E., 76
CAT-PD (Computerized Adaptive Test of Personality Disorder), 278
Cattell, R. B., 37
Center for Epidemiological Studies Depression Scale (CES-D), 3, 23–27, 67, 67*t*, 68, 84, 84*t*, 85, 86*t*, 104, 193, 194, 268*t*
CFI (comparative fit index), 15
Chapman, L. J., 143
Checking factor, 35, 242, 242*t*, 243, 244*t*
Checking scale (IDAS-II)
  and anxiety symptoms, 249*t*
  Big Five Inventory correlations with, 43*t*, 44
  convergent/discriminant validity analyses, 120, 120*t*
  correlations with *DSM* diagnoses, 251, 251*t*, 252*t*, 253, 254*t*, 257, 266*t*
  correlations with EPSI, 277*t*
  correlations with IMAS, 240*t*, 241, 241*t*, 261*t*
  correlations with ISDI, 273*t*, 274*t*
  correlations with MIHT, 283*t*
  correlations with other measures, 239*t*
  correlations with PID-5, 280*t*
  correlations with SPQ, 282*t*
  creation of, 35
  descriptive statistics across respondent types, 51*t*
  development of, 238
  factor structure for, 48*t*, 49*t*
  group comparisons for, 52, 52*t*
  as indicator of internalizing, 162
  intercorrelations of other scales with, 45*t*, 46
  internal consistency of, 38*t*, 39
  logistic regression analyses, 257, 258*t*
  normative statistics for, 54*t*, 57*t*

and OCD symptoms, 247, 247*t*
and social anxiety, 105
test-retest analyses of, 40*t*
Checking symptoms
correlations of measures for, 238, 239, 239*t*
diagnostic specificity of, 253–55, 256, 256*t*
factor analyses of, 243, 244*t*, 245
in interview measures, 240*t*–242*t*, 241, 243
relations of anxiety symptoms and, 248, 249, 249*t*
relations of depression symptoms and, 246*t*, 247*t*
in structure of OCD symptoms, 235–38, 236*t*, 237*t*
Children, ratings of anxiety and depression in, 3
Chmielewski, M., 20–21, 281
Chorpita, B. F., 12
Clara, I. P., 16
Clark, L. A., 4–9, 23, 88–89, 92, 108, 208
Claustrophobia scale (IDAS-II)
and anxiety symptoms, 209, 220–21, 223, 224*t*
Big Five Inventory correlations with, 43*t*, 44
construct validity of, 220–21
correlations with APPQ and FQ, 213, 213*t*
correlations with *DSM* diagnoses, 223, 224*t*, 226, 227*t*, 228, 228*t*, 229, 266*t*
correlations with EPSI, 277*t*
correlations with IMAS, 219, 219*t*, 220*t*, 261*t*
correlations with ISDI, 273*t*, 274*t*
correlations with MIHT, 283*t*
correlations with PID-5, 280*t*
correlations with PSRS, 211, 212, 212*t*
correlations with SPQ, 282*t*
creation of, 35
descriptive statistics across respondent types, 51*t*
development of, 209, 210
factor structure for, 48*t*, 49, 49*t*
group comparisons for, 52, 52*t*
intercorrelations of other scales with, 45*t*, 46
internal consistency of, 38*t*, 39
normative statistics for, 54*t*, 57*t*
test-retest analyses of, 40*t*, 42
Cleaning factor, 35
Cleaning scale (IDAS-II)
and anxiety symptoms, 249, 249*t*
Big Five Inventory correlations with, 43*t*, 44
correlations with *DSM* diagnoses, 251, 251*t*, 252*t*, 253, 254*t*, 257, 267*t*
correlations with EPSI, 277*t*
correlations with IMAS, 240*t*, 241, 241*t*, 261*t*
correlations with ISDI, 273*t*, 274*t*
correlations with MIHT, 283*t*
correlations with other measures, 239*t*
correlations with PCCP, 242, 242*t*, 243, 244*t*, 245
correlations with PID-5, 280*t*
correlations with SPQ, 282*t*
creation of, 35
descriptive statistics across respondent types, 51*t*
development of, 238
factor structure for, 48*t*, 49*t*
group comparisons for, 52, 52*t*
as indicator of internalizing, 162
intercorrelations of other scales with, 45*t*, 46
internal consistency of, 38*t*, 39
logistic regression analyses, 257, 258*t*
normative statistics for, 54*t*, 57*t*
and OCD symptoms, 247, 247*t*
and social anxiety, 105
test-retest analyses of, 40*t*, 42
Cleaning symptoms. *see* Washing and cleaning symptoms
Clinician ratings
and co-occurrence of symptoms, 2–3
depression symptoms, 65–66, 66*t*
of depression symptoms, 65–66, 66*t*
Clinician Rating Version of the IDAS (IDAS-CR)
anxiety symptoms on, 217–19, 221*t*, 222, 223*t*, 229, 230
and depression symptoms, 101, 101*t*

Clinician Rating Version of the IDAS (IDAS-CR) (*Cont.*)
 diagnostic specificity of, for depression, 97, 98*t*
 and externalizing psychopathology diagnosis, 166
 in IDAS-II discriminant validity tests, 262
 and internalizing psychopathology diagnosis, 158, 159*t*
 in primary samples for validity evidence, 55, 58–60, 59*t*
 and social anxiety/social phobia symptoms, 106–7, 107*t*
 in validity analyses of Ill Temper scale, 147–49, 148*t*
 in validity analyses of Mania scale, 119–21, 120*t*
Coefficient alphas, 36–37, 38*t*, 39*t*
Cohen, A. S., 109, 111
Cohen's *d*, 51
Collaborative Psychiatric Epidemiological Surveys, 17
Community Mental Health Center of Mideastern Iowa, 55
Comorbidity(-ies) (generally)
 definition of, 1
 diagnostic, 3–4
 direct modeling of, 15
Comorbidity of emotional disorders, 2–18
 and definition of comorbidity, 1
 and diagnosis-based structural analyses, 15–18
 integrative hierarchical model of, 12–15
 as problem, 2–5
 tripartite model of, 7–12
 two-factor affective model of, 5–7
Comparability coefficients, for bipolar symptom factors, 127–28, 128*t*
Comparative analyses, for anxiety symptoms, 224–26, 225*t*, 226*t*
Comparative fit index (CFI), 15
Comprehensiveness, of traditional depression scales, 24
Compulsive Activity Checklist (CAC), 233
Computerized Adaptive Test of Personality Disorder (CAT-PD), 278
Congruence coefficients, for bipolar symptom factors, 127
Content validity, of traditional depression scales, 24–25
Convergent validity, 10–11
 of IDAS depression scales, 72–75, 73*t*, 74*t*
 of IDAS-II anxiety scales, 211–21, 218*t*
 of IDAS-II/IDAS-CR positive mood scales, 89–90, 89*t*
 of IDAS-II OCD scales, 238–45, 244*t*
 of IDAS-II PTSD scales, 184–94
 of IDAS-II scales, 260–62, 261*t*
 of Ill Temper scale, 147–49, 148*t*
 of Mania scale, 119–21, 120*t*
 of SCOPI scales, 235–38
 of specific IDAS scales, for depression, 69, 69*t*, 70
Co-occurrence of symptoms, 2–3
Core Depression dimension, 30
Cox, B. J., 16
Criterion validity
 differential, 265, 266*t*–267*t*, 267
 of IDAS depression scales, 83–85, 84*t*
 of IDAS-II anxiety scales, 221–27
 of IDAS-II Euphoria scale, 114
 of IDAS-II Mania scale, 122, 122*t*
 of IDAS-II OCD scales, 250–57, 251*t*, 252*t*, 254*t*, 256*t*
 of IDAS-II PTSD scales, 194–204
Curious Experiences Survey, 284
Current manic episodes
 correlation of anxiety measures with, 221*t*, 223*t*, 224*t*
 correlation of PTSD measures with, 204*t*
 correlations of PTSD measures with, 195*t*, 196*t*
 criterion validity of symptom scales for, 266*t*

Dependability coefficients, 37
Depressed Mood scale, 6
Depression
 diagnostic specificity of positive affect measures for, 95–100, 96*t*, 98*t*–100*t*

and generalized anxiety disorder, 1, 3
general measures of, 67, 67*t*, 68
integrative hierarchical model of, 13–14
and Positive Affect, 93–102, 94*t*, 96*t*, 98*t*–102*t*
sex differences in, 85, 86, 86*t*
and social anxiety/social phobia, 104
specialized measures of, 67*t*, 68–69
specific IDAS scales, convergent validity of, 69, 69*t*, 70
specificity of hedonic deficit in relation to, 111–12
Depression composite, 161, 162, 163*t*, 164*t*
Depression factor
and indicators of externalizing psychopathology, 168, 168*t*, 169*t*
and indicators of internalizing psychopathology, 161–63, 163*t*, 164*t*
and psychoticism indicators, 172*t*, 173*t*
Depression scales (IDAS-II)
and Beck inventories, 75–76
convergent/discriminant validity of, 72–75, 73*t*, 74*t*
correlations of depression symptoms with, 101–2, 102*t*
criterion validity of, 83–85, 84*t*
diagnostic specificity of, 76–82, 78*t*–80*t*
differential criterion validity of, 265, 266*t*, 267
differential diagnostic specificity of, 268*t*, 269, 269*t*, 270
and Hamilton Rating Scale for Depression (HRSD), 70–72, 71*t*
incremental validity of, 82, 82*t*, 83
logistic regression analyses of, 82, 82*t*, 83
specificity of, to depression, 75–82
Depression scales, limitations of traditional, 23–25
Depression symptoms, 61–86
in children, 3
clinician ratings, 65–66, 66*t*
differential organization of, 263–64
general factor of, 61–62
and IDAS vs. *DSM* scales, 62, 62*t*, 64*t*
and OCD symptoms, 245–47, 246*t*, 247*t*
overlap of PTSD symptoms and, 182–84, 183*t*, 184*t*
relations among, 64–66, 65*t*, 66*t*
relations of positive affect measures to, 100–102, 101*t*, 102*t*
self-report data, 64, 65, 65*t*
specific IDAS scales, 62–64, 63*t*
Depressive disorders, convergent validity of IDAS-II for, 261*t*
Depue, R. A., 116
Descriptive statistics
for IDAS, 49, 50*t*
for IDAS-II, 51, 51*t*
Diagnosis-based structural analyses, 15–18
direct modeling of comorbidities in, 15
early structural data, 16
of emotional disorders, 15–18
recent studies, 17–18
and Watson's 2005 model, 16–17
Diagnostic and Statistical Manual of Mental Disorders (DSM)
anger measures and internalizing psychopathology in, 156–60, 157*t*–160*t*
depression scales in, vs. IDAS, 62, 62*t*
depression symptoms and IDAS vs. content scales of, 62, 62*t*, 64*t*
OCD in, 232
PTSD diagnosis in, 175
specificity of measures compared to (*See* Diagnostic specificity)
Diagnostic and Statistical Manual of Mental Disorders, first edition *(DSM-I),* precursors to PTSD diagnosis in, 176
Diagnostic and Statistical Manual of Mental Disorders, second edition *(DSM-II)*
precursors to PTSD diagnosis in, 176
Diagnostic and Statistical Manual of Mental Disorders, third edition *(DSM-III)*
exclusion rules in, 19
PTSD diagnosis in, 176–77
Diagnostic and Statistical Manual of Mental Disorders, third edition-revised *(DSM-III-R),* 4
and Mood and Anxiety Symptom Questionnaire, 9
PTSD diagnosis in, 177, 179
three-factor diagnosis model of, 16

Diagnostic and Statistical Manual of Mental Disorders, fourth edition *(DSM-IV),* 1, 4
  Anxiety Disorders Work Group, 7–8
  bipolar disorders in, 18
  correlation of PANAS-X and internalizing psychopathology on, 154–56, 155*t*, 156*t*
  HICs and depressive symptoms on, 29
  IDAS scales and, 31, 32
  PTSD diagnosis in, 177–81, 178*t*
  relevance of depression measures to, 24, 28
  and tripartite model, 12
Diagnostic and Statistical Manual of Mental Disorders, fifth edition *(DSM-5),* 1
  anger as symptom in, 146–47
  anxiety symptoms in, 206
  diagnostic reliability of, 21–22
  IDAS scales and, 31, 32
  PTSD symptoms in, 180–81
  relevance of depression measures to, 24
  and tripartite model, 12
Diagnostic comorbidity, 3–4
Diagnostic heterogeneity, in disorder-based analyses, 22
Diagnostic reliability, in disorder-based analyses, 20–22
Diagnostic specificity
  of anxiety scales, 221–27, 221*t*, 223*t*–225*t*, 227*t*
  of bipolar symptom factors, 140–41, 141*t*
  differential, 267–70, 268*t*, 269*t*
  of HPS subscales, 144, 144*t*
  of IDAS depression scales, 76–82, 78*t*–80*t*
  of IDAS-II OCD scales, 250–57, 250*t*–252*t*, 254*t*, 256*t*
  of Mania scale, 122, 122*t*
  of positive affect measures, for depression, 95–100, 96*t*, 98*t*–100*t*
  of PTSD and depression symptoms, 267–71, 268*t*, 269*t*
  of PTSD symptom scales, 194–204, 195*t*–197*t*, 199*t*, 201*t*–204*t*
Differential criterion validity, 265, 266*t*–267*t*, 267
Differential diagnostic specificity, 267–70, 268*t*, 269*t*
Differential incremental specificity, 270–71
Differential specificity, of PTSD symptoms, 182–84, 183*t*, 184*t*
Direct modeling, of comorbidities, 15
Disappointment, feelings of, 3
Discriminant validity
  of IDAS depression scales, 72–75, 73*t*, 74*t*
  of IDAS-II anxiety scales, 211–21, 218*t*
  of IDAS-II/IDAS-CR positive mood scales, 89*t*, 90
  of IDAS-II OCD scales, 238–43, 239*t*–242*t*
  of IDAS-II PTSD scales, 184–94
  of IDAS-II scales, 262
  of Ill Temper scale, 147–49, 148*t*
  of Mania scale, 119–21, 120*t*
  of OCI and OCI-R scales, 233, 234
  of SCOPI scales, 236–38, 236*t*, 237*t*
  of traditional depression scales, 23–24
Disorder-based analyses, of social anxiety/social phobia, 103
Disorder-based analyses of emotional disorders, 18–22
  diagnostic heterogeneity in, 22
  diagnostic unreliability in, 20–22
  hierarchical exclusion rules in, 19–20
  low base rates in, 18–19
Dissociation symptoms
  comparative analyses of, 200
  correlations for measures of, 191–94, 192*t*, 193*t*
Dissociative Processes Scale (DPS), 192*t*, 193, 193*t*, 284
Dozois, D. J. A., 85
Drug Use Survey (DUS), 167, 168, 168*t*, 169*t*
DSM. see Diagnostic and Statistical Manual of Mental Disorders
DUS. *see* Drug Use Survey
Dysphoria
  correlations with *DSM* diagnoses, 228, 228*t*, 229, 229*t*
  correlations with PSRS, 230, 230*t*
  as general depression factor, 61–62
Dysphoria factor

differential specificity of, 182–84
in PTSD models, 179
Dysphoria scale (IDAS and IDAS-II)
Big Five Inventory correlations with, 42–44, 43*t*
as bipolar symptom scale, 123, 124*t*, 134, 135
convergent/discriminant validity analyses, 73*t*, 74, 74*t*, 120, 120*t*, 148, 148*t*, 217, 218, 218*t*
convergent validity analyses of, 67–69, 67*t*, 69, 69*t*, 70
correlations self-report measures, 125*t*
correlations with Beck inventories, 75, 76, 95
correlations with *DSM-5* diagnoses, 79*t*
correlations with *DSM* diagnoses, 266*t*, 268*t*, 269*t*
correlations with *DSM-IV* diagnoses, 78*t*–80*t*
correlations with EPSI, 277*t*
correlations with HRSD and, 71, 71*t*
correlations with IMAS, 261*t*, 265, 267
correlations with ISDI, 273*t*, 274, 274*t*
correlations with ITRI, 192, 192*t*, 193*t*, 194
correlations with MASQ, 208, 208*t*, 209
correlations with MIHT, 283*t*
correlations with PANAS-X, 90, 90*t*
correlations with PCL, 186, 187, 187*t*
correlations with PID-5, 280, 280*t*
correlations with SPQ, 281, 282*t*
creation of, 32
criterion validity of, 84, 84*t*
as depression scale, 62, 64–66, 65*t*, 66*t*
and depression symptoms, 101, 101*t*, 102, 263, 264
descriptive statistics across respondent types, 50*t*, 51, 51*t*
and diagnostic specificity, 79, 80
and externalizing, 166
factor structure for, 47–49, 47*t*, 48*t*, 49*t*
group comparisons for, 52, 52*t*
intercorrelations of other scales with, 44, 45*t*, 46
internal consistency of, 38, 38*t*, 39*t*
logistic regression analyses, 257, 258*t*
normative statistics for, 54*t*, 56*t*
and OCD symptoms, 247*t*
and psychoticism, 170
as PTSD scale, 185
and PTSD symptoms, 199*t*, 200, 202, 202*t*, 203, 203*t*
sex differences on, 86, 86*t*
and social anxiety, 104
test-retest analyses of, 40*t*, 41, 42
Dysphoria symptoms
comparative analyses of, 199–200
correlations for measures of, 191–94, 192*t*, 193*t*
predictive power of, 202, 268–69
in PTSD models, 177, 178*t*, 179
Dysphoric arousal, 178*t*, 180
Dysphoric Arousal factor, in PTSD models, 180
Dysthymic disorder, tetrachoric correlations, 4*t*, 5
Dysthymic disorder symptoms, and negative trait affect scales, 163*t*, 164*t*

Eating Pathology Symptoms Inventory (EPSI), 69*t*, 70, 275*t*–277*t*, 276–78
Eaton, W. W., 4
Eckblad, M., 143
Edinburgh Postnatal Depression Scale (EPDS), 67*t*, 68, 71, 71*t*, 84, 84*t*, 85
Edinger, J. D., 76
Emotional disorders, 1–22
diagnosis-based structural analyses of, 15–18
disorder-based analyses of, 18–22
modeling symptoms within, 22
research on structure of, 1–2
as term, 1
See also specific headings, e.g.: comorbidity of social disorders
Enns, M. W., 16
EPDS. *see* Edinburgh Postnatal Depression Scale
EPSI. *see* Eating Pathology Symptoms Inventory
ESI (Externalizing Spectrum Inventory), 284
ESI-BF (Externalizing Spectrum Inventory-Brief Form), 284
Euphoria dimension, 35, 263

Euphoria scale (IDAS and IDAS-II)
  and bipolar disorders, 114
  as bipolar symptom scale, 122–23, 124*t*, 129, 134, 134*t*, 136*t*
  convergent/discriminant validity analyses, 120, 120*t*
  correlations self-report measures, 125, 125*t*, 126
  correlations with *DSM* diagnoses, 266*t*
  correlations with EPSI, 277*t*
  correlations with IMAS, 99, 99*t*, 100, 100*t*, 121, 261, 261*t*, 262
  correlations with ISDI, 273*t*, 274*t*
  correlations with MIHT, 283*t*
  correlations with PANAS-X, 90*t*, 91, 91*t*, 92
  correlations with PID-5, 113–14, 113*t*, 280, 280*t*
  correlations with SPQ, 282*t*
  and diagnostic specificity, 97, 98*t*
  diagnostic specificity of, 122
  factor analysis of, 126, 127*t*, 136, 137, 137*t*
  as indicator of psychoticism, 172, 172*t*, 173*t*
  and positive mood dysfunction, 89, 89*t*
  as positive mood scale, 265
  and specific negative affects, 94, 94*t*
Euphoria scale (IDAS-II)
  Big Five Inventory correlations with, 43*t*
  creation of, 35
  descriptive statistics across respondent types, 51*t*
  factor structure for, 48*t*, 49, 49*t*
  group comparisons for, 52, 52*t*
  intercorrelations of other scales with, 45*t*, 46
  internal consistency of, 38*t*, 39
  normative statistics for, 54*t*, 57*t*
  test-retest analyses of, 40*t*
Exclusion rules, hierarchical, 19–20
Experiential deficit, in schizophrenia/schizotypy, 108
Expressive deficit, in schizophrenia/schizotypy, 108
Externalizing psychopathology, 165–70
  IDAS-CR correlation to diagnosis of, 166
  IDAS-II correlation to diagnosis of, 165–66
  IMAS correlation to diagnosis of, 166
  NEO correlation to diagnosis of, 166–67
  PANAS-X correlation to diagnosis of, 165
  trait negative affect analysis of, 167–69, 168*t*, 169*t*
Externalizing Spectrum Inventory (ESI), 284
Externalizing Spectrum Inventory-Brief Form (ESI-BF), 284
Extraversion, and positive emotionality, 92–93

Faceted Inventory of the Five-Factor Model (FI-FFM), 151, 152, 152*t*, 153*t*, 154, 160, 161, 161*t*
Factor analysis
  of bipolar symptom scales, 133–34, 136–37, 137*t*
  for internalizing psychopathology symptoms, 160–61, 1651*t*
  for OCD symptoms, 243, 244*t*, 245
Factor structure
  for ESPI, 276, 276*t*, 277
  for IDAS-II, 47–49, 47*t*–49*t*
  for ISDI, 272
  for PID-5, 278, 279, 279*t*
Failure, feelings of, 3
Fearfulness, 3
Fear Questionnaire (FQ), 104, 162, 212, 213, 215–17, 219–21, 225–27, 248
FI-FFM. *see* Faceted Inventory of the Five-Factor Model
Fit indices, 15
Five-factor dysphoric arousal model of PTSD symptoms, 180
Foa, E. B., 234
Forbush, K. T., 17–19, 70, 276
Four-factor dysphoria model of PTSD symptoms, 179
Four-factor numbing model of PTSD symptoms, 179
FQ. *see* Fear Questionnaire
Friedman, M., 180–81

GAD. *see* Generalized anxiety disorder
GADQ-IV. *see* Generalized Anxiety Questionnaire-IV

GAD symptoms
correlation of anxiety measures with, 221*t*, 223*t*–225*t*, 225, 226, 227*t*
correlation of PTSD measures with, 195*t*–197*t*, 198, 199*t*, 201*t*, 204, 204*t*
correlations of anger measures with, 154, 155, 155*t*–160*t*, 156*t*, 157, 160
negative trait affect scale and, 162, 163*t*, 164*t*, 165
Gamez, W., 87
Garbage in garbage out (GIGO) problem, 25
Garbin, M., 26
Gard, D. E., 111
Gard, M. G., 111
GBI (General Behavior Inventory), 123–24, 125, 125*t*, 126, 127*t*, 142
GDS (Geriatric Depression Scale), 67*t*
General Depression scale (IDAS and IDAS-II)
Big Five Inventory correlations with, 43*t*, 44
convergent validity analyses of, 67–69, 67*t*
correlations with HRSD and, 71, 71*t*
creation of, 32
criterion validity of, 83–85, 84*t*
descriptive statistics across respondent types, 50*t*
group comparisons for, 52, 52*t*
as indicator of internalizing, 161
intercorrelations of other scales with, 44
internal consistency of, 38, 38*t*, 39*t*
normative statistics for, 54*t*, 55, 58*t*
sex differences on, 86*t*
test-retest analyses of, 40, 40*t*, 41
General factor, for PTSD, 181–82, 263
Generalized anxiety disorder (GAD)
and depression, 1, 3
in integrative hierarchical model, 13, 14
irritability in, 146
and OCD symptom measures, 250*t*–252*t*, 254*t*, 255, 256*t*
and social anxiety/social phobia, 104
tetrachoric correlations, 4*t*, 5
Generalized Anxiety Questionnaire-IV (GADQ-IV), 104, 162, 163, 163*t*, 164*t*, 226, 227, 248, 249*t*
Genetic risk factors, 16
Geriatric Depression Scale (GDS), 67*t*, 68
Gootzeit, J., 182, 191, 194, 263
Gotlib, I. H., 3, 24
Green, M. F., 108, 111
Gross stress reaction, 176
Group comparisons, for IDAS-II, 50*t*–52*t*, 51–53
Gruber, J., 115

Hamilton Rating Scale for Depression (HRSD), 59*t*, 60, 70–72, 71*t*
HCL-32. *see* Hypomania Checklist-32
Hedonic deficit
in schizophrenia and schizotypy, 108–9, 110*t*, 111
specificity of, in relation to depression, 111–12
Heterogeneity, diagnostic, 2, 22
Hickling, E. J., 178
HICs. *see* Homogeneous item composites
Hierarchical exclusion rules, 19–20
Hierarchical models of mood disorders
Barlow's, 13
integrative, 12–15
Histrionic personality disorder (HPD), 117–18
Hoarding symptoms
diagnostic specificity of, 253, 255, 256, 256*t*
in structure of OCD symptoms, 235–38, 236*t*, 237*t*
Homogeneous item composites (HICs)
for anxiety, 185
defined, vii, 28
in IDAS, 29, 29*t*, 30
in IDAS II, 33, 33*t*, 34
Horan, W. P., 108, 111
Hotelling test, 149
HPD (histrionic personality disorder), 117–18
HPS. *see* Hypomanic Personality Scale
HRSD. *see* Hamilton Rating Scale for Depression
Hyperarousal factor, differential specificity of, 182
Hyperarousal scale, and PTSD symptoms, 199, 199*t*

Hyperarousal symptoms
comparative analyses of, 198, 199
correlations for measures of, 191–94, 192*t*, 193*t*
predictive power of, 202
in PTSD models, 177, 178*t*
Hypervigilance factor
in PTSD models, 179, 180
relations of IDAS-II and other measures for, 187
Hypervigilance symptoms
comparative analyses of, 198, 199
in PTSD models, 177, 178*t*
Hypomania Checklist-32 (HCL-32), 125, 125*t*, 126, 127*t*
Hypomanic Personality Scale (HPS), 115, 124–26, 125*t*, 127*t*, 129–30, 133, 134, 134*t*, 136, 137, 137*t*, 142–44, 144*t*

IDAS. *see* Inventory of Depression and Anxiety Symptoms
IDAS-CR. *see* Clinician Rating Version of the IDAS
IDAS-II. *see* Inventory of Depression and Anxiety Symptoms (second version)
Ill Temper scale (IDAS and IDAS-II)
Big Five Inventory correlations with, 43*t*, 44
convergent/discriminant validity analyses, 120, 120*t*, 148*t*, 217, 218*t*
correlations with *DSM* diagnoses, 156–58, 157*t*, 158*t*, 159*t*
correlations with EPSI, 277*t*
correlations with HRSD and, 71*t*
correlations with IMAS, 149, 149*t*, 261*t*
correlations with ISDI, 273*t*, 274*t*
correlations with MIHT, 283*t*
correlations with PANAS-X, 150, 150*t*, 151
correlations with PCL, 186, 187*t*
correlations with PID-5, 280, 280*t*
correlations with SPQ, 281, 282*t*
correlations with trait measures of negative affect, 151–53, 152*t*
descriptive statistics across respondent types, 50*t*
development of, 31
and externalizing, 165–66
and externalizing psychopathology diagnosis, 165–66
factor structure for, 47*t*, 48*t*, 49*t*
group comparisons for, 52, 52*t*
intercorrelations of other scales with, 45*t*
internal consistency of, 38, 38*t*, 39*t*
and internalizing psychopathology diagnosis, 156–58, 157*t*–159*t*
normative statistics for, 54*t*, 56*t*
and psychoticism, 170
test-retest analyses of, 40, 40*t*
validity of, 147–53, 148*t*–150*t*, 152*t*
ILPP (Iowa Longitudinal Personality Project), 41–42
IMAS. *see* Interview for Mood and Anxiety Symptoms
Inappropriate content, on traditional depression scales, 24
Incremental specificity
differential, 270–71
Incremental validity
of IDAS depression scales, 82, 82*t*, 83
of IDAS-II anxiety scales, 228–30
of IDAS-II OCD scales, 257, 258, 258*t*
of negative affect scales, 155–58, 156*t*, 158*t*
of positive mood scales, 97
of PTSD symptoms, 200–204, 201*t*–203*t*
Ingram, R. E., 25
Insomnia factor, 30, 31
Insomnia scale (IDAS and IDAS-II)
Big Five Inventory correlations with, 43*t*
convergent/discriminant validity analyses, 72, 73*t*, 74, 74*t*
convergent validity analyses of, 69, 69*t*, 70
correlations with Beck inventories, 75, 76, 95
correlations with *DSM-5* diagnoses, 79*t*
correlations with *DSM* diagnoses, 266*t*, 269*t*
correlations with *DSM-IV* diagnoses, 78*t*–80*t*
correlations with EPSI, 277*t*
correlations with HRSD and, 71, 71*t*
correlations with IMAS, 261*t*

correlations with ISDI, 272, 273t, 274, 274t
correlations with MIHT, 283t
correlations with PCL, 186, 187t
correlations with PID-5, 280t
correlations with SPQ, 282t
as depression scale, 62, 64–66, 65t, 66t
and depression symptoms, 101, 101t, 263, 264
descriptive statistics across respondent types, 50t
development of, 31
and diagnostic specificity, 81
factor structure for, 47t, 48t, 49t
and General Depression scale, 32
group comparisons for, 52, 52t
intercorrelations of other scales with, 45t
internal consistency of, 38, 38t, 39t
normative statistics for, 54t, 56t
sex differences on, 86t
test-retest analyses of, 40t
Integrative hierarchical model, 12–15
of anxiety, 13–14
and Barlow's hierarchical model, 13
of depression, 13–14
modeling of comorbidity in, 14–15
and tripartite model, 12
Integrative hierarchical model of comorbidity, 12–15
Intermittent explosive disorder, 147
Internal consistency, of IDAS-II, 37–39, 38t, 39t
Internalizing psychopathology, 154–65
IDAS-CR correlation to diagnosis of, 158, 159t
IDAS-II correlation to diagnosis of, 156–58, 157t, 158t
Ill Temper scale and diagnosis of, 156–58, 157t–159t
IMAS correlation to diagnosis of, 159, 160t
NEO correlation to diagnosis of, 159, 160
PANAS-X correlation to diagnosis of, 154–56, 155t, 156t
trait negative affect analysis of, 160–64, 161t, 163t, 164t
Internalizing symptoms, of PTSD, 177, 178t
Interview data, on social anxiety/social phobia, 106–7, 107t
Interview for Mood and Anxiety Symptoms (IMAS), 114, 154, 173
anxiety scales of IDAS-II and, 219t, 220, 220t, 221
anxiety symptoms on, 219, 219t, 220t
correlations of IDAS-II scales and, 261, 261t, 262
depression and, 99–100, 99t, 100t
depression scales of IDAS-II and, 79t
depression symptoms on, 73–75, 74t
diagnostic specificity of items on, 269, 269t
differential criterion validity for items on, 265, 266t, 267t
externalizing psychopathology and, 166
Ill Temper scale and, 149, 149t
internalizing psychopathology and, 159, 160t
Mania scale and, 121, 121t, 122
OCD symptoms on, 239–42, 240t, 241t, 251, 251t
positive mood scales of IDAS-II and, 99–100, 99t, 100t
primary samples using, 59, 59t, 60
psychoticism and, 170
PTSD symptom scales of IDAS-II and, 189–90, 189t, 190t, 203, 204, 204t
PTSD symptoms on, 196, 196t, 197
Interview measures
and anxiety symptoms, 217–20, 218t
convergence of IDAS-II OCD scales and, 239–43, 240t–242t, 244t, 245
Intrusions factor
differential specificity of, 182, 183
in PTSD models, 179
relations of IDAS-II and other measures for, 188, 188t, 190, 190t
Intrusion symptoms
comparative analyses of, 198
correlations for measures of, 191–94, 192t, 193t
predictive power of, 201–2
in PTSD models, 177, 181
self-rated, 195–97

Inventory of Depression and Anxiety Symptoms (IDAS), vii, 23
  descriptive statistics for, 49, 50*t*
  Phase1 in development of, 28–30, 29*t*
  Phase2 in development of, 30–32
  in primary samples for validity evidence, 55, 58, 59*t*, 60
  schizophrenia and schizotypy analyses, 112–14, 113*t*
  See also specific scales
Inventory of Depression and Anxiety Symptoms (second version) (IDAS-II), vii, 23
  anxiety scales, creation of, 34–35
  basic analytic strategy in development of, 34
  bipolar scales, creation of, 35–36
  correlations of depression symptoms with, 100–101, 101*t*
  correlations of psychoticism with, 170
  correlations of schizophrenia/schizotypy symptoms with, 112–14, 113*t*
  descriptive statistics for, 51, 51*t*
  diagnostic specificity of, for depression, 97, 98*t*
  and externalizing psychopathology diagnosis, 165–66
  factor structure of, 47–49, 47*t*–49*t*, 49*f*
  group comparisons, 50*t*–52*t*, 51–53
  internal consistency, evidence of, 37–39, 38*t*, 39*t*
  and internalizing psychopathology diagnosis, 156–58, 157*t*, 158*t*
  internal structure of, 44–49
  item-level analyses of bipolar symptoms on, 122–23, 124*t*
  methodology, 33–34, 33*t*
  norms, nationally representative, 53–55, 54*t*, 56*t*–58*t*
  and personality, 42–44, 43*t*
  preliminary analyses in development of, 34
  primary samples as validity evidence of, 55, 58–60, 59*t*
  PTSD symptoms on, 184–86
  rationale for, 32–33
  reliability of symptom measures, 36–37
  retest evidence for reliability of, 39–42, 40*t*
  scale intercorrelations, 44, 45*t*, 46
  See also specific scales
Iowa Longitudinal Personality Project (ILPP), 41–42
Iowa Sleep Disturbances Inventory (ISDI), 272, 273*t*–275*t*, 274–76
Iowa Traumatic Response Inventory (ITRI), 191–94, 192*t*, 193*t*, 198, 199*t*, 200–202, 201*t*, 268, 268*t*, 269
Item-level analyses, of bipolar symptoms, 122–23, 124*t*

Johnson, S. L., 117
Joiner, T. E., 112
Joiner, T. E., Jr., 36, 37

Kashdan, T. B., 103, 104
Kendall, P. C., 3
Kendler, K. S., 16
Kessler, R. C., 4
Kimhy, D., 111
Knauss, F., 76
Koffel, E. ., 272
Koffel, E., 272
Koopman, R. F., 25
Kotov, R., 17, 19, 20, 87, 103
Kring, A. M., 108, 111
Krueger, R. F., 16, 278

Lambert, M. J., 24
Lassitude factor, 30, 31
Lassitude scale (IDAS and IDAS-II), 28
  Big Five Inventory correlations with, 43*t*
  convergent/discriminant validity analyses, 72, 73*t*, 74, 74*t*, 148, 148*t*
  convergent validity analyses of, 69, 69*t*, 70
  correlations with Beck inventories, 75, 76, 95
  correlations with *DSM-5* diagnoses, 79*t*
  correlations with *DSM* diagnoses, 266*t*, 269*t*
  correlations with *DSM-IV* diagnoses, 78*t*–80*t*
  correlations with EPSI, 277*t*
  correlations with HRSD and, 71, 71*t*

correlations with IMAS, 261*t*
correlations with ISDI, 273*t*, 274, 274*t*
correlations with MIHT, 283*t*
correlations with PID-5, 280, 280*t*
correlations with SPQ, 282*t*
as depression scale, 63, 64–66, 64*t*, 65*t*, 66*t*
and depression symptoms, 101, 101*t*, 102, 263, 264
descriptive statistics across respondent types, 50*t*
development of, 31
and diagnostic specificity, 80, 81
factor structure for, 46, 47*t*, 48*t*, 49*t*
and General Depression scale, 32
group comparisons for, 52, 52*t*
intercorrelations of other scales with, 45*t*
internal consistency of, 38, 38*t*, 39*t*
normative statistics for, 54*t*, 56*t*
sex differences on, 86, 86*t*
test-retest analyses of, 40*t*

Leckman, J. F., 233
Lewinsohn, P. M., 85
Leyton Obsessional Inventory (LOI), 232–33
Logistic regression analyses, of IDAS depression scales, 82, 82*t*, 83
Longley, S. L., 283
Lorenzo-Seva, U., 127
Lutz, C. J., 170

Magee, W. J., 4
Major depression
criterion validity of symptom scales for, 266*t*
differential incremental validity for symptoms of, 270
predictive power of anxiety measures for, 228*t*, 229, 229*t*
symptom dimensions in, 263
tetrachoric correlations, 4*t*

Major depressive disorder (MDD)
negative trait affect scales and, 163*t*, 164*t*
and OCD symptom measures, 250*t*–252*t*, 254*t*, 255, 256*t*, 257
specificity of IDAS-II depression scales for, 268*t*, 269, 269*t*, 270

Major depressive disorder (MDD) symptoms
correlation of anxiety measures with, 221*t*, 222, 223, 223*t*–225*t*, 225, 227*t*
correlation of PTSD measures with, 195*t*–197*t*, 198–200, 199*t*, 201*t*, 204, 204*t*
correlations between, 263
correlations of anger measures with, 154, 155*t*–160*t*, 156, 157, 159, 160

Major depressive episode, Dysphoria scale and criteria for, 32
Mania dimension, 35, 263
Mania factors, differential correlates of, 264–65
Mania scale (IDAS-II)
Big Five Inventory correlations with, 43*t*
as bipolar symptom scale, 122–23, 124*t*, 134, 134*t*
convergent/discriminant validity analyses, 119–20, 120*t*, 148, 148*t*
correlations self-report measures, 125, 125*t*, 126
correlations with *DSM* diagnoses, 122*t*, 266*t*
correlations with EPSI, 277, 277*t*
correlations with IMAS, 121, 121*t*, 261, 261*t*, 262
correlations with ISDI, 273*t*, 274*t*
correlations with MIHT, 283*t*
correlations with PID-5, 280, 280*t*
correlations with SPQ, 281, 282*t*
creation of, 35
and depression symptoms, 264
descriptive statistics across respondent types, 51*t*
diagnostic specificity of, 122
factor analysis of, 126, 127*t*
factor structure for, 48*t*, 49, 49*t*
group comparisons for, 52, 52*t*
as indicator of psychoticism, 172*t*, 173*t*
intercorrelations of other scales with, 45*t*, 46
internal consistency of, 38*t*, 39
normative statistics for, 54*t*, 57*t*
test-retest analyses of, 40*t*
validity of, 119–22, 120*t*, 121*t*

Mania symptoms, differential organization of, 264
Manic Distress (factor)
 described, 126, 264
 differential correlates of, 264–65
 See also Two-factor structure of bipolar symptoms
Manic Elation (factor)
 described, 126, 264
 differential correlates of, 264–65
 See also Two-factor structure of bipolar symptoms
Markon, K., 182, 191
Markon, K. E., 20–21
MASQ General Distress (MASQ GD), 245, 246*t*
Massachusetts General Hospital Hair Pulling Scale, 284
Mataix-Cols, D., 233
Maudsley Obsessive-Compulsive Inventory (MOCI), 233
McGonagle, K. A., 4
mDES (modified Differential Emotions Scale), 134–36
MDQ. *see* Mood Disorder Questionnaire
Mechanical Turk sample, 53, 133–36
Mental neutralizing symptoms, diagnostic specificity of, 253, 255–57, 256*t*
Merikangas, K. R., 18
Metalsky, G. I., 112
MIDAS (Rhode Island Methods to Improve Diagnostic and Assessment Services), 17
MIHT. *see* Multidimensional Inventory of Hypochondriacal Traits
Miller, C. J., 20–21
Milwaukee Inventory for Subtypes of Trichotillomania, 284
Milwaukee Inventory for the Dimensions of Adult Skin Picking, 284
Mineka, S., 13, 14
Mini-International Neuropsychiatric Interview (M.I.N.I.), 58, 59*t*
Mini-MASQ, 208, 208*t*
Minor, K. S., 109, 111
MOCI (Maudsley Obsessive-Compulsive Inventory), 233
Modified Differential Emotions Scale (mDES), 134–36
Mood and Anxiety Symptom Questionnaire (MASQ), 162, 248, 268*t*
 anxiety scales of IDAS-II and, 208, 208*t*, 209, 216, 217
 correlations of ITRI scales and, 193, 193*t*, 194
 depression scales of IDAS-II and, 67, 67*t*, 68
 development of, 9, 10
 DSM diagnoses and, 225, 226, 227
 Panic scale and, 220
 relations among scales of, 10–12, 11*t*
 sample items from, 9*b*
 social anxiety/social phobia and, 104, 105
Mood Disorder Questionnaire (MDQ), 133, 134, 134*t*
Moran, E. K., 108
Moran, P. W., 24
MOVES, 285
Multidimensional Inventory of Hypochondriacal Traits (MIHT), 275*t*, 282–84, 282*t*, 283*t*
Multiscale Dissociation Inventory, 284
Multivariate relations, for trait negative affect scales, 163–64, 164*t*, 168, 169, 169*t*, 172, 173, 173*t*
Myers, J., 16
Myin-Germeys, I., 111

Naragon, K., 92
Naragon-Gainey, K., 93, 104
Narcissistic personality disorder (NPD), 117–18
Narcissistic Personality Inventory (NPI), 117
National Comorbidity Survey (NCS), 4, 5, 18, 20
National Institute of Mental Health (NIMH), vii
NCS. *see* National Comorbidity Survey
NCS Replication (NCS-R), 18
Neale, M. C., 16
Negative affect, and positive affect measures, 93–94, 94*t*

Negative Affect dimension, 5–7
Negative symptoms, of schizophrenia/schizotypy, 108–9, 110*t*
NEO Personality Inventory-3 (NEO-PI-3), 137, 138*t*, 143, 144, 151, 152*t*, 153*t*, 154, 160, 161, 161*t*, 264
NEO-PI-R, 159, 160, 166, 167, 169–70, 170–71, 173, 174
Netherlands Mental Health Survey and Incidence Study (NEMESIS), 5, 18
Norms, on IDAS-II, 53–55, 54*t*, 56*t*–58*t*
NPD (narcissistic personality disorder), 117–18
NPI (Narcissistic Personality Inventory), 117, 139
NSMHWB (Australian National Survey of Mental Health and Well-Being), 5, 16
Numbing factor
  differential specificity of, 182
  in PTSD models, 179, 180
Numbing symptoms
  comparative analyses of, 199–200
  predictive power of, 202
  in PTSD models, 177, 178*t*, 181

Obsessing symptoms, diagnostic specificity of, 253, 255, 256, 256*t*
Obsessive-compulsive disorder (OCD)
  convergent validity of IDAS-II for, 261*t*
  criterion validity of symptom scales for, 266*t*–267*t*
  diagnostic heterogeneity with, 22
  in *DSM*, 232
  negative trait affect scale and, 162, 163*t*, 164*t*
  and social anxiety/social phobia, 104
Obsessive-Compulsive Inventory (OCI), 233–34
Obsessive-Compulsive Inventory-Revised (OCI-R), 105, 162, 234, 245, 260
  anxiety symptoms on, 248, 249*t*
  factor analysis of, 243, 244*t*, 245
  OCD diagnosis and, 252–55, 252*t*, 254*t*
  and OCD symptoms, 234, 258–59
  OCD symptom scales of IDAS-II and, 238, 239, 239*t*, 257–59, 258*t*
  OCD symptom specificity on, 246, 246*t*, 247*t*
  and SCOPI, 235, 235*t*, 236
Obsessive-Compulsive Symptoms factor, 30
OCD. *see* Obsessive-compulsive disorder
OCD composite, 162, 163*t*, 164*t*
OCD symptoms, 232–59
  and anxiety symptoms, 247–49, 249*t*, 250*t*
  correlation of anxiety measures with, 221*t*, 223*t*–225*t*, 225, 227*t*
  correlation of PTSD measures with, 201*t*, 204*t*
  correlations of anger measures with, 154, 155*t*–160*t*, 156, 158, 160
  correlations of PTSD measures with, 195*t*–197*t*, 199*t*
  and depression symptoms, 245–47, 246*t*, 247*t*
  diagnostic specificity of, 250–57, 250*t*–252*t*, 254*t*, 256*t*
  differential organization of, 263
  factor analyses for, 243, 244*t*, 245
  IDAS-II scales, 238–39, 239*t*
  IMAS analyses, 239–42, 240*t*, 241*t*
  incremental validity of scales, 257, 258, 258*t*
  Obsessive-Compulsive Inventory (OCI), 233–34
  PCCP analyses, 242–45, 242*t*
  revised OCI (OCI-R), 234, 258–59
  Schedule of Compulsions, Obsessions, and Pathological Impulses (SCOPI), 234–38, 235*t*–237*t*, 239*t*, 258
  self-report measures, 232–33
  specificity of, 245–57
  structure of, 233
OCD symptom scales (IDAS-II), 262
  convergence of interview measures and, 239–43, 240*t*–242*t*, 244*t*, 245
  development of, 238
  diagnostic specificity of, 250–57, 251*t*, 252*t*, 254*t*, 256*t*
  differential criterion validity of, 265, 266*t*–267*t*
  incremental validity of, 257, 258, 258*t*
  relations of SCOPI and OCI-R to, 238, 239, 239*t*

OCI (Obsessive-Compulsive Inventory), 233–34
OCI-R. *see* Obsessive-Compulsive Inventory-Revised
O'Hara, M. W., 6
Oppositional defiant disorder, 146–47
Ordering factor, 35
Ordering scale (IDAS-II)
- and anxiety symptoms, 249, 249*t*
- Big Five Inventory correlations with, 43*t*
- convergent/discriminant validity analyses, 120, 120*t*
- correlations with *DSM* diagnoses, 251*t*, 252*t*, 253, 254*t*, 257, 266*t*
- correlations with EPSI, 277*t*
- correlations with IMAS, 240*t*, 241, 241*t*, 261*t*, 265
- correlations with ISDI, 273*t*, 274*t*
- correlations with MIHT, 283*t*
- correlations with other measures, 239*t*
- correlations with PCCP, 242, 242*t*, 243, 244*t*, 245
- correlations with PID-5, 280*t*
- correlations with SPQ, 282*t*
- creation of, 35
- descriptive statistics across respondent types, 51*t*
- development of, 238
- factor structure for, 48*t*, 49*t*
- group comparisons for, 52, 52*t*
- as indicator of internalizing, 162
- intercorrelations of other scales with, 45*t*, 46
- internal consistency of, 38*t*, 39
- logistic regression analyses, 257, 258*t*
- normative statistics for, 54*t*, 57*t*
- and OCD symptoms, 247*t*
- and social anxiety, 105
- test-retest analyses of, 40*t*

Ordering symptoms and rituals
- correlations of measures for, 238, 239, 239*t*
- diagnostic specificity of, 253–55, 256, 256*t*
- factor analyses of, 243, 244*t*, 245
- in interview measures, 240*t*–242*t*, 241, 243
- relations of anxiety symptoms and, 249*t*
- relations of depression symptoms and, 246*t*, 247*t*
- in structure of OCD symptoms, 235–38, 236*t*, 237*t*

Osman, A., 24

Padua Inventory, 233
PANAS (Positive and Negative Affect Schedule), 88
PANAS-X. *see* Positive and Negative Affect Schedule–Expanded Form
Panic Attack Symptom Questionnaire (PASQ), 105, 162, 193, 193*t*, 194, 215, 216, 220, 225–27, 248
Panic composite, 162, 163, 163*t*, 164*t*, 248, 249*t*
Panic disorder
- and OCD symptom measures, 250*t*–252*t*, 254*t*, 255, 256*t*
- predictive power of anxiety measures for, 228*t*, 229, 229*t*, 230
- tetrachoric correlations, 4*t*, 5

Panic disorder symptoms
- correlation of anger measures with, 154–56, 155*t*–160*t*, 158–60
- correlation of anxiety measures with, 221*t*, 222–24, 223*t*–225*t*, 226, 227*t*
- correlation of PTSD measures with, 195*t*–197*t*, 198–200, 199*t*, 201*t*, 204*t*
- negative trait affect scale and, 162, 163*t*, 164*t*

Panic factor, 30, 31
Panic scale (IDAS and IDAS-II)
- and anxiety symptoms, 248
- anxiety symptoms on, 207–9, 220, 222–23, 223*t*
- Big Five Inventory correlations with, 43*t*
- construct validity of, 220
- convergent/discriminant validity analyses, 120, 120*t*, 148, 148*t*, 217, 218, 218*t*
- correlations with APPQ and FQ, 213, 213*t*
- correlations with ASI, 214, 215*t*
- correlations with *DSM* diagnoses, 222–23, 223*t*, 226, 227*t*, 228–30, 228*t*, 229*t*, 266*t*
- correlations with EPSI, 277*t*

correlations with HRSD and, 71*t*
correlations with IMAS, 219, 219*t*, 220*t*, 261*t*
correlations with ISDI, 273*t*, 274*t*
correlations with ITRI, 192–93, 192*t*
correlations with MASQ, 208, 208*t*, 209
correlations with MIHT, 283*t*
correlations with PCL, 186, 187, 187*t*
correlations with PID-5, 280, 280*t*
correlations with PSRS, 211, 212*t*
correlations with SPQ, 281, 282*t*
descriptive statistics across respondent types, 50*t*
development of, 31, 207–8
factor structure for, 46, 47*t*, 48*t*, 49*t*
group comparisons for, 52, 52*t*
as indicator of internalizing, 162
intercorrelations of other scales with, 45*t*
internal consistency of, 38, 38*t*, 39*t*
normative statistics for, 54*t*, 57*t*
structural analysis, 216, 217*t*
test-retest analyses of, 40*t*, 42
Panic symptoms, correlation of anxiety measures with, 215–17, 215*t*, 216*t*
Paranoid personality disorder, anger symptoms in, 147
PASQ. *see* Panic Attack Symptom Questionnaire
Pathological component, of Euphoria scale, 92
Patient Health Questionnaire-9 (PHQ-9), 104, 161, 193, 193*t*, 246, 247*t*, 268*t*
PCCP. *see* Personality, Cognitions, Consciousness, and Perceptions Interview
PCL. *see* PTSD Checklist
Peritraumatic dissociation, 191
Personality, and IDAS-II scales, 42–44, 43*t*
Personality, Cognitions, Consciousness, and Perceptions Interview (PCCP), 58–60, 59*t*, 106–7, 107*t*, 242–45, 242*t*, 244*t*, 245, 253–55, 254*t*, 261, 261*t*, 262, 267*t*
Personality disorders
anger in, 147
and elevated positive mood, 117–18
Personality Inventory for *DSM-5* (PID-5), 112, 113*t*, 275*t*
externalizing psychopathology and, 167, 168*t*, 169*t*
IDAS-II vs., 278–81, 279*t*, 280*t*
Ill Temper scale and, 151, 152, 152*t*
internalizing psychopathology and, 160, 161, 161*t*
Mania factors on, 264, 265
OCD symptoms and, 246, 247*t*
personality disorder and, 117–18
and personality pathology, 139, 140*t*
psychoticism and, 170, 171, 172*t*, 173*t*
trait negative affect scales and, 153*t*, 154
Personality measures
facet-level relations of bipolar symptom factors with, 137–38, 138*t*
relations of bipolar symptom factors and, 134–36, 136*t*
Personality pathology measures, relation of bipolar symptom factors with, 138–39, 140*t*
Phobic Stimuli Response Scales (PSRS), 103–4, 211–12, 212*t*, 220, 221, 224, 225*t*, 227, 230, 230*t*
PHQ-9. *see* Patient Health Questionnaire-9
PID-5. *see* Personality Inventory for *DSM-5*
Positive affect, elevated, disorders associated with, 114–18
Positive Affect dimension, 6, 7, 87–88
Positive and Negative Affect Schedule (PANAS), 88
Positive and Negative Affect Schedule–Expanded Form (PANAS-X), 6, 42, 109, 264
depression scales of IDAS-II and, 69, 69*t*, 70, 101–2, 102*t*
diagnostic specificity of, for depression, 95–97, 96*t*
disorders of positive affect and, 115, 115*t*, 117, 118
and externalizing psychopathology diagnosis, 165
and internalizing psychopathology diagnosis, 154–56, 155*t*, 156*t*
as measure of positive emotionality, 88–89

Positive and Negative Affect Schedule–Expanded Form (PANAS-X) (*Cont.*)
with MTurk sample, 134, 135, 136*t*
relation of negative and positive affects on, 94, 94*t*
relations of IDAS-II scales and, 90–92, 90*t*, 91*t*
social anxiety/social phobia and, 103–5
in validity analyses of Ill Temper Scale, 150–51, 150*t*
Positive emotionality, 88–93
and extraversion, 92–93
IDAS-II scales as measure of, 89–90, 89*t*
PANAS-X Scales as measure of, 88–89
relations of PANAS-X and IDAS-II scales for, 90–92, 90*t*, 91*t*
Positive mood component, of Euphoria scale, 92
Positive mood dysfunction, 87–118
bipolar disorders, 114–17
depression, 93–102, 94*t*, 96*t*, 98*t*–102*t*
elevated positive affect, 114–18, 115*t*
and measurement model for positive emotionality, 88–93, 89*t*–91*t*
personality disorder, 117–18
schizophrenia/schizotypy, 108–14, 110*t*, 113*t*
social anxiety/social phobia, 102–7, 106*t*, 107*t*
Positive mood scales (IDAS-II)
and Beck inventories, 95
diagnostic specificity of, for depression, 95–100, 96*t*, 98*t*–100*t*
differential correlates of, 265
relations of, with depression symptoms, 100–102, 101*t*, 102*t*
relations of specific negative affects and, 93–94, 94*t*
Positive Schizotypy composite, 171, 172, 172*t*, 173*t*
Positive symptoms, of schizophrenia/schizotypy, 108–9, 110*t*
Positive Urgency Measure (PUM), 135, 136
Posttraumatic stress disorder (PTSD)
correlations of anger measures with, 154–58, 155*t*–160*t*
criterion validity of symptom scales for, 266*t*
diagnostic heterogeneity with, 22
historical background of diagnosis, 175–78, 178*t*
irritability in, 146
and OCD symptom measures, 250*t*–252*t*, 254*t*, 255, 256*t*
in three-factor diagnosis model, 16
Predictive power, of PTSD symptoms, 200–203, 201*t*–203*t*
PROC CALIS, 15
PSRS. *see* Phobic Stimuli Response Scales
Psychometrics, and symptom co-occurrence, 3
Psychomotor Problems factor, 30
Psychoticism, 170–74
PTSD. *see* Posttraumatic stress disorder
PTSD Checklist (PCL), 105, 186–89, 187*t*, 188*t*, 191–94, 192*t*, 193*t*, 194, 197, 197*t*, 198, 199*t*, 200–202, 201*t*, 248, 268, 268*t*, 269
PTSD Checklist-Civilian Version, 105, 162
PTSD composite, 162, 163, 163*t*, 164*t*, 248, 249*t*
PTSD scales (IDAS-II), 262
convergent and discriminant validity of, 184–86
criterion validity of, 194–204
differential criterion validity of, 265, 266*t*
differential diagnostic specificity of, 267–69, 268*t*, 269*t*
relations of IMAS analyses with, 189–90, 189*t*, 190*t*
relations of ITRI analyses with, 191–94, 192*t*, 193*t*
relations of PCL analyses with, 186–89, 187*t*, 188*t*
PTSD symptoms, 175–205
comparative analyses across multiple measures, 198–200, 199*t*
convergent/discriminant validity of scales, 184–94
correlation of anxiety measures with, 221*t*, 223*t*–225*t*, 227*t*
criterion validity of scales, 194–204
differential incremental validity for, 270–71
differential organization of, 263

differential specificity of, 182–84, 183*t*, 184*t*
in *DSM*, 176–78
historical background of PTSD diagnosis, 175–78, 178*t*
IDAS-II scales, 194–95, 195*t*
IMAS analyses, 189–90, 189*t*, 190*t*, 203, 204, 204*t*
intrusion/avoidance symptoms, self-rated, 195–97, 196*t*
ITRI analyses, 191–94, 192*t*, 193*t*
negative trait affect scale and, 162, 163*t*, 164*t*, 165
PCL analyses, 186–89, 187*t*, 188*t*, 197, 197*t*, 198
predictive power, incremental, 200–203, 201*t*–203*t*
and social anxiety/social phobia, 104
strong general factor for, 181–82
structure of, 178–81

PUM (Positive Urgency Measure), 135, 136

Questionable content, on traditional depression scales, 24

R01 grant, vii
Radloff, L. S., 26
RADS-2 (Reynolds Adolescent Depression Scale–Second Edition), 67*t*, 68
Reexperiencing symptoms
comparative analyses of, 198
in PTSD models, 176–77, 178*t*
Regier, D. A., 21–22
Regression analyses
of ESPI factors and IDAS-II scales, 277, 278
of IDAS depression scales, 82, 82*t*, 83
of ISDI factors and IDAS-II scales, 274–76, 275*t*
of MIHT factors and IDAS-II scales, 283, 284
of PID-5 factors and IDAS-II scales, 280–81
of SPQ factors and IDAS-II scales, 281, 282
Reliability
defined, 36
in disorder-based analyses, 20–22
of IDAS-II, 39–42, 40*t*
of IDAS-II symptom measures, 36–37
Request for Applications (RFA), vii
Reynolds Adolescent Depression Scale–Second Edition (RADS-2), 67*t*, 68
Rhode Island Methods to Improve Diagnostic and Assessment Services (MIDAS), 17
Rituals. *see* Ordering symptoms
RMSEA (root-mean-square error of approximation), 15
Root-mean-square error of approximation (RMSEA), 15
Rosario-Campos, M. C., 233
Ross, S. R., 170, 173–74
Ruiz, M. A., 166

Sampling issues, with traditional depression scales, 24–25
Samuel, D. B., 117, 166, 171, 173
Satisfaction with Life Scale (SWLS), 135, 136
Saulsman, L. M., 117
Schedule of Compulsions, Obsessions, and Pathological Impulses (SCOPI), 105, 162, 234
anxiety symptoms on, 247–50, 249*t*, 250*t*
OCD symptom scales of IDAS-II and, 252–54, 252*t*, 254*t*, 257–60, 258*t*
OCD symptom specificity for, 245–47, 246*t*, 247*t*
and OCI-R, 235, 235*t*, 236, 236*t*
and PCCP analyses, 242*t*, 243, 244*t*
relation of IDAS-II OCD scales to, 238, 239, 239*t*
and Y-BOCS, 236–38, 237*t*
Schinka, J. A., 166
Schizophrenia and schizotypy, 108–14
hedonic deficit in, 108–9, 110*t*, 111
IDAS analyses of, 112–14, 113*t*
specificity of hedonic deficit, in relation to depression, 111–12
Schizotypal Personality Questionnaire, 248
Schizotypal Personality Questionnaire (SPQ), 109, 110*t*, 162, 171, 275*t*, 281, 282, 282*t*

Schizotypal Traits Questionnaire-Short Form, 171
Schizotypy. *see* Schizophrenia and schizotypy
Schmidt. F., 87
SCID-IV. *see* Structured Clinical Interview for *DSM-IV*
SCOPI. *see* Schedule of Compulsions, Obsessions, and Pathological Impulses
Seashore Psychology Clinic, 55
Self-report data
  and co-occurrence of symptoms, 2
  depression symptoms, 64, 65, 65*t*
  on depression symptoms, 64, 65, 65*t*
  on social anxiety/social phobia, 104–6, 106*t*
Self-report measures, of OCD symptoms, 232–33
Self-report scales, anxiety symptoms on, 211–17
Sex differences, in depression, 85, 86, 86*t*
Short Michigan Alcoholism Screening Test (SMAST), 167
SHS (Subjective Happiness Scale), 135, 136
Simms, L. J., 179–80
Skin Picking Scale, 284
Slade, T., 16
SMAST (Short Michigan Alcoholism Screening Test), 167
Social Aloofness composite, 171, 172, 172*t*, 173, 173*t*
Social anxiety, 102–7
  disorder-based analyses of, 103
  interview data on, 106–7, 107*t*
  prior evidence on, 103–4
  self-report data on, 104–6, 106*t*
  symptom-based analyses of, 103–7
Social Anxiety composite, 162, 163, 163*t*, 164*t*, 248, 249*t*
Social anxiety disorder, and negative trait affect scale, 162, 163*t*, 164*t*
Social Anxiety factor, 30, 31
Social Anxiety scale (IDAS)
  anxiety symptoms on, 206–7, 220, 221–22
  Big Five Inventory correlations with, 43*t*, 44
  convergent/discriminant validity analyses, 217, 218, 218*t*
  correlations with ASI, 214, 215, 215*t*
  correlations with *DSM* diagnoses, 228*t*
  descriptive statistics across respondent types, 50*t*
  development of, 31, 206–7
  factor structure for, 46, 47*t*
  group comparisons for, 52, 52*t*
  internal consistency of, 38, 38*t*
  test-retest analyses of, 40*t*, 41, 42
Social Anxiety scale (IDAS-II)
  and anxiety symptoms, 248
  Big Five Inventory correlations with, 43*t*, 44
  construct validity of, 220
  convergent/discriminant validity analyses, 120, 120*t*, 148, 148*t*, 218
  correlations with APPQ and FQ, 213, 213*t*
  correlations with *DSM* diagnoses, 221, 221*t*, 222, 225, 225*t*, 226, 227*t*, 228, 228*t*, 229, 229*t*, 266*t*
  correlations with EPSI, 277*t*
  correlations with HRSD and, 71*t*
  correlations with IMAS, 219, 219*t*, 220*t*, 261*t*
  correlations with ISDI, 273*t*, 274*t*
  correlations with MIHT, 283*t*
  correlations with PID-5, 280, 280*t*
  correlations with PSRS, 211, 212, 212*t*
  correlations with SPQ, 281, 282*t*
  descriptive statistics across respondent types, 51*t*
  development of, 207
  factor structure for, 48*t*, 49, 49*t*
  group comparisons for, 52, 52*t*
  as indicator of internalizing, 162
  intercorrelations of other scales with, 45*t*
  internal consistency of, 38*t*, 39, 39*t*
  normative statistics for, 54*t*, 56*t*
  structural analysis, 215–17, 216*t*, 217*t*
  as symptom-based analysis, 105, 107
  test-retest analyses of, 40*t*, 41
Social anxiety symptoms, correlation of anxiety measures with, 215–17, 215*t*, 216*t*

Social phobia, 102–7
criterion validity of symptom scales for, 266*t*
disorder-based analyses of, 103
interview data on, 106–7, 107*t*
and OCD symptom measures, 250*t*–252*t*, 254*t*, 255, 256*t*
predictive power of anxiety measures for, 228*t*–230*t*, 229, 230
prior evidence on, 103–4
self-report data on, 104–6, 106*t*
symptom-based analyses of, 103–7
tetrachoric correlations, 4*t*, 5
Social phobia symptoms
correlation of anxiety measures with, 221*t*, 222, 223*t*–225*t*, 225, 226, 227*t*
correlation of PTSD measures with, 195*t*–197*t*, 198, 199*t*, 201*t*, 204*t*
correlations of anger measures with, 154, 155*t*–160*t*, 160
Specific phobia
and anxiety symptoms, 209–10
criterion validity of symptom scales for, 266*t*
and OCD symptom measures, 250*t*, 251, 251*t*
predictive power of anxiety measures for, 228*t*–230*t*, 230
Specific phobia symptoms
correlation of anxiety measures with, 221*t*, 223*t*–225*t*, 224, 227
correlation of PTSD measures with, 204*t*
correlations of anger measures with, 154, 155, 155*t*–160*t*, 159
correlations of PTSD measures with, 195*t*, 196*t*
SPQ (Schizotypal Personality Questionnaire), 216, 217, 226, 227
Stability coefficients, 37, 39–42
Standardized root-mean-square residual (SRMR), 15
Stanton, K., 208
State associations, in bipolar disorders, 114
State-Trait Anxiety Inventory, 3
Steer, R., 26, 85
Steer, R. A., 26
Stony Brook University, 59, 60
Structural analyses
for anxiety symptoms, 215–17, 215*t*, 216*t*
for OCD symptoms, 233
Structured Clinical Interview for *DSM-IV* (SCID-IV), 20, 21, 55, 58–60, 59*t*, 165
Stuart, S., 6
Subjective Happiness Scale (SHS), 135, 136
Substance use disorder, 165, 166, 167*t*, 168*t*
Sub-Work Group on Posttraumatic and Dissociative Disorders, 180
Suicidality factor, 30, 31
Suicidality scale (IDAS and IDAS-II)
Big Five Inventory correlations with, 43*t*
convergent/discriminant validity analyses, 72, 73*t*, 74, 74*t*, 148, 148*t*, 217, 218*t*
convergent validity analyses of, 69, 69*t*, 70
correlations with Beck inventories, 75, 76, 95
correlations with *DSM-5* diagnoses, 79*t*
correlations with *DSM* diagnoses, 266*t*, 269*t*
correlations with *DSM-IV* diagnoses, 78*t*–80*t*
correlations with EPSI, 277*t*
correlations with HRSD and, 71, 71*t*
correlations with IMAS, 261*t*
correlations with ISDI, 273*t*, 274*t*
correlations with MIHT, 283*t*
correlations with PID-5, 280, 280*t*
correlations with SPQ, 281, 282*t*
as depression scale, 62, 64–66, 65*t*, 66*t*
and depression symptoms, 101, 101*t*, 102, 263, 264
descriptive statistics across respondent types, 50*t*
development of, 31
and diagnostic specificity, 81
factor structure for, 46, 47*t*, 48*t*, 49*t*
and General Depression scale, 32
group comparisons for, 52, 52*t*
intercorrelations of other scales with, 45*t*
internal consistency of, 37, 38, 38*t*, 39*t*
normative statistics for, 54*t*, 56*t*
sex differences on, 86*t*
test-retest analyses of, 40*t*

Suspiciousness composite, 171, 172*t*, 173*t*
SWLS (Satisfaction with Life Scale), 135, 136
Symptom-based analyses, of social anxiety/social phobia, 103–7
Symptom-based model of psychopathology, 260–85
  development of, 271–85
  and differential criterion validity, 265, 266*t*–267*t*, 267
  and differential diagnostic specificity, 267–70, 268*t*, 269*t*
  and differential incremental specificity, 270–71
  and differential symptom correlates, 264–65
  and Eating Pathology Symptoms Inventory (EPSI), 276–78, 276*t*, 277*t*
  further extension of, 284–85
  and Iowa Sleep Disturbances Inventory (ISDI), 272, 273*t*–275*t*, 274–76
  and Multidimensional Inventory of Hypochondriacal Traits (MIHT), 282–84, 283*t*
  multiple symptoms within disorders, 262–64
  and Personality Inventory for *DSM-5* (PID-5), 278–81, 279*t*, 280*t*
  robust symptom dimensions, identification of, 260–62
  and Schizotypal Personality Questionnaire (SPQ), 281, 282, 282*t*
Symptom measures, reliability of IDAS-II, 36–37
Symptoms
  co-occurrence of, 2–3
  differential correlates for, 264–65
  differential organization of, 263–64
  modeling, within emotional disorders, 22
  specific dimensions of, 262–63
Sypher-Locke, H., 108

Tellegen, Auke, 5
Temperament and Affectivity Inventory (TAI), 131–35, 132*t*, 136*t*, 151, 152, 152*t*, 153*t*, 154, 160, 161, 161*t*, 265
Ten Berge, J. M. F., 127
Test-retest analyses, 21, 37
Tetrachoric correlations, 4, 4*t*, 5
Three-factor diagnosis model, 16
TLI (Tucker-Lewis Index), 15
Trait associations, in bipolar disorders, 114–15, 115*t*
Trait measures, and Ill Temper Scale, 151–53, 152*t*
Trait negative affect scales
  bivariate relations for, 162–63, 163*t*, 167, 168, 168*t*, 171, 172, 172*t*
  indicators of externalizing psychopathology on, 167–68, 168*t*, 169*t*
  indicators of internalizing psychopathology on, 160–64, 161*t*, 163*t*, 164*t*
  initial factor analysis for, 160–61, 1651*t*
  multivariate relations for, 163–64, 164*t*, 168, 169, 169*t*, 172, 173, 173*t*
  psychoticism indicators on, 171–73, 172*t*, 173*t*
  validity of, 153, 153*t*, 154
Trauma-based disorders, 175–76. *See also* Posttraumatic stress disorder (PTSD)
Traumatic Avoidance factor, 35
Traumatic Avoidance scale (IDAS-II)
  and anxiety symptoms, 248
  Big Five Inventory correlations with, 43*t*
  comparative analyses, 198
  correlations with *DSM* diagnoses, 196, 196*t*, 197, 199*t*, 266*t*, 268*t*
  correlations with EPSI, 277*t*
  correlations with IMAS, 189, 189*t*, 190, 190*t*, 261*t*
  correlations with ISDI, 273*t*, 274, 274*t*
  correlations with ITRI, 193*t*, 194
  correlations with MIHT, 283*t*
  correlations with PCL, 186, 187, 187*t*, 188*t*, 189, 197, 197*t*
  correlations with PID-5, 280*t*
  correlations with SPQ, 282*t*
  creation of, 35
  descriptive statistics across respondent types, 51*t*
  factor structure for, 48*t*, 49*t*

group comparisons for, 52, 52*t*
as indicator of internalizing, 162
intercorrelations of other scales with, 45*t*, 46
internal consistency of, 38*t*, 39
normative statistics for, 54*t*, 57*t*
as PTSD scale, 186, 195, 195*t*
and PTSD symptoms, 202, 203, 203*t*
and social anxiety, 105
test-retest analyses of, 40*t*, 42

Traumatic intrusions, as PTSD symptom, 177, 178*t*
Traumatic Intrusions factor, 30, 31
Traumatic Intrusions scale (IDAS and IDAS-II)
and anxiety symptoms, 248
Big Five Inventory correlations with, 43*t*
comparative analyses, 198
convergent/discriminant validity analyses, 148, 148*t*, 217, 218*t*
correlations with *DSM* diagnoses, 196, 196*t*, 199*t*, 266*t*, 268*t*
correlations with EPSI, 277, 277*t*
correlations with HRSD and, 71*t*
correlations with IMAS, 189, 189*t*, 190, 190*t*, 261*t*, 265
correlations with ISDI, 273*t*, 274, 274*t*
correlations with ITRI, 192, 192*t*, 193*t*, 194
correlations with MIHT, 283*t*
correlations with PCL, 186, 187, 187*t*, 188*t*, 189, 197, 197*t*
correlations with PID-5, 280, 280*t*
correlations with SPQ, 282*t*
descriptive statistics across respondent types, 50*t*
development of, 31
factor structure for, 47*t*, 48*t*, 49*t*
group comparisons for, 52, 52*t*
as indicator of internalizing, 162
intercorrelations of other scales with, 45*t*, 46
internal consistency of, 38, 39*t*
normative statistics for, 54*t*, 57*t*
as PTSD scale, 184–85, 194–95, 195*t*
and PTSD symptoms, 202, 203, 203*t*
and social anxiety, 105
test-retest analyses of, 40*t*, 42

Tripartite model, 7–12
development of, 7–8
and development of Mood and Anxiety Symptom Questionnaire (MASQ), 9, 9*b*, 10
early testing of, 8–9
implications of, 12
importance of symptoms in, 12
problems with, 12
and relations among MASQ scales, 10–12, 11*t*

Tucker-Lewis Index (TLI), 15
Two-factor affective model, 5–7
and "big two" dimensions of affect, 5
and Negative Affect dimension, 5–6
and Positive Affect dimension, 6

Two-factor structure of bipolar symptoms, 126–33
assessment implications of, 143–45
Big Five Inventory, factor correlations to, 128–30, 129*t*
BIS/BAS scales, factor correlations to, 130–31, 131*t*
factor analyses of the bipolar scales, 126–27
factor similarity in, 127–28, 128*t*
future research directions for, 141
research implications of, 142–43
TAI, factor correlations to, 131–33, 132*t*

Unhappiness, feelings of, 3
University of Buffalo, 62
University of Iowa, 28, 33, 41, 55, 60, 62, 191
University of North Texas, 41, 42, 278
University of Notre Dame, 41, 42

Validity
content, 24–25
convergent (*see* Convergent validity)
criterion (*see* Criterion validity)
discriminant (*see* Discriminant validity)
of IDAS-II, 55, 58–60, 59*t*
of Ill Temper scale, 147–53, 148*t*–150*t*, 152*t*
incremental (*see* Incremental validity)

Validity (*Cont.*)
  of Mania scale, 119–22
  of trait negative affect scales, 153, 153*t*, 154
Vollebergh, W. A. M., 16

Washing and cleaning symptoms
  correlations of measures for, 238, 239, 239*t*
  diagnostic specificity of, 253, 255, 256, 256*t*
  factor analyses of, 243, 244*t*, 245
  in interview measures, 240*t*–242*t*, 241, 243
  relations of anxiety symptoms and, 248, 249, 249*t*
  relations of depression symptoms and, 246*t*, 247*t*
  in structure of OCD symptoms, 235–38, 236*t*, 237*t*
Watson, D., 1, 5–11, 16–19, 23, 62, 70–71, 87–89, 92, 103–4, 125*n*1, 126, 182, 185, 187, 191, 207, 208, 210, 234–36, 242, 245, 246, 272, 281
Well-Being factor, 31
Well-Being scale (IDAS and IDAS-II)
  Big Five Inventory correlations with, 43*t*, 44
  and bipolar scales, 32
  as bipolar symptom scale, 123, 124*t*, 134, 136*t*
  correlations with Beck inventories, 95
  correlations with *DSM* diagnoses, 266*t*, 269*t*, 270
  correlations with EPSI, 277*t*
  correlations with extraversion, 93
  correlations with HRSD and, 71*t*
  correlations with IMAS, 99, 99*t*, 100, 100*t*, 261*t*
  correlations with ISDI, 273*t*, 274*t*
  correlations with MASQ, 208, 208*t*, 209
  correlations with MIHT, 283*t*
  correlations with PANAS-X, 90*t*, 91, 91*t*, 92
  correlations with PID-5, 112, 113, 113*t*, 280*t*
  correlations with SPQ, 282*t*
  and depression scales, 100, 101, 101*t*
  descriptive statistics across respondent types, 50*t*
  development of, 31
  and diagnostic specificity, 97, 98*t*
  factor analysis of, 136, 137, 137*t*
  factor structure for, 47*t*, 48*t*, 49, 49*t*
  and General Depression scale, 32
  group comparisons for, 52, 52*t*
  intercorrelations of other scales with, 45*t*, 46
  internal consistency of, 38, 38*t*, 39*t*
  normative statistics for, 54*t*, 56*t*
  and positive mood dysfunction, 89, 89*t*
  as positive mood scale, 265
  and specific negative affects, 94, 94*t*
  test-retest analyses of, 40*t*
WHIIRS (Women's Health Initiative Insomnia Rating Scale), 69*t*, 70
Widiger, T. A., 117, 166
Wittchen, H.-U., 4
Women's Health Initiative Insomnia Rating Scale (WHIIRS), 69*t*
Worry, 210
Worry Domains Questionnaire–Short Form, 104
Wu, K. D., 234–36

Yale-Brown Obsessive-Compulsive Scale (Y-BOCS) Symptom Checklist, 236–38, 237*t*
Yale Global Tic Severity Scale-Self Report, 285
Yufik, T., 179–80

www.ingramcontent.com/pod-product-compliance
Lightning Source LLC
LaVergne TN
LVHW011911200926
848484LV00002B/591

9780199301096